A HISTORY OF THE HOLOCAUST

For my brothers Earl, Harvey, Norman, Kendall and Sheldon
– for all the dreams we shared and all that we have done

A HISTORY OF THE HOLOCAUST

Saul S. Friedman
Youngstown State University

VALLENTINE MITCHELL
LONDON • PORTLAND, OR

Published in 2004 in Great Britain by
VALLENTINE MITCHELL
Suite 314, Premier House,
112–114 Station Road, Edgware, Middlesex HA8 7BJ

and in the United States of America by
VALLENTINE MITCHELL
c/o ISBS, 920 NE 58th Avenue, Suite 300
Portland, Oregon 97213-3786

Website: http://www.vmbooks.com

British Library Cataloguing in Publication Data

Friedman, Saul S.
A history of the Holocaust
1. Holocaust, Jewish (1939–1945)
I. Title
940.5'318

ISBN 0-85303-435-4 (cloth)
ISBN 0-85303-427-3 (paper)

Library of Congress Cataloging-in-Publication Data

Friedman, Saul S., 1937–
A history of the Holocaust/Saul S. Friedman.
p. cm.
Includes bibliographical references and index.
ISBN 0-85303-435-4 (cloth)
1. Holocaust, Jewish (1939–1945) 2. Jews–Persecutions–Europe. 3.
Germany–History–1933–1945. 4. Germany–Ethnic relations. I. Title.

D804.3.F755 2003
940.53'18–dc21

2003057169

Typeset in 10.5/12.5pt Times NR by Vitaset, Paddock Wood, Kent
Printed in Great Britain by
MPG Books Ltd, Bodmin, Cornwall

Contents

Illustrations

Maps

Preface

Holocaust is the term applied to the Nazi scheme of genocide in Europe between 1933 and 1945. From the Greek *holocauston* meaning burnt whole or a great fire, the word derives from the Hebrew *oleh* (עהל , to go up, Lev. 1:9) or *kurban* (קרבן , burnt offering, Lev. 1:14) used to describe sacrifices offered by high priests in ancient Jerusalem.[1] In the wake of World War II, survivors, seeking purpose in the horrors of Auschwitz and Dachau, suggested that six million Jews who perished in ghettos and concentration camps may have been objects of a divine test as unfathomable to us as that experienced by Job. More recently, Jewish historians have taken to calling the event *Shoah* (שאה , destruction, Ps. 35:8).[2]

Some scholars believe that five million Gentiles from Poland, Ukraine, France, Greece and Yugoslavia should also be included in this saga. A distinction must be made, however, between individuals, *some* of whom were sent to forced labor camps (*Zwangsarbeitslager*) or were executed before a firing square, and Jews, *all* of whom were to be slain in extermination camps (*Vernichtungslager*). Yisrael Gutman and Shmuel Krakowski of the Yad Vashem Institute in Jerusalem stressed this point when they contrasted the plight of Jews and Polish Gentiles during World War II. 'In spite of the Nazi terror,' they wrote, 'the great majority of Poles still lived in their pre-war apartments and worked at their pre-war jobs. Although they were subject to exploitation and terror, they never faced total extermination. Although they had lost their independence, they could still look for help to the Polish Government-in-London, the Polish Armed Forces in exile and the constant support that the Allied powers extended to the Polish underground.'[3]

The only groups treated like Jews by the Nazis were the insane, congenitally handicapped, Jehovah's Witnesses, gays and Gypsies. Much as the Nazis despised these groups, however, they were more concerned with purging their territory of what they termed *Lebens unwertes Leben* (Life unworthy of Life) than killing all of them. Some religious offenders were invited to recant and embrace the New Order. Himmler wanted to preserve some Gypsies as evidence of an earlier Aryan civilization. Nazi doctors entertained notions of 'curing' the handicapped and homosexuals through surgery or drugs. In the final analysis, only one group was to be eliminated wherever they were found – the Jews.

Over 50 million people died as a result of total war between 1939 and 1945.

Of these, 12 percent were Jews. Half of the victims in Nazi concentration camps were Jews. At the time, Jews constituted less than one-quarter of 1 percent of the world's population. The Holocaust was unique within the context of Jewish history. While Jews endured persecution throughout history, Roman procurators, Saracen holy warriors, and Inquisitors usually held out the prospect of survival to those who would convert. Not so the Nazis. It mattered little whether the Jewish captive was an atheist, an orthodox rabbi, a mother or small child. They all had to die. As Emil Fackenheim once declared, the Holocaust was a unique descent into hell.[4] In five years, two-thirds of the Jews in Europe were murdered, a thousand-year-old civilization was destroyed. Where the previous massacres had been implemented by people derided as barbarians, the killing of the Jews took place in the heart of twentieth-century Europe, drawing its inspiration from modern science, its method from the most recent technology. The plan also entailed a unique form of slavery. Until the Nazis, slaves in the mines of Laurium or plantations in Louisiana were deemed to have value. In this system, every Jewish slave was designated for death.

A contemporary event, the Holocaust brings into question the foundations of Western civilization. As Elie Wiesel explained, 'Whenever you touch that period, you touch the core of history. All questions become very poignant.' Questions like how could a cultured people like the Germans embrace Hitler? What of the complicity of the free world which appeased the Nazis before the invasion of Poland? What of the Soviet Union which sent vast supplies of grain and petroleum to Hitler before his conquest of western Europe in 1940? Why did Latin American republics refuse sanctuary to refugees? How do we measure the response of the United States and President Franklin D. Roosevelt? What of the Papacy and the International Red Cross? Is it fair to liken the behavior of Jews in Europe to sheep as H.R. Trevor-Roper, Bruno Bettelheim, Hannah Arendt and Jesse Jackson have done? How are the guilty to be punished? How long must perpetrators be sought? What is the connection between Holocaust and the state of Israel? Can people believe in God after Auschwitz?

Much as some would have it otherwise, the subject of the Holocaust refuses to go away.[5] When Germany debated capping the statute of limitations on war crimes in 1978, broadcast of the NBC docudrama 'Holocaust: The Story of the Family Weiss' prompted the government to reverse its decision. Ronald Reagan's visit to the military cemetery at Bitburg in West Germany in 1985 and Ernst Nolte's article in *Die Frankfurter Allgemeine Zeitung* a year later calling for a *Schlusstrich* (a bottom line) on German guilt revived debate on the Holocaust, as did the publication of *Hitler's Willing Executioners* by Jonathan Goldhagen in 1996. As Berliners dedicate a park in memory of Jews killed in the Holocaust, the words of Primo Levi ring true. Said Levi, '*Wer keine Erinnerung hat, hat keine Zukunft*' (He who has no memory, has no future). Minorities that believe the Holocaust has no relevance for them should understand that when the Allies overran the death camps at the end of World War II, they found enough Zyklon B (hydrogen cyanide pellets) to kill another 20 million people. There were less than three million Jews left in all of Europe.

My own involvement with Holocaust studies goes back to 1949 when I took Bar Mitzvah lessons from a survivor in Berea, Ohio. Since then, my understanding of what transpired in World War II has been enriched by a number of courageous souls (Jim Elder, Esther Shudmak, Eva Fugman Jacobs, Bill Vegh, Sonja Schwartz, Robert Clary) who endured that other planet, and scholars (Nora Levin, Emil Fackenheim, Jacob Marcus, Ben Halpern, Marie Syrkin) who influenced my thought.

Academics may be disappointed to find no great philosophy of history spun in these pages. The question that still baffles is why so many people behaved in such a perverse manner during the Holocaust. Human beings are flawed creatures, and a number of excuses have been offered to account for what happened – religious bias, frustrated nationalism, ethnocentrism, chauvinism, economic rivalry, personal spite and aggression, sadism, and the charisma of one particular demagogue. According to this last rationalization, generals and privates, men and women across Europe were simply following orders from Adolf Hitler. The Nazi leader, too, has been analyzed by conventional historians, psychohistorians, and deconstructionists. Some attribute his hatred of Jews to a provincial Catholic upbringing, a brutal father, his adoration of his mother (treated for cancer by a Jewish doctor in her last years), his failure to gain entry to the Viennese Academy of Fine Arts, the influence of professional anti-Semites, alienation from society, or madness. Some scholars, unable to cope with the magnitude of the Holocaust tragedy, simply throw up their hands and declare the tragedy to be metahistory – beyond human comprehension. I prefer the view of Rabbi Zvi Yehuda of the Cleveland College of Jewish Studies. For Rabbi Yehuda, the Holocaust was neither mystical nor inevitable. It was 'just the culmination of evil'.

While developing this text my principal commitment has been to students, lay persons and other teachers who still need to understand basic facts before they graduate to a different level of Holocaust studies. Sadly, the shelf-life of good textbooks like those authored by Leon Poliakov, Gerald Reitlinger and Nora Levin is rather short. My own book is offered as a synthesis of sources and issues, a primer in the study of genocide. I trust it is readable. I accept responsibility for errors in fact.

Finally, a word of appreciation to those who assisted in the completion of this work – Sally Green, editor at Frank Cass Publishers; Bonnie Harris of the YSU History Department and Kathy Leeper of the Graphic Center; Professors William Fishman and Martin Berger, who offered suggestions for the manuscript; my wife Nancy (my inspiration for 40 years), and our children Jason (who helped with illustrations), Molly (who shared her sadness with me as we toured Dachau in 1988) and Jonathan (my peer and colleague).

Maps

BALTIC SEA

LITHUANIA

GDYNIA

DANZIG

EAST PRUSSIA

VILNA

SUWALKI

GRODNO

BARANOVITCH

RUSSIA

BYDGOSZCZ   TORUN

LOMZA   BIALYSTOK

GNIEZNO

POSEN   PLOCK

TREBLINKA

BUG

KUTNO

WARSAW   SIEDLCE

PINSK

CHELMNO

BREST-LITOVSK

KALISZ

LODZ

SOBIBOR

PIOTRKOW   LUBLIN

RADOM   CHELM

MAJDANEK

BELZEC

WLODZIMIERZ

GERMANY

CZESTOCHOWA   ZAMOSC

LUCK   ROWNE

SOSNOWIEC

VISTULA   SAN

KATOWICE

LWOW

AUSCHWITZ

RZESZOW   JAROSLAV

TARNOPOL

CRACOW   TARNOW

BIELSK

PRZEMYSL   SAMBOR

NOWY SACZ

DROHOBYCZ

STRYJ

STANISLAWOW

KOLOMYJA

NAZI CONCENTRATION CAMPS

GOVERNMENT GENERAL

WARTHEGAU/ANNEXED BY GERMANY

OCCUPIED BY SOVIET UNION 1939–1941

1. Poland 1939–44

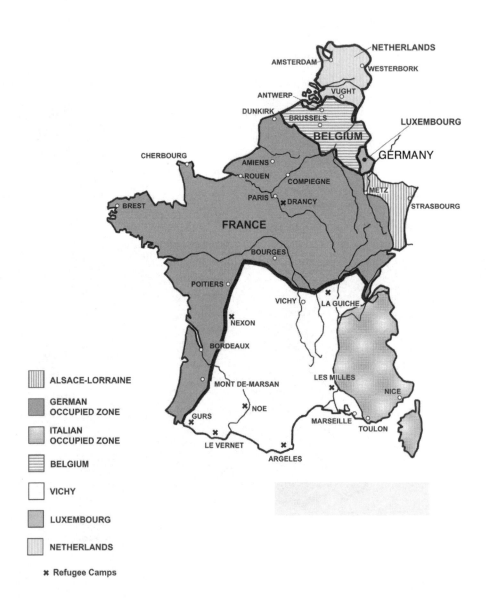

NETHERLANDS

AMSTERDAM
WESTERBORK

ANTWERP
VUGHT

DUNKIRK
BRUSSELS

LUXEMBOURG

BELGIUM

GERMANY

CHERBOURG

AMIENS
ROUEN
COMPIEGNE

METZ

PARIS
DRANCY

STRASBOURG

BREST

FRANCE

BOURGES

POITIERS

VICHY
LA GUICHE

NEXON

BORDEAUX

MONT DE-MARSAN

LES MILLES

NICE

NOE

GURS

MARSEILLE

TOULON

LE VERNET

ARGELES

ALSACE-LORRAINE

GERMAN
OCCUPIED ZONE

ITALIAN
OCCUPIED ZONE

BELGIUM

VICHY

LUXEMBOURG

NETHERLANDS

✕ Refugee Camps

2. Vichy France and Western Europe 1940–44

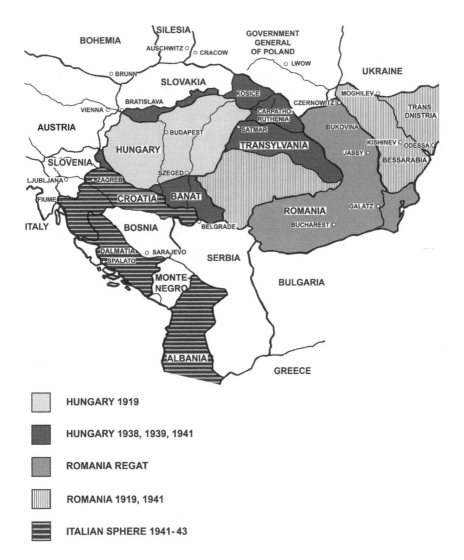

BOHEMIA

SILESIA

AUSCHWITZ ○ ○ CRACOW

GOVERNMENT
GENERAL
OF POLAND

○ LWOW

UKRAINE

○ BRUNN

SLOVAKIA

KOSICE

CZERNOWITZ

MOGHILEV ○

TRANS
DNISTRIA

BRATISLAVA

VIENNA ○

AUSTRIA

CARPATHO-
RUTHENIA

BUKOVINA

KISHINEV ○ ○ ODESSA

SATMAR

○ BUDAPEST

TRANSYLVANIA

JASSY ○

BESSARABIA

HUNGARY

SLOVENIA

SZEGED ○

LJUBLJANA ○

● ZAGREB

FIUME

CROATIA

BANAT

ROMANIA

GALATZ ○

BELGRADE

BUCHAREST ○

ITALY

BOSNIA

○ SARAJEVO

DALMATIA
● SPALATO

SERBIA

BULGARIA

MONTE-
NEGRO

ALBANIA

GREECE

☐ HUNGARY 1919

■ HUNGARY 1938, 1939, 1941

▦ ROMANIA REGAT

▥ ROMANIA 1919, 1941

▤ ITALIAN SPHERE 1941-43

3. Central Europe 1941–45

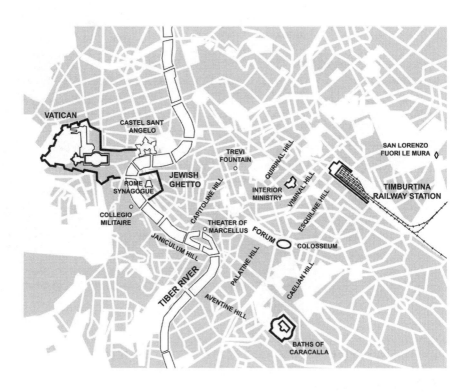

4. Rome 1943

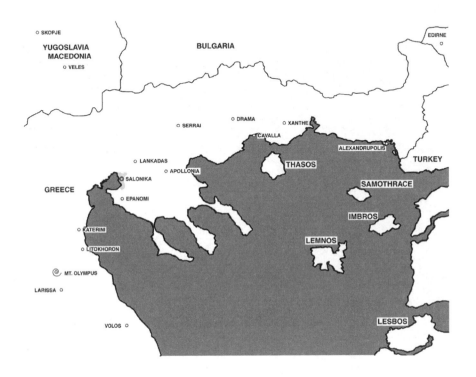

5. Salonika and Macedonia 1941–45

6. The Baltic States 1941–45

1

The Jews: A History of Persecution

An old Hessian legend tells of a servant who worked for a wealthy, but penurious lord. After three years, the servant was compensated with three pennies and dismissed. As he made his way through a forest, the servant met a dwarf who granted him three wishes in exchange for his pennies – a gun that would hit everything he aimed at, a fiddle that would make everyone dance, and the ability to compel people to speak the truth. The servant then encountered another man 'with a long goatee' marveling at a songbird in a tree. The servant shot the bird and it fell into a mass of prickly shrubs, where-upon he commanded the man, 'All right, you dog, go in and get it if you want it.' The old man fell on all fours and proceeded into the brambles. As the barbs tore at his face, the servant picked up the fiddle and started to play, forcing the old man to dance till he was bloody. 'You've skinned plenty of people,' chided the servant, 'now the brambles can skin you.' The old man pleaded for his life, offering to forfeit a bag of gold. When the servant released him, the old man rushed to a nearby village, charging that he had been robbed of his ducats. The judge and townsfolk agreed and ordered that the servant be hanged. Granted a last request, the servant used his fiddle to put the people into a dancing frenzy. Then he forced the old man to confess that he had stolen the money, at which point the townsfolk hanged the old man from the gallows.[1]

There is no mistaking the identity of the knavish old man in the *Kinder-märchen* of Jakob and Wilhelm Grimm. 'The Jew in the Brambles', as the story is titled, reflects a culture which for centuries taught its children to fear the *Judel* (a Jewish demon that inhabited stoves), the *Judenblick* (evil eye), *Judensau* (offspring of a Jew and a pig), *Judenloch* (hole where Jews resided), *Judenpech* (fuel of the hellfire), *Judenspiess* (the lance that pierced the side of Christ and which, as usury, continues to torment Christians) and *der ewige Jude* (the eternal Jew, a frightening old man who was cursed forever for his role in the murder of God's son).[2] In a land of passion plays, the brothers Grimm recounted other tales where Jews are righteously punished ('A Good Stroke of Business' and 'The Bright Sun Will Bring It To Light'). They repeated accusations of ritual murder[3] and introduced a range of definitions in their *Deutches Wörterbuch*, including *judeln* or *juden* (a verb, to Jew, 'as the way some Jews often act in business'), *Judenbengel, Judenlummel* and *Juden-mauschel* (Jewish boors), *Judenhaus* ('he is as welcome as a piglet in a Jewish house'), *Judenkopf* ('cleverness lives in a Jew's head') and *Judenseele* ('lost as a Jew's soul').[4]

To please their nationalist friends in the *Christliche-Deutsche Tracht-gesellschaft* in Berlin, the Grimms included off-color Jewish tales in all seven editions of their folktales. While generations of children around the world delighted in sanitized versions of the sagas of Snow White, Cinderella, Little Red Riding Hood and Rapunzel, scholars like Maria Tatar, Bruno Bettelheim, Carl Jung and Sigmund Freud wrestled with the salacious content and hidden symbolism of the Grimm fairy tales.[5] Louis Snyder has warned that the ultimate goal of such literature was to inculcate 'respect for order, belief in the desirability of obedience, subservience to authority, respect for the leader and the hero, veneration of courage and the military spirit, acceptance without protest of cruelty, violence and atrocity, fear of and hatred for the outsider, and virulent anti-Semitism'.[6] Ruth Bottigheimer also cautioned: 'Unable to vent their frustration on the immediate sources of their grinding poverty (like the miserly master in "The Jew among Thorns"), [the Grimms] invented scapegoat figures like the Jew, who in the words of the text even has a goat's beard to identify him with the scapegoat (*Sündenbock*). Attacking the egregious Jew whom numerous regulations kept outside the social fabric not only diverted disruptive feelings from socially related figures like the servant's master, but it also united the poor in hatred of a common enemy for whom no epithet was bad enough.'[7]

To those who recite the nursery school mantra that name-calling cannot hurt, Gordon Allport notes that hatred begins with verbal rejection and proceeds to discrimination, physical separation, boycotts and, ultimately, violence.[8] Desmond Morris, Konrad Lorenz, Helmut Schoeck, Robert Ardrey, Anthony Storr and Clyde Kluckhohn have written on the universal danger of envy, projection, transference, displacement and aggression.[9] Arthur Miller articulated this concern in his play *Incident at Vichy*. Taken to Gestapo headquarters, Doctor Leduc tells a German, 'Each man has his Jew; it is the other. And the Jews have their Jews. And now, now above all, you must see that you have yours, the man whose death leaves you relieved that you are not him, despite your decency. And that is why there is nothing and will be nothing – until you face your own complicity with this … your own humanity.'[10]

Gustave LeBon, Theodor Adorno, Wilhelm Reich and Stanley Milgram have all warned of the herd instinct among people and how differently people act when they are alone or in a mob.[11] Through rage or frustration, normal men and women create a world populated by demons whose evil can only be combated by equal malice.[12] The German psychoanalyst Irenaus Eibl-Eibesfeldt has called man's ability to transform his opponent into a 'devil' more serious than the invention of weapons. 'In the last analysis,' wrote Eibl-Eibesfeldt, 'it is this capacity to switch off pity that makes him into a cold-blooded murderer.' People convince themselves that their enemies are not merely objects of fear and mistrust, but monsters or vermin which must be killed.[13] Killing becomes a mystical ritual, an 'orgy of destruction', putting the killer in a state of ecstasy.[14]

THE JEW AS SCAPEGOAT

The Jew has long been a favorite of those who seek scapegoats. In 1873, Wilhelm Marr, a German journalist, coined the term synonymous with Jew-hatred – anti-Semitism. Shortly after, a Russian Jew, Leon Pinsker, concluded that Jews were not a chosen people, but 'a people chosen for universal hatred'.[15] A physician, Pinsker wrote that 'Judaeophobia is a psychic aberration. As a psychic aberration, it is a hereditary and as a disease transmitted for 2,000 years, it is incurable.' Jewish history in the *Galut* (Hebrew for exile) has been drenched with blood because societies that did not punish wrongdoers encouraged them. As Hans Toch has written, 'the Ghost of Riots Past hovers like a friendly specter over each new outbreak; it provides historical sanction, and it furnishes vivid images of how and why to proceed'.[16]

Massacres left two million Jews dead during the Roman conquest of Judaea (63 BC–AD 135) Perhaps 250,000 died under the Byzantines, another 250,000 during the Arab conquest of the Middle East. Thousands were drowned or scalped when Visigoths conquered Spain; another 50,000 died as a result of excesses perpetrated by self-proclaimed Crusaders in the Rhine-land after 1095. The Inquisitions may have added 25,000, expulsions from European lands another 200,000. Medieval superstition gave rise to three libels – host desecration (the charge that Jews stole the Eucharist wafer for the purpose of stabbing it), ritual murder (belief that Jews recreated the passion of Christ, killing a Christian child to secure blood as an ingredient for Passover matzos) and well poisoning (Jews were blamed for the Black Death) – which resulted in 250,000 more Jewish victims from Savoy to Syria. Some 100,000 Jews died in the wars of the Reformation, and 250,000 between 1648 and 1656 during a national insurrection in the Ukraine. Jews perished in a second uprising under Catherine the Great, 50,000 in Russian pogroms of 1881–82. Any recapitulation must also include 30,000 victims of riots in Germany between 1815 and 1830, 100,000 slain in eastern Europe during World War I, 150,000 in the struggle for Ukraine in 1919, 50,000 in Romania, Poland and Hungary amid inter-war pogroms, 200,000 at the hands of Muslims in different periods of history and 100,000 miscellaneous victims.

Jews made ideal scapegoats for several reasons. Numerous enough to be visible and resented, they were few enough to be vulnerable. Historically an urban people, they clustered in towns or cities where the Jewish quarter could be easily identified. On the eve of World War II, 60 percent of 270,000 Jews in France lived in Paris; 60 percent of the 140,000 Dutch Jews lived in

Amsterdam; 90 percent of Belgium's 90,000 Jews lived in Antwerp or Brussels; 73 percent of the 80,000 Greek Jews lived in Salonika; nearly 50 percent of Hungary's 500,000 Jews lived in Budapest; 33 percent of Germany's 600,000 Jews lived in Berlin; 92.5 percent of the 190,000 Jews in Austria lived in Vienna. It was much the same in eastern Europe: 40,000 in Riga, 50,000 in Bialystok, 60,000 in Minsk, 65,000 in Cracow, 80,000 in Vilna, 85,000 each in Kharkhov, Lwow and Kishinev, 140,000 in Kiev and Leningrad, 200,000 in Lodz, 350,000 in Warsaw.

In Poland, Slovakia and Romania, Jews could often be distinguished by the way they looked. Jewish women made use of traditional *sheytls* or wigs. Men and boys, devotees of the Hasidic movement, wore dark gabardine outfits topped with a cap, *shtreiml* (fur head piece) or flat-brimmed hat. In eastern Europe beards were a sign of religious reverence. Not only did *Ostjuden* look and dress differently, they subscribed to a peculiar diet. Jews spoke and wrote an alien tongue. When they communicated among themselves they retreated into the twang of Yiddish or what some Gentiles perceived as the demonic script of Hebrew. Jewish rituals – *tashlich* (blessing of waters), *mikveh* (ritual bathhouse), *kashrut* (rites of purity), and *shehitah* (a method of slaughtering) likewise were perceived as arcane or evil.

Gentiles simultaneously loathed and feared Jews. Thus, while the Church banned intermarriage at the Council of Elvira in 313, Jews were denounced for their alleged 'exclusivism'. In 1808, an assemblage of rabbis explained to the French that biblical injunctions against intermarriage operated only against Canaanite pagans. In the years following emancipation, Christians resented Jews for retaining their identity and for prospering. Anti-Semites, pointing to Jewish accomplishments (Jews with less than 0.3 percent of the world's population contributed 15 percent of the Nobel laureates), could not allow that such achievements came from natural ability.

THE OL FUN YIDDISHKAYT

Dr Pinsker spoke of 2,000 years of hatred, but such disdain dated to the time of Abraham. Initially, the conflict among Israelites, Amalekites, Edomites and Canaanites was over land. Monotheism added new elements of friction. Where the gods of Egyptians, Philistines and Greeks were many and tangible, Jehovah stood alone, non-anthropomorphic, immanent. Carrying the *ol fun yiddishkayt* (the yoke of Jewishness), Jews refused to embrace the gods of their conquerors. If the masses venerated Baal, Moloch or Zeus, such back-sliding was condemned by prophets and mainstream Jewry which, in turn, was attacked by Gentiles for disloyalty. When Judaeans refused to acknow-ledge Antiochus IV as a god, the Seleucid monarch issued a set of decrees (*Gezerot*) bent on their extermination.

Gentile polemicists spared Jews no accusations in the Graeco-Roman period. According to Apollonious Malo, Moses was a criminal, Mosaic law nothing but abominable precepts. Tacitus claimed Jews were descended from lepers. Dio Cassius labeled them cannibals. Cicero, Lemprias and Juvenal called them misanthropes, cowards and business cheats. Added Apion, Jews could not lay claim to the invention of one thing that benefited mankind. Throughout the centuries, anti-Semites have claimed that Jews are repugnant, ill-mannered and avaricious.[17]

For 1,000 years, Europeans portrayed Jews as money-grubbing Shylocks. Shakespeare, Karl Marx and Werner Sombart created the impression that Jews venerated Mammon and directed prosperity wherever they pleased. As Sombart wrote in 1911, Jews were 'atoms of molten money which flow and are scattered but which at the least inclination reunite into one principal stream'.[18] Millionaires like Moses Montefiore and Maurice de Hirsch, the Rothschilds in Paris, Vienna and London and the Brodskys in Russia confirmed the notion that Jews were responsible for capitalism. They were also the sponsors of worldwide revolution: communism allegedly was the handiwork of Karl Marx (who converted to Christianity at the age of 12), Leon Trotsky, Karl Radek, Maxim Litvinov, Lazar Kaganovich, Lev Kamenev and Grigory Zinoviev, all prominent Bolsheviks who dissociated themselves from their Jewish roots.

THE EUGENICISTS

The nineteenth century added another rationale for Jew-hatred. In the age of Darwin and Mendel, Francis Galton (1822–1911) proposed solutions to England's population problems through the pseudo-science of eugenics (race improvement). According to Galton, heredity, not environment, determines ability and character. Three-fourths of an individual's genetic package comes from grandparents (the Law of Ancestral Heredity) and offspring of superior and inferior individuals are always inferior (the Law of Retrogression). Galton argued that society had a right to protect itself from asocials: criminals and the insane. 'Quality families' should be encouraged to have more children. Intelligent refugees should also be welcomed. As Galton wrote in 1908, the first object of eugenics 'is to check the birth rate of the unfit, instead of allowing them to come into being, though doomed in large numbers to perish prematurely'. In his last work, *Kantsaywhere*, completed months before his death in 1911, Galton fantasized about an island society ruled by intellectuals who not only regulated marriage, but also subsidized the birth and education of gifted children. The dark side of his utopia was that individuals deemed inferior were expelled. Those who refused to leave or proved mentally incompetent would be shut away in asylums.[19]

Galton at least had legitimate credentials. Not so some of his contemporaries. Polygenists like Christoph Meiners disputed the concept that all

people were descended from a common ancestor. Meiners, Voltaire and the
Swiss naturalist Louis Agassiz argued that the races could be traced to
different primate ancestors (whites to chimpanzees, Asians to orangutans
and blacks to gorillas.) Edward Tyson maintained there was a different
'liquor' in black blood, a notion once advanced by Johann Meckel.[20] The
Dutchman Pieter Camper suggested that only persons who were tall or whose
jawlines were set at an angle of 100 degrees with their skulls could be civilized.
Carl Carus indicated that noses were the key to character; for Andre Retzius
it was cephalic index. Johann Lavater argued that the entire face should be
read like a book. ('Every forehead which above projects, and below sinks in
towards the eye, in a person of mature age,' wrote Lavater, 'is a certain sign
of incurable imbecility.') To Lorenz Oken, it mattered only whether an
individual could blush.[21]

In 1850, Robert Knox, the Scottish anatomist, declared: 'Race in human
affairs is everything' and two years later Count Arthur de Gobineau published an *Essay on the Inequality of the Human Races*. A royalist who despised
the revolutions of 1830 and 1848, de Gobineau analyzed ten empires and
concluded that each collapsed because of miscegenation. 'The human race
in all its branches has a secret repulsion from the crossing of blood,' wrote
de Gobineau. There were three races, each with its own attributes. Blacks,
who possessed physical energy and artistic talent, were descended from
Hamites. They suffered from limited intellect and were easily enslaved. The
Yellow race (including Finns and Altaic peoples) were natural merchants who
formed the core of societies. They tended to apathy, lacked strength, were
mediocre and obstinate. Whites were marked by reflective energy, intelligence,
physical power and perseverance. In the fabric of men, the black and yellow
were cotton and wool, while whites were silk. In this human tapestry, Aryans
were gold and silver threads and among Aryans, the noblest of all were the
Germans. Broad-shouldered heroes of blond hair, de Gobineau's Frankish
ancestors preserved classical civilization. Only the Jews have been able to
master the blending of blood. Jews of the nineteenth century, a hybrid race
that never possessed a culture of its own, were virtually indistinguishable
from their ancestors.[22]

THE ULTIMATE SIN: DEICIDE

The principal reason Jews have been so unpopular in the last 2,000 years is
the charge of deicide – Christ-killing. They had brought persecution upon
themselves in the book of Matthew (where a mob chants to Pilate, 'His blood
be on us and our children') and the book of John (where they spared Barabbas
over Jesus). Until the papal encyclical *Nostra Aetate* declared in 1965 that
Christ's death was a necessary sacrifice, responsibility for which falls upon all
mankind, Jews in every generation were punished for the crucifixion of Jesus.

Christians were instructed to pray for their perfidious souls. The first image of Jews that a child learned from catechism was that they were responsible for the death of the son of God.

Attacks upon the Jewish people and their religion figure prominently in the polemics of the earliest church fathers. Justin Martyr, Tertullian and St Ignatius of Antioch denounced the synagogue as a center of lies and obsolete practices. Theophilus, Irenaeus and Hippolytus accused Jews of killing Christ, and Origen warned that Jews would never return to their ancestral land. Eusebius, Bishop of Caesarea, castigated Jewish character. St Jerome compared Jewish prayers to the braying of donkeys, St Ambrose called the synagogue 'a house of impiety', St Cyril referred to the 'shameful' rabbinate and St Ephraim likened Judaism to 'a harlot'. St Augustine described the way Jews held Jesus, debased and flogged him, then 'nailed him to a tree'. But it was left to another saint, John Chrysostom (Archbishop of Constantinople, 344–407) to summarize the misery of Jews in terms of divine malediction. Said St John 'the Golden Mouthed', 'God hates you.'[23]

Before the Visigoths arrived, Jews enjoyed prosperity in western Europe. In Italy Jews served as physicians, craftsmen, farmers and judges prior to the Lombard invasion. Some German tribesmen regarded Jews as bearers of Roman culture. Charlemagne (768–814) authorized their trade in wine, switched the major market day in his domains from Saturday and intervened on their behalf in legal disputes.[24] Such prosperity did not go unchallenged. Agobard, Archbishop of Lyons (779–84), denounced the special status of Jews and plotted with Lothair, son of Louis the Pius, to depose the King. Over the next centuries, Jews were barred from practicing law, medicine, farming or holding public office. They were not to be seen in public during Holy Week or the last days of Advent. Interference with conversion to Christianity, circumcising a Christian slave or intermarriage was punishable by death. The Church adopted two devices that would be revived by the Nazis. Jews were marked with a badge stitched on the breast. Originally a circle (*rouelle*), representing coins Judas received for his betrayal of Jesus, the badge might take the form of a miniature decalogue, yellow armband or a wizard's peaked hat. Jews were segregated in the most dilapidated section of a town – ghettos – a term derived either from the Italian *borghetto* (little town) or the Hebrew *get* (separation/divorce). Forced to pay protective taxes and attend conversionary sermons, they were locked in at night and periodically subjected to massacres.

MARTIN LUTHER

One Christian who saw the unfairness in all of this was Martin Luther (1483–1546). The godfather of the Protestant Reformation studied Hebrew with rabbis in Württemberg and on the day he posted his critique of the Church (31 October 1517) Luther was visited by two Jews who suggested that he convert to Judaism. Sympathetic to their plight, Luther believed the answer was for Jews to follow him. The Danish pastor Poul Borchsenius has written: 'Probably he believed that the purified Christianity that he preached, and that was inspired by the Bible, which the Jews had first possessed, would lead them [the Jews] in large numbers into his fold.'[25] Thus in May 1523 Luther issued a homily, titled *That Jesus Christ Was Born a Jew*. In it, he wrote: 'We [Christians] must receive them [the Jews] cordially, and permit them to trade and work with us, that they may have occasion and opportunity to associate with us, hear our Christian teaching and witness our Christian life.'[26] According to Luther, for Jews Christianity was nothing but 'Popishness and monkery'. It was illogical to condemn Jews for usury when Christian law had forbidden them to own land or engage in manual labor. Christians, who were supposed to be working for their salvation, alienated Jews by condemning them as 'stiff-necked', 'slandering them' with charges of poisoning wells, stealing the Host or using Christian blood. 'If the apostles had dealt with Gentiles as we with Jews there would be no Christians among the Gentiles.'[27]

Few Jews were won over by Luther's arguments. Meanwhile, Luther underwent his own transformation. Fearful of Ottoman Turkish advances into central Europe and excesses of peasant rebellions, Rhenish freebooters and Anabaptist crusaders, Luther doffed the cloak of reformer, and revealed 'the appalling nakedness of the one-time monk with deep-rooted hatred of the Jews'.[28] Within a year of publishing his friendly essay, Luther argued that God's covenant with the Jews had been broken. Their miserable state was retribution for killing God's son. Jews could only cling to the Bible by perverting the meaning of scripture. By November 1527, Luther devoted 17 sermons to the Jews as 'blasphemers', 'stubborn', 'intractable', 'idolaters' and 'wiseacres' who surpassed the Greeks in their mythology.[29] In 1529, Luther charged the Jews with preaching 'openly false doctrines'.[30] Three years later in *Table Talk*, he told Veit Dietrich, 'the Jews go astray so often in the Scriptures because they do not know the [true] contents of the books'.[31] Ultimately, he claimed that the Bible was purely a German book. The only scripture to which the Jews had a right, Luther declared, was 'that contained in a sow's tail; the letters that drop from it, you are free to eat and drink'.[32]

In more moderate days, in the spring of 1525, Luther had been content to charge that the hearts of Jews were 'full of wicked wiles'.[33] Over the next 15 years, he attacked some of his peers who were urging Christian–Jewish dialogues. Luther was revolted by the practice of permitting Jews to pass through or settle in duchies which previously had barred them. When the *Shtadlan* (intercessor) Josel von Rosheim requested safe conduct through the Electorate of Saxony, Luther exploded: 'Why should these rascals, who injure people in body and property and withdraw many Christians to their superstitions, be given permission?'[34] From innocents who were to be saved in 1523, the Jews were now 'usurers, adulterers, drunkards, and fanatics'.[35] Luther determined to write one last great essay that would protect Germans from Jewish perfidy. In the fall of 1540, he announced that he planned to write against the Jews because they slandered the Virgin Mary, calling her 'a stinkpot, a hag, and a monstrosity'.

Luther's essay, *Concerning the Jews and Their Lies*, appeared in 1543. It was no less chilling than the aforementioned *Table Talk*. Plagiarizing freely from his old rival Johannes Eck, Luther charged that the Talmud taught it was no sin to break an oath with, rob or kill a Gentile. He accused Jews of poisoning springs, mutilating Christian children and securing blood for the consecration of their priests. Jews had no reason to complain about their state, as Christians suffered for more than 300 years after the death of Christ. Most important, in *Concerning the Jews and Their Lies*, Luther outlined a ten-point program to resolve Germany's 'Jewish Question'. He suggested:

1. Their synagogues ... should be set on fire, and whatever does not burn up should be covered or spread over with dirt so that no one may ever be able to see a cinder or stone of it ...
2. Their homes should likewise be broken down and destroyed ... They ought to be put under one roof or in a stable, like Gypsies ...
3. They should be deprived of their prayerbooks and Talmuds in which such idolatry, lies, cursing and blasphemy are taught ...
4. Their rabbis must be forbidden under threat of death to teach any more ...
5. Passport and traveling privileges should be absolutely forbidden to the Jews ...
6. All their cash and valuables of silver and gold ought to be taken from them and put aside for safekeeping ...
7. Let the young and strong Jews and Jewesses be given the flail, the axe, the hoe, the spade, the distaff and spindle, and let them earn their bread by the sweat of their noses as is enjoined upon Adam's children ...
8. Let us apply the same cleverness [expulsion] as the other nations, such as France, Spain, Bohemia, etc.
9. If I had power over the Jews, I would assemble the best and most learned among them, and under penalty of having their tongues cut out, force them to accept the Christian teaching.
10. To sum up, dear princes and nobles who have Jews in your domains, if this advice of mine does not suit you, then find a better one, so that you and we may all be free from this insufferable devilish burden – the Jews.[36]

POLIN! HERE THOU SHALT REST

By the middle of the sixteenth century many Jews had had their fill of western Europe and determined to head east. A few merchants may have filtered into Poland with the decline of Rome or as a result of trade with Byzantium.

More followed when Jews were expelled from England, France, Cologne, Strasbourg, Spain and Sicily. They came, as Moses Isserles wrote to a friend in Germany, because, 'You may have to be content with dry bread, but you will be able to eat it without fear.' They came after Grand Duke Boleslaw issued the Statute of Kalisz in 1264 which guaranteed personal protection and equality in trade. In 1551 another decree created the *Vaad Arba Arazot* (Council of Four Lands), an assembly of 76 Jewish representatives that met twice each year to discuss matters of common concern and appoint delegates to the Sejm (national parliament) in Warsaw.[37]

A special invitation had been extended to Jews in the fourteenth century from Casimir III (1330–70) and his successor Jagiello (1386–1434) who hoped to strengthen a backward economy.[38] Jews played a significant role in Poland's three-tiered society. At the top were Poles, landowners (*szlachta*), burghers and free farmers who were Catholics. At the bottom were Ukrainians, a mix of frontier warriors, descendants of Kievan Rus, dirt farmers and herdsmen from the steppes who acknowledged papal authority. Jews were employed by Poles as middlemen, collecting taxes from the Ukrainians, holding keys to their churches.

In 1648, Ukrainian frustrations exploded when their Hetman Bogdan Chmielnicki called for a war of national liberation. For eight years, Cossack freebooters besieged cities and massacred the inhabitants. On 10 June 1648, 6,000 Jews were slain at Nemirov where the Scottish-born 'Krivonos' (Broken-Nose) distinguished himself breaking the backs of infants. Women jumped to their deaths from a bridge rather than submit to rape. The head of a Yeshiva in Nemirov, Rabbi Jechiel Michal, was clubbed to death as he walked to the cemetery. Two weeks after, Poles abandoned their defense of Tulcyzn and permitted the massacre of 2,000 Jews. Gangs, dubbed the *Chern* (scum of the earth), continued killing in Bar, Brody, Ostrow, Kremenetz, Mezevicz, Polonnoie and Dubno. Jews and Poles were beheaded or tied to horses and dragged along the road (what Cossacks called 'presenting the red ribbon'). At Zaslav, Jews were led to a cemetery chapel which was then set afire, Catholic priests were skinned alive and the corpses of Polish nobles disinterred. At Moghilev, 1,500 men, women and children, 800 Gentiles and 700 Jews were ordered to dig their own graves. In some communities, children were thrown into wells.

When the armies of the Swedish King Carl Gustav invaded Poland in 1655, Polish patriots turned on the Jews, slaughtering anyone who would not convert. Before the killing stopped, virtually every Jewish community from Podolia to Lithuania had been touched by the *Gezerah* (catastrophe).[39] Two hundred and fifty thousand Jews were murdered in the worst massacres in Jewish history since the Roman conquest. For Ukrainians the rebellion was a failure. At Pereaslav in 1654, Cossack leaders swore allegiance to Tsarist Russia, unwittingly forfeiting independence for another 340 years.

THE GHETTO AND THE SHTETL

The *Gezerah* reminded Jews that, no matter how they tried to blend into a Gentile world, inevitably they were regarded as *Luftmenschen* (rootless wanderers). Children grew up stunted, rickety and sallow in the depressing confines of ghettos.[40] Conditions were not much better in *shtetls*, little towns that dotted the map of eastern Europe. As Casimir had hoped, Jews became the middlemen in Poland. By 1939, between 52 percent and 76 percent of the small shops (taverns, grocery stores) were run by Jews and 80 percent of the tailors were Jews. So, too, were 80 percent of Poland's furriers, capmakers and bookbinders, 75 percent of the barbers, 60 percent of the watchmakers, tinsmiths, carpenters and upholsterers, 40 percent of the shoemakers, 33 percent of the glaziers, butchers and bakers.[41] Jews served as coachmen, street cleaners, knife grinders and musicians. Jewish society also had its share of the unemployed, including a whole class of *schnorrers*, beggars whose curses were not to be believed.

At the center of every Jewish town was the *kehillah* (the organized Jewish community), obligated to uphold people's dignity from the cradle to the grave. This included providing meals and clothes for the needy, a dowry for indigent brides (pans, bed linen, etc.), hospitality for students or the homeless on the sabbath, visiting the sick and watching over a dead body before its burial, comforting mourners. Because Jews could expect little help from the state, the *kehillah* was supposed to maintain orphanages and hospitals, house the aged, mediate differences between husbands and wives, supply tools to artisans and offer technical assistance and 'free' loans to those who sought to emigrate either to the West or to Palestine.

What sustained those who remained behind was their faith. The synagogue served as a place of study, assembly and worship. Jewish sanctuaries took many forms: elegant Romanesque structures like the Tlomackie Square Synagogue in Warsaw and the 3,000-seat temple in Florence; smaller *daven-shuls* like the Saul Wahl Synagogue in Poland (named for a Jew who as President pro tem of the Sejm technically was King of Poland for one day) and the *Altneushul* in Prague (said to be the resting place of the *golem*, a monster who protected Jews from massacres); *shtibls*, small houses of Hasidic sects; stone fortresses like the synagogue in Tarnopol that supplied protection from pogromchiks and the fragile wooden structure at Woldowa that did not.

For many in eastern Europe, Judaism was defined in terms of Hasidism, an evangelical movement that arose as a reaction to the failed claims of Sabbatai Zevi, a pseudo-messiah who appeared after the Chmielnicki massacres. The Jewish masses were drawn to the teachings of Israel ben Eliezer (1698–1759), a wonder-working healer known as the *Baal Shem Tov* ('master of the good name') who used homeopathic herbs and primitive psychology to treat the delusional. The Baal Shem Tov taught that the world was based on love of God, love of Israel, love of Torah. At a time when rabbis reproached the masses for their ignorance of *Halacha* (Jewish law), the Baal Shem Tov stressed

1. Altneuschul in Prague,
where the Golem, a creature
of fantasy that protected the
Jews from pogroms,
supposedly resided.

sincerity of prayer, humility and service to God. God permeated everything
with his holy spirit. The human experience is in reality a joyous, mystical one.

Followers of the Baal Shem Tov, dubbed *Hasidim* (pious ones), were taught
to seek a model (*tikkun*) in a *rebbe* or *tsaddik*, living saints. The latter need have
no formal training in Torah or Talmud, just possess a divine spark that would
show the proper way to union with God. Sects cropped up throughout Europe
– at Belz in Galicia where the Rokeah family established a dynasty of sages,
at Ger near Warsaw with the Alter family, at Bratzlav in the Ukraine, at Satmar
in the Carpathians, at Liady in Lithuania, then later at Liubavitch, a village
near Moghilev where the Schneersons were practically treated as royalty.[42]

THE EXPLOITATION OF THE DAMNED

When the Nazis controlled Europe, they exploited Jewish institutions and
history. Jacob Presser noted that German predators used 'an almost scientific
method for milking millions of physically and economically defenseless
people as a stepping-stone towards their extermination'.[43] In September 1939,
when the Nazis conquered Poland, they transformed the *kehillahs* into 24-
man Jewish councils responsible for implementing orders within the Jewish
community. By replacing popular leaders with a second-tier clique, the Nazis
hoped to neutralize independent action. As Rudolf Kastner of the Budapest
Vaad (Council) declared: 'Step by step they [the Jewish leaders] were made
tractable. In the beginning relatively unimportant things were asked of them,

replaceable things of value like personal possessions, money and apartments. Later, however, the personal freedom of human beings was demanded.'[44]

Jewish dress and beards and residence made it easier to identify the intended victims. Some Holocaust survivors swear that Jews carried themselves differently, stoop-shouldered, eyes downward, as they walked in the streets. Like the Cossacks before them and Bosnian murder gangs after, the Nazis knew they could always find Jews gathered at a cemetery for a funeral. They timed major roundups to coincide with Jewish holidays such as Tisha B'Av in Warsaw (1942), Rosh Hashanah in Denmark (1943), Passover in Hungary (1944). Occasionally, the Nazis forced groups of Jews into fragile, wooden synagogues which were then turned into raging infernos. The Nazis duped Jews, who stressed the importance of personal hygiene, by lining up men, women and children outside of places marked 'shower chambers'. They also exploited the lesson of Jewish history which taught that people survived through compliance rather than resistance. As Zisia Friedman advised his colleagues in the Warsaw Ghetto, 'If we go along, some of us will survive. The Germans can't kill all of us.'[45]

There were also historical reasons why the Nazis established extermination camps in eastern Europe. This was where most of the nine million Jews of Europe were concentrated. Railway lines were in place, criss-crossing industrial regions. The Nazis also appreciated the deep-rooted anti-Semitism of peoples in the East. Few peasants objected to the arrival of the death trains. As James Glass has written, 'It is disingenuous to suggest that the Nazis set up the extermination camps in Poland only because the country contained a large number of Jews. The Germans were aware of the vastness of Polish anti-Semitism. They knew that little, if any, resistance to the death camps would come from local populations. Polish resistance groups and partisans rarely had anything to do with Jewish fighters and would, on occasion, murder Jews.'[46] Miriam Kuperhand survived by hiding in the woods outside Siemiatycze. She noted that Polish partisans 'spent more energy hunting Jews than harassing the German occupiers'. Her husband Saul, a survivor of Treblinka, agreed, labeling Germans and Poles ('with a few glorious exceptions') the enemy.[47]

German forces were greeted as deliverers in the Baltic states, Ukraine and White Russia. Reports of the Einsatzgruppen indicated that the reaction of local populations to mass killing of Jews ranged from 'indifferent' in Mogilev to 'gratefully susceptible' or 'friendly' in Brest-Litovsk. The Nazis pretended to be champions of frustrated nationalists against Jewish Bolsheviks and in return received extensive cooperation from Polish, Latvian, Estonian, Romanian, Lithuanian, Ukrainian and White Russian peasants. But even this, noted Ronald Headland, could not account for the way systematic killing proceeded. 'The extent and brutality of collaboration in the east,' he wrote, 'must surely be some barometer of the anti-Semitism as it existed generally among the population.' Anti-Semitism, Headland concluded, was 'endemic to eastern Europe'.[48]

2

Rehearsal for Destruction: The Jews of Tsarist Russia

THE LAND OF THE FLEA AND THE HOME OF THE SLAVE

Much of the hostility directed against Jews in eastern Europe may be traced to Russia, which served as a proving ground for anti-Jewish massacres in recent centuries. Even before Ukrainians accused them of ritual murder at the Pechera monastery in 1096, Jews were an unwelcome caste in Russia. Resented by the merchants of Kievan Rus, tracked down and impaled by the Brooms (state police) of Ivan the Terrible, Jews were equally unwelcome to the Romanovs. Said Peter the Great: 'I prefer to see in our midst nations professing Islam and paganism rather than Jews. They are all rogues and cheats. It is my endeavor to eradicate evil, not multiply it.'[1]

Despite Peter's aversion, his domains counted 250,000 Jews by 1700. Russia's share in the partitions of Poland (1772, 1793, 1795) added another million. In her last years, Catherine the Great attempted to confine Jews to the Polish regions (known as the Pale of the Settlement). Through bribes and guile, Jews managed to live outside the Pale, even in the capital, St Petersburg. In 1815, Catherine's grandson, Alexander, the enigmatic tsar whose forces wore down Napoleon, inherited 200,000 more Jews when he annexed the Grand Duchy of Warsaw. A religious zealot, Alexander planned to force Jewish villagers into larger ghettos and send Jewish boys to military settlements where they would be converted to the Christian faith.[2]

It was left to Nicholas I to implement the so-called canton concept. Government child-snatchers known as *khappers* seized 40,000 boys between 1825 and 1855 as families said *kaddish* (the Hebrew prayer of mourning). Whipped, starved and doused with water, some committed suicide rather than submit to baptism. Derided as *zhidy* (kikes), Jews endured discrimination in employment and schooling. One hundred and fifty thousand were shoved back into the Pale by Nicholas's Third Section (state police). Their holy books were censored and burned.[3] Jews were 'poor white slaves' who lived in filthy hovels, five or six families to a building. Twenty percent of Vilna's Jews lived off the dole from the *kehillah*. In Berditchev, Grodno, Kovno and Odessa, cadaverous Jews ate farina paste and died 'like flies'. In St Petersburg (where Jews were not supposed to live), John Foster, the

American ambassador, found 1,800 crammed in a barn. Foster reported: 'All of these sufferers are in rags, most are barefoot, many bear marks of mutilation upon their faces, their heads bound-up, their expressions blanched and glazed.'[4]

Russia's hapless performance in the Crimean War prompted Alexander II (1855–81) to embrace reform. Alexander encouraged investment in mines, railroads, banks and factories. The new tsar opened schools to applicants based upon ability, not background. He revamped the army, instituting literacy programs and wiping out deferments based on class. He permitted the creation of *zemstvos*, local councils with quasi-legal standing. A law of 20 November 1864 promised fair, public trials. Restrictions on movement and residence were eased for Russia's Jews and serfs. In 1867, noting that 'it is better to abolish bondage from above than to wait for the time when it will begin to abolish itself spontaneously from below', Alexander II emancipated 47,000,000 of his subjects.[5] Despite these efforts, the one decent tsar that Russia produced remained the object of assassins. Seven attempts were made on his life before he was killed as he drove through the streets of St Petersburg on 13 March 1881.

ORTHODOXY, AUTOCRACY AND NATIONALISM

Alexander's death ended the experiment in assimilation for his nation's Jews. Now Russia would be led by less admirable men. The reformer tsar was succeeded by his younger son, Alexander III, a dour man who once said, 'We must not forget it was the Jews who crucified our lord and spilled his precious blood',[6] then the effete Nicholas II who, for a time, was under the sway of the monk Rasputin. Over the next three decades policy would be dictated by reactionaries like Interior Ministers Nikolai Ignatiev (1881–82), Dmitri Tolstoy (1882–89), I.N. Durnovo (1889–95), D.S. Sipiagin (1895–1902), Wenzel von Plehve (1902–4) and Peter Stolypin (1904–11). These bigoted officials were committed to a program of orthodoxy (one true faith – Russian Orthodox Christianity), autocracy (revocation of reforms) and nationalism (the forging of a single Russian identity).

The inspiration for this ideology was Constantin Pobedonostsev, once tutor to the crown prince, then Procurator of the Holy Synod (a kind of ministry of religious affairs) from 1880 to 1905. A gaunt, reserved man who taught law at the University of Moscow, Pobedonostsev was a committed pan-Slav and Slavophile who peppered Alexander III with unctuous letters contrasting the peasants' love of the tsar with corruption in so-called Western democracies.[7] 'The whole secret of Russia's order and progress', he had written in October 1876, 'is in the person of the monarch. The day may come when flatterers will try to persuade you that it would suffice to grant Russia a so-called constitution on the Western model, and all difficulties would disappear and the government could live in peace. This is a lie, and God forbid that a true Russian shall see the day when this lie will become an accomplished fact.' Three years later, he wrote from St Petersburg, 'What I hear here from highly placed and learned men makes me sick, as if I were in the company of half-wits or perverted apes. I hear everywhere the trite, deceitful and accursed word – constitution. This word, I fear, has made its way into high circles and is taking roots. But I also meet and talk with the sane Russian people who are full of apprehension. They fear primarily that basic evil, a constitution.'

The reactionaries were able to wipe away the progress of 30 years in the course of a few summers. On 29 April 1881, Alexander III issued a manifesto threatening to use 'absolute power' against all assaults on the government. On 13 August universities were placed under the supervision of the Ministry of Education. Public schools in Poland, Estonia, Finland and East Prussia were staffed with Russian teachers. The next day, 14 August 1881, the government proclaimed a state of emergency, restoring a system of arrest and detention without appeal. This law, which was supposed to last three years, operated until March 1917. On 27 August, the government established preliminary censorship for all newspapers. By 1890, the former system of the officers corps was restored. Electoral rolls in municipal corporations and *zemstvos* were again restricted.[8]

The common denominator among the reactionaries was Jew-baiting. As Minister of Education, Tolstoy tried to block entry of Jews into colleges. Known as 'Liar Pasha' when he served as Russian ambassador to Turkey, Ignatiev once declared there was nothing he could do about his people's animosity toward Jews, then suggested to Baron Horace de Gunzburg that persecution might cease if a million rubles were deposited in his bank account. Count Plehve was a supporter of groups like the Order of the Archangel Michael and the Order of the Double Eagle, superpatriots known as 'Black Hundreds' who were committed to pogroms.[9] When one of Alexander's assassins, Jessie Helfman, proved to be Jewish, reactionaries seized the opportunity to drown reform in Jewish blood. Pobedonostsev summed up their mood when he predicted that one-third of Russia's Jews would die out, one-third would leave the country and one-third would be absorbed by the surrounding population.[10]

THE POGROMS OF 1881–1882

Reports of organized anti-Jewish massacres began filtering out of Russia in the spring of 1881. Six months later, *The Times* of London ran a series of articles detailing what the editors called 'scenes of medieval horror'. Placards appeared throughout the country telling how the new tsar had given his blessing to pogroms. Christians were instructed to place crosses before their houses to protect themselves from misdirected violence. Disturbances were to take place on Sunday or saints' days when peasants and workers had free time. From Crimea in the south to Byelorussia and Poland in the north, Jews were attacked while Cossack units of the government stood by.

The troubles started at Elisavetgrad, a Ukrainian town of 30,000 (one-third of them Jews), on 27 April. Men swilled liquor at a 'dram shop', then marched upon the Jewish neighborhoods. When the Jews defended themselves, troops called to quell the disturbance joined the rioters. In two days 500 homes and 100 shops were looted. After one man was pitched from his roof, his daughter was raped by 20 soldiers. At Smielo on 7 May, 13 died and 1,000 were made homeless. The next day 20,000 Jews in Kiev were assaulted, including a three-year-old child who was thrown from a window and another infant who was stoned to death. On 9 May, Jews in Berezowka were driven from a synagogue and forced to stand for hours in a stream of water up to their necks; nine drowned. Three young women died after being raped. Meanwhile, the town constable rode about shouting, 'Beat the Jews!' The pogroms spread to Konotop and Wassilkov on 10 May. In the latter town, a tavern keeper named Rykelmann, his wife and six children had their throats cut after the man opened his liquor cellar to rioters. Mobs attacked Jews in Taurida, Ekaterinoslav, Alexandrovsk, Znamenka and Poltava. When pogromchiks in Balka could not locate a Jew named Allowitz, they raped his wife and burned his house. At Gregorievk, an innkeeper named Ruffmann was cooped in a barrel and pitched into the Dnieper. At Kitzkis, a couple and their two children were burned alive. Jewish settlements at Golaypol and Orjechow were pillaged, farm implements destroyed. Three million rubles worth of damage was done at Odessa, where 150 Jews were arrested by authorities when they tried to defend themselves.[11]

Over the next six months, the Russian sky was aflame with the 'crowing of the red cock'. Reports told of 30 Jews wounded at Saratov in June. New massacres were reported in Kiev, Ouchow, Konotop and Penjaslaw in July, Koretz, Njezin, Lubny and Borzny in August, Suwalki, Moghilev, Vitebsk and Slonim in October, Zhitomir in November, Smika and Kishinev in January, Balta and Walegojulawo in April. Six thousand Jews lost their homes to fire in Minsk and more in Pinsk in July. Three hundred homes and 600 shops were destroyed in Warsaw at Christmas. Jews who were not expelled from their hometowns (Liebenthal, Podolak, Dubno, Charkoff, Wolinsk, Constantinov Orel, Pereaslav) fled to refugee camps in regions bordering Austria or Prussia. There were 1,500 men, women and children starving outdoors at Podwoloczyska, 2,000 huddled in the cellars of Brody. All told there would be 50,000 deaths and 100,000 families reduced to beggary in 167 locales following the assassination of Alexander II.[12]

Tsarist apologists blamed the victims for inviting misery upon themselves. A Countess Ragozin, writing in *Century Magazine*, accused Jewish grocers of selling rotten meat, tavern keepers of keeping Gentile customers drunk on vodka and 'Talmudist' Jews of perverting Biblical texts, engaging in loan-sharking and plotting with revolutionaries to overthrow the monarchy. Henry Edward Cardinal Manning of New York responded by asking: 'How can citizens who are denied the right of naturalization be patriotic? How can men, who are only allowed to breathe the air, but not to own the soil under their feet, to eat only a food that is doubly taxed, to be slain in war, but never to command – how shall such a homeless and exiled race live of the life of the people among whom they are despised, or love the land which disowns them?'[13]

THE MAY LAWS

Embarrassed by protests in Berlin, London, Philadelphia and New York, Russia's reactionaries authorized a special Committee for Revision of the Jewish Question late in 1881. Not surprisingly, the commission, composed of reliable functionaries, blamed the Jews for inciting the massacres. To rectify the situation, the commission proposed several 'temporary' resolutions in the spring of 1882: barring Jews from making new settlements outside the Pale; restricting the right of Jews to execute legal documents; and forbidding business on Sundays or Christian holidays. Over the next decade, these so-called May Laws were supplemented by a host of decrees evocative of America's Black Codes. Thousands of people were expelled from Kiev and St Petersburg. Moscow was purged at Passover 1891 when Grand Duke Sergei rounded up 20,000 Jews in three days. Special exemption was offered to Jewish girls who registered as prostitutes.

Jews could not reside within 35 miles of the German or Austrian borders. They were unwelcome in Finland, Livonia, Kuban (with its mineral spas) or Yalta (a favorite resort of the royal family). The Tsarist state barred Jews from using Christian names. In 1892, Jewish soldiers lost the right to live anywhere they chose. Jewish artisans also lost their exemptions. A watchmaker who sold a fob or a baker who sold coffee in his shop were now deemed merchants and could be expelled. Jews living in cities or villages were disfranchised. They could not join the police force, become actors, serve as foremen of juries or on the boards of orphanages. Jewish tavern owners could no longer sell whiskey. Jewish financiers could not acquire interest in mines or oil fields and the number of Jews permitted to sit on the stock exchange was limited.

In July 1894, the Ministry of Education advised that only children of parents who could prove they possessed the right of domicile could attend state schools. (In the chaos of the 1880s and 1890s many Jewish schools had closed.) Within a year, a number of technical schools and universities institutionalized the *numerus clausus*, capping the number of Jews at 10 per-cent of the student body. The legal profession was closed to Jews for 15 years in 1889. In 1893, the number of Jewish pharmacy students was limited to

5 percent. That same year, Jewish veterinarians were informed they could not practice in Russia. By 1900 every educational institution in the country had some form of quota that operated against Jews.[14]

Russian Jews responded in various ways to such intimidation. Perhaps two million packed their possessions and fled westward to Germany, England and the United States. Others like Dr Pinsker, Peretz Smolenskin, Eliezer ben Yehudah, Achad ha-Am, Chaim Bialik, Max Lilienblum, Shmul Mohilever, Menachem Ussishkin, Nachman Syrkin, Aaron David Gordon, David Ben Gurion, Joseph Trumpeldor and Zev Jabotinsky embraced the Zionist movement. Trotsky, Zinoviev, Radek and Kamenev stayed behind, hoping to change the system by revolution. The remainder prayed that the persecution would pass.

DUMAS, KISHINEV AND BEILISS

They were wrong. As Nicholas II assumed the throne in 1894, practically every sector of Russian society was in turmoil. The tsar's coronation festival at Khodnyka Field in May 1896 was marred by a panic that left 1,300 people dead. There were workers' strikes, riots in oil fields, mutinies and assassinations. Education Minister Bogolepov was shot by a student in February 1901. Pobedonostsev was the target of a *zemstvo* statistician a month later. Interior Minister Sipiagin was shot in 1902, his successor Count Plehve killed by a bomb in 1904 and his successor Peter Stolypin shot to death in Kiev in 1911 after a bomb detonated at his summer home failed to kill him. A Los Angeles reporter offered a poetic envoi for the regime: 'Twinkle, twinkle little Czar. How I wonder where you are. Hope you're locked up good and tight. In your bomb-proof for the night.'

When Japan attacked the Russian fleet docked at Port Arthur, Manchuria, in February 1904, Nicholas's advisers were presented with an opportunity to rally the nation while extending their imperialist program. Few government leaders believed that Russia could lose such a conflict. Within a year, however, Kaiser Wilhelm was pressing his beleaguered cousin to accept mediation offered by the United States. Russia sustained the destruction of a second fleet (the Baltic under Rozhdezventsky), a naval mutiny (led by the battleship *Potemkin* in the Black Sea) and a full-scale revolution (the Petrograd Soviet in the winter of 1904–5). Fearing collapse of his dynasty, Nicholas reluctantly issued a manifesto in October 1904, providing for civil liberties (freedom from arrest, press, assembly, opinion) and summoned the first of four *dumas* (parliaments) that would meet before World War I.

Russia's experiment with constitutional government was a sorry one. The 26 political parties in the first duma refused to cooperate with one another. Two hundred deputies, including many leftists and Constitutional Democrats, fled to Finland in December 1907 when the government refused to compromise on questions of capital punishment and police misconduct. A second duma, elected in February 1907, lasted four months. Parliament shut down when Social Democrat headquarters was raided by the state police who accused the party of planning a rebellion and the assassination of Nicholas II. The election process for the third duma (the only one to complete its five-year term) favored landowners, industrialists and merchants. The fourth duma, elected in November 1912, was, by all accounts, even more conservative.

Nicholas and his aides were aware of the depth of Gentile antipathy toward Jews and knew how to exploit it. Even before the Russo-Japanese War, a ritual murder accusation occurred in the Bessarabian town of Kishinev. A young woman had disappeared in January 1903. On 6 April, after Easter Sunday services, Christians poured out of their churches bent on mayhem. Fifteen hundred stores and homes were looted, 86 people were wounded or mutilated, and 45 were slain (including babies, old men and women). Drawing upon the same dark emotions, Tsarist officials instigated widespread pogroms that left 900 people dead and 200,000 homeless two weeks after the issuance of the October manifesto.[15]

Tsarist autocrats cynically exploited anti-Semitism one last time in 1911. Mendel Beiliss, a Jewish workman living illegally in Kiev, was accused of having killed a boy and using his body for ritual purposes. Evidence suggested that a gang of robbers were the actual culprits, but it did no good. Beiliss was kept in prison until he could be presented in full beard and black caftan. The case became an international cause célèbre, with statesmen, attorneys and churchmen condemning the proceedings. In the end, Beiliss was acquitted by a semi-literate jury which, nevertheless, held that ritual murder had been done.[16]

THE PROTOCOLS OF THE ELDERS OF ZION

In its final stages of decay, Tsarist Russia promoted an insidious piece of anti-Jewish propaganda. A hundred-page pamphlet, the *Protocols of the Elders of Zion*, told of a purported Jewish conspiracy to seize control of the world's governments.[17] Portions of this anti-Semitic standard appeared for the first time in the columns of Paul Krushevan's tabloid *Bessarabetz* between 1903 and 1907. Krushevan, one of the instigators of the Kishinev pogrom, did not reveal who supplied him with what he claimed were the minutes of secret meetings between the World Union of Freemasons and the Elders of Zion. In all probability, his source was Serge Nilus, a landowner and member of the Black Hundreds. Nilus, who spent some time in France after he had gone bankrupt, was also vague about how he acquired these documents.

A doctored version of an 1864 political tract published in Brussels (Maurice Joly's *Dialogue in Hell between Montesquieu and Machiavelli*), the

Protocols eventually would be declared *Schundliteratur* (trash) by a Swiss court in 1935. But at the turn of the century there was sufficient hostility against Jews to warrant belief in their authenticity. Bigots like Eduard Drumont in France, Vladimir Soloviev in Russia and Hermann Goedsche in Germany had warned of an alliance among Rothschilds, Mongols, Freemasons and Jews. The creation of the socialist Jewish Bund in 1897, Herzl's call for a World Zionist Congress that same year and the success of Bolshevism all seemed to confirm the worst.

The appeal of the *Protocols* lies in their simplicity. Jews, identified with the perfidious serpent, have been scheming to place power in the hands of a group of elders representing the 12 ancient Israelite tribes. Because of their small numbers, Jews exploit the naivete of *goyim* (a Hebrew word for non-Jews used in a derogatory manner). The first stage in world conquest is to compromise those institutions that served as the foundation of Western civilization: the Church, nobility and aristocratic government. Rather than attack Christianity directly, it is more effective to call for toleration of all faiths, then espouse the merits of Darwinism, Marxism, agnosticism and atheism. The elders seek the downfall of existing governments by advocating individual rights and constitutions which are 'nothing but abstractions devised by Jews to mislead the Goyim'. Jews instigate labor disputes, pitting working men against society's elite. They delude the middle class to achieve monopolies. Money enables Jews to control the media, promoting sexual depravity, crime and drunkenness. Money gives Jews political influence. Proof of Jewish control of elected officials comes from the anomalous statement in the *Protocols*, '*Per me reges regnant*', 'through me, kings rule'. Jews promote warfare between nations to profit from the sale of war *matériel* and to kill off the best Anglo-Saxon stock. Once the white world has been sufficiently weakened, the Elders, allied with Freemasons and the Japanese, will proclaim a Davidic King-Pope who will impose a police state. In this New Order, Jews will determine what may be taught or thought. Classical education will be outlawed. The masses, dulled by full employment, games and pornography, will not care. Opponents of the regime will be placed in concentration camps. If these secret instructions fall into the hands of sensible Gentiles, the Elders will destroy civilization. For the Jews have mined the subway systems in the world's largest cities.

The *Protocols* were declared defamatory by a Swiss court 70 years ago, yet they have been recycled in virtually every language. Henry Ford pilfered ideas for his *Dearborn Independent* between 1920 and 1925. Ford's essays, collected as *The International Jew* are still favored readings of anti-Semites. Alfred Rosenberg came into possession of the *Protocols* while living in Estonia. The concept of a Jewish conspiracy was acknowledged by the German High Command which declared in the fall of 1944 that 'Jewish plutocracy and Jewish communism are out to hunt down the German people which has escaped from slavery'. The conspiracy was promoted by Goebbels's

Propaganda Ministry which warned in December 1944 that 'the central issue of this war is the breaking of Jewish world-domination'. Said Goebbels, 'If it were possible to checkmate the 300 secret Jewish kings who rule the world, the peoples of this earth would at last find their peace.' Adolf Eichmann believed in the conspiracy, denouncing Hitler in 1961 as a marionette of 'satanic international high finance of the western world'.[18]

POST-WAR POGROMS

If Jews were manipulating warfare in the twentieth century, they were going about it in an inexplicable fashion. During World War I, Jews in eastern Europe were attacked by every retreating army save one. Ninety-six thousand Jews served in the Imperial German Army; 35,000 were decorated for valor; 12,000 died for the Fatherland. By way of contrast, 650,000 Jews were conscripted into the Tsarist military; 60,000 were decorated and 100,000 lost their lives under the Romanov red, white and blue standard. Yet most Jews in eastern Europe preferred the presence of Germans to that of any other military force. The Kaiser's generals arrested and publicly executed any soldier found guilty of rape, murder or robbery. Some Jews fantasized a cultural bond with the Germans based upon similarities of language. Jewish schoolchildren peddled newspapers to coreligionists in the German Army. German military units deloused Jewish housing and German military bands serenaded Jews in the *shtetls*. Memories of these contacts would come back to haunt Jews in 23 years.[19]

Hoping to undermine the Romanov Empire, Wilhelm and his advisers cultivated separatist movements within Russia. Initially, this meant supporting Ukrainian Hetman Peter Skoropadsky, then an independent Central Rada in Kiev. Germany continued to encourage nationalist elements after the Bolshevik Revolution in November 1917, after the Treaty of Brest-Litovsk took Russia out of the war in February 1918 and after the armistice-capitulation in November 1918. Not surprisingly, a collateral result of the chaos generated by battles among Red, White, Polish, Ukrainian and anarchist armies was more bloodshed against the Jews.

According to the *New York Times* of 7 April 1919, 'Cable dispatches received yesterday by the *Jewish Morning Journal* of this city tell of the massacres of Jews in the Ukraine even more horrible than the massacres under Czarism. The dispatches assert that a systematic effort is being made to annihilate the Jewish population in the Ukraine, and that in the city of Felshtin alone, soldiers killed 800 Jews and wounded 400, while the killed and wounded in Proskurov numbered more than 4,000. The surviving Jews in both these cities, according to the dispatches, have been pillaged and robbed of all they possess, and their plight is pitiable.'[20]

In fact, the troubles had begun almost as soon as the Great War ended.

Between 14 December 1918 and mid-February 1919, Jewish relief agencies in Russia counted 55 separate pogroms. Many of the incidents were spontaneous acts of rage as in Poltava and Kherson where Jews were thrown from moving trains. In Ziadkovtzy, 15 Jews were pitched into a well. Near Kiev, 103 were tossed from an excursion boat into the Dnieper. At Tschernobyl, armed mobs drove Jews into a stream and shot those who tried to escape. In the Ukrainian countryside, children threw rocks at the corpses of Jews hanging from trees. And in Elisavetgrad veterans of the Tsarist Army pitched hand grenades into cellars filled with Jewish refugees.

Defeated soldiers passing through a village would demand food and drink. They abused bearded Jews and extorted tribute and weapons. Jews that complied would be denounced as Bolsheviks by right-wing troops, as Tsarists by the Red Army. The tatterdemalion heroes would then demand Jewish women, and when opposed, resorted to rape and murder. At Bratzlav and Kamenetz-Podolsk, Jews had their limbs chopped off. In Brailov, victims had their tongues pulled out, eyes gouged and noses cut off. In Uman, pogromchiks seeking bracelets, brooches and earrings hacked off the hands, feet, ears and even breasts of victims. Cases of multiple rape were common. In Smotrich, some of the girls were attacked by as many as ten Cossacks. In Potapovichi, two girls who resisted had their faces beaten to bloody pulps. Two girls from Ladyzhenka were brought to a hospital in Kiev. One's nose was broken. Both were terribly mutilated and suffering from venereal disease. Children were killed before their parents. Of 168 deaths at Petschanka, an infant taken from its mother's breast was beheaded. Seventy-two died at Kopai-Gorod where a father was forced to lick the blood of his dead son. At Kitai-Gorod, a mother and child were dragged through the streets by horses.

A favorite method of killing was to line people up and see how many could be killed with a single bullet. (According to *The Times*, the record was six or seven.) At Trostianetz in Podolia, hundreds of Jews who sought refuge in the community house were attacked by a mob using pickaxes, knives and clubs. In Tetiev, 70 people, including children, were flung against a basement wall and slashed to death. More than 500 Jews hiding in the rafters of the synagogue were burned alive. In Dubovo, the killing place was the home of a man called Feldman. A Moravian and a Russian armed with sabres kicked people down an outside staircase to the cellar where other pogromchiks beheaded them.[21] In Zhitomir, Koziatyn, Fastov and Berditchev, pogromchiks attacked survivors who came to bury their dead in the Jewish cemeteries. A survivor recalled the carnage at Cherkassy where 800 had died:

> Dead bodies lay near me. I rose, my underwear was all soiled with blood and near me I heard the groans of a dying man. I summoned all my strength to get to the dying person. All around there was no one, it was quiet and the groaning was distinctly audible, but I could not find the man. Again, I lost consciousness. How long I lay there unconscious I do not know. But when I woke up, I realized I was lying next to Kanevsky and it was he who

was groaning. 'Kanevsky,' I said, 'Maybe you can get up and we will try to go home.' 'No,' he replied, 'I am dying. I beg you, find my son and put him next to me. I should like to embrace him before I die.' I found his son. He was dead. I moved the father near the son. He embraced him, burst into tears, heaved a deep sigh, and died.[22]

Some of the worst excesses were perpetrated at Proskurov, a town which hitherto had been spared. Tradition held that a Hasidic *tsaddik* said no pogromchik would cross its threshold. That held true until 15 February 1919. That Friday evening, troops under the direction of Ataman Semosenko unleashed a week-long assault against Proskurov's Jewish quarter. Reports of the Red Cross and the French-based *Comité des Délégations Juives* tell of victims hacked down in the streets or as they cowered in their homes. Students who tried to assist the wounded were also killed. Young women became deranged as a result of multiple rape. An infant was seized from its mother and repeatedly lanced on a pike. An old man was pitched out of a window by his beard. The paralyzed son of a rabbi was murdered as he lay helpless in bed. Two young children were cast alive into a burning fire. Whole families – 14 in the house of Averbach, 21 in the house of Semelman, five in the house of Blechman, eight in the house of Krotchak and 25 in the house of Kligerman – were slaughtered and lay unattended for days. The list of survivors included individuals with 'two wounds to the posterior and left wrist', 'contusions and bayonette wounds to the foot', and one marked '28 wounds in the breast, back, hands and feet'.[23]

Fifteen hundred Jews were killed in Proskurov. The exact number of victims who died elsewhere in the Ukraine between 1917 and 1921 is unknown. The cautious, low figure of between 50,000 and 60,000 with an equal number of wounded is offered by N. Gergel (a member of the Bund who worked for the Russian Red Cross).[24] In August 1920, representatives of 29 nations meeting at Karlsbad were informed that more than 138,000 Jews had been massacred and 130,000 children orphaned as a result of the pogroms.[25] Many of the massacres were perpetrated by forces associated with the Ukrainian National Republic. Others were perpetrated by Tsarist armies under Generals Denikin and Yudenich, disgruntled Bolshevik forces, Polish legionnaires, anarchist bands or rogue units.[26]

NON-PERSONS AND INDIFFERENCE

Between 1917 and 1919, typhus afflicted every third person in Ukraine. While thousands of square miles of grain were left to molder, fruit rotted on trees and livestock strayed untended, families were identified as 'cat', 'dog' or 'horse' families depending on the nature of their regular diet. Jews slept on floors among the rats and scrambled for a potato, onions, a pitcher of milk or a sack of corn meal. As Henry Alsburg wrote of the region in 1920: 'All that one can say is that Ukraine is perhaps one of the nearest places imaginable ... to Hell.'[27]

Two decades before the Russian Revolution, the labor Zionist Nachman Syrkin warned, 'In Russia, where Jews are not emancipated, their condition will not be radically altered through an overthrow of the present political regime. No matter what new class gains control of the government it will not be deeply interested in the emancipation of the Jews.'[28] Lenin condemned pogroms and the Beiliss affair, claiming that the barbarous treatment of Jews surpassed that of Negroes. But like Karl Kautsky, Lenin viewed Jewish nationalism (Zionism) and Jewish socialists who sought autonomy (the Bundists) as a hindrance to human progress.[29]

Stalin had even less use for Jewish culture or identity. At one point, Stalin offered Jews their own *oblast* (territorial home) in Birobidjan, north of the Amur River. Subsequently, Stalin purged the Politburo of its Old Guard Jews. Sharing many of Hitler's racist views, Stalin suppressed criticism of the Nazis on the eve of World War II. There was some easing of anti-Semitism during World War II, as Stalin encouraged all nationalities to unite in the 'Great Patriotic War'. Then in 1948, following the death of his friend A.A. Zhdanov, the Soviet dictator massacred or deported hundreds of Jewish professionals and intellectuals. Before his death in 1952, Stalin succeeded in making more than three million Jews non-persons in his country. Where the *Large Soviet Encyclopedia* of 1932 devoted 117 pages to Jewish history and culture, a revision 20 years later offered just two pages on these anachronisms.[30]

3

The Witches' Brew of Fascism

By the end of the nineteenth century, groups proclaiming themselves anti-Semitic had cropped up in Romania, Austria, Germany, Hungary and the state that regarded itself as the handmaid of liberty – France. On 1 November 1894 *La Libre Parole*, a racist scandal sheet published by Eduard Drumont, bannered a story 'Jewish Traitor Arrested'. French investigators, pursuing a leak of information to the German military attache in Paris, had arrested Captain Alfred Dreyfus. That was all Drumont needed to know, for Dreyfus was a Jew. In an instant, the editor, who had gained fame in 1886 by publishing *La France Juive*, a two-volume diatribe against Jews, judged and convicted Dreyfus. His behavior was not much different from generals charged with resolving the affair. On 22 December 1894, Dreyfus was court-martialled and found guilty of treason, on the basis of what proved to be forged documents. Two weeks later, this lone Jewish officer on the high command was degraded in the courtyard of the École Militaire. On 22 February, he was banished to Devil's Island.[1]

The Dreyfus Affair plunged France into a decade of public strife. Everyone had an opinion not only on his guilt, but also about the role played by Jews in French society. *La Croix*, a popular Catholic journal, blamed Jews for the creation of the republic, for socialism, and anticlericalism. Its editors needed no proof of Dreyfus's guilt, because 'all Jews are guilty'. One reader expressed the hope that Dreyfus might be innocent so he would suffer more. As Drumont called for 'a man of the people who will take up our campaign, who will refuse to be bought off by the Synagogue', Jules Guérin founded *La Ligue antisemitique française*. The next year, Maurice Barres introduced the concept of 'socialist nationalism' to French politics. Max Regis, whose followers chanted '*a mort les juifs! Il faut les pendre! Par leur pif!*' (Death to the Jews! They must be hung! By their snouts!), was elected mayor of Algiers. In that single year, 1898, there were anti-Jewish riots in 70 French towns and 22 openly professing anti-Semitic representatives were elected to the Chamber of Deputies.[2]

Assigned to cover the trial of Dreyfus for *Die Neue Freue Presse* of Vienna, Theodor Herzl observed: 'In France, in republican, modern, civilized France, a hundred years after the Declaration of the Rights of Man.

Until that time most of us believed that the solution of the Jewish question was to be patiently waited for as part of the general development of mankind. But when a people which in every other respect is so progressive and so highly civilized can take such a turn, what are we to expect from other peoples which have not even attained the level France attained a hundred years ago?'[3]

NAPOLEON AND NATIONALISM

The Dreyfus Affair capped a century of war and revolution that left France enervated. More important, the affair symbolized the failure of the Enlightenment. Since the middle of the seventeenth century, Baruch Spinoza, Rene Descartes, John Locke, Isaac Newton, Immanuel Kant and Jean-Jacques Rousseau had taught that human beings were inherently good, born with equal capacity to think and develop. The key to freedom was man's intellect. Just as laws of thermodynamics were revealed by empirical observation, so governments, should be the product of reasonable men acting in a social compact to protect 'inalienable rights'.

England's 'Glorious Revolution' in 1688 and the American revolution a century later seemed to confirm the sanctification of reason. The rise of the bourgeoisie had brought freedom to slaves, serfs, proletarians and Jews. As Erich Fromm wrote, 'The more the middle class succeeded in breaking down the power of the former political or religious rulers, the more men succeeded in mastering nature, and the more millions of individuals became economically independent, the more did one come to believe in a rational world and in man as an essentially rational being.'[4] Instead of a cosmopolitan world based on liberty, equality and fraternity, however, the French Revolution paved the way for Napoleon Bonaparte and tyranny.

Although he boasted of 'consecrating ... the kingdom of reason',[5] Napoleon only ushered in an era of reaction. The rulers of Europe rejected constitutions, popular assemblies and social reform. Just as Pobedonostsev, they stressed stability and rule by the 'best' people. Guided by Austria's Count Metternich, Europe's monarchs suppressed revolts in Spain, Piedmont, Poland, Hungary and Slovakia. In the West, they endorsed Ultramontanism, loyalty to the Pope. In England, unpopulated villages continued sending absentee landlords to Parliament while children chained to carts toiled in coal mines. Millions died of starvation in Ireland while peasants living in wattle huts in Calabria came down with pellagra. The Industrial Revolution with its depersonalization of work and growth of cities diminished the worth of individuals. Isolated and insecure, man was an automaton, a cog in mass production,[6] enduring what Bruno Bettelheim called a *Karteimensch* (punchcard) existence.[7]

ROMANTICISM: MAZZINI AND GARIBALDI

From exile, Napoleon taunted, 'Europe is marching toward inevitable change. There are national aspirations that must be satisfied, sooner or later, and toward this we must march.'[8] The deposed emperor sounded much like Giuseppe Mazzini who envisioned an 'association of nationalities' based not upon reason but instinct and emotion.[9] Mazzini exhorted the young men of Italy to appreciate the 'grand and holy mission confided to you by God'. Such work could be achieved 'only through long effort, and through the living example of austere virtue given to the multitude; by the sweat of the soul; by the sacrifice of your blood; by the ceaseless preaching of truth; by the boldness of faith; by the solemn, unfailing, unchanging enthusiasm, superior to every sorrow that informs the spirit of men who acknowledge no master save God; no instrument but the people; no path save the straight line; no aim but the future of Italy'.[10]

By mid-nineteenth century every European nationality and many in the Western hemisphere were celebrating group virtue in this manner. Hampden Clubs in England, Young Italy, Young America, Decembrists and *Narodniks* in Russia, the Philike Hetaria in Greece, and Burschenschaften in Germany believed that providence had assigned a special place to their people. Eugene Delacroix, Joseph Turner, Franz Schubert, Robert Schumann, Hector Berlioz, Johann Strauss, Peter Tchaikovsky, Ljudevit Gaj, Francis Palacky, Taras Shevchenko, Adamandios Korais, Adam Mickiewicz and Frédéric Chopin were defying conventions in the arts and literature.[11] What began as passionate experiment (what scholars call Romanticism) often devolved into chauvinism, tribal nationalism or something worse.[12] Romanticism died alongside the millions of workingmen, members of international brother-hoods who marched off to kill one another in World War I. As post-war Europe tried to come to grips with new political and economic arrangements, a Danish critic pronounced the death of Romanticism 'in a sort of witches' sabbath in which the philosophers play the part of the old crones, amidst the thunders of the obscurantists, the insane yells of the mystics, and the shouts of the politicians for temporal and ecclesiastical despotism'.

Shortly before his death in Pisa in 1872, Giuseppe Mazzini lamented, 'I had thought to evoke the soul of Italy, but all I find before me is its corpse, rotten with materialism and egoism.' Fifty years of labor culminated in the unification of Italy under Victor Emmanuel in 1870, but Mazzini shuddered at Italy's future.[13] Many of his countrymen seemed captivated by Giuseppe Garibaldi, a professional soldier of fortune, who espoused *putschism*. Though his red-shirted followers yielded conquered territory to the new Italian state, Garibaldi disparaged idealists like Mazzini and Count Camillo Cavour, noting that 'dictatorship, like Machiavellianism, has been wrongly under-stood'. Said Garibaldi: 'Is it not easier to find one honest man than to find five hundred? [i.e. in a parliament]'[14]

Thousands of people in Garibaldi's Italy lived in caves, huts or cellars, subsisting on black barley bread. There were ten people to every room in the working-class district of Rome. More than half of the 10,000 laborers in Sicily's sulphur mines were children. Disease and illiteracy were rampant. Garibaldi spoke directly to these 'unhappy people' from a balcony, reminding them that their husbands and sons had been snatched from the workshop and plough by aristocratic brigands, 'that den of assassins' (the Papacy) and 'that Babylonian anarchy' which 'makes Europe the battlefield for a perpetual strife between misery and luxury'.[15] Garibaldi called for separation of church and state, an end to privileges based on property, a single tax, universal suffrage, free education, and peace through strength. When he died in 1882, the task of inflating the Italian ego fell to Gabriele D'Annunzio, an author-poet who was a disciple of Nietzsche. After spearheading Italy's entry into World War I on the Allied side in 1915, D'Annunzio served as a flyer and naval commander. In September 1919, emulating Garibaldi, he led 1,000 legionnaires in the occupation of the Adriatic port city of Fiume.[16]

MUSSOLINI AND THE MARCH ON ROME

Like much of Europe, post-war Italy was crying for leadership. The nation lost 500,000 men on the battlefields. Prime Minister Vitorio Orlando had gone to Versailles touted as the leader of one of the Big Four powers and returned in a funk. Orlando's successor, Giovanni Giolitti could not unite dissidents in Italy's parliament. Military expenses left the nation bankrupt. Strikes crippled its industry, peasant uprisings threatened its food supply. Italy seemed primed for a Bolshevik revolution.

The man who stepped forward to end this chaos was a 36-year-old political adventurer – Benito Mussolini. The son of an anarchist blacksmith, Mussolini had attended a Catholic seminary – until he was expelled for stabbing a fellow student. In 1902, he went to Switzerland to avoid service in the Italian army. While attending the University of Lausanne, he gravitated toward socialist circles and was twice expelled from the university for political activities. Returning to Milan, he served as editor of the Socialist journal *Avanti* and was jailed in 1911 for denouncing the so-called Macaroni War in Libya. A pacifist, he opposed D'Annunzio's war propaganda, then served in combat. No longer a socialist, in March 1919, Mussolini brought together veterans, irredentists and anti-Bolsheviks and founded his *Fascio di combattimento* (Union of Combat) in Milan. Mussolini's black-shirted *Squadristi* acquired a reputation as strike-breakers and auxiliary police.[17] When in the autumn of 1922, the government of Luigi Facta proved unable to deal with a general strike proclaimed by the Socialists, the fascists took to the streets, seizing control of town councils in Ferrara, Cremona, Parma and Ravenna, burning buildings in other cities, and threatening to march on Rome. When King Victor Emannuel II refused to sanction Prime Minister Facta's call for martial law, Mussolini proceeded to Rome by railway coach. Decked out in spats and walking coat, on 30 October 1922 he was designated Italy's Prime Minister.[18]

Mussolini consolidated his dictatorship along lines suggested by Garibaldi and Napoleon. In his first speech as Prime Minister, Mussolini pointed out that he 'could have chastised all those who ... defamed and tried to injure Fascism', but did not. Shrewdly and methodically, he employed constitutional processes to destroy the constitution. His first cabinet counted only three fascist ministers. At the end of 1923 a new electoral bill awarded two-thirds of the seats in parliament to the party with the largest number of votes in national elections. By this time, the *Squadristi* had been incorporated into the state militia and the fascists triumphed in the 1924 elections. When opposition leader Giacomo Matteotti was assassinated in June, non-fascist representatives walked out of the parliament. Mussolini's response was to dissolve opposition parties, impose censorship and create a state police; so much for parliamentary debates which he dismissed as 'boring masturbation'. Apparently the Italian people agreed. In 1929, 8.6 million cast ballots in support of Fascist party candidates, only 136,000 voted no. Napoleon advised the modern tyrant to make his people feel good by evoking military greatness and pageantry. Posturing from a window to his strutting troops, *il Duce* (the leader) had done just that.[19]

DUCISMO

Fascism is derived from *fasces*, rods tied about an axe carried by lictors as symbols of civil and military authority in ancient Rome. Mussolini was hard-pressed to define fascism, calling it 'the nursling' of action. To Hermann Rauschning fascism was 'the revolution of nihilism', for Hans Morgenthau 'a conglomeration of fragments of ideas'. According to Stanley Payne, a variety of right-wing groups emerged in Europe after World War I – those who were committed fascists (Nazis, Falangists, Arrow Cross, Thunder Cross), conservatives who adopted authoritarian method to maintain the status quo (Carolists in Romania, Croix de Feu in France, Fatherland Front in Austria), and military extremists who embraced violence that bordered on nihilism (Zbor in Yugoslavia, Tautininkai in Lithuania).[20] More recently, Payne has constructed a fascist typology which includes a 'vitalist' ideology, authoritarian state, a series of negations (antiliberalism, anticommunism) and mass organization under a charismatic leader.[21]

Perhaps Helmut Kuhn came closest to defining the totalitarian movement when he called fascism 'the revenge of Passion frustrated and degraded'.[22]

Fascism was an ever-mutating hybrid, taking what was useful from other political ideologies, developing its own mythology, and accepting help from sympathetic clusters of the people. Its overriding principle was expedience. Mussolini was especially indebted to the syndicalist Georges Sorel for his program. For Sorel, violence, direct action and the general strike were the weapons of liberation, not false humanitarianism which stupefied liberal parliaments. Honor, not justice, was the goal of mankind and it could be achieved by individuals combining with others and sacrificing their lives for the state.[23]

For Mussolini, the state embodied the will to power of the people, its creative energies. 'Fascism', he had written, 'rejects ... the conventional life of political equalitarianism clothed in the dress of collective irresponsibility'. Mussolini rejected the socialism of his youth because it was atheistic (he made a point of respecting the special relationship between church and state; the Concordat in 1929 was a model for subsequent dealings between authoritarian governments and clergy) and because it pitted workers against owners. Instead, fascism devised the concept of corporatism where industrialists, workers and consumers collaborate under the direction of the government. Mussolini's 'productionism' aimed at surpassing the per capita output of workers in France and the United States by 1938.[24]

Mussolini understood that for the masses, myth was as important as bread, and so his speeches stressed traditional virtues (honor, truth, courage, obedience) that had given Rome domination over the Mediterranean, and a *horror libertatis* common to fascists. The Duce stressed that fascism was not pacifist ('fascism believes now and always in heroism'). Ever vigilant against its enemies, fascism recognized that 'war alone brings up to their highest tension all human energies and puts the stamp of nobility upon the peoples who have the courage to meet it'.[25]

Initially, anti-Semitism was not a tenet of fascism. Mussolini derived his knowledge of socialism from Angelica Balabanov, a Russian Jew, and co-edited the fascist journal *Gerarchia* with his Jewish mistress Margherita Sarfatti. Five Jews sat among the 119 men who founded the fascist movement in Milan on 23 March 1919 and 225 Jews marched with Mussolini when he seized power. There were 1,770 Jewish members of the *Partito Nazionale Fascista* (PNF) in 1938, nearly 5,000 by 1933. Before Adolf Hitler imbued fascism with his brand of racism, Mussolini restored Italian national pride, put people back to work, and caused trains to run 'on time'. As Payne has written, 'Thus by the 1930s [Italy] had become a sort of model or example for a new kind of syncretistic, semipluralist dictatorship, at least theoretically based on a single state party.'[26] If communism represented a poison to western civilization, fascism seemed to be the antidote. Mussolini's jumble of expedience had great appeal to the disaffected in France, the Low Countries, Central Europe and the successor states of eastern Europe where all sorts of *fascisant* groups were emerging.[27]

HUMAN DYNAMITE

The peacemakers at Versailles hoped to confer self-determination upon a host of frustrated nationalities in eastern Europe. The task proved impossible in a region where 22 million people were identified as minorities. Poland was restored as Wilson promised, but among its 30 million citizens were six million Ukrainians and Russians and three million Jews. Poland's access to the sea came at the expense of one million Germans who lived in a strip (the Polish Corridor) that bifurcated the Old Reich. The seven million people of Romania, who had fought alongside the Allies, were rewarded with Transylvania and 11 million Hungarians, Saxon Germans, Gypsies and Jews, most of whom wanted no part of Romanian rule. Czechs and Slovaks were joined in an artificial republic with three million Sudeten Germans. Six million Orthodox Serbs were granted dominion over three million Catholic Croats, 1.1 million Slovenes, 700,000 Bosnian Muslims, and tens of thousands of Montenegrins, Albanians, Germans, Italians and Jews. Hungary and Austria quarreled over the Burgenland; Lithuania, Poland and Germany over Memel; Russia and Finland over Karelia; Romania and Bulgaria over Dobrudja; Italy, Austria and Yugoslavia over Carinthia-Styria; Bulgaria, Yugoslavia and Greece over Macedonia; Yugoslavia, Italy and Albania over Trieste-Fiume; Romania and Hungary over Banat. Nationalist tensions were so great that one writer termed the situation 'human dynamite'.[28]

Poland, Lithuania, Czechoslovakia, Estonia, Yugoslavia and Latvia were created, in part, to serve with Hungary, Romania and Bulgaria as a *cordon sanitaire* against Bolshevism. To win approval from the peacemakers, the successor states pledged respect for freedom of speech, freedom of the press, trade unions, civil and religious rights of minorities. Each experimented with multi-party parliaments and land reform. Because none of these peoples had experience with republican government, there were riots in the streets and national assemblies, even assassination. (Bulgarian reform leader Alexander Stamboliski was mutilated in 1923; Ion Duca, Prime Minister of Romania, was killed in 1934; Prime Minister Ante Radić was slain on the floor of the Yugoslav parliament in 1928; King Alexander was slain in Paris in 1934.) With the exception of Czechoslovakia each nation ended up embracing some form of quasi-fascist dictatorship.

THE SPOOR OF FASCISM

Aping Mussolini, east European nationalists preached the myth of historical greatness and virtue. They spoke of the need to reclaim historic patrimony, by force if necessary. They warned of enemies (foreign minorities, Jews, trade unionists, plutocrats and communists) and of the need to defend capitalism and Christianity. They talked of the need for unity and loyalty to a single leader, what Italians cheered as *Ducismo*. In Poland, Marshal Josef Pilsudski (*Dzjadek*/Grandpa) seized control of the government in May 1926 and ruled as Minister of War until his death in 1935. In Hungary, Admiral Miklos Horthy established a regency that lasted for 25 years. President Antanas Smetona led Lithuania for 14 years following another coup in 1926. Propped up by the Fatherland Front, Engelbert Dollfuss was Chancellor of Austria between 1929 and 1934. Ante Pavelić was the Croatian *Poglavnik*. *Conducator* Ion Antonescu seized control in Romania in 1940. Monsignor Josef Tiso served as head of the Slovak Republic.[29]

The concept of dictatorship was bolstered by a monolithic political structure. The Farmers Party in Estonia, the Falanga in Poland, the Zbor movement in Serbia all preached chauvinism, irredentism, militarism and anti-Semitism. Most adopted a symbol based on some variant of a cross. In 1937, Poland's major parties the National Radicals (*Naras*) and National Democrats (*Endekis*) formed the Camp of National Unity, an anti-Semitic coalition that supported the militarists. In Hungary power was vested in Horthy's National Unity Party. Horia Sima was the leader of the Iron Guard in Romania, Pavelić of the Croatian Ustashis. Tiso's base in Slovakia was the Hlinka Guard, named for ultra-nationalist priest Andrei Hlinka.

Fascism touched a responsive chord in many segments of the population. Superstitious peasants (50–80 percent in Slovakia and Ukraine were illiterate) looked to village priests or landlords for direction.[30] Fear of peasant unrest prompted landed gentry and industrialists to support a movement that diverted hostility away from themselves. In Italy, the *Confindustria*, a confederation of industrialists, functioned alongside state syndicates. The 1934 Austrian constitution spoke of seven national corporations that were to represent every aspect of the nation's population. In Poland the *pans* (nobles) created the Leviathan, an economic cartel that controlled mines, textile trades, coal fields and lumber production. When squabbles erupted among his police, Alexander of Yugoslavia assumed a royal dictatorship in 1929. After a decade of civil strife, Boris of Bulgaria took control of his army and police in 1935. Carol of Romania, living in exile till 1926, returned to his homeland to serve as regent, then dictator. Monsignor Hlinka attacked Germans and Jews for the plight of Slovaks in the 1920s. From Gnieszno, Poland in 1936, Primate August Hlond called for a boycott of Jewish businesses. In Romania, Miron Christea, patriarch of the Orthodox Church, said in 1937, 'One feels like crying with pity for the good Romanian Nation whose very marrow has been sucked from its bones by the Jews. To defend ourselves is a national and patriotic duty, not anti-Semitism.' His aide, Archdeacon Jon Mota, called for 'drastic treatment on the lines of the grand master Hitler'.[31] Russian émigrés who had lost everything to the Bolsheviks, unemployed veterans like the *Heimwehr* in Austria, *Legionnaires* in Romania and *Vlajka* in Czechoslovakia, Bulgarian youth groups, lawyers, shopkeepers and members of the civil service all rallied to the fascist cause, eager to identify the enemy responsible for their own plight and that of their nation.

GOVERNMENT BY PERSECUTION

Hitler's rise to power caused little sensation in central and eastern Europe because most governments there had already experienced flirtation with dictatorship. During the inter-war period, conservatives, right-wing militarists and fascists adopted the following anti-Jewish decrees: [32]

1. **Restriction of citizenship.** In Romania and Hungary, Jews were required to provide written proof of residence dating beyond World War I. This was particularly onerous since such documentation would likely be found in government buildings, prime objects of attack in wartime. In Latvia, Jews were permitted to seek naturalization after 20 years. Poland restricted Jewish participation in elections for the Sejm and barred them from 'Polonizing' their names.
2. **Deportation and emigration.** Lithuanians fretted about the presence of so many Jews in 'our cities'. Slovaks complained that Jews were responsible for the Germanization of their culture. Every session of the Polish Sejm debated expelling Jews. Some 185,000 Jews left between 1921 and 1925, and another 86,000 between 1927 and 1931. As late as 1935, the Poles dispatched a commission to explore the possibility of shipping thousands of Jews to Madagascar.
3. **Trade restrictions.** State monopolies in Poland and Romania made it impossible for Jews to engage in the trade of tobacco, liquor, salt, matches or public transport. If the Leviathan in Poland had its way, Jews would have been eliminated from the textile industry as well. The idea was to impoverish Jews or drive them from the country. Twelve thousand Romanian Jews lost their businesses in the inter-war period.
4. **Sponsorship of anti-Semitic literature.** Anti-Semitic pamphlets, including *The Protocols of Elders of Zion*, were distributed by state printing offices. The governments of Poland, Latvia or Romania also posted placards lampooning Jews as economic bloodsuckers or rats responsible for joblessness, war and disease.
5. **Boycotts, pickets and mass demonstrations.** Jewish businesses were picketed and boycotted with official approval. Governments sponsored massive street rallies like that in Bucharest in 1936 which attracted 280,000 Iron Guardists, thousands of Endekis in Warsaw in 1938, and thousands more among the Arrow Cross in Budapest in 1944.
6. **Interference with Jewish religious liberties.** Jews were forced to observe Sunday as a day of rest, losing an additional day of work. After 1936, Poland emulated Switzerland by banning *shehitah*. Between 1918 and

1939, Jewish cemeteries and houses of worship were desecrated in Romania, Poland, Hungary and the Baltic states.

7. **Abrogation of minority rights guarantees.** Before 1939, there were no ministers of Jewish affairs, no Jewish consistories to represent the rabbis before the government, no special currency privileges, no special rules governing the travel of Jews out of the land, no state documents or newspapers published in Yiddish or Hebrew.

8. **Numerus clausus.** Hungary instituted a quota system in 1938, limiting the number of Jews in professions to 20 percent. A year later the number was reduced to 6 percent in the professions, 12 percent in the work force. Bulgaria restricted them to 1 percent of the professions. In Poland, they were allotted only 1 percent of the civil servants. The number of Jewish students declined from 9,000 in 1922 to 4,000 in 1938. In the academic year 1938/39 six Jewish students were killed at the University of Lemberg as some Poles joked about the need for a *numerus nullus*.[33]

9. **Deliberate impoverishment and unfair taxation.** Poland's Jews (10 percent of the population) paid 35 percent of their nation's taxes. Leather Street in Vilna, the Nalewki district in Warsaw and Poddenbem in Lemberg were among the worst slums in Europe. Eighty percent of the Jewish children in a Vilna school were tubercular or anemic, 57 percent in Grodno. As families starved, parents offered to sell their children in return for food. In Romania, Jews were required to help underwrite Orthodox schools that they could not attend.

10. **Pogroms.** Thirty thousand Jews were killed in the so-called 'Cold Pogrom' conducted by forces of Marshal Pilsudski in 1920–21, thousands more in massacres in 1936. Five thousand Jews died in the 'White Gloved Pogroms' of 1920 carried out by reactionary forces of Admiral Horthy. There were assaults against Jewish homes, businesses and synagogues in Czechoslovakia and Romania. Many who defended themselves were arrested and thrown into jail as provocateurs.

Ultimately all of the successor states caved in before totalitarianism. 'Liberated' by German troops in the summer of 1941, the Baltic states supported massacres of what they deemed Jewish Bolsheviks. At first Tiso's puppet regime unhesitatingly shipped out Jews. Then, worried about the treatment of converts and lacking sufficient labor, the government of Slovakia delayed deportations. Croatia and Bosnia supported 'ethnic cleansing' not only of Jews but of Serbs as well. Romanian anti-Semites, particularly in the region of Transnistria, were more vicious and thorough than some of their Nazi counterparts. And while some leaders in Hungary expressed concern about the disposition of their countrymen, 400,000 Jews would be shipped out to their deaths in Auschwitz.

Jewish survivors who straggled home after World War II found that the attitudes of their countrymen had not changed. Jimmy Elder spent the final year of the war in four concentration camps. He saw his mother and sister selected for the gas chamber. When he returned to school in Hungary in the fall of 1945, his classmates asked nonchalantly, 'Where were you?' He tried to explain, but the students were not interested. Esther Bitman went back to her family's home in Rachov, a small town in the Carpathians. Her parents and several siblings were dead. The house was empty. When she visited her neighbors, she discovered her mother's doilies decorating their table. Sixteen-year-old Eva Fugman returned to Pionki where she grew up in a family of six children. Only she and one sister survived. Her neighbors greeted them with: 'You're still alive? So many Jews still alive?' Eva Fugman left Poland never to return. By April 1946, 800 Polish Jews had been killed in post-war pogroms. Deep-rooted hatreds erupted in another massacre at Kielce on 4 July 1946. More than a year after the end of World War II, months after the world knew that Jews had been gassed at Auschwitz, a ritual murder accusation resulted in the deaths of 41 Jews.[34]

4

The Metapolitics of Nazism

Fascism in the Mediterranean and eastern Europe might be ascribed to puffery and poorly educated masses. The question that has befuddled scholars for some 70 years, though, is how could Nazism captivate a sophisticated nation like Germany? This was the land that produced composers like Bach, Mozart, Handel and Haydn, a land whose philosophers – Kant and Hegel – extolled world peace. The poet Wolfgang Johann Goethe had written, 'Noble let man be, helpful and good – for that alone distinguishes him from all creatures of our knowledge', and Beethoven had adapted the words of his friend Friedrich Schiller's *Ode to Joy* as the central theme to his Ninth Symphony.

Some scholars see in Adolf Hitler the epitome of a Germany that never produced a national humorist, never learned to laugh at itself, and instead cleaved to authority and paternalism. Fromm suggests that Germans were a people in disequilibrium, suffering a national psychosis.[1] Jay Gonen and John Weiss speak of immutable national characteristics which include a Manichaean world outlook, infantile myths, suicidal sacrifice, and a predisposition for totalitarian organization.[2] Daniel Goldhagen painted broad strokes of 'ordinary Germans' – civilians who rampaged through the streets on Kristallnacht, middle-aged policemen who joined killing squads at Lomazy in 1942, and concentration camp guards who abused prisoners even when the war was lost. Goldhagen discerned an 'eliminationist anti-Semitism' in nineteenth-century Germany, a country he found to be more anti-Jewish than France or Russia.[3] In that same century, the poet Heinrich Heine offered a melancholy assessment of the Germans' love of war. According to Heine, Christianity temporarily subdued the 'brutal warrior ardor' of ancient tribesmen. But, one day, when the talisman rots, the 'frantic berseker rage whereof Northern poets have said and sung so much' would break forth again and 'Thor with his giant hammer … will shatter the Gothic cathedrals'.[4]

Through the Napoleonic Wars, a hodgepodge of 38 German principalities, free cities and leagues were sustained by prophets like Achim Arnim, Theodor Koerner, Ernst Arndt, Heinrich von Kleist and Johann Fichte.[5] These zealots taught that Germans were a god-blessed people. The foremost spokesman of these early Teutomaniacs was the citizen soldier Fichte. In the winter of 1807–8, Fichte delivered a series of *Addresses to the German Nation* at Berlin's Academy of Sciences. Speaking under the scrutiny of an occupation army, Fichte condemned contemporary morality. National regeneration could be accomplished by a dynamic spirit which the German people alone possessed. According to Fichte, Germans were an *Urvolk*, a primal people that could be traced to the beginning of time. 'To have character and to be German', he wrote, 'undoubtedly mean the same. All comparisons between the German and the non-German are null and void. We are a chosen people. Chosen by God with a moral right to fulfill our destiny by every means of cunning and force.' One year after the Holy Roman Empire was dissolved, Fichte called upon Germans to unite in a patriotic state that would be a force in international diplomacy and commerce. 'If ye sink', he told them, 'humanity sinks with you, without hope of future restoration.'[6]

The French represented the principal, though not exclusive, obstacle to the revival that Fichte preached. A century before, Andreas Eisenmenger warned the German people of a more insidious enemy in his 2,000-page study *Entdecktes Judentum* (Judaism Uncovered). Trained in Semitic languages, Eisenmenger cited passages from Hebrew texts that supposedly illustrated the corrupt nature of Judaism.[7] By the time Napoleon destroyed the ghetto walls in western Europe, other German academics were demanding that Jewish tradesmen be forced to wear a 'national cockade' or expelled to British colonial plantations. Fichte was not oblivious to the negative image of the Jew. Writing in the midst of Jacobin terror (1793), he declared that Jews were loyal not to their respective states but to an invisible empire. 'A mighty state stretches across almost all the countries of Europe, hostile in intent and engaged in constant strife with everyone else', said Fichte, 'this is Jewry.' Reluctant to withdraw emancipation, he nevertheless inspired subsequent Jew-baiters when he said, 'The only way I see which civil rights can be conceded to the Jews is to cut off all their heads in one night and to set new ones on their shoulders which should contain not a single Jewish idea'.[8]

Like many German intellectuals, Fichte had difficulty reconciling images of Spinoza and Mendelssohn with Jewish street peddlers.[9] Kant denounced Judaism as a set of putrefied legal concepts, but he maintained contacts with individual Jews (Markus Herz, Solomon Maimon, Lazarus Bendavid) whom he admired. Goethe and Schiller enjoyed the camaraderie of Jewish salons in Berlin. Friedrich Schleiermacher and Friedrich Schlegel spurned any connection between Jesus and Judaism, yet such bigotry did not prevent Schlegel from marrying the daughter of Mendelssohn. Clemens Brentano publicly equated Jews with Philistines and privately adored Rahel Varnhagen. Ernst Arndt worked for more than 40 years to block the granting of civil rights to Jews who were cheating, destructive vermin. Yet, he too, was fascinated by the Jewess Henriette Herz.[10]

THE BURSCHENSCHAFTEN: JAHN

In Germany romanticism and nationalism were kept alive by professors and students, dueling societies and bully clubs that attacked religious and national minorities. The godfather of these *Burschenschaften* was Friedrich Jahn (1778–1852). A professor of philology from Leipzig, Jahn despised everything French. 'The father who lets his daughter learn French', he said, 'is as good as a man who apprentices his daughter to whoredom'. Accompanying allied armies into Paris in 1815, Jahn clambered to the top of the Arc de Triomphe and defaced the statue of the goddess Victory. Dressed in a beard and medieval costume, Jahn glorified German culture. He coined the term *Volkstum* (what people have in common in thinking, feeling, loving, hating and faith) and declared, 'the holiest moment in history is when the masses awaken to an awareness of the eternity of their own Volkhood'. Jews and Gypsies, lacking visible roots, had no *Volkstum*. Jahn called for the unification of all Germans (including the Swiss, Dutch and Danes) by a leader with a new capital called Teutonia.[11]

In the fall of 1817, elements of the *Burschenschaften* gathered at the Wartburg castle to mark the 300th anniversary of Luther's Reformation consigned two dozen texts to a bonfire. Among the condemned works were the Code Napoleon, Kotzebue's *German History*, the journal *Alemannia*, and books by the Jew Saul Ascher and Prussian Minister Schmalz. Of such actions, Heine warned, 'When they burn books, it is men they will burn next'. Over the next 15 years, mobs of students, soldiers and burghers chanting HEP! HEP! (an acronym for *Hierosolyma est Perdita*, Jerusalem is destroyed) ran amok through the former ghettos of Bavaria, Saxony, Austria, Lübeck and Bremen, hoping to purge the Fatherland of its enemies.

THE GLORIFICATION OF WAR: TREITSCHKE

Germany was united not by self-proclaimed Crusaders, but through the 'blood and iron' policies of its chancellor Otto von Bismarck. Heinrich Treitschke at the University of Berlin became an enthusiastic supporter of the Chancellor's militarist policies. Treitschke argued that the state was an organic entity embodying the aspirations of its people. Born in violence, the state was entitled to seize *Lebensraum* by any means. Said Treitschke,

> War is the test whereby the weak and cowardly are recognized and punished justly. Without war, no state could be. All those we know of arose through war and the protection of their members by armed force remains their primary and essential task. The grandeur of war lies in the utter annihilation of puny man in the great conception of the state and it brings out the full magnificence of the sacrifice of fellow countrymen for one another. In war, the chaff is winnowed from the wheat.

A believer in the 'bravery of the Aryan race', Treitschke looked to a time when Germany, allied with Spain, and ruling most of central Europe, would succeed Great Britain as the dominant world empire.[12]

Initially ambivalent toward Jews, Treitschke hoped that restraint on the part of Germans might lead to their assimilation. He declined to sign an anti-Jewish petition and even praised the contributions of Mendelssohn, Veit and Neander. In November 1879, however, this man who had been disparaged as a philo-Semite, reversed himself. Writing in the *Preussische Jahrbücher*, he resurrected Luther's credo that 'the Jews are our national misfortune'. Like Drumont in France, Treitschke blamed Jewish speculators for the worldwide financial panic in 1873. Wrote Treitschke, 'From the East frontier there pours year by year from the inexhaustible Polish cradle a huge number of ambitious, trouser-selling youths, whose children and children's children, in times to come, will dominate Germany's stock exchanges and newspapers.'[13] As he explained in his *History of Germany*, such Jews remained devoted to 'huckstering and usury' and 'the fanaticism of the Talmud faith'. Jews were guilty of 'parochial narrowness', 'morbid arrogance', 'crude intolerance' and 'cosmopolitanism'. Jews who owed no loyalty to any nation and who declined to serve in the military were responsible for the disintegration of the national spirit. It was the Jews who welcomed the French and their culture into Germany even after the defeat of Napoleon. 'Never before in history', wrote Treitschke, 'had the victor bent his neck thus willingly beneath the yoke of the vanquished.' Jews had penetrated literary circles, seized control of the press, and saturated Germany with their hatred of Christianity and 'shameless disrespect of the fatherland'. Treitschke took comfort in the knowledge that most German sages since Luther despised the Jews. And though he did not endorse a campaign of retribution, Treitschke warned Jews of 'the old *furia tedesca* – the savage wrath of the northern beserkers'.[14]

THE WILL TO POWER: NIETZSCHE

Friedrich Nietzsche shared Treitschke's aversion for Jews, disdaining teachings that produced a slave morality of *ressentiment*.[15] He ridiculed Jews as *chandala* (a hybrid race) that invented nothing. In letters to Richard Wagner, Nietzsche railed against French-Jewish superficiality and noted how Jews everywhere wanted to be in the vanguard.[16] But this son of a Lutheran minister from Leipzig also praised Jews as the principal spreaders of rationalism. He refused to break with Paul Ree, even when the Wagners made an issue of his friendship with a Jew in 1877.[17] Before he was institutionalized in a mental asylum in 1888, Nietzsche made it clear that he wanted little to do with *Kultur-Philistines*, blockheads who gorged themselves on nationalist pamphlets and Wagnerian music. He despised Treitschke, denounced Wagner as decadent and called Eugen Dühring 'a foaming fool'.[18] According to Nietzsche, the Wagnerites were leading Jews 'to the slaughterhouse'.[19] The extremists reciprocated, calling him unpatriotic, unmanly, and, as Wagner intimated, the deranged product of masturbation. And yet, in a letter to Franz Overbeck dated 24 March 1887, Nietzsche delighted in pointing out how he enjoyed a 'strange and mysterious respect among all radical parties'. Hardly an issue of an anti-Semitic journal appeared without some interpretation of his philosophy 'which gave me a good laugh'. His final judgment of the German nationalists scribbled in that hospital in Basel stated simply, 'I want to have all anti-Semites shot.'[20]

In two works written before his mental collapse – *Thus Spake Zarathustra* (1883) and *Beyond Good and Evil* (1886) – the disciple of Schopenhauer outlined a world view devoid of grand scheme or deity. 'This universe', he wrote, 'is a monster of energy, without beginning or end; a fixed and brazen quantity of energy which grows neither bigger nor smaller, which does not consume itself, but only alters its face.' Nietzsche's Dionysian world was one of eternal self-creation, self-destruction. In short, 'this world is the will to power and nothing else! And even ye yourselves are this will to power and nothing besides!' Said Nietzsche, 'One should not suppose the mission of a higher species to be the leading of inferior men; but the inferior should be regarded as the foundation upon which a higher species may live their higher life, upon which alone they can stand.' Then, invoking a term that would appeal to the Nazis, he advised, 'I teach you the Superman. Man is something that is to be surpassed. What have ye done to surpass man? All beings hitherto have created something beyond themselves: and ye want to be the ebb of that great tide, and would rather go back to the beast than surpass man? What is the ape to man? A laughing stock, a thing of shame. And just the same man shall be to the Superman: a laughing stock, a thing of shame. Lo, I teach you the Superman! The Superman is the meaning of the earth. Let your will say: the Superman shall be the meaning of the earth!'[21]

Beyond Good and Evil contains numerous epigrams that sound as if they come from Hitler's speeches: 'You, I advise not to work, but to fight. You I advise not to peace, but to victory. Let your work be a fight, let your peace be a victory.' 'Ye say it is the good cause which halloweth even war? I say unto you it is the good war which halloweth every cause.' 'War and courage have done more great things than charity.' 'Write with blood and you learn that spirit is blood.'[22] In 1940 Crane Brinton conceded, 'Nietzsche wrote much the Nazis find delightful; he also wrote much they cannot bear to hear, and certainly cannot bear to have repeated.'[23] More recently, Steven Aschheim has concluded that Nietzsche's teachings could be fitted into practically any ideology.[24] In a sense, Nietzsche was hijacked by the very nationalists he despised.[25] His sister Elisabeth altered letters addressed to his mother to make it appear that he was writing to her and that he shared her brand of fanaticism. Elisabeth's husband, Bernhard Förster, a minor figure in anti-Semitic circles, circulated Nietzsche's writings and made Elisabeth a celebrity among the Nazis after she returned from a failed colonial venture in

Paraguay. Earlier, Nietzsche made it clear that his brother-in-law played no role in his personal or professional life. 'My dealings with him are very polite but aloof', he wrote in 1887, 'and as infrequent as possible.'[26]

THE ARYAN MYTH: HOUSTON STEWART CHAMBERLAIN

There was nothing ambiguous about the writings of Houston Stewart Chamberlain, an English dilettante who married the daughter of Richard Wagner. In 1899, Chamberlain published a ponderous, two-volume study of civilization, *The Foundations of the Nineteenth Century*. Chamberlain's claim of objectivity[27] was contradicted in a long chapter, 'The Entrance of the Jews into the History of the West', which was a primer on anti-Semitism. For Chamberlain, Jews were parasites, eternal aliens, a people that created no art or philosophy. With the exception of a few positive characteristics, 'all the meanness of which men are capable seem concentrated in this one nation; the grinning mask of vice stares out in unveiled nakedness'. Whenever Jews were treated with kindness, they responded with intolerance.[28] Like Eisenmenger, Chamberlain charged that Judaism was 'a disintegrating force', polytheistic and materialistic, 'the arrest of development'. The Torah was the product of 'demoniacal power and will', the Talmud a dreary collection of rubbish and abominable sayings. The goal of Judaism, expressed in the Book of Ezekiel, was to consume and enslave all other nations.[29]

In Chamberlain's view, Jews were Semites, by nature one-sided and fanatical. Descended from Bedouin, they were lazy, deceitful, cruel, greedy, cowardly, rightly regarded by all nations as the scum of mankind. Some were Syrians, roundheaded, poor soldiers, easily vanquished. At least half possessed the Hittite nose and were unintelligent. The Ashkenazim were a vulgar crowd, fickle, wretched and filthy.[30] From these convoluted notions of anthropology, Chamberlain concluded, 'The Jewish race is a permanent but mongrel race which retains its mongrel character.'[31] The Jewish master plan was that one day there would only be one pure race, the Jews, and all the rest would be 'a herd of pseudo-Hebraic mestizos, a people beyond all doubt, degenerate physically, mentally and morally'.[32] Chamberlain advised his readers: 'A man can very soon become a Jew without being an Israelite. Often it needs only to have frequent intercourse with Jews, to read Jewish news-papers, to accustom himself to Jewish philosophy, literature and art.'[33]

One figure definitely not a Jew was Jesus Christ. According to Chamberlain, Jesus was good-looking, friendly, idealistic, independent, a leader, all qualities foreign to Jews. 'Whoever makes the assertion that Jesus was a Jew is ignorant or insincere', said Chamberlain.[34] The only ray of light in the chaos of the Roman empire came from the north. The Teutons warded off the Asiatic peril. The Teutons' thirst for knowledge and love of freedom preserved classical law codes. Mentally and physically superior to other races in Europe, the Teutons were entitled to dominate wherever they chose. The best nations (Italy, Spain, France, Germany) were descended from Teutonic stock. On his deathbed in 1923, Chamberlain was introduced to Adolf Hitler and called him heaven-sent. 'My faith in the Germans has never wavered for a moment', he said, 'but my hope, I must own, was sunk to a low ebb. At one stroke you have transformed the state of my soul. Now I may go to sleep because you have been born.'[35]

PAMPHLETEERS OF HATE

Adolf Hitler was familiar with Treitschke, Nietzsche and Chamberlain, but the Nazi leader preferred brief, strident articles like those in the *Linzer Fliegender* and the Vienna *Alldeutsche Tagblatt*. The Austrian *Bauer* also favored racist pamphlets like August Röhling's *Talmud Jew* (1871); Eugen Dühring's *The Jewish Question as a Problem of Racial Character* (1880); Theodor Fritsch's *Handbuch der Judenfrage* (which went through 26 printings by 1907) and Julius Langbehn's *Rembrandt as Educator* that stressed hatred of Jews for Germans. Guido List and George Lanz urged their people to rally behind a *Führer* who would carry the fight against *Rassenschande* (racial shame) and *Mischlingsblut* (mixed blood) 'as far as the castration knife'.[36] According to Paul de Lagarde, Jews were diseased, usurious vermin, they had to be exterminated as quickly as possible. 'With trichinae and bacilli, one does not negotiate, nor are trichinae and bacilli subject to education', he said. Long before the Nazis fired ovens in Upper Silesia with human bodies, de Lagarde advised, 'There can be no doubt that a Kingdom of Lodomeria or a Duchy of Oswieczyn (Auschwitz) or a Grand Duchy of Ruthenia are impossible.'[37]

These crude ideas found support in Alfred Plotz whose Race Hygiene Institute condemned the creation of a *Mischmashvolk*,[38] and Arthur Dinter whose *Sünde wider das Blut* (1921) preached the concept of telegony (one sexual contact with an inferior male permanently taints a superior female). Hitler was especially fond of Otto Weininger whose *Sex and Character* (1903) went through 18 editions. For Weininger, temperament, intelligence, even body smells confirmed the superiority of men and whites over women and blacks. There was another inherently inferior group. The Jewish race, an anthropological hybrid ('the readily curling hair points to the Negro; admixture of Mongolian blood is suggested by the perfectly Chinese or Malay formation of face and skull') engendered its own problems. According to Weininger, no one was more likely to be anti-Semitic than Jews themselves, for daily they came into contact with other Jews and they understood 'that no one who has had experience of them considers them lovable'.[39] Considering their character and physical flaws, Jews should not exist. Weininger, a Jew who converted to Protestantism, earned Hitler's admiration, by committing suicide.

RICHARD WAGNER: *JUDAISM IN MUSIC*

The Teutomaniac who had the greatest influence upon Hitler was the classical composer Richard Wagner (1813–83). Said Hitler: 'For me, Wagner is something godly and his music is my religion. I go to his concerts as others go to church.' Other critics were more severe. According to Max Nordau, Wagner was 'the last mushroom on the dunghill of Romanticism'.[40] Nietzsche called him 'an oracle from the other world' and asked 'Is Wagner a man? Is he not a disease?'[41]

Scholars trace some of Wagner's pan-Germanism to the confusion surrounding his childhood. His father, Carl Friedrich, died in Leipzig six months after Richard was born. There was some delay in having the infant Wagner baptized. Subsequently, his mother married a painter-actor named Ludwig Geyer. Until he was 14, Wagner carried the name and stigma of his stepfather as Geyer was a name associated with Jews. For the remainder of his life, Wagner was attacked by music critics and racial demagogues for having 'Jewish blood', even though there is no evidence to suggest that Geyer was Jewish or that he was the composer's natural father.[42]

The young Wagner was a member of the *Burschenschaften*. In 1839, inspired by Polish émigrés, he traveled to France. Deemed a radical during the revolution of 1848, Wagner fled to Switzerland with his collection of French colognes and satin dressing gowns.[43] He picked up something else while in Paris – an intense hatred of Jews. The words of anarchist Pierre Joseph Proudhon inspired him:

> Write an article against this race which poisons everything by butting in everywhere ... Demand their expulsion from France, except for Jews married to Frenchwomen: liquidate their synagogues; deny them any kind of employment; work for the abolition of their religious practices. Not for nothing did the Christians call them Godkillers. The Jew is the enemy of mankind. This race must be sent back to Asia or else be exterminated.[44]

There was a professional element in Wagner's anti-Semitism. He expected to be hailed as a second Beethoven when he went to Paris. Instead, accolades went to Giacomo Meyerbeer, Jules Halevy, Jacques Offenbach and Felix Mendelssohn, all of whom he identified as Jews.[45] Wagner especially resented Mendelssohn, whose artistry was celebrated at age 17. At first, the two were on polite terms. Wagner expressed admiration for Mendelssohn's 'Hebrides Overture' and submitted a copy of a symphony for his evaluation.[46] In time, Wagner turned against Mendelssohn and Meyerbeer, dismissing their works as boring travesties, caricatures of synagogue chants or archaic compositions which he labeled 'foreign, cold, strange, listless, unnatural and distorted' (*fremdartig, kalt, sonderlich, gleichgüeltig, unnatürlich und verdreht*).[47]

Wagner's hostility toward Jews generally was revealed in two articles he contributed to the *Neue Zeitschrift für Musik* in September 1850. Intended as cultural essays, they were republished in pamphlet form as *Das Judentums in der Musik*. Like Franz Liszt's *Gypsies and Their Music in Hungary* (1861), *Das Judentums* was nothing but a tired recitation of anti-Semitic charges made by Fichte, Jahn, de Gobineau and Marx. Wagner exulted the virtue and collective will of the Volk. The people had fallen from a state of grace because they had naively accepted un-German concepts like democracy, equality and freedom of the press. The culprits who managed to dominate German media, business and arts were Jews. Some, like the Rothschilds, used wealth to insinuate themselves into positions of influence. As Wagner declared, 'He [the Jew] rules and will rule, so long as money remains the power before which all our doings and our dealings lose their force.'[48]

Wagner was especially upset with the success of Jewish musicians and writers. 'Disagreeably foreign', 'art-fiends', 'freaks of nature', Jews contributed nothing to civilization. They could not share the *Leidenschaften* (passions) of the nation, had no claim on *Volksgeist* (national spirit). Jews were soulless wanderers hostile to European art and civilization. Whether the poems of Heine or the speech of a Jewish tradesman, Jews were incapable of artistic expression because of their inability to speak German or any other language properly. 'The first thing that strikes our ear as quite outlandish and unpleasant, in the Jew's production of the voice sounds is a creaking, squeaking, buzzing, snuffle ... an intolerably jumbled blabber' (*zischender, schrillender, summender, und murksender Lautausdruck ... eines unerträglich verwirrten Geklappers*).[49]

In 1850 and again in 1869 when *Das Judentums* was republished, Wagner called for an end to constitutional monarchy. The draft-dodger of 1833 called for universal military training to mold a nation of true Germans. Echoing Marx, he called for the Jews to cease revering Mammon. He also urged Germans to recognize that baptism could not erase the biological and spiritual differences between Jews and Germans. The only thing that could save both peoples was a conversion in spirit, the abandonment of Judaism. As Wagner advised, 'Remember that only one thing can redeem you from the burden of your curse: the redemption of Ahasuerus – going under.'[50]

WAGNER IN BAYREUTH

The middle decades of the nineteenth century were productive ones for Wagner. It was in this period that he composed *Rienzi*, *Lohengrin*, *Das Rheingold* and *Die Walküre*, *Tristan and Isolde*, *Die Meistersinger von Nürnberg* and the *Siegfried Idyll*. Lush, melodic works, these compositions glorified fair-haired Nordics and disparaged dark, alien intruders. Wagner portrayed the interaction of gods with humans, destruction and rebirth, eternity in Valhalla. His ultimate goal was to stage a perfect blend of Germanism and Christianity (*Parsifal*).[51] Scholars debate the political implications of these works. Said Thomas Mann: 'I go farther than Peter Viereck. I find an element of Nazism not only in Wagner's questionable writings. I find it also in his music.'[52] Michael Tanner scrutinized Wagner's operas and found them free of anti-Semitism.[53] Marc Weiner believes that Wagner's librettos and the screechy music ascribed to villains like Mime, Alberich, Hagen, Beckmesser, Hagen and Klingsor served as an outlet for his bigotry. Indeed, the large noses, beards, foul odors, awkward gait, clubfeet and other deformities, love of money, sexual threat, and treachery associated with these characters are evocative of the medieval image of Jews.[54]

Through the patronage of Ludwig II, King of Bavaria, after 1876 Wagner's operas were staged in a spacious theater at Bayreuth.[55] He settled here after marrying Cosima Liszt, the daughter of Franz Liszt. It was in Haus Wahnfried, his baronial mansion in Bayreuth, that Wagner spun his weird blend of metapolitics. Well into the night he regaled guests with theories of German nationalism, vegetarianism, yearning for a folk-deliverer, contempt for rationalism, hatred of Catholics, bankers, democrats and Jews. In this last regard, he was cheered by his wife Cosima, descended on her mother's side from the house of Simon Bethmann, a Jewish banker from Frankfurt.[56]

Wagner was unrelenting in his Judaeophobia. As he told Liszt, anti-Semitism was 'as necessary to my nature as gall is to blood'. He blamed Jews for his financial problems while working on *Das Rheingold* in 1854. A year later, responding to negative reviews in London (Wagner had worn gloves while conducting Mendelssohn's 'Italian Symphony'), he scored the British press as a 'pack of vagabond Jews'. When *Tannhäuser* was hissed at its Paris debut in 1861, he blamed German Jews in the audience. A similar reaction to the first performance of *Meistersinger* in Vienna in 1877 was written off to collaboration of Austrian Jews and Catholics. In 1881, Wagner wrote to King Ludwig asking that the Kappellmeister Hermann Levy should not conduct the premier of his 'most Christian of works', *Parsifal*. (Wagner had tried in vain to convert Levy who conceded his Jewish background was 'a walking anachronism'.) Ludwig's response ('there is nothing so nauseous, so unedifying as disputes of this sort; at bottom all men are brothers whatever their confessional differences') so enraged Wagner that he exploded at the Bavarian king, denouncing Jews as 'the congenital enemies of humanity and all that is noble' (*dass ich die jüdische Race fur den gebornen Feind der reinen Menscheit*). To his credit, Ludwig did not back down, insisting that if his orchestra performed, so would Levy.[57]

In 1877, Wagner helped establish the *Bayreuther Blätter*. Ostensibly a cultural publication, the journal served as another outlet for Wagner's personal tantrums. Between 1879 and 1881, he published a series of articles espousing vegetarianism (Nietzsche called them 'a vegetable affair'). For Wagner, vivisection was an anti-Christian act. Jesus had died for all breathing things, including little animals. Northern climates encouraged meat-eating, violence, warfare. According to Wagner, if men emigrated to warmer areas, they could live on fruits and vegetables, become less violent, like vegetarian tigers and panthers he claimed inhabited parts of Canada, or the peaceful Japanese.[58] In 'What is German?' (February 1878) Wagner decried the effrontery of Jews who raised opulent synagogues in German cities. In 'What Boots this Knowledge' (December 1880) he called upon the people to prepare for war.[59] Three months later in 'Know Thyself', he denounced German culture as 'a barbaro-Jewish medley'. He blamed the concept of property which benefited only Jews, pretenders to a 'Mosaic confession', but in reality the only race which appreciated the importance of blood. While Germans were weakened by intermarriage with Walloons, Croats, Spanish, French and Swedes, Jews, 'the plastic demon of man's downfall', remained 'unaltered'.[60]

THE LEGACY OF WAGNER

Wagner's moral collapse can be seen in *Heldentum und Christentum* (Heroism and Christianity) published in September 1881. Originally, Aryans, the seed of the gods, capable of heroism, metaphysics, self-control, had been the chosen race. Their golden age of peace and prosperity was eroded through intermarriage and the eating of meat. Those responsible for this fall of man were Jews, 'former cannibals, educated to be the business leaders of our society'. As proof, he offered Adam and Eve, expelled from the garden of Eden not because they tasted flesh, but because they ate from forbidden fruit. Cain struck his brother dead because the Jews' bloodthirsty deity found Abel's fatted lamb *shmackhafter* – tastier. The Jew was outside the cycle of racial betterment. Their pleas for toleration, assimilation, were nothing but covers for sexual indulgence and the fouling of blood. For, in the end, 'racial decline through wrong marriage' has been more pernicious to the human race than any other thing.[61] Germans could submit to *Untergang* (downfall) and 'simply croak in the gutter'. Or they could fight back like gods. Christ's blood was 'the divine substance to preserve Aryans and elevate lower races'. The blood of the savior, 'the quintessence of free willed suffering and godlike compassion', 'the procreative force' that would redeem those who understood the importance of racial purity.[62]

Adolf Hitler's debt to Wagner is clear. The *Führer* claims to have been inspired to become an artist when he attended his first opera (*Lohengrin*) at the age of 12. Hitler told friends that the Nazi dream was born in Vienna when he saw *Rienzi*. He saw *Meistersinger* at least 100 times. *Mein Kampf* was dictated to Wagnerian music. Said Hitler, 'Whoever wants to understand National Socialist Germany must know Wagner.' And again: 'Nearest to the heart of the Volk is Wagner.' For Hitler, Wagner was 'the greatest philosopher in Germany'.[63] German tradition spoke of a folk-king deliverer who would be raised from the masses on a shield and the Austrian corporal never tired of speaking of his humble roots. The site of this coronation: Berchtesgaden in the Bavarian Alps, where Hitler located his personal retreat. Ninety miles away was Nuremberg, home to the sixteenth-century cobbler Hans Sachs, the poet who supposedly saved the west from Asian hordes. Nuremberg hosted the annual Nazi party rallies. Like Wagner, Hitler and his cronies exploited great crowds, with spectacles, torchlight parades, medieval costumes, emotional cries of *Dolchstoss* (betrayal) or *Deutschland Erwache* (a party slogan borrowed from a chorus in *Meistersinger*). It was no coincidence that Germany's western wall of forts was dubbed the Siegfried Line or that Hitler approved of a 1937 painting of himself in white armor as Lohengrin reincarnate.

There was something else. Wagner suggested that Jews redeem mankind from the 'curse of Ahasuerus' through *Selbstvernichtung* (self-destruction). Since they refused to do so, Wagner suggested his countrymen undertake a *Grosse Lösung* (a great solution). Any doubts as to what he meant should have been clarified in December 1881. Informed that 460 Jews had died in a Vienna theater fire during a performance of Gotthold Lessing's *Nathan der Weise*, Wagner pronounced a curse: 'All Jews should burn to death.'[64]

5

Hitler and the End of Weimar

WEIMAR: A CANDLE BURNING AT BOTH ENDS

Germany emerged from World War I psychologically battered, but relatively unscathed. Bombarded with propaganda that targeted the Kaiser as the enemy and weakened by an Allied blockade which cut food imports by 90 percent, Germany asked for an armistice. When sailors at the Kiel Naval Base mutinied and Kaiser Wilhelm fled the country, the Great War ended. Soldiers and civilians packed the war memorial in Berlin chanting *Nur die vierzehn Punkte* (only the 14 Points). Germany was now a republic, its rump parliament sitting in Weimar. Instead of a permanent cessation of hostilities, however, government leaders discovered that the Allies intended to prolong the blockade until a formal peace treaty could be devised. While diplomats at Versailles squabbled for seven months, Germans subsisted on turnips, ersatz bread and horse meat. Some sent their children to families in Denmark or Holland.[1]

When the terms of Versailles were revealed, General Erich von Ludendorff, speaking for most Germans, called the treaty 'a bastard *Diktat*'. Instead of general disarmament, the document limited German forces to 100,000 men. The *Reichswehr* was forbidden any tanks or aircraft nor could it maintain fortifications 40 kilometers east of the Rhine River. Germany's navy was scrapped and its shipbuilders ordered to compensate the Allies with one million tons of shipping. Formally blamed for the war, Germany had to turn over thousands of railway cars, trucks and pieces of farm equipment to the French. Colonies valued at $9 billion were parceled to the Americans, British and Japanese. None of this counted against reparations ($32 billion), the largest sum ever demanded of a vanquished nation. If Germany managed to pay, the indemnity escalated to $50 billion. Social Democrats who traveled to Paris had no choice but to sign this capitulation as Marshal Foch stood ready to invade the Fatherland with one million troops.[2]

To guarantee payments, the French sent troops (including Senegalese colonials) into the Ruhr in 1919–20. The Weimar government gave the Allies what they wanted – more Deutsche marks – stamping them out on 1,783 printing presses. Valued at 4.2 to the dollar in 1914, the mark dipped to 2.5 trillion to one dollar by the end of 1923.[3] In the process, Weimar alienated its *Stehkragenprolet* (starched-collar proletariat), the people who were the backbone of the republic.

The Weimar government was ultimately flawed. Any one of the 30 assorted parties that secured 1.5 percent of the national vote was entitled to representation in parliament. Since all seats in the Reichstag (over 600 by 1932) were selected at large, the slate system favored party hacks.[4] In the event of public disorder, Article 48 of the constitution provided for rule by decree. Germany's armed forces could monitor postal and telephone communication and conduct wholesale arrests. Political idealists adopted *Deutschland über Alles* as the national anthem and approved steel helmets, jackboots and the goose step for the army. As right and left-wing freebooters fought in the streets, intellectuals likened Weimar to a candle burning at both ends.[5]

It took the army two weeks to restore order when the Spartacists (communists) attempted a revolution in January 1919. A second Berlin rising in March left 1,500 dead, including Spartacist leaders Rosa Luxemburg and Karl Liebknecht. With leftists attempting coups in Bremen, Halle, Wilhelmshaven, Leipzig, Dresden, Magdeburg, Düsseldorf and Munich,[6] the *Reichswehr* sought help from veterans in paramilitary groups. These *Stahlhelm* and *Freikorps* then created their own threat. In March 1920, General Walther Lüttwitz refused to dismiss several brigades in Berlin. Captain Hermann Ehrhardt, Ludendorff and Wolfgang Kapp conspired with Lüttwitz to overthrow the republic. Ebert directed his Chief of Staff, General Hans von Seeckt,[7] to suppress the rebels. When the latter refused, Ebert and the Social Democrats fled to Dresden. The Kapp putsch failed when Berlin's trade union councils proclaimed a general strike. Unable to overcome such opposition, the putschists abandoned Berlin. Ludendorff went to Sweden, while Lüttwitz, Kapp and Ehrhardt fled to the haven of dissident right wingers – Munich.[8]

The capital of Bavaria endured its own post-war turmoil. With the collapse of imperial armies in November 1918, Kurt Eisner proclaimed a socialist government in Munich. This republic lasted until elections in January 1919. Eisner, who garnered less than 3 percent of the vote, was assassinated as he was about to tender his resignation. His regime was succeeded by an anarchist clique which for one week issued a host of bizarre decrees. On Palm Sunday the communists established a Soviet headed by Max Levien, Towia Axelrad and Eugen Leviné.[9] Finally, in March 1920, the Bavarian diet elected Gustav von Kahr, an admirer of Mussolini, premier.

One group that flourished in von Kahr's Munich was the National Socialist German Workers Party (NSDAP). Founded in 1919 by the engineer Gottfried Feder and Anton Drexler, a railway mechanic,[10] the Nazis gathered at street corners, encouraging listeners to embrace their program. Some of their ideas seemed innocuous: the state should promote livelihood of citizens, provide old age care and educational opportunity for gifted children, raise standards of health, and implement land reform. Several points appealed to nationalists: union of all Germans in a Great Germany; curtailment of non-German immigration; colonies to accommodate 'surplus population';

revocation of the treaties of Versailles and Saint German. Other points were more problemmatic: nationalization of department stores (many of which were owned by Jews), freedom of religion except for Jews. Only persons of German blood might be citizens of the state. Jews could reside in the state as aliens. They should not vote, lend money or publish newspapers.[11]

ADOLF HITLER: THE PSYCHOPATHIC GOD[12]

One of those who joined the Nazis in September 1919 was a drifter named Adolf Hitler.[13] Born in the town of Branau-am-Inn, near Linz, Austria on 20 April 1889, Hitler struck Dorothy Parker as the embodiment of 'the Little Man'. Five feet seven inches tall, the Nazi *Führer* favored padded uniforms and jackboots because of his slight build and mincing walk. His eyes were ice blue, cold and penetrating. He affected a Charlie Chaplin style mustache and his dark brown hair was combed back with a forelock in a manner reminiscent of a painting of Wotan, the Teutonic god of wolves and the hunt, done by Franz von Stuck in Munich in 1889, the year of Hitler's birth.[14]

The Nazi leader tried to impress people with his power and fearlessness. His favorite dogs were Alsatian wolfhounds. During World War II, he dubbed various field headquarters the *Wolfschlucht* (Berlin), *Wolfsschanze* (East Prussia) and *Werwolf* (Ukraine). Though he once snapped at a servant, 'I am the wolf and this is my den', Hitler was beset with a host of phobias. He dreaded assassination, treason, decapitation and being poisoned by coffee, cigarettes or meat. He never wore a watch because time was an enemy. Obsessive about cleanliness, he repeatedly washed his hands and raged against human filth. He trembled at the notion of needles, anesthetics or operations. Conversely, he enjoyed being in crowds, staying up into the middle of the night, talking, watching movies and ridiculing his colleagues – what Germans term *Schadenfreude*, taking pleasure in the misery of others.

Occasionally, sleep would end in nightmares, with Hitler waking in a cold sweat, muttering about 'Him!'[15] In all probability, 'him' was his father, Alois Schicklgruber, a gruff, pipe-smoking official in Austrian customs who changed his name to Heidler/Hitler in 1877. Schicklgruber's checkered ancestry included cousins who were retarded, hunchbacks, high-grade morons and a suicide in a mental institution. His mother was a semi-literate peasant woman from Graz named Maria Anna. Legend had it that Schicklgruber's father was a Jew named Frankenberger and that the family paid Jewish relatives to suppress the facts. Census records indicate no residents of Graz by that name. Jews had been barred from living in Graz since 1500. Bank records show no transfer of funds to a family named Frankenberger.[16] Such rumors, however, probably exacerbated the anti-Semitism the young Hitler imbibed in the parochial schools of Austria.

The family owned property (nine acres) and employed household domestics.[17] Alois Schicklgruber was a brutish man who terrorized his spouses and children. Two wives succumbed to tuberculosis before he married Klara Pölzl, Hitler's mother. Schicklgruber was 23 years older than this girl who entered his household at age 16 as his foster daughter and second cousin. Not only did she witness the deaths of her predecessors, Klara could do nothing as four of her own children – Gustav (1885–87), Ida (1886–88), Otto (1887) and Edmund (1894–1900) – died of diphtheria or measles. A devout Catholic, pregnant with her first child before she married Alois, Klara believed God was punishing her. She pampered and protected Adolf, possibly suckling him to age three, shielding him from beatings administered by Alois or Adolf's elder half-brother Alois Jr.[18]

The young Hitler was a fair student with a good, but selective, memory. Later he would challenge his generals to recite names of their subalterns and field commanders. He was fascinated by reports of Boer resistance against the British in South Africa and western tales spun by German author Karl May. Some time around 1900, Hitler's schoolwork tailed off. This change has been traced to 'primal scene trauma' or the death of Alois Sr in 1903.[19] A likelier explanation is that the small-town boy had difficulty adjusting to the pressures of a *Realschule* in Linz.[20]

HITLER IN VIENNA

In 1907, the 18-year-old youth made his way to Vienna. Later, he would talk of building a new German capital and constructing the greatest monuments in Europe. A new Arch of Triumph would rise 400 feet. His Nazi meeting hall would have a dome 16 times the size of St Peter's and accommodate 180,000 persons. The party stadium at Nuremberg would seat 400,000. Meanwhile, in Vienna Hitler slept till noon, painted postcards and water-colors and was rejected twice by the Academy of Fine Arts.[21] That same year, 1907, Hitler lost his mother to cancer. Klara had been treated for several years by the family doctor Eduard Bloch. The thought of a Jew administering painful iodoform to his sainted mother must have disturbed the aspiring artist, yet Bloch lived out his life undisturbed after Hitler annexed Austria.[22]

Depressed and short on funds, Hitler volunteered as a porter at the main *Bahnhof*. Few people hired the thin young man in a lice-ridden blue suit. He subsisted on a diet of rice and chocolate. When he had money, he slept in a flophouse on Meldemannstrasse.[23] Some nights, his home was a bench in parks along the Danube cleared for Vienna's homeless by Mayor Karl Lueger. Hitler learned a great deal by observing 'Handsome Karl' who managed to stay in office by flaying eastern Jews, Marxist radicals and Slavic revolutionaries.[24] When critics pointed out the incongruity of his friendship with the Rothschilds, Lueger declared, 'I will decide who is a Jew'. He was not the first German politician to exploit Jews. After 1882, Otto Böckel, Adolf

Stoecker, Karl Ahlwardt and Georg Schönerer directed anti-Semitic move-ments.[25] Felix Salten might have been describing Hitler when he wrote of Lueger: 'He validates Vienna's lower class in all its qualities, in its lack of intellectual wants, in its distrust of education, in its tipsy silliness, in its love of street songs, in its adherence to the old-fashioned, in its boisterous smugness; and they rave, they rave blissfully when he talks to them.'[26]

Hitler would later recount how his experience in Vienna transformed him into an anti-Semite. Although some of his friends in the flophouses and many of the patrons who purchased his paintings were Jews,[27] Hitler claimed to be repelled by bearded Jews who crowded the Leopoldstadt district. There were more than 175,000 Jews living in Vienna in 1910, most of them Orthodox, many of them poor street peddlers.[28] Stories of Jewish usury, greed and crowding of universities were highlighted by the 'gutter press' of Vienna, which was the impressionable would-be artist's favorite reading.[29]

In May 1913 Hitler emigrated to Bavaria to avoid being conscripted into the Austrian army where he might be forced to serve alongside Jews. He was photographed smiling at the Feldherrnhalle (war memorial) in Munich when Germany declared war in August 1914. The military provided Hitler with a sense of belonging. Those who served with him recalled a serious young man who despised war profiteers, Marxian defeatists and Jewish slackers.[30] In four years on the Western Front, Hitler rose to the rank of Lance Corporal and was awarded the Iron Cross first class, Germany's highest decoration.[31] Scholars debate whether the distinction was merited or the medals distributed en masse. There is also a question whether Hitler suffered a mustard gas attack near Ypres.[32] Whether Hitler's temporary blindness was hysterical or the result of a gas attack gone awry, he believed it had happened. He would later tell how while recovering at Pasewalk he underwent a vision to save Germany and the world.[33]

When the war ended, Hitler was left to continue his quest for the idyllic family life.[34] Like Stalin, his idea of good art was one where happy children cavorted before robust parents. He planned housing for villagers, a people's car (the *Volkswagen*) and a string of highways useful to military and civilian traffic. Germany was his family and its children precious to Hitler. They were to be enrolled in the *Pimpfe* (Hitler Youth) or the *Bund Deutscher Mädel* for National-Socialist indoctrination. Children recited a grace prais-ing, '*Führer*, my *Führer* sent to me from God, protect and maintain me throughout my life. Thou who has saved Germany from deepest need, I thank thee today for my daily bread. *Führer*, my *Führer*, my faith, my light. Heil my *Führer*.'[35]

Obsequious toward elderly women like Frau Bechstein who served as a surrogate mother, Hitler was ambivalent toward younger women. In his view, women should be helpmates to their husbands and bear many children. To encourage births, the Nazis created the Honor Cross of German Mother-hood, rewarding women who had four or more children with a bronze, silver or gold medal. Three million women received the last award. Hitler's personal life was a disaster. His first love, Geli Rabaul, a niece who served him as house-keeper, died in 1932 under suspicious circumstances. Subsequently, three women involved with him (Renate Müller, Frau Inge Ley and Suzi Liptauer) committed suicide. Three others (Mimi Reiter, Unity Mitford and his long-time companion Eva Braun) tried to kill themselves. None of the theories about his sexuality – that he supposedly suffered from syphilis, was a sadomasochist, voyeur, bisexual, or had only one testicle – are proven. In simplest terms, Hitler was a sociopath who, notwithstanding his reverence for his mother, had an abiding contempt for women.[36]

HITLER ON THE JEWS

In October 1918, Hitler returned to Munich as a guard in a prisoner of war camp. In the spring, he was sent to Lechfeld near Augsburg to serve as a *Vertrauensmann* (undercover agent). He reported on pacifists, socialists and *Freikorps* until his discharge in March 1920.[37] Membership in the Nazi party changed everything. Lueger spoke of politics as magic – 'The masses will obey he who knows how to appeal to them' – and Hitler quickly realized that he possessed *Fingerspitzengefühl*, the ability to hold an audience at one's finger-tips. His message was simple:

1. The old Germany suffered from forces of decay – senility, a malignant tumor, alien virus, chronic disease, plague, a poisonous bacillus, cancerous ulcer or pestiferous carrier.[38]
2. Those responsible for Germany's weakness were the November criminals (Weimar politicians), intellectuals, Marxists and Jews.
3. The *Volk* must guarantee the strength and growth of the state through union with Austria and acquisition of land at the expense of the Slavs.
4. To achieve greatness Hitler urged sacrifice and resistance, *Weltmacht oder Niedergang* (world power or destruction).

Hitler reserved his fiercest condemnations for 'the filthy' Jews. It was almost impossible for him to utter the word Jew without attaching some derogatory adjective. He raved against the smell of caftan wearers and their dirty clothes, little Jews who acted like maggots in a rotting corpse.[39] Left alone, Jews would ultimately smother in 'filth and offal'.[40] Like Voltaire and Wagner, Hitler accused Jews of transforming civilizations into 'dirt and dung'. The Jew could never become a German or a Frenchman for to do so would mean he must 'surrender the Jew in him'.[41] The Jew wants no healthy, sturdy race before them, but 'a rickety herd capable of being subjected'. He dupes the goyim with talk of trade unions, social democracy, Marxism. But, warned Hitler:

With satanic joy in his face, the black-haired Jewish youth lurks in wait for the unsuspecting girl whom he defiles with his blood, thus stealing her from her people ... he does not shrink back from pulling down the blood barriers for others, even on a large scale. It was and it is Jews who bring the Negroes into the Rhineland, always with the same secret thought and clear aim of ruining the hated white race by the necessarily resulting bastardization, throwing it down from its cultural and political height, and himself rising to be its master.[42]

Using 'the tactics of the hyena', these Orientals manipulated nation against nation in an effort to kill off hundreds of thousands of people. 'Only a few wars and revolutions, that was enough to put the Jewish people into possession of the Red gold and thereby make them masters of the world.' The Jew was an eternal bloodsucker, the best example of which was Russia where 'he killed or starved about 30 million people with positively fanatical savagery, in part amid inhuman tortures, in order to give a gang of Jewish journalists and stock exchange bandits domination over a great people'. Said Hitler: 'The end is not only the end of the freedom of the peoples oppressed by the Jew, but also the end of this parasite upon the nations. After the victim, the vampire sooner or later dies too.'[43]

There was room for traditional bigotry in Hitler's anti-Semitism:

In boundless love as a Christian and as a man I read through the passage which tells us how the Lord at last rose in his might and seized the scourge to drive out of the Temple the brood of vipers and adders ... With deepest emotion I recognize more profoundly than ever before in the fact that it was this that he had to shed his blood upon the cross. As a Christian, I have no duty to allow myself to be cheated, but I have the duty to be a fighter for truth and justice.[44]

In one apocalyptic revelation, he advised: 'We have faith that one day Heaven will bring the Germans back into a Reich over which there shall be no Soviet star, no Jewish star of David, but above the Reich there shall be the symbol of German labor – the Swastika.'[45]

HITLER'S HENCHMEN

Hitler surrounded himself with a group of devoted apparatchiks.[46] Some, like Hitler, had not been born in Germany proper. Many were convinced that Germany had been betrayed in the Great War. All were anti-Semites, anti-democratic Teutomaniacs convinced of Germany's special position in the family of nations and committed to the concept of racial purity. Physically or psychologically blemished, few evoked images of Aryan perfection. Most were fairly bright, relatively young men[47] like Adolf Hitler who was 44 years old when he became Chancellor.

Ernst Röhm (1887–1934) was a stumpy man who distinguished himself in the battle of Verdun. Forty-six years old when the Nazis seized power, the scar-faced Röhm helped organize the Nazi party's Gymnastic and Sports Section. The *Sturmabteilung* (SA) or Brown Shirts were streetbrawlers whose job it was to protect Nazi speakers from rival political gangs. By 1933 the SA counted more than one million members and Röhm considered himself the heir apparent to the *Führer*'s job.[48] **Paul Joseph Goebbels** (1897–1945), a Catholic from the Rhineland, was a short, frail man with a clubfoot. Goebbels was dark (some even joked Semitic) in appearance. Educated at Heidelberg, Goebbels was unable to obtain a literary position after the war. Thirty-six years old in 1933, Hitler's propaganda minister was with the *Führer* in a Berlin bunker at the end of World War II.[49] **Hermann Wilhelm Goering** (1893–1946), the last commander of the Richthofen Flying Circus, was 40 when Hitler became Chancellor. The portly Goering, who weighed 280 pounds and was nicknamed *der Dicke* (Tubby), started as an aerial observer in World War I. Before the conflict was over, he shot down 22 Allied planes. A lover of pomp, Goering served as President of the Reichstag, head of the Luftwaffe, and Deputy *Führer*.[50]

Heinrich Himmler (1900–45) was a near-sighted Catholic from Munich. Himmler served in the last days of World War I, then on the barricades in 1919–20. Believing that Germany would never revive, he joined the Artamanen movement, a back-to-the-earth group that preached emigration

2. *Reichsführer* Heinrich Himmler, architect of forced population transfers (Holocaust Memorial Museum).

to South America. In 1929 he was entrusted with the creation of the *Schutz-staffeln*, an elite inner guard that could prove purity of ancestry back to 1750. Originally numbering 280 members, the SS grew to more than two million by 1942 including 30,000 in the Gestapo, 800,000 in combat divisions and others in security units.[51] **Reinhard Heydrich** (1904–42) was Himmler's right hand man in the Reich Central Security Office (RSHA). Court-martialled from the Navy in 1930, Heydrich later became a central figure in Germany's Jewish Question. Ironically, Heydrich, one of the few Nazis to approximate a blond Aryan, may have had some Jewish ancestry. Himmler eulogized this 'god of death' in June 1942 saying, 'He had overcome the Jew in himself by purely intellectual means and he had swung over to the other side. He was convinced that the Jewish elements in his blood were damnable.'[52]

Born in Egypt, **Rudolf Hess** (1894–1987) served first as Hitler's personal, then party, secretary. In the spring of 1941, believing he could arrange a common front with the British against Russia, Hess flew to Scotland. His erratic behavior convinced his jailers that he was demented. Sentenced to life imprisonment after the war, he allegedly hanged himself in 1987.[53] **Martin Bormann** (1900–45) assumed Hess's duties as Director of the Party Chancellery. A bull-necked street brawler from Halberstadt, Bormann shared Himmler's dream of breaking the power of the clergy and returning Germany to a pagan state. Unpopular with his comrades, Bormann disappeared when the Russians entered Berlin.[54]

Julius Streicher (1885–1946) was a Nuremberg schoolteacher who once headed up his own nationalist party. Bald, thick-necked and slackjawed, Streicher was, perhaps, the most virulent anti-Semite in the Nazi hierarchy. His tabloid, *Der Stürmer*, specialized in pornography and outlandish tales about Jews.[55] **Alfred Rosenberg** (1893–1946), the party intellectual, came from Estonia. His *Myth of the Twentieth Century* was a clumsy imitation of Houston Stewart Chamberlain's earlier work. In 1941, Rosenberg became Minister for the Occupied Eastern Territories.[56] **Joachim Ribbentrop** (1893–1946) was an ex-champagne salesman who emigrated to Canada after World War I. The Nazis' foreign affairs specialist because he could read English and French, the arrogant Ribbentrop played a significant role in the murder of Jews.[57]

Hans Frank (1900–46) was 29 when Hitler picked him to lead the Nazi legal section. As Governor-General of Poland, Frank served as overseer for more than three million Jews in the Lublin Reservation. **Albert Speer** (1903–81) joined the Nazi party in 1931 and later gave form to Hitler's dreams of a convocation center in Nuremberg, the Tempelhof Air Field and Olympic Sportspalast in Berlin.[58] Other early notables included **Robert Ley** (1890–1945), who headed the Nazi labor front; **Ernst Kaltenbrunner** (1903–46), Heydrich's successor at the RSHA; **Baldur von Schirach** (1907–74), the half-American leader of the Nazi youth; and **Wilhelm Frick** (1877–1946), Minister of Interior in Hitler's 1933 cabinet.

THE BEER HALL PUTSCH OF 1923

Failed painter, journalist, soldier and airman, butcher, commercial clerk and architect; the Nazi movement did include one grand figure – General Ludendorff. Three years after the failed Kapp Putsch, the aging Ludendorff returned to Germany. The German economy was in chaos and French troops had reoccupied the Ruhr. For Hitler and the Nazis, the time seemed ripe to duplicate the feat of Mussolini and his Black Shirts who had seized power in Rome. On the night of 8 November 1923 von Kahr and other Bavarian officials held a town hall meeting in Munich's *Bürgerbräukeller* (a public dining hall). Von Kahr had given a speech denouncing communism when Hitler, wearing an ill-fitting morning coat, broke into the room accompanied by storm troopers. The Nazi leader clambered atop a table, fired a shot into the ceiling and declared the Reich and Bavarian governments overthrown. Von Kahr, General von Lossow of the Bavarian *Reichswehr*, and Colonel Seisser of the Munich police were taken aside and informed that Hitler and Ludendorff would head the new government.

The next day, Hitler and Ludendorff led their minions through the cobbled alleys of Munich to the Feldherrnhalle. At the spot where the declaration of war was announced in 1914, they were confronted by troops of the Bavarian Provincial Police. Using lances and sidearms, the loyalists quickly dispersed the Nazis. Fourteen storm troopers were killed, several more wounded (including Goering, who attributed his drug addiction to wounds sustained in Munich). A bewildered Ludendorff was taken into custody. Not Hitler. At the first sign of trouble, the decorated war hero ran to a waiting automobile which took him 35 miles into the country. Hitler spent the next two days sniveling under a blanket in the home of a comrade, Ernst 'Putzi' Hanfstaengl.[59]

Charged with treason, the putschists could have been subjected to capital punishment. Instead, Nazi partisans filled the courtroom with cheers of 'Heil Hitler'. Emboldened, Hitler offered not apology but petulance.[60] He and his comrades had tried to save Germany from the real traitors – pacifists, communists and Jews. Apparently this warmed-over polemic appealed to the tribunal for the judges freed Ludendorff and Goering and sentenced Hitler to five years in Landsberg prison. His jail cell was decorated with party emblems and pictures. Other prisoners cleaned his facilities and arranged flowers and presents sent by admirers. Hitler slept as late as he liked and received visitors in his unlocked cell. These included his pet shepherd dog, party leaders and Rudolf Hess, who helped draft *Mein Kampf*. Hitler was released after serving thirteen months in jail.

Such lax law enforcement was not remarkable. Weimar's judiciary repeatedly demonstrated right-wing sympathies. Of 775 army officers implicated in the Kapp Putsch, 91 received leaves, 57 were transferred, 48 were relieved of duties, and 486 had their proceedings suspended. In 1921, German courts were unwilling to punish the assassins of Matthias Erzberger, the Social Democrat who signed the capitulation at Compiègne. When Foreign Minister Walter Rathenau was assassinated in June 1922, judges handed down light sentences to 11 conspirators. Between 1919 and 1933 there were 22 political assassinations attributed to the left. Four (18 percent) went free. In the same period, there were 354 murders committed by the right, and of these 326 (92 percent) went unpunished.[61]

GERMANY IN THE PROSPEROUS YEARS

In Hitler's absence, Gregor and Otto Strasser pushed the Nazi movement into the Rhineland and Prussia with moderate success. They hired Goebbels to edit the *Völkischer Beobachter*, the official party journal. Still, there were only 27,000 members on party rolls when Hitler was released from prison. In the next four years, the Nazi party was restructured from local *Gruppe* and *Ortsen*, through *Kreise* (circles), to *Gaue* (districts), each with their own officers. At the same time, Hitler established special units for teachers, physicians and lawyers. Still, the Nazis made little headway between 1925 and 1929 because times were good. Germany's mills hummed with activity. American loans and investments helped Germany pay reparations which, in turn, offset Allied war loans.[62]

Germany's revival could be attributed, in large measure, to Gustav Stresemann. The leader of the small People's Party, he served as Foreign Minister for most of the period 1923–29. It was Stresemann, together with Reichsbank advisers Hjalmar Schacht and Hans Luther, who managed to bring the runaway inflation of 1923 under control. In 1924 Stresemann and the American Charles Dawes rearranged the reparations schedule. That same year at Locarno Stresemann convinced the British and French to settle boundary disputes through mediation. In 1926, Germany joined the League of Nations. Three years later, it signed the Kellogg–Briand Pact, renouncing aggressive warfare. In 1929 Stresemann restructured reparations once more. Then the American stock market crashed in October and with it came the house of cards that sustained the German economy. Stresemann was not around to witness the destruction of all he had worked for. He died the same month that Wall Street crashed.[63]

Weimar had already lost another icon. Ebert passed away on 28 February 1925 of a ruptured appendix. He was 54 years old, relatively young by political standards. His death gave Germans the opportunity to elect a president for the first time. They blundered. Wilhelm Marx of the Social Democrats received 13.75 million votes. A Communist, Ernst Thälmann, garnered 1.9 million. But an independent candidate – Field Marshal Paul von Hindenburg – won 14.65 million votes and the top office in Germany. A worse choice could not be imagined. The descendant of Prussian aristocrats,

Hindenburg had been a soldier for 40 years. Commander of the Eastern Front in World War I, Hindenburg originated the charge of a *Dolchstoss* (betrayal) causing Germany's defeat. Testifying before a Reichstag panel in 1920 Hindenburg said: 'Like Siegfried, stricken down by the treacherous spear of savage Hagen, our weary front collapsed.' Urged to run by Admiral Tirpitz, this foe of Weimar was 78 years old when he was elected to a seven-year term in 1925.[64]

MÜLLER, BRÜNING, PAPEN, SCHLEICHER, HITLER

As long as the German economy was sound there was little danger from fringe groups. Worldwide Depression brought with it unemployment, 1.4 million in 1929, 3.1 million in 1930, then 5.7 million in 1931. For the masses who had been devastated twice in ten years, the sight of soup kitchens after a taste of prosperity was too much. In droves, they abandoned moderate socialists and old-fashioned nationalists in favor of parties with radical programs. There were only 12 Nazis in the Reichstag in May 1928. Two years later there were 107. The only other party that registered substantial gains were the Communists. In July 1932, with six million Germans out of work, the Nazis won six million votes and 230 seats in the Reichstag. They constituted the largest political party in Germany.[65]

The Nazis promised jobs, respect for values, restoration of pride. But what especially boosted them was their promise to do something about Weimar and the Jews. Party membership increased among blue and white collar workers, as well as authoritarian types. The Nazis were popular among peasants in Silesia, Franconia, Saxony, Schleswig-Holstein, Brandenburg, East and West Prussia. Before 1933, they controlled the state police of Anhalt, Brunswick, Thuringia and Mecklenburg. Brown Shirts clashed with partisans of the communist Red Front or the Socialist Reichsbanner.[66] Some were injured. A few, like Horst Wessel, a 23-year-old street brawler attacked by a communist over a prostitute, were killed.

In March 1930 the coalition government of Social Democrat Hermann Müller resigned. For the next two years, Germany was led by Dr Heinrich Brüning. A member of the Center (Catholic) party, a nationalist with a sterling war record, Brüning hoped to get Germans working again through a customs union with Austria and a program of rearmament. When the Allies would permit neither, he cut government spending, earning the title of 'Hunger Chancellor'. To make matters worse, presidential elections were held in April 1932. Hitler won 11 million votes (30.1 percent of the total) but ran second to Hindenburg, who was reelected with 49.6 percent of the vote. Because of Nazi violence, the government invoked Article 48. Considered a weakling by German Chief of Staff Kurt von Schleicher, Brüning was replaced by Franz von Papen. A reactionary who directed espionage in the

United States in 1915, von Papen served six months as Chancellor. In the summer of 1932 he persuaded the Allies at Lausanne to scale down reparations to $714 million. Despite this, he too was gone in November 1932, a victim of von Schleicher's ego. Next, von Schleicher tried to rule. Lacking a popular base, he was ousted in January 1933.

Hindenburg was faced with a dilemma. Germany's two major political parties were the Nazis and the Communists. Not only was Bolshevism repugnant to the Prussian aristocrat, the Nazis held nearly three times as many seats in the Reichstag as the Communists. The military feared Russia and Poland which had 40 armed divisions to Germany's ten. Steel magnates Fritz Thyssen and Alfried Krupp had been making secret contributions to Nazi party coffers. Early in January 1933 a group of bankers and industrialists met with Hindenburg's son Uskar at the Cologne home of Baron Kurt von Schroeder. They convinced him that Hitler should head a new government assisted by Von Papen as Deputy Chancellor. Most Germans accepted the appointment as 'an expression of non-ideological protest'. It would ruin Hitler's career, quipped Social Democrat leader Otto Wels. There were even a few nationalistic Jews who welcomed the move, believing it would restore German pride.[67] Without violating the Weimar constitution, Adolf Hitler became Chancellor on 30 January 1933.

6

Gleichschaltung: The Nazi Consolidation of Power

THE REICHSTAG FIRE

The Nazis held only two posts in Hitler's first cabinet (Frick as Minister of Interior, Goering Minister without portfolio), but behaved as expected. They enrolled 50,000 men, mainly members of the SA and SS, as police auxiliaries to harass political opponents. Then, on 27 February 1933 an event occurred that would forever change Germany: the Reichstag erupted in fire. In minutes, Germany's parliament building became a tangle of twisted steel and embers. In the show trial that followed, Goering acted as prosecutor. Alone among four accused communists, Marinus van der Lubbe, a Dutch half-wit, was found guilty and sentenced to death. He had been charged with the same crime – treason – brought against Hitler and Goering when they staged the Munich putsch. The Nazis were slapped on the wrist. On 10 January 1934 van der Lubbe was beheaded.

Hindenburg invoked Article 48 – the suspension of civil rights – and approved the arrest of communist leaders. Hitler asked Parliament to transfer legislative authority – including power to initiate constitutional amendments and make treaties – to the cabinet for four years. On 23 March 1933, what was left of the Reichstag gathered in the Kroll Opera House to vote on this Enabling Act. The resolution required approval from two-thirds of the 647 representatives. The Nazis could count on 288 of their own members and 52 nationalists. Ninety-four Social Democrats who had not been arrested or had remained home did oppose the law. Most of the 66 Center Party (Catholic) delegates registered 'ja', only a handful abstaining or voting no. Later, these politicians explained they were concerned that their families might be harmed if they voted the wrong way. Hitler was strong enough to do what he wanted anyway and this was one way to check communism.[1]

Such rationalizations helped the Nazis implement their program of *Gleichschaltung* (taming of independent bodies). When enemies of the regime were placed under *Schutzhaft* (protective custody) 'good people' thanked God it was not happening to them. Villagers residing near new concentration camps deluded themselves that the *Haftlinge* (prisoners) must have done something to merit punishment. As the Evangelical pastor Martin Niemoeller declared upon his arrest: 'First they came for the Jews and I did not speak out because I was not a Jew. Then they came for the Communists and I did not speak out because I was not a Communist. Then they came for the trade unionists and I did not speak out because I was not a trade unionist. Then they came for me and there was no one left to speak out for me.'

DACHAU: THE FIRST FORMAL CONCENTRATION CAMP

The Enabling Act opened the way to a concentration camp system that ultimately counted more than a million inmates, of various origins, from Riga in Latvia to Malines in Belgium. Initially, there were three large camps with a capacity of 20,000, complemented by 65 smaller units totalling 85,000 prisoners. The longest lived Nazi *Katzets* was Dachau, nine miles northwest of Munich. Opened in late March 1933, what had once been a munitions camp became the model for *Zwangsarbeitslager* (forced labor camps) under SS *Oberführer* Theodor Eicke. Prisoners stumbled through gates inscribed *Arbeit macht frei* (work gives freedom). Shaven, tattooed with numbers and wearing ill-fitting uniforms, they were assembled on a gravelled *Appelplatz* (roll call area), where they listened as guards harangued them about the consequences of breaching camp rules. 'Legal punishments' included hanging from the gallows, standing at attention, carrying loads of cement at the double, confinement to a yard-square dungeon, or whipping with a club. The guards devised their own amusements, including exposure of naked victims to the cold, forcing them to climb trees and sing, or *Sportmachen*, forcing exhausted prisoners to push heavy rollers across the parade grounds or perform calisthenics after work.[2]

Everybody worked in Dachau, in shifts as long as 12 hours. There were carpenters, electricians and stonemasons who built the initial camp with its 30 barracks; artists, tailors and toymakers who crafted Christmas gifts for the SS; and all sorts of professionals who provided slave labor for Messcherschmitt and BMW factories. Fed wormy meat, cabbage soup, slivers of cheese, prisoners rooted in the garbage for potato peelings. They shared *Pritschen* (tiered bunks), trying to keep warm with a single blanket. People in higher bunks were admonished not to throw live lice. Hygiene was primitive, dysentery and typhus rampant. A trip to the *Revier* (hospital) was virtually a death sentence, for the only medications were aspirin and castor oil.[3]

In the woods behind the main camp guards used prisoners for target practice. Inmates who could no longer work were drowned in a lake. Some new arrivals never made it into the barracks. A survivor made the following entry for 21 November 1942:

> 500 invalids came yesterday from a camp near Danzig ... 51 of these 'invalids' came in dead, but their bodies had already been partly eaten by the others, the remains and bones were thrown out of the chink in the cattle-

truck door during the journey. Only a few unrecognizable parts of the body remained. The whole side was missing from one body, from others the nose or cheek or genital organs ... All the corpses were photographed. Most likely the camp authorities did this to send evidence to Berlin. The prisoners during the six days that their journey lasted, received only one piece of bread, six hundred grams, I believe. Hunger delirium broke out among them as they suffered for a long time from under feeding.[4]

Beyond the main camp stood two brick buildings. The larger structure contained a delousing chamber for clothing and a white-tiled gas chamber that was built too late to be put into operation. Both buildings contained furnaces installed by J.A. Topf and Sons of Erfurt. Ashes from these cremataria were turned over to families at the cost of 75 marks per urn. Some 230,000 prisoners passed through the gates of Dachau. When the camp was liberated late in April 1945 there were 32,000 survivors in huts designed for 5,000. In 12 years, 30,000 prisoners, nearly two-thirds of them non-Jews, died here.

SACHSENHAUSEN

The nerve center for the camp system was Sachsenhausen, located outside Oranienburg, 20 miles north of Berlin.[5] Early in July 1934, *Reichsführer* Himmler appointed Eicke to the post of *Inspekteur der Konzentrationslager*. Within a year, *Gruppenführer* Eicke reorganized 3,000 camp guards as *Totenkopfverbände* (Death's Head Units). Shortly after, a number of 'wild' (unofficial) camps, including Columbia House in Berlin, Fuhlsbüttel in Hamburg, Esterwegen in Friesland and Oranienburg, were closed. Lacking a facility in the north, the SS opened Sachsenhausen in September 1936. Subsequently, all Gestapo and *Totenkampfverbände* were given hands-on training at Sachsenhausen.[6] For many recruits, the camp system represented an opportunity for access and advance within the SS. As in Dachau, the SS administration was divided into five *Abteilung – Lager Kommandant* and his cronies, guards and inmates, food and housing, transport, and a medical section. The Nazis created a hierarchy that mirrored their own even among their prisoners. Each block and *stube* (cell) had its own senior (*kapo*) and scribe reporting to a *Lageraltester*, prison elder. The latter, charged with coordinating clerical staff and order police, was usually a criminal or a communist with influence in labor allocation.

Inmates built satellites at Neuengamme outside Hamburg and Gross Rosen in Lower Silesia. Skilled workers were assigned to plants operated by Heinkel, Daimler, Hentschel-Maschinenbau, Siemens and *Auer A.G. Gasmasken-Demagpanzerwerk*. Late in the war, the Nazis assembled a group of artists to counterfeit currency with a view to destabilizing the economies of Great Britain and the United States. Slave labor was so profitable (perhaps

100,000 DM per day) that in 1938 Himmler turned Sachsenhausen over to SS *Gruppenführer* Oswald Pohl and the SS *Wirtschaft und Verwaltungshauptamt* (WVHA, SS Economic and Administrative Office).[7] When the Russians liberated the camp in April 1945, they found 3,000 people alive. Nearly half of the 200,000 persons who passed through the main gates did not survive.

BUCHENWALD

Situated on a slope of the Ettersberg near Weimar, Buchenwald was opened in 1937. The camp was built around a huge oak once frequented by Goethe, Germany's poet of freedom. (In 1944, Commandant Koch ordered the tree to be cut down.) Buchenwald's main gate taunted newcomers with the inscription *Jedem das seine* (to each his due). Inmates, immortalized in the song 'Peat Bog Soldiers', toiled in quarries, arms factories, on railway lines, as tailors and gardeners. They were required to offer 'the Saxon salute' (hands behind the head while doing kneebends) at a distance of three paces. In July 1943, 2,000 French deportees were dumped into the camp, without food or blankets. They all died of starvation and disease. Another time, 800 Soviet prisoners were brought to a special barrack for what they thought was to be a physical examination. Each man was shot in the back of the head.

There were barracks for 'doll boys' (in the spring of 1945 there were 877 minors in the camp, including a 3½-year-old boy who was labeled a 'partisan') and *Prominenz* (figures like French Premier Leon Blum, Weimar Social Democrat Rudolf Breitscheid, industrialist Fritz Thyssen, Italian Princess Mafalda Hesse, six members of the Stauffenberg family, and leaders of the Hungarian and Romanian fascist parties). Conditions were especially bad in Little Camp, where 10,000 Gypsies, Jews and political prisoners were housed in shacks and tents. Not far from the camp crematorium, Kommandant Koch maintained a zoo with four bears, five monkeys and a rhinoceros. Koch fed steak to his pet bears while the inmates subsisted on 'Viking Salad' (rotten liver sausage, fish heads and potatoes), and tea made from acorns. By the fall of 1944 the daily death toll in Buchenwald reached 150–200. Some prisoners were executed for their skin tattoos which were then removed, tanned and made into riding crops, handbags and lampshades. On 11 April 1945, 21,000 inmates were liberated. In eight years, Buchenwald had counted 65,000 dead, more than 40,000 of them Jews.[8]

MAUTHAUSEN

In the Nazi system Dachau was listed as a Class I camp. Before the war, it was possible for inmates to secure their release. Until April 1944, when it was upgraded to Class I, Buchenwald was listed as Class II, a more punitive institution. Prisoners assigned to Class III camps were never supposed to return. When the Nazis annexed Austria, Himmler decided that granite quarries at Mauthausen would make an ideal location for a new camp. Situated in the mountains, 20 miles from Linz, Mauthausen opened in August 1938. Before the creation of the charnel houses in Poland, Mauthausen was listed as a Class III concentration camp, the only one of its kind at the time.

The life expectancy for workers in the *Wienergraben* (granite quarries) was three months. To expedite the killing process, the Nazis had Spanish Republican refugees cut a stone staircase to the quarry pit. The SS guards forced prisoners to trundle stones up and down the 186 'Spanish Stairs' until the inmates collapsed and died. In 1944, 47 Allied fliers walked the path barefoot lugging 50 pounds of stones on their backs. None survived. In 1941, a group of Dutch Jews made the Sisyphean trek for three days. Then, as Konnilyn Feig reports, 'Driven by despair, the remaining Jews joined hands and leaped over the precipice to their death in the quarry below.'[9]

Under its third commandant, Franz Ziereis, Mauthausen counted 18,000 inmates working in the quarries and a Messerschmitt factory. Four miles west were the subsidiary camps of Gusen, underground tunnels with 24,000 prisoners producing machine guns and aircraft fuselages. At Ebensee, Melk, Fernberg, Passau, Gross-Reming, Lobelpass and St Valentine village children taunted arrivals, 'You'll soon be up the chimney on Totenburg'.

3. Mauthausen. Granite quarries where Jews, anti-Nazi Germans and allied prisoners of war were worked to death between 1938 and 1945 (Holocaust Memorial Museum).

Ziereis admitted that his guards killed hundreds with whips, axes and fatal injections.[10] Mauthausen was the last of the major Nazi concentration camps to be liberated. When American troops entered the main site on 8 May 1945, they found 16,000 walking skeletons of various nationalities. A total of 206,000 persons passed through the main camp. More than 110,000 died there, 3,000 after liberation.[11]

TAMING OF INDEPENDENT BODIES

The terror generated by concentration camps, enabled the Nazis to convert Germany into a totalitarian state within a year. Many Communists were already in camps by the end of March. In June 1933, the Social Democrats were declared subversive. The following month, the Catholic Center Party, Bavarian People's Party and Democrats voluntarily dissolved. By July 1933, the Nazis were the only legal party in Germany. In April, Hitler dismissed the state governments and replaced them with more pliant officials. The Nazis mounted a simultaneous attack against the trade unionists, arresting a number of leaders in May 1933. That summer, Robert Ley was named chief of the new Labor Front. With thousands of 'interlopers' in *Katzets* and Germany engaged in rearmament, unemployment shrank to less than one million by 1936.

In March 1933 the Nazis established special tribunals (*Sondergericht*) to hear political cases. School teachers were encouraged to join the Nazi party. Baldur von Schirach replaced youth groups like the *Wandervogel* with Hitler Youth, while Gertrud Scholtz-Klink, mother of 11, organized the NSF (association of Nazi women). By 1942, the National Socialist People's Welfare Organization subsumed many of the functions of the German Red Cross, assisting Aryan victims of bombardments, maintaining 600 kindergartens, and distributing winter relief to its 16 million members.[12]

Persuaded by Cardinal Eugenio Pacelli, Nuncio in Berlin, the Catholic church signed a concordat with Hitler in July 1933. Just as the 1929 pact with Mussolini, this agreement guaranteed the Church its position in Germany – provided prelates did not meddle in politics. Cardinal Erich Faulhaber of Munich showed the way at Advent in 1933 when he declared: 'From the Church's point of view, there is no objection whatever to racial research and race culture.'[13] Faulhaber's colleagues 'consistently showered gratuitous and unsolicited declarations of loyalty upon Hitler'.[14] Still, Nazi hooligans harassed Catholic youths to get them to quit church organizations. They berated priests in song and attacked church offices. Claiming vicissitudes of war, the Nazis shut down the Catholic press and confiscated churchbells in 1939. Hitler's relationship with Protestants was not much better. In July 1933, he issued a new constitution for the Protestant Church blending 28 provincial branches into a Reich church under a Nazi bishop.

THE NIGHT OF LONG KNIVES

One major embarrassment for Hitler during that first year was the behavior of Ernst Röhm and the Brown Shirts. It was common knowledge that Röhm and his top associates were homosexuals. During the first days of the Nazi regime, the SA trashed stores, whisked people away and bludgeoned them in cellars, sheds or garages that the Brown Shirts called concentration camps. For Hitler, the undisciplined behavior of Röhm and his group was hampering efforts to restore trade. Röhm also infuriated the military by demanding that SA officers who received commissions as street brawlers be equated with Germany's professional soldiers.

An overconfident Röhm railed against 'Beefsteak Stürme' (communist converts) and threatened aristocrats that a second revolution was yet to come. Warned Röhm: 'We will extirpate the old bureaucratic spirit of the petit bourgeois. We will clean up this pigsty.' As for Hitler, 'If I can't work with Hitler, we shall get on without him. Hitler is a traitor.'[15] With Hindenburg's blessing, Hitler met with Generals von Blomberg and von Fritsch and Admiral Erich Raeder aboard the battleship *Deutschland* in April 1934. In exchange for their support, Hitler promised to end talk of a merger in ranks and to stop SA units from bringing weapons into the Rhineland.[16]

The purge that followed was remarkably simple. Hitler instructed the SA leadership to go on holiday and on 30 June 1934 Röhm and his cronies did just that. While they drank themselves into a stupor at Bad Wiesse, Hitler dispatched SS units to the southern health spa. In the middle of the night, the SS surprised and killed their victims in bed. A sobbing Röhm was given a chance to shoot himself before he was executed.[17] The Night of Long Knives provided Hitler with the opportunity to even a number of old scores. In Berlin, Gestapo agents murdered General von Schleicher in his dining room. In Bavaria, Gustav von Kahr was taken into the woods and hacked to pieces. Other victims included Otto Strasser, Father Bernhard Stämpfle (a priest who helped edit *Mein Kampf*) and two of Von Papen's closest advisers. When Hindenburg died on 2 August 1934, Hitler fused the positions of Chancellor and President into one. He was now *Führer* of Germany.

AXIS AND APPEASEMENT

In the next five years fear of German strength prompted diplomats to yield before Hitler's bluster. The Allies made no protest when Hitler pulled Germany out of the League of Nations in October 1933. He also withdrew from disarmament discussions at Geneva, but continued to dangle the issue of 'offensive weapons' before the democracies. Periodically, Hitler stunned western chancelleries with a series of 'Saturday surprises'. On 8 March 1935, he revealed a commitment to revive the air force, which already was as large as Britain's. A week later, Hitler announced the existence of a 550,000-man army. French, British and Italian officials met to consider responses. The so-called Stresa Front disintegrated when Mussolini invaded Ethiopia in October 1935. British Prime Minister Stanley Baldwin not only yielded to Hitler's military demands, in June 1935 he granted Germany's navy 35 percent parity with England.

While most of Europe was occupied with the fate of Haile Selassie's countrymen, Hitler moved to reclaim German soil. The Saar was taken in January 1935. A year later (March 1936), the *Führer* tested the free world's resolve (England was occupied with the marital problems of Edward VIII) by sending troops into the Rhineland. That summer, Spain dissolved in civil war. Although 26 nations, including Italy and Germany, pledged themselves to non-intervention, Hitler and Mussolini actively supported General Francisco Franco until the Falangists achieved victory in April 1939. In 1937 Hitler renounced the war guilt clause of the treaty of Versailles and Germany, Italy, Japan announced the formation of an anti-Comintern Axis as France and Britain tried to conceal their impotence behind the fig leaf of appeasement. Five years of *Gleichschaltung* seemed to confirm what Hitler had been saying on street corners. He was Siegfried, triumphant over Germany's enemies – the communists, lying lawyers and weak-willed generals, and the corrupt democracies. Hitler's *Nibelungenlied* contained one more group of monsters – the Jews.

A SHORT HISTORY OF GERMAN JEWRY

There may have been Jews in parts of Germany before there were Germans. Livy, Plutarch and Polybius wrote of long-haired, blue-eyed warriors from the north who brandished great swords and were accompanied to battle by shrieking women and children. But the barbarians who vexed Hannibal were Celts who traced their lineage to prehistoric settlements.[18] Jewish merchants followed Roman legions along the Rhine, Moselle and Danube Rivers centuries before the arrival of Ostrogoths, Visigoths, Franks or Lombards. Originally regarded as equals with the Romans, Jews were stripped of privileges wherever the Germans and the Catholic church became more secure. In 880 a church synod in Metz barred Jews from eating with Christians. In 1266 another council at Breslau forbade Jews from living next door to Christians. Jews were restricted to *Judengasse* (gated quarters). They could not own slaves, build synagogues or appear in public during Holy Week. Those who would not abjure Judaism in a 'blood-curdling' oath were expelled to Poland. More fled when brigands claiming to be holy warriors ravaged Rhenish towns during the Crusade period. Others followed when thousands of their coreligionists from Alsace to Vienna were burned at the stake on charges of ritual murder, host desecration and well-poisoning.

Denied land tenure, Jews could be neither *Ritter* (lord) nor *Knecht* (knight). They were *fidei inimici* (enemies of the true faith), *vogelfrei* (rootless men cursed to wander the earth), *fremde* (aliens). Payment of a *Leibzoll* (annual head tax) enabled a few to stay within a specific realm as dealers in tobacco, textiles, lenses or cattle, or as treasury agents (*Kammerknechte*). But the rights of *Schutzjuden* (protected Jews) were so limited that the Jewish code of Frederick the Great was referred to as a 'law worthy of cannibals'.[19] It was not until July 1869 that the North German Confederation granted equality to all confessions. Now intellectuals who favored Jewish assimilation demanded that Jews convert to Christianity. German nationalists agreed to let Jews attend state-sponsored schools but would not hire Jewish instructors. Germans sought out Jewish lawyers but not judges.[20] Many Germans were upset with the success of families like the Oppenheims in Cologne, the Goldschmdits and Rothschilds in Frankfurt, and the Seligmanns, Hirsches, Bleichroeders, Meyers and Liebermanns in Berlin.[21]

In the course of the struggle to gain acceptance as *Inlandern* (residents) or *Staatsburger* (citizens), Jews produced philosophers Moses Mendelssohn and Martin Buber, generals Max Hoffman and Liman von Sanders, scientists Fritz Haber and Albert Einstein, physicians Otto Warburg, Otto Meyerhof, Otto Loewi and Karl Landsteiner. Jews were accepted in regional ecclesiastical associations and Jews and Gentiles shared houses of worship in Leipzig, Stettin and Hamburg. The *Centralverein* (Central Association of German Citizens of Jewish Religion) established in 1893 was mainly concerned with defamation suits between 1893 and 1915.[22] As Shulamit Volkov and Peter Pulzer observed: 'Imperial Germany had no Dreyfus Case, no Russian-style pogroms and no publicly-elected anti-Semitic mayors as in Austria.'[23]

Karl Jaspers, Leon Poliakov, Hermann Cohen and Golo Mann claimed that the assimilation of Jews in Germany was more complete than anywhere else.[24] Said Hugo Preuss, 'We want to be German. We can be nothing else.' From Alfred Wiener: 'Fatherland is no empty word for us.' Sociologist Franz Oppenheimer: 'My Germanism is as sacred to me as my Jewish forefathers. I combine in me the German and Jewish national feeling.' And Walter Rathenau: 'My people are the Germans, nobody else.' Bernhard Dernburg, Minister of Finance in 1919, resigned when he learned of the terms of Versailles. Albert Ballin, one-time financial aide to the Kaiser, committed suicide. And while most Jews considered Weimar to be the logical product of Lessing, Goethe and Herder, another Jewish war veteran, Max Naumann, organized an anti-Zionist League of Nationalist German Jews in 1921. Naumann and his Jewish storm troopers applauded Hitler's appointment as Chancellor in 1933. The following year, the Berlin attorney died in Dachau.

GREUELPROPAGANDA AND BOYCOTTS

When Hitler came to power there were fewer than 600,000 Jews in Germany, 0.76 percent of the total population. Because of emigration, intermarriage and a low birth rate, their relative numbers had actually been decreasing since 1890. Nazi screeds reminded the faithful that it was the Jews who had crucified Christ and were plotting world domination beginning with a Zionist base in the Middle East. For the Nazis, Jews were a *Giftpilz*, a poisonous mushroom that cropped up everywhere – 160,000 Jews in Berlin, 26,000 in Frankfurt, 20,000 in Breslau. The Nazis claimed that most retailers, bankers, chiseling plutocrats were Jews. In fact 3.5 percent of the middle-class jobs in Germany were filled by Jews, many of whom were recently arrived tradesmen from eastern Europe. Only 200 of 5,000 professors and none of the major capitalists were Jews.[25]

When the Brown Shirts ruled the streets, they attacked Jews and destroyed books unacceptable to them. The works of Remarque and Werfel, Marx, Bebel and Lassalle, Heine and Kafka, Goethe and Schiller were consigned to bonfires. Goebbels delighted over the destruction saying: 'The soul of the German people can again express itself. These flames not only illuminate the final end of our era. They also light up the new age.'[26] In the United States, Rabbi Stephen Wise, head of the American Jewish Congress, urged President Roosevelt to open America's doors to political and religious refugees. Wise also proposed a boycott of German goods. His efforts were countered by Eric and James Warburg who convinced Roosevelt that reports of persecution were exaggerated.[27] German newspapers dismissed accounts of brutality as *Greuelpropaganda* – atrocity mongering. Wise's rally against Nazism at Madison Square Garden on 27 March and the appearance of Jewish pickets in New York City were too much for Hermann Goering, who was directing Germany's economic recovery. Goering summoned Max Naumann, Heinrich Stahl (president of the Berlin Jewish community) and Julius Brodnitz (chairman of the German Citizens of Jewish Faith) and warned that German Jews would not be safe unless Wise's boycott was canceled. The German Jewish leaders dutifully asked their American counterparts to cease such activities.[28]

Instead of a hoped-for concordat with Hitler, Germany's Jews suffered economic retaliation. Approved by President Hindenburg, the scheme called for a national boycott of Jewish shops, doctors and lawyers on Saturday, 1 April 1933. Soundtrucks roved the streets barking a simple message: as a response to *Greuelpropaganda*, buy only from Germans. Proclaiming a boycott was easier than executing it. There were clashes with storeowners, civilians, even members of the army. A more significant problem was the determination of a Jewish enterprise. Was a business Jewish according to its name, clientele, board of directors? How much Jewish blood was needed to label someone a Jew? In the confusion, Hitler had to extend a government loan to bail out Tietz department stores, one of the very chains he loathed, because the company employed 14,000 Germans.

THE NUREMBERG LAWS

Boycott Day demonstrated to the Nazis that there was a need for a better way to regulate Jewish activities in Germany. On 7 April 1933 the civil service and legal profession were closed to Jews. Two weeks later, Hitler barred Jewish physicians from the National Health Service. Jews were ousted from agriculture in September, journalism and other cultural activities in October. They were banned from parks, shrines, sporting clubs, public baths and recreational facilities. One exemption asked for by Hindenburg on 4 April, proved troublesome. Until the Field Marshal's death individuals who had won the Iron Cross in combat, and their families, were immune from such laws.[29]

On 25 April 1933, the Nazis carried their crusade into the classroom with a law against overcrowding of German schools. Jewish texts and instructors had already been purged. Jews could only account for 1.5 percent of the students at gymnasia, technical institutes and universities. Those who managed to graduate were awarded degrees by number, after all other students had received their honors.[30] Those who elected to remain in public schools were separated from Aryans by rows at the back of the room. *Rassenkunde* (racial science) was mandated from elementary school (with Jews portrayed as lechers or thieves) to nuclear physics (derided by Goebbels as 'an instrument of world Jewry for the destruction of Nordic science'). Few Jewish parents sent their children back to schools in the fall of 1933.

According to the *Völkischer Beobachter* of 8 April 1933, 'Our aim is the biological separation of the Jewish and German races.'[31] The Nazis especially fretted over Jewish intermarriage, 27 percent in Berlin, 39 percent in Hamburg by 1930. In 1934, the process of defining a Jew was assigned to Dr Gerhard Wagner, director of the German Medical Association. Dr Wagner and his cronies in the Society for Racial Hygiene welcomed the task of confronting Judaism which was, for them, was 'a disease incarnate'.[32] In September 1935 their handiwork was revealed to more than 500,000 Nazis at the annual party jamboree in Nuremberg. On 15 September, the Nazis declared that only those of German blood could be citizens of the state. Jews were stripped of citizenship. Officially, they were now *Staatsangehöriger* (dependents of the state). They were not to participate in public functions, salute the swastika flag, or play music by German composers. A second decree passed the same day struck against miscegenation. Marriages between Jews and Aryans were now forbidden and the Public Prosecutor's office was instructed to encourage annulments. Sexual relations outside of marriage was punishable by a fine and/or imprisonment. Jews were forbidden to employ German females between the ages of 14 and 45. Those who committed *Rassenschande* (racial shame) were shamed publicly.

On 14 November 1935, the Nazis finally declared that a Jew was anyone who had three Jewish grandparents or who had one Jewish grandparent, if that individual belonged to the Jewish faith. Individuals who had one or two Jewish *Eltern* (*Mischlings* Second Grade and First Grade) need not be deemed Jews if they did not practice Judaism. Religion, therefore was a determinant of race. Using the Nazi scheme, it was estimated there were 500,000 full, three-quarter or one-half Jews, another 300,000 *Mischlings* in Germany in 1935.[33] There would be more elaboration of the racial decrees that winter. Couples seeking to be married had to undergo physical examinations and certify Aryan ancestry through *Sippenförscher* (genealogists). For the moment, Hitler chose to moderate enforcement of the Nuremberg laws. Germany had been awarded the Olympic Games for 1936 and stung by foreign criticism, the Nazis reasoned that cash was more important than ideology.

THE OBERAMMERGAU TERCENTENARY

A year before the Nuremberg Laws were enacted, another spectacle demonstrated the importance of tourism to a sick economy. In the summer of 1934 villagers in the Bavarian town of Oberammergau staged a tercentenary of their famous passion play. Far from being a 'hymn of reconciliation' as touted by its author Alois Daisenberger, the Oberammergau's script was branded anti-Semitic by Deems Taylor, Tom Driver, Eric Bentley, Markus Barth and Krister Stendahl.[34] Audiences were treated to horned priests who debated the fate of Jesus, Pharisees chanting '*Er muss sterben! Er muss sterben!*' and a mob of Jews shrieking, '*Kreuzige Ihn! Kreuzige Ihn!*' Jews were described as 'a race oppressed by God's curse', 'treacherous', 'inhuman', 'killers of prophets' and 'hypocrites'. In a series of living tableaus, Jews were identified with the murder of Abel, the sale of Joseph into bondage, and Abraham's sacrifice of his own son. Small wonder that at the turn of the century rabbi Joseph Krauskopf called the Oberammergau Passion 'unhistoric in fact, false in interpretation and cruel inference'.

As bad as the traditional play had been, it was impossible for the 1934 Passion to remain free of Nazi taint. In June 1934 Goebbels informed the German Theater Association that art must conform to politics. Hitler also stressed blood and race as the source of artistic intuition. For Hitler, the Passion was an *Anschauungsunterricht für Rassenunterschiede* (an instruction for racial distinction). In July 1942, he praised Pontius Pilate, 'a Roman racially and intellectually superior', standing out 'like a firm, clean rock in the middle of the whole muck and mire of Jewry'.[35]

Visitors to Oberammergau in 1934 found the village 'different in particulars' (more men in Brown Shirts, swastika signs, the Hitler salute), but they agreed with the London *Times* correspondent that there was no friendlier place in Europe. A new preface thanked God for sparing the German people the plague of 'Bolshevism, this pestilence of abandonment of the race created by God'. And further, 'instead of the imminent ruin we experienced the fortune of a new life which unites us all in our race. Is there any time more favorable than these days of the suppression of the anti-Christian powers in our fatherland to remember the price the Son of God Himself paid for His people, the people who adhere to Him and to His banner.'[36]

Frederick Birchall of the *New York Times* attributed changes due to 'current tendencies in Germany'. Where Anton Lang stressed Christ's humility in 1930, Alois Lang wanted to offer a heroic fighter in the mold of Hitler. Wrote Birchall, 'Never have Oberammergau's Jewish mobs been more virulent, never have the Pharisees and scribes who invoke the mob been more vehement than this year.' Other correspondents found the play to be an epic of sustained enmity, bitterness and vengeance. The inspiration for these changes was director Georg Lang, who in 1935 would direct *The Harvest*, a drama depicting the rape of an Aryan girl by a Jew. One of the first Nazis in Oberammergau, Georg Lang served Goebbels's propaganda ministry until the end of World War II. Of 714 persons who took part in the the 1934 pageant, 152 were Nazi party members. Many others were Catholics who believed that Jews had been rejected by God.[37] Eighty-four performances of the Passion in 1934 generated more than $1 million in profits for the villagers.

THE NAZI OLYMPICS

Hitler anticipated an even more lucrative windfall in 1936. The International Olympic Committee had awarded the summer games to Germany in 1931. The Nuremberg Laws complicated the work of the IOC which was trying to explain away years of anti-Semitism. After March 1933, 250 Jewish clubs were disbanded and Jews were denied the use of recreational facilities. Wrote SA leader Bruno Malitz: 'We can see no positive value for our people in permitting dirty Jews and Negroes to travel throughout our country and compete in athletics with our best.'[38] In response, French bobsledders Philippe Rothschild and Jean Rheims indicated they would bypass the winter games at Garmisch-Partenkirchen. They were joined by Prince von Starhemberg, head of the Austrian sporting association, and athletes from Poland, Czechoslovakia and Hungary.

The fate of the Berlin Games depended upon America's actions. In June 1933, members of the IOC threatened a boycott unless the Nazis reinstated Theodor Lewald to the German Olympic Committee and pledged non-discrimination in competition. (Lewald's paternal grandmother converted to Christianity when she was 17.) Five months later, the American Amateur

Athletic Union voted to boycott the 1936 games unless Germany changed its attitude toward Jewish athletes 'in fact and theory'. Anticipation of tourist dollars and the opportunity to demonstrate the superiority of the Aryan race tempered German response to these and other provocations. Lewald was reinstated with an honorific title and the half-Jewish Captain Wolfgang Fuerstner organized the Olympic Village. Twenty-one Jewish athletes were 'nominated' for Olympic tryouts (including world champion high jumper Gretel Bergmann). No full-blooded Jews were 'invited' to training camps although two half-Jews (hockey star Rudi Ball and fencer Helen Mayer) were. Said Avery Brundage, a prominent member of the American Olympic Committee (AOC): 'Frankly, I don't think we have any business to meddle in this question. We are a sports group, organized and pledged to promote clean competition and sportsmanship.' Brigadier-General Charles Sherrill of the AOC concurred. In 1933, Sherrill had promised Rabbi Wise that the AOC would take a firm stand on the rights of Jews in Germany.

Returning from Germany in 1934, Brundage declared that Jews there assured him the government was observing the letter of the Olympic spirit. He failed to mention that discussions were conducted in the presence of the Gestapo. Through 1935 Brundage warned he would sponsor a 'rump' American team if the AOC did not call off its threatened boycott. He was supported by William Henry, director of the 1932 games, General Sherrill, and AOC Secretary Frederick Rubien. Said Rubien: 'The Germans are not discriminating against Jews in their Olympic tryouts. The Jews are eliminated because they are not good enough as athletes.' Sherrill was more blunt, declaring in the age of Hank Greenberg, Sid Luckman and Barney Ross, 'There never was a prominent Jewish athlete in history.' At a meeting of the AOC in New York in December 1935, Brundage and his cronies managed to defeat a resolution calling for an investigation of Germany. Judge Jeremiah Mahoney, a Catholic who served as President of the AOC, and several supporters angrily submitted their resignations. When the Berlin games opened, the US had its largest contingent and a rare cash surplus.

The 1936 games are remembered for the accomplishments of Jesse Owens. Less than a month after German heavyweight Max Schmeling knocked out Joe Louis, Owens avenged the honor of minorities by winning four gold medals. People recall that he was snubbed by Hitler, who refused to greet the black athlete. Hitler's actions stemmed, in part, from a flurry during the first day's activities, when he greeted three Germans who had swept the shotput competition. Instructed by IOC officials that he would have to show the same courtesy to other winners, the Nazi leader left the stadium rather than greet three American blacks who won medals in the high jump. Subsequently, he remained aloof from all winners.

If anyone had cause to be angered by what transpired in the Sportpalast it was Marty Glickman and Sam Stoller. The only two Jews on the American track team, Glickman and Stoller had qualified for the 400-meter relay team, considered to be the best in the world. On the day of competition, they were summoned to the locker room and informed by coaches Lawson Robertson and Dean Cromwell that they were being replaced. The coaches claimed the Germans were going to spring a 'surprise' team upon the Americans.[39] Back in 1936, Stoller said, 'It was a shock to get the bad news after being assured until Saturday morning that I was certain to compete.' Glickman told reporters he felt Cromwell 'was looking out for Southern Californians'. Speaking from a freer vantage in 1978, Glickman explained what really happened. The day after the 400-meter finals, Robertson told him: 'I did a terrible thing. I want to apologize.' According to Glickman: 'It is my opinion they did it to save the Nazis further embarrassment. So many blacks were winning – we won the high jump and all the sprints from the 100 through the 800 meters – they couldn't keep the blacks off the American team because there were so many. But in order to spare their friends having Jews compete and win, they kept the Jews off the team.'

That the games went on in Berlin is a testament to Brundage, a man Glickman described as 'a horror, an arrogant, autocratic American Nazi'.[40] The result was a lucrative pageant for the Nazis. Tourists spent millions in Germany and came away lauding clean, safe streets and inexpensive hotels. Athletes were impressed with the accommodation and food at the Olympic Village, and the atmosphere at the Sportpalast where a chorus proclaimed the brotherhood of man. German technology outdid itself with new timing devices and special movie cameras which enabled Leni Riefenstahl to edit the epic film 'Olympia'. Meanwhile, as marathon runners were plodding along treed boulevards in Berlin, prisoners were being tortured in nearby jails. Thousands more were languishing in concentration camps run by the *Sicherheitsdienst*. And while Jesse Owens may have been immortalized as the champion of minorities, the Nazis celebrated the fact that more medals were won by athletes from Germany than any other nation.[41]

7

The Year of Decision: 1938

THE JEWS WHO FLED GERMANY

In 1933, 37,000 Jews emigrated from Germany and another 23,000 in 1934. Incredibly, 10,000 returned in 1935. Those who left were rebuked by their co-religionists as 'deserters'. Many Jews felt that the Nazi persecution was a passing phenomenon, no worse than conditions in Poland or Romania. Besides, these were Germans, not barbaric tribesmen from the steppes. In 1936 no one could have imagined what would transpire in the ghettos and concentration camps of World War II. Some Jews dreaded trying to blend in with a new culture. Social workers in the United States and England commented about a *bei-uns* (yearning for past comforts) syndrome among refugees that contrasted one-time wealth and possessions with current poverty.

Once the Olympics were over, the Nazi regime redirected its energies to forcing Jews out of the German economy. Verbal intimidation gave way to physical assault, as the government encouraged 'voluntary' transfer of Jewish businesses to Gentiles. Between 1936 and 1938 more than 10,000 businesses were 'Aryanized', including the Petschek coal fields, Orenstein-Koppel locomotive works, department stores, textile companies, paper mills, chemical works, cigar manufacturers and steel mills, all for a fraction of their actual worth. In the process, 60,000 Jews were reduced to poverty. Those who tried to emigrate faced additional obstacles. In the last three months of 1938, Jewish emigrants paid 92,000,000 DM ($37,000,000) in flight taxes.[1] In 1937 the Nazis permitted Jews to purchase German goods that could be taken out of the country. The wrinkle was finding some place that would accept Jews. Flotsam, Erich Maria Remarque called them, the debris of humanity, shunted from one border to another without any hope.[2]

ANSCHLUSS: THE FIRST VICTIMS OF NAZI AGGRESSION

The obvious choice of German refugees was Austria. Nearby and familiar, there was no need to learn another language. After 1929, the Fatherland Front steered the nation along a neutralist course, suppressing a Socialist revolution in February 1934, shunning the call for an economic union with

Germany.[3] When the Nazi party was outlawed in Austria in June 1933, the *Führer* required German tourists bound for the south to deposit 1,000 marks against their return. Following the Röhm purge, he called upon party loyalists to act in his native land. On 25 July 1934, Austrian Brown Shirts staged their own putsch, killing Dollfuss and temporarily seizing the chancellery in Vienna.[4]

Reacting nervously to such threats in 1934, Mussolini dispatched four divisions to the Brenner Pass. The crisis passed and Austria's new Chancellor, Kurt von Schuschnigg, resisted Hitler until 1938 when he was summoned to Berchtesgaden. As Hitler lectured him on the suffering of ten million Germans in Graz and Styria, Schuschnigg knew he could no longer count on the Italians. Instead, he called a plebiscite for 13 March on the question: 'Are you in favor of a free and German, an independent and social, a Christian and united Austria?'[5] Schuschnigg believed that workers, peasants, Jews and monarchists would approve the question by 70 percent.[6]

Refusing to be outmaneuvered, Hitler delivered an ultimatum to the Austrian government on Friday morning, 11 March: postpone the plebiscite or face military intervention. A second warning was delivered to Schuschnigg at 3p.m.: resign or face attack. All through that fateful day, Schuschnigg sought support from European governments. Though upset at Hitler's threat of force, British Prime Minister Neville Chamberlain expressed understanding of the German position. Because of a cabinet crisis, there was no functioning government in France. The only nation that offered assistance (knowing it would be the next victim of Nazi imperialism) was Czechoslovakia.[7]

Lieutenant Walter Beck, a 23-year-old Jew from Vienna, welcomed a tussle with the Germans: 'The Austrian Army could have held up the Germans for four years if they wanted.'[8] Schuschnigg and his advisers saw it differently. Austria's army (consisting of 150 artillery pieces, a few tanks, no air force, two anti-aircraft guns) could resist the invasion for perhaps two days.[9] At 8p.m. on 11 March, Schuschnigg addressed the nation from the Ballhausplatz. Speaking a few feet from the spot where Dollfuss had been assassinated, he announced that Austria was yielding to prevent the shedding of German blood. It was a lie, he said, that Austrian authorities were no longer in control of events. Claims of riots all over the country were invented from A to Z. In stepping down, he called upon Austrians not to resist the forced annexation of their nation.

Shortly before dawn on Saturday, 12 March, patrols of the German 8th Army entered Passau, Salzburg, Kiefersfelden. Later in the afternoon, Hitler crossed the border in an open-air Mercedes to visit the grave of his mother. 'Special Case Otto' (the code name for the invasion of Austria) was achieved. On Sunday, 13 March 120,000 persons turned out to greet Hitler at Linz. On the day when Austrians were supposed to be voting to retain their freedom, President Wilhelm Miklas transferred power to Arthur Seyss-Inquart, the Minister of Interior. The next day a million Austrians assembled at the

Heldenplatz as Cardinal Theodor Innitzer welcomed Hitler to Vienna. Thirty years before the aspiring artist had frequented flophouses. Now the *Führer* proclaimed, 'This land is German, it has recognized its mission, it will fulfill it and will never be surpassed by anyone in loyalty to the great German national community.'[10] The provisional government authorized two measures: (a) the Re-Unification Law which declared Austria to be a province of the German Reich; and (b) a plebiscite on re-unification. Some 4,453,000 voters (99.73 percent) approved the *Anschluss* in this 'free and secret' election on 10 April 1938.[11]

GLEICHSCHALTUNG IN AUSTRIA

'You think it [terror] takes months to prepare,' said Walter Beck, 'but it happens overnight.' In 24 hours, 76,000 persons were arrested, including Dr Otto Loewi (winner of the 1936 Nobel Prize for medicine), Baron Louis Rothschild, 82-year-old Sigmund Freud and the novelist Felix Salten. Six thousand officials were dismissed from the Ministries of Public Safety and Education. General Zehner, the last Austrian Minister of Defense, and 20 of his colleagues were executed. Vienna bloomed with anti-Jewish caricatures and public invitations for Jews to come to the only place where they were welcome – the cemetery. Homes were plundered and people beaten on the streets while the police stood by. Professors were dismissed and the works of Stefan Zweig, Franz Werfel, Gustav Mahler, Georges Bizet, Mendelssohn and Arnold Schoenberg were proscribed.[12] Two months after the *Anschluss*, the daily mortality rate among Austrian Jews rose from 6 to 50. Many of these deaths were suicides. In a three-day period, authorities reported 131, 201 and 205 self-inflicted fatalities. By March 1939, Jewish suicides totaled 3,741.[13]

At this point, the Nazis were talking openly about forcing Jews to leave German territory.[14] Adolf Eichmann came to Vienna to coordinate refugee matters. From his abode in the former Rothschild mansion, Eichmann boasted that he arranged the emigration of 100,000 of Austria's Jews by May 1939,[15] but the reality was that a world unwilling to shelter German refugees in 1933 was even less inclined to welcome Austrians. Walter Beck recalled the lines of people ('longer than the lines at "Jaws"') who crowded the US consulate seeking visas. 'Some of them never got in. They stood all day. Some people would break down and beg, "At least let my children go".'[16]

AMERICA CALLS FOR A REFUGEE CONFERENCE

In 1933 Hitler taunted: 'Why does the world shed crocodile tears over the richly merited fate of a small Jewish minority? I ask Roosevelt, I ask the American people: are you prepared to receive in your midst these wellpoisoners of the German people and the universal spirit of Christianity? We would willingly give everyone of them a free steamer-ticket and a thousand-mark note for traveling expenses if we could get rid of them.'[17] On 23 March 1938 FDR, concerned that Nazi excesses might spark imitation in eastern Europe, instructed Secretary of State Cordell Hull to issue a call for a conference on refugees that summer. There were certain stipulations: no group should be equated with the refugee problem; there must be no interference with existing relief agencies; funding should come from voluntary sources; and no nation would be required to alter existing immigration laws.[18]

Use of the term 'refugees' was unfortunate. Officials offered a feeble defense that not all those in need were Jews. In 1938, the League of Nations estimated there were 300,000 stateless White Russians, 120,000 Armenians, 20,000 Nestorian (Christian) Iraqis, 30,000 Italians, 400,000 Spanish Republicans in French detention camps, another 3,000,000 deemed 'internal refugees', and millions of Chinese who had been uprooted by the Japanese.[19] The fact remains that the number of projected 'refugees' (600,000) was identical with the Jewish population of greater Germany. Harold Willis Dodds, chief US delegate to the Bermuda Conference in 1943, related: 'Everyone knew that when you talked about refugees in those days, you were talking about the Jews.'[20] Roosevelt knew it, too, for he wrote of the proposed conference that 'the policy of the German Government toward Jewish minorities was the prime cause of the entire problem'.[21]

Reference to existing relief agencies was also regrettable, for it implied that such organizations were effective. The League of Nations resettled 2,000,000 Greeks, Turks and Bulgarians after World War I. Faced with the prospect of more émigrés from Bolshevism and nationalist squabbles in the Balkans, the League established the Nansen Office in 1921. Headed by the polar explorer Fridtjof Nansen, the agency issued an international passport, enabling the bearer to work in one of the 52 nations that subscribed to the program. The problem was that the Nansen passport guaranteed a person's right to return to his country of origin. Hitler was unwilling to make such a stipulation. To prevent disruption of labor markets, in October 1933 the League created the Office of High Commissioner for Refugees from Germany. To appease US isolationists, the office was made autonomous and an American, James McDonald, became its first director. During the Austrian crisis, the Nansen Office was issuing fewer than 5,000 documents per year, the High Commissioner's Office aiding 50 refugees a week.[22] McDonald resigned in December 1935, stating that philanthropy could not resolve refugee problems.[23]

By stressing that no nation would be required to alter existing laws, the US was not just placating its friends in Europe, Roosevelt and Hull were also responding to the restrictionist spirit of America. In 1938 Americans overwhelmingly disapproved Nazi treatment of Jews (94 percent expressed disgust in a December Gallup poll) but a like number (83 percent according to a *Fortune* poll) rejected changes in the nation's immigration laws.[24] When immigration threatened to soar past one million at the end of World War I, American nativists succeeded in capping arrivals at 154,000 each year. Entry visas were parceled out to nationalities based upon their numbers in the census of 1890. Under the Johnson–Reed Law of 1924, 120,000 visas went to west and north Europeans (England, Ireland, Scandinavia). Germany and Austria were allotted 27,000 each year, Poland 6,524, Japan none at all. The system proved lethal for victims of fascism. For example, a Hungarian seeking entry to the US in 1938 would have to wait 25 years for one of the 869 visas allotted his nation.[25]

Notoriously inefficient in the best of times, American consular offices demonstrated a remarkable penchant for detail during the Depression. If a refugee had little cash in 1938, officials could reject him because he might become a public charge. If he had a job waiting in the States, he could be turned down for violating the alien contract labor law. Short of having investments in the US or possessing a professional degree, the only way a refugee could obtain a visa was to have someone in America offer a financial affidavit on his behalf. Until 1937, applicants with criminal records – including those from concentration camps – could be rejected.[26] The same policy applied to anyone with a physical impairment or suffering from starvation. Said Martin Gumpert: 'Surely the American consular officers are today the world's most skilled experts in misery.'[27] Between 1933 and 1937, 174,067 persons entered the US, while 221,239 departed, a net loss of 47,172. The immigration total for 1933 (23,068) was the lowest since 1831. Perhaps 1.5 million visas went unused during the Holocaust.

EVIAN AND THE IGCR

Thirty-two nations accepted Hull's call to attend a conference on refugees. Italy declined out of a sense of loyalty to Germany. Ireland maintained a flatline neutrality. France hosted the meeting in the resort town of Evian-les-Bains on the shores of Lake Geneva. Before the first session, the western powers added a stipulation. No 'sender' nation (countries with minority problems) could participate, only 'receiver' states. That meant east European nations (Hungary, Romania, Poland, Latvia and Lithuania) would only be accorded observer status. Without their cooperation or that of Nazi Germany, chances of formulating a workable plan of emigration were slim. Actually, once Assistant Secretary of State George Messersmith briefed the President's Advisory Committee on Political Refugees on 16 May, no one should have expected anything to come of Evian. Messersmith indicated that the goal of such a meeting was to create a third committee to deal exclusively with Austrian refugees.[28]

When the conference opened on 6 July, America's spokesman Myron Taylor recited the government's line and managed to do so without once using the word Jew.[29] The other delegates were relieved. One after another they came forward to boast of their humanitarian efforts – 25,000 refugees admitted in 1938 said France's Henry Berenger, 40,000 to Palestine according to Britain's Lord Earl Winterton. M.A. LeBreton of Argentina pointed out that his country had taken 32 Jewish immigrants for every 48 who entered the US since 1935. Chile's Garcia Oldino noted that his nation accepted 14,000 refugees since 1933. Bolivia, Peru, Cuba, Paraguay and Uruguay also boasted of double digit increases in their Jewish populations.[30] The worst case of self-promotion came on 9 July 1938, when the representative of the Dominican Republic, Virgilio Trujillo-Molina, announced that his government would accept 100,000 'agriculturists with an unimpeachable record' from Austria and Germany. Hailed as a breakthrough by Roosevelt, the Dominican offer was an empty gesture. Few, if any, of the Jews of Austria were farmers. By the end of 1941, the Dominican Republic Settlement Corporation had taken 500 Jewish families.[31]

There was another flurry of excitement when Heinrich Neumann, a surgeon from Vienna, arrived at Evian. According to Hans Habe, Neumann, a frail, 65-year-old Jew, was sent to the conference by Seyss-Inquart. The Nazis were prepared to release all 600,000 Jews in the Reich for a price of $250 apiece, $1,000 per family, a total of $150,000,000. Rabbi Wise's World Jewish Congress had rejected a similar scheme in January 1936, calling it 'blackmail'. Lucy Dawidowicz discounts the actuality of such a proposal, but Habe's wife, Licci, swears that her husband never fabricated anything and that the reason he told the story in the form of a novel (*The Mission*) was to add a dramatic touch.[32] In his book, Habe recounted how the delegates at Evian dismissed the Nazi offer as medieval ransom, a form of slavery, a ploy to obtain cash for Germany's war machine.[33] The delegates discussed and rejected a number of potential sanctuaries (West Australia, French North Africa, Shanghai, Angola, Alaska, Madagascar, Tanganyika, Rhodesia, Mindanao, Guiana and Central America). The Free World dreaded having to deal with 600,000 Jewish refugees cast adrift, with more to follow.[34]

After a week of haggling the Evian conference adjourned on 15 July 1938. As predicted, a final communiqué called for the creation of an Inter-governmental Committee on Refugees (IGCR) based in London. Independent of the League of Nations, its director was George Rublee, once a member of the US Federal Trades Commission. As Rublee and Hjalmar Schacht of the *Reichsbank* traded proposals to regulate the departure of 50,000 Jews each year from Germany, Argentina, Chile and Brazil withdrew from the IGCR. France, Belgium and Holland enacted new laws barring immigration from Germany. The British admitted 'Aryan' refugees while denying access to 'non-Aryans'. Rublee did wrest promises from the Nazis to reduce flight taxes and control the issuance of bogus visas, but he, too, offered his resignation in February 1939.[35]

In the last summer of peace, Herbert Emerson, League commissioner for all refugee questions, informed the IGCR that 500,000 Europeans were in need of relocation. Of these, 167,000 were confessional Jews from pre-Hitler Germany, 42,000 confessional Jews from Austria, 127,000 were non-Aryan Christians from greater Germany (Jews by Nuremberg definition), 140,000 were Jews in European countries of temporary refuge, and 16,000 (mostly Jews) were persons in non-European countries of temporary refuge.[36] Emerson reported that the IGCR had less than $10,000,000 in assets, all of which had been contributed by the American Joint Distribution Committee (JDC), a Jewish relief agency. Taking note of the 'lukewarm attitude' of many governments, Roosevelt urged the IGCR to continue operations with a skeletal force. When war broke out in September, Emerson, who deemed his titles to be 'purely honorary', suspended activities on behalf of refugees.

THE SUDETENLAND CRISIS AND THE MUNICH CONFERENCE

While Western diplomats wrestled with fallout from the *Anschluss*, Hitler turned his attention to Czechoslovakia. In April 1938 Hitler met with Nazi leader Konrad Henlein to outline plans for the Sudetenland. Henlein then relayed Hitler's demands to Czech President Eduard Beneš. When German troops moved toward the border in mid-May, the Czechs mobilized. France, which had a mutual security pact with Czechoslovakia, pressed the British for support. But Neville Chamberlain, aware that the Soviet Union would be of no help, temporized. Against the advice of Generals Beck and Blomberg,[37] Hitler promised 'deliverance' to Sudeten Germans at the Nuremberg rally on 12 September. When Lord Runciman, Britain's emissary in Prague, blamed the Czechs for heightening tensions, Chamberlain decided to negotiate directly with Hitler. On 15 September, the two leaders agreed that the Sudetenland should have autonomy. Six days later, Beneš gave in. In a second meeting with Chamberlain at Godesberg, Hitler made new demands: annexation by Germany of specific areas; plebiscites in other portions of Czechoslovakia; and settlement of Polish–Hungarian claims on Czech terri-tory. Shaken, the British Prime Minister departed. In the next several days, England, France and Russia prepared for war. Images of his people digging bomb shelters and distributing gas masks were too much for Chamberlain. On 29 September, he made one last effort at negotiation. Calling upon Mussolini to mediate, Chamberlain and French Premier Eduard Daladier flew to Munich.[38]

The Munich Conference rubber-stamped Hitler's demands from Godes-berg. Czechoslovakia was dismembered. The Sudetenland was awarded to Germany. Beneš resigned and went into exile on 6 October.[39] Slovakia declared its independence on 16 March 1939. Ruthenia went to Hungary on 13 March. Poland annexed the coal fields of Teschen about the same time. Germany completed the destruction of Czechoslovakia by declaring a protectorate over Bohemia and Moravia on 14 March. The last action finally convinced Chamberlain that Hitler's territorial appetite was insatiable. But in October 1938, the British Prime Minister returned from Munich with a scrap of paper that supposedly guaranteed 'peace in our time'.

REFUGEES IN NO-MAN'S-LAND: THE GRYNSZPANS

The rape of Czechoslovakia complicated efforts of IGCR and Reichsbank officials to regulate the flow of refugees. No-man's-land, once the desolate zone between two trenchlines, acquired a new meaning over the winter of 1938/39. In Austria, Nazis loaded a vermin-infested barge with Jews from the Burgenland and set it adrift in the Danube. Slovak authorities dumped hundreds of freezing Jews into fields between Mischdorf and Bratislava, at Nitra, Tapocany, Lilina, Michalovce, Prestany and Zilino. Following their annexation of Carpatho-Ruthenia, Hungarian bigots expelled 10,000 Jews over the border at Kosiće.

All of this was noted by the Camp of National Unity in Poland which won 90 percent of the seats in the Sejm that fall. On 6 October, the day Beneš stepped down, the government of Colonel Joseph Beck, General Edward Rydz-Smygly and Premier Felicjan Slawo-Skladkowski issued a seemingly innocuous edict. The new law advised Poles residing outside the country and carrying passports older than five years that they had to secure special visas by 29 October or forfeit their citizenship. Many Jews had been sent to Germany during World War I or emigrated during the Weimar period. Polish anti-Semites hoped that as many as 50,000 would ignore the instructions and become wards of Germany.[40]

The ploy almost worked. Beginning with the night of 27 October, Gestapo officials swooped down upon Polish Jews residing in Germany. In the next week, 18,000 men, women and children were dumped over the border. Families were separated, people killed, and a few went mad. Demoralized Jews clustered in makeshift camps near Poznan, Lodz, Lemberg, Cracow and Zbaszyn. They slept on the streets, in stables and under blankets draped over tree limbs. As typhus became rampant, the Joint Distribution Committee supplied soup in huge vats and the impoverished Jews of Poland contributed 2,000,000 zlotys ($400,000) for refugee relief.[41]

One of the families living in a boxcar near Zbaszyn was that of Zindel Grynszpan. The father of eight, Grynszpan had come to Hanover in 1911. Never naturalized, he eked out a living first as a tailor, and then as a grocer. His sixth child, Herschel, was born in Germany in 1921. At 17, the younger Grynszpan went to live with an uncle in Paris. During the first week of November 1938 Herschel received a postcard from his sister Berta describing conditions in Zbaszyn. Grynszpan crafted an appeal to President Roosevelt.[42] Distraught, he decided to avenge his family's suffering. Somehow, he obtained a revolver. On the morning of 7 November, he penned a last note ('My dear parents. I could not do otherwise. May God forgive me. My heart bleeds at the news of 12,000 Jews' suffering. I must protest in such a way that the world will hear me. I must do it. Forgive me. Herschel.')[43] and went to the German Embassy.

Incredibly, this short, swarthy Jew, who claimed to be carrying a letter for Ambassador von Welczek, was permitted to go upstairs and rove the halls of the embassy. By mistake, Grynszpan entered the office of legation Third Secretary Ernst vom Rath. Asked for the message, he shouted, 'You are a filthy *Boche* and here in the name of 12,000 persecuted Jews is your document.' Vom Rath was shot five times. He lived two days. Grynzspan was taken into custody by embassy porters who turned him over to the French police. Because of legal delays, Grynszpan remained in prison till the summer of 1940 when Goebbels demanded a show trial to prove he acted as an agent of 'World Jewry'. That trial was postponed when Grynszpan threatened to claim a failed homosexual relationship with vom Rath.[44]

KRISTALLNACHT

Hitler had long wanted to address lingering resentment among the Brown Shirts for his purge of Röhm. The assassination of Swiss Nazi leader Wilhelm Gustloff at Davos in February 1936 alerted the Nazis to the possibility of channeling popular rage against Jews. Hitler mused how the murder of Henlein might justify an invasion of Czechoslovakia. During the summer of 1938 facilities at Buchenwald and Sachsenhausen were expanded in anticipation of Jewish prisoners. Jews were barred from serving as financial advisers, salesmen, publishers, realtors and tourist guides. Two hundred Jewish-owned banks were closed and all Jews were ordered to add 'Israel' or 'Sarah' to their given names. On 8 June, the 51-year-old Munich synagogue was destroyed by arson. Two weeks later, US Ambassador Wilson reported how Nazi gangs smeared the word 'Jude' across the windows of shops along the fashionable Kurfürstendamm in Berlin. On 10 August, Streicher presided over the partial destruction of the Nuremberg synagogue that had been chartered by Ludwig of Bavaria in 1872.[45]

Vom Rath's death on 9 November provided the excuse for the Nazis' bloodbath against Jews. Coincidentally, that day was the anniversary of Hitler's 1923 putsch. Goebbels, addressing an audience assembled in the same Munich beer hall, made it clear that the regime would not oppose spontaneous expressions of rage.[46] *Kristallnacht* (the Night of Broken Glass) began at 1 a.m. with attacks against synagogues and Jewish shops in Breslau. Police and firemen stood by, as mobs smashed glass, started fires, and chanted, 'You should all die in the fire.'[47] Within the hour, 10,000 rioters torched seven of Berlin's temples, using hatchets against the Potsdam synagogue because it was too close to other structures. In Leipzig human remains were exhumed and strewn about the Jewish cemetery. At 3 a.m. Jews in Furth were driven to a stage in a public theater. In Emden, residents of a Jewish old folks home also were beaten and marched through the square. Children from an orphanage in Dinslaken were forced to witness the burning of their home.[48] Twelve-year-old Sonja Schulmann had experienced anti-Semitism in her hometown of Neustadt. Her schoolteacher had hung the little girl by her coat collar to a peg in the cloakroom. Her mother had died of pneumonia when she was denied medical treatment. While her father sought visas to America, Sonja was at a boarding school outside Frankfurt. On *Kristallnacht*, Sonja and her classmates were forced to watch as blackshirts burned Jewish prayer books in the schoolyard.[49]

That night, Gestapo agents in *Rauberzivil* (rubberized raincoats) arrested Leo Sonnenborn, a haberdasher from Frankfurt. His widow, Settie related what happened in Buchenwald: 'They beat them all, especially the big ones. One day, it was snowing. They were standing outside. They had no shoes on. A brother-in-law of my aunt was standing in front of Leo and had a heart attack. He was sitting down, and they thought he just didn't want to stand up. They beat him to death. My aunt got an urn with his ashes.'[50] To obtain her husband's release, Settie Sonnenborn renounced claims to her father's cattle estate. 'Leo was four weeks in the concentration camp. I didn't know he was coming home. In the evening, at 11 o'clock, the bell rang. I opened the door and I heard his footsteps. He had lost weight and his head was shaved. He looked awful and he stank. He said, "I didn't have my suit off in four weeks." So he took his suit off, and I took it down to the garbage.'

The Nazi firestorm swept through Germany and Austria. Twenty-one synagogues burned in Vienna where 50 persons committed suicide that night.[51] More synagogues burned in Freiburg, Stuttgart, Karlsruhe, Heidelberg, Heilbrunn, Bingen and Tübingen. At Worms, a synagogue dating to 1034 was leveled. In Dusseldorf, one man was stabbed with a pitchfork, another had his jaw broken, a 70-year-old suffered a shattered pelvis. In the resort town of Baden-Baden, religious leaders were forced to sing the 'Horst Wessel Lied', then watch as their synagogue was set afire at midday on 10 November. It was much the same in Dortmund, an industrial center north of Düsseldorf. Among Dortmund's 300 Jews were the Grunfelds, Czech nationals with four young sons. When vom Rath died, Herman Grunfeld, *gabbai* at the Dortmund synagogue, brought the Torah scrolls home. His son Eli who was 15 at the time recalled:

> It was about midnight. All of a sudden, we heard the windows downstairs being shattered. At least a half-dozen SS men came up to our apartment, wearing black coats. Father and mother told us to hide under the bed. Then he opened the door when they knocked. They came in and started beating him. He was bleeding all over, shouting in German and Yiddish, 'Don't hit

me!' My mother was crying, so we went to help our father, shouting. 'Leave my father alone!' They pushed us aside and hit my mother. They must have thrown her at least ten feet. They were breaking the furniture with heavy truncheons. We had a grandfather's clock which they broke. They destroyed my father's Yiddish books. But they didn't find the Sefer Torahs. They were behind the door to the bedroom and when the SS opened the door, they didn't see it.[52]

A Gentile neighbor intervened, pointing out that Grunfeld was a citizen of Czechia. The next day Eli's parents decided to send the two older boys to England as yeshiva students. Bertha Grunfeld accompanied Eli and Leib to the Czech consulate in Cologne, then to Amsterdam. She stayed with them two days before returning to Germany. In June 1943 the elder Grunfelds were deported to Theresienstadt. They were murdered that summer.

ATONEMENT

Nearly 600 synagogues were burned or confiscated during the 'Night of Breaking Glass'. Several thousand stores and businesses were demolished.[53] Twenty thousand Jews were thrown into concentration camps.[54] Captain Erich Wolf, a half-Jew who commanded Goering's squadron in World War I, was beaten to death at the entry gate to Buchenwald.[55] Perhaps 2,500 Jews died as a result of *Kristallnacht*. The Nazis may have anticipated the universal rebuke that followed, but they failed to consider that Jewish businesses and houses of worship were insured. Aping Tsarist anti-Semites who turned responsibility for the pogroms of 1881–82 back upon the victims, the Nazis blamed the Jews who not only committed 'dastardly murders', but were guilty of an 'inimical attitude' toward the German people. On 12 November, the government called for the elimination of Jews from the economic life of Germany. Jewish businesses and real estate were to be Aryanized by 1 January 1939. The Jewish community was ordered to pay an 'atonement fine' of one billion marks ($400,000,000) and to divest itself of stocks, bonds, gold, platinum and silver within the week.[56]

The governments of Holland, Great Britain, Sweden, Denmark, even the Soviet Union denounced *Kristallnacht*. In America, Herbert Hoover, Alf Landon, Thomas Dewey and Gerald Nye chastised the Nazis. They were joined by Al Smith, Interior Secretary Harold Ickes, John L. Lewis, William Green, Sinclair Lewis, Harry Emerson Fosdick, Henry Sloane Coffin, Episcopal Bishop William Manning and Bishop Edwin Hughes of the Methodist Church. The National Conference of Christians and Jews set aside two days for prayer and the Reverend Ralph Sockman of New York warned: 'Christianity must save the Jews if it is to save itself'. When Nazi thugs attacked the palaces of Cardinal Faulhaber in Munich and Innitzer of Vienna (both of whom had condemned *Kristallnacht*), Archbishop Michael Curley of Baltimore denounced Hitler as a madman and dared the Nazi to meet him at the State Department.[57]

Criticism came from unexpected sources. *The New Yorker Staats-Zeitung*, the foremost German-language daily in the US, editorialized: 'In the name of our dear ones do we protest against the desecration of the German name through fanatics in the ranks of the party in power who are trying to drag a great people into the mire of their degradation.'[58] The national executive of the American Legion deplored 'the unconscionable policies now being pursued by the German Government with respect to racial and religious minorities'. Columnist Westbrook Pegler denounced 'this Nazi thing' as 'the final act in the debasement of the German nation'.[59] Henry Ford agreed with the editors of *Commonweal*, *Nation* and *New Republic* calling for the issuance of 100,000 to 500,000 emergency visas. Said Ford, 'I believe that the United States cannot fail at this time to maintain its traditional role as a haven for the oppressed. I am convinced not only that this country could absorb many of the victims of oppression who must find a refuge outside of their native lands, but that as many of them as could be admitted under our selective quota system would constitute a real asset to our country.'[60]

On 15 November FDR recalled Ambassador Hugh Wilson and suspended trade talks with the Nazis. Roosevelt told reporters: 'I myself could scarcely believe that such things could occur in a twentieth century civilization.' Asked if he favored a mass transfer of Jews, Roosevelt hedged: 'I have given a great deal of thought to it', then added, 'the time is not ripe for that'.[61] Three days later, Roosevelt dashed any hope that the government might take some initiative. The President noted there were nearly 15,000 refugees from Germany and Austria in the country under visitors' visas. Conceding that such people would in peril if they went home, the President said the US would extend visas another six months, then another if necessary. Eventually, they would have to return to their place of origin. 'They cannot be here and then come in under a later quota under the present law. They would have to go.'[62]

THE SS *ST LOUIS*: VOYAGE OF THE DAMNED

Sonja Schwartz came to the United States with her father at the end of the summer of 1939. Walter Beck, Eli Grunfeld, Leo and Settie Sonnenborn also managed to reach safety before the start of World War II. However, 907 Jews aboard the Hamburg-American liner SS *St Louis* were less fortunate. When the *St Louis* sailed from Germany for Cuba on 15 May 1939, its passengers knew there were problems with their landing permits. Each had paid $150 to the Cuban Director of Immigration for their papers. These were voided ten days before the vessel sailed. Aboard the *St Louis*, officials reassured passengers that their permits would be honored. Passengers were hopeful because representatives of the JDC and the National Coordinating

Committee (NCC) on Refugees were meeting with Cuban President Laredo Bru and strongman Fulgencio Batista. They created a Jewish council aboard ship with attorney Josef Josef as its head. One man was less optimistic. Just released from Dachau, Aaron Pozner bore the razor cut of a camp inmate. Fearful of being rearrested, he spent the night before sailing hiding in a warehouse. While his fellow passengers sunned themselves on deck, Pozner remained in his cabin during the ocean voyage.

When the *St Louis* docked at Havana on 27 May, only a handful of passengers were permitted to land. Bru, responding to an outcry in the Cuban press, ordered the vessel out of harbor, threatening to have it towed by gunboats if necessary. On 2 June, the *St Louis* began a week-long odyssey through the Caribbean. Three days later, Bru reversed his decision, announcing that Cuba would grant temporary refuge to the passengers if relief organizations put up $500 guarantees for each. The total amount required ($500,000) had to be raised within a specific time. When neither the JDC nor the NCC could collect such a sum, Bru broke off negotiations. Meanwhile, as the *St Louis* passed within view of Miami Beach, the US Coast Guard was alerted to the possibility that its captain might try to beach the ship on American soil. That very thought had crossed Captain Gustav Schroeder's mind. It returned as the vessel sailed by the coast of England on its way to the North Sea and a melancholy welcome in Hamburg. At the last moment, England, France, Holland and Belgium agreed to divide the 900 Jewish passengers, provided relief agencies guaranteed their maintenance. At the same time, officials from the JDC, NCC and the League advised that action on behalf of the *St Louis* passengers did not 'constitute a precedent for other ship-loads'. Most of the passengers of the *St Louis* were eventually sent to concentration camps when the Nazis occupied western Europe between 1940 and 1942. Perhaps 240 of the original 907 passengers survived World War II. Aaron Pozner, the man who had just been released from Dachau and was so worried about his freedom, ultimately died in the gas chambers of Auschwitz.[63]

World War II Begins: The Polish Ghettos

THE MOLOTOV-RIBBENTROP PACT

Once Czechoslovakia was safely tucked away, the *Führer* launched a campaign on behalf of the million Germans living in the Polish Corridor. Such bombast was by now too much for British Prime Minister Chamberlain, who made it clear that his government was prepared to go to war to protect Poland. The same was true for France and even the USSR. When Germany's generals again warned that the nation could not sustain a two-front war, Hitler conceded the point. The Nazi leader dispatched Ribbentrop to Moscow while Britain and France relied upon low level representatives to shore up the détente with Russia. The democracies did not appreciate the stakes involved until it was too late. On 23 August 1939, Hitler and Stalin announced the signing of a ten-year non-aggression pact. Secret protocols later revealed that in the event of a political rearrangement in eastern Europe (i.e. Germany's conquest of Poland and Lithuania), Russia was to have a free hand in Finland, the Baltic states, Bessarabia and eastern Poland.[1]

One week after the signing of the Nazi–Soviet Pact, Germany claimed Polish troops attacked a radio station at Gleiwitz in Upper Silesia. Invoking the right of self-defense, Hitler declared war on Poland on 1 September 1939. In a rambling speech, he promised not to make war on women or children and vowed not to rest until the conflict was successfully concluded.[2] Wagering that the Allies would sit on the Western front, the *Führer* threw 44 infantry, six motorized and six Panzer divisions, plus 1,500 combat aircraft into the Polish campaign. Germany overran Poland in 28 days.

BLITZPOGROM

Speaking to the Reichstag on 30 January 1939, Hitler warned: 'If the international Jewish financiers in and outside Europe should succeed in plunging the nations once more into a world war, then the result will not be the Bolshevization of the earth, and thus the victory of Jewry, but the annihilation of the Jewish race in Europe!' At the same time, the Nazi leader told Czech Foreign Minister František Chvalkovsky, '*Die Juden würden bei uns vernichtet*' (the Jews will be destroyed by us).[3]

The *Blitzkrieg* spawned its own *Blitzpogrom*. German troop trains headed east with signs chalked, *Wir fahren nach Polen, die Juden zu versohlen* ('We're traveling to Poland to thrash the Jews'). Wehrmacht units assisted the SS with the desecration of Jewish houses of worship, cemeteries and community houses. At Wloclawek, Sochaczew and Kutno they knocked over tombstones. In Orle, Przemysl and Lodz, they used heavy artillery to pummel synagogues into rubble. The Nazis celebrated the expulsion of Jews from Bydgoszcz by ripping the Star of David from the synagogue roof. Horses were tethered at the ark in the Bedzin synagogue. Some of these buildings were used as latrines or dormitories. Regular troops were photographed laughing while their comrades kicked Jews in the streets, forced them to goose step, offer the Hitler salute, sweep off tanks or pray over fallen companions.[4] Jews were forced to straddle one another like horses, bark like dogs, or use their prayer shawls to clean toilets. Unlike World War I, German soldiers were not punished for misdeeds. In October Hitler issued a general amnesty, removing them from jurisdiction of regular courts martial.[5]

The Nazis delighted in tormenting Orthodox men. They set fire to the beards of Jews in Zgierz. At Aleksandrov, near Lodz, they simply ripped off half the facial hair. As an observer in Warsaw noted:

> It was the practice of Nazi officers to cut off the beard of any bearded Jew they saw. It made no difference whether the wearer was an old and venerable rabbi or a young man with a stubby growth. Sometimes the shearing was done at home, when the Nazis came round to take a census. Sometimes it was done summarily on the street. An officer driving along in his car would sight a bearded Jew in the distance. The car would put on speed and draw up alongside the unfortunate Jew and off would come the beard. A common variation of this was to cut only half of the beard taking care to pull off bits of flesh with it. If scissors were by chance not at hand an ordinary knife was used, and in that case a swastika would be cut in the victim's hair.[6]

German troops were joined in these activities by Polish anti-Semites. Polish *schmaltzovniks* (informers) served in the auxiliary Blue Police, and pointed out Jews who attempted to secure food from public soup kitchens and betrayed Jews trying to pass as Aryans.[7] At Kalisz, the Nazis assembled several hundred Jews in the synagogue. After burning the torah scrolls, they torched the building, killing most of the people inside. On Rosh Hashanah, 35 Jews were burned alive in the slaughterhouse of Mielec. In the industrial town of Bielsko 2,000 Jews were taken to a local school. There they were hanged by their arms, beaten, scalded with hot water, and finally killed by having garden hoses thrust down their throats till their stomachs ruptured. At Ostrowe, on 3 September, male Jews were ordered to dig their own graves and were then shot.[8]

Those murdered at Gdynia included judges, bankers, men who oversaw the operation of the port. Among the dead at Inowroclaw were a count and a chemist. In Radom, Lublin, Kielce, Warsaw, Olkusz, Otwok, Mlawa, Rybnik and Lodz the Nazis murdered 80-year-old priests, book publishers, high-school students, hoteliers, physicians, engineers, factory cashiers and policemen. Some were beaten to death with rifle butts or lead pipes. Others were left hanging from lamp posts.[9] Heydrich labeled the practice 'housecleaning'. No justification was offered for the following atrocity:

> Zosia was a little girl, the daughter of a physician. During an 'action' one of the Germans became aware of her beautiful diamondlike dark eyes. 'I could make two rings out of them,' he said, 'one for myself and one for my wife.' His colleague is holding the girl. 'Let's see whether they are really so beautiful. And better, yet, let's examine them in our hands.' Among the buddies exuberant gaiety breaks out. One of the wittiest proposes to take the eyes out. A shrill screaming and the noisy laughter of the soldier-pack … What happens next is that the fainting child is lying on the floor. Instead of eyes two bloody wounds are staring. Two weeks later I met the girl by chance. It was a quiet day, the girl was lying in her bed. A handkerchief was tied around her eyes. The girl was stroking her mother's hand and comforting her: 'Don't cry, mother dear, it probably had to happen this way. It is still better that they took my eyes instead of killing me.' At one of the next 'actions' little Zosia was taken away. It was, of course, necessary to annihilate the blind child.[10]

CREATION OF *JUDENRATS*

Under the New Order, a little less than one-third of Poland, chiefly the old German territories from Danzig down to Silesia, was reincorporated into the Reich. The eastern third, from Bialystok to Lwow, was awarded to Russia. The leftovers, including the provinces of Warsaw (ruled by SS Police Chief Ludwig Fischer), Lublin (under Odilo Globocnik), Kielce (SS Police Chief Friedrich Krüger) and Cracow (*Brigadeführer* Otto Wachter), known as the Government-General, were placed under the command of Hans Frank who ruled from Wawel Castle in Cracow. It was here that the Nazis intended to deposit the bulk of Europe's Jews.[11]

In a gesture designed to confound the Jews, late in September, Heydrich ordered the creation of *Judenrats* in towns with populations exceeding 10,000. Jews could not be suspicious of councils whose functions were reminiscent of their own *Kehillahs*. What they did not realize was that these 24-man councils would be chaired by men like Adam Czerniakow in Warsaw, Chaim Rumkowski in Lodz, Jacob Gens in Vilna, and Moshe Merin in Sosnowiec, second-tier leaders who fancied themselves as *Shtadlanim* (respected intercessors) and who in fact were regarded by Jews and Germans alike as *Hofjuden* (court Jews).[12]

The Warsaw *Judenrat* counted 6,000 employees, 12 times the number who held jobs with the old *Kehillah*.[13] Tracking births, deaths and locations of Jews in a town was not so different from what the *Kehillah* had done. Concern about so many idle Jews prompted Friedrich Krüger to put male Jews between the ages of 12 and 60 to work removing the debris of war, shoveling snow, and constructing the new Otto Line between the Bug and San Rivers.[14] As the Nazis debated the fate of the Jews, *Judenrat* officials tried to impress them with their productivity. By the summer of 1942 the *Arbeitsamt* in Warsaw listed 70,000 furriers, hatters, tailors and shoemakers, along with workers in saw mills, bakeries, tanneries and factories that manufactured socks, gloves, cardboard boxes, brushes, kerchiefs, mattresses, toys, rubber, and pots and pans.[15]

Each community was permitted to organize an *Ordnungs dienst* (order service/police). These volunteer units directed traffic, supervised sanitation, and disposed of dead bodies. Strutting about in caps, uniforms and boots, the Jewish police hoped that such service would protect them from deportation. According to Emmanuel Ringelblum, archivist of the Jewish Historical Institute, nearly half of the 2,000 men in Warsaw's public safety force were non-Jews, including chief Josef Szerynski who had converted before the war.[16] They were, said Ringelblum, men of 'the lowest class', 'underworld people', 'the scum come to the top'.

The *Judenrat* and police were responsible for implementing decrees issued by Nazi authorities. In November 1939, this meant that Jews over the age of 12 were required to wear a white band marked with a blue Star of David on their right arms. Jewish places of business were to be identified with a star. Jewish physicians were not to treat Aryan patients, nor were Jews to attend Aryan doctors. The Nazis blocked Jewish bank accounts and confiscated savings over 2,000 zlotys ($100). They seized books, pianos, even commodes from Jewish apartments, while forcing *Judenrats* to turn over stocks of soup and rice. When Polish hooligans attempted pogroms in the spring of 1940, Jews were barred from certain streets and parks. They could sit in sections marked 'for Jews only' on streetcars. When, in April 1941 they were barred from buses or taxis, creative thinkers jerry-rigged rickshaws out of bicycles. In Warsaw, the trading house of Kohn and Heller serviced Jewish neighborhoods with horse-drawn wagons (dubbed 'Uncle Kohn's Cabins').

NISKO

Heydrich's *Schnellbrief* of 21 September 1939 spoke of creating a *fremdsprächigen Gau Krakau*[17] but that was deferred while diplomats resolved 'secret' aspects of the Molotov–Ribbentrop pact.[18] The Nazis sought guarantees for *Volksdeutsch* (ethnic Germans) residing in the Baltic states and Volhynia. On 6 October 1939, Hitler announced that the Warthegau would be integrated into the Reich. The territory abutting Russian Galicia would be made over into a Jewish Reservation. Non-Germans would have to leave

German territory to make room for ethnic Germans, a shift of five million people.[19] The task of *Festigung deutschen Volkstums* (consolidation of the German people) was entrusted to Heinrich Himmler. An enthusiastic advocate of the *Heim ins Reich* program, Himmler had been trying to persuade 200,000 South Tyroleans to come home since May. (The Tyroleans rejected land in the Beskid foothills near Crakow.) Now Himmler had to deal with 60,000 *Volksdeutsch* refugees from Lithuania, Latvia and Estonia, 200,000 from eastern Poland, several hundred thousand more from Bessarabia, Bukovina and Transylvania. And while the *Reichsführer* greeted several transports,[20] it was virtually impossible to maintain the stated goal of three non-Germans displaced for every repatriated German. Polish farms were too small for Germans, some of whom could speak Polish and understood that the confiscations were arbitrary.[21]

Deportations of Jews, Poles and Gypsies from the Warthegau began in October 1939. Four months later military governors in Bromberg, Kalisz, Graudenz and Posen proclaimed their cities free of Jews.[22] Sixty thousand Jews already had been displaced as a result of the German invasion of Poland. Thousands more were sent to Lublin, Cracow, Czestochowa and Warsaw that winter. The *Kultursgemeinde* in Vienna advised the city's remaining 55,0000 Jews to prepare for deportation for what was being called 'the Lublin Reservation'.[23] The site of the proposed reservation was Nisko, a town on the San River, south of Lublin. Ultimately one million Jews were to be squeezed into this desolate region. SS officers painted a grim picture for Jews: 'The *Führer* has promised Jews a new homeland. There are no houses. If you build there will be a roof over your head. There is no water; the wells around carry disease. There is cholera, dysentery and typhoid. If you bore and find water, you will have water.'[24] The first work details at Nisko froze behind barbed wire in subzero temperatures. A handful of craftsmen from the second gang were permitted to remain in the camp. The rest were marched through a heavy rain to the Soviet border where they were warned: 'Anyone who tries to come back will be shot.' Because Hans Frank opposed the dumping of Jews in his realm, only 4,000 persons had been deported to Nisko by April 1940.[25]

THE FIRST GHETTOS: WARSAW

Despite the failure of Nisko, the Nazis continued to move people from reclaimed German soil. Only now these Jews were dumped into cities like Katowice, Bedzin, Kalisz, Sosnowiec, Czestochowa and Lodz. Stripped of their nationality, deportees were placed in a Yiddish-speaking milieu that was alien to many of them. They sat on straw in cavernous halls, subsisting on cabbage soup and potatoes supplied by the *Judenrats*. Observed *Die Deutsche Polizei*:

4. Warsaw Jewish cemetery. Gravesite of the great Yiddish writer, Yitzhok Leibush Peretz.

Wherever we looked, we saw Jews. And what figures! Filthy, ragged and with an expression in which a perpetual grin mingled with hesitation and uncertainty. The stones in the streets resemble caverns and holes. They were thick with dirt. The deeper we went into the ghetto, the more dismal it became. The streets grew narrower, the dirty houses with their filthy windows without curtains became smaller. In the rooms which were on the ground floor the Jews had hung cardboard or newspapers over the windows so that one should not be able to look into their filthy stables. *Mögen Sie in Ihrem Dreck ersticken – uns soll es recht sein* (Let them choke in their filth. It's all right with us).[26]

This was Warsaw, one of the greatest cultural centers in Jewish history. Eighty Jewish newspapers and magazines were published here in 1939. In 1920 Dr Samuel Goldflamm and Jacob Apenszlak founded the Jewish Art Society, preserving religious treasures and paintings by Mane Katz, Artur Szyk, Jacob Apfelbaum and Maurycy Minkowksi. Fifty Jewish libraries indexed more than 260,000 volumes of Jewish literature and Warsaw was the home of the great Yiddish writer Yitzhok Leibush Peretz. The Jewish district beyond Krasinski Park was a labyrinth of yeshivas and synagogues. The Methibtha Institute headed by Rabbi Solomon Joskowicz had 400 students. Dr Moses Tauber's Seminary for Teachers of Jewish Religion supplied Poland's public schools with skilled educators. And here in Warsaw was the Institute for Science of Judaism, a university offering courses in bible, Jewish History, archaeology, sociology, homiletics. The faculty included Professor Meir Balaban, Rabbi Abraham Heschel and Dr Arieh Tartakower.[27]

In the winter of 1939/40 the Nazis began squeezing Jews back into traditional neighborhoods. Ghettos in all but name, these *Judenwohnbezirken* (Jewish dwelling sections) were supposed to be epidemic zones. On Rosh Hashanah (16 October 1940) the Nazis informed Warsaw's Jews that they would be separated in one month. Some people were relieved that they would not have to deal with Polish thugs. The *Judenrat* favored compliance. Lacking arms or organization for resistance, there was no alternative. One-third of the city, 80,000 Gentiles, 150,000 Jews had to relocate. When the ghetto was closed on 15 November, the people realized they were penned.

A wall 11 miles long ringed 100 city blocks in the oldest section of north central Warsaw. Where a pre-war mix of 150,000 poor Jews and Gentiles once lived, 445,000 Jews would eventually be closeted. Thirty percent of the city's

5. Warsaw 1942. A dead Jewish child from the ghetto (Holocaust Memorial Museum).

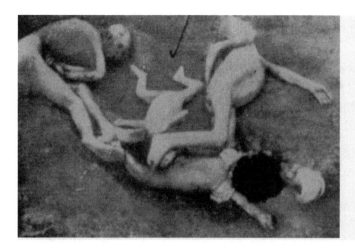

6. Warsaw 1942. Jewish children, victims of edema and starvation (Holocaust Memorial Museum).

population occupied 2.4 percent of its space.[28] The Warsaw Ghetto had no streetcar connection with other parts of the city, no parks, no playgrounds, and few trees. Members of the Jewish Police, Polish Blues and SS monitored 13 gates. Jews roved the ghetto, fondling used books on Leszno Street, hawking rags on Chlodna or Zelazna streets. For most, the only exit from the ghetto was via the Jewish cemetery off to the northwest. Later, it would be the *Umschlagplatz* (railway center due north).

The epidemic zone became a self-fulfilling prophecy. When the Nazis created the ghetto, they excised the 1,200-bed Warsaw Jewish Hospital and the 300-bed Jewish Children's Hospital, two of the largest health facilities in eastern Europe. Physicians struggled to contain outbreaks of exanthematic typhus (a flea-carried plague that afflicted as many as 100,000 persons and which proved fatal for 15 percent of its victims), tuberculosis, typhoid or colitis (a virulent form of dysentery that could kill within two days of onset). Records show 750 of 784 people were sick at No. 3 Pawia, 252 of 287 at No. 7 Ostrowska, 190 of 190 at No. 14 Ostrowska. Children suffering from contagious diseases were placed two or three to a bed in the hope that body heat might keep them alive. About 43,000 persons died in 1941, a death rate of 10 percent.[29]

Many were victims of one of the cruelest starvation programs in human history. In 1941, the Nazis sacked Poland of 800,000 tons of bread, 150,000 tons of sugar, 40,000 tons of meat, 1,000,000 tons of potatoes, 700,000 head of swine, plus countless eggs, chickens, etc.[30] At the same time, the Nazis decreed rationing in the conquered territories. A German living in Poland was entitled to 2,083 calories per day. A Polish Gentile received 1,355. A Jew was eligible for 209 calories per day.[31] The Nazis disagreed about the enforcement of rationing (Civil Administrator Heinz Auerswald and his aide Max Bischoff were more humane than 'attritionists' like *Gruppenführer* Bruno Streckenbach). All concurred with Commandant Fischer who predicted that the Jews would disappear from hunger and 'nothing will remain of the Jewish Question but a cemetery'.[32]

Jews could purchase food at sites operated by the *Judenrat* at 12:30 and 4:30 p.m. The only meat available (horsemeat) was not kosher and sold at 75 cents a pound. Bread that was 33 percent sawdust, chestnuts and other ersatz materials sold at $1.20 a pound, potatoes and groats at $5, sugar $7, a single egg cost 35 cents.[33] A ration card cost 3.5 zlotys (less than 20 cents). Desperate people tunneled under or climbed over the walls in an effort to smuggle. Many children turned to begging. A popular song in the kingdom of hunger was *Hot Rachmones*, the words for which were: 'Have pity, have mercy, good people. Drop me a piece, a piece of bread. A tiny, tiny piece of bread. Why a few crumbs, some crumbs of bread. Have mercy, have pity, good people. Tra la, la, la, la.'[34]

There was plenty of food, champagne and caviar for collaborators and their women in cafes like the Melody Palace, Gypsy Tavern, Hotel Britannia and the Quiet Corner.[35] Meanwhile, the *Judenrat* operated 141 soup kitchens. Members of *Toropol*, *Hashomer Hatzair* and *Tkumah* planted vegetable gardens. Until Pearl Harbor, the Joint Distribution Committee, HIAS, ORT (vocational training), TOZ (Jewish medical society) and CENTOS (child welfare) had agents in the ghetto. YIKOR (the Jewish Cultural Organization) started a children's chorus, five theaters in Polish and Yiddish, and a chamber orchestra. The latter showcased Marysia Ajzensztat ('the Nightingale of the Ghetto') and Ludwik Holcman (a violin prodigy who was murdered at Treblinka). And there was the ONEG SHABBAT, a literary group that sponsored lectures and gathered documents as evidence of Nazi war crimes.[36]

Despite such efforts, people died in droves. A few simply lay down on the sidewalk and never woke up again. The next morning they were covered with newspaper, until work details collected the bony cadavers in pushcarts and wheeled them to common graves. Children, some of whose parents were dead, huddled in rags on the streets. In November 1941, Dr Ringelblum wrote of shoeless children with blue hands standing dumbly on Nowolipki Street weeping. 'I heard a tot of three or four yammering. The child will probably be found frozen to death tomorrow morning, a few hours off. Early October, when the first snows fell, some 70 children were found frozen to death on steps of ruined houses.'[37] Dr Janusz Korczak, who maintained an orphanage for 196 children on Sienna Street lamented in his diary, 'Why can't I calm this unfortunate, insane quarter?' And later, 'What matters is all this did happen.'[38]

LODZ GHETTO: JUDGMENT DAY

Often called 'the Manchester of Western Poland', Lodz was an industrial center that was home to 200,000 Jews in 1939. Shortly after the occupation, the Germans renamed Lodz Litzmannstadt in honor of a World War I hero. During a visit, Baldur von Schirach promised that German youth would 'uproot' Jews from the city. On 8 October 1939 Nazi storm troopers conducted a house-to-house pogrom. A month later, eleven synagogues were set afire. On 8 February 1940 the Nazis declared the Baluty district a *Wohngebeit der Juden*, the first formal ghetto in Poland.[39] As the ghetto population swelled to more than 150,000 and temperatures fell to 15 degrees below zero, Sam Eilenberg and his bride Nadja considered themselves lucky to have a single room:

> We were freezing to death. There was no coal. We got a little ration of wood. People burned everything made of wood. They took everything apart, even the outside lavatories. Every tree was cut down. People were taking doors out. I got two main wires, one positive and one negative. Over there, all the cables were 220-volt lines. I rolled the wire on a broom handle and hung these on two nails on the wall. Then I tapped into the outside high-tension wire. The whole thing probably used 10,000 watts of electricity, but we had a heating machine and a hotplate as a result. I had to stop, though, because the poles outside were getting red. You could see the wire glowing on the wall in our room in the dark. It could have caught fire.[40]

Chaim Rumkowski, a former social worker who was Chairman of the *Judenrat*, declared: 'Here in the ghetto, we are all workers, we are all equal.'[41] That was not the case. *Judenrat* officials, police and teamsters dressed and ate better than the common folk. For most, the diet consisted of potatoes, cabbage, radishes and ersatz coffee. Soup was made of potato peels, barley and turnips. Ration coupons provided 300 grams of meat or 200 grams of sausage per month. Milk, cheese and sugar were virtually unobtainable.[42] As more people were forced into the ghetto and the bread ration was cut, doctors performed abortions for a single loaf of bread. Meanwhile, the death rate increased from 40 to 45 cases per week in 1939 to 360 in May 1941.[43]

Rumkowski met periodically with Nazi officials. Afterward, the *Judenrat* would decry sabotage and warn parents of children who peddled on the streets that they might be deported. Ten thousand were 'resettled' in January 1942, hundreds of children in May. Asked what resettlement meant, Rumkowski replied, 'If I told everything, you would not sleep. This way I alone cannot sleep.' On 1 September 1942 the Nazis ordered the Jewish Police in Lodz to clear ghetto hospitals of their patients. After three days of bloodshed, the *Judenrat* announced that Rumkowski would deliver an address on Friday afternoon, 4 September, Rosh Hashanah. Fifteen hundred Jews assembled at Fire Brigade Square to hear their Chairman. It was one of the most agonizing spectacles in Jewish History. Rumkowski explained that his superiors had insisted that the ghetto be thinned out again. Originally, they demanded 24,000 people, 3,000 per day for eight days. But he succeeded in reducing the number to 20,000. If 20,000 unproductive Jews were not supplied, the entire population would be deported. The haggard *Judenältester* informed his audience:

A grievous blow has struck the ghetto. They are asking us to give up the best we possess – the children and the elderly. I was unworthy of having a child of my own, so I gave the best years of my life to children. I've lived and breathed with children. I never imagined I would be forced to deliver this sacrifice to the altar with my own hands. In my old age I must stretch out my hands and beg: Brothers and sisters, hand them over to me! Fathers and mothers, give me your children![44]

As men and women wailed, Rumkowski commiserated, 'I must perform this difficult and bloody operation – I must cut off limbs in order to save the body itself! I must take children because if not others may be taken as well, God forbid.' As for the sick, 'in their place, we can save the healthy'. In closing, Rumkowski admitted:

A broken Jew stands before you. Do not envy me. This is the most difficult of all the orders I've ever had to carry out at any time. I reach out to you with my broken, trembling hands and I beg: Give into my hands the victims, so that we can avoid having further victims, and a population of a hundred thousand Jews can be preserved. So they promised me: if we deliver our victims by ourselves, there will be peace.[45]

For the next eight days the Gestapo, aided by Jewish Police and the *Judenrat*'s White Guard (teamsters) dragged the sick, anyone over 65 and children to waiting trucks. People offered bribes, to no avail. A newborn infant, 33 hours old, was taken and counted against the quota. An SS man gave a Jewish mother three minutes to leave her 4-year-old daughter, and when she refused, he shot both of them in the head. Sam Eilenberg lost his mother in these Aktions. Though only 53, she was led off with a five-year-old grandson, screaming, 'Children, please help me! Get me out of here!'[46] When the curfew was lifted, over 15,000 Jews had been deported. Those who lost loved ones told themselves that the deportees were actually being resettled. There were rumors that the children were playing in the gardens at Helenowek. Some parents offered prayers for the dead. As winter drew near, survivors of 'Judgment Day' turned their thoughts to bread, coal and the ceaseless tirades of Chairman Rumkowski.

There were rumors (that the deported children had returned, that the Pope intended to visit the ghetto) and taunts (Polish anti-Semites paraded on 3 May, with signs proclaiming, 'Kill the Jews'). When the Nazis decided to clear the Lodz ghetto in August 1944, Rumkowski informed the population that they must assemble or face the prospect of deportation without personal belongings. Five thousand persons per day were shipped out over 20 days. Munitions workers under the protection of Nazi leader Hans Biebow went to Germany. Non-essential persons like the 70-year-old Rumkowski and his *Judenrat* cronies were sent to Auschwitz. Sixty thousand persons died in the Lodz Ghetto, another 130,000 were killed in concentration camps. Only 10,000 survived.[47]

THE CRACOW GHETTO

No formal ghetto was proclaimed in Cracow until 3 March 1941, but the inhabitants of this medieval town experienced hardship from the moment German troops entered the city on 6 September 1939. Cracow had had a Jewish street since 1304. Its Kazimierz district, was famed for archways and yeshivas captured on canvas and in photographs by Lionel Reiss and Roman Vishniac. Moses Isserles authored an Ashkenazic religious code here. Cracow's pre-war Jewish population of 65,000 grew to 72,000 in the first days of the war, an intolerable situation for the Nazis who had selected Cracow, not Warsaw, as the seat of the Government-General. German troops perpetrated the usual mayhem in Cracow during the *Blitzpogrom*. In September, 20 Jews were sent to their deaths. 17 more were shot in November. On the night of 3 December, the SS attacked Jews from the Dietel Parkway to the Vistula, tearing up furniture and killing 61 people. At the end of August 1940 30,000 were expelled to Kielce or Warsaw. Another 20,000 were deported by the end of October, leaving 20,000 skilled workers, *Judenrat* officials (headed by Dr Arthur Rosenzweig) and their families.[48]

In the winter of 1940/41, Cracow's Jews were confined to the Podgorze district across the Vistula, connected to the city by two bridges. The blue-jacketed Jewish police cooperated when SS Police Chief Waechter ordered the expulsion of 11,000 unproductive Jews in November 1940 and when the Nazis formally proclaimed a ghetto on 3 March 1941. Initially confined to 320 apartments in Jozefinska, Lwowska, Brodzinska and Salinarna streets, Cracow's 16,000 Jews were forced into less than a third of a square mile on 25 June 1942. Five months later (28 October) 1,800 men and women were sent to Plaszow, a former Jewish cemetery that was converted into a forced labor camp. Inmates worked in quarries, *Julags* (exempted factories), and on roadways. They also endured the caprice of SS Commandant Amon Goeth, a sadist who, armed with a hunting rifle, sniped at persons moving across the *Appelplatz*.

In December 1942, the Nazis split the Cracow ghetto into two zones at Plac Zgody (Peace Square). Essential workers went to Zone A, all others to Zone B. Jews from nearby towns were brought to Zone B. Tadeusz Pankiewicz, a Gentile who ran a pharmacy in Podgorze, recalled the latter: 'They were figures in tattered garments, barefoot, hungry, infested with lice, with faces unshaven for a long time, with dazed expressions in their eyes, terrified … The majority of them had never been anywhere outside of the villages where they were born; they had never seen a larger town in their lives.'[49]

At 11 a.m. on the morning of 13 March 1943, the SS, accompanied by Lithuanian, Latvian, Ukrainian and Polish auxiliaries, surrounded Ghetto A. The *Judenrat* was instructed to deliver all useful workers to Plaszow. No children would be permitted in the camp. During the next 24 hours, some

Jews tried to escape through the sewers to Aryan sections of Cracow. Others despaired and poisoned their children. Once Ghetto A was liquidated, residents of Ghetto B were to present themselves for transports taking them east. On 14 and 15 March, the streets of Ghetto B were packed with dazed, terrified Jews moving to Plac Zgody. A handful of SS men, supported by *Sonderdienst*, randomly shot doctors and their patients, individuals with foreign passports, wagons filled with children from the kindergarten on Jozefinska street. Elderly men were shot in the back of the head with dum dum bullets. In a single day, 3,000 people were deported, 1,500 murdered.[50]

It took several months for the Nazis to clear Cracow. Some Jews tried to elude the SS by hiding in basements or attics. The SS conducted daily sorties into apartments, looting furniture, silver, iron and copper objects. Any Jews found were instantly shot. In December 1943 the remnants of the *Judenrat* and Jewish Police were moved to Plaszow, where, following a dispute between Gestapo officials (who wanted some of their toadies spared) and Commandant Goeth (who made little distinction between Jews), most were executed.[51]

RADOM PROVINCE: THE SMALL TOWN OF PIONKI

Pionki was a small town in Radom province 90 miles south of Warsaw. Eva Fugman was the daughter of a grocer. An independent man, Mr Fugman was jailed twice by the Nazis (for slaughtering a cow and refusing to surrender fur coats). When he returned in January 1942, the Nazis confined the Jews to a row of houses along Leschnitza Street. The Fugmans had a kitchen and a bedroom for a family of nine. Their ranks increased to 19 with the addition of friends and an orphan boy of 10 rescued by Eva's father:

> He came into our ghetto wormy from head to toe. I don't know how he got out of his own ghetto. This Jewish police commandant wouldn't let him in. My father almost had a fist fight with him and said, 'You're not throwing this child out.' He bathed him and shaved his hair, burned his clothes, and put him in the stables with the cows. He coughed so horribly, we were afraid it was tuberculosis or something. We made a little bunk for him in the stable, gave him milk from the cow three times daily. Eventually he ate at the table. You should have seen this child three or four weeks later. A beautiful youngster.[52]

On the morning of 18 August 1942, the Jews in Pionki were trucked to Treblinka. Eva and her sister Genia were spared, to work in what had been a plastics factory. The girls laid the foundation for a *Werkschutz*, mixing cement with their hands and carrying blocks ten hours a day. Depressed and weak, Eva contracted typhus and was dumped into a crowded sickroom. Two uncles intervened and spared her life:

We had triple decker bunks in a room about 18 by 12. Some of them couldn't even walk. They took them out with the beds. One of the girls whose name was Eva from Koschnitz. She couldn't get her boots on. When the Ukrainian guards came around, one named Janczek told this man Halbert who used to have a drugstore before the war, 'We have orders to leave Eva and Chaim here. They're not going to the hospital.' So Halbert said, 'What do you mean they are not going. Everybody's going.' Then Janczek picked up his rifle, aimed at him and said: 'I told you to leave those two here.' When the others heard that I'm not going, you could see right away, we're not going to any hospital. This other girl named Eva didn't even try to pull her boots on anymore. She said, 'I don't care. I can go without boots.'

The sick youngsters were taken to another area of the camp and shot. In August 1944, the Nazis closed the work camp and shipped everybody, including Eva and her sister, to Auschwitz.

KIELCE: A WOMAN WHO SAW HER CHILD SELECTED

Helen Rosenzweig was a dressmaker married to a young carpenter from Skarzysko. Their son, Moshe Shaya, was born in 1937.[53] When Nazi officials ordered a deportation early in 1940, Helen took her boy to Kielce. As the cost of a loaf of bread soared to 200 zlotys ($10), Helen volunteered to work at a leather factory in Zhidlovtsa. There were rumors that the Nazis were going to make Zhidlovtsa into a *Judenstadt* or Jewish city. Instead, late in 1942, they announced the clearing of the Skarzysko ghetto. Helen, her husband and son hid behind a false wall in a basement bunker. When they emerged, most of the town's Jews were gone. Helen walked back to Kielce with her son in freezing weather. In May 1943, the Nazis ordered a roundup. At the time, Samush was six years old:

Where could I go with him? I was lost. I didn't expect this to happen. I didn't know it would happen again. Once, twice, *drei*, again now. I remember when we were in the home the last time. he asked, 'They shoot people? They kill people? In the heart?' He showed me, pointing to his heart. He was smart. He said, 'Mother, I can work. I will go out. I can make something.' But they didn't want children of six or seven. I was dressed and the child was dressed, in a little warm coat. The Gestapo and Gendarmerie banged on the doors downstairs, *Aufstehen! Aufstehen!* There was a platz with at least a thousand people standing there. My little boy was standing near me and I was helpless. I didn't know what to do. While the selection was being made, I went to the toilet to hide. The toilet was by the *Werkschutz*. A gendarme came in and told me to leave. I left my child in the toilet. I went out and said to myself, 'Maybe this way I can save him.' But they said to the children under twelve, *Alles abzugeben*. The boy came out. I hadn't told him anything in the toilet and he came out. I tried to run to him, but it was already too late. They took him away. I thought maybe he would be safe over there because there were a lot of children. I never saw him again. Later on, we heard they killed all of the children. They gave them some bread to eat and they shot them. They killed them in Kielce and made one grave.[54]

Helen Rosenzweig spent the next 18 months working in the ammunition factory of Pionki. Late in 1944, she escaped along the sewer drains with a fellow inmate. She spent the last eight months of the war in the basement of a Polish baker in Skarzyskö: 'I was always crying. In Pionki, they almost wanted to send me away because I was crying. The last moment, when I heard the war was over, I started to cry so much. I knew I would never see my boy, but I dreamed about him. He was always in my head.' The sole memento of her little blond boy was a pink woolen scarf knitted for him by his grandmother.[55]

STATISTICS

During the first three years of the Nazi occupation, more than a million Jews lost their lives in Poland. They included 150,000 murdered at the beginning of the occupation, 341,938 who perished as a result of sickness and epidemics, and 769,938 who were victims of deportations.[56]

After the war, many people rationalized that the free world did not know the extent of the Nazi murder plan. Perhaps not the details, but a great many people knew, and not merely from statements published in obscure reports that lay untouched till war's end. Articles in the *New York Times* and *Collier's* detailed what was happening in Lodz or Warsaw long before 1945. One striking example was a two-page pictorial essay titled 'Germans Impose Mass Death on Red Prisoners and Poles'. Published by *Life Magazine* (a journal with the nation's second-largest circulation, 6,000,000 readers), this article showed Russian PWs, some dead after forced marches, others strung on electrified barbed wire, whole stacks of starved victims gathered for burial. A second collection of photos revealed the carcasses of Jews in the Warsaw Ghetto being counted and buried in trenches. Some were children, their bellies bloated with edema. One particularly horrifying picture was of a man holding by the throat what appeared at first glance to be a chicken. In reality, the victim of 'slow starvation' was a Jewish infant. The date on *Life*'s article was 23 February 1942, one month after the proclamation of the Final Solution at the Wannsee Conference, three full years before the concentration camps were finally shut down.[57]

9

Blitzkrieg in the West: Holland

THE PHONY WAR

For many observers, Hitler's astonishing victory in Poland seemed to remove any reason to continue the war. David Lloyd George suggested that serious consideration be given to Hitler's peace proposals. Pope Pius XII, King Gustav of Sweden and President Roosevelt were mentioned as possible mediators between the Allies and Axis. In the last week of February, FDR sent Sumner Welles on a tour of Europe's capitals. Within a month 55 nations informed Secretary of State Hull that they would be interested in attending a peace conference. When Finland ceded East Karelia to the USSR in March 1940, Avery Brundage and the International Olympic Committee suggested that the Olympics might yet be held in Helsinki that summer.

Through the winter of 1939/40, French commander Maurice Gamelin kept his troops behind the 'impregnable' Maginot Line, an 87-mile stretch of barbed wire and pillboxes, complemented by 400,000 troops of the British Expeditionary Force). Gamelin would not repeat mistakes of World War I when tens of thousands of soldiers were lost in senseless assaults. The number of casualties sustained by the French during the first four months of war (2,000) seemed to vindicate that policy. Some observers dubbed the conflict 'the Twilight War', the *drôle de guerre* or the 'Phony War'. Buoyed by a two to one advantage in manpower, the normally cautious Chamberlain commented that Hitler had 'missed the boat'.[1] French Premier Paul Reynaud was even more confident, ridiculing German peace offers as counterfeit.[2]

The test of wills came in Norway. Half of Germany's iron came from Sweden. Because the Kiruna orefields were so far north, it was easier to ship material via train to Narvik in Norway where it was loaded onto German freighters. The British often filled their ships next to those of the Nazis. Through the winter, Norway's Prime Minister Johann Nygaardavold pleaded with belligerents to respect his nation's neutrality.[3] On Sunday, 7 April, the British navy began mining sea lanes from Trondheim to Bergen to prevent German U-boats from operating out of Norwegian fjords. The British planned to occupy these cities, but were preempted when Hitler launched his own invasion of Norway and Denmark on 9 April 1940. The Danes surrendered in two hours. Norway took longer – five weeks. On 7 May, Neville

Chamberlain stepped down. Three weeks later, the British left Narvik. The Phony War was over.

CASE RED, CASE YELLOW

On the very day Winston Churchill became Prime Minister (10 May), German paratroops began dropping into Holland and Belgium. The ensuing campaigns (*Fall Gelb* for the Low Countries, *Fall Rot* for France) were surprisingly short and marked by blunders. The Dutch military attache in Berlin learned of the impending assault on the evening of 9 May, but Holland refused to believe that the Nazis would violate its neutrality. The Dutch tried to blow bridges and flood the plain, but these actions were only an inconvenience to the swift-moving Wehrmacht. When a German force failed to capture government leaders at the Hague, Rotterdam was fire-bombed on 14 May. Eight hundred persons were killed, thousands made homeless. As Queen Wilhelmina fled to England, Holland capitulated.[4]

Belgium was alerted to the Nazi onslaught earlier than Holland. A pair of Luftwaffe officers carrying invasion plans were captured by Belgian militia on 9 January. The Belgians called up their 700,000 man army, but refused to share information with or permit British and French troops on their soil until it was too late. The Belgians relied upon their own 'state of the art' fortifications that stretched from Antwerp to the Meuse River. The Nazis made short shrift of these. On the night of 10 May, 80 paratroops dropped atop Fort Eben Emael and wiped out most of the gun positions and killed or captured 1,500 men in 30 hours.

Next it was France's turn to stumble. Generals Gamelin, Alphonse Georges, René Billotte and Jean-George Blanchard were old, slow-moving and predictable. They enjoyed numerical superiority in tanks but failed to appreciate that many of their vehicles were inferior in speed, range and fire power. French intelligence reckoned it would take nine to ten days for an army to move through the Ardennes: Stuka dive bombers, artillery and daring infantry strikes blasted the French from their positions above the Meuse in three. In desperation, Reynaud replaced Gamelin with another septuginarian, Maxime Weygand, who tried to patch together a defense along the Somme and Aisne rivers. It was too late. When Heinz Guderian's tank brigades reached Calais on 20 May, more than one million Allied troops were trapped.

Somehow, a slapdash flotilla of ships pulled 338,000 troops from the beaches of Dunkirk between 26 May and 4 June. The Allies were so desperate for good news that Dunkirk was hailed as a kind of victory. People ignored 44,000 French soldiers abandoned on the quays. Belgium's King Leopold surrendered on 28 May. The Nazis pierced Weygand's hedgehog line at Belleau Wood and Château-Thierry on 10 June. The same day Mussolini declared war, occupying Provence and the Riviera. On 11 June, Churchill visited Tours and implored the French to fight in the streets. Instead, Paris was declared an open city. On 12 June, 40,000 more Allied soldiers and 12 generals surrendered. Two days later, Nazi troops goose-stepped through the streets of Paris. On 17 June, Reynaud resigned in favor of Marshal Henri Philippe Pétain, hero of the battle of Verdun. The 84-year-old Marshal sued for an armistice.

Hitler enjoyed the fullest measure of revenge on 21 June 1940. French representatives were summoned to the railway coach in the forest of Compiègne where peace terms had been dictated in 1919. This time German demands were non-negotiable: the northern departments of France, including Paris, and a coastal strip running to Spain, were to be occupied; a puppet government would be permitted in Vichy; anti-Nazi agitators were to be turned over to the occupation authorities; and the French navy would be neutralized. Hitler had won his third campaign and Berlin celebrated the victory of fascism with a flower-strewn parade on 19 July 1940.[5]

THE JEWS OF WESTERN EUROPE

Germany's triumph in the West brought with it control over another 500,000 Jews. Many were refugees from Nazism. Most were Jews whose lifestyle differed significantly from that of their eastern brothers. The Union of Utrecht in 1579 promised Jews religious liberty, but it was not until 1791 that the French National Assembly granted Ashkenazic and Sephardic Jews civil rights. Napoleon tantalized the Jews when he summoned a Sanhedrin of Europe's sages in 1808, then channeled their efforts into a Jewish Consistory. Western civilization was enriched by philosophers like Baruch Spinoza, Henri Bergson, Marcel Proust and Herman Heijermans, composers Paul Dukas and Darius Milhaud, and the works of Jewish Bohemians in Paris (Camille Pissarro, Marc Chagall, Chaim Soutine, Amadeo Modigliani, Abraham Mitchine and Jacques Lipchitz), collectively known as the 'École Juive', built hospitals and research institutes where Fernan Widal and Alexander Besredka worked in infectious diseases. Paul Hyams (whose father was Jewish) served as Belgium's Prime Minister as well as the first President of the League of Nations. Leon Blum served as Premier of France and Lodewijk Visser was President of the Dutch High Court.

Most Jews in the Low Countries and France were laborers, craftsmen, merchants or street vendors. They lived close to kosher butcher shops and synagogues. They prayed in Hebrew but were fluent in the language of their neighbors. They dressed no differently. Men shaved. People kept businesses open on Shabbat. Some even ate shellfish. At one time four of the seven Aldermen in Amsterdam were Jews. Immigrants from Poland prided themselves on being French, Belgian or Dutch. It was a feeling reciprocated by Gentiles. Siep Jongeling, who was a teenager in Kinderdiik in 1940, recalled:

'We got along very well. There was a large normal working community in what was called Joordaam. They were Jews, but they were not any different from us. They were part of our people.'[6]

Jews in the West were unprepared for what lay before them in the death camps. Prior to deportation, some inquired whether they would be traveling first or third class. Esther Bittman, who came to Auschwitz from the Carpathians, believed that deportees from the West died in greater numbers because they lacked a toughness acquired from exposure to anti-Semitism. Eva Fugman concurred: 'The French girls were so concerned about the way they looked. When they came, they traded food rations for makeup. You cannot live on lipstick and rouge. Dutch girls were the opposite. They were very quiet and never had the energy to come back to life. I guess they were children from rich homes who never knew any hardship. For them, the Germans did not have to use crematoria. Every few days one of them would get close to the electrified wire. This was the quickest way to solve her loneliness and suffering.'[7]

In 1939 100,000 of 140,000 Jews living in Holland were killed by the Nazis. The mortality rate of over 70 percent is unmatched anywhere save among Polish Jews. France lost 90,000 (33 percent) of its 270,000 Jews, Belgium 35,000 (40 percent) of its 90,000. The irony is that Jews fared worse in the west where resistance to the Nazis was greatest.

HOLLAND: THE ARYAN ATTESTATION

The first Jews to settle in the Low Countries were refugees from the Inquisition who came to Antwerp in 1512.[8] A century later, there were 800 Jews in Amsterdam, less than one percent of the population. The Jews were poor, second-class citizens, excluded from guilds and government posts until 1796. After Napoleon, Michael Godefroi and Van Ralte served as Ministers of Justice and Henri Pollack helped establish Holland's first trade unions. Rabbinical councils cleaved to orthodoxy while business and political leaders favored assimilation. There was a Zionist federation which stressed philanthropy. On the eve of World War II, 65 percent of Holland's Jews were concentrated in Amsterdam, the rest living in the Hague, Groningen, Rotterdam or Arnhem. At least 20,000 were by Nazi racial definition *Mischlinge*. Forty thousand were refugees.[9]

The persecution of Dutch Jews began innocently enough. On 29 May 1940 Artur Seyss-Inquart was installed as *Reichskommissar*, assuming powers normally vested in the Queen and Parliament. In his first public address, Seyss-Inquart promised to respect Dutch political institutions. Parliament would continue to meet and Holland's 200,000 civil servants would remain in office. That same summer, Seyss-Inquart informed a rally of 80,000 supporters of the *Nationaal-Socialistische Beweging der Nederlanden* (NSB),[10] that 'the Jews, for us, are not Dutch. They are those enemies with whom we can come to neither an armistice nor to peace. The *Führer* declared that the Jews have played their final act in Europe, and therefore they have played their final act.'[11]

Without prompting, in August 1940 the government of Prime Minister Gerbandy moved to define and stigmatize Jews in Holland. According to an October decree, a Jew was anyone with three Jewish grandparents or, if he or she were observant, two Jewish grandparents. On 18 October, all gainfully employed persons had to fill out forms listing racial background. As a result of the Aryan Attestation, Jews were dismissed from the police, universities, unions, newspapers, orchestras and film industry. Academics, jurists and journalists shrugged their shoulders, signed the attestation, and moved into positions vacated by their colleagues. Jacob Presser noted, 'The Press had been among the first Dutch professions to allow itself to be forced to toe the Nazi line ... Some Dutch papers tried to out-Stürmer *Der Stürmer* itself.'[12] As for the average citizen, 'Quite a few Dutchmen failed to "notice" or when they could no longer close their eyes, found all sorts of excuses for standing aloof. They felt sorry for Jews and congratulated themselves for not being one of them. They did not know, they did not want to know. And when Hitler made it very easy for them – they did not have to know.'[13] Meanwhile, the Nazis commended the 'exemplary behavior' of the Dutch Census Office which registered 160,820 persons and hundreds of businesses.[14]

HOLLAND: THE *JOODSE RAAD*

Responding to the crisis, in December 1940 Dutch Jews created a Jewish Coordination Committee (*Joodse Coordinatie-commissie*). Headed by 69-year-old Lodewijk Visser, recently dismissed from the High Court,[15] the Coordination Committee served as a counterweight to the Committee for Special Jewish Affairs (*Comite voor Bijzondere Joodse Belangen*, CBJB) and the Committee for Jewish Refugees (*Comite voor Joodse Vluchtelingen*, CJV) both established in 1933 and perceived as servile to the Nazis. David Cohen, professor of ancient history at the University of Amsterdam, chaired the CJV while the CBJB was headed by diamond merchant Abraham Asscher.[16] Despite friction, the committees managed to prevent the imposition of a 'closed ghetto' (segregation by walls) or a 'visual ghetto' (signs warning of a Jewish Quarter). Instead, they were subjected to a 'spiritual ghetto'.

Following a series of anti-Jewish incidents in Arnhem, the Hague and Utrecht, NSB toughs tried to make a pogrom in the Jewish quarter of Amsterdam on 8 February 1941. They were rebuffed by Jewish youths armed with clubs. The Germans had to send three battalions of infantry and tanks to extricate the local Nazis. Four days later, city commandant Boehmcker summoned Asscher, Rabbi L.H. Sarlouis and Rabbi David Frances and ordered them not only to surrender all arms but to create a *Joodse Raad voor Amsterdam* within 24 hours. Asscher agreed to share leadership with Professor Cohen. Justice Visser refused to participate, but designated Izak Kisch as his representative. The latter was not overjoyed, noting, 'This council will bring the hatred of the Jews upon itself and will be the laughing-stock of the non-Jews.'[17]

On 15 February, SIPO-SD forces destroyed a Jewish cafe in the Rembrandtplein which, they claimed, was a center of underground agitation. A week later, they arrested 425 men between the ages of 20 and 35 and sent them to Buchenwald. Three hundred men were rounded up in Amsterdam and sent to Mauthausen in June, another 300 were taken from Arnhem and Enschede in the fall of 1941. Only one survived.[18] In September, the German Kommissariat barred Jews from public buildings, parks, art exhibitions or musical performances, shopping in public venues, attending public schools or changing their place of residence.[19] Until his death in February 1942, Visser badgered officials of the Dutch College of Secretaries-General and SS leader Rauter about the deported Jewish youths. He urged the *Joodse Raad* not to abide by the Nazi decrees. Visser's aide, Kisch resigned from the *Judenrat* on 21 September, accusing the council of 'deliberate[ly] misleading the Jewish public'. Cohen conceded, 'Every time I make a decision, I have Mauthausen before my eyes – weeping mothers, crying children, trembling men and Jewish youngsters killed.'[20] *Joodse Raad* officials should have had no illusions about what deportation meant. In March 1941 Eichmann sent Jacob Edelstein and Richard Friedmann from Vienna to coax the Dutch to volunteer for re-location. The two men instead warned of mass executions in the east.[21]

In the summer of 1941, Cohen and Gertrud van Tijn turned over a list of college students to the authorities. After a brief debate in March 1942, the *Joodse Raad* agreed to supply 1,400 Jewish men for forced labor. When Eichmann announced his plan to deport 40,000 Jews from Holland in June 1942, the *Joodse Raad* sacrificed the majority to save a minority.[22] The council temporarily managed to exempt diamond cutters, radio technicians, citizens of neutral states, the US or Britain, Jews who claimed Portuguese or Spanish ancestry, Jewish spouses in an intermarriage, those who agree to be sterilized, and employees of the *Joodse Raad*.[23] On 20 March 1943 Nazi officials commended the Council for its 'distinguished service during the dejudaization of the Netherlands'. After the war, Dutch and Jewish scholars conducted separate inquiries into the role of the *Joodse Raad*. The Dutch commission concluded that the Jewish Council 'let itself be used for the liquidation of Dutch Jews'.[24] The Jewish group found such behavior 'dishonorable', particularly in lending support to anti-Jewish measures and cooperating in deportations. The post-war Jewish commission recommended that Cohen and Asscher be barred from any further office. For his part, Asscher left the Jewish community and was buried in a Gentile cemetery.[25]

HOLLAND: THE GENERAL STRIKE

On the morning of 25 February 1941, an event of singular importance took place in Holland. Along the coast from Middelburg to Alkmaar, Dutch shipyard workers refused to report for work. In the cities of Rotterdam, Amsterdam, the Hague and Utrecht, banks and schools closed, and trolleys sat idle in the street. No noise came from the giant Smit complex that turned out diesel and steam engines. Outraged at the treatment of the Jews, Holland was observing a general strike. The call came from the Communist Party, but 20,000 Dutch men and women responded.[26] Siep Jongeling was one of the first to walk out: 'We went into the shops and said, "Hey, we're going on strike. We have to do something about this. We are going to stop it."'[27] The Nazis reacted instantly. The mayors of three cities (Amsterdam, Hilversum and Zaandam) were removed, their governments fined more than $9 million. Within 24 hours 1,000 workmen were arrested. Some were executed on the spot:

> They declared martial law, a curfew. The next day, the security or military police were in full force at the shops. That same afternoon, they started rounding up fellows who printed leaflets to go on strike. The first was Hank DeGroot and the other one was Smit. His father was a superintendent at the shipyard. The third one was from Alblasserdam. All they did was type up a little note about what the Germans did to the Jews and distributed it. The German SS took them to Dodrecht, one of the oldest cities in the Netherlands, about 10 miles away, to a military school. They shot them that same afternoon, simply for printing those bulletins. That same day, their parents got the bodies back. The next day we went back to work. You weren't that brave.[28]

The general strike lasted two days, and when it ended, so did German cordiality. The Nazis, who employed 3,000 special Order Police in all of France, brought 5,000 to Holland. Now it was illegal to own radios or congregate in groups of more than three. In the next four years, Holland would be looted of vast supplies of clothing, industrial machinery, agricultural goods.[29] Any Dutchman could be drafted into the *Wehrmacht*: 25,000 were recruited to fight in Russia, the largest contingent from any occupied country. When resistance surfaced, as in the town of Putten where a German officer was killed by the underground, 580 of the 590 men in the town were shot.[30]

The change was welcomed by NSB 'bloodhounds', informers who exposed Jews living in illegal areas.[31] Dutch banks blocked Jewish funds. In 1942 Puls moving vans took more than $200,000,000 worth of property from Jewish apartments and businesses 'on permanent loan'. Wrote Raul Hilberg, 'In no occupied territory of the great semicircle from Norway to Rumania did the Germans manage, in one form or another, to collect so much Jewish wealth.' Dutch police escorted Jews to the transit camps of Vught and Westerbork.[32] The Dutch Red Cross sent parcels into Vught once – at

Christmas 1943.[33] Said Hilberg, 'Holland was the one territory of the occupied West in which the Jews did not have an even chance to live.'[34]

DURCHGANGSLAGER: WESTERBORK AND VUGHT

The *Joodse Raad* did protest when the Nazis started herding Jews from Zaandam and Hilversum into Amsterdam early in 1942 and when they confiscated wedding rings, watches, table silver and gold teeth. The Council also objected to the movement of Jews to detention camps closer to the German border.[35] Opened to German refugees in the winter of 1939–40, Westerbork was located 50 miles northeast of Amsterdam in a region noted for ancient megaliths. When the camp was transferred to Nazi control in the summer of 1942, Westerbork consisted of wooden barracks, administrative offices, storage halls and workshops covering 65 acres. A Jewish Council maintained an index of inmates, distributed food, assigned housing, supervised children's education and holiday observances. In the 'Big Barrack', camp residents enjoyed boxing matches, classical concerts and revues.[36] Westerbork also contained one of the largest hospitals in Europe (1,800 beds) with a well-stocked pharmacy and modern surgical equipment, testimony to the influence of its chief physician, Dr F.M. Spanier, one of 181 Jewish passengers from the SS *St Louis*.[37]

Like Spanier, Kurt Schlesinger was a German Jew who arrived in 1939. A burly man, Schlesinger worked his way up from ditch digger to a seat on the camp council. He ingratiated himself to the various commandants, especially Albert Gemmeker, the SS officer who ruled Westerbork during its major deportations. Schlesinger would testify for Gemmeker in 1949, noting that he brought 'order, calm and humanity' to the camp. Survivors recall a different Nazi, who screaming with rage over the escape of two inmates, ordered 50 sick Jews onto a transport in the middle of a downpour. The commandant hanged four inmates who tried to escape in September 1944. When one of the men survived the noose, Gemmeker ordered him killed by lethal injection.[38]

Dressed in a black army shirt, riding breeches, boots and a Nazi-style cap, Schlesinger gathered about him 180 young men directed by Arthur Pisk, an Austrian who favored a Hitler-style mustache. Charged with keeping order in the camp, the *Ordnungsdienst* plundered luggage and helped load the death trains. In a camp where numbers determined importance, they answered only to 'No. 1', Kurt Schlesinger. After 15–16 July 1942, when other members of the Jewish Council were deported, 'there was now a one-man Jewish council who spoke German'.[39]

In the summer of 1942, Willi Zopf, Eichmann's personal adjutant, informed the Amsterdam *Joodse Raad* that Dutch Jews would be moved east for 'labor service'. On 26 June, Professor Cohen protested what he called a violation of international law. The Nazis simply ignored him. The *Joodse Raad* caved in, designating all persons who did not hold *Sperrstempel* (exemptions).[40] Among those involved in these 'razzias' were Security Chief Rauter, his aides Fritz Schmidt, Friedrich Wimmer and Dr Wilhelm Harster, Gestapo officials Willi Lages and Ferdinand aus der Funten, and Gertrude Slottke. The latter, 'an old parchment bag, an inhuman automaton, an unfeeling witch', was responsible for clearing castle Barneveld of 400 Jews. Even the Wehrmacht Commander in Holland, General F.C. Christiansen, regarded as a decent man, ordered a 78-year-old Jew and another legless Jewish veteran to 'labor service' in Auschwitz, saying, 'A Jew is a Jew, legs or no legs.'[41]

Once they reached Westerbork, deportees discovered that being Dutch was a liability. Schlesinger and other German Jews would not allow a repeat of an earlier selection that resulted in the expulsion of 400 German Jews. Every Sunday the Westerbork council made selections. Two thousand people were shipped off every Tuesday. The process was interrupted once, at Christmas 1943. On Monday nights, camp Service Men would enter a barrack, read a list of names and order these people to report the next morning with their possessions. On transport day, barracks doors were locked and there was no roll call. The work day, which normally started at 7:30 a.m., was pushed back to 11. During those four hours, the Service Men performed their ghoulish tasks of rounding up the sick, disabled and orphaned.[42]

Westerbork was a 'sluice', ever filling with arrivals from Amsterdam and Rotterdam and ever emptying to the East. Between 17 July 1942 and 3 September 1944, 93 trains left Holland on a 450 mile journey to Poland. There were no survivors in 26 of these transports. There were no trains from France and Belgium between March and July 1943 because of a backlog of Salonika Jews who were being 'processed' at Auschwitz. The trains never stopped running from Holland. Nineteen transports carried 34,313 Dutch Jews to Sobibor in that period. Nineteen persons survived.[43] An admiring Adolf Eichmann declared, 'The trains ran like a dream.'[44]

THE TRAIN FROM APELDOORN

On the night of 21 January 1943, Ferdinand aus der Funten, chief of the security police, carried out a raid against the Jewish mental hospital in Apeldoorn, 30 miles east of Amsterdam. The Nazis had their eyes on this facility which housed 1,100 patients for some time. When a group of Service Men from Westerbork showed up on 20 January, physicians and nurses prepared for the worst, setting aside stocks of food, linen and scopolamine. But even they were shocked by what took place on 21 January.

According to eyewitnesses, Major aus der Funten acted like the 'devil incarnate', barking orders at the ODs and his own troops. Patients, some in strait-jackets, some naked, were forced out into the night. As aus der Funten screamed, 'They are all asocial elements', the patients were thrown onto trucks with 100 retarded boys and girls from the nearby Achisomog training institute. The trucks deposited their loads before freight trains waiting at the Apeldoorn rail station. Dutch trainmen watched as the SS beat their charges into the cattle cars. Some of the deranged resisted to the end, sticking their hands in the path of metal doors.

A Dutch Jew described what happened to the Apeldoorn transport when it reached Auschwitz. 'I was on the station when the train arrived. It was one of the most horrible transports from Holland that I saw. Many of the patients tried to break through the barrier and were shot dead. The remainder were gassed immediately, but I remember that the doctors and nursing staff who were in a separate wagon, were not taken to the gas chambers, but to the camp.' Ordered to carry the dead to crematoria, the health care staff that refused were tossed into a pit and burned alive. Not a single patient or member of the hospital staff from Apeldoorn survived.[45]

HOLLAND: A HIDING PLACE

After the general strike of February 1941, many Dutch civilians were disgusted with the persecution of Jews. Farmers warned of raids by setting their windmills to a particular position. Communists, members of the Christian Reform Church, and independent groups printed pamphlets decrying the occupation.[46] When the Nazis decreed the wearing of the Yellow Star on 29 April 1942, some Gentiles placed carnations in their lapels or pieces of yellow paper in their shirt pockets as a gesture of sympathy for Holland's Jews.[47] The Dutch underground distributed 300,000 paper stars bearing the words 'Jews and non-Jews united'. The Nazis ignored these forms of civil disobedience, but not the illegal distribution of ration cards. From his bank outside Haarlem, Paul van Kessel and four colleagues distributed 50,000 ration cards to *Onderduikers* (people in hiding). When the Nazis caught on, they arrested and executed the ringleader in Amsterdam. Three assistants were sent to concentration camps. Only van Kessel, who fled to the countryside, survived.[48]

Escape from Holland was virtually impossible. If the Nazis could not mount an invasion of England across the stormy waters of the North Sea, it was unlikely that a boatload of refugees could elude coastal patrols. There were a few attempts to flee by land. Joachim 'Shushu' Simon, a young Zionist, conceived the idea of leading Jewish children on hikes across Belgium and France to the borders of Spain. He made three crossings with his 'scouts' before the Nazis arrested him in January 1943. In prison, Simon committed suicide by slashing his wrists. His place was taken by an anarchist, Joop Westerweel who was flogged and shot in 1944.[49]

Hiding in wooded areas was also out of the question. Three hours from the coast there were dense forests, the Velowe in Gelderland province, in parts of Utrecht, down south in Limburg. Siep Jongeling dismisses the notion that people could have run to the woods. 'The climate is something fierce – cold and wet. The Germans would have loved it, because they would have surrounded the woods, gone in and killed them all.'[50] The only hope for Jews and anti-Nazi resisters was to go into hiding with their Dutch neighbors. Perhaps as many as 20,000 were concealed on farms or in false rooms. Some of these served as temporary shelters, until people were able to move on. Sometimes a farmer turned people out when they could no longer pay. More than a few Dutchmen yielded to threats. And yet Jews were helped by Christians like Paul van Kessel:

> It was 1943. My first wife and I had been married for just one year. We lived 500 meters from the headquarters of the Dutch green Police in Blumenthal, five miles from the sea. We took in a widow, her sister, and the widow's two children, aged 16 and 14. Don't ask why. We were young and didn't calculate the risk. The woman had been a neighbor of my parents. Before the war, she was always good, generous, prepared to help people. They stayed with us about a year and then they left. They had to stay in all day. We told them not to move around. They were four of them in this little room. At night, they could go out in the garden and get some fresh air, for just a quarter of an hour. They couldn't stand it any longer. After a year, they said, 'We go to the ghetto in Amsterdam. We can live, walk in the street, speak.' Jews were victims of their own character.[51]

ONE OF ONE HUNDRED THOUSAND: ANNE FRANK

One of those victims was a young German-Jewish refugee named Anne Frank. Born in Frankfurt in 1929, Anne was four years old when her father Otto took his wife and two daughters out of Nazi Germany and resumed trade in commodities in Amsterdam. Anne received a bright-colored plaid diary from her father on her thirteenth birthday in June 1942, A month later, the family went into hiding in an attic concealed behind a false door at 263 Prinzengrachtstrasse. For two years, the little girl recorded events that went on about her. Addressing an imaginary friend (Kitty), Anne complained about the crowding caused by opening the annex to four other Jews and the tension of sharing a room with a crotchety old refugee. She told of having to sit quietly during the day to avoid being detected by workers downstairs. Anne posted pictures of movie stars on the wall of her cubicle and told how her sister Margot wanted to go to Palestine after the war. She knew about Stalingrad, the Allied invasion of North Africa, and the end of Mussolini. She watched as families were marched away and and wondered how the Dutch people could let this happen. She said of Westerbork that it 'sounds terrible'. She wrote of gassings in Poland and admitted she was afraid of concentration camps. Nevertheless, when the Allies landed at Normandy, she wrote, 'I may yet be able to go back to school in September.' Most important, two years changed her attitude toward the teenaged boy whose family had taken refuge with the Franks. Fifteen-year-old Anne had fallen in love with Peter van Damm.

On 4 August 1944, the Dutch Green Police, acting on a tip, knocked aside the bookcase concealing access to the attic. The Franks and their friends were taken to Westerbork. Following a brief stay, they were deported to the East. The destination of the family was Auschwitz. Separated from their parents, Anne and Margot were shipped back to Germany when the death camp was abandoned in January 1945. Both girls perished of typhus in Belsen in March 1945. Of the eight persons who hid in the annex, only Otto Frank survived. After the war, he found the memoirs of his daughter scattered about the floor of the attic. Two years later he granted permission for their publication. Through her diary, Anne put a face to the countless, anonymous victims of the Holocaust.[52]

Amazingly, some critics begrudged this girl and her family their moment in history. In 1960, child psychologist Bruno Bettelheim declared, 'Hers (Anne's) was certainly not a necessary fate, much less a heroic one; it was a senseless fate.' Bettelheim offered four objections: the family jeopardized survival by staying together instead of separating; conducting 'business as usual' (having the teenagers study during the day), was a form of acceptance of their degraded status; lacking a second exit, the group could easily be trapped; and they failed to take a gun with them. As Bettelheim wrote, 'The loss of an SS with every Jew arrested would have noticeably hindered the functioning of the police state.'[53] Asked in October 1986 if he still held such views, Bettelheim (who committed suicide in 1990) responded, 'Absolutely. Hers was a senseless fate.'[54]

Bettelheim's criticisms do not hold up. There was no guarantee that anyone, let alone a 13-year-old girl, could outwit the Nazis and survive. Many Jewish children were hidden successfully, as Bettelheim suggests. Many more were betrayed and deported. The Franks did what they thought was best, going into hiding together. Once in the attic, they had no choice but to remain silent during the day, just like Paul van Kessel's Jewish family. The only way to keep three teenagers quiet was to have them study mathematics, read history, and write essays in a foreign language. Two doors to a hideout might have doubled the chances of discovery. As for guns, few people in Holland owned such weapons. Had they been used when the police came, the entire family would have been killed instantly. The Franks hoped to survive by complying with the Nazis' demands. That was the very method of survival advocated by Bettelheim, who was detained in Buchenwald in 1938.

Following the publication of his daughter's diary, Otto Frank permitted a stage adaptation in Israel by Meyer Levin. This version was performed a few times, before Mr Frank authorized a different production. The new performance of the diary reflected a more 'internationalist' view. Anne's references to the Zionism of her sister and her own appreciation of a Jewish homeland[55] were deleted. Entries on behalf of Jews were also emended. In November 1942 she lamented, 'I get frightened when I think of close friends who have now been delivered into the hands of the cruelest beasts that walk the earth. And all because they are Jews!'[56] Then in April 1944 she wrote at length:

Who has inflicted this upon us? Who has made Jews different from all other people? Who has allowed us to suffer so terribly up till now? It is God that has made us as we are, but it will be God, too, who will raise us up again. If we bear all this suffering and if there are still Jews left, when it is over, then Jews, instead of being doomed, will be held up as an example. Who knows, it might even be our religion from which the world and all peoples learn good, and for that reason and that reason only do we have to suffer now. We can never become just Netherlanders, or just English, or representatives of any country for that matter, we will always remain Jews, but we want to, too.

Be brave! Let us remain aware of our task and not grumble, a solution will come. God has never deserted our people. Right through the ages there have been Jews, through all the ages they have had to suffer, but it has made them strong too; the weak fall but the strong will remain and never go under![57]

This eloquent statement was altered in the stage production to read 'We're not the only people that've had to suffer. There've always been people that've had to … Sometimes it is one race, sometimes another.'[58] If Anne Frank's words could be changed and the family demeaned, why not call into question the entire story? When the *Diary of Anne Frank* was staged in Germany and Austria in 1958, neo-Nazi groups contended that the entire tale was a fabrication and demonstrated outside theaters. Reacting to such criticisms, Simon Wiesenthal tracked down the SS *Unterscharführer* responsible for leading the raid against the Franks. In 1963 Karl Silberbauer was working for the Vienna police force. Following a brief suspension, *Inspector* Silberbauer was back at work at the *Erkennungsamt* (Identification Office).[59]

From her little room, Anne Frank had written in the summer of 1944, 'In spite of everything, I still believe that people are really good at heart.'[60] In Jerusalem there is a winding road to Yad Vashem, the center of historical research that includes a museum as well as memorials dedicated to children, resistance fighters, destroyed communities. Known as the Avenue of the Just, the road is ringed with trees planted in honor of non-Jews who aided Jews during the Holocaust.[61] By 1976, the state of Israel had recognized 1,500 Righteous Gentiles from World War II. Nearly half, 683, were Dutch citizens.[62]

10

Belgium and Luxembourg

BELGIUM: THE INCIDENT AT THE REX

The defining moment for Belgian Jews during World War II occurred in Antwerp on 14 April 1941. Officials of the German Propaganda Ministry were promoting two anti-Jewish films that spring. 'Jud Süss' had already been shown in Bruges, Ghent and Antwerp. On 6 April, 'Der Ewige Jude', with its crude images of rats, kosher butchering and Jewish millionaires, opened in Antwerp. Four days later, Belgian anti-Semites marched through Lange Kievitstraat, smashing windows of Jewish stores. On the evening of 12 April, fist fights disrupted a performance at *L'Ancienne Belgique*, a music hall. Order was restored only after several patrons began singing a patriotic hymn, 'Vlaanderen'.[1]

Authorities should have expected trouble when *La Ligue de la Defense du Peuple* scheduled a second showing of 'Der Ewige Jude' at the Rex Cinema for the morning of 14 April. Other pro-Nazi organizations helped fill the 1,500-seat movie theater. There were militia from the *Vlaamsch National Verbond* (Flemish National Front) which claimed 100,000 followers; members of the Black Brigades, Belgians who hunted Jews living in Aryan sectors; SS volunteers from *De Vlag* movement; and Rexists, drawn from French-speaking Walloons in the south. These groups were united against Free Masonry, bolshevism and especially the Jews, who 'should be exterminated'.[2]

The emotionally charged audience cheered as René Lambrichts spoke of the day when the last Jew along with occult forces would be expelled from Flanders and Wallonia. More applause followed as Hitler's image flashed upon the screen. When the film ended, several hundred people milled about, some brandishing clubs and iron bars. A few spoke of cracking the heads of 'scummy Jews'. Emboldened by the presence in their ranks of German *Feldgendarmerie* (military police) the crowd started chanting, '*Ein Volk! Ein Führer!*' and began plundering Jewish shops. On Somerstraat, an old woman was thrown through a window. On Koornstraat, a furrier fled with his child in his arms as his shop was looted. Police reinforcements arrived but were unable to stop the mob from proceeding toward two synagogues on Oosten-straat. Before the buildings were set afire, looters carried away furniture, religious garb, books and symbols. The mini-*Kristallnacht* lasted 15 minutes. Over the next several weeks, victims of the attack were indemnified. Police units and tradesmen squelched another pogrom on 17 April. As the clandestine newspaper *Le Temps Nouveaux* declared, 'the population of Antwerp refuses to give ear to Nazi propaganda'.[3]

What happened in Antwerp caught the Nazi leadership by surprise. *Militärbefehlshaber* Alexander von Falkenhausen, the military governor of Belgium,[4] Eggert Reeder (his chief administrator), Gunther Heym (political head of the administration) and Constantin Canaris (head of the security police) had not anticipated such an incident.[5] The Germans talked about extending the 'velvet paw' to Belgium. While fascist groups dreamed of a Greater Flanders or Wallonia united to Germany, most Belgians harbored feelings of *Deutschfeindlichkeit* – enmity toward Germans. Belgians had not forgotten that 'the Fritz' violated their nation's boundaries twice during the century. Nearly 50,000 of their countrymen died in combat in World War I, another 8,500 were killed in 1940. During the 18-day war, 10,000 homes were destroyed, 13,000 civilians were killed, and four million Belgians (half the population) became refugees.[6]

German soldiers acted as if Belgium were 'a great department store'. Supplied with military scrip good only in occupied territories, these luxury-starved 'potato bugs' shipped cartons of food, clothing and jewelry back to Germany.[7] German businessmen 'fixed their eyes like vultures' on Belgian steel mills, coal mines, textile factories and diamond works.[8] Once a minor trading partner of Belgium, during the war Germany accounted for 88 percent of its export trade. Firms like Karges-Hammer-Lecluye, Société Générale de Belgique, Brevets van Burkel, AEG Brussels, SEM Brussels and Ford Motors Antwerp contributed railway cars, trucks, mortars, howitzers, small arms and ammunition to the Nazi war effort.[9]

Life under the occupation was miserable. Belgians were entitled to 11 pounds of potatoes monthly, no fats, white flour or coffee. As in Warsaw, children sang songs about ration cards and students risked arrest by making caricatures of Hitler. Lacking medical supplies, one physician likened the situation to 'the great epidemics of the Middle Ages'. Still, the spirit of the Belgians was not broken. As one elderly housewife quipped about British air raids in a letter to an American friend in 1941, 'When our English friends cause a little breakage, we really do not mind. In fact, we are only too anxious for them to do so, more and more. You know, when one is fond of children, one likes them to be noisy; noise is a sign of health.'[10]

THE JEWISH QUESTION IN BELGIUM: THE FIRST PHASE OF PERSECUTION

The Nazis hoped to deflect resentment toward the nation's Jewish minority which supposedly dominated Belgium's banking and diamond trade. The list of plutocrats who fled the country in 1940 includes Camille Huysmans,

Antwerp Burgermeister Romi Goldmuntz, the Zionist Numa Torczyner, textile producer Max Gottschalk, Raphael de Bauer who headed up the Belgian branch of the Banque de Paris, Paul and Jules Philippson, and Dannie Heinemann, the creator of SONFINA (an industrial cartel)[11] as well as hundreds of Jewish diamond cutters and officials of the *Fédération Générale des Travailleurs Diamantaires*, whose pre-war president was Isidore Lipschutz.[12] The roads out of Belgium were also clogged with simple folk. Anita Maroko's family were among the millions who were trapped:

> There were a lot of refugees running away from the Germans. Wherever we could sleep overnight, we did. The people suffered. It was hard to find food. French and English soldiers would throw away canned food to the people – corned beef. We saw a lot of fights in the air. Planes would fall down in fire. We didn't know whether they were English, French or German. The people would say, 'Oh, those are the English. Don't worry. We can walk. We don't have to run away.' The Germans machine-gunned people. We were walking, and all of a sudden the planes went 'put-put-put'. It was a miracle. We threw ourselves in a ditch. We got up. We didn't know if we were alive or dead.[13]

There were 90,000 Jews (including refugees) in Belgium when the war began, 1.1 percent of the population. Those who traced their ancestry back several generations were fiercely patriotic. Before the turn of the century, Rabbi Armand Bloch exalted the Jews' loyalty to Belgium, a pledge restated by Rabbi David Berman in 1930 on the occasion of the nation's centennial. As the situation of Jews in Germany and eastern Europe deteriorated, Rabbi Berman, Alfred Errera and Max Gottschalk forged an alliance of Jewish groups in Belgium. A council for refugees was established in October 1935. Two years later *Le Foyer Israélite de Bruxelles* served as the central agency for Jews in Belgium.[14]

Most Belgians never bought into the notion that Jews were responsible for their misfortunes. In 1942, military authorities bemoaned that 'only a tiny fraction [of the Belgian people] understands the significance of this question'. When the Nazis refused to issue food ration cards to Jewish children, the Belgian Red Cross fed them. When the Nazis attempted to ostracize Jews, their Belgian neighbors affirmed friendships with the victims.[15] As one teacher wrote to a friend,

> F. and his other Jewish colleagues have been deprived of their work, for the Germans have brought into force a 'Jewish status', i.e. the first step toward the Nuremberg Laws. I can scarcely describe our indignation. Needless to say, F. has grown very old. But he nurses no wrath, for he well knows that Germans and Germans only are to blame. Besides, he has had occasion to rejoice last week: you remember that delightful girl who became engaged to his son, just before the invasion? Well, she insisted on marrying him, not only because she loves him, but to show that the Belgian spirit is in no way contaminated by the odious Nazi doctrine.[16]

As in Holland, that doctrine was spelled out in a series of ordinances introduced in the fall of 1940. On 23 October, the Nazis banned kosher butchering. Five days later, Jews (defined as anyone with three Jewish grandparents) were required to carry identity papers stamped *Jood-Juif.* They were ordered to register their home addresses and property. Jews were ousted from the bar, teaching, journalism and public employment.[17] The collaborationist press hailed these measures as 'a prelude to great cleansing' and Nazi militiamen attacked Jewish shops crying, 'All Jews to Palestine.'[18] Most Belgians were outraged. Following the promulgation of the first statutes, the Conseil de Legislation protested 'the most flagrant violations' of the Belgian Constitution which guaranteed equality before the law.[19] Citing the Hague Convention of 1907, judges argued they were obligated to enforce their nation's laws, not foreign decrees. On one occasion, every member of the Supreme Court as well as lower civil and criminal courts walked out as a protest against military meddling in a case in Antwerp.[20]

Educational institutions proved to be especially troublesome. The rector of the Free University of Brussels protested restrictions against Jewish students. When the Nazis insisted upon replacing five Jewish professors at the University of Louvain, Rector H. van Weeyenbergh claimed the Belgian constitution granted autonomy to academic institutions. Like Police Commissioner Beauprez of Ostend, who refused to cooperate with the Germans, van Weeyenbergh was thrown into prison for 18 months.[21] He was released through the intervention of Cardinal Joseph Ernest van Roey. The primate of Belgium intervened so often following the first spate of anti-Semitic decrees that he was denounced by collaborators as one of three persons responsible (along with Churchill and Leon Blum) for Belgium's misfortunes.[22]

L'ASSOCIATION DES JUIFS EN BELGIQUE

The Nazis enacted a second wave of anti-Jewish laws on 31 May 1941. Bank deposits and stocks held by Jews were diverted to financial institutions designated by the authorities. Jewish shops and homes were to bear signs designating ownership. Jews were fired from the boards of larger commercial firms and the staffs of Jewish community organizations were also dismissed. According to the invaders, Jews controlled 47 percent of commercial and industrial firms and 34 percent of Belgian banks. In fact, Eggert Reeder lamented 'the feeble importance of Jewish influence' in his first annual report to Berlin.[23] When the Nazis decreed the firing of Jews in 1940, Reeder discovered he could only dismiss 60 public servants. Forty of 1,300 university professors in Brussels were Jews, 14 of 1,500 lawyers, 35 of 2,100 financial agents at the bourse in Brussels and Antwerp.

The Nazis achieved moderate success in the *désenjuivement* of 7,700 businesses. Twelve Jewish administrators for the Electrobel trust resigned before the enactment of the discriminatory laws. A few individuals married to Christians were granted exemptions. Because of the importance of diamonds and copper, the Nazis did not meddle with holdings in the Congo. So many Jewish diamond cutters had fled, occupation authorities complained that Aryan gem experts in Belgium were 'a totally, useless resource'.[24] The Germans estimated the value of Aryanized businesses at 12 million Rentenmarks (150 million Belgian francs). Jews and Belgians place the figure eight times higher.[25]

In September 1941, the Nazis restricted Jews to four towns (Antwerp, Brussels, Liège and Charleroi) and subjected them to a curfew.[26] It was only a matter of time before they got around to creating a central *Judenrat* for all of Belgium. The proclamation of an Association of Jews in Belgium (*Joden vereeniging in Belgie*, AJB) was announced on 25 November 1941. The AJB assumed responsibility for religious, charitable and educational institutions, as well as 'other duties'. Technically under the Belgian Ministries of Interior and Health, the Association answered to the Chief of the Military Administration and 'the service delegated by him to this end'. That service was the SD.[27] The men who served on the AJB – including its president Rabbi Salomon Ullmann, administrative chief Martin Benedictus, Robert Holzinger of the labor department, Salomon Van den Berg of Brussels, N. Nozyce of Liège, J. Mehlwurm of Charleroi and M. Blum of Brussels – thought they would be able to manipulate the Nazis. In reality, they could do only what they were commanded.[28]

One week after the committee came into being, Jewish students were expelled from public schools. In April 1942, Jews of German origin were informed that their property was being confiscated without compensation. On 1 June, Jews were barred from practicing medicine. The same day, the military administration decreed the wearing of the badge. Reeder and Falkenhausen had resisted the imposition of this device, arguing it would provoke hostility toward Germans. They yielded when Berlin insisted that the step was necessary for 'the solution of the Jewish question in Europe'. On 5 June, several Belgian mayors met with German officials to protest the rule. In Antwerp, then Brussels, city councilors announced they would not support such a measure. Within several days, however, Jews throughout Belgium were wearing the badge.[29]

Confronted with a shortage of industrial workers, Germany called upon its 'liberated' neighbors to help. During the first months of the occupation, 125,000 Belgians responded to the offer of jobs in Germany. Then word filtered back about working conditions. Food was meager, the workday grueling, and pay inadequate. Contracted 'over an indefinite period', volunteers endured the terror of armed guards and British bombers. Small wonder that Belgians spurned the Todt Organization which sought 5,000 workers for Atlantic fortifications in 1942. The Nazis responded by 'drafting' 20,000 men off the street and from movie theaters before the Belgian Secretary General for Labor protested such actions as 'unwarranted' and 'above the needs of the army'.[30] To appease his subjects, General Falkenhausen ruled that Belgian workers would be used only on Belgian soil. Such provisions did not apply to Jews. Compulsory labor was decreed for all profiteers (e.g. Jews, communists and saboteurs). On 8 May 1942 Falkenhausen announced that Jewish workers could be isolated from other personnel in 'centers reserved for them'. As Lucien Steinberg concluded, 'In sum, the concentration camp received legal sanction.'[31]

Between 13 June and 12 September 1942, 2,252 Jews were shipped to northern France. They were rounded up by Belgian police, examined by Belgian doctors, then placed in trains guarded by Belgian troops until they reached the French border. The Belgians made a serious mistake in the first transport from Antwerp on 13 June. Detrained at one railway terminal (Gare de Nord) in Brussels, 300 men marched through the streets in broad daylight to the Gare du Midi. The 'pathetic cortège' made a profound impression upon the population. There would be no slip-ups in the seven transports from Antwerp (13 June, 14 July, 15 August and 12 September), Brussels (26 June), Charleroi (31 July) and Liège (2 August).[32]

The German policy of forced labor evoked protests from a wide range of Belgians, none more influential than Cardinal Van Roey. In a letter to Falkenhausen dated 15 August 1941, Van Roey expressed his outrage over punishments that 'offend human psychology'.[33] Pressed by Falkenhausen to endorse the Nazis' fight against Bolshevism, the Cardinal explained he could not support such a crusade as long as the Church and its bishops were in 'mortal anguish'. The primate made repeated inquiries to the Ministry of Labor on behalf of deported workers.[34] Then, on 12 December 1942, he issued an episcopal letter to be read in all churches in Belgium decrying the 'desolation' of those who were being deported.[35] Such denunciations were most appropriate as the Nazis had decided to ship Jews from Belgium to death camps in the East. And the principal transit camp would be the old Dossin Kaserne located in the center of Malines, not far from the Cardinal's palace.

THE RAZZIAS OF SUMMER 1942

On 15 July 1942, Maurice Benedictus, administrative chief of the AJB, was summoned to SS headquarters in Brussels. One of Adolf Eichmann's top aides, Major Anton Burger, informed him that 10,000 Jews were needed to offset the shortage of workers in the Reich. The task of selecting deportees would fall to the executive of the AJB. If the council failed to cooperate, Burger hinted authorities 'would use methods proven in other countries'.[36] Burger assured Benedictus that everything would be done in a humane fashion. Once the quota was filled (from refugee Jews) Burger promised there would be no further *rafles* (roundups).[37]

There were four roundups at the end of summer – 15 August, 28–29

August, 3–4 September and 11–12 September. On 22 July, members of the *Feldgendarmerie* and Belgian militia groups began seizing Jews and taking them to Breendonck prison.[38] The first raid took nearly 1,000 victims. The Nazis and their allies managed to send 1,305 persons from Antwerp to Malines as a result of the second razzia. The Nazis rewarded their Flemish auxiliaries by allowing them to ticket Jewish businesses that did not display required signs. During a five-month period, more than 2,800 Jewish shops were visited. In 1942, the Belgian Nazis were authorized to arrest Jews who broke the law.[39]

While Antwerp was beleaguered, Brussels seemed to enjoy a charmed existence, even after an incident that normally would have triggered a pogrom. On the afternoon of 29 August 1942, Robert Holzinger, who headed the labor office for the AJB, was shot four times by a bicyclist as he left his home. He died four hours later. The assassin, Vladek Rakower, was a member of the Jewish underground. The socialist journal *Le Drapeau Rouge* justified the killing as a punishment for Holzinger's collaboration. The Jewish council, dreading reprisals, issued a statement expressing 'great sadness' over the death of its colleague. Salomon Van den Berg called Holzinger 'a brave man' and said he was the victim of 'cowardly assassins'. While members of the Association wrestled with personal grief, Lieutenant Asche visited AJB offices on 30 August and warned if Holzinger's killer was not found in 24 hours, the Jews would experience something that would 'not be a child's game'.[40]

The next few days passed quietly. A number of Jews (57) were taken to Malines on 31 August, 46 on 1 September, 82 on 2 September, 22 on 3 September. The AJB was assured that labor transports to France were temporarily suspended. Starting on the night of 3 September, the Jews of Brussels experienced four days of torment. Germans and their auxiliaries (no Belgian police were involved) cordoned off streets in the middle of the night, breaking into apartments and beating people from their beds. A 72-year-old woman was thrown into the night. At Avenue Clemenceau and Rue de la Clinique, a woman carrying a new-born baby was struck in the face when she asked an SS man for some milk. Hundreds of people were stuffed into moving vans where they waited for hours before being transferred to Malines.[41]

As the razzia in Brussels continued, members of a Jewish resistance group headed by Theodore Angeheloff decided to retaliate. On 6 September six persons were injured when a bomb exploded during a meeting of Rexists and the de Vlag movement at the Marivaux Cinema. Van den Berg and the AJB condemned such acts. For their part, the Nazis responded by imprisoning 50 prominent hostages, including Jean Herincks, the Bürgermeister of Uccle. They also punished the Belgians by seizing 5,000 bicycles.[42] Through inform- ants and chance arrest, the Germans managed to eliminate Holzinger's assassin and leaders of the group that had engineered the Marivaux bombing.[43]

There would be one more major roundup in Antwerp that September.

The city was calm for two weeks prior to 11 September – Rosh Hashanah. Jews asked if they might peacefully observe their holiday. They received assurances from Eric Holm who had just returned from Brussels. Instead, Jews who ventured into the street were stopped and interrogated. Anyone of foreign nationality was arrested. This surprise razzia netted 1,422 persons, the largest catch ever.[44] By the end of the month, the Nazis achieved their goal of sending 10,000 Jews east. And still the transit camp of Malines was overflowing.

MALINES: THE DOSSIN KASERNE

Unlike most Nazi concentration camps, the Dossin Kaserne, the fortress that served as the main collection center for transports leaving Belgium, was located in the heart of Malines on the Rue de Stassart. Malines lay equidistant (30 kilometers) from Antwerp and Brussels in the most heavily populated region of Belgium. In the early days when men were sent to France for forced labor, the Association of Jews in Belgium instructed individuals to report with identity papers. Later, workers were advised to carry with them food for two weeks as well as work shoes, stockings, shirts, pants, a change of underwear, one pullover, a bowl, two cups and a spoon. The Nazis warned that failure to report would result in deportation to a concentration camp in Germany. Officials of the AJB added their own warning of 'the sad consequences' for the person, his family and all Jews in Belgium.[45]

If a convoy lacked the complement of 1,000, Jews would have to remain in the stark halls for a week or longer. Henri Sonnenbluck was 16 years old when he and his mother were arrested in Antwerp. In the transit camp, they were offered a soup so foul that only a few of the newcomers would touch it. During the nine months Sonnenbluck was in Malines, some of his companions organized cultural and social activities. An Austrian gave a course on philosophy, a Polish Jew tried to interest others in politics, and a boxer named Perez offered instruction in self-defense. Henri's mother befriended a 15-year-old girl (Rosa Erlich). On 15 January 1944, all three were among 657 persons packed into Convoy XXIII. Upon arriving at Auschwitz, 420 of these (including Sonnenbuck's mother and Rosa) were gassed.[46]

All told, 17 convoys left Malines between 5 August and 3 November 1942. Not 10,000, but nearly 17,000 Jews were sent east. The Association of Jews in Belgium could not prevent the deportation of school teachers, members of the council or their families.[47] In the last week of October, Kurt Asche assured officials of the AJB that the transports were suspended. A week later, he announced the return of Jewish workmen from France. By this time Jews no longer believed what the Nazis promised. Many went into hiding or attempted to break free of the transports which began moving from Malines again on 18 January 1943. Nachum Mittelsbach and his wife evaded authorities with forged papers for seven months before a 'tracker' betrayed them. The night before their departure from Malines, in April 1943, 1,400 people designated for Convoy XX sang and danced the hora. When Mittelsbach learned that everyone would be killed, he stripped boards away from a window of his cattle car and leaped to freedom with his wife and several others.[48]

Situated in the midst of an anti-German populace and visited by delivery men who smuggled letters, parcels and tools, Malines was never hermetically sealed. In the summer of 1943, Maurice Heiber (who worked in the SS mess) learned that 2,000 new spots were being prepared in Malines. By this time, most foreign Jews had either been deported or gone into hiding. The only conclusion Heiber could reach was that despite pledges made to Dowager Queen Elisabeth and to the leaders of the AJB, the Nazis intended to round up Jewish citizens of Belgium.[49]

VAN ROEY AND THE CATHOLIC CHURCH

All of this took place in the seat of the highest ranking church official in Belgium – Cardinal van Roey. When the Nazis began their roundups of the Jews, van Roey was bombarded with appeals from leaders of the AJB, converts, Gentiles with Jewish spouses, or their children. On 3 August, Edmond-Francis Leclef, Van Roey's secretary, asked German authorities where Jews were going in Poland or Ukraine. The curt response indicated that males between the ages of 17 and 40 would be employed in labor enterprises. Beyond that, 'the military was not competent in this area'.[50]

Cardinal Roey would express his personal anguish over the treatment of Jews in letters to the Papal Secretary in Rome, Cardinal Maglione. On 4 August, he wrote: 'Actually, the treatment to which the Jews have been subjected is truly inhuman and evokes general pity and indignation. Catholic converts who were born Jews are also subjected to these measures. I have tried to secure mitigation, but, unfortunately, have not obtained anything.'[51] In December, Van Roey wrote again: 'The seizure and deportation of the Jews, about which I wrote you last August 4th, has been pursued without letup, and I believe there won't be much rest in Belgian territory. These measures have been executed with a brutality and cruelty that has profoundly revolted the Belgian people. I have intervened in several cases, but generally in vain. Likewise baptized Jews and converts haven't been spared.'[52] Documents attest to Van Roey's efforts on behalf of a 52-year-old Jewish woman from Antwerp who was, nevertheless, deported from Malines on 14 August.[53] The Primate did manage to save the life of Rabbi Ullmann who was twice imprisoned at Malines.[54] Canon Leclef also credits Van Roey with the rescue of hundreds of Jewish children who were sheltered in Belgian convents and monasteries during the war.[55]

Jean Herinckx offers a different image of the Belgian Primate, noting that the Cardinal refused to authorize emergency baptisms of Jewish children unless parents or the nearest relatives specified that the child would truly practice Catholicism.[56] If anything, Van Roey seemed as exercised by the Nazis' seizure of 4,568 churchbells in the summer of 1944 (the Nazis wanted to recast 1.7 million pounds of iron into ammunition) as he was by their treatment of the Jews.[57] Van Roey opted for statesmanship while lesser church figures saved lives. The Bishop of Liège sheltered several Jews, including a rabbi and his family, in his palace for months, the curate of Brussels secured hiding places for 250 Jewish children and 125 others, and Abbé Rauch, the curate of Felennes, permitted several dozen children to stay in his building. Abbé Louis Cells raised four Jewish children whose parents had been deported and even arranged for their Bar Mitzvahs. Father Édouard Froidure ran an underground camp for 300 Jewish children. Father Joseph André, vicar of Saint-Jean Baptiste at Nâmur, assisted an impoverished Jewish family from Germany in 1941. Thereafter, hundreds of Jews came to the 'Home of the Angel' who rarely slept for fear that some of his charges might be betrayed. Père Bruno, from the abbey of Mont-César, was supposed to care for children in a house for the blind. Père Bruno was surprised to find a number of Jewish children who could see in their midst. These were some of the 316 Jewish children protected by the priest during the war.[58]

ACTIVE RESISTANCE: THE FIL AND CDJ

From the start of the occupation, individual Belgians resisted German rule. Major E. Calberg in the department of Food and Supply managed to distribute 1,000 food parcels to Jews in hiding. Mlle Yvonne Nevejaean headed up *Oeuvre national de l'Enfance*, which served as a liaison between Jews and the Belgian government-in-exile. The *Marraines* (Godmothers), a group of university women organized by Nelly Lameere, collected money, food, clothing and sweets for Jews in hiding. More, they supplied 'a human presence' to the children who were separated from their parents.[59] One group that especially bedeviled the Nazis was the Belgian railway workers. In 1941, the Nazis ordered 200 engines from Belgium. A year later, not a single machine had been delivered. In Liège 32 locomotives were smashed and eight rail stations set on fire. At one time 50 percent of Belgium's freight cars were laid up. Underground flyers instructed how to burn out an axle with a mixture of sand and grease, how to sever airbrake lines with a straight razor. During the first three months of 1942, there were 25 major train accidents in Belgium. Railway sabotage was so extensive that the Nazis had to post guards at every 50 feet along some of the lines.[60]

The umbrella organization for Belgium's resistance was *Le Front de l'Indépendance* (FIL) formed in March 1941 by journalist Fernand Demany,

Abbé André Boland and Dr Albert Marteaux of the communists. FIL consisted of a National Council, a secretariat headed by Demany, the *Armée Belge des partisans* directed by communists Jean Terfve and Raoul Baligand, and a host of other committees formed by young people, lawyers, doctors, etc. One of the latter was the *Le Comité de Défense des Juifs* (CDJ) organized late in 1941 as a counterbalance to the Association of Jews in Belgium.[61] The CDJ forged documents, exposed collaborators, arranged hiding places for children, and may have saved the lives of 30,000 persons.[62] It tried to convince German authorities that an exchange might be made of Jews who held 'certificates' to Palestine for interned German nationals.[63] Some of the Maquis groups associated with the CDJ engaged in acts of sabotage, such as the one that enabled Nachum Mittelsbach to escape from a death train and the bombing at the Marivaux Cinema. Of the eight founders of the CDJ, six were deported.[64]

Despite repeated promises that no transports would leave after November 1942, 11 more trains carried 9,000 people from Malines to Auschwitz before the end of the war. Five smaller transports went to Buchenwald, Ravensbrück, Belsen and Vittel. Some Belgian Jews had been apprehended during razzias in the summer of 1942, but were separated from less fortunate kinsmen and detained in Malines. Frustrated by their lack of success in rooting out refugees, the Nazis mounted 'Operation Iltis' in September 1943. A total of 750 Jews of Belgian nationality were arrested in Brussels and taken to Malines. Another 250 were taken into custody in Antwerp. The roundup collapsed in a sea of public protests, however, when it became known that 145 persons had been sealed in a furniture van leaving nine dead, 80 unconscious and several others insane.[65] 'Operation Iltis' was a failure, but the SS continued to deport diamond workers, tailors and other persons with protected status. Only the lack of railway cars stopped Anton Burger from deporting members of the AJB and their families in August 1944. Of 25,257 Jews who went to Auschwitz in 28 convoys, 1,204 returned.[66] Nearly one-third of Belgium's Jews perished in the Holocaust.

LUXEMBOURG: GAU MOSELLAND

Following the Blitzkrieg in the West, Germany retook territory lost to Belgium in the settlement of 1919. The Nazis simply annexed Luxembourg: 324,000 people who lived in Gau Moselle were offered German citizenship and invited to change their names.[67] Posters reminded the Luxembourgeois of their historical enmity for the French and the German eagle replaced the lion in popular heraldry. In August 1940, Gauleiter Gustav Simon proclaimed German the official language of the state, declaring, 'Enough of foreign language. Your speech should be German and only German.' As another German propaganda release declared in 1941, '*Hinweg mit separatismus.*

Luxembourg, you are Germany, your motherland is Germany, you ought to be with us.'[68]

Most people in this small nation quietly endured their shame, clinging to their identity as *Letzebuergesch, Letzebuergesch, Letzebuergesch* (Luxembourgers). A few could not contain their anger and joined resistance groups like the the LPL (*Ligue patriotique luxembourgeoise*), the LRL (*Lion Rouge Luxembourgeois*), LVL (*Volkslegion*) and *League du peuple*.[69] In 1940 the underground helped escaped prisoners of war cross into French territory. Pierre Grégoire and Abbé Jean-Baptiste Esch were sent to Sachsenhausen for their anti-Nazi articles in *La Parole luxembourgeoise*. They were more fortunate than Willy Seidler, Demy Dondliger and Gabriel Richetta, resistance leaders who were executed at Klingelputz, a prison in Cologne. Heinrich Adam also perished in Klingelputz. A German by birth, he worked in Luxembourg for 30 years and married a Luxembourg woman. In September 1942, Adam went to the police and disavowed his German nationality. 'I am ashamed to be German', he declared. 'I am solidly with the Luxembourg people.'[70] For this, he, like Seidler, Dondliger and Richetta, was beheaded.

What prompted Adam's outburst was imposition of martial law throughout Luxembourg on 31 August 1942. The day before, Gauleiter Simon, speaking from the Grand Ducal Palace had announced the call up of men between the ages of 20 and 24 for service in the *Wehrmacht*. When factory workers arrived at their jobs in the town of Wiltz on 31 August, somebody pulled the whistle and they walked off. Within hours the strike had spread to Esch in the south. As one adviser explained to Simon, 'The people have chosen honor, loyalty to independence.'[71] Simon proclaimed a state of siege which lasted for six days. Placards appeared in every city warning: *Todesurteile gegen Streikende werden sofort durch Erschiessen vollstreckt* (The death sentence will be immediately imposed by shooting against strikers). Storm troopers arrested strike leaders. Then, true to his word, Simon announced the executions of men who were postal workers, engineers, teachers and roofers.

The families of the rebels were sent to Hinzert, a transit camp at Trèves. In the fall of 1941, 512 Luxembourg Jews were among 20,000 Jews from the Reich shipped to the ghetto of Lodz. Two thousand more Jews would be detained in the lightless barracks of Hinzert before going to Treblinka or Auschwitz.[72] One Luxembourger who could comment on the treatment of Jews in concentration camps was Monsignor Jules Jost. Taken to Dachau in August 1943, Jost was liberated in April 1945 along with 26,000 Jewish survivors from Auschwitz, Ravensbrück, Belsen. 'The horror of their condition was indescribable', said Jost:

> One night at a camp named Kaufering IV, I was called into a barrack where a Hungarian Jewish woman had given birth. I found her lying on the ground, on a little straw. Her face was lit up with joy and her little child, she called him Gyorgy, was at her breast. The baby was given a number by

the SS. The next day, the mother and her newborn left the camp with a card carrying the reference 'Sonderbehandlung', signifying that these two deemed useless mouths by the SS Economic Service were to be liquidated.[73]

Luxembourg owns the dubious distinction of having been liberated twice in World War II. Prince Felix and Crown Prince Jean accompanied the Americans on 10 September 1944. Three months later, Nazi panzers split the Allied line in what became known as the Battle of the Bulge. Five thousand American soldiers are buried in the cemetery of Hamm two miles east of Luxembourg City. The number is virtually identical to Luxembourg's civilian losses during the war. Jewish losses were even more devastating. An estimated 700–800 persons, perhaps 20 percent of the Jews of Luxembourg, survived World War II.[74]

11

Vichy France

Before World War II, republican France generated its own copycat fascist groups. Outfitted in jodhpurs and jackboots, members of the Parti Populaire, the Front Paysan, Cagoulards and Croix de Feu paraded through the Arc de Triomphe. Despite the *loi Marchandeau* which in 1881 prohibited religious or racial defamation, zealots like Jacques Doriot, Marcel Déat, Eugene DeLoncle, Henri Dorgères and Colonel François de La Roque spewed hatred against foreign workers, refugees and Jews.[1] When Eduard Daladier became Premier in May 1938, some aliens were assigned to detention camps. Six months later, the government withdrew rights from individuals 'unworthy of the title of French citizen'.[2] Under Vichy, French nationalists resurrected the *françisque* (a double-headed axe used by ancient Gauls) as their symbol and adopted the fascist salute. Marshal Pétain's image graced propaganda offices everywhere.[3] Newsreels shrilled 'His name rings out like a shot. Pétain! He is full of energy and good will, his soul is ready, this great victor who is even greater in defeat.' Teenagers swore an oath 'to unite and to gather all our forces, our faith, our ardor, at the service of the marshal, at the service of France'.[4]

Despite assertions that the Vichy government was sovereign (at least in the south), there was a good deal of confusion over who actually made policy, especially where Jews were concerned. Reasonable estimates placed the number of Jews in France at 270,000, half of them stateless. About 150,000 Jews lived in Paris, mostly in the vicinity of the rue de Rosier.[5] After Compiègne, it was illegal for Jews or blacks to move between the Occupied and Unoccupied Zones. Yet the Nazis expelled 22,000 Jews (including veterans of the Kaiser's army) from Alsace, Baden, Württemburg and the Saarpfalz to refugee camps in the south until protests from Vichy's Minister of Interior to the Armistice Commission at Wiesbaden halted the transfers.

The highest ranking German in France was General Otto von Stülpnagel. Hailed as an anti-Nazi because of his involvement in the 1944 plot to kill Hitler, Stülpnagel was hardly a moderate on the Jewish question. In September 1940 he ordered the registration of Jewish businesses to facilitate Aryanization of Jewish property. When communists began attacking German soldiers in Paris in the summer of 1941, Stülpnagel authorized reprisals. One hundred hostages were executed for an assassination attempt against a Luftwaffe major in December 1941. At the same time 1,100 Jews were deported to the East and a billion franc fine was imposed upon Jewish communities of France. Before being replaced by his cousin Karl Heinrich in February 1942, Stülpnagel favored use of the Jewish badge in France.

Stülpnagel was advised by a number of 'experts' on Jews. Dr Werner Best worked with Dr Elmar Michel of the Economic Section trying to lure workers to Germany. Ambassador Otto Abetz called for the enactment of a comprehensive Jewish ordinance. Officials of *Einsatzstab Rosenberg* were mainly concerned with looting paintings and antiques from Jewish homes.[6] The Eichmann Office sent *Haupsturmführer* Theodor Dannecker to serve as *Judenreferat* in France. One of Eichmann's top men, Dannecker was assisted by *Obersturmführer* Heinz Röthke, SS *Brigadeführer* Carl Oberg, *Sturmbannführer* Herbert Hagen, *Standartenführer* Helmut Knochen of the Security Police (SD) and *Obersturmführer* Kurt Lischka, a brutish man from the Gestapo.[7]

As in the Low Countries, the Nazis moved slowly before imposing a racial state. Jews were required to register with authorities, turn in radios, observe a curfew, and mark their businesses with bilingual signs. Eager to involve the French in the spoilation of the Jews, the Nazis approved the creation of the *Service de Contrôle des Administrateurs Provisoires* (SCAP) in the fall of 1940. Funds from Aryanized transfers were supposed to go into special accounts of Vichy's Treasury Department, but did not. In June 1941 all pretense of legality was dropped when a new decree permitted SCAP to seize Jewish businesses. By May 1944, 42,000 Jewish enterprises had been assigned to Aryan trustees, some of whom redirected sales to third parties to block their return to Jewish owners.[8]

In August 1940, the law against defamation was repealed. So, too, the Cremieux decree which accorded Jews rights in North Africa. French anti-Semites were pleased when on 3 October, the government issued its first *Statut des Juifs*. The decree went further than Nuremberg, declaring anyone with *two* grandparents to be a Jew. Excepting war veterans, Jews were barred from all public positions.[9] Over the next few months Jews would also be barred from banking, entering restaurants, using public telephones or riding any but the last coach of the metro. A 2 percent quota was imposed upon the legal, architectural and medical professions. School enrollment was capped at 3 percent. Through it all, Vichy officials promised that 'the persons and belongings of Jews will be respected'.[10]

THE COMMISSARIAT FOR JEWISH AFFAIRS

In February 1941, Dannecker outlined the need for a specific bureau to regulate Jewish activity. A month later, the puppet French cabinet established a General Commissariat for Jewish Affairs (*Commissariat général aux questions juives* or CGQJ). Xavier Vallat, who had lost an eye and leg in World

War I, was selected to head the agency. Once a member of *Action Française*, Vallat was an outspoken anti-Semite. The Jew, he claimed, was a parasitic foreigner belonging to a cursed race. Vallat endorsed what he called a national solution of the Jewish question, that is, allowing each country to determine the fate of its Jews at war's end. He criticized Nazi reprisals, roundups and the introduction of the badge.[11] Because of his perceived weakness, Vallat was replaced in March 1942 by Louis Darquier, a coarse bigot who headed his own racist movement. Despised by most Vichy officials (Pétain referred to him as *Monsieur le tortionnaire* – Mr Torturer), Darquier was the perfect man to execute the Nazi program.[12]

In the spring of 1941, Vallat approved a special cachet ('Juif') for identity cards. That June, a second Jewish statute extended restrictions to all of France and subjected recent conversions to government review. After 1940 the CGQJ received over three million letters of *délation* (denunciation) from informants.[13] Auxiliary police (*Sections d'Enquête et Contrôle*, SEC) and Doriotist militia groups exposed Jews in hiding, torched seven Paris synagogues, and assisted in the deportation of Jews from France. In May 1941, the CGQJ founded an Institute for the Study of the Jewish Question (*l'Institut d'études des questions juives*, IEQJ). The propaganda institute published brochures ('The Cancer that Undermined France', 'French-Jewish Colonization'), and posted placards that blamed Jews for tuberculosis, syphilis and cancer. It promoted right-wing newspapers like *Au Pilori* that declared on 14 March 1941:

> Death to the Jew! Death to villainy, duplicity, to Jewish trickery! Death to Jewish argument! Death to Jewish usury! Death to everything that is false, ugly, filthy, repugnant, Negroid, mongrel, Jewish! Death! Death to the Jew! Yes. Let us repeat. Repeat it! Death! M.O.R.T. AU JUIF! There! The Jew isn't a man. He is a stinking beast. You fight the pox, you fight epidemics. You fight against the invasion of microbodies. You fight against sickness, against death, therefore against the Jews.[14]

The Commissariat sponsored a major anti-Semitic exhibition (*Le Juif et la France*) in September 1941. Crowds entering the Palais Berlitz were greeted by a giant spider suspended from the ceiling representing Jewry feasting on the blood of France. Rooms were filled with grotesque images of Jewish eyes, noses, mouths, 'scientific proof' of their inferiority. Others revealed Jewish sexual perversion, Jews as criminals, speculators, subversive writers and diseased refugees. The exhibition played to crowds in Paris for 16 weeks before going on to Marseille, Nice, Cannes, Toulouse and Lyons.[15] The CGQJ also underwrote two chairs on Judaism at the Sorbonne. The first lecture was given on 15 December 1942 by Henri Labroué. The one-time deputy informed his audience that it was improper to identify ancient Israelites with contemporary Jews. 'The Jews have a particular odor', said Labroué, 'which shows ancient Negro connections. Jews aren't physically like other men. Their religion is the opposite of Christianity.' Subsequent lectures were so poorly attended that the Nazis shut down the institutes in the spring of 1943.[16]

THE UGIF

Despite the creation of the CGQJ, there were still 67 Jewish organizations in France and Dannecker wanted to deal with a central *Judenrat*. On 29 November 1941. Vichy ordered the creation of a *Union générale des Israélites en France* (UGIF) The concept was resisted by the Central Consistory of Jews, the Federation of Jewish Societies in France, the Amelot Committee (including refugee Jews) and the communist *Solidarité*, as well as Zionist groups. Nevertheless two agencies came into being in January 1942 – the UGIF-S based in Vichy under Albert Lévy and the UGIF-N headed by André Baur which operated out of Paris. Technically one agency, the two bodies acted independently of one another. There were no Jewish police in France outside of detention camps. Neither organization selected individuals for deportation to the east. As Dr George Wellers noted, the element essential to collabora-tion – 'the desire for final success of persecutors' – was missing.[17] The twin UGIFs served mainly as conduits for humanitarian agencies such as the Joint Distribution Committee and American Friends Services Committee. They would also pay fines imposed upon the Jews community (over 485 million francs, \$200 million, by 1943) for damage caused by the resistance or Allies.[18]

The UGIF was the link to the outside world for many Jews in French detention camps. There were 26 such sites in the Unoccupied Zone (includ-ing Rivesaltes, Barcares, Argelès, Le Vernet, Rieucros, Les Milles, Sept-fonds, Agde, Noe, Gurs, La Guiche and Venissieux), 15 (notably Royallieu, Pithiviers, Beaune-la-Rolande and Drancy) in the Occupied Zone.[19] These *camps de concentration* housed 53,610 inmates (foreign Jews, Spanish Republicans, Gypsies, Poles and anti-Nazi Germans) in the fall of 1940.[20]

The *Sûreté National* began arresting stateless Jews in October 1940. The first mass arrests occurred on 14 May 1941, when 4,000 foreign Jews were 'invited' to Beaune-la-Rolande and Pithiviers. Because of a shortage of SS Order Police, this roundup, like that conducted against workers in the 11th Arrondisement on 20 August and one involving Jewish notables in Paris on 12 December 1941, were conducted by French gendarmes.[21] On 27 March 1942, 558 men from the Royallieu camp were taken to the railway station at Compiègne where they boarded third-class passenger trains with 554 men from Drancy. This was the first French transport bound for Auschwitz. Of 1,112 relatively healthy men, 19 survived the war.[22]

LA GRANDE RAFLE

That first trainload of deportees was viewed more as an anomaly than a harbinger of doom. In the spring of 1942, Jews in France were feeling optimistic. Hitler's 'final' offensive against Russia had ended with disaster at Kursk and people hoped that an understanding might be achieved with corrupt leaders like Laval and Darquier. Such hopes proved unfounded. In June, the Nazis ordered Jews in the Occupied Zone over the age of six to wear the yellow star. Some Gentile students tried to buoy their comrades by declaring themselves 'JUIF' (*Jeunesse Universitaire Intellectuelle Française*) and sporting yellow kerchiefs from their pockets. Several were arrested and sent to Drancy where they languished for three months.[23]

As Jews resigned themselves to wearing the badge, the Nazis prepared an even more disastrous surprise. On 11 June 1942 Adolf Eichmann convened a meeting of race specialists in Berlin where he outlined plans for Jews in western Europe. Eichmann called for the removal of 100,000 Jews from France. These numbers were only 'a quota', as he envisaged the deportation of all Jews between the ages of 16 and 40 except those married to Aryans.[24] Lacking the manpower to effect mass arrests, the Nazis had to rely upon French security forces who had cooperated in earlier roundups. Thousands of gendarmes, detectives, CGQJ auxiliaries, Dorotist militiamen, bailiffs and student trainees would be needed. Darquier, his director of police for Jewish questions (Schweblin), commissioner Leguay and Vichy police chief Bousquet promised their fullest cooperation for *Opération Vent Printanier* (Spring Wind) that was to occur on 13 July.[25]

Out of deference to Bastille Day (the French national holiday on 14 July) the roundup was postponed till 16–17 July. The French police were told that only foreign Jews of specific nationality (German, Austrian, Polish, Czech, Russian) were to be arrested. Males between the ages of 16 and 60 and females between 16 and 55 (except those who were pregnant and near delivery, nursing, or had children under the age of two) were to go.[26] Remarkably, when Darquier tried to place stateless children in orphanages around Paris, he was overruled by Premier Pierre Laval. Laval argued that the children would present a burden to France. The premier was prepared to send children from the Unoccupied Zone. His position was endorsed by the Council of Ministers and Pétain.[27] On 20 July, Eichmann authorized the deportation of children, regardless of age.[28]

On the morning of 16 July, 9,000 French police and auxiliaries began their sweep through the 20 Arrondisements and 25 suburbs of Paris. They were seeking 27,388 foreign Jews and they had been instructed to act quickly, with a minimum of force. Once police were in an apartment, the Jews were allowed to take only personal items and food for two days. Individuals were escorted to Renault buses which carried them to prefect headquarters. The roundups lasted from 4 to 9:30 a.m. and 12 to 3:30 p.m. on 16 July, 4 a.m. to 1 p.m. on 17 July, enabling the police to have time for meal breaks.

Even before 16 July, some officers leaked the news to Jewish acquaintances. Many fled their homes, hiding with friends and relatives. Others refused to believe the roundup would take place. At the last moment, they barred doors or hid in basements. Angry French officers took whoever they found, French citizens, the sick and dying. To increase the tally, one dead newborn was carried away in a sheet that first night. Eyewitnesses told of a mother who threw her children from a fourth-story window as gendarmes broke into her apartment. Elsewhere a ten-year-old girl leaped to her death from a third floor. At Montreuil, a physician administered lethal injections to himself and his family.[29]

On 16 July 9,800 Jews were arrested, 3,000 on 17 July. Of these, 3,031 were adult males, 5,082 females. There were also 4,051 children under the age of 16, making a total of 12,884 Jews netted by the *Grande Rafle*. Six thousand adults were sent directly to Drancy.[30] The rest were taken to an indoor bicycle arena near the Pont de Bir Hakeim. Before the war, the Vélodrome d'Hiver had been used for political rallies. During the *Grande Rafle*, people sat on the floor, in seats, along the rafters, waiting in despair. There was no food for two days and the only water available came from an outside hydrant. The building had ten lavatories most of which soon malfunctioned.[31] Near the main entry tunnel, doctors set up a primitive clinic in the loges with people lying on stretchers. Many children in the arena were suffering from measles, chicken pox, whooping cough, scarlet fever or typhus. A 16-year-old girl recalled, 'It was a veritable slaughterhouse. The sick ones spit up blood. People passed out endlessly. The screams of the children were deafening. People went mad.' There were at least 30 suicide attempts. That first night several Jewish leaders toured the facility and promised to send additional medical supplies. They appealed to Darquier's aide Pierre Gallien, who waited till Saturday to reject their offer. According to Gallien, everything in the Velodrome was 'perfect and sanitary'.[32]

After five days, the building was cleared and most of the people were sent to Drancy. Some women and children were funneled to Pithiviers and Beaune-la-Rolande, two camps of Loiret which until July 1942 held 1,500 inmates, all of them adult male Jews. In the week following the *Grande Rafle*, the population of Pithiviers and Beaune-la-Rolande swelled to 7,500. No provision was made for the new arrivals, no beds, no food. Reports told that both camps reeked – 'the closer you come the more the air seemed infected'.[33] During the first week of August, Mothers and young girls were forced into boxcars that went directly to Auschwitz. Five hundred children, aged 2 to 13, had to endure another level of hell before going east.

DRANCY

Eight miles northeast of downtown Paris, Drancy is a suburb filled with flea markets, apartments and a blue/white collar population mix. The U-shaped buildings of the transit camp are flanked by the Joliot Curie Recreation Center and an expanse of green grass and playgrounds. Today the complex houses 1,000 persons of low income. Opened in the fall of 1940 as a detention camp for French prisoners of war, Drancy housed civilians from England,

Yugoslavia and Greece until August 1941 when it was used almost exclusively for Jews. Gendarmes patrolled the perimeter. This infamous site functioned as an *Abwanderungslanger* (emigration camp) in the Nazi scheme of genocide and French officers answered to Dannecker, Röthke and *Hauptsturmführer* Alois Brunner (who assumed command after July 1943).

In August 1941, the dormitories had no room dividers, few beds, no blankets, no spoons and a primitive supply of water. The only thing in readiness for 3,500 men was a set of regulations prepared by Dannecker. Under these rules, it was forbidden to smoke, communicate with the guards, receive parcels, or to look out the windows when the SS visited the camp.[34] The inmates did wrest some concessions from their jailers. After weeks of a bland diet of soup, coffee and 250 grams of bread, in October they broke up a morning Appel (roll call), chanting, 'Food! Food! We want to eat! We want to eat!' Shortly after, 800 of the weakest prisoners were freed. The rest received permission to receive two postcards per month as well as a single food parcel and a change of 'linen' every two weeks.[35]

Periodically, the Nazis reminded their prisoners how capricious life could be. On 12 December 1941, Dannecker selected 308 men to leave the camp. The inmates were convinced they were going to be executed, but they went instead to Compiègne where they joined 750 hostages taken in Paris. Two days later, a Wehrmacht detachment shot 44 of these men at Mont Valérien along with a similar number of communists. At the end of January, Dannecker reappeared in Drancy, calling for agricultural workers. Fifty young volunteers spent the next two months at Compiègne, in cold and hunger. On 27 March, 554 Jewish men from Drancy were chosen for the first transport to Auschwitz. A month later (29 April) 500 more were sent to Compiègne to join deportees from Pithiviers and Beaune-la-Rolande.[36] Early in July the camp was told to expect 3,000 new inmates. Jews from housing projects, prisons, alien refuges and nursing homes swelled the actual count to more than 6,000.

The children who had been arrested in the *Grande Rafle* began arriving in August. 'Devoured by vermin' and 'macerated in excrement' some of these youngsters did not even know their names. Wooden tags about their necks did not help because the children sometimes exchanged these. Older siblings or friends helped the younger ones find assigned rooms, even carried them to fourth floor dormitories.[37] In Drancy, female volunteers washed the children with what little soap was available, and gave them food and drink. The children could not digest cabbage soup. They developed terrible diarrhea and, being unable to get to the toilets, soiled their clothes and mattresses where they lay. The women would wash them again, but each time the children ate, the vicious cycle resumed. At night the rooms were filled with sobs and shrieks brought on by nightmares. Dr Wellers and René Blum, brother of the former French premier, visited a room which housed 110 children.[38] The men found sisters (aged 12 and 5), sitting on mattresses. Blum struck up a conversation with the older girl who was reading an issue of *le Cri du Peuple*. When he noted that it was an anti-Semitic newspaper, the girl exploded:

> I don't want to be French. The French are wicked, wicked, and I detest them. It was the French who came to our house. They searched everywhere for my little sister because my mother hid her. They found her because the little one cried. Afterward, they came to school to take me. At Beaune-la-Rolande, it was the French customs agent who took my mother and father ... and here it is the gendarmes who guard us.

When Blum said it was all due to the war, the young girl replied, 'And why can't they do anything? They were able to hunt for my sister! They were able to let us go with our parents. They are evil, disgusting.'[39]

On 18 August 1942, members of the PQJ (auxiliary police) made a search of the children's barracks, tearing apart bundles, confiscating pendants, bracelets and earrings. The next morning, the children were awakened at 5 a.m. They dressed in the dark and were told to assemble in the courtyard. Some refused to budge. Dr Wellers recalled: 'It happened sometimes that a whole roomful of a hundred children, as if seized with ungovernable panic and frenzy, no longer listened to the cajoling of the grownups who could not get them downstairs. It was then that they called the gendarmes, who carried the children in their arms, screaming with terror.'[40]

As their names were called, the children reboarded the buses that brought them to the camp. At the Bobigny railway station, they were given bread and a can of condensed milk. Some of their attendants accompanied them as they entered the freight cars. They spoke of a wonderful land of Pichipoi where Jews, reunited with their families, would laze in green pastures. In Pichipoi the sun shone every day. There would be no hunger, no cold, no sickness and no Germans.[41] The children wanted to believe in this land of bliss, but instinctively they knew it was a fantasy. As Mlle Monod, a Red Cross nurse, noted:

> Many of the children were too small to climb into the freight cars without a footboard. The bigger ones climbed in first and helped pull in the smaller ones. The gendarmes lent a hand, taking the youngest, practically infants, and passing them to those already inside, among whom were a few women, who were breast-feeding. It was then that the children were seized with fear. They did not want to leave and began to sob, calling on the social workers and sometimes even the gendarmes to help them. I remember little Jacquet, aged five, who was particularly fond of me. Begging for my help he cried, 'I want to get down, I want to see the lady again, I don't want to do pipi on the floor. I want the lady to help me down to do pipi' ... The door of the wagon was closed and padlocked, but he still stuck his hand out through a crack between two planks; his fingers moved; he continued to cry out, 'I don't want to do pipi on the floor, I want the lady to help me do pipi.'[42]

In the transport of 19 August 1942, 4,500 Jewish children were shipped east. A memorandum of Belgian railway workers dated 11 November 1942, described cattle cars that returned from Auschwitz still containing the corpses of 25 Jewish children.[43]

MORE TRANSPORTS

Every Sunday, Tuesday and Thursday 1,000 people were loaded into the cattle cars. For those charged with making up the lists, the task was 'painful and depressing'. In the summer of 1943, the Nazis deported the top officials of the UGIF – Andre Baur, Armand Katz, Fernand Musnik, Raymond-Raoul Lambert and their families. Drancy was replenished on Monday, Wednesday and Saturday. Many of the newcomers hailed from the Unoccupied Zone. Late in August 1942, detention camps in the south were cleared to meet a goal of 32,000 deportees. Distinctions between the two zones in France were erased when, following the Allied invasion of North Africa in November 1942, German troops marched into territory reserved for Vichy. Another 35,000 Jews were sent out in 1943–44. Many of these people had sought sanctuary in the Mediterranean departments awarded to the Italians in 1940. SS units surprised 20,000 Jews in Nice, another 22,000 in the port of Marseille.[44]

Perhaps 30,000 Jews managed to flee from the Unoccupied Zone to Switzerland or Spain before the Nazis closed off these escape routes. More than 50,000 were seized along the Riviera. Among them were 5,000 Jewish children, the subject of discussions between Vichy and American officials during the summer of 1942. At the same time, Laval was encouraging the Nazis to take Jewish children in the *Grande Rafle*, he was prepared to let all 5,000 go to America. Talks meandered over the next several weeks as State Department officials fretted about violating American immigration law and Laval demanded assurances that the children would not be used for propaganda. When the Nazis occupied southern France, such questions became moot. The children were sent to Drancy.[45]

Much of the suffering in Drancy could be attributed to new camp commandant SS *Hauptsturmbahnführer* Alois Brunner.[46] A runty salesman from Rohrbrünn, Austria, Brunner joined the Nazi party in 1931. Following the *Anschluss*, he attached himself to Eichmann's Security branch in Vienna. Eichmann praised him as 'my most consistently effective aide'. Acquaintances recalled an extremely violent person, one who could not speak to Jews without cursing. Dieter Wisliceny described him as 'a man with bad posture, black, kinky hair, dark eyes, thick lips and a hooked nose. He must have had some Gypsy or Jewish blood.' After his arrival in Drancy in June 1943, it was not unusual to see Brunner strutting through the camp, lashing at inmates with a horsewhip.

Brunner replaced French gendarmes with 25 of his own SS security men. He also ordered the UGIF to supply 40,000 index cards for record keeping and 500 armbands to be used by Order Police in the camp. When two prisoners escaped, he sent the Jewish elder and 65 aides to Auschwitz. When a tunnel was discovered in November 1943, Brunner had 14 inmates fill it in. Then he tortured the men before shipping them off to Auschwitz. Brunner cooperated with Klaus Barbie, the Gestapo chief of Lyons, when Barbie arrested 41 Jewish children and ten adults in the village of Izieu in April 1944. Brunner put the children on a train to the east, just as he would send 500 children designated 'future terrorists' from Paris in June 1944. Brunner saw off his last transport from Drancy in August. Unable to commandeer a complete train from the Wehrmacht, he procured a cattle car to hold 50 prominent Jews (including the family of banker Armand Kohn and members of the underground). When he turned Drancy's 1,400 inmates over to the International Red Cross, Brunner declared, 'To hell with the camp.'

By official count, the total number of 'racial deportees' from France in World War II (including Gypsies) was 120,000.[47] Most of these were Jews who passed through Drancy. The camp was supposed to accommodate 5,000 persons. At its peak, it counted 15,000. Sixty-seven of the 79 transports from France to Nazi death camps originated from Drancy. Today a monument stands before the complex. It tells how 100,000 Jews passed through the camp on their way to the east. Of these, 258 were shot as hostages. Only 1,582 survived. There is also an inscription which reads: 'Passer-by, meditate and never forget. "Behold and see if there be any pain like unto my pain."'

MADAGASCAR

Before the Nazis decided that all Jews should be exterminated, another concept suggested by Luther and Goethe was considered – expulsion. Himmler outlined such a scheme in a report to Hitler in the summer of 1940. The Gestapo chief declared, 'I hope that thanks to the possibility of a large emigration of all Jews to Africa or some other colony, I shall live to see the day when the concept of Jew will have completely disappeared from Europe.' Hitler's initialed evaluation was 'Very good and correct'.[48]

The territory that fascinated the Nazis was Madagascar, an island 1,000 miles long, 300 miles wide, larger than the state of Texas. A French possession 500 miles east of Africa, Madagascar attracted many nations with population problems. Napoleon dreamed of enticing Frenchmen with offers of plantations. Foreign Minister Georges Bonnet wanted to dump 200,000 refugees here in 1938. The Japanese made a study of Madagascar in 1927, the Poles did the same in 1926 and 1937. Hjalmar Schacht mentioned it in discussions with the IGCR after Evian. In February 1939, Alfred Rosenberg told the press that the island might accommodate 15 million Jews. Months later, both South Africa's Foreign Minister Oswald Pirow and Italy's Mussolini expressed support for a Jewish colony in Madagascar.[49]

Some scholars (Lucy Dawidowicz, Hannah Arendt) discount the notion that the Nazis considered the huge island a serious option.[50] Shielded by mountains rising nearly a mile in height, the western half of the island was a Savannah as hot as 'a furnace door'. The eastern side was equatorial, dotted with crocodile-laden marshes. The Poles found the soil to be poor, and unlikely to support extensive farming. Only 2 percent of the island was under cultivation. Most of Madagascar's rivers were navigable only by canoe. There were few good roads in 240,000 square miles. Syphilis, malaria and yellow fever were endemic and few Europeans stayed longer than five years.[51]

Such difficulties notwithstanding, Simon Wiesenthal, Gerald Reitlinger and Raul Hilberg maintain that such a project appealed to the Nazis.[52] Even as he was celebrating his victory over France, Hitler informed Mussolini that 'A Jewish state could be created in Madagascar.' Vichy's transfer of the island would restore Germany's colonial presence in Africa. Moving Jews would place them among their own kind. These disease-carrying creatures would be isolated in a region where the British traditionally quarantined lepers and political troublemakers. Removing them from Europe would ease pressure on the Government-General in Poland. Confinement in Africa under Nazi control might also convince American Jews to cease agitation on behalf of the Allies.[53] The plan called for 25,000 Europeans to leave the island and be replaced by four million Jews. Jews eventually would enjoy limited autonomy, their own postal service, railways. The Nazis would maintain naval and air bases at strategic points on the island. Perhaps two million Jews would perish in what Eugene Hevesi called the greatest pogrom in history.[54]

There was no way the Nazis could transfer Jews from Europe while the war continued. Hitler expected the British to capitulate after the fall of France. Once that happened, freighters could start carrying Jews through the Suez Canal into the Indian Ocean. When Germany's aerial Blitz failed to subdue England by the end of 1940, Hitler decided to attack the Soviet Union. That invasion rendered the subject of Madagascar moot. As Rademacher reported in February 1942: 'The war with the Soviet Union has in the meantime created the possibility of disposing of other territories for the Final Solution. In consequence, the *Führer* has decided that the Jews should not be evacuated to Madagascar, but to the East. Madagascar need no longer therefore be considered in connection with the Final Solution.'[55]

THE RESISTANCE MYTH

According to popular legend, virtually every man, woman and child in France opposed the German occupation.[56] Such tales were nurtured by Charles de Gaulle who, eager to protect the name of France, suppressed films such as Marcel Ophuls's *Sorrow and the Pity* and Alain Resnais's *Night and Fog*, both of which portrayed the French in a less favorable light. Many

Frenchmen did belong to the Maquis but estimates are that 40 percent of the organized underground was Jewish.[57] The Nazis stressed this when they published the names of captured resistance leaders (Fingerweiss, Grieswachs, Elek, Lifschitz, Reiman).[58] Frenchmen did harass German units when Allied troops were on the outskirts of their towns in the summer of 1944. Some risked their lives early on, opposing the application of anti-Jewish decrees. Pastor Marc Boegner, president of the Protestant Federation, and René Gillouin denounced the Statut des Juifs in the fall of 1940.[59] Villagers in Chambon-sur-Lignon sheltered Jews.[60] Members of CIMADE (Protestant underground committee) escorted Jews to Switzerland and Spain. Monsignor Valerio Vateri, the papal Nuncio in Paris, tried to secure the intervention of Pius XII or Vatican Secretary of State Cardinal Maglione on behalf of baptized Jews or those involved in intermarriage.[61] Jules-Gérard Saliège, Archbishop of Toulouse, was joined in his denunciation of the roundups in 1942 by church leaders from Marseille and Montauban.[62]

By February 1943 French Christians had their own deportations to worry about. The Laval government agreed to supply the Nazis with 700,000 industrial workers for the duration of the war. The French saw little difference between Gentiles drafted into the *Service du Travail Obligatoire* (STO) and Jews bound for 'labor camps' in the east. Pétain did not intervene for decorated veterans, the wives of close companions or his own speech writers.[63] Laval thought he was saving France by sacrificing foreign Jews, but biologist Claude Levy sees it differently:

> The fact that a French government agreed to surrender French nationals and even refugees who sought its protection – thus denying the traditional right to asylum in France – proved that it was not a government worthy of being labeled French, or worthy of what is loved about this country, about France. France collaborated. It is the *only* country in Europe which collaborated. Others signed armistices, capitulations in the field and so on, but France is the only country in Europe which had a government which collaborated, a government which introduced laws on the racist level that went even further than the Nuremberg Laws.[64]

12

Fear of Fascism: America before Pearl Harbor

In July 1940 radio stations across the US crackled to the sound of Wagnerian music interspersed with harsh German accents. An hour-long program titled *Sieg im Westen* ('Victory in the West') celebrated the Nazi triumph over the Allies. Directed toward an estimated 20 million German hyphenates and their families, *Sieg im Westen* reflected a disturbing trend in American society. Just as in Europe, fascist pretenders emerged from the economic dislocation of the Great Depression, offering easy solutions to complex problems. Although they were unable to seize control of the government, they did delay America's response to the threat of Hitler.

According to the House Un-American Activities Committee, there were 135 groups subscribing to neo-fascist programs in the US in January 1939.[1] These included George Deatherage's Knights of the White Camellia, Gerald L.K. Smith's Committee of One Million, Gerald Winrod's Defenders, Joe McWilliams's Christian Mobilizers, Joseph Kamp's Constitutional Education League, Harry Jung's American Vigilant Intelligence Federation, Allen Zoll's American Patriots, Yankee Freemen, Citizens Protective League, American Nationalist Party and American Vindicators.[2]

One of the more important fascist blocs was rooted in the German population. The Teutonia Society, German American National Alliance, Einheitsfront, Steuben Society, Friends of the New Germany and German-language newspapers maintained close relations with the Fatherland. Patriots like the publisher George Sylvester Viereck, who had been indicted for sedition in World War I, felt vindicated by the resurgence of the Third Reich. In 1936, leaders of several groups banded together as the German–American Bund. Its declared purpose was 'to exterminate with all power the stinking poison of red Jewish infection in America'.[3]

Heavily subsidized by the Nazi Ministry of Propaganda, the Bund was headed by Fritz Kuhn, a 40-year-old engineer from Munich. A pudgy veteran of the German army in World War I, Kuhn entered the US illegally via Mexico before finding a job with the Ford Motor Company. Flanked by bodyguards attired in American Legion style uniforms, Kuhn made an unlikely

American *Führer*. He raved against 'di Joos' (e.g. J.P. Morgan, Franklin Roosevelt and Fiorello LaGuardia) and was greeted with Hitler salutes and the chant of 'Frei Amerika!' In 1936 Kuhn led a contingent of American Nazis to the Olympic Stadium in Berlin and presented Hitler with a memorial book inscribed with blessings. The Bund was one of several agencies that benefited from $300 million expended by the *Deutsches Ausland Institut* before 1941. American Nazis helped establish chairs of German Studies at several universities. German-American journals reprinted releases from World Service (the Nazi press service). A German-American Business League urged members to boycott Jewish businesses and to bank assets in the Fatherland. In turn, the Nazis helped operate 24 Bund summer camps where children learned to sing, hike and imbibe the spirit of Hitlerism. Before Kuhn was indicted for tax fraud in 1942, his followers filled Madison Square Garden with rallies. On other occasions they joined with members of the Ku Klux Klan, Knights of the White Camellia and Christian Mobilizers in a show of solidarity.[4]

SILVER SHIRTS AND CHRISTIAN FRONT

According to the McCormack Committee, the largest, best financed, best publicized fascist group in America was the Silver Shirt Legion. Founded by William Dudley Pelley, a publisher from Ashville, North Carolina, on 31 January 1933 (the day after Hitler took power in Germany), the Silver Shirts claimed a membership of 100,000 in 22 states. The movement enjoyed popularity among sailors, marines and national guardsmen on the West Coast and law enforcement officers in the South. Families from Seattle to Boston gathered to discuss articles from the *Liberator*, Pelley's 'fearlessly anti-Jewish' weekly. An erstwhile anti-Communist missionary, California restaurateur and screenwriter, Pelley moved to Washington in the late 1920s and made a small fortune in spiritualism. According to his autobiography, in August 1928 he died and went to heaven for seven minutes. Transformed and with an invisible oracle at his side, Pelley then founded the movement which, he said, would redeem the United States by 1962. In September 1934, Pelley issued a 'new emancipation proclamation' calling for: registration of persons of Hebrew blood; quotas on Jews in professions; renunciation of Jewish nationalism; prohibition of the use of Gentile names by Jews; creation of ghettos; and confiscation of Jewish property. Two years later, he formed his own Christian Party and ran for President under a slogan of 'Christ or Chaos'. Before he was indicted for sedition, Pelley flooded the nation with more than three and one-half tons of hate literature per year.[5]

More influential than Pelley was Father Charles E. Coughlin, a priest from Royal Oak, Michigan. Coughlin was welcomed to his parish outside Detroit in 1928 by members of the Ku Klux Klan who burned a cross on the church-grounds. Subsequently, he demonstrated a flair for radio. Coughlin's sermons broadcast weekly inspired listeners during the darkest moments of the Depression. When Franklin Roosevelt (FDR) became President in 1933, Coughlin was a welcome guest at the White House. Shortly after the New Deal program took shape, Coughlin broke with the President. His radio programs became more critical, hinting at insidious influences around FDR. Calling for 'social justice', Coughlin created the Christian Front. In 1936, Coughlin linked forces with what was left of Huey Long's presidential campaign and Francis Townsend's social security movement to create the Union Party. Their candidate, christened in Cleveland, was North Dakota's William Lemke. Coughlin was so confident of victory that he promised to retire from broadcasting if Lemke did not win nine million votes. Lemke won 883,000 out of the 46 million cast.

Instead of abiding by his threat/promise, Coughlin launched a vitriolic campaign against Jews, offering a commentary on the *Protocols of the Elders of Zion*. While not certifying the Protocols, Coughlin asked his listeners, 'Is it not true that the synagogue of Satan, under the leadership of anti-Christ, has hindered and hampered the activity of the Mystical body of Christ? Is it not true that some unseen force has taken Christ out of government, business, industry, and to a large degree, education? Is it not true that a force over which we Christians seem to have no control, has gained control of journalism, motion pictures, theatres and radio?' Although he was being broadcast over 46 stations, Coughlin was angered that his program was not heard in the west or south, and for that he blamed Jewish control of the networks. He claimed that the Bolshevik revolution was staged by 25 Jews close to Lenin and was financed by the Jewish banking house of Kuhn-Loeb.[6]

To those who criticized such statements, Coughlin replied he was unafraid of being labeled anti-Semitic since that was a favorite device of communists. Somehow, he always found time to defend Nazi Germany. Hitler's persecution of Jews was termed defensive because a worldwide 'sacred war' had been declared upon Germany 'by the race of Jews'.[7] Coughlin excused Hitler's seizure of Austria and the Sudetenland and offered the incredible challenge after *Kristallnacht*: 'Let he who is without sin cast the first stone.' This bigot priest warned a throng at Briggs Stadium in Detroit of a ten-year conspiracy against the American people that 'robbed you of your bank savings account, then of your jobs, and in many cases of your homes'. His magazine *Social Justice* had a circulation of one million readers. Between five million and 15 million Americans listened to his weekly sermons and more than half agreed with what he was saying. They contributed $100,000 each week to a nonprofit corporation which, in the heart of the Depression, listed assets of more than $1.5 million.[8]

Coughlin stopped commenting on public issues after Pearl Harbor. Other fascist leaders were not as wise. Those not done in by their own quarreling were indicted for sedition. It is a mistake, however, to minimize Coughlin's legacy or that of the other neo-fascists. These men did have influence with government and business leaders. Their literature left an impression on the consciousness of America. As Gustavus Myers wrote: 'Organizations of the character described may and do have a transient existence, but their published matter sinks into many a receptive mind, there to abide long after the perpetrators responsible have disappeared and their malodorous methods have been forgotten.'[9]

THE MAN ON THE WHITE HORSE: THE CONSERVATIVE RIGHT

There had always been conservatives who believed that American society was only a step away from sliding into godless Bolshevism. They were horrified as longshoremen tied up the docks of San Francisco, teamsters shut down Minneapolis, and rubber workers occupied plants in Akron in 1934–35. They disapproved of the killings of workers at the Electric Auto-Lite factory in Toledo and Republic Steel outside Chicago. They were also troubled when national guardsmen were posted behind sandbagged machine guns outside GM plants in Flint, Michigan in February 1937.[10]

Foremost among these self-proclaimed patriotic organizations were the Crusaders for Economic Liberty, a million-member group originally conceived as a bulwark of prohibition. The Crusaders received support from J. Howard Pew of Sun Oil, Irenee, Pierre and Lamont DuPont, and Sewell Avery of Montgomery Ward. These same persons, along with Alfred Sloan of General Motors and E.T. Stotesbury of the House of Morgan, contributed to the Sentinels of the Republic, whose President Alexander Lincoln wrote that the fight for Western civilization could only be won 'if we recognize that the enemy is worldwide and that it is Jewish in origin'. James Rand, president of Remington Rand, J.H. Alstyne, president of Otis Elevator, Sloan and the DuPonts contributed to Merwin K. Hart's New York State Economic Council which Supreme Court Justice Robert Jackson labeled fascist. Mrs A. Cressy Morrison of the Daughters of the American Revolution and Colonel McCormick of the *Chicago Tribune* endorsed Elizabeth Dilling's 'Mothers March on Washington' (which opposed Lend-Lease) and Dilling's outrageous little pamphlet *The Red Network* (an index of individuals and organizations in the United States accused of being communists).[11]

The million-member American Legion and its night-riding cousin, the Black Legion helped arouse fear, suspicion and race hatred. The American Legion consistently opposed immigration reform and astounded even its staunchest supporters when it endorsed vigilantism, 'but not in uniforms', at its 1937 convention in New York City.[12] John Trevor's 2.5 million member American Coalition (which counted the DAR and Sons of the American Revolution among its 115 affiliates) lobbied against any modification of this nation's immigration laws. Francis Kinnicutt's Allied Patriotic Societies, the

150,000-man Junior Order of American Mechanics, the American Medical Association, the BPOE (Elks' clubs) and Chambers of Commerce all fretted over America's 12,000,000 unemployed, 443,000 World War I veterans without jobs, the 660,000 children on social security rolls. They were joined by the American Federation of Labor and its offshoot, the CIO, both of which were concerned about job security for Americans. More amazing, right-wing elements were supported by members of the American Communist Party, which between 1939 and 1941 parroted the pro-German party line from Moscow.

Restrictionists led by Senator Robert Rice Reynolds (Democrat, North Carolina) convinced Americans it was not in their interest to welcome victims of Nazism.[13] Using phenomenal projected birth rates, they defeated the Wagner–Rogers bill that would have admitted 20,000 'refugee' children in 1938. Two years later, they helped block efforts of the Committee for the Care of European Children headed up by Eleanor Roosevelt. Created in the spring of 1940 in response to an appeal from the American Red Cross, the Committee intended to bring 70,000 refugee children to the US. Four separate bills were introduced in Congress to facilitate the admission of these children, but none passed. Former President Herbert Hoover set the tone for opponents of rescue, warning that within a year 18,000,000 Europeans might be in need of assistance. Said Hoover, 'For one hundred and fifty years America was this refuge and this sanctuary. Sanctuary must be found elsewhere.'[14]

Isolationists raised objections based upon the experience of World War I. If U-boats attacked ships carrying children across the Atlantic, the US might be dragged into war. To avoid such a scenario, Congress amended the Neutrality Law of August 1940, requiring American ships sailing from France or Portugal to be clearly marked with huge flags and the Stars and Stripes painted on both sides of the vessel and on deck. All told, 10,000 children and 1,100 adults reached the US and Canada before the rescue plan was abandoned in the fall of 1940.[15] Most of those who reached safety were British subjects who would have entered the US anyway under normal immigration procedures. In November 1940, FDR asked a restructured National Coordinating Committee for Aid to Refugees to draw up a list of eminent refugees who might be granted temporary visas to the US. Marc Chagall, Max Ernst, Jacques Lifschitz, Lion Feuchtwanger, Franz Werfel and Konrad Heiden were among the 1,236 fortunates who escaped from France before this program too was terminated in January 1941.[16]

The Right cringed when the President denounced Mussolini's attack on France as a 'stab in the back'. They opposed the creation of a western-hemispheric security arrangement which tied the US through Canada to England. Conservatives, Republicans, socialists and pacifists criticized the swap of 50 destroyers to England for trusteeship over British Caribbean islands, the sale to Great Britain of aircraft stamped 'obsolete' as they rolled off the assembly line, the training of British pilots in south Florida, the enactment of a billion-dollar military preparedness bill and America's first peacetime selective-service law in September 1940, Lend-Lease, the blocking of assets of conquered European states, the convoying of war *matériel* to the British Isles in the spring of 1941, and ultimately the order of November 1941 permitting 'shoot on sight' attacks against German U-boats, not to mention the suspension of shipments of steel and oil to Japan.

To preserve the American way of life, some foes of FDR and the New Deal were prepared to sacrifice constitutional rights to a military savior like General Douglas MacArthur, George Van Horn Moseley or Smedley Butler. In 1935, ex-marine General Butler told the McCormack Committee that a group of unnamed Wall Street bankers had suggested he attempt a Mussolini-style coup in August 1934. They offered to supply the cash ($3,000,000) and personnel (500,000 men) for a march on Washington to topple Roosevelt. If Butler declined, they were prepared to ask MacArthur or Hanford MacNider of the American Legion.[17] In May 1939, George Van Horn Moseley testified that he had been asked to repulse an 'invasion' of 150,000 Spanish mercenaries who were being brought to the country by rich Jewish communists. This hare-brained scheme was the work of Baron Manfred Freiherr von Killinger, German Consul General in San Francisco, who intended to unite Irish nationalists, the KKK, Bund, Silver Shirts and 'Park Avenue Patriots' in a nationalist junta. The plot was quashed and von Killinger and his chief associate, Mrs Leslie Fry, fled the country.[18]

MESSIAH OF AMERICA FIRST: CHARLES LINDBERGH

What these groups lacked was a charismatic leader who could appeal to a broad cross-section of the American people. The necessary party apparatus was set in place in the spring of 1940 when law students at Yale University created America First, Inc. The credo of this organization: no binding alliances; non-intervention in European affairs; war as a last resort. The students understood that if America went to war, their lives would be at stake and they did not believe the struggle was worth it. For his part, Roosevelt, who was pursuing an unprecedented third term as President, dismissed their objections, referring to anti-war students as 'Shrimps!'[19] By the end of summer 1940, real power brokers took control of the movement. The new chairman was General Robert Wood of Sears, Roebuck. His board included Henry Ford, Hanford MacNider of the American Legion, actresses Dorothy and Lilian Gish, World War I ace Eddie Rickenbacker, Avery Brundage, Roosevelt's Ambassador to England Joseph Kennedy, Alice Roosevelt Longworth, Robert Hutchins of the University of Chicago, and Oswald Garrison Villard, socialist editor of *Nation* magazine. America First drew its 15 million members from pacifists, academics, fascist sympathizers and reactionary politicians such as Gerald Nye (Republican, North Dakota),

Ernest Lundeen (Republican, Minnesota), Rufus Holman (Republican, Oregon) and Clare Hoffman (Republican, Michigan).

The movement found its messiah in the fall of 1940. Charles Lindbergh became an international celebrity when he crossed the Atlantic in a single-engine aircraft in 1927. Lindbergh and his poet wife Ann Morrow avoided the spotlight following the kidnap-murder of their infant son in 1931. Charles began making public appearances in 1936, commenting on the state of aviation. Impressed with the technology, training and superior 'natural psychology' of the Luftwaffe, Lindbergh believed that the German military was invincible.[20] In 1940, he began speaking against what he believed to be the disastrous policies of the Roosevelt administration.

For Lindbergh the war in Europe was not a struggle between good and evil. There was no Genghis Khan marching against civilization, no parachutists dropping on the streets of New York, no enemy aircraft crossing the Arctic Circle to bomb the Midwest. This was simply another war 'in that age old history of wars' that erupted periodically on the continent. The United States had no crucial interest in the war, especially after Germany invaded Russia in June 1941. Better to let the two behemoths of Europe destroy one another than come to the aid of the USSR, a nation whose record of 'cruelty, bloodshed and barbarism was without parallel in modern history'.[21]

Imperialist England which denied self-determination to peoples in India, the Middle East and Africa was hardly better than Germany. The British, suffering 'dry rot democracy', would fight to 'the last drop of American blood'. Lindbergh mocked British assurances that the war had reached a turning point in France, then Yugoslavia and Crete, declaring, 'Always the same story – one defeat after another since this war began and always the demand for more assistance from America. First they said, "sell us the arms and we will win." Then it was "lend us the arms and we will win." Now it is, "bring us the arms and we will win." Tomorrow it will be "Fight our war for us and we will win."'[22] Speaking against Lend-Lease, Lindbergh declared, 'I do not believe that the danger to America lies in an invasion from abroad. I believe it lies here at home in our midst and that it is exemplified by the terms of this bill – the placing of our security in the success of foreign armies and the removal of power from the representatives of the people in our land.'[23]

Lindbergh could not see how the United States with its woefully prepared armed forces stretched over two-thirds of the world could vie simultaneously with the Nazis and Japanese. When the Nazis were overrunning the Maginot Line, Lindbergh accused FDR of blustering like some western cowboy with an empty gun. Instead of encouraging the British and French to wait for help we could not send, he urged the government make a powerful hemispheric defense its first priority.[24] Arming to attack Europe would 'necessitate that the lives and thoughts of every man, woman and child in this country be directed toward war for the next generation, probably for the next several generations.'[25]

In the fall of 1940, 80 percent of Americans polled indicated they wanted no part of war. America First hoped to create a new party that would capture the Presidency in 1944, possibly with a ticket of Lindbergh and Hoover. In the months preceding Pearl Harbor, Lindbergh attracted standing room only audiences at New York's Madison Square Garden, Philadelphia's arena, San Francisco's Civic Auditorium and the Hollywood Bowl. Then, on 11 September 1941, Lindbergh stumbled. Speaking to the nation from Des Moines, Lindbergh attacked three groups that had deceived Americans – 'the British, the Jewish [sic], and the Roosevelt Administration'.[26] Lindbergh excused the British because they were 'desperate'. England simply did not have the population, geographic position or air force sufficient to win the war. He also expressed sympathy for the 'Jewish race' which had been so cruelly persecuted by the Nazis. Of all peoples, however, Jews should oppose involvement in war because 'they will be among the first to feel its consequences'. Lindbergh added that the greatest danger to Jews 'lies in their large ownership and influence in our motion pictures, our press, our radio and government'.[27] The Des Moines speech was denounced by spokesmen for the Roosevelt Administration and major newspapers in the country.

When Japan attacked Pearl Harbor Lindbergh volunteered his services to the military and was assigned to the Pacific theater. Distrust of this remarkable man was confirmed when Lindbergh's wartime journals were published in December 1969. While allowing that 'we won the war in a military sense', Lindbergh declared 'in a broader sense' western civilization was the loser. The defeat of Germany and Japan unleashed the still greater menaces of Russia and China. Poland was not saved. France and England were reduced to second rate powers. Lindbergh lamented about much more than 'breakdown' of western civilization. Sounding much like America's opponents in that conflict, he also bemoaned the loss of 'the genetic heredity formed through aeons in many million lives'.[28]

BRECKINRIDGE LONG AND THE FIFTH COLUMN

Many Americans shared Lindbergh's concern that this nation was being undermined by sinister forces. Unlike Lindbergh, however, they were more concerned about the threat of a fascist 'fifth column'. Hitler's former colleague Otto Strasser painted a gloomy picture of imminent fascist takeovers in Argentina, Chile, Ecuador and even Mexico. Writers in popular journals (*America, Saturday Evening Post*) brought the menace closer, charging that Hitler was forcing persons who had relatives in European concentration camps to do his bidding.[29] Hollywood offered images of espionage in films like *Saboteur, Confessions of a Nazi Spy* and *Notorious*. The fear was fed by government leaders. In the summer of 1940, Martin Dies of the House Un-American Activities Committee warned there were six million communist and Nazi sympathizers in the US.[30] Colonel William Donovan, director of the Office of Strategic Services lamented that foreign agents like Frederich Ried, German consul in New York who had masterminded Nazi activity in Brazil, French anti-Semite Pierre Massin, John Makkari, author of Hungary's anti-Jewish laws, and a host of other foreign agents were free to operate in the US.[31] President Roosevelt himself warned Americans to be alert to the fifth column menace that summer.

Not all Americans believed that aliens and Jews were fifth columnists, but many did, and one of those who had the power to do something about it was Breckinridge Long, who served as Assistant Secretary of State beginning in January 1940. Described as 'a narrow, limited man',[32] he had little sympathy for the common man. Having contributed generously to FDR's campaign chest in 1932, Long was rewarded by being named Ambassador to Italy. Over the next four years, he lavished praise upon Mussolini. Recalled for reasons of health, he went into private practice until 1939 when he was asked to negotiate trade with Italy. That same year, Sumner Welles welcomed him back to the State Department.

As Assistant Secretary, Long supervised 23 of the 42 divisions of State, including those bureaus which dealt with overseas relief, transport, civilian internees, prisoners of war and the all-important visa section. An old-fashioned nativist, Long surrounded himself with aides who were equally insensitive, and biased. Avra Warren, the head of the Visa Division, rejected a proposal from Harold Ickes permitting 12,000 'German' refugees in Portugal to come to the Virgin Islands. Warren also rejected as impractical a scheme to open Alaska to refugees arguing that 'nearly all of them belong to a particular race' and that admission in large numbers might create 'serious problems'. Robert Alexander, Warren's assistant in the Visa Division, opposed the idea of lumping unused visas into what he called 'a jackpot for the Jews'. Alexander implied that Jewish pressure only served to confound the Allies. European Division Chief Elbredge Durbrow dismissed reports of mass extermination as atrocity tales. Robert Borden Reams, Long's chief adviser on Jewish questions in the Division of European Affairs, believed most refugees coming to the United States were fifth columnists. 'Naturally it can't be made public knowledge, but some are getting in and some have been apprehended as agents', Reams later commented.[33]

In his eagerness to prevent America from falling to the very fascists for whom he had once expressed admiration, Long did everything he could to impede the rescue of the victims of fascism. He crippled efforts to save British children during the summer of 1940, charging that there were no American vessels available and adding that 'the very surest way to get America into this war would be to send an American ship to England and put 2,000 babies on it and then have it sunk by a German torpedo'. Long refused to approve visas for scholars and scientists stranded in France because they had no French exit visas (which could not be obtained without an American entry visa!). He abandoned his own limited effort to grant visas to rabbis and yeshiva students saying that there was no definite assurance that the persons to whom passports would be delivered were actually the ones whose names appeared on consular lists. On 17 June 1940, he noted in his diary that the American-Canadian border was a 'sieve' through which alien agents could walk. On the same day, he instructed Avra Warren that the naturalization laws of the US had to be tightened.[34]

After the collapse of France, Long called for alien registration and a narrower interpretation of the nation's LPC (likely to become a Public Charge) clause. He fretted about '2,000 saboteurs' who supposedly were employed in shipping and aircraft industries. Long departed from the State Department's tradition of silence on legislative matters and asked Attorney General Francis Biddle to co-sponsor a measure that would bar aliens whose admission would be 'inimical to the interests of the United States'. The Smith Act (28 June 1940) required registration of 'enemy aliens' over 14 and detailed penalties for subversive activities. Still, Long's fears about 'the insidious infiltration of whispering agents ... the agents of trouble and discord ... the saboteurs [who] throw monkey wrenches into the machinery' persisted.[35] He was miffed when, during the winter of 1940–41, Hull advised him to be as lenient as possible toward 450,000 Jews that the Nazis were supposedly sending to Portugal. He had even more cause for worry when in May 1941 he received a cable from Laurence Steinhardt, America's Ambassador in Moscow. Steinhardt charged that many persons had come to the US under fraudulent pretenses and intended to 'engage in activities inimical to our interest'.[36]

On 5 June 1941, the State Department instructed consuls to submit visa applications of persons with close relatives in occupied territory to Washington for final approval. Refugees leaving Vichy France were required to submit four photographs instead of the usual three. The extra picture went to the files of the Second Bureau, responsible for espionage activity. Visas were granted on the condition that the emigrant serve as a Vichy agent upon reaching the United States. Representative Sol Bloom introduced a bill blocking admission of individuals whose relatives were potential hostages. The practical result of this 'Relative Rule' was that one-half of the 69,604 visa applications received by the State Department during the fiscal year of 1941/42 were turned down.[37]

On 26 July 1941, Albert Einstein appealed to Eleanor Roosevelt, denouncing the 'wall of bureaucratic measures' that was making it all but impossible to assist victims of fascism. Six weeks later, James McDonald, once League High Commissioner, wrote to the President, saying, 'The so-called relative rule should be canceled or substantially modified. Our experience with refugees has convinced us that it is unnecessary, illogical, ill-adapted to the purposes, claimed for it, and cruelly burdensome on the refugees affected by it.'[38] Meanwhile, the State Department prided itself on having spared the nation what Long termed 'the pernicious activities against the Unites States by German agents in the guise of refugees.' Testifying before Congress in the winter of 1943, Long said, 'I think the records of the FBI will show that there was quite a good deal of that at one time and that there were in this country certain persons to whom those persons were under instructions to report when they arrived.'[39]

Far from discovering any anti-democratic conspiracy among refugees, the FBI testified to the loyalty of America's immigrants. After the war, J. Edgar Hoover declared: 'The experience of the FBI in coping with foreign agents, spies and saboteurs has conclusively illustrated that the great mass of aliens are loyal to America, devoted to the principles of democracy. The vast majority of aliens have remained true to the land of their adoption.'[40] Some 23,000 'enemy aliens', less than 0.5 percent of all such people in the US in 1940, were taken into custody for questioning. A fraction of these received jail sentences – generally for minor violations of immigration regulations. During World War II, 300,000 foreign-born served in the US Army, among them 109,000 noncitizens and 30,000 'enemy aliens'. Thousands more labored, without incident, in defense plants. Long and his cronies should have considered the record of the foreign-born in World War I when four million aliens, 60 percent of whom had not even sworn declarations of intent to become naturalized citizens, registered for the draft. Three months before Pearl Harbor, Immigration Commissioner Earl Harrison concluded that aliens were reliable persons with strong ties in the US and that they had never conducted themselves as 'enemies' of the United States.[41]

Officials at State may have been alarmed by the thought of refugee conspirators, but it is noteworthy that of 30 persons indicted for sedition by the Attorney General's office in the spring of 1942, not one was an alien.[42] Many months before Pearl Harbor the FBI and various municipal police had shattered every one of the major Nazi espionage networks in the United States, Hans Thomsen, German Chargé in Washington, lamented in 1941: 'American authorities knew of the entire network, which was no work of art in view of the naive and, to a certain extent, stupid manner in the way these people carried on.'[43] Long was worried about spies sneaking into the United States at a time when Pelley, Coughlin and Lindbergh were openly undermining the confidence of Americans. The Germans moved staff personnel back and forth to their Washington embassy till 30 June 1941. The Japanese and Italians did the same until December; Vichy France and its Second Bureau, the very agency that caused Long and the FBI so much consternation, continued to maintain offices in the US capital until November 1942.

13

Germany: Purge of the Contragenics

LIFE UNWORTHY OF LIFE

In July 1940, jubilant Berliners showered victorious Wehrmacht units with confetti and flowers. The time seemed ripe for the Nazis to deal with the last of their domestic enemies – the contragenics. This last term, coined by Richard Deppe, included anyone deemed an impediment to the creation of a *biologisch* state. Not just considered to be asocial, it was a crime in Germany to be a Gypsy, homosexual, Jehovah's Witness, mentally ill or physically handicapped person or Jew.

Two years before the enactment of the Nuremberg Laws (14 July 1933), the Reichstag passed a law devised by 'racial hygienists' Fritz Lenz, Alfred Ploetz, Ernst Rudin and Gerhard Wagner. The Law for Prevention of Progeny with Hereditary Diseases provided that individuals deemed unfit by any of 181 Genetic Health Courts would have to undergo sterilization. (Lenz estimated that could mean as much as 10 percent of the German population.[1]) The Nazis claimed that healthy individuals were having one or two children while inferior people were 'reproducing unrestrainedly'. In Germany, hereditary diseases encompassed mental illness (schizophrenia, manic depression), retardation, physical deformity, epilepsy, blindness, deafness and alcoholism.[2]

That definition was still less inclusive than one embraced by the Eugenics Center on Long Island which pushed for the sterilization of 'shiftless, ignorant, and socially inadequate' elements in America. By 1920 25 US states ordered sterilization for the criminally insane and people determined to be genetically inferior. Fritz Lenz wrote enviously of the work being done by Charles Davenport's facility at Cold Harbor, New York, and the Carnegie Institute in Washington. Then in 1927, the US Supreme Court acknowledged the right of the state to act in the case of *Buck v. Bell*. Writing for the majority, Oliver Wendell Holmes declared, 'Three generations of imbeciles is enough.' Between 1904 and 1972, 70,000 Americans, most of them poor, young misfits and run-aways were sterilized.[3]

The Nazis acknowledged their debt to American eugenicists. Richard Walther Darré, founder of the Artamanen movement, likened *Zuchtung* (breeding) to keeping a garden free of weeds and praised the writings of Lothrop Stoddard. In July 1936, Davenport, Harry Laughlin and Dr Foster

Kennedy were given honorary degrees from the University of Heidelberg. Several German scientists were, in turn, invited to participate in the 200th anniversary of Harvard. By this time, the forced sterilization program was in full swing in Germany. Judgments were made by a panel of two physicians (usually psychiatrists) and a district judge who had never seen the subject. Many of the victims were beggars, juvenile delinquents or criminals referred to the Department of People's Health by social workers or the police. Sterilization was accomplished by vasectomy or tubal ligation. Before Hitler attacked Poland, over 300,000 Germans were sterilized. Several thousand died as a result of the procedures.[4]

Jews and Gypsies were not formally included in the program, but children of mixed African and German descent were. 'Rhineland bastards' were offspring of French colonial troops who occupied the Rhineland in 1923 and German women. No one knows how many there were (Goering ordered a tally from Düsseldorf, Aachen, Cologne and Koblenz in April 1933). The concept of sterilization had been rejected as 'demoralizing' by the Bavarian Ministry of Interior in 1927. Four years later, Professor Oswald Bumke warned of a greater danger: 'Pretty soon we will no longer hear about the mentally sick but instead about Aryans and non-Aryans, about the blonde Germanic race and about inferior people with round skulls.'[5] Between 500 and 800 mixed-race children were sterilized by the Gestapo's Special Commission #3 in 1937.[6]

The shift from sterilization to *Gnadentod* (euthanasia) was relatively easy for Hitler. In 1935, the *Führer* warned that he would not feed 'useless eaters' or *Lebensunwertes Lebens* (life unworthy of life) in any future war. He could cite enough authority for his position. Wilhelm Schallmeyer, Alfred Ploetz, Alfred Grotjahn and Arthur Dinter had long warned of the clash between the *höherwertig* (healthy, superior peoples) and *minderwertig* (chronically ill, inferior).[7] In 1920, the psychiatrist Alfred Hoche and Karl Binding, a jurist from Leipzig, published *Die Freigabe der Vernichtung lebensunwerten Lebens* ('Permission to Destroy Life Unworthy of Life'). Binding argued that *Sterbenhilfe* (death assistance) was a healing duty. Hoche claimed that many of the people in asylums were nothing but 'empty shells'.[8] The naturalist Ernst Haeckel, too, had sympathized with the plight of thousands of 'cripples', 'deaf and dumb' and 'cretins' born every year. Rather than underwriting 'fathomless costs' in extending their existence, Haeckel suggested, 'How much of this loss and suffering could be obviated if one finally decided to liberate the totally incurable from their indescribable suffering with a dose of morphia.'[9]

After 1935, Goebbels's propaganda ministry produced motion pictures intended to elicit support from the public. The insane were trundled before the camera, giggling, twitching, screaming. Children with Down's Syndrome or macrocephaly were backlit to exaggerate their deformities. Then a 'professor' speaking to a class of 'university students' would explain how in the realm of nature the weak die out. In 1939 two films challenged the healthy to consider what they might do if they fell ill. *Dasein ohne Leben* (Existence without Life) and *Geisteskrank* (Mental Illness) played to the fear of people losing their wits as they age. In 1895 Adolf Jost had argued for the right of an individual to determine when he should die in *Das Recht auf den Tod*. In 1941, 15 million Germans agonized over the tale of a pianist afflicted with multiple sclerosis in *Ich Klage An* (I Accuse). Many agreed the state should decide when to end life for those who could not decide for themselves.

EUTHANASIA: THE T-4 PROGRAM

In October 1939 Hitler signed an order permitting physicians to terminate patients. Backdated to coincide with the outbreak of war, the decree authorized Dr Karl Brandt (one of Hitler's personal physicians) and chancellery chief Philip Bouhler to grant mercy death to 'those suffering from illness deemed to be incurable'.[10] The process required a series of assessments by physicians and representatives of the Ministry of Interior. Dubbed T-4, because its headquarters were located at Tiergartenstrasse 4 in Berlin, the program mandated a review of all patients in government or church-sponsored sanitariums.

Children were among the first victims of T-4. Informed that an idiot child named Knauer was born blind, with a leg and part of an arm missing, Hitler sent Brandt to the clinic at Leipzig where the child was hospitalized.[11] Action by physicians spared parents responsibility for its death. It was unnecessary to submit dossiers of children under the age of three for review. Older children suffering from cleft palates, epilepsy or schizophrenia were brought to a hospital and given overdoses of luminal. If this did not induce death, they were injected with morphine and scopolamine. At Eglfing-Haar, Dr Hermann Pfannmüller devised a starvation diet which led to a slow death of children. Some of Pfannmüller's 'patients' were Jews who were not mentally ill.[12]

It was just a matter of time before such techniques were applied to adults. Individuals were transported to killing centers in special busses manned by the SS. Six facilities were available at Hartheim near Linz, Sonnenstein, a nursing station in Saxony, castle Grafeneck south of Stuttgart, Bernburg, Brandenburg and Hadamar. Initially, killing was done by injection, but in 1940 the SS built a gas chamber disguised as a shower at Brandenburg. The system was efficient and clean, and could dispose of 18–20 individuals in less than an hour. It was also, SS doctors believed, 'the most humane form of death'.[13]

The dead were examined for gold teeth, then taken to crematoria. Their families received ashes and a letter listing the cause of death as heart failure, septicemia or bacterial infection. Mistakes were made in the shipment of ashes (one patient's family received two urns, another was informed that their loved one, who long before had his appendix removed, died of appendicitis). Everything was supposed to be done in secrecy, but hospital personnel talked about what went on beyond the high walls and townsfolk could smell what was in the air.[14]

When it became evident that the Nazis were killing their own people, protests mounted. The psychiatrist Karl Bonhoeffer was ousted from his position at the Berlin University because he opposed sterilization and *Gnadentod*. Professor Hans Gerhard Creutzfeld of Kiel and Professor Gottfried Ewald of Göttingen tried to prevent the transport of their patients to the killing centers. Dr Heinrich Hermann, warden of the Wilhelmsdorf asylum, declared that killing certain patients was 'acting against God's will'.[15] Relatives badgered hospital staffs and party functionaries for information. Else von Löwis mobilized the Nazi women's organization against the program. Werner Mölders, a Luftwaffe war hero, wrote to his superiors threatening to return his medals because of the euthanasia program. Paul-Gerhard Braune, director of the Hoffmunstal Institution of Berlin, and the Reverend Fritz von Bodelschwingh, director of the Bethel Institution for epileptics at Bielefeld, used their influence in the Confessional Church to oppose the policy.[16]

On 6 July 1941, the Catholic bishops of Germany issued a pastoral letter which denounced the taking of innocent life. Clemens Count von Galen, bishop of Münster, elaborated in another sermon on 3 August 1941. Von Galen directed his remarks to the frail, the mentally ill, and severely disabled soldiers as he warned, 'If it is once accepted that people have the right to kill "unproductive" fellow humans – and even if it only initially affects the poor defenseless mentally ill – then as a matter of principle murder is permitted for all unproductive people.' Added Galen, 'Woe to mankind, woe to our German nation if God's holy commandment Thou Shalt not Kill ... which God our Creator inscribed in the conscience of mankind from the very beginning of time is not only broken, but if this transgression is actually tolerated and permitted to go unpunished.'[17]

The T-4 program officially ended on 24 August 1941. At that point 70,273 persons had been 'disinfected'.[18] Responding to public outcry, Hitler instructed Brandt to 'stall' the operation. The murder of the innocents never really stopped.[19] The Nazis killed mental patients in Poland, Holland and elsewhere. Twenty thousand hospital patients in Pomerania were terminated in the spring of 1940 to provide accommodations for Baltic Germans.[20] Between 200,000 and 250,000 persons died as a result of the Nazi euthanasia programs. That figure included 5,000 Jews, children in mental asylums and adults described as 'insolent', 'Marxist' or 'anti-German agitator'.[21] In 1940, the Nazis brought in Polish Jews for gassing experiments. In 1941, the Nazis reconstituted T-4 as 14f13 and simply shifted the vans, gas chambers and doctors to death camps in Poland.

THE KINGDOM OF GOD: THE JEHOVAH'S WITNESSES

Jews were not the only religious group tormented by the Nazis. When Hitler came to power, there were perhaps 20,000 Jehovah's Witnesses in Germany. During World War I, their refusal to fight made them unpopular. Germans did not accept the argument that they were soldiers in Jehovah's army, hence unable to swear allegiance to any worldly government. Nazis not only questioned the American origins of the movement, but were suspicious of connections with Zionists and communists.[22] The Nazis were exasperated when Witnesses refused to volunteer at the start of World War II like members of 40 other religious groups (including the Mormons).

On 1 April 1933, Hitler banned their publications. A few weeks later, storm troopers sacked Jehovah's Witnesses' buildings in Magdeburg, burning books worth two million marks. In October 1934, congregations across Germany petitioned the government for relief. It made no difference. When the Magdeburg group continued to import literature from Switzerland, the Nazis imprisoned its leaders. Witnesses lost their jobs and pensions. Their children were expelled from school. Finally, on 1 April 1935, the group was banned altogether. The following year, Himmler established a special Gestapo unit to infiltrate groups and compile lists of 'publishers' (as Witnesses refer to themselves). Four hundred Witnesses were sent to Sachsenhausen where they were distinguished by a purple triangle on their jackets. By the end of 1939 there were 6,000 Witnesses in Nazi concentration camps.[23]

On Easter Sunday, 1939, the roll call officer at Buchenwald demanded that the Witnesses acknowledge the rule of the *Führer*. They were again called on Whit Sunday. When they failed to demonstrate the requisite patriotism, they were subjected to more than a hour of heavy calisthenics. When Buchenwald's Witnesses refused to serve in the army at the start of the war, the SS beat and robbed them at the gatehouse. On New Year's Day, 1942, they were summoned to the Appelplatz and denounced for not having contributed to German Winter Relief. Said one Roll Call Officer: 'You arch criminals, you heavenly sons of bitches, you'll slave tonight until dark at four degrees below. Take off your underwear at once!' They also had to trade leather shoes for wooden ones. On 15 February 1942, Jehovah's Witnesses were forced to stand for hours in eight inches of snow as punishment for having listened to radios. At Buchenwald, some of their number were periodically murdered in the trenches that served as cesspools.[24]

Between 2,500 and 5,000 Jehovah's Witnesses died behind barbed wire. Two hundred were executed by wartime tribunals.[25] What sustained the survivors was their extraordinary faith and a support system unlike any other in the camps. From the start, Witnesses held secret prayer services and baptisms, and smuggled literature. Himmler expressed envy of their 'unshakable faith'.[26] As Eugen Kogon declared, 'Psychologically speaking the SS was never quite equal to the challenge offered them by Jehovahs' Witnesses.'[27]

THE ASSAULT AGAINST HOMOSEXUALS

Another group frustrated and frightened the Nazis. According to one estimate there were 1.2 million gay men in Germany in 1928. Though Röhm's clique held leadership positions in the SA, the party rejected homosexuality as something that 'emasculates our people and makes it a plaything for our enemies'.[28] Most Nazis agreed with Himmler that homosexuality was a crime which must be exterminated 'root and branch'.[29] The ancient Teutons drowned homosexuals. In 1851, the Prussian legal code outlawed 'unnatural' sexual acts between men. The Prussian precedent was adopted as Paragraph 175 of Bismarck's Criminal Code. Any male who *committed* a lewd or lascivious act with another male might be imprisoned for ten years.[30] Paragraph 175 used the words lewd and lascivious nine times without offering a definition of either term.

Homosexuality was legally condemned but privately condoned under Weimar. The public tolerated lesbian balls and the existence of 40 gay bars in Hamburg, Berlin, Munich and Bremen. For more than 20 years, Dr Magnus Hirschfeld, founder of the Institute of Sexual Science, tried to repeal Paragraph 175. Hirschfeld, who was gay, enlisted the support of Martin Buber, Albert Einstein, Max Liebermann, Karl Kautsky, Käthe Köllwitz, Engelbert Humperdinck, Karl Jaspers, Thomas Mann and August Bebel.[31] Still, the hint of homosexuality was enough to send shock waves through German society. The Social Democrats temporarily deserted Hirschfeld, feigning shock when the industrial baron Alfried Krupp was discovered in the company of young men at Capri and when an exposé linked Prince Philipp zu Eulenburg with Count Kuno von Moltke. In 1919, Germans were stunned by the release of *Different from the Others*, an openly gay film starring Conrad Veidt. Four years later, they were horrified by revelations at the trial of Fritz Haarmann, a police informer from Hanover. Haarmann confessed to having lured 120 young boys to his rooms. He then abused and killed them, grinding up their flesh and selling it as fresh horsemeat.[32]

Hirschfeld endured personal rebuke as he labored to bring about reform. In 1920 he was attacked while lecturing in Munich. The following year, he suffered a fractured skull. In 1923 a man fired a pistol into an audience in Vienna. Nazi thugs ransacked Hirschfeld's offices in Berlin on 6 May 1933, burning his library four days later. That first year, Hitler outlawed homosexual and lesbian organizations, but he did not proceed against gays until after the Röhm purge. Drawing upon information garnered from torture and address books, police started arresting male gays in the fall of 1934. The law against homosexuality was expanded to include lewd glances and made retroactive. Now a person could be condemned for a wink or an act committed years before the Nazis came to power.[33]

In October 1936, Himmler established a special office of the Gestapo for the purpose of stamping out abortions and homosexuality. Headed by SS

Captain Joseph Meisinger, this division worked closely with Baldur von Schirach purging the Hitler Youth. In 1937, Meisinger conducted a witch hunt against the lay brothers of Waldbreitbach. In 1938 he helped bring down generals von Blomberg and Fritsch. By threatening to smear Blomberg's wife (her mother had worked in a massage parlor and she had posed for nude photographs), Goering and Meisinger forced Blomberg's resignation as Minister of Defense. Von Fritsch resigned as chief of staff of the *Wehrmacht* after winning a libel suit against a Gestapo informant who claimed a homosexual liaison with the general.[34]

HOMOSEXUALS IN CAMP: THE PINK TRIANGLE

Until 1941, members of the military found guilty of homosexual activity were sent to punishment battalions. On 4 September 1941 the Ministry of Justice issued a decree stating that 'deviant criminals' who threatened the health of the German people would be put to death. Two months later, Himmler warned that any member of the SS engaging in such acts would be executed. In February 1942, the rule was extended to all males found guilty of homosexuality.[35] Marked with the number 175 (violators of Paragraph 175 of the criminal code) or an A (for *Arschficker*), homosexuals were assigned a pink or lilac triangle. This insignia aroused fear and loathing not only from the SS guards but other prisoners as well. Segregated in their own barracks, few gays achieved the rank of Kapo, let alone any other position of authority in the prisoner hierarchy. Cooperation among homosexuals was rare for fear other inmates might resent this friendship.[36]

The men with the pink triangles carried snow from the campgrounds of Sachsenhausen with their bare hands. They risked the loss of fingers and feet while pushing carts from the Klinker brick works or dragging blocks of granite from the pits of Mauthausen. They were beaten about the head with horse whips and buckets as they labored in the quarries of Dora, Natzweiler, Nordhausen and Gross-Rosen. Some were castrated or became the unwitting objects of hormonal experiments conducted by Dr Carl Vaernet in Buchenwald. Others were given lethal injections at Flössenburg.[37] A 60-year-old priest from a prominent family in the Sudetenland was beaten when he arrived at Sachsenhausen in February 1940. The next morning his fellow prisoners had to carry him to the parade grounds. A student recalled:

> When our block senior reported to the SS block sergeant, the latter came over to the priest and shouted: 'Can't you stand up, you arse-hole,' adding: 'You filthy queer, you filthy swine, say what you are!' The priest was supposed to repeat the insults, but no sound came from the lips of the broken man. The SS man angrily fell on him and was about to start beating him once again. Suddenly the unimaginable happened, something that is still inexplicable to me and that I could only see as a miracle, the finger of

God: From the overcast sky, a sudden ray of sunshine that illuminated the priest's battered face.[38]

At that point, even the SS sergeant walked away and the priest murmured with a dying voice: 'Thank you Lord ... I know that my time has come.'[39]

In 12 years of Nazi rule, 100,000 homosexuals were arrested. Fifty thousand were convicted under Paragraph 175. Between 5,000 and 15,000 were sent to concentration camps. An estimated 60 percent of these died.[40] The Nazis did not pursue prominent gay artists, actors or west European homosexuals. (Jews, Poles or Russians who happened to be gay were twice-cursed.) Heinz Heger writes with some bitterness, '*Only* some tens of thousands of homosexuals were killed, as against six million Jews.' Amazingly, for a long time in the post-war period, the two Germanies gave tacit approval to this persecution by their inaction. In neither the east nor the west were homosexuals recognized as victims of Nazi persecution. Gays received no reparations. The Nazi statute of 1935 which expanded Paragraph 175 remained on the books in East Germany until 1967, in West Germany until two years later.[41]

THE GYPSIES: VICTIMS OF UNIVERSAL DISCRIMINATION

There was another group of contragenics whose fate was nearly as hopeless as the Jews. Europe's Gypsies were also irredeemable. In their telling, the Gypsies originated in India before Muslim conquerors displaced them westward about AD 800–950. They were craftsmen, metal-workers, shoe-makers, blacksmiths. Different tribes were known as Rom (a cognate of the Hindi Dom), Sinti (implying a connection with the province of Sind) or Kale. The Greeks referred to them as *atsingani* (heretics or untouchables), hence the Hungarian or German term *Zigeuner*. Gypsies claim that their more familiar name derives from Egypt where they were persecuted and finally expelled for their Christian beliefs.[42]

In Germany, England and Holland they were regarded as heathens, unwelcome in church, unfit for burial in Christian cemeteries. Intermarriage was discouraged and Gypsy children were not to be baptized. A litany of accusations made them as unpopular as Jews. Gypsies were spreaders of disease, horse thieves, child-stealers, dishonest businessmen, magicians in league with Satan.[43] Coming from the East they were denounced as spies for the Turks.[44] In his 1876 text, *L'uomo dellinquente* (Criminal Man), Cesare Lombroso typecast Gypsies as vain, shameless, shiftless, violent and canni-balistic.[45] In popular German literature, Karl May lampooned 'Gitanos' as vengeful, hateful dogs.[46]

Before the end of the sixteenth century anti-Gypsy statutes were enacted throughout Europe. Such laws not only denied Gypsies citizenship, they also ordered them out of the country. 'Gypsy Hunts' were organized in Austria, Swabia and Denmark, and bounties paid for chasing bands away. Those who did not leave might be sent to galleys or lose their children to other Christians. Some of the men were burned at the stake. The German county of Lippe-Demond decreed in October 1770: 'All Gypsies caught will be hanged and shot.'[47] Under Joseph II of Austria, Gypsies were ordered to send their children to schools and attend regular church services. In Romania, tens of thousands were reduced to serfdom, where many wore iron clamps on their foreheads, metal collars about their necks, shackles on their feet and yokes over their shoulders. Not until 1856 did the 400,000 Gypsies of Romania enjoy *desrobirejar* (emancipation).[48]

Under Bismarck, the various Länder tolerated 'sedentary' Gypsies and expelled those who moved about in caravans. In 1783, the ethnologist Heinrich Grellmann proclaimed Gypsies 'repellent'. A century later, Alfred Dillman founded the first Gypsy Information Service in Munich to track *die Zigeunerplague*. By 1906 the Prussian Ministry of Interior concluded bilateral agreements with nine European nations aimed at 'combating the Gypsy nuisance'. The British, too, tried to impose settlement upon so-called Travelers by the turn of the century.[49] In France, Gypsies were forced to secure a *carnet anthropométrique*, a 100-page document containing the photograph and vital statistics of the bearer along with his fingerprints, head size, chest measurements, and length of right ear and left foot. The German provinces of Baden and Prussia adopted this certificate during the Weimar years.

THE PRE-WAR PERSECUTION OF THE GYPSIES

In 1933, Achim Gercke established the Center of Genealogical Research in Berlin to deal with the Gypsies as well as Jews. Three years later, the work was taken over by Dr Robert Ritter and the Racial Hygiene Unit of the Ministry of Health. Gypsies, like Jews, were ousted from the Civil Service and Armed Forces in the first wave of Nazi legislation. Under the Nuremberg Laws, Gypsies (defined as anyone with one or two Gypsy grandparents) were barred from sexual contact with Aryans. In January 1940, Ritter concluded: 'The Gypsy question can only be solved when the main body of asocial and good-for-nothing Gypsy individuals of mixed blood is collected together in large labor camps and kept working there, and when the further breeding of this population of mixed blood is stopped once and for all.'[50] Before the Berlin Olympics, 600 Gypsies were detained in a camp at Marzahn, outside Berlin. The next year the Nazis established a series of *Zigeunerrastplatz* (barbed wire enclosures) near Cologne, Düsseldorf, Essen, Frankfurt and Hamburg. More sizable camps were established at Salzburg and Lackenbach following the annexation of Austria.[51] Dr Ritter and his assistants, Eva Justin, Adolf Würth and Sophie Einhardt took blood samples in the various camps. Eighteen thousand persons were sent to Auschwitz as a result of the broad definition of what constituted a Gypsy.[52]

Forty thousand Gypsies should have been easier to dispose of than 600,000 Jews. And though racial experts proposed a decree titled *Bekämpfung der Zigeunerplage* (Combating the Gypsy Plague), no Gypsy law was ever enacted.[53] The 1933 Law for the Prevention of Hereditary Diseased Offspring was presumed to include Gypsies and 400–450 were sterilized before 1939.[54] There was discussion of sending the Gypsies to Polynesia or Abyssinia under a 1934 decree which permitted the expulsion of 'undesirable foreigners'. Miscegenation was covered under the Nuremberg Laws. In 1937, Germany's criminal code was amended to permit the imprisonment of individuals guilty of anti-social behavior (e.g. beggars, tramps, prostitutes, the 'workshy' and Gypsies). After Germany invaded Poland, several thousand Gypsies were dumped over the Polish border. They were warned if they attempted to return to Germany, they would be sterilized.[55] Some Gypsies and half-Gypsies were permitted to remain in their jobs, but thousands more were interned in Ravensbrück, Buchenwald, Neuengamme and Dachau.

THE FINAL SOLUTION TO THE GYPSY PROBLEM

Kenrick and Puxon write, 'It has not been established with certainty when and by whom the decision was made to annihilate the Gypsies alongside the Jews.'[56] In 1933 some Nazi ideologues suggested that the Roma and Sinti be loaded into barges, taken out to sea and drowned.[57] In mid-summer 1942 the Nazis began placing Gypsies in detention camps in western Europe. In the east, the Nazis were more ruthless. The Germans massacred Gypsies in Olcyce, Berna, Radom, Kormorow and Lohaczy. Dogs were set against the Gypsies of Poznan. In Volhynia, the SS murdered Gypsy children by smashing their heads against tree trunks. They dealt more kindly with the 13,000 Gypsies of Bohemia and Moravia, confining them to camps at Lety and Hodonin until the summer of 1943. In Slovakia, Tiso mandated forced labor for 80,000 Gypsies. In Romania, Antonescu called for their elimination, saying, 'Mice, rats, crows, Gypsies, vagabonds and Jews don't need any documents.'[58] Virtually all of the Gypsies in Lithuania and Estonia were annihilated.[59]

On 31 January 1942 Gypsies like Jews were declared *Schutzangehörigen*.[60] In a meeting held on 18 September 1942, Himmler, General Bruno Strecken-bach, Minister of Justice Otto Thierack and two other SS legal experts agreed that 'persons under protective arrest, Jews, Gypsies and Russians would be delivered by the Ministry of Justice to the SS to be worked to death'.[61] Correspondence with Himmler dated from October confirms that Gypsies serving sentences in prison, including women, were to be turned over to the SS.[62] On 16 December 1942, Himmler signed a decree authorizing the shipment of German Gypsies to Auschwitz. Consistent with his arcane interests in 'Indo-German life', the *Reichsführer* tried to save the Sinti (13,000 Gypsies he considered to be Aryans) and Lalleri Gypsies (a smaller, but nevertheless Teutonic sect). Himmler's intervention angered Goebbels, Bormann and Hitler and he was forced to restrict his list of exemptions to essential war workers, Gypsies with war decorations or those married to Germans.[63] By the spring of 1943 distinctions were wiped away. The work of the SIPO was so complete that Himmler conceded in March 1944: 'As far as Poles, Jews and Gypsies are concerned, the accomplished evacuation of three groups by the Chief of Police has made the publication of special decrees for them meaningless.'[64]

GYPSIES IN THE DEATH CAMPS: THE MEN WITH THE BROWN TRIANGLES

After 1942, Gypsies were sent to the death camps of Chelmno and Treblinka. Virtually all the Gypsies in Croatia were massacred in Jasenovac when their Italian protectors capitulated in September 1943. Others died alongside Jews in Belgrade.[65] By 1944 they were being expelled from Hungary. In many locales, the Gypsies were taken to synagogues before being sent to concentration camps. The only countries where Gypsies were spared were Bulgaria, Denmark, Finland and Greece. In 1943 Gypsies from the Greater Reich were sent to 40 barracks in Birkenau known as the Gypsy family camp.[66]

Word had come down from Berlin that the Gypsies were not to be treated the same as Jews, and Commandant Hoess confessed to being fond of his prisoners who wore brown triangles. During the pogroms against Jews in Romania, Poland and Ukraine, Gypsies discovered they were no longer Europe's most loathed population. As Christians, they shared the booty of the hated Jews. That new-found status carried into the camps where some became Kapos. Ten thousand men, women and children lived in Section BIIe in Birkenau. There was a playground and a special school. More than 300 births were recorded here during that first year. Gypsy men were permitted to let their hair grow back, a privilege denied other prisoners. Musicians were excused from heavy labor. Some men did no work at all.

It should be stressed that conditions in the Gypsy Camp were relatively better than in the rest of Auschwitz. Individuals who were deemed unfit for work were sent to the gas chambers. In 17 months, 23,000 persons passed through the Gypsy Camp. Many died of starvation and disease. Outbreaks of typhus, smallpox, scurvy, dysentery, a leprosy-like condition called Noma, and a virulent form of chicken pox killed thousands. Gypsy twins were included in the experiments of Dr Mengele. At least 140 Gypsy women were sterilized by Dr Clauberg. Many men and women died as a result of beatings, long roll calls in inclement weather and heavy labor in forests, canals and stone quarries.[67]

According to Hoess, Himmler decided that the Gypsy Camp should be eradicated after visiting Auschwitz in July 1943. The *Reichsführer* was put off by overcrowding, 'the unhygienic conditions', and high mortality rate.[68] The ranks in the Gypsy Camp were thinned as young men were sent to Mauthausen. Gypsies were used for sea-water, typhus and gas experiments at Natzweiler, in Block 47 and the Little Camp of Buchenwald. Their women were sterilized at Ravensbruck. Like other victims of Nazism, they were dumped into the crowded camps of Majdanek, Flossenburg, Dora and Belsen, simply to die. For 4,000 persons remaining in the Gypsy Camp at Birkenau, the end came on the night of 2–3 August 1944. Hans Schwarz-huber, commandant of Birkenau, told Hoess that the operation was more difficult than any he had undertaken.[69] The Nazis told the inmates they were being shifted to another camp and supplied them with special rations of bread and salami. The Gypsies were not deceived. When the trucks pulled up before their barracks, people tried to hide. Others begged for mercy, declaring that they were Germans. The SS responded with clubs and curses. When the night was over, 2,897 Gypsies were murdered. The rest were sent to other concentration camps.[70]

The end of World War II did not bring with it an era of tolerance in Europe. Whether under Soviet puppet states or NATO democracies, Gypsies again reverted to a pariah people. Scholars dispute the number of Gypsy deaths (219,700 say Kenrick and Puxon, much less according to Michael Zimmermann) reported in World War II. Those numbers influence the debate over whether the Nazis intended genocide against the Gypsies. (Yehuda Bauer, Jack Eisner and Stephen Katz claim the persecution of Gypsies was not genocide.) According to Brenda and James Lutz, the Nazis targeted Gypsies not because of what they did, but because of who they were. The Nazis destroyed whole Gypsy communities. The Lutzes concluded, 'Ultimately the Gypsies were subject to persecution under the Nazis for racial reasons.'[71]

14

The Last Jews of Germany

By the summer of 1940, there were 200,000 Jews left in Germany and Austria. Since Hitler came to power 10,000 had committed suicide.[1] For the most part, they were elderly, more women than men. Too sick or poor to risk escape, they consoled one another with the slogan that 'everyone stays at his post'. For Otto Hirsch, Dr Arthur Lilienthal, Dr Paul Eppstein, Moritz Henschel, Dr Julius Seligmann, Philip Kozower, Cora Berliner, Hanna Karminski and Heinrich Stahl that post was the *Reichsvereinigung der Juden in Deutschland*. Created by Nazi decree on 4 July 1939, the Association of Jews in Germany operated 142 schools, 90 homes for the aged, 26 children's homes, 14 hospitals and countless soup kitchens.[2] It maintained training centers for Zionist youth and encouraged cultural activities. During the first years of the war, the association passed along government instructions to Jews. Later, the *Reichs-vereinigung* reluctantly drew up lists for deportation and assigned Jewish 'wardens' to assist in roundups.

Like their colleagues in Poland's *Judenrats*, members of the *Reichs-vereinigung* were under tremendous psychological pressure. No one typified this 'profound emotional disturbance'[3] more than Dr Leo Baeck, chief rabbi of Berlin. Head of the association of German rabbis, Grand Master of B'nai B'rith until the Nazis banned that Jewish fraternal organization in 1937, leader of the Central Verein, the Jewish Agency for Palestine, *Keren Hayesod*, and the old *Reichsvertretung*, Rabbi Baeck was the obvious choice to head the *Reichsvereinigung*. Nicknamed 'the Cardinal', this sage refused to leave Germany.[4] Said Baeck, 'As long as one Jew lives in Germany – my place is beside him.'[5]

Baeck's presence gave German Jews hope that they might outlast this terrible interlude. Following Kristallnacht, the Nazis issued one piece of anti-Jewish legislation after another. Jews had to turn over bonds, stocks, jewelry and works of art. They were not permitted to own automobiles. Jews were barred from going to movies, entering parks, serving on boards of trade. Jewish men were called to forced labor. By 30 April 1939, families were instructed to move into Jewish-owned housing.[6] With the outbreak of war, Jews were subject to a curfew. Possession of radios was forbidden. They might be ordered to report daily at 7 a.m. to do calisthenics for the Gestapo or SD.[7]

In January 1940, the *Reichsvereinigung* was told that the Jewish community must pay a special war tax. A month later, Jews were denied ration coupons for shoes and clothing. In July, private telephones were confiscated. A year later Jews could not use public telephones.

On 1 September 1941 the Nazis ordered Jews in Germany over the age of 6 to wear the yellow star. Jewish businesses also had to be clearly marked. Some Germans believed that their countrymen in the United States were being forced to wear the swastika with the letter G.[8] E.D. Oswalt, a 65-year-old half-Jewish publisher who was married to a Jewish woman, frequently forgot to wear the star. He was summoned before the Frankfurt Gestapo and never returned.[9] In the Hessen town of Giessen a Jew was denounced by a neighbor for not wearing the yellow badge. His family later received his ashes in an urn.[10]

A small percentage of Germans were enthusiastic about the anti-Jewish laws.[11] Some Gentile doctors refused to treat Jewish patients. Lawyers and policemen enforced laws which they knew were unjust. An equally small number of Germans opposed the racial laws. In Düsseldorf and Geisenheim, they brought food and blankets to their Jewish neighbors. In Sonderburg, a blind woman brought food parcels to her neighbors across the street until the last 12 Jews were ousted in July 1942. In Würzburg, Ilse Totzke continued to affirm her friendship for Jews until she was sent off to a concentration camp.[12] A few Germans risked prison by hiding Hebrew prayer books and Torah scrolls. The average citizen reacted with pity and shame to the decree mandating the wearing of the yellow star, but 'people became used to it'. As Cardinal Adolf Bertram of Breslau declared in a letter to bishops, Jewish concerns must be sacrificed to more pressing interests.[13] After a while, when children uttered anti-Semitic remarks, adults simply turned away.[14]

Rabbi Baeck told his people to wear the yellow star with pride. But with the enactment of the badge, Jews were alienated from Gentiles and, to a certain extent, their own people. There was little commercial contact between the two peoples since most Jewish businesses had been Aryanized or forced to close by 'silent boycott' of Gentile customers. After Kristallnacht, Jews who kept the Sabbath or holidays did so privately. Jewish social and educational groups no longer were permitted to function. Childhood acquaintances, card-playing friends and neighborhood women no longer acknowledged one another. If fire broke out in a Jewish house, the residents were left to their own resources.[15] Jews sat in rooms with decaying furniture, their only contact with the outside world the few letters they sent or received.[16] As Henry Huttenbach phrased it, the sense of isolation created a 'psychological claustrophobia'.[17]

Early in 1942, German Jews were ordered to surrender winter coats and blankets for troops on the Russian front. They were barred from using public rest rooms or public transport (unless they were traveling more than 7.5 kilometers to work). Now the doors of their homes had to be marked with the yellow star and they were not permitted to shop on the Kurfürstendamm. In February, the Nazis decided that Jews no longer could purchase newspapers. In May, Jews were instructed to turn in all pets, electrical appliances, cameras, typewriters and bicycles. Two months later all Jewish schools and journals were shut down. Jews were not permitted to buy milk, eggs, fish, smoked meats, cheese, white bread, cake, alcohol or cigarettes. Most disturbing, they were only permitted to shop for potatoes, beets, cabbage and coarse black bread between the hours of 4 and 5 p.m. in special 'Jew stores'.[18]

A NAZI FANTASY: POPULATION EXCHANGE

On 15 February 1940, Heydrich resumed deportations of Jews from Stettin and southwest Germany. Jews from Schneidemühl in West Prussia and Breisach am Rhein were also sent East over protests of the *Reichsvereinigung*. Seventy-two Jews died marching 14 hours through a blizzard from Lublin to Piaski. A five-year-old child suffering from frostbite had both hands and feet amputated. Hundreds more perished in the next month.[19] The Jews of Schneidemühl and Breisach were eventually allowed to return to their homes.[20] Between 1933 and 1940 340,000 Jews left the Reich while 530,000 Germans returned. As of May 1940 there were 315,000 Jews on German soil and over 8,000 *Volksdeutsche* housed in temporary camps.[21] Meanwhile, the Nazis discovered they needed Jewish skilled laborers for bridge building, armaments and electrical works. By the fall of 1940 more than 50,000 German and Austrian Jews (as well as 200,000 Jews from the occupied territories) had been drafted into the German labor service.[22]

On 2 October 1940, Hitler presided over a meeting of unhappy Nazi leaders in Berlin. Baldur von Schirach, Gauleiter of Vienna, complained that there were still 60,000 Jews in his city. Hans Frank, Governor-General of Poland, moaned that he was being swamped with Jewish deportees. Frank was supported by population experts (who warned the region would be a breeding ground of disease), Germany's generals (concerned about security in eastern Poland) and Goebbels (who declared, 'Everyone wants to unload their rubbish into the Government-General').[23] On 4 November, Hitler informed Frank he would have a free hand in carrying out 'political assignments'. Then speaking to General Jodl, Hitler declared: 'The political assignments in the Government-General take precedence over the military ones.' There could be no doubt what Hitler meant by 'political assignments'. On 5 October, Heydrich submitted several options for the resolution of settlement problems in Bohemia and Moravia. Hitler approved one which read: 'To be excepted from assimilation are those Czechs against whom any racial reservations exist or those with anti-Reich sentiments. This category is to be wiped out.'[24]

At Hitler's urging (*der Führer wunscht, dass möglichst bald das Altreich und das Protektorat vom Westen nach dem Osten von Juden geleert und befreit werden*), Himmler resumed shipments of German Jews on 18 September 1941.[25] A month later, Kurt Daleuge, chief of the Order Police, directed the deportation of 19,827 Jews to the Lodz ghetto. Over half of these came from Vienna and Prague, the rest from Berlin, Cologne, Hamburg, Dusseldorf and Frankfurt. Even though Lodz had been annexed in 1939, the Nazis argued that the Jews, by 'taking up residence abroad', had renounced their status as *Staatsangehöriger*. This permitted the legal fiction that it was not Germans who were being removed, but stateless persons of Jewish descent.[26]

Twenty-five transports, each carrying 1,000 Jews, left Berlin in the next ten weeks. There were several convoys from Frankfurt in the same period.[27] Lina Katz was among 1,251 Frankfurt Jews who were deported. They were paraded through the Great Market Hall at 7 a.m. 'Right and left stood people [Gentiles] who looked on silently in dense queues.' Their guards assured the Jews that Lodz was 'a very orderly and pretty ghetto'.[28] Of five convoys that left Frankfurt before May 1942, only one reached Lodz. As soon as the trains reached the Warthegau, SS guards forced the deportees from the cattle cars, stripped and shot them.[29] Jews who did reach the ghettos between the Vistula and Bug arrived 'humiliated, half starved, without energy and weary to death'.[30] Crowded in filthy rooms and unable to speak the local language, Jews from the Old Reich suffered starvation, disease and despair.

RIGA AND RUMBULA

With the Lodz ghetto filled to overflowing, the Nazis decided to send Jews farther east. On 24 October 1941 Daleuge issued another deportation order calling for removal of 50,000 Jews to Riga and Minsk. To accommodate 10,000 Jews from Hamburg, the Germans staged a mock demonstration among the Jews of Minsk on the anniversary of the Bolshevik Revolution. They then shot all 12,000 participants.[31] Still, Himmler was displeased with Heinrich Lohse, Kommissar for the Baltic Provinces and Byelorussia, who was committed to economic exploitation of Jews. There were also complaints that Wilhelm Kube, commandant of Minsk, was too lenient toward Jews.[32] In order to make room for the incoming transports of German Jews, the *Reichsführer* sent General Friedrich Jeckeln to Riga in mid-November. Jeckeln and his staff had distinguished themselves murdering Jews in the Ukraine earlier that year. Jeckeln devised the system of killing which became standard for the Nazis: force Jews into trenches and shoot them in the skull, layer after layer. The Nazis even had a word for it: *Sardinenpackung* (sardine-packing).

It only took Jeckeln a day or so to determine the site of his projected massacres. The Rumbula forest (the forest of crows) was less than ten kilometers from the ghetto in Riga. For two weeks, Jeckeln methodically planned the operation, lining up trucks to transport the aged and sick to the woods and using the same trucks to return clothing. Seventeen hundred men would be needed, to police the ghetto, escort the deportees, and patrol the Rumbula perimeter. These included forces of the German *Ordnungspolizei, Schutzpolizei* and *Gendarmerie* in Riga as well as 1,000 Latvian police, army reserves and auxiliaries. On 20–21 November, Russian prisoners of war carved six pyramidal trenches out of the sandy soil. One week later, the Nazis split the Riga ghetto along Liela Kalna Street. Some 4,000 able-bodied men were placed in a small ghetto. They were joined by several hundred women listed as seamstresses. The rest of the population was told they would be relocated to another camp for light work. Since there had been no real persecution for weeks, Riga's Jews thought they had nothing to fear.[33]

At 4a.m. on Sunday, 30 November 1941, German and Latvian units, accompanied by 80 Jewish policemen moved into the larger ghetto, ordering people to assemble with 20 kilograms of belongings. The apartments and streets soon became littered with bodies of those who did not move quickly enough. Between 600 and 1,000 corpses were picked up by Jewish men detailed from the small ghetto later that day. The chaos continued throughout the day, in full view of Riga's Gentile population.[34] The first contingents of Jews reached Rumbula at 9a.m. They were told to deposit valuables in a large wooden box placed at the entry of the perimeter. Stripped to their underwear, the Jews ran a gauntlet that funneled them toward the deep trenches. The actual killing was done by 12 of Jeckeln's men. As the day wore on, their marksmanship declined, leaving some of those in the pits half-dead. Jeckeln insisted that Latvian officials share the responsibility. Lohse and Dr Otto Drechsler, *Gebietskommissar* for Latvia, were here. So, too, Viktors Arajs, the one-time lawyer who headed a Latvian detachment that murdered thousands of Jews, Gypsies and Soviet officials.[35] Swaggering drunk, Arajs shouted down to those in the pits, 'Today Jewish blood must flow!'[36]

Thousands more were hustled out to Rumbula on 8 December 1941. When the operation was over, 24,000 Jews lay dead. To that number must be added 1,000 German Jews, the first transport from the Old Reich, who were liquidated at Rumbula even before the Latvians, on the morning of 30 November. Later when German Jews arrived in Riga, they were placed in blood-smeared buildings. There were now two ghettos, one for Latvian Jews, one for the Germans, separated by Ludzas/Leipzigerstrasse. Anyone attempting to make contact between the two ghettos was shot.[37]

The Nazis planned to send 240,000 Jews from the Reich to Riga. The actual figures were more like 20,000.[38] On 22 December, 500 young people were taken to a wooded area 20 kilometers from the center of Riga. They were joined by 500 prisoners from the Jungfernhof camp. Their task was to create a new concentration camp – Salaspils. The small camp (originally 44 buildings) may have been intended as an extermination center. Jews in the construction commando witnessed mass hangings and shootings of runaways.

While they were excavating burial sites, the graveyard detail uncovered hundreds of bodies of Russian soldiers and civilian women who had been shot. Salaspils was converted into a forced labor camp for Gentiles when the last Jews returned to Riga in January 1943.[39]

In their absence, conditions in the ghettos had deteriorated. In January 1942, 1,050 Czech Jews passed through Riga. Only 70 arrived at Salaspils. Wagons filled with soiled clothes and shoes offered insight into the fate of the others. On 13–14 March 1942 the Nazis selected 4,000 older Jews from the populations of Riga and Jumpravmuiza for a special transport to Dunamunde, 200 kilometers south of Riga. They never arrived. Aided by Arajs's Latvians, the SS massacred the entire lot in the Bickernicker Forest. Transports from Frankfurt, Königsberg and Berlin met a similar fate. Two thousand persons were sent to Auschwitz when the Riga ghetto was closed in November 1943.[40]

THE JEWS OF BERLIN

Deportations from the Reich directly to extermination camps began during the summer of 1942. The Hamburg Jews, living a seemingly charmed existence in the Minsk ghetto, were exterminated in gas vans at the end of July.[41] There were by this time 40,000 Jews in Berlin, perhaps half of all the Jews in Germany. That fact was not lost upon the Gauleiter of Berlin, Joseph Goebbels. Hitler's faithful Minister of Propaganda filled his wartime diaries with complaints against the Jews. They were 'riffraff [who] must be destroyed', 'potato bugs', 'parasites', who corrupted public life.[42] The Jewish question could only be resolved by 'brutal methods'. In March 1942, Goebbels declared that Jews were being punished for the belligerence of their kinsmen in England and America. 'It's a life-and-death struggle between the Aryan race and the Jewish bacillus.'[43]

Goebbels was especially upset with the 'insolence' of Jews in Berlin.[44] The problem was that too many Jews enjoyed protection in the armaments industry. As evidence he could point to an incident which took place on 18 May. Goebbels had arranged for an exhibit titled 'The Soviet Paradise' at the Lustgarten. The exposition, designed to deflect attention from German losses on the Russian front, was too much for members of the Jewish resistance. A number of young men and women banded together under the leadership of Herbert Baum, an engineer at the Siemens electrical motor plant. For four years, the Jews, mostly Left Zionists, circulated anti-Hitler handbills, forged documents, and prevented works of art from being confiscated by the Nazis. Using incendiary devices, the Baum group sabotaged Goebbels's exhibit, injuring 11 visitors and destroying some of the displays. In retribution, the Gestapo seized two dozen members of the Baum group and 500 Berlin Jews; 250 of the latter were executed at an SS airfield in Berlin, the rest sent off to

Sachsenhausen. Baum was tortured to death in June. Following a series of trials before *Sondergericht* (special courts), 21 of his companions were beheaded.[45]

Goebbels was delighted when in September 1942 the *Führer* promised to rid the capital of Jews. The *Reichsvereinigung* was ordered to draw up transports of the usual 1,000 persons. The deportees were to bring bedding and rations for five days. Their destination was Theresienstadt, the fort outside Prague that served as a way station to Auschwitz. Some Jews committed suicide. Perhaps as many as 5,000 became 'U-Boats', hiding with friends, relatives or officials who did not support the regime's racial policies. Bernard Lichtenberg, provost of St Hedwig's Church in Berlin, publicly prayed for the Jews and asked to be sent to Lodz along with them. (He was deported to his death in Dachau in November 1943.) White Russian émigrés, police constables, the sister of Horst Wessel and the son of Field Marshall Reichenau risked their lives helping Jews. The underground, led by Erik Wessen, a German architect, and Erik Perwe and Erik Myrgren, ministers of the Church of Sweden, secured false baptismal records and bribed German trainmen to secrete Jews in crates bound for Sweden. Together they saved hundreds of lives.[46]

At the start of 1943, the Nazis continued to drain the ghettos of Frankfurt, Bingen, Mainz and Darmstadt. Spirits plummeted in Berlin when three of the top figures in the *Reichsvereinigung* – Rabbi Baeck, Dr Eppstein and Philip Kozower – were sent to Terezin in January 1943. To expedite roundups, the Gestapo set up a special Jewish Bureau of Investigation on Iranienstrasse. Staffed with Jewish 'catchers' (spies promised exemption from deportation), the Bureau rooted out Jews and turned them over to the Nazis.[47] A jubilant Goebbels could note: 'We are now definitely pushing the Jews out of Berlin.' 'With regard to the Jewish question he [Hitler] approved of my measures and specifically ordered me to make Berlin entirely free of Jews.'[48]

On 19 April 1943, a number of Zionist youths, girls and boys, were transferred from their training camps to the holding facility on Grosse Hamburg Street. It was Passover, the very moment when Jews in the Warsaw Ghetto were initiating armed resistance against the Germans. Locked in their rooms, these young Jews kept up their regimen, exercising and chanting Hebrew songs for several days. They sang: 'We form a new generation, a strong generation! Our demand – honor for the Jew! We are fighting for liberty, equality, the reign of law!' On Sunday, the *Hechalutz* held a seder. The next day they were assembled at dawn and placed in trucks which took them again to the freight station. Before being sealed in cattle cars, they hugged one another and said their goodbyes. Said Annaliese Borinsky: 'We spent that night without sleeping a wink. From time to time we see people working on the tracks. Amongst them – star-bearers. Many of them in P.O.W. uniform. We ask them, where, what is the probable target of our trip. They shrug their shoulders. One of them points to the sky. We fail to understand the hint.' The transport of young, healthy Jews was bound for Auschwitz.[49]

THE *FABRIK AKTION*: THE ISSUE OF MIXED MARRIAGE

A major roundup of Berlin's privileged factory workers was planned for 27 February 1943. Goebbels hoped to snare 4,000 Jews in this *Fabrik Aktion*. Units of the *Leibstandarte Adolf Hitler* division surrounded the factory district in the middle of the night. People were taken from their jobs and dumped into open cattle cars. Some protested, showing their work passes which no longer offered protection. Others committed suicide, taking veronal or potassium cyanide.[50] Some workers had been warned in advance. As Goebbels complained, 'The scheduled arrest of all Jews on one day has proven a flash in the pan because of the shortsighted behavior of industrialists who warned the Jews in time.'[51]

Frustrated with the count, the SS swooped down on Jewish apartments, taking 100 Jews married to Aryans and other exempted persons to the jail on Rosenstrasse. The next day, 6,000 people, wives, children and their supporters gathered near Gestapo headquarters on Burgstrasse, chanting, 'We want our men!' The demonstrations continued for several days. Eventually, the men in the Rosenstrasse Center were released and 35 others who had actually arrived in Auschwitz were returned.[52] Goebbels attributed the protests to 'actors' or 'Bohemians', and noted angrily 'If a German still finds it possible to live with a Jewess as his legal wife, that's a point against him, and it's out of place to be too sentimental about this question in wartime.'[53]

On 19 May 1943, Himmler proclaimed Berlin *Judenrein*. It was not so. Just four weeks earlier, Goebbels made the following entry in his journal:

> The Jewish question in Berlin has not found its final solution yet. There still remain a considerable number of Jews by law, Jews in privileged mixed marriages, and even Jews in simple mixed marriages, here in the city. This presents grave problems ... I do not want any more Jews wearing the Jewish star to be seen walking around in the capital of the Reich. They should either be allowed to go without the star and granted the rights of privileged ones, or be deported for good from the capital.[54]

There still were 18,515 Jews in Berlin as of 13 March. Many of these were officials charged with transferring Jewish property to the state or supervising patients in the Jewish hospital on Iranienstrasse. Several hundred Jews were deported between 10 and 16 June 1943. The Nazis were still sending out transports from the Charlottenburg depot at the end of 1943.[55]

The roundups depleted, but did not eliminate Jews from Germany's largest cities. The Nazis could not decide what to do with Jews married to non-Jews and their *Mischling* offspring.[56] *Mischling* first grades enjoyed recourse to courts until April 1943. Eight months later, the Nazis removed exemptions for Jews whose Aryan spouses had died or divorced them (unless their offspring had died in combat). Following the attempt on Hitler's life on 20 July 1944, *Mischlings* in the civil service or military were purged. Himmler protected some first-degree cross breeds by conscripting them for forced labor in October 1945, then decreeing that Christians of non-Aryan descent be sent to Terezin. The Nazis were deporting intermarried Jews from Frankfurt as late as February 1945.[57]

By the time the Russians closed in on Berlin in the spring of 1945, the German capital had been pounded into rubble. As Leonard Gross wrote, 'Death was everywhere now. Bodies lay in doorways after every raid, dragged there by survivors. Hours later burial details would appear to cart the bodies off, not to graves but to funeral pyres. There were too many dead for the graves.'[58] There were no Jews left in Geisenheim or Massbach, only seven racial Jews in Rashi's Worms, 20 in Giessen, no more than 145 in Frankfurt. Perhaps 110,000 German Jews lost their lives in the Holocaust. When it was all over, there were still 1,123 Jews in Berlin.[59]

VIENNA: CITY OF LOST DREAMS

Before the *Anschluss* 90 percent of Austria's 198,000 Jews were concentrated in Vienna. Within a year, more than 80,000 fled to England, the US, Palestine, France, Belgium, South Africa and Shanghai. While Austria succeeded in portraying itself as the first victim of German aggression, the nation produced not only Hitler but such prominent Nazis as Odilo Globocnik (coordinator of Einsatzgruppe activities in Russia), Ernst Kaltenbrunner (Heydrich's successor at the RSHA), Artur Seyss-Inquart (Reichskommissar for the Netherlands), Hans Rahm, Siegfried Seidl and Anton Burger (commandants of Terezin), General Alexander Loehr (commander of the Southeast Front), Amon Goeth (commandant of Plaszow) and Alois Brunner, butcher of Drancy. Austria contributed a disproportionate number of volunteers for the SS (14 percent), and even more of the death camp guards (30 percent). Simon Wiesenthal estimates that Austrians bear responsibility for at least half the deaths of Jews in the Holocaust.[60]

According to George Berkeley, the average Austrian was far more vicious in his hatred for Jews than Germans.[61] While many Germans were embarrassed by public assaults against Jews, Austrians not only enjoyed ogling such incidents but were more likely to participate in physical assaults against Jewish neighbors. Seeing his janitor wearing a swastika lapel pin, Ernst Ruzicka commented: 'These are the people who cheered the Emperor and then cursed him, who welcomed democracy after the Emperor was dethroned, and then cheered [Dollfuss's] fascism when that system came to power. Today he is a Nazi, tomorrow he will be something else.'[62]

Within days, if not hours, of the *Anschluss*, Vienna's streets were filled with people proclaiming their Nazi allegiance. Wrote one observer: 'The city gave the impression of a nation on the march. Marching columns of brown uniforms (the regular storm troops), black uniforms (the party's elite troops), gray uniforms (of the Great German Army), exotic uniforms (the Madman's future colonial army), exercising columns of civilians, marching columns of the party's youth organization, down to grade school level. Everywhere the sound of shrill commands and stomping boots filled the streets.'[63] Carl Zuckmayer compared the behavior of the Viennese on 11 March to a scene from Hieronymous Bosch. He had witnessed the Nazi putsch in Munich and the first days of Hitler in Berlin, but 'nothing compared to the first days of Vienna' with its hysterical men and women, and the 'wild, hate-filled crowds'.[64]

Like their German counterparts, Austria's Jews felt the wrath of Kristallnacht and the 'cold pogroms' (legislative persecution) which followed. Six Viennese synagogues were torched, only one left standing as a result of the Night of Glass. Four thousand businesses were looted that night, then Aryanized. Ten thousand Jews were sent to Buchenwald and Dachau in 1938. Thousands more were concentrated in Vienna's old Leopoldstadt district. Jewish schools were closed, veterans deprived of the right to wear uniforms. Jewish physicians and lawyers were only permitted to serve as 'aides'. By September 1939, the *Gemeinde* (Jewish community) was feeding most of the Jews of Vienna and tending for 2,300 orphans.[65]

OBERSTURMBANNFÜHRER EICHMANN

From the moment Austria was absorbed by Germany, the Viennese *Gemeinde* had to reckon with its own particular demon. Adolf Eichmann, a member of the Nazi Party since 1932, was assigned the task of expediting Jewish emigration from Austria. Born in Solingen, Germany in 1906, Eichmann joined the security forces in 1934. With a limited knowledge of Yiddish and Hebrew, he became the party's specialist on Jewish affairs. In the fall of 1941 Eichmann was promoted to head Section IVB4 (Jewish Affairs) under Heinrich Müller and Reinhard Heydrich in the Reichs Security Office. Psychiatrists would later claim that Eichmann was 'a perverted sadistic personality', 'a man obsessed with a dangerous and insatiable urge to kill'.[66] Himmler considered him 'overbearing'.[67] Jewish leaders found him mean-spirited (they called him *des Teufels Vertreter*, the Devil's Deputy).[68] No monster, Eichmann was 'a leaf in the whirlwind of time' who was blown 'into the marching columns of the Thousand-Year Reich'.[69]

Immediately after the *Anschluss*, Eichmann packed officials of the *Gemeinde* off to Dachau and reconstituted it under a different leadership.[70] Until the Nazis banned voluntary emigration in November 1941, Josef Loewenherz, Aron Menczer and William Perl negotiated with Eichmann to allow a few Jews emigrate to Palestine. Several boatloads were authorized, mainly to create friction between Jews and England. Eichmann's feelings were revealed when he informed Dr I.H. Koerner, *Aus diesen Transporten wird nichts. Wir brauchen keine Verbrecherzentrale in Palaestina, die Juden werden atomisiert* (Nothing will come of these transports. We don't need a center for criminals in Palestine. The Jews will be atomized).[71]

Once America entered the war, Austria's Jews were sent to Theresienstadt. By the end of summer 1942, 14,000 old people, disabled war veterans, patients, and families of mixed marriages were sent to the transit ghetto. That left 6,300 Jews, mainly foreigners or those with special connections like the Jewish daughter-in-law and half-Jewish grandchildren of Richard Strauss. As Jews departed, Austrians joked about how they would become soap.[72] Only a handful of Gentiles offered assistance. Henrietta von Schirach, wife of the city's Gauleiter, asked Hitler to alleviate the suffering of children and was told to mind her own business. Wehrmacht Sergeant Anton Schmidt saved hundreds in Vilna ghetto by smuggling food and acting as a go-between for partisans. Sentenced to death by the Gestapo, Schmidt declared, 'Everyone must die some day. If I can choose to die as a killer or a helper, then I choose to die as a helper.'[73]

Eventually, not even the leaders of the *Gemeinde* or the JUPO (the Jewish police force) were spared. Five thousand Jews (less than 3 percent of the pre-war population) remained in the city in the spring of 1945. As in the rest of Austria and Germany, the Jewish community of Vienna was moribund.[74]

15

The Invasion of Russia: Einsatzgruppen

OPERATION BARBAROSSA

On 10 May 1941, the German *Luftwaffe* conducted its last conventional attack against London. The fire-bombing (the same night that Rudolf Hess flew to Scotland on his wayward peace mission) left more of the city demolished than the Great Fire of 1666. Herman Goering had boasted that his air force would spearhead the first conquest of the British Isles in 900 years. After nine months of aerial combat and 2,698 downed German aircraft, 'Operation Sea Lion' was postponed indefinitely. Instead, Hitler decided to implement 'Operation Barbarossa', the invasion of Russia.

Relations between the signatories of the Molotov-Ribbentrop pact had never been warm, especially after the Soviets annexed 175,000 square miles of land in 1940. Hitler's scheme was to strike at Russia with three army groups that would envelop Soviet forces with swift-moving columns of panzers. To avoid pitfalls encountered by Napoleon, Hitler wanted the attack to begin in mid-May 1941. Allowing eight to ten weeks for German troops to reach the Volga, they could pause, with sufficient food, *matériel* and slave labor before the onset of winter. What was left of the Russian army could freeze in Siberia.[1]

'Barbarossa' was one of the world's worst kept secrets.[2] In February Russia's embassy in Berlin reported that large numbers of Wehrmacht troops equipped with German–Russian handbooks were being sent east. In March, Cordell Hull handed the Soviet ambassador in Washington what proved to be a fairly accurate outline of Nazi invasion plans. Soviet agents in Tokyo and Switzerland added verification. Before the end of spring, the Germans began pulling diplomatic personnel and shipping from cities in the Soviet sphere. Amazingly, Stalin continued to send grain and petroleum and even turned over some German communists to the Nazis. He refused to believe that Hitler would break a treaty that still had eight years to run. Even if he had, there is little he could have done to prevent an assault. A purge by the Soviet dictator four years earlier had wiped out 35,000 of the Red Army's best officers.

Fortunately for Stalin, Hitler had to postpone his spring attack. On 28 October 1940 (the 18th anniversary of the Black Shirt march on Rome), Mussolini attacked Greece from Albania. His plans for the conquest of Egypt from Libya stymied, Mussolini thought his army would handily subdue the forces of Greek dictator John Metaxas. When Greek mountain fighters repulsed his first units in November, Mussolini personally directed a second invasion in March 1941. This time the Italians lost one-third of Albania before Hitler decided to rescue them. The *Führer* dismissed the Greek invasion as *Schweinerei* (a dirty little mess), but it gave Germany an excuse to press Yugoslavia into an alliance. King Paul granted German troops permission to cross his boundaries on 25 March. Two days later, army officers favorable to the Allies ousted Paul in favor of his nephew Peter. On 5 April, Prime Minister Simovich signed a non-aggression pact with the Soviets. The next day, Belgrade was bombed and German forces invaded both Yugoslavia and Greece. Officially the campaign in Yugoslavia lasted until 17 April, that of Greece until the conquest of Crete on 30 May. These digressions delayed the German assault upon Russia by six weeks. 'Barbarossa' did not begin until 22 June 1941. That Sunday 150 German divisions accompanied by 14 Romanian and 20 Finnish divisions struck across the 2,000-mile border with the Soviet Union.[3]

PREPARATIONS FOR THE FINAL SOLUTION

Hitler charged 'this greatest army in history' to set aside notions of morality and act ruthlessly. Russia was not a signatory to the Hague Agreement of 1907 or the Geneva Convention, therefore 'Bolshevik fanatics' were not to be treated as normal prisoners of war, but were to be liquidated. As Field Marshal Wilhelm Keitel explained, in a clash between 'two opposing political systems', the army could execute political commissars or turn them over to the Gestapo.[4]

Nazi officials knew the invasion would have ramifications upon four million Jews who lived east of the Curzon Line. Hitler made no effort to conceal what he planned to do with the *Ostjuden*. In November 1940 Hans Frank and General Jodl had been instructed to give priority to 'political assignments' (e.g. the eradication of certain racial categories).[5] That same month, Hitler told Himmler that the Final Solution of the Jewish Question was now within his *Umfeld* (jurisdiction),[6] although the *Führer* did not formally assign Himmler *Sonderaufgaben* (special tasks) until March 1941.[7] On 3 December 1940, Hitler informed a Bulgarian delegation that 'the Soviet intelligentsia led by Jews will be evacuated'. On 17 July 1941 he told Croatian Marshal Slavko Kvaternik of his intention of approaching all European countries with the demand for the removal of every last Jew from Europe.[8]

On 31 July 1941, six weeks after the invasion of Russia, Hermann Goering wrote to Reinhard Heydrich:

> In completion of the task which was entrusted to you by the Edict dated 24 January 1939, of solving the Jewish question by means of emigration or evacuation in the most convenient way possible, given the present

conditions, I herewith charge you with making all necessary preparations with regard to the organization of practical and financial aspects for a total solution of the Jewish Question in those territories of Europe which are under German influence.[9]

Two weeks later Goering expressed the opinion that 'the Jew in the territories dominated by Germany had nothing more to seek'. He added that where Jews were allowed to work, it should only be in closely guarded concentration camps and that he preferred Jews be hanged rather than shot, as the latter was too honorable a death.[10]

Heydrich was the RSHA's specialist on Jewish affairs and Goering owned a galaxy of impressive titles (Reichsmarschall, Prime Minister of Prussia, Minister Plenipotentiary for the Four-Year Plan and Luftwaffe commander). Neither they, nor anyone else (Himmler, Keitel or Eichmann), however, would have presumed to issue such orders on their own. Indeed, Keitel prefaced his instructions on commissars with the words 'by order of the *Führer*'. It was common for Himmler, Goering and other Nazi leaders to preface orders with the words *des Führers Wunsch* (the *Führer*'s wish).[11] Gerald Fleming maintains Hitler 'painstakingly avoided being in any way associated personally with the implementation of the liquidation orders he himself had originated'. Hitler was concerned that the German people, who protested against the euthanasia program, might not tolerate the murder of millions of innocents because of race.[12]

No rational scholar doubts that such orders were given or that they came from a man who was untroubled by the misery in Poland's ghettos or the murder of Germany's handicapped.[13] Fleming and Eberhard Jaeckel believe that genocide was an objective from the start of the war.[14] Helmut Krausnick argues that the decision to liquidate Jews came during the planning of the Russian invasion (March 1941).[15] Raul Hilberg and Christopher Browning see that decision coming in July 1941, while Uwe Dietrich Adam, Martin Broszat and Arno Mayer insist that the Final Solution resulted from the realization that the war against Russia was lost.[16] Lucy Dawidowicz maintains the decision must have been reached between 18 December 1940 and 1 March 1941. Hitler notified his generals that he intended to attack Russia a week before Christmas. On the March date, Himmler visited Auschwitz and advised commandant Rudolph Hoess to expect a huge expansion of the Silesian concentration camp.[17]

It may be that the fate of Europe's Jews was determined earlier than Dawidowicz suggests. In July 1940, Hitler asked his generals to develop plans for the invasion of Russia. He declared: 'Russia is the factor by which England sets the greatest store. If Russia is beaten, England's last hope is gone. Germany is then master of Europe and the Balkans. Decision: As a result of this argument, Russia must be dealt with. Spring 1941.'[18] On 29 July Jodl relayed the *Führer*'s 'expressed wishes' to his field commanders. Two months later (September 1940) as Hitler conceded the battle of Britain was over, Heydrich informed Hans Luther that the Jewish question was no longer capable of being solved by emigration.[19]

It seems unlikely that Hitler issued any order to kill all Jews in the late summer/fall of 1940. With Europe at his feet, there were a number of options available for the *Umsichtung* of Jews, including ghettoization, starvation or the reservation at Madagascar. Over the winter of 1940/41 Lublin SSPF *Gruppenführer* Odilo Globocnik suggested the creation of a forced labor camp where Jews would die out while draining swamps and making rivers navigable.[20] There was even talk of taking over Russian camps in the White Sea area.[21] Impressed with the success of the T-4 program, Himmler requested assistance from Dr Bouhler for the elimination of 'human ballast' through sterilization.[22] As Henry Friedlander writes, 'The success of the euthanasia policy convinced the Nazi leadership that mass murder was technically feasible, that ordinary men and women were willing to kill large numbers of innocent human beings, and that the bureaucracy would cooperate in such an unprecedented enterprise.'[23] For the moment, however, another method would be explored.

THE EINSATZGRUPPEN

Nazi population and security experts repeatedly came back to a scheme suggested by an officer named Kuensberg in January 1941 – the formation of mobile killing squads that would operate in tandem with frontline troops.[24]

7. Remnants of synagogue cupola from Bialystok. The synagogue was destroyed on 26 June 1941 and members of the congregation burned alive.

8. Jedwabne, Poland. Barn door memorial, with the outline of a barn where 1,500 Jews were burned alive on 10 July 1941, by their Gentile neighbors.

Meeting with Generals Keitel and Jodl in March of 1941, Hitler demanded that the elimination of the 'Jewish-Bolshevik intelligentsia' be given the highest priority.[25] Within the month Heydrich, General Halder and General Eduard Wagner, head of the army Quartermaster Corps, developed the protocol for these special units. The Einsatzgruppen were not limited to anti-partisan activity but would also 'carry out executive measures against the civilian population', especially Jews. *Flurbereinigung* (clearing the field) of the Jews was essential to pacification.[26] When the plan was recirculated on 20 May it was retitled 'The Final Solution of the Jewish Problem' and bore the signatures of Eichmann and Himmler's intelligence chief Walter Schellenberg.[27]

There were 3,000 specially-trained SS in the Einsatzgruppen. Drawn principally from the Gestapo, Kripo and Security Service, their numbers also included members of the Waffen SS and Order Police. Einsatzgruppe A under SS *Brigadeführer* Franz Stahlecker, then Heinz Jost, operated in the Baltic region. Einsatzgruppe B, commanded by Arthur Nebe, was assigned to White Russia. Einsatzgruppe C under Otto Rasch operated in Ukraine, while Einsatzgruppe D under Otto Ohlendorf worked in the Crimea. Many of these leaders were veterans of the SIPO or SD.[28] They understood their mission was not simply to 'root out' but destroy Soviet commissars, Jews, Gypsies and other racial undesirables. Guidelines furnished by Heydrich's office empha-sized that 'wild, subhuman' Jews had tormented native populations in the East by serving in the communist NKVD secret police.[29] Schooled in murder at centers in Poland or rifle ranges at Pretsch, Saxony, the Einsatz groups were praised by Himmler in a series of morale-boosting speeches between 1941 and 1943. Said Himmler: 'Most of you know what it means when 100 corpses lie there or 500 or 1,000 – to have gone through this and apart from exceptions caused by human weakness – to have remained decent, that has hardened us. That is a page of glory in our history never written and never to be written. We had the moral right to exterminate this people which intended to destroy us.'[30]

One who did know of their actions was Hitler. In August 1941, Heinrich Müller instructed the heads of the four groups 'the *Führer* [was] to be kept informed continually from here about the work of the Einsatzgrupppen in the East' and that materials of special interest (e.g. photographs) were to be delivered with the greatest dispatch.[31] Responding to complaints from the Quartermaster Corps in October 1941 about disruptions caused by deportations, Hitler curtly informed his staff, 'The Jewish question takes priority over all other matters.'[32] Two weeks later, on 21 October 1941, Hitler issued a statement through Bormann which read: 'When we finally stamp out this plague, we shall have accomplished for mankind a deed whose significance our men out there on the battlefield cannot even imagine yet.'[33]

German forces moved so quickly during the first weeks of the Russian campaign that hundreds of thousands of Jews were trapped behind enemy lines and were 'killed like sleeping flies'.[34] Thirty thousand Jews died at Kovno that summer, 75,000 in Minsk. Another 40,000 at Riga, where girls were raped and drowned in a well. And 50,000 died in Vilna during seven nights of terror between 4 September and 28 October. The figures from the south were equally depressing: Lwow (30,000), Tarnopol (5,000), Kamenetz-Podolsk (23,600), Chernigov (10,000), Stanislavov (15,000), Dniepropetrovsk (11,000), Odessa (26,000), Kharkov (14,000) and Rovno (15,000). When they occupied Kovno, the Lithuanian capital, on the night of 25–26 June, the Nazis opened the prisons and encouraged inmates to make a pogrom. In a few hours, several synagogues and 60 houses were set on fire and 1,500 Jews were 'eliminated'. Over the next two nights, 2,300 more Jews were 'rendered harmless'. SS troops ringed a gas station as Lithuanians pummeled Jews with wooden clubs and lead pipes. Women hoisted their children to watch as 45 people were beaten to death in the space of an hour. A German soldier observed, 'After each man had been killed, they [the crowd] began to clap and when the [Lithuanian] national anthem started up they joined in singing and clapping.'[35]

In Vilna, the shock squads were joined in street attacks against rabbis by Poles and Lithuanians. In Lwow, *Oberstürmführer* Wilhaus shot at Jewish infants tossed in the air while his 9-year-old daughter squealed 'do it again, Daddy'. In March 1942 Wilhelm Kube, commandant of Minsk, had Jewish children taken from an orphanage to an open trench. Then, as they were buried alive, Kube tossed candy into the pit.[36] Eventually, the Einsatz groups adopted the method of killing devised by Jeckeln at Rumbula and Ohlendorf in Odessa. The Nazis would summon Jews to the public square. The Germans claimed they were moving the Jews from the front. (Einsatzgruppe leaders testified that Jews seemed remarkably ill-informed about how the Germans regarded them.)[37] Jews were marched out of town to a ravine, cemetery, a park like Ponar outside Vilna where people once picnicked.[38] Stripped of their clothing, the Jews would run a gauntlet of dogs and armed men. Unable to escape, they were marshaled to a ledge above a trench. Thirty yards away stood machine guns. As each group filed into the death trap, the SS took turns manning the guns.

THE ROLE OF THE WEHRMACHT

The Einsatzgruppen were assisted by local militia and police forces. They also received cooperation from the Wehrmacht which agreed to a split chain of command on 4 April 1941.[39] German combat troops has the same mindset as the Einsatz units. They absorbed the first casualties from the hated Bolsheviks. Once the army rounded up Jews, they transformed them into 'garbage' that had to be cleared away by the Einsatzgruppen.[40] German soldiers stood by, transfixed by what Willi Dressen called 'execution tourism',[41] then they joined in the killing. Their generals encouraged them to kill. Two weeks before the invasion of Russia, the Wehrmacht Command approved the 'unobtrusive' killing of political commissars. On 18 August 1941, *Reichskommissar Ostland* Hinrich Lohse specifically called for the countryside 'to be cleansed of Jews'. On 10 September 1941, Major General von Bechtolsheim, *Kommandant in Weissruthenien*, noted that because Jews were 'capable of any treachery' there were no guidelines for how they were to be treated. Two weeks later Lieutenant General Walter Braemer declared that all elements endangering peace in Byelorussia (e.g. communists, Jews and circles friendly to Jews) 'be rendered harmless'. On 10 October, Field Marshal Walther von Reichenau ordered the destruction of 'sub-human Jewry'. A month later, Colonel-General Hermann Hoth also called for the merciless eradication of Bolshevik-Jewish agitators.[42]

From the Baltic to Crimea, Einsatzgruppe leaders praised the Wehrmacht. In July, regular army units of the 221st Infantry Division helped clear the towns of Baranovichi and Novogrudok in White Russia. A month later, the 350th Regiment killed all Jewish males in the vicinity of Bialowiza. The 354th and 727th Infantry participated in the 'mopping up' of 1,000 men, women and children outside the village of Krupka in October. Before the German offensive broke down in December, Wehrmacht troops were involved in the shooting of 1,338 Jews in Smolevici, 1,000 in Koidanovo, 15,000 in Slutzk, 7,000 in Borisov, 4,500 in Nesvizh, 1,000 in Turec and Swierzna, 1,800 in Mir. Hannes Heer estimates that 20,000 of the Jews murdered in White Russia were killed by Wehrmacht troops.[43]

Einsatzgruppen in Ukraine enjoyed enthusiastic support of regular army units. Propaganda Company 637 of the Sixth Army supplied music at Zhitomir where General Reinhardt's troops assisted Einsatzgruppe C in 'combing out' the town and in Kremenchug where the Seventeenth Army actually urged the mobile killing squads on. An infantry platoon participated in a massacre of 1,160 Jews at Luck. Military police assisted in the execution of 2,200 Jews at Gorky. Field Police killed 156 Jews in Tospo. Wehrmacht units also participated in massacres at Vitebsk, Poltava, Borisov, Kharkov and Gornostaipol.[44] As German troops advanced into East Galicia, Abwehr units smothered the countryside with flyers that read: *Werft die Waffen auch jezt nicht weg. Nimm sie in Deine Hand. Vernichte den Feind. Volk! Wisse! Moskau, Plen, die Ungarn, das Judenthum – das sind deine Feinde. Vernichte sie.*[45] When major pogroms erupted in Lemberg, Zloczow and Tarnopol that summer, the Wehrmacht did not intervene.[46]

BABI YAR

Army units assisted in the single worst atrocity perpetrated by the Einsatz-gruppen. Reacting to a series of explosions that rocked the Krestchiak, the business center of the Ukrainian capital on 24 September, Major General Eberhard authorized a *Vergeltungsmassnahme für Brandstiftungen* (reprisal action for arson). Kiev's Jews were ordered to report to the intersection of Melnikov and Dokhturov Streets on the morning of 29 September. Their destination was Babi Yar, the Old Widow's gully several miles outside of Kiev.

A Jewish actress, Dina Pronicheva, described what happened. Thousands of Jews scooped up what goods they could carry in their arms or carts and reported to the authorities. As they marched out of town, old-timers recalled

9. Dina Pronicheva testifies on Babi Yar (Soviet Photographic Exhibition).

the behavior of German troops in World War I and speculated that Jews were being moved out of concern for their safety. When the columns reached a cemetery near Babi Yar, it was apparent that there was no railway depot. People were told to leave their belongings and sit down. Then in groups of ten, 20 or 50, they were marched out of sight. Forced through a cordon of men and dogs, the victims were stripped and beaten. As they ran, some were laughing hysterically. The faces of others turned gray. Dazed and in shock, they had no time to recover when they emerged upon a narrow precipice that overlooked a gully filled with bloody bodies. Using her labor card which gave no indication she was Jewish, Dina Pronicheva avoided being sent to her execution. Like several others, she insisted she had come to see friends off. The ruse worked temporarily. At twilight, a Nazi officer drove up to the small group that had been exempted and ordered all of them killed immediately or 'no Jew would report tomorrow'. Dina's group was given no time to undress. Across the gully she saw the machine guns. Before the tracers came near, she fell into the pile of warm, wet humanity below. The mass was still shifting, moving. Not all of the victims were dead yet. SS guards wandered through the pit striking at those who seemed suspicious. Dina was hit in the breast. Then the word was given to start shoveling. As dirt filled her mouth, the Jewish woman flailed away and managed to crawl out of the death pit. In the dark, she encountered a young boy who had lost his parents in the massacre. Together they tried to sneak away. Early the next day the boy, Motya, was trapped and shot.[47] When the forces of Einsatzgruppe C completed their work, they called upon units of the army engineers to dynamite the rock face of the ravine to cover traces of the murder operation.[48]

10. Dead at Babi Yar (Soviet Photographic Exhibition).

There were 33,771 Jews killed at Babi Yar on 29–30 September 1941. At least five of the victims were newborn infants who had not yet been named. One was 111 years old.[49] More Jews were killed at Babi Yar in two days than US Marines at Iwo Jima in 26 days of fighting in March 1945 or at Okinawa in the summer of 1945. The death toll overshadows Auschwitz which processed 10,000 bodies per day. For the next two years, Babi Yar was in continuous use, as a construction site, a training camp for SS guards, and as a forced labor camp. More than 200,000 people would be buried here before the retreating Nazis tried to erase evidence of what they had done.[50]

Long after World War II, there were no monuments at Babi Yar, just a simple plaque that spoke of Russian deaths. Nothing about Jews, only a caretaker who spoke Yiddish. The Soviets tried making the area into a soccer field in 1959, an apartment complex the following year. Construction was halted when bulldozers exposed bones and when a landslide of mud and water dredged up other human remains. In 1961, the poet Yevgeny Yevtu-shenko wrote: 'Here together with Russians and Ukrainians lie Jews. I am proud of the Russia which stood in the path of bandits.' His words were denounced in the official press as a 'monstrous insult' and 'pygmy's lick-spittle'. A year later, Dmitry Shostakovich dedicated his Thirteenth Symphony to Babi Yar. After a few performances, it was banned. Soviet reaction to this kind of notoriety was summed up by Khruschev who in 1962 informed Yevtushenko, 'Comrade, this poem has no place here.'[51]

AKTION PETLURA

Hitler spoke of Ukrainians as *Untermenschen* who were to be dispersed or enslaved. Three million Ukrainians were taken by the Nazis for forced labor. An equal number died in concentration camps or in reprisals. According to Taras Hunczak, the Nazis established killing centers in 250 locations and wiped out 16.7 percent of the Ukrainian population, a higher percentage of deaths than in any nation other than Poland.[52] For the Russian campaign, however, the Nazis recruited four divisions of combat SS from among Germans and Herrenvolk (Dutch, Norwegians, Balts, Ukrainians, Roman-ians, Walloons and Hungarians). Among those units were the 600 man Nachtigall and Roland Battalions, formed in West Galicia under the Central Ukrainian Committee (OUN). Ukrainian nationalists under Yaroslav Stetsko mistakenly believed that a Nazi victory would restore their independence. Warned Stetsko: 'I have the opinion that in the struggle against Judaism in the Ukraine the German methods will be used.'[53] When German troops invaded the USSR, they were greeted by jubilant peasants who tossed floral bouquets in their paths and by local politicians who welcomed the Nazis to the town square.[54]

Elements of the OUN which had denounced Jews as 'the vanguard of

Muscovite imperialism', now mounted a hate campaign against moderate Ukrainian politicians and Jews. Anti-Semitic posters, journals and exhibitions calling for a Ukraine without Poles or Jews appeared in city after city.[55] On 25 June, Stetsko called for the creation of a militia to 'help remove the Jews'.[56] When the Wehrmacht returned to Lwow on 30 June, Ukrainian rage exploded. *Nachtigall* troops forced Jews to kneel before their captors on the street or carry garbage from building to building in their mouths. In Zloczow Ukrainian nationalists led by Ivan Klymiv-Lehenda forced Jews to exhume the corpses of 649 NKVD victims at the citadel with their bare hands. Bodies littered the streets of the inner city as a result of the four-day pogrom in Zloczow. At least 1,000 Jews were beaten to death at Brygidki prison. Six hundred Jewish men were executed at a bathhouse by the SIPO and militia following the discovery of 200 corpses in the NKVD prison at Tarnopol. Ukrainian *Schutzpolizei* carried out actions in Dubno, Tuchina and the Rovno areas in 1941.[57] At least 10,000 Jews died in pogroms which some Ukrainian nationalists labeled 'Aktion Petlura'.[58] Fifteen years late, Ukrainians made the Jews pay for the assassination of their Hetman in Paris.

Even after the Nazis made it clear that they had no intention of permitting the Ukrainians to set up an independent state, they still received cooperation. Ukrainian police 'guarded the ghettos as well as the Aktions, accompanied the transports to the death camps, and participated directly in the Ausrottung of the Jews'.[59] Ukrainians from the SS-102 punitive battalion wiped out 27,000 Jews in the Shumsk, Kremenetz, Pochayev and Veliko-Dederkalasky districts in 1941. Ukrainian militia operating with Einsatz groups C and D in southern Russia became self-sustaining (drawing their salaries from confiscated Jewish goods) and specialized in shooting children.[60] William Kornbluth, a survivor from Tarnow, described the carnage of 12 September 1942:

> Young children fared the worst. The Ukrainians smashed their heads on the cobblestones which lined the Marketplace. Much of the area was covered with blood and the curbsides turned into red rivulets. Some of the blood flowed over the cobblestones into adjacent streets and had to be hosed off, later in the evening, to disinfect the area. The place resembled a slaughterhouse, where the victims were not chickens or cattle, but helpless little children. The O.D. [Jewish auxiliaries] had the job of collecting their battered little bodies, some still showing signs of life, and loading them on horsedrawn wagons. The corpses were taken to the Jewish cemetery to be dumped in a mass grave.[61]

Fifty-eight Jewish communities in the Ukraine endured pogroms in the summer of 1941.[62] Many Jews in the smaller Bukovina towns like Radauz and Czaudin were killed by Ukrainian bands from Russian-held Galicia. Ukrainian troops helped clear the ghettos of Rovno (1942), Molotivka, Visnitza, Brody and Warsaw (April 1943), Lwow and Chortkiv (July 1943). In November 1943 Ukrainian SS killed 500 Jews near Dorucow and Wawrzice.

Ukrainians trained as *Wachmänner* (policemen) at Trawniki near Lublin formed the bulk of guards employed at Pawiak Prison in Warsaw and the concentration camps of Ostrow, Poniatow, Plaszow, Janow, Monowitz, Sobibor and Treblinka.[63] Kurt Gerstein told how he watched as 200 Ukrainian guards at Belzec used leather whips to clear a trainload of Jews from Lwow and then drove them to their deaths in August 1942.

THE HALYCHYNA DIVISION

While many of their countrymen were dying in Majdanek, thousands of Ukrainians volunteered to fight for the Nazis in the 14th Waffen SS Grenadier Division.[64] Formed by Gustav Wächter, Nazi governor of Galicia in May 1943, the Halychyna Division swore an oath of allegiance to Hitler and was sent off by the President of the Ukrainian Aid Committee Dr Volodymyr Kubijovyc.[65] Five thousand Ukrainians were sent to France where they hunted members of the resistance and downed Allied flyers. In February 1944, two regiments were reorganized as a *Kampfgruppe* in eastern Poland. They were reprimanded by their own executive officer Wolf-Dietrich Heike for 'unseemly behavior'.[66] The Nazis were upset with attacks against Polish Catholics slaughtered with knives in Palikrowy, Malinska, Czernicy and Moderowka. In the town of Huta Peniacka, Ukrainian forces rounded up farmers and their families, placed them in barns and burned them alive. Valery Strykul claims that the Halychyna tortured more than 2,000 civilians to death, shipped 20,000 persons to Germany and burned 20 villages in Poland.[67] The figure does not include casualties from six Polish villages wiped out in the Hrubieszow-Lublin district. Such deeds prompted the Polish Armia Krajowa to complain to its leaders in exile of 'the terrorist actions of the SS Halychyna Division and UPA'.[68]

The Halychyna lost two-thirds of its men in the defense of Brody in the spring of 1944. Its numbers were replenished at Neuhammer by youths and veterans from the Volhynia-based 31st SD brigade which helped suppress the Polish uprising in Warsaw that summer. In October, the division was sent to Slovakia where it aided the Tiso dictatorship in squelching a democratic rebellion. Three months later (January 1945), the Halychyna was transferred to Slovenia where more atrocities took place. In May, the division hunkered down in Austria, hoping to avoid capture by the Soviets. Arrangements were made for surrender to the British. The latter swallowed the tale of freedom fighters struggling for their homeland and admitted 15,000 veterans of the division to England and its dominions. Among those who reached America were Simon Ridtschenko, interpreter for the Gestapo at Biela Tserkov and Cherkassy; Joseph Marusiak, a policeman who killed Jews in Bolekhov; Fedir Hrinchuk and Stary Okesinets of the SS-102 Battalion; Nikifor Lukhaninov, responsible for the burning of 500 people; Wasyl Shkvarko, who supervised the deaths of hundreds at a trench in Chortkiv; Johann Dostkotzynski, guard at Tarnow and Treblinka; Hryhorij Tsebrii, accused of gouging eyes at Malij Plavuchi in July 1942; Yuri Torbech, who participated in massacres at Strahoveta, Rawa Ruska and Turka; Serge and Mykola Kowalchuk of Lubomliva; Fedor Federenko, guard at Treblinka; and Ivan Chrabatyn, second in command of the police at Stanislav where 10,000 Jews were murdered.[69]

Many Ukrainians actively opposed the Nazi occupation. More than 200,000 participated in the resistance after the Nazis incorporated Eastern Galicia into the Government General and turned the administration of other Ukrainian territories over to Kommissar Erich Koch. Ukrainians point to Metropolitan Andreas Szeptycki of Lwow as an example of resistance. Not only did the Archbishop of the Uniate church hide Jews (including Lwow's chief rabbi Lewin) in convents and monasteries, he threatened 'divine punishment' upon persons who shed innocent blood.[70] Says Philip Friedman, 'There are many records about simple Ukrainian people, peasants, housemaids, workmen who saved or helped Jews.'[71] Dieter Pohl also notes that the civilian government in Lwow opposed pogroms and that the Nazis had to rely upon outsiders or their own agents to execute attacks on Jews after August 1941.[72]

Ukrainians were not the only ethnic forces that committed war crimes in the East. Hundreds of Lithuanians volunteered to serve as police, militia or in regular SS battalions. Smaller numbers volunteered in Latvia and Estonia.[73] The behavior of *Selbstschutz* (police auxiliaries) embarrassed their Nazi superiors. Einsatzgruppe A recruited several hundred Lithuanians to help with sweeps through Vilna, Raseinyai, Rokishkis, Perzai and Prienai districts that resulted in the deaths of 47,000 persons in three months. There was no anti-Nazi partisan movement in Lithuania, the only country beside Germany which conducted book-burnings during World War II, a country where 200 Jewish communities were obliterated.[74] Latvian 'Askaris' were described as 'able helpers' whose only drawback was their tendency to loot from the dead. In Estonia, the *Selbstschutz* were entrusted 'to do the entire dirty work' of shooting whatever Jews were left following the Soviet retreat.[75] A Lithuanian journalist named Klimatis organized the first pogrom that resulted in the deaths of nearly 5,000 people in the last week of June 1941. Vincent Brizgys, one-time auxiliary bishop of Kaunas, forbade any assistance to Jews during the roundups. Karl Linnas was sentenced to death *in absentia* by the Estonian government for killing inmates at the Tartu concentration camp. Edgars Laipineks was listed as a war criminal in 1949 for murders perpetrated at the central prison in Riga, Boleslaw Maikowskis was sentenced to death *in absentia* by the Latvian government for his actions as chief of police in Reshnitza. All of these individuals were living in the United States after World War II.

The reason so much emphasis is placed upon Ukraine is that this region of the USSR had the largest number of Jews – 1.5 million in Soviet Ukraine, 600,000 more in Volhynia and Western Galicia. It was a region where Jews who fled to the woods faced dangers as great as the Nazis. Nora Levin has written: 'For those who got past these hazards [actions, pogroms], there was the likelihood of being turned in by peasants who were paid or frightened, or just hated Jews. There were also Polish, Lithuanian or Ukrainian guerrilla bands who were generally as hostile as the Nazis themselves and freely killed Jews in the forests.'[76] Only 17,000 of the 870,000 Jews who lived in the Ukraine in 1939 survived the war, barely 2 percent.[77]

On 16 March 1944, Heinrich Himmler addressed the officers of the Halychyna Division at Neuhammer. Said Himmler, 'Your homeland has become so much more beautiful since you have lost – on our initiative, I must say – those residents who were so often a dirty blemish on Galicia's good name, namely the Jews.'[78]

16

Wannsee: The Saga of Czech Jewry

PROTEKTOR OF BOHEMIA AND MORAVIA

In September 1941, Reinhard Heydrich, was named *Protektor* for Bohemia and Moravia. The man who described himself as 'the chief garbage collector' of the regime,[1] was determined to make his territory 'a showplace of the New Order'.[2] There had been 250,000 Jews in Czechoslovakia, 120,000 in the west. Jews served on the city council in Prague where 70,000 lived before the war. Jews were listed on the boards of 900 companies in Bohemia where the intermarriage rate by 1933 was 23 percent.[3] Still, American diplomat George Kennan warned Washington that hostility toward Jews was so great that if the Nazis introduced their racial program they would not encounter significant resistance.[4] Among the proto-fascist elements in pre-war Czechoslovakia were the Slovak People's party, the Svatopulk Guards, *Vlajka*, the Czech National Camp for Aryans, Jiri Skibrny's National Socialist Party, the Agrarian Party of Rudolf Beran, and Gen. Rudolf Gadja's Czech legion (groups described by Josef Korbel as 'pathological scum'[5]).

There was no outcry when the Nazis marched into Prague in March 1939 and extended their discriminatory laws to Bohemia. In August 1939 Adolf Eichmann established a *Zentralstelle fur jüdische Auswanderung* (Central Office for Jewish emigration) in Prague. On 26 January 1940 von Neurath ordered the transfer of Jewish enterprises to Aryan *Treuhandler* (trustees). (During the war $500,000,000 in assets were transferred to non-Jews through 'fraudulent bullying'.)[6] In April 1940 a *numerus clausus* capped the number of Jews in professions at 2 percent. In April 1941, Czech Jews were ordered to register and carry identity cards. Four months later, the Nazis decreed the wearing of the yellow star.[7] That same summer, a delighted Heydrich informed Eichmann, 'The *Führer* has ordered the physical extermination of the Jews.'[8]

Three weeks after assuming office in Bohemia (17 October 1941) Heydrich called a group of SS leaders to Prague to discuss implementation of Goering's Final Solution communiqué. Eichmann, General Karl Hermann Frank, Colonel Gerhard Mauer, Hans Gunther, Horst Bohme and Dr Karl Freiherr von Gregory attended the meeting. Heydrich proposed that 5,000 Jews, leave for the Lodz ghetto immediately.[9] The remainder under his control could be processed through transit camps such as Terezin. *Von dort aus kommen die Juden nach dem Osten*. (From there, the Jews would be sent to the East.)

Heydrich warned that any Gentile interfering with these actions would be deported alongside the Jews. As for what would occur in the East: *Die Juden haben sich die Wohnungen in die Erde hinab zu schafen.* (Jews will have to build their dwellings under the ground.)[10]

Heydrich's plan to meet with SS leaders in Berlin on 9 December was deferred when Japan attacked Pearl Harbor. On 11 December 1941, Hitler declared war against the United States. Almost lost in Hitler's hour-long rant about American provocations was his reference to the Jews. Said Hitler, 'We know, of course, that the eternal Jew is behind all this; Roosevelt himself may not realize it, but then that only shows his own limitations. Indeed, we all know the intention of the Jews to rule all civilized states in Europe and America. We know this is a time when for nations it is the question of "to be or not to be."'[11] The next day (12 December), Hitler reminded Goebbels: *Die Vernichtung des Judentums muss die notwendige Folge sein. Diese Frage ist ohne jede Sentimentalitat zu bretrachten.* (The destruction of Judaism must be the necessary consequence. This question must be considered without sentimentality.)[12] When Heydrich and his aides finally got together, they would not have to debate whether the Jews should die, but how.[13]

VANS OF DEATH

The first death convoys left Germany at the end of October 1941. In the next two years, more than than 50 transports would make the journey to killing fields outside Minsk, Kovno and Riga. Many of these Jews were exterminated in what the Czechs called *dushegubky* ('soul destroyers'). On 25 October 1941, Dr Erhard Wetzel of the Ministry for Occupied Eastern Territories sent a message to General Lohse, *Reichskommissar Ostland.* Wetzel stressed that the goal was *Beseitigen* (elimination) of the Jews. Most important: 'Given the present situation, Jews who are not fit for work can be eliminated without qualms through use of the Brack device.'[14]

SS *Oberführer* Viktor Brack was an official in the Chancellery. His superior Philip Bouhler had been in charge of the T-4 euthanasia program. 'Brack's device' was an adaptation of the killing procedure suggested by Drs Walter Heess and Albert Widmann of the *Kriminal-technische Institut* – carbon monoxide. Exhaust from a van or truck was piped to kill passengers sealed in the back. Over the winter of 1940/41, SS *Obersturmführer* Herbert Lange commanded a unit of 75 men which murdered patients from German and Polish asylums. The victims were forced into gray-green vans marked 'Kaiser Coffee Company'. These were driven about until the passengers died. Although several thousand persons were eliminated in this manner, the process proved to be clumsy, time-consuming and, in view of petrol consumed, wasteful.[15]

When the Nazis invaded Russia, they confronted more 'useless' civilians.

An attempt to blow up an insane asylum in Minsk miscarried, leaving body parts hanging from trees. Einsatzgruppe B commander Arthur Nebe recalled how he nearly died when he fell asleep in his own garage with the motor of his car running following a drunken revel. The task of designing a reliable gas van or *Saurerwagen* was given to Walter Rauff and his aides in the SD motor pool. After refinements were made to the flooring and rear ramp, the vehicles produced by Firma Gaubschat in Leipzig resembled furniture trucks, five meters long, two meters wide. Tested on Russian prisoners at Sachsenhausen, they could kill 50 adult passengers within a half hour. Ultimately 30 large vans and 20 smaller Opel models along with two Dodge conversion vans were deployed.[16]

'The Brack Device' accounted for at least 2,000 Jews murdered by Einsatzgruppe A in Riga in December 1941. Drivers in Moghilev, Orel, Maly Trostinec and Minsk helped clear ghettos in the area controlled by Einsatzgruppe B. Einsatzgruppe C only needed two vans at Poltava in November 1941. By midsummer 1942, vans were in use throughout Ukraine, Crimea, Lublin and Yugoslavia. There still were problems. The *Saurerwagens* bogged down on muddy roads. Leaks developed, prolonging the agonies of those trapped inside. There was one case where a truck exploded when the pipe was improperly attached. Civilians pressed into service to deposit the dead in trenches found bodies covered in excrement, vomit and urine.[17] In the fall of 1941, Eichmann described the procedure as 'the most horrifying thing I had ever seen in my life'.[18]

Eichmann's visit to Chelmno, a small town in the Polish Corridor, had a greater significance. On 16 July 1941, SS *Sturmbahnführer* Rolf-Heinz Hoppner wrote Eichmann recommending the elimination of all Jews in the Warthegau by 'some fast-working poison'. Hoppner's suggestion that 300,000 Jews be killed quickly was seconded by Wilhelm Koppe, SS police chief for the region. Chelmno was selected because it was accessible to a number of cities with Jewish populations, including Lodz. Because of his experience, Lange was placed in charge of operations. Over the next three years, Jews arrived at the Chelmno train station and were moved by trucks to a castle on the town square that served as a holding facility. Polish volunteers and SS men wielding whips forced groups into the death vans. Three kilometers off in the Lubartow forest lay the actual *katzet* populated by clothing sorters, jewelers, tailors, shoemakers and burial teams. The SS averaged six to nine trips daily to the trenches. In this way, the Nazis achieved their goal of killing 300,000 people, including large numbers of children, Russian prisoners of war, even a bus filled with nuns at Chelmno.[19]

When two *Saurerwagens* arrived in the fall of 1941, Chelmno became the first permanent extermination camp in World War II. Using technology developed at Hadamar and Hartheim, the SS experimented with a fixed gas chamber at Lublin. In September, Dr Widmann demonstrated in Moghilev how carbon monoxide chambers could be combined with crematoria. Before the year was out, many physicians associated with T-4 were transferred to the Nazi concentration camps. They helped sterilize prisoners in Mauthausen and Buchenwald and gave lethal injections to brain-damaged German soldiers. Most important, they were gassing Russian prisoners with Zyklon B (hydrogen cyanide) in Belzec and Auschwitz. All that was needed now was an official imprimatur for *Beseitigung*.[20]

THE WANNSEE CONFERENCE

On 20 January 1942, Heydrich assembled 15 Nazi specialists on the Jewish question at the offices of Interpol in the Berlin suburb of Grossen Wannsee. Joining him were Eichmann, Wilhelm Stuckart (State Secretary in the Ministry of Interior), Justice Roland Freisler (President of the *Volksgerichthof*), Heinrich Müller (of the Gestapo), Alfred Meyer (Gauleiter for the Occupied Eastern Territories), Georg Leibbrandt (Reichsamtsleiter for Eastern Territories), Erich Neumann (State Secretary for the Four Year Plan), Josef Buhler (from the Government General), Martin Luther (for the Foreign Office), Wilhelm Kritzinger of the Reich Chancellery, Otto Hoffmann of the Race Settlement Office; Eberhard Schoengarth (head of the Gestapo in the Government General) and Rudolf Lange (representing the Gestapo in the eastern territories).

This very much was Heydrich's show.[21] He began by telling how Goering had placed him in charge of the *Endlösung* of the Jewish question. After nearly a decade of confrontation, there were still 11,000,000 Jews in the world. Employing the euphemism of choice, he suggested that Jews be brought east for 'labor utilization', roadbuilding, slaving in mines, and other physically grueling work. A large part would then 'fall away through natural reduction'. As for the rest, history showed that they represented 'a dangerous germ cell of new Jewish development'. Heydrich proposed that a handful, war veterans with the Iron Cross, people over 65 years, politicians and celebrities could be housed temporarily in an Old People's Ghetto.[22]

There followed a country by country review. Representatives of the Government General repeated Frank's opposition to more Jews being moved to Poland. Kritzinger and Luther expressed concern over relations with the Vatican, the Italians and in Scandinavia where anti-Semitism was not widespread. Kritzinger wondered how military priorities would be reconciled with the removal of Jews. How would the operation be financed?[23] There were also questions about Aryan spouses in mixed marriages and their *Mischling* offspring, perhaps as many as 72,000 half-Jews and 100,000 dependents. Several officials, while committed to sterilization, nevertheless expressed concern for the loss to the Aryan gene pool.[24]

Heydrich conceded there might be resistance in 'Nordic areas', but there would be none in the south and east where most Jews were located. The plan had the approval of the highest authority (Hitler). Friendly nations (Croatia, Romania, Slovakia) were supportive. The church presented no problem. Apart from a protest over shootings in Belgrade, the Nuncios had not objected to Nazi policy. As for logistics, Heydrich explained Jews would travel on trains bringing back Russian prisoners of war. The operation would be financed by funds confiscated from Jews themselves. As for Aryans in mixed marriages, the government was restoring privileges to those who divorced their spouses. *Mischlings* First Grade (those with two Jewish grandparents) or *Mischlings* Second Grade (one Jewish grandparent) would be excused, provided they held vital positions (as physicians, scientists, etc.). Those who looked Jewish would be treated as Jews, unless they submitted to sterilization. In that case, they might be sent to the Old People's Ghetto.[25]

The conference proceeded cordially, casually. At his trial in Jerusalem, Eichmann testified that the atmosphere was quite relaxed. Afterward, the Nazi leaders broke into small groups for a buffet lunch, drinking and joking loudly. The Wannsee protocol contains no reference to specific methods of killing. Eichmann vaguely recalled subsequent discussion with Heydrich and Müller about shooting. The war with Russia having dragged on more than six months, everyone in the room understood what was meant by 'labor utilization'.

THE END OF HEYDRICH: LIDICE

Heydrich had wanted to be the first governor to purge his territory of Jews. He nearly succeeded. In a matter of months, residents from 123 of Bohemia's 131 Jewish communities were transferred to ghettos in Prague. Between 24

11. Ghettoization. Jewish deportees arrive in Theresienstadt (Yad Vashem).

November 1941 and 16 March 1945, 122 trains carried these people to Terezin/ Theresienstadt and beyond. In all, 93,952 Czech Jews were deported to the east. Of these 424 managed to elude the roundups by hiding and 3,371 survived the death camps.[26] By May 1942 Heydrich believed his work in Bohemia to be finished and was ready to offer his services in France.

Heydrich would not see his dream of genocide come to fruition. On the morning of 27 May 1942, the Reichsprotektor was ambushed by Czech commandos as he motored into Prague. The assassins, Jan Kubish and Josef Gabschik, had been parachuted into the country by the RAF several months before. Their attack almost miscarried. Gabschik's gun jammed, but a bomb planted by Kubish exploded as Heydrich's car crossed the Moldau bridge. In shock and suffering broken ribs, the Nazi leader emerged from the debris. Taken to a hospital, he was expected to survive. Legend has it that he lingered in pain with a broken spine. In fact, metal fragments lodged in his body caused his death on 4 June 1942.

The Czech town of Lidice would suffer for Heydrich's assassination. According to rumor, the commandos had been sheltered here. (In fact, they stayed in the village of Lezhaky.) On 9 June, Waffen SS units forced the residents of Lidice to the town square: 195 women were shipped to Ravensbruck where half perished; 100 small children were given to Germans in the region; 191 men and boys over the age of 16 were simply executed. Family pets also were shot. The SS plundered the village, blowing up all the houses, sparing only useful livestock. Two weeks later (25 June) the Nazis tracked down the remaining partisans at the Karel Boromaeus Greek Orthodox Church in Prague. They used water hoses, machine guns and tear gas against the commandos, who commited suicide rather than surrender. About the same time, the SS razed Lezhaky and two trains, each carrying 1,000 Jews, left Terezin for the east. There were no survivors of these transports.[27]

SLOVAKIA: THE JEWISH CODE

The Czechs never again mounted a serious resistance movement. There was opposition, however, in Slovakia. Since 1938, this state had been a model Nazi satellite. Once there were more than 135,000 Jews in Slovakia. By 1942 the number was down to 89,000. Mainly Hasidic, these eastern Jews were alienated from their Gentile neighbors. Their intermarriage rate was less than 2 percent.[28] Jews owned 6 percent of the land (250,000 acres) worth $135 million. Organized in the *Zidovska Ustredna Udradnovna pre Slovensku Krajinu* (Central Jewish Office for the Region of Slovakia), Jews debated whether their future lay in assimilation or Zionism. Seven thousand Slovak Jews were permitted to emigrate to Palestine between March 1939 and 1941. Those who stayed were stunned when the independent Slovak nation imposed all kinds of restrictions upon them.

In April 1939 the Tiso government proclaimed the broadest definition of a Jew in Europe. Anyone with a single Jewish parent would be considered Jewish. That summer, the practice of shehitah was banned. Slovakia imposed a 4 percent quota on professions and demanded the Aryanization of Jewish businesses. Following a meeting with Tiso at Salzburg in the summer of 1940, Hitler sent Eichmann aide Dieter von Wisliceny to Slovakia to assist with the Jewish question. In September 1940 the Slovak Central Economic Office consolidated Jewish community groups into a central *Judenrat* (*Ustredna Zidov*) headed by hand-picked *Starosta* (Jewish elders). Over the next few months, the Ministry of Interior encouraged elements of the Hlinka Guard and *Freiwillige Schützstaffel* to attack Jews.[29]

On 9 September 1941, the government issued a comprehensive Jewish Code. At 270 articles, the Code ran longer than the Slovak constitution.[30] A special division on Jewish Affairs, was established under the brutal Sano Mach. In Slovakia the badge was required of Jews over the age of six. The Code made no exceptions for 10,000 'racial' Jews who were converts to Catholicism. Males between the ages of 18 and 60 were subjected to a draft as *Robotnik Zid* (Work Jews). Thousands of blue-uniformed slaves died in camps at Poprad, Zhilina, Novaky and Sered. By the end of 1941, Jews were ordered out of Bratislava and Pressburg. In March 1942 parliament discussed how all Jews could be banished from Slovakia in accordance with 'Christian ethics'.[31]

On 10 March, a few thousand were thrown across the border into Galicia. Between 26 March and 5 April, eight transports carried 8,000 youth east. In the process, members of the Hlinka Guard plundered the belongings of deportees and abused Jewish women at the loading zones.[32] There would be 57 transports (19 to Auschwitz, 38 to Lublin) before the deportations were temporarily halted in October 1942. By then, fewer than 20,000 Jews were left in Slovakia.[33]

THE WORKING GROUP AND THE EUROPA PLAN

There were no further deportations from Slovakia for more than a year, in part because of opposition from the Catholic and Evangelical churches and some politicians. Cardinal Karel Kaspar in Prague protested about the treatment of Jews as early as November 1939. In May 1942, again in August, Slovakia's Protestant clergy issued pastoral letters denouncing Jew-bating as a violation of the teachings of Jesus. The Vatican and its Nuncio inquired about the welfare of converts in the summer of 1942. Education Minister Dr Jozef Sivak, Justice Minister Dr Gejza Fritz, Finance Minister Dr Mikulash Pruzhinsky, even the aged Prime Minister Vojtech Tuka urged a reassessment of the Jewish Code in September 1943. Nothing could be done to help those who had been deported. As Eichmann explained, the Jews who had been sent to Poland were no longer alive.[34]

What triggered the conscience of clergy and officials were the frantic appeals of Slovakia's Jews. An unofficial Jewish cabinet headed by Gisi Fleischmann of the WIZO and Rabbi Michael Dov Weissmandel contacted the underground in Slovakia, Poland and Hungary, hoping to arrange escapes from the transports. Known as the *Pracovna skupina* or *Nebenregierung*, the Working Group bribed officials and sheltered a handful of Jews who crossed into Slovakia from Poland after 1942. When the Nazis seized Hungary in 1944, the Working Group secured the return of 7,000 Slovak Jews. Slovakia's Jews confirmed the operations of Auschwitz and urged the Allies to bomb the death camp.[35]

In June 1942 Weissmandel approached Wisliceny, offering $50,000 if he would help Slovakia's Jews. Three months later, the Working Group proposed a payment of $2,000,000 in return for the cessation of all deportations in Europe. The Jews also promised to come up with supplies of food and medicine. Under a 15-day deadline on what was dubbed 'the Europa Plan', Weissmandel appealed to Rabbi Stephen Wise, Saly Mayer of the Joint Distribution Committee, Nathan Schwalb of the Jewish Agency in Geneva, and Jewish leaders in Budapest. A year later, when Hungarian Jewry came under the Nazi knife, Rabbi Wiessmandel urged Jewish leaders in Budapest to pay a similar bribe to the Germans.[36] When several of Himmler's aides were arrested and Wiscliceny was transferred to Greece in the fall of 1943, hopes for the Europa Plan were dashed.[37] It is questionable whether the scheme could have worked. Jewish organizations were unwilling to offer the Nazis any goods or cash[38] and the sum negotiated ($2,000,000) was only a fraction of the cost for visas to Switzerland at the time.[39]

When Slovakia erupted against the Nazis on 29 August 1944 Jews constituted 10 percent of the partisans.[40] While the rebels waited in vain for reinforcements from the Soviet army 100 miles away, SS Generals Gottlob Berger and Hermann Hoefle regained control of the Tatra mountains within a month. There would be no negotiations with, no exemptions for, Slovakia's Jews. Himmler declared that deportation of Slovakia's Jews was a priority. To accomplish this, he transferred Alois Brunner from Drancy to Slovakia. Brunner personally directed manhunts and was at the Sered railway station when the first deportees from Slovakia left on 30 September.[41] Using five security police details, Brunner shipped nearly 9,000 Jews to Terezin, Auschwitz, Stutthof, Sachsenhausen and Belsen by the end of the year.[42]

Among those arrested by the Gestapo were Gisi Fleischmann and Rabbi Weissmandel. Fleischmann was tortured by Brunner, but refused to disclose the location of people she was hiding from deportation. She died in Auschwitz. Weissmandel also boarded a transport, but managed to escape (his wife and five children were gassed). On 4 April 1945, the Red Army liberated Bratislava. By that time more than 90 percent of Slovakia's Jews were dead. President Tiso was hanged two years later. Considered an anti-communist hero by some, he offered an epitaph to Slovakia's Jews in 1942 saying, 'In deporting Jews we have simply acted in accordance with the command of God: Slovak, get rid of your enemy!'[43]

THE PARADISE GHETTO OF TEREZIN

Most of the Jews in Slovakia went directly to death camps in Poland. Bohemia's Jews were taken to Terezin, a military town located 40 miles northwest of Prague. Constructed by Joseph II and named for his mother, Terezin was an example of Hapsburg *Schlamperei* (disorder). The fortress with eight ramparts and 30-foot thick walls was never besieged, never defended. Used as a prison for political radicals and war captives, Terezin was opened to civilians in 1888.[44] In December 1941 Jewish workmen arrived from Prague to remodel the fort. Gentiles were ordered out in the summer of 1942. Headquarters for the SS Commandant and his troops were established on the edge of a wooded park. The Nazis made use of a nearby building (*Kleine Festung*) as a punishment block. In July 1943, concentration camp dossiers and other documents from the Reichs Main Security Office were transferred to Terezin. These incriminating records, many of them bearing the inscription *an KLA* (deported to Auschwitz) were burned in April 1945. Between November 1941 and March 1945, 122 trains traveled to Terezin, carrying more than 140,000 Jews from Bohemia, Germany, Denmark and Holland.[45]

Until tracks were extended along Sudstrasse in the spring of 1943, deportees had to trudge two kilometers from the railway junction of Bohusovice. Rena Rosenberger came from Westerbork in 1944. 'We saw spiratic, livid faces, full of curiosity', said Mrs Rosenberger. 'These people had an uneasy expression on their faces and their complexion had a color I have never seen before.'[46] The new arrivals looked no better. Egon Loebner described a group of sick old men and women that arrived from Vienna in September 1942. One woman suddenly shrieked. 'Do you know who I am? I am the daughter of Herzl!' Trude Herzl-Neumann, at 55 the youngest daughter of Theodor Herzl, had come to Terezin from a mental hospital in Vienna where she had been confined for 11 years. On 18 September, this woman, who had been a critic of the Zionist movement, wrote to leaders of the Altestenrat requesting assistance 'in these difficult times'. The note was signed *mit Zionsgruss ergebenst*. Five months later, Trude Herzl-Neumann died. Her ashes were mingled in the crematorium with 23 others who perished that day.[47]

Terezin was governed by a 13-man *Altestenrat*. Headed by a Czech Jacob Edelstein (until November 1943), a German Dr Paul Eppstein (until July 1944) and an Austrian Benjamin Murmelstein (until the camp was liberated) the council shared power with a 200-man Jewish police force under the direction of Karl Lowenstein, a police captain from Minsk. The *Altestenrat* maintained a bank that issued ghetto scrip. It supervised the kitchen staff, women's service, children's homes, medical and sanitation services, a ghetto newspaper and *Freigestaltung* (lectures on Spinoza or ancient Assyria, jazz bands, performances of 'Carmen' and Verdi's 'Requiem').[48]

Excepting Lowenstein (an arrogant man who was thrown into the Kleine Festung in 1943 for trafficking in meal tickets), most of the councilors were men of high principle. Edelstein was a Left Zionist who was universally respected. His deputy, Otto Zucker, had been the head of the Zionist emigration office in Prague. Dr Erich Osterreicher of the labor department, Dr Erich Munk, chief medical officer, Dr Leo Janowitz of the Secretariat, Fredy Hirsch and Gonda Redlich of the *Jugendfursorge* all have been praised by survivors. Originally, Terezin was to house prominents like Rabbi Baeck and Heinrich Stahl of Berlin, Professor Cohen of Amsterdam, and people over 65. When the commandants learned they could profit from Jewish labor in machine shops, mines and construction sites, they retained young, healthy Jews. Then for no apparent reason, the young Jews were deported. When it was decided that Terezin could be used to impress the International Red Cross, the aged and sick were sent off. Still later, officials of the *Altestenrat*, *Feuerwehr*, *Krankenfürsorge*, *Korperhinderte* were deported because they knew too much. Edelstein visited Nisko in the fall of 1939. In March 1941 he advised the *Joodse Raad* in Holland and his own colleagues, 'We have to develop a delaying tactic, only gaining time is our motto. Time is on our side. And we have to preserve human dignity.'[49]

It was a daunting task. Terezin's *kasernes* were supposed to accommodate 7,000 soldiers. There were 58,491 Jews in the summer of 1942.[50] The Housing Office parceled space in multi-tiered bunks to families of five to ten persons. The Raumwirtschaft computed space available to people – 2.4 meters for sick persons, 0.9 for those who were healthy.[51] As Zdenek Lederer noted, 'If Prague had been as densely populated as Theresienstadt its population would have totaled 22.5 million and not one million.'[52] Water from antiquated wells was rationed, four gallons per person per day. There were few functioning lavatories. Workers and their families subsisted on a diet of coffee and bread in the morning, soup, sauerkraut or dumplings at lunch, potato soup for supper. The starvation rations caused disorientation, even suicide. 'You see only old, white-haired people, slowly slinking through the city', reported Dr Ruth Ornstein, 'the signs of death all about them.'[53] When people staggered to their *kasernes*, they found foul-smelling rooms teeming with flies, lice and bedbugs. 'You were bothered by bugs,' said Rena Rosenberger. 'It was a hobby to count the bugs you killed during the night.'[54]

Conditions in the women's *kaserne* were actually better than those in the Hanover barracks, next to the new rail junction. Built for draft animals, the Hanover's stalls served as the *Schleuse* (floodgate or locks) for persons being deported. The blind and mentally deranged lay naked on stone floors in 'ice cold and total darkness' in the Kavalier *kaserne* till the SS whisked them away in September 1942.[55] Five hundred doctors and 1,300 nurses labored in makeshift sick wards in the Sudeten, Dresden and Frontier barracks. For nurse

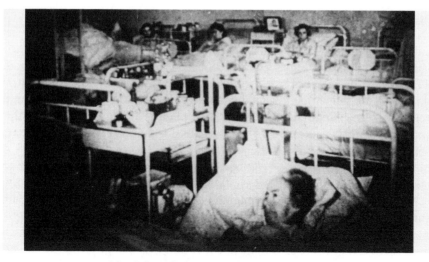

12. A hospital at Terezin (Yad Vashem).

Resi Weglein, the most frightful sight was of 'millions of agonizing spirits' covered with insects, lying in the sick rooms, dying, as 'we nurses knew we could not help them'.[56] In its four years as a transit ghetto, Terezin experienced outbreaks of scarlet fever, typhoid, polio, spotted typhus, diphtheria, dysentery, septicemia and cerebrospinal fever. As the number of sick climbed to 30 percent and the death toll passed 190 per day in the summer of 1942, a confident Commandant Siegfried Seidl gloated, 'The clock ticks well.'[57]

In November 1943, the Nazis found another way to kill – by counting. There were 134 so-called deserters from September transports, another 55 persons missing from Terezin registries. Commandant Burger ordered a counting (*Zahlappel*) of the ghetto's population. On the morning of 11 November 1943, 36,000 persons, some two years of age, were marched out to a meadow that once served as a military campground. They stood, in groups of 100, as they were counted and counted again. Only the critically ill were exempted.[58] From 7 a.m. until 11 p.m., 16 hours, the Jews stood without food or water. '36,000 submissive people, like little children or lambs', wrote Gonda Redlich. 'It was awful. There, outside, men were stripped of their shame, each acting according to his needs, relieving themselves before strange women like animals.'[59] Three hundred persons collapsed and died during the Zahlappel.

TEREZIN: A PERFORMANCE FOR THE RED CROSS

Over the winter of 1943/44 rations inexplicably improved and the ghetto was transformed. Barracks were cleaned and painted, the postal building was refurbished, and a prayer hall was constructed in the gymnasium. Commandant Rahm ordered a sign 'Boy's School' placed over the entry to a former hospital.[60] The ghetto's hospitals were purged of terminal cases and the few patients found themselves in modern beds with fresh linens. A special children's pavilion was laid out, replete with cribs, toys, sandboxes and swings. Checkered tablecloths appeared at street cafes. Store windows boasted sugar, margarine, liver sausages, sardines and canned meat. The *Stadtplatz* (central plaza) was sodded with grass and benches were placed for the few elderly that were left. Twelve hundred rose bushes were planted and in the middle of this wonderful park a pavilion fit for 25 musicians was raised. Twice daily concerts were given to appreciative audiences.[61]

It was all part of the *Verbesserung* (the Embellishment), a scheme to deceive a deputation of the International Red Cross that visited the ghetto in June 1944. By filming Jews lounging to twilight concerts, mending clothes, wandering in and out of Terezin's *Bucherei* (library), the Nazis could energize their own people who were enduring all sorts of privations. The task of supervising 'Aktion Z', as the project was dubbed, was given to SS *Hauptsturmführer* Hans Gunther. Only 40 yards of the documentary survive. The visit of the Red Cross is not on the surviving film. Neither was the deportation of 7,500 persons sent to Poland in the spring of 1944 as part of what the Nazis called the *Auflockerung*, thinning of the ghetto population.[62]

On 23 June, members of the commission, consisting of Frants Hvass of the Danish Red Cross, Dr Juel Henningsen of the Danish Foreign Ministry, Dr M. Rossel from the Swiss Red Cross, and D. Heidenkampf of the German Red Cross, were escorted through the ghetto by Everhard von Thadden of the German Foreign Office, Gunther, Commandant Hans Rahm and Dr

13. The Embellishment, 1944. Terezin children pose for representatives of the International Red Cross (Yad Vashem).

Eppstein who had been supplied with a car and driver.[63] In their reports, Hvass, Hennigsen and Rossel described Terezin as an *Endlager* (final camp) where conditions were 'relatively good'. After the war, representatives of the IRC explained they had not been deceived.

The Embellishment, like the Nazi propaganda film, was a fraud, *irrsinnig Vorbereitungen, irrsinniger Humbug* ('insane preparations, insane humbug') said Edith Ornstein.[64] 'We wanted so much to believe', wrote Resi Weglein, 'that now the terrible hunger would be past. But we saw our hopes dashed to the ground. Two days after this commission disappeared, our meals were stripped back for two weeks. The common cry resounded: *Nie wieder Kommission!*' (Never again commissions).[65] On 16 September 1944, Yom Kippur, Dr Eppstein announced that the Nazis were resuming transports. Men between the ages of 18 and 50 had to go to work in Germany. Inexplicably, they were not to take washbowls, water containers or tools. Eight days after making this announcement, Eppstein was thrown into the Little Fortress. He was shot in October.

Twelve transports carrying nearly 20,000 persons, would leave for Auschwitz that fall. Of 2,038 aboard the last train, 137 survived. The deportations from Terezin had a ripple effect upon Jews already in concentration camps. In Auschwitz, there had been a special section, 30 wooden stables occupied by 5,000 Jews deported from Terezin in September 1943. Another 5,000 people were squeezed in in December 1943. Known as the Czech family camp, its chief kapo was Arno Boehm, a criminal who was not Jewish. The Jewish spokesman was Fredy Hirsch. Although the Czech family camp was less than a kilometer from the crematoria, the inmates believed they were protected by the International Red Cross. On 5 March 1944 the people were told they were being relocated. Apart from minor scuffles and a few suicides (Hirsch took poison), on 7 March inmates in the Family Camp were taken by truck to gas chambers number 2 and 3. As they went to their deaths, they sang 'Hatikvah' and the Czech national anthem. Only 70 persons survived.[66]

TEREZIN: LIBERATION

In the last days of war, Terezin's population swelled to more than 30,000. Thousands of men and women in striped pajamas came stumbling in from labor camps in Germany and the death camps of Poland. According to Kathe Goldschmit Starke, many fell to their deaths when the cattle cars were opened. 'And what came to life was hardly human.'[67] They were, said Leo Holzer, 'heavily infested with typhus, full of vermin, half and completely starved, human ruins'. Some were in convulsions, *der Koerper gluehte in schweren Fieber* (their bodies burning in heavy fever).[68] Adds Rena Rosenberger: 'They were emaciated, starving, half-dead, wild animals. They begrudged their fellow man of his bread and hit each other for a little bit of food.'[69] 'Now for

14. Corpses at the so-called 'Paradise Ghetto' of Terezin (Yad Vashem).

the first time', wrote Leo Holzer, 'we learned for real what fate had befallen our poor brothers and sisters, where our parents, our children had lost their lives. Now for the first time we learned the ghastly truth which earlier, from various pieces of information, we should have guessed, but did not know for certain.'[70]

The Nazis had plans for these survivors. Hans Günther instructed Terezin Commandant Karl Rahm to dig a huge pit near the Litomerice Gate. Once completed, the pit would have been larger than those at Buchenwald where 10,000 Jews were shot to death days before liberation. Rahm also wanted workmen from the ghetto joinery to seal off doors and ventilation ducts in underground passages near the Litomerice and Bohusovice gates. Once completed, the passages could have held about 4,000 people. Said Rena Rosenberger, 'The Germans planned to gasify all of the inhabitants of the ghetto.'[71]

When the Russians entered Prague in the first week of May 1945, they encountered 3,000 Jewish survivors. They also discovered 54 warehouses filled with thousands of religious articles, pianos, carpets and books. The Nazis intended to use synagogues for a state museum on the vanished Jews.[72] At 7:45 p.m. on 8 May 1945, the first Soviet tanks reached the ramparts of

Theresienstadt. A total of 140,000 Jews had passed through these gates. Of these, 33,419 died here, another 86,934 perished in camps and forests of the east. Many of the inmates were children. Counselors and teachers organized education, encouraged religious study, Zionism and Hebrew. They played ping pong, soccer and ghetto monopoly. Youngsters ran food from the soup lines to the weak and elderly in attics. They were encouraged to draw and write poetry. In the midst of this misery, they were bold enough to perform an opera by Hans Krasa, a Czech-Jewish composer who was a disciple of Stravinsky and Schoenberg.

'Brundibar' tells how two children struggle to obtain milk for their sick mother. Pepicek and Aninka go into the streets, not to beg, but to sing for charity. Chased from the corner by the mean organ-grinder Brundibar, Pepicek and Aninka are helped by a dog, a cat and a sparrow – who join them in song and earn a small fortune. Brundibar tries to steal the money but is foiled by the animals and other local children. In the end the children proclaim, 'He who loves justice and will abide by it and who is not afraid is our friend and can play with us.' Brundibar was staged 55 times in the Magdeburg *kaserne* in 1943–44. In September 1944 the composer, Krasa, was deported to Auschwitz. Some 15,000 Jewish children passed through Terezin. Only 100, less than one percent, survived. Speaking for all the survivors, Leo Holzer declared, '*Unsere Angehörigen kamen nicht mehr zurück*' (Our families did not return).[73]

Aktion Reinhard

ORDINARY GERMANS

Throughout the year 1942, Jews were purged from Lodz, Cracow, Kielce, Rzeszow and Pionki in what the Nazis, honoring the memory of their fallen comrade Heydrich, dubbed *Aktion Reinhard*. Himmler appointed SS *Brigadeführer* Odilo Globocnik to assume command of the extermination of Poland's Jews.[1] The 500 reservists of SS Police Battalion 101 were typical of those who carried out the actual killing. Veterans of the earlier campaign in Poland, they were older (mean age 36.5 years) married men drawn from the lower middle class. Three-fourths were fathers who had no affiliation with official Nazi organizations.[2] The unit conducted its first action in Jozefow during the last week of June 1942. The police cordoned off the town and sent 400 men to a labor camp near Lublin. The rest of Jozefow's Jews were marched into the woods where they were shot. Each policeman had to account for five or ten victims. When the massacre was over 1,500 Jews lay dead.[3]

A month later, on the morning of 19 August 1942, the men of Battalion 101 carried out another operation in Lomazy. The battalion herded the town's Jews, many of whom were from Germany, to an athletic field near the school. They sat in the sun for hours while off in the woods 60 Jewish men were digging a pit 30 yards wide by 55 yards long. When a contingent of Ukrainian auxiliaries arrived, the waiting Jews were lined up in columns of six or eight. Twenty-five old men were stripped, clubbed and ordered to crawl on the ground. The rest were beaten into the woods. As they tumbled into the pit, the Germans and Ukrainians shot them. Later, they raked the victims with rifle fire. Seventeen hundred Jews perished at Lomazy that hot August day.[4]

The men of SS Order Police Battalion 101 helped deport nearly 50,000 Jews from Parczew, Miedzyrezec, Radzyn, Lukow, Bila, Komarwoka, Wohyn and Czermierniki. They killed another 33,000 Jews in Serokomla, Talcyn, Kock, Parczew, Konskowola, Majdanek and Poniatowa.[5] Few of these men, or other members of the SS were psychopaths. Einsatzgruppe leaders Arhur Nebe and Otto Rausch had been police inspectors, Otto Ohlendorf an economist, Ernst Biberstein a Protestant minister. Like the men of Police Battalion 101, they were, as Christopher Browning put it, 'ordinary men', whose indoctrination convinced them that the extermination of Jews was a prophylaxis. Karl Frenzel, one-time commandant of Sobibor, declared, 'I was no anti-Semite, but we had to do our duty'.[6] Rudolf Hoess, commandant of Auschwitz, said virtually the same thing at Nuremberg, 'From our entire training the thought of refusing an order just didn't enter one's head, regardless of what kind of order it was.'[7]

TISHA B'AV 1942

The Jews in Warsaw felt the impact of *Einsatz Reinhard* in July 1942. Through the month of June rumors circulated of a transfer of 60,000 persons from the ghetto. On 2 July, more than 100 Jews, including ten members of the *Ornungsdienst* were taken from the ghetto and shot. Between 15 and 20 July, 700 Jews with foreign documents were detained at Pawiak Prison. The Nazis also arrested Abraham Gepner, the respected head of the *Judenrat*'s ration office. On 20 July, *Judenältester* Czerniakow learned that the ghetto had been transferred to the jurisdiction of SS *Oberscharführer* Hans Hoefle and the *Transferstelle*. Most ominous, 500 Ukrainian and Lithuanian militia replaced older Germans patrolling the ghetto.

On 19 July, Himmler issued written instructions to *SS Obergruppenführer* Friedrich Kruger calling for the resettlement of the Jewish population of the Government General by the end of December.[8] At 10 a.m. on 22 July 1942, Hoefle informed Jewish officials that all non-essential persons in the ghetto were to be sent east. Exemptions would be granted to council members, their aides and families, the Jewish Police and Ambulance Service, patients in hospitals, and persons working for German companies. Deportees were to take 15 kilograms of belongings and food for a three-day journey. Anyone failing to report or trying to disrupt the transports would be shot. Six thousand persons per day were to be transferred from the Umschlagplatz (collection station) at Stawki Street. The German order to clear the ghetto was issued on the ninth of Ab, the date that commemorates some of the greatest tragedies in Jewish history.[9]

Only one member of the *Judenrat* paused to ask, 'Gentlemen, before you pass to the technical means of executing the order, stop and think should this be done.' Several days later a conference was held at the headquarters of ZTOS (the Jewish Society for Social Welfare) with representatives from most political and religious groups attending. Sadly, they concurred with the recommendations of Rabbi Zishe Friedman and historian Israel Schipper. Said Friedman, 'To fight the Germans is absolutely senseless. The Germans can liquidate us all within a few days. And if we do not fight, the ghetto will last longer and then perhaps the miracle will occur.' God would not permit the extermination of the Jewish people. The Allies, the Red Army, one day would bring freedom. Taking note of the Jewish experience during the Crusades, Schipper also counseled non-violence. 'Self-defense means the destruction of the whole Warsaw Ghetto!' In war everyone must make sacrifices, 'So, we, too, have to sacrifice to save a certain number of people.'[10]

Ghetto residents wanted desperately to believe Nazi promises that children who were registered would be sent to Palestine. Some felt that conditions in a new work camp could not be any worse than the ghetto. At the end of the month, several thousand ragged, broken souls were lured to the Umschlagplatz by the offer of bread and marmalade. Polish observers indulged in none of this wishful thinking. On the day Hoefle visited the *Judenrat*, Anton Syzmanowski, an officer in the *Armia Krajowa*, told his superiors that it made no sense for the Germans to create a blissful work camp for the Jews. In reality, they were telling them, 'Line up in rows so that we can kill you, but have your jewelry ready to save us trouble!'[11]

The Jewish police faithfully performed their duties. Like their chief Josef Szerynski, a notorious anti-Semite who had been an inspector in the Polish police before the war, many were converts to Christianity, designated Jews by the Nuremberg Laws. Warsaw's Jews described 'Colonel' Szerynski as prominently wearing a cross. One of his top aides (Schmerling) was an apostate. The Jewish underground tried, unsuccessfully, to assassinate Szerynski and his successor Jakob Leikin. Both were undone by their own greed. Szerynski was arrested for stealing a batch of fur coats intended for the Wehrmacht in Russia. Leikin and another policeman named Furst peddled exemptions for 5,000 zlotys. Leikin's wife and child were executed by the Germans.[12]

These jackbooted collaborators tried to impress the Nazis during the daily 'Aktions'. The SS, Ukrainian/Lithuanian auxiliaries and Polish Blues would cordon off a neighborhood in the morning. Then Jewish police, armed with batons, chased people from their apartments. Those without work permits were taken to the Umschlagplatz. Craftsmen were deported while Orthodox Jews who recently shaved their beards were excused. Children who tried to hide were shot when the Ukrainians and SS combed the Jewish living quarters. Staircases and streets were littered with broken window glass, prams, cribs, musical instruments, bedding, suitcases, abandoned sewing machines and the most precious, yet worthless of personal belongings – family photographs.[13]

Emmanuel Ringelblum, the chronicler of the Warsaw ghetto, deplored the cruelty of the Jewish police as they scurried about seeking their daily quota of five heads. Wondered Ringelblum, 'Where did Jews get such murderous violence?'[14] Adam Czerniakow had no illusions about what these deportations meant. On 24 July, he committed suicide. On his desk was a note to his wife asking forgiveness. There were also several scraps of paper. On one was scratched a number '7,000'. The Nazis were raising the quota. There is a dispute about what was written on the other slip. Some witnesses maintain it read 'to the end'. Czerniakow was succeeded by Marek Lichtenbaum. That same day, the *Judenrat* tried to counter rumors by issuing a notice that affirmed 'resettlement of the unproductive population in the Jewish quarter of Warsaw is really to the East'.[15]

THE UMSCHLAGPLATZ

The Umschlagplatz was a gloomy set of buildings surrounded by barbed wire where people waited for the trains that would carry them away. They waited in darkened rooms where the stench was unbearable. The halls echoed with the cries of children and choking sounds of the aged. There were protests from hundreds of persons who had been baptized shortly before the war. The Ukrainian and SS guards patrolled with attack dogs. To maintain terror, they randomly shot individuals on the platform. One Gestapo man allegedly was credited with more than 1,000 kills at the Umschlagplatz.

On one occasion, a Jewish man grabbed a German by the throat as he was being loaded into a cattle car, another snatched a Ukrainian's rifle. They were both shot dead. Some young people tried to escape from the fifth floor of the warehouse across a plank stretched to a building on Niska Street. Survivors recall how the poet Hillel Zeitlin, a copy of the Zohar in hand, marched with dignity through a path of Ukrainian guards to take his place in one of the boxcars in September 1942. Rabbi Zwi Michelson, at 86 the oldest rabbi in Warsaw and the author of 43 books, was deported earlier. A colleague, Rabbi Yitzhak Meir Kanal, refused to be led away. He snatched the gun of a German soldier and was shot on the spot. Rabbi Kanal was 82 years old.

Perhaps the most audacious case of heroism involved *Judenrat* officials Nahum Remba and Ala Golomb-Grinberg. They established a two-room 'clinic' complete with hospital beds near the wire of the Umschlagplatz. Dressed in white, Remba roamed the platform, picking individuals who supposedly were incapable of travel. These people (invariably healthy young men and women) would be whisked back to the ghetto. Hundreds were saved by Remba before the Nazis caught on to this ruse and deported him.[16] Marek Edelman of the Jewish Fighting Organization offered special praise for the ghetto's medical personnel who supplied injections of cyanide or morphine. Said Edelman, 'Cyanide is now the most irreplaceable thing. It brings a quiet, peaceful death, it saves from the horror of the cars.'[17]

Every morning and at about five in the afternoon, locomotives pulled away from the Gdansk railway station. At a time when the Nazis had problems securing transport for troops and military supplies, 200 freight cars were diverted to *Aktion Reinhard*.[18] One hundred men, women and children were stuffed into boxcars fit for eight horses. Instinctively, the frightened crowds made for the higher floors in the holding centers. As Marek Edelman recalled, 'Just to get away, higher up, further from the chase. One might be lucky enough to miss one more transport, to save another day of life.'[19] It did not help. Fifty thousand Jews were shipped out on 5–6 September 1942 during what was dubbed 'the Kettle'. (SS Officer Witasek who directed the operation supposedly exclaimed, 'Ah, but we had a fine pot!')[20] Two months later, 1,300 members of the Jewish Police who assisted in the Kettle, were loaded, along with their families, into boxcars at the Umschlagplatz.

THE SAGA OF JANUSZ KORCZAK

Henryk Goldszmit was a Jew born in 1877 when much of Poland was still part of Russia. Trained as a physician, he served in both the Russo-Japanese War and World War I. In inter-war, republican Poland, Goldszmit became a celebrity, as a neurologist who gave advice over the radio and as a writer of children's stories under his pen name 'Janusz Korczak'. During the inter-war years, Korczak set up several orphanages in Warsaw. Nondenominational institutions, they flew the red and white flag of Poland, a tree or four-leaf clover, the Jewish Mogen David. The doctor surrounded himself with nurses and counselors, including his friend Stephania Wilczysnka, all of whom were advocates of the Montessori system of education. Children made rules, meted out rewards and imposed punishments in the homes. Adults were there to prepare each child to become self-sufficient at the age of 14.

Korczak would write later of a dream he had at age five – to create a world

15. Memorial to Janusz Korczak (Henryk Goldszmit), Jewish pediatrician who tried to protect children in the Warsaw Ghetto.

where 'there wouldn't be any dirty, ragged and hungry children with whom one was not allowed to play in the backyard'.[21] On one occasion, he took a group of visitors through a dormitory and declared, 'Listen. You will never hear anything as lovely as the symphony of a sleeping child's breathing.' In the ghetto, he offered all kinds of advice. Never leave a child alone after he/she had a bad dream.[22] Never refuse to tell a story 'over and over and over again'. 'The same fairy tale endlessly repeated [is] like a sonata, a favorite sonnet, like a sculpture without the sight of which the day seems colorless.'[23]

Like Emmanuel Ringelblum, Korczak was a Zionist. He had been to Palestine in 1932–33 but returned to Warsaw. When the Jews were confined to 'the District of the Damned', he established a home for 195 children on Krochmalna, then Gesia, and finally Sienna streets. Korczak and his aides organized lectures, games, concerts for their wards. The doctor risked beatings to obtain food for his orphans. When one merchant informed him it was illegal to sell such goods to Jews, Korczak replied, 'In that case give it to me as a gift.'

When the Nazis ordered the ghetto be cleared, the doctor was suffering from heart and bladder trouble, pleurisy, a chronic eye infection and swelling of the legs. Often, he was so weary after soliciting supplies, he had to lay in bed for extended periods of time. Korczak had no illusions about what would happen to his children. In a long passage in his diary on euthanasia, Korczak mused how easy it would be to kill the children with a dose of poison. 'One spoonful will alleviate the pain like medicine.' But just as quickly, he added: 'When during the dark hours I pondered over the killing (putting to sleep) of infants and old people of the Jewish ghetto, I saw it as a murder of the sick and feeble, as an assassination of the innocents.'[24]

What happened next is clouded with myth. In its simplest telling by Ringelblum, when Korczak was informed that his orphanage was being closed, he 'built up the attitude that everyone [including directors of the home] should go to the Umschlag together'.[25] According to Aaron Zeitlin, Korczak was visited by an SS officer who told him that his orphans were to be evacuated but that the doctor and his staff would be exempted. (In another version, the officer supposedly was a racial German who had been protected in one of Korczak's orphanages as a child.) Zeitlin embellishes his tale with a discussion between Korczak and the more practical Wilczynska where the latter suggests fleeing the ghetto.[26]

Genia Silkes, a courier to the Aryan sector of Warsaw, maintains that Korczak told the children, 'You are going to summer camp, a vacation. Dress in your best clothes. Please sing.' They put cookies in their pockets. The children were not deceived. One asked him: 'Tell me, teacher, will it be very painful?'[27] As the children marched along Sliska Street, dressed in middy blouses, yellow stars stitched to blue jackets, Joseph Hyams claims the procession reminded onlookers of a 'field of buttercups'. Igor Newerly claims the children marched in fours under their flag – 'the gold four-leaf clover on a field of green ... because green is the symbol of everything that grows'.[28] For Hillel Seidman, the line of children was 'small, tiny, rather precocious, emaciated, weak, shriveled and shrunk'. Seidman allows that the children were orderly, as Korczak moved from one child to another, straightening a cap, buttoning a coat, wiping a tear. 'The children are calm', wrote Seidman, 'but inwardly they must feel it. They must sense it intuitively, otherwise how could you explain the deadly seriousness on their pale little faces?'[29]

Perhaps the most accurate portrayals of those final moments came from Wladyslaw Szpilman, the pianist who managed to survive on the Aryan side of Warsaw, and an account left by Nahum Remba with Ringelblum's secret archives. On the day of the deportation, Szpilman was walking through Gesia Street when he happened upon Korczak and his aides leading the orphans to the Umschlagplatz. Wrote Szpilman:

> The column was led by an SS man who, like most of the Germans, liked children, even those whom he was shortly going to kill. Particularly he seemed to be fond of a twelve-year-old violinist, who carried his instrument under his arm. He ordered him to take his place at the head of the column and to start playing – and so they marched.
>
> When I met the procession on Gesia street, all the children were singing together, with beaming faces, while the little violinist was playing. Korczak marched with two of the youngest children in his arms. Their faces were also smiling, apparently he had been telling them funny stories.[30]

According to Remba, the scene at the freight cars was 'an organized silent protest against this barbarism'. There was no chaos. 'All of the children had formed ranks in rows of four, with Korczak at their head, his eyes lifted to the sky; holding two children by their small hands, he led the procession. The second unit was led by Stefania Wilczynska, the third by Broniatowska – her children had blue backpacks – the fourth unit was led by Szternfeld from the boarding school on Twarda Street. Even the Police stood still and saluted. When the Germans saw Korczak, they asked: 'Who is this man?'[31]

MAJDANEK

Jewish deportees in Poland did not have to travel far. The Nazis had been developing a series of penal camps since early 1940. In the summer of 1941, Himmler instructed Globocnik to develop a slave labor facility on the outskirts of Lublin. The camp, known as Majdanek, measured 675 acres, much of it serving DAW (*Deutsche Ausrustungswerke*, the German Supply Establishment) and the SS WVHA as a clearing house for property taken from prisoners. Majdanek was no more than two miles from the center of Lublin. Satellite camps operated on Lipowa Street within the city and at a nearby airfield. A five-story building on Chopin Street served as a veritable

16. Memorial sculpture at Majdanek (seen close up), only a few hundred
yards from Lublin.

department store of confiscated goods. There were thousands of safety razors
and pen knives in one room, mountains of yarn in another. One floor contained women's dresses and blouses, another 800,000 pairs of shoes, boots
and bedroom slippers. There were rooms filled with gold watches, diamond
pins, furs, quilts and underwear. Majdanek even had a children's floor, replete
with notebooks, pen holders, erasers, domino sets, jigsaw puzzles, marbles,
celluloid dolls and teddy bears.[32] As of December 1943 the WVHA collected
more than $70 million from the prisoners of Majdanek.[33]

Majdanek's 144 barracks were subdivided into seven so-called fields.
Whether in Fields I and II or V and VI, guards like Anton Tuman, Helen
Braunsteiner and Lena Donat beat the prisoners mercilessly. Konnilyn Feig
claims that the killing was so extensive that prisoners welcomed a transfer to
Auschwitz.[34] The Jews of Lublin were purged on the night of 23–24 March
1942 when 108 children under the age of nine were taken to the outskirts of
town and shot. A total of 2,500 people died that night, another 25,000 were
deported to concentration camps at Belzec and Trawniki, and 3,000 were
taken to barracks in Majdanek.[35] Guests witnessed the gassing of 8,000 Cracow
Jews in the spring of 1943. Before the Nazis constructed a crematorium, they
disposed of the remains by burning stacks of corpses saturated with gasoline.

Over 18,000 Jews were murdered in Majdanek on 3 November 1943.
Operation *Erntefest* (Harvest Festival) was retribution for Jewish rebellions
in Warsaw, Bialystok, Sobibor and Treblinka. At the end of October a group
of Soviet PWs were assigned the task of digging a set of zigzag trenches
behind Fields V and VI. On the night of 2–3 November, Jews in Fields III
and IV were rousted from their barracks. They were joined by women and
the sick, many of whom came from the typhus barrack. The actual killing
lasted from 6 in the morning to 5 in the afternoon. Jews in Poniatow, Trawniki

17. Memorial sculpture at Majdanek seen from a distance.

and other nearby camps were also killed that day. When it was over, there were only 311 Jewish women and 300 men alive in Majdanek.[36] Some 350,000 people representing 50 nationalities would die in Majdanek before the Russians overran Lublin in July 1944.[37]

VERNICHTUNGSLAGER: BELZEC

When the Nazi hierarchy decided to exterminate all Jews in the winter of 1941/42, SS *Oberführer* Christian Wirth, a policeman from Stuttgart was given the task of constructing Vernichtungslager that would achieve the goal. Wirth's Kommando developed three extermination camps: Treblinka northeast of Warsaw, Belzec and Sobibor near the Bug River in the East. Each of these camps was small, no more than a mile square. Located in relatively isolated areas, they operated amid a sympathetic populace. As Itzhak Lichtman later testified, when his group marched to Krasknystaw station on their way to Sobibor, Polish adults and children mocked them, *Hey, Zydzi, idziecie na spalenie* (Jews you are going to burn).[38]

The experience of the Einsatzgruppen and police units demonstrated that shooting was wasteful and psychologically taxing. Use of carbon monoxide, while effective to a point, was still inadequate in view of the millions of Jews and other racial undesirables that had to be liquidated. At Belzec the Nazis devised a different form of mass murder. Deportees who survived the trip to this camp 60 miles northeast of Lublin were driven by Ukrainian guards into what appeared to be a large delousing chamber. In fact the room had a metal floor. Once the victims were locked in, a current of electricity was released, killing most instantaneously. Like carbon monoxide, electrocution was a messy, cumbersome form of execution. A Polish policeman testified how he saw prisoners laying naked, jerking convulsively in the barracks:

> The guards keep on shooting at the throng. Corpses are scattered every-where ... Every few minutes the guards pick a number of men to clear the dead which are piled up alongside the fence. This, too, is done without any emotion, without a single expression in their faces as though they are completely oblivious of what they are doing. these are no longer normal beings but one large convulsive mass breathing its last.[39]

A post-war commission in Poland estimated 600,000 Jews perished in Belzec.

SOBIBOR

Where Chelmno, Belzec and Majdanek evolved into death camps, Sobibor, located between Wlodawa and Chelm, was designed solely for killing. Opened in April 1942, the camp was commanded by SS *Haupsturmführer* Franz Stangl, another veteran of the T-4 program. Sobibor's five gas chambers were tested with the execution of 150 Jews from nearby Wlodawa followed by thousands from Hrubieszow, Mielec and Krasnystaw. Out of 7,000 people who left Hrubieszow, three were permitted to live.[40]

Sobibor functioned as a charnel house for Jews from Poland, Ukraine, Byelorussia and, in the summer of 1943, Holland. Survivors told how 300 new arrivals from Majdanek were doused with chlorine causing some to burn and peel before they died. Another 1,500 Jews from Majdanek were starved

18. The loading platform at the death camp of Sobibor, where 350,000 Jews were murdered.

to death because the gas chambers were not operating.[41] Sometimes deportees did not reach the camp. On the way from Opole and Wanwilice, peasants stood with shovels as Jews passed by. When they saw one who was well-dressed, they would hand the German or Ukrainian guards a liquor bottle. The man would then be shot and the Polish peasants could take his shoes and clothing.[42]

In the camp, prisoners were beaten, degraded and shot. Women were raped before they were executed. *Oberwachmann* Paul Groth set his Saint Bernard dog on Jews. Groth organized flogging parades, where inmates had to run a gauntlet of Ukrainians armed with whips and rubber clubs. Inmates who begged for water were shot in the head by Hermann Michel, a *Volksdeutsch* nicknamed 'the Preacher'. When a newborn baby was discovered in one of the barracks, *Oberscharführer* Gustav Wagner ordered it be drowned in a latrine.[43] Sobibor had a small gauge railway that was supposed to carry the sick to a 'Lazaret' (hospital). In fact, the cars took their loads to a giant pit 200 meters beyond the Appelplatz where Ukrainians, directed by *Oberscharführer* Bredov, shot and dumped the Jews.[44] A survivor, Moshe Bahir, recalls a poignant moment in 1943 when Franz Reichleitner served as camp commandant:

> Once there was an old Jew who was brought in a transport of thousands and who did not allow them to drag him forcibly so they threw him into the freight car. By chance, camp commander Franz Reichleitner was present. The Jew declared that he did not believe the lies that had been told to the arrivals about a 'hospital, light work and good living conditions.' By his own effort he got out of the car, bent down and in his trembling hands scooped up two fistfuls of sand, turned to Karl Frantz, the SS man, and said, 'You see how I'm scattering this sand slowly grain by grain, and it's carried away by the breeze? That's what will happen to you; this whole great Reich of yours will vanish like flying dust and passing smoke!' The old man went along with the whole convoy, reciting 'Hear O Israel' and when he said the word, 'the Lord is one,' he again turned to Frantz and slapped him with all his might. The German was about to attack him, but Reichleitner, who was standing by, enjoying the whole performance, said to Frantz, 'I'll settle the account with him. You go on with your job.' The camp commander took the old man aside and killed him on the spot, in front of his family and all the people in the convoy.[45]

More than 350,000 Jews perished in Sobibor before the camp was put out of commission by a revolt of prisoners on 14 October 1943.

TREBLINKA

Most Jews from the Warsaw Ghetto were sent to Treblinka, a camp located off the Bialystok line near Malkinia, 50 miles northeast of the Polish capital. Treblinka A was opened in 1940 to house Polish troublemakers, mainly farmers who slacked in their production for the New Order. In November

1941 saboteurs and criminals were brought here under orders from Ludwig Fischer, SS Police Chief in Warsaw. Four months later, a second camp, Treblinka B, was carved out amid the poplars and sandy hills. Transports began arriving at Treblinka in May 1942 and continued through 2 August 1943, bringing Jews not just from Warsaw but other parts of Poland and the Reich. Relentlessly they came, for 396 days, three or four trains daily, each consisting of 50 or 60 wagons, each in turn holding 80 to 150 human beings. Officials of the *Reichsführer*'s office and the German Ministry of Transport exchanged compliments on the efficiency of the convoys.[46] Peasants profiteered by selling the deportees water at 100 zlotys ($5.00) a bottle as they neared the camp.

As the music of Strauss, Lehar or Offenbach blared from loudspeakers, members of a 200-man *Sonderkommando* wearing coveralls and blue neckerchiefs marshaled the passengers out to the Appelplatz. They listened as an SS man welcomed them to what seemed to be a bona fide station. To the left stood a cashier's booth with signs proclaiming 'Trains to Bialystok, Siedlce, Warsaw' and a station master's office. There was a restaurant (closed), a baggage room, even a false hospital off to one side. Treblinka had neatly trimmed gardens, a zoo, heavy-duty cranes and several oversized chimneys. There were placards designating areas for tailors, shoemakers and other skilled workers to assemble. Smiling guards instructed the deportees to leave their belongings on the platform and proceed to a delousing barrack. Paper money, coins, watches, jewelry were to be deposited with the cashier's office.[47] While some of the deportees were skeptical (why did the railway line end at the camp, what was the stench pervading the camp, why were the *Sonderkommando* so uncommunicative, why were the strongest men and women separated from the rest of the arrivals) most were taken in by the Nazi *trompe l'oeil*. All of this happened so quickly. There were only a few SS men and Ukrainians

19. Memorial at the death camp of Treblinka.

20. Symbolic steles at Treblinka, where 700,000 Jews were murdered.

patrolling the entire area. There was nothing to fear. Later arrivals would be forewarned. Two trainloads that refused to unload were massacred by automatic weapons.

Just prior to the march to the baths, kapos distributed soap. The deportees lined up ten abreast and walked along a cinder path dubbed 'the Path of Heaven' that took them into Treblinka B. Two hundred meters from the main square and concealed by trees the Nazis had constructed two large, innocent-looking brick structures. They were the gas chambers. Death House II contained three gas chambers. Death House I was substantially larger, 40 yards by 25 yards consisting of ten chambers each approximately 35 square meters. Treblinka could 'process' 2,000 persons per day. All pretense of tenderness was dropped in those last moments:

> At the head a group of women and children is driven, beaten by the accompanying Germans, whips in their hands. The group is driven ever quicker; ever heavier blows fall upon the heads of the women who are together with the shouts and curses of the Germans interrupt the silence of the forest. The people finally realize that they are going to their death. At the entrance of death-house No. 1 the chief himself stands, a whip in his hand; beating them in cold blood, he drives the women into the chambers. The floors of the chambers are slippery. The victims slip and fall, and they cannot get up for new numbers of forcibly driven victims fall upon them. The chief throws small children into the chambers over the heads of the women. When the execution chambers are filled the doors are hermetically closed and the slow suffocation of living people begins, brought about by the steam issuing from the numerous vents in the pipes. At the beginning, stifled cries penetrate to the outside; gradually they quiet down and 15 minutes later the execution is complete.[48]

Yankel Wiernik was one of the few survivors from Treblinka. As a *Sonder-kommando*, he witnessed the brutality of two Ukrainian guards known as Nikolai and Ivan 'the Terrible'. These men operated the machinery for the death houses. They also delighted in tormenting lines of naked people standing in the cold. Recalled Wiernik, 'Tiny tots stood barefoot and naked in the open. For a long period they awaited their turn in the gas chambers. The children's feet froze to the earth. They wept and shuddered. Ivan's favorite victims were the little ones. He would tear a child from its mother's grasp, then holding it by feet or hand, smash its head against a wall.'[49] When the doors to the buildings were opened Ivan, wielding a pipe, Nikolai, armed with a sabre, would force people in.

At Treblinka, the Nazis killed by suffocation (pumping air out of death chambers), pumping steam into the rooms, and with carbon monoxide generated by diesel engines. While the killing took place, members of the *Lumpensortierung* (sorting barracks) went through belongings of the depor-tees. When the gassing was finished, the *Sonderkommando* would hose down the tangled bodies, making it easier to separate the dead. The prisoner detail deposited corpses in four large burial pits carved out in Camp B by the cranes or burned them in stacks of cordwood known as 'the Roast'. According to Leon Poliakov, 800,000 Jews were murdered in Treblinka.[50]

KNOWLEDGE AND DENIAL

The novelists John Hersey and Leon Uris claim that Warsaw's Jews learned the destination of the transports by marking boxcars with chalk and monitoring their return. Acting upon the advice of a Polish railway worker, Zalman Friedrych tracked the trains to Sokolow, where he learned from villagers, 'terrible things were happening in Treblinka'.[51] While in Sokolow, he encountered Azriel Wallach, nephew of Soviet diplomat Maxim Litvinov. Weak and in rags, Wallach related how he witnessed mass gassings in Treblinka before escaping.[52]

It is clear from reading journal entries in 1942 that the Jews of Warsaw knew about Treblinka. Ringelblum talks of the methods of killing in the 'bath' – gas, steam, electricity. He mentions Jewish grave diggers with 'yellow patches on their knees', and tractors that plowed under the ashes of burned Jews. He scores the naivete of Jews from western Europe who believed Treblinka to be an industrial factory.[53] Yet even Ringelblum laments the response of his fellow Jews in Warsaw. Writing on 15 October 1942, he asked: 'Why didn't we resist when they began to resettle 300,000 Jews from Warsaw? Why did we allow ourselves to be led like sheep to the slaughter? Why did everything come so easy to the enemy? Why didn't the hangmen suffer a single casualty? Why could 50 SS men with the help of a division of some 200 Ukrainian guards and an equal number of Letts, carry the operation out so smoothly?'[54]

Late in August 1942 Leon Feiner, chairman of the central committee of the Bund, tried to explain Jewish behavior to Shmuel Zygelboim, one of two members of the Polish National Council in London. Feiner noted the lack of support from abroad, the absence of hope inside the ghetto. He spoke of illusions nurtured by the enemy, feelings of self-preservation common to officials of the *Judenrat*.[55] Polish Jews had been physically abused, psychologically battered for centuries. Three years of Nazi occupation weakened their will to live. Many were starving or sick. Lacking training and resources, armed resistance seemed futile. Secular Jews placed their faith in civilization. The Orthodox consoled themselves reading the book of Job. Mothers and fathers did everything they were told in the misguided notion that compliance would save their children.

In June 1942, Ringelblum wrote: 'Does the world know about our suffering? And if it knows, why is it silent? Why is the world not stirred when tens of thousands of Jews are shot in Ponari? Why is the world silent when tens of thousands of Jews are poisoned in Chelmno? Why is the world silent when hundreds of thousands of Jews are massacred in Galicia and other newly occupied areas?' Ringelblum dismissed the notion that the world was inured to suffering by the rivers of blood (Russian, Chinese, English) that were being spilled daily. His conclusion was that London 'didn't know what was happening in detail'.[56] In fact, the free world obtained information on the death camps in the spring of 1942. Letters from the ghetto told how members of the family *Akhenu* (our people, the Jews) with the exception of *Miss Eisenzweig* (iron workers) had been invited by *Mr Jaeger* (hunter, i.e. the Germans) to his mansion called *Kever* (in Hebrew, the grave). People felt lonely because Uncle *Gerusch* (deportation) and his friend *Miso* (death) worked in Warsaw. Other letters spoke of difficult times when *Ami* (our people) marries Miss *Harigevich* (*harog* – to kill) or when *Alifowski* (from alofim, thousands) moves to *Kiloyon* (annihilation) or *Adamowski* (earth) streets.[57]

As western diplomats and strategists debated the nuances of such codewords, trains moved inexorably to Belzec, Chelmno, Sobibor, Majdanek and Treblinka. Meanwhile, the Nazis failed to realize that by taking away the weak they were creating conditions that would give rise to armed rebellion. By the end of 1942, the ghettos were populated, for the most part, with young men and women stripped of any illusions.

18

Jewish Armed Resistance

WARSAW: THE JEWISH FIGHTING ORGANIZATION

On 16 February 1943, Heinrich Himmler issued the following instructions to SS *Gruppenführer* Friedrich Kruger in Cracow:

> For security reasons I order the destruction of the Warsaw Ghetto after having transferred the concentration camp to another place. On execution you will salvage the material to be found there and those buildings which are still serviceable. The destruction of the Ghetto and the transfer of the camp are necessary; without such measures it is impossible to restore calm to Warsaw and put an end to all the criminality which will continue as long as the Ghetto exists. Kindly furnish me with a detailed plan for the destruction of the ghetto. The district today inhabited by 500,000 persons of low degree, and which therefore cannot be used by Germans, must be absolutely razed to the ground. Warsaw, a city of a million inhabitants, a dangerous center in a continual state of ferment and rebellion, must absolutely be reduced in size.[1]

Himmler's order was prompted by an armed clash that had occurred when the Nazis attempted another roundup of Jews on 18 January. Ten German troopers were killed before the SS secured control of the ghetto.[2] Responding to this challenge, Himmler decreed that the ghetto be obliterated. In its place he suggested a housing development for Aryans or a park with a monument celebrating the destruction of the Jews. All of this to be accomplished by 20 April, in time for Hitler's 54th birthday.

The Nazis had been opposed by units of the Jewish Fighting Organization (*Zydowska Organizacja Bojowa*). The ZOB evolved from several Zionist groups – *Hashomer Hatzair, Dror, Gordonia* and *Akiba* – which had begun to strike back at the Nazis with illegal newspapers in August 1940. Mimeographed sheets like *El Al* (Upwards), *Neged Hazerem* (Against the Current), *Poletarischer Gedank* (Proletarian Thought) kept Jews in the ghetto informed of the invasion of Yugoslavia, America's entry into war, and the assassination of Heydrich. The journals quoted Peretz, who 'taught us to love and appreciate our life', André Maurois's rule that 'a people that is not ready to die for freedom will lose that freedom', and the simple message from Sholom Asch's *Kiddush Hashem*. In that book, we meet a Lublin Jew standing near a shop.

A passerby asks him: 'Your shop is empty, what are you selling?' The Jew replies, 'I sell faith.'[3]

In October 1941, Warsaw's Jews contacted the resistance in Bialystok and Vilna. In January 1942, again in March, other political parties in the ghetto were invited to join with the *Hechalutz*. When the deportations began in 1942, Bundists and General Zionists agreed to coordinate their activities with the ZOB. A central committee headed by Yitzhak Zukerman, Menahem Kirschenbaum and Abrasza Blum created units for propaganda, finance and supplies, intelligence and combat. The latter numbered 22 groups, four from the Bund, two from Poale Zion, four from leftist organizations, the rest from *Hechalutz*. The leader of the ZOB was a 23-year-old member of Hashomer Hatzair, Mordecai Anielewicz.[4] Revisionist Zionists led by Paul Frenkel and the communists led by Jacob Berman formed their own combat squads.[5]

In December 1942, the ZOB purchased ten pistols from the Polish Home Army at a cost of 12,000 zlotys each ($600). Two months later, the Polish Government-in-Exile shipped the Jews 50 revolvers, 50 hand grenades and four boxes of explosives. The Jews in the ghetto added rifles, Molotov cocktails, mines, supplies of benzine, hydrochloric acid and potassium for chemical bombs, even a few gas masks and German uniforms to their arsenal. Men, women and children tunneled bunkers, carved out hiding places beneath trapdoors, behind walled up alcoves, in attics. Buildings were linked by passageways cut through walls.[6] Jews also became familiar with escape routes to the Aryan side through the sewers at Prosta, Ogrodowa and Franciszanska streets.

All of these groups endorsed goals declared by the ZOB in December 1942: opposition to resettlement and punishment of collaborators.[7] Jews and Poles averaged more than 200 acts of sabotage monthly. Ghetto fighters assassinated six collaborators and three SS policemen that same winter.[8] When Walter Toebbens, the principal employer in the ghetto, tried to persuade men working in his shops to relocate voluntarily, they responded by burning a warehouse filled with furniture. Several factories that produced mattresses, beds and blankets for the SS were torched on 6 March. Members of the Jewish Fighting Organization clashed with the SS on 13 March. That same day, 10,000 persons were cleared from the Cracow ghetto and sent to Plaszow.[9] Jews in Warsaw were warned that the Nazis planned a similar action for their ghetto.[10]

There were 70,000 Jews left in the city, distributed over four ghetto areas. According to David Wdowinski, a Revisionist leader, the Gestapo tried to sow dissension among Jews by sponsoring their own 'Association of Free Jews'. Commanded by a convert, Captain Lonsky, the Association published its own journal and tried to promote rebellion before Jews were prepared militarily or psychologically.[11] Much as the *Judenrat*, it was ignored, As

Chairman Marek Lichtenbaum told his German handlers, 'I have no power in the ghetto; another government rules here!'[12]

THE BATTLE OF THE WARSAW GHETTO

The truth of those words became evident when SS police chief Friedrich Von Sammern-Frankenegg sent troops to clear the ghetto on Monday, 19 April – the first day of Passover. The SS, assisted by Ukrainian auxiliaries and Polish Blues, 850 men in all, began assembling outside the ghetto at 2 a.m. Two light French tanks and artillery were also moved into position.[13] About 4 a.m. the Nazis began moving into the larger ghetto in small groups. By 7 a.m., they had coalesced into larger, confident units. As they strutted, singing to the intersection of Mila and Zamenhofa streets, the site of the 18 January uprising, they were again attacked. This time, however, the Jews were better armed.

Jewish commentators maintain 'bodies flew everywhere' when a mine beneath the main gate was detonated.[14] The attack inflicted such great injuries, writes Israeli historian Yisrael Gutman, that 'the Germans retreated and dispersed, leaving their casualties lying on the street'.[15] Chaim Frimmer, a survivor of the clash, agreed: 'The battle lasted for about half an hour. The Germans retreated leaving many dead and wounded in the street.'[16] Several waves of attacks were repulsed before the Nazis asked for a truce. Dr Lautz, one of the directors of the brush firm, tried to convince the Jews to surrender. When his pleas were rejected, the Nazis sent in their two tanks. These were set afire by Molotov cocktails. A frustrated von Sammern-Frankenegg, believing that only dive bombers could dislodge the Jews, pulled out of the ghetto, telling his colleague SS *Gruppenführer* Jurgen Stroop, *Alles ist verloren.*[17]

Unquestionably, this telling, along with the claim of 250 Germans dead or wounded in that first encounter, is exaggerated. Then the diffident von Sammern-Frankenegg was replaced by General Stroop. Forty-eight years old, from a Prussian middle-class family, Stroop had joined the SS in 1932. As an SS *Oberführer* in the Sudetenland, he helped subdue the Czechs in 1939. When war broke out, he was made commander of the Poznan region, where he killed 2,000 Poles. Promoted to *Brigadeführer*, Stroop assisted in massacres of Jews from Lwow and Cracow. At his trial in Poland in 1953, Stroop declared, 'All my life I have behaved in a gallant manner. This is the treasure I leave to my wife and to my sons.' As for Jews, 'Throughout my life I have made no distinction between a Catholic, a Protestant or a Jew. I grew up in a small city of 14,000 inhabitants and among my next-door neighbors there were also Jews.' Those who knew him described Stroop as possessing 'an idiotic sense of Prussian discipline, a type who would have carried out with equal determination a massacre of fleas, goats or human beings'.[18]

Stroop prepared for battle with the Jews meticulously. He could call upon 2,000–3,000 troops, including 800 SS Panzer grenadiers and reserves from an SS cavalry unit in Warsaw, 140 SS police, 100 Wehrmacht engineers and medical personnel, 500 Polish Police and firemen, and 335 Ukrainian trainees from the Trawniki concentration camp. His weapons included one captured French tank, two heavy armored cars, several howitzers and cannon, flame throwers and machine guns. His strategy was to keep the Jews confused. One day he would mass his forces at the western end of the ghetto at 7 a.m. and begin the attack. The next day he would come from the north at 9 a.m., 10 a.m. or even at 1 o'clock in the afternoon. To minimize his own casualties, he would unleash an artillery barrage without warning against an apartment complex. Only after a block had been set afire or reduced to rubble would he send in his foot soldiers.

All of this was recorded in daily dispatches and a 75-page summary Stroop prepared for his superiors.[19] To force Jews from their underground hiding places, the Nazis flooded the sewers, dumped creosote in the water, tossed gas bombs and used flame throwers. As Stroop reported on 26 April, burning was 'the sole and final method for forcing this rabble and subhumanity to the surface' (*Dieses ist die einzige und letzte Methode, um dieses Gesindel und Untermenschentum an die Oberflache zu zwingen*).[20] A 24 April dispatch noted: 'Over and over again we observed that Jews and bandits, despite the danger of being burned alive, preferred to return into the flames rather than fall into our hands' (*Immer wieder konnte man beobachten, dass trotz der grossen Feuersnot Juden und Banditen es vorzogen, ieber wieder ins Feuer zuruckzugehen, als in unsere Hande zu fallen*).[21] On 22 April, he reported, 'Masses of them – entire families wreathed in flames – jumped from the windows or tried to let themselves down by means of sheets tied together' (*In Massen – ganze Familien – sprangen die Juden, schon vom Feuer erfasst, aus dem Fenster oder versuchten sich durch aneinandergenupfte Bettlaken usw., herabzulassen*).[22] Charred bodies lay everywhere and the stench of burning flesh permeated stairways and alcoves. By 25 April, the ghetto was 'a giant sea of flame'.

Anielewicz and the ZOB issued their own communiqués. They told how Jews dressed in Nazi uniforms attacked Pawiak prison seizing arms and releasing criminals. The communiqués spoke of the executions of Chairman Lichtenbaum and other *Judenrat* officials by the Nazis on 23 April. That same day, the ZOB issued a special appeal 'to the Polish People'. It read:

> Poles! Citizens! Soldiers of Liberty! To the thunder of the German guns which are destroying our homes, the homes of our mothers, wives and sons, to the rattle of the machine guns which are being fired at us in the battle by the German police and the SS, in the midst of the columns of smoke, the flames and the blood of the Warsaw Ghetto, we prisoners of the Ghetto, send you our heartfelt greetings. We know that you are following with heavy hearts, with tears of compassion, with admiration and anxiety, the last

phases of our desperate struggle against the terrible invader. With your own eyes you see how the Ghetto has been completely transformed into the fortress which it will remain. We shall all die in this struggle but we shall never surrender. We, like you, wish to take our revenge on our common enemy and make him pay for all his crimes. It is a struggle for our liberty and yours! For your human dignity and ours! We shall avenge the crimes of Oswiecim, Treblinka, Belzietz, and Poland! Long live the fraternity of the bloody struggle of fighting Poland! Long live liberty! Death to the assassins and butchers! Long live the struggle against the invader to the last drop of our blood!

The Jewish Combatant Organization[23]

The evocation 'for our liberty and yours' had been the rallying cry of Polish nationalists against the tsars. Now Jews were calling upon the Polish underground to help them. Their common fight was symbolized by two tattered flags flying over Muranowski Square – the red and white of republican Poland and the blue and white of Zion. The ghetto fighters would be disappointed. As the ZOB lamented on 27 April, 'the Ghetto has not yet received the slightest help in munitions and military equipment'. The Home Army possessed large quantities of arms which they would use in their own uprising in 1944, but the Poles 'obstinately refused the request for weapons made by the Ghetto organization'.[24] Twenty Poles under the command of Jozef Pszenny, a captain of the engineers, tried, unsuccessfully, to break into the ghetto to assist the Jews.[25] Most Poles, however, were bemused by what was happening. As Zvia Lubetkin wrote:

The ghetto is afire. It is burning, night and day, the fire consuming house after house. Streets go up in flame. Columns of fire shoot skyward, sparks flying, and the skies are ablaze with a red, horrifying brightness. Very close by, behind the wall, life goes on as usual. Citizens of the metropolis take walks, play, enjoy themselves and see at close hand the smoke by day and the fire at night. A merry-go-round with children is circling to their innocent joy, village girls who come to the city also come here, waddle by and watch the flames; they know that 'the Jews are burning.'[26]

Lubetkin described the despair of the dwindling number of Jews in the ghetto. 'There were scarcely any bullets left. We were oppressed by hunger. A slow death awaited us all. What would tomorrow bring? No one knew.'[27]

As the Nazis uncovered more hiding places in May, Stroop complained about the behavior of women in the resistance. On 8 May, he noted, 'Today we again caught quite a number of Jewesses who carried loaded pistols in their bloomers with the safety catch released' (*Heute wurden wiederum eine ganze Anzahl Judinnen erfasst, die in ihren Schlulpfern entsicherte und geladene Pistolen trugen*).[28] On 13 May: 'One of the females searched swiftly put her hand under her shirt and withdrew a pineapple, hand grenade, drew the safety catch, threw the grenade among the men who were searching her and ran quickly for cover' (*Eins der Weiber wie schon so oft blitzschnell unter ihren Rock und holte aus ihrem Schlupfer eine Eierhandgranate hervor, die sie abzog und unter die sie durchsuchenden manner warf, dabei blitzschnell selbst in Deckung sprang).*[29]

With the assistance of an informer, the Nazis located the headquarters of the ZOB at No. 18 Mila Street. This subterranean complex consisting of dormitories and a kitchen covered three blocks. On 8 May the Nazis tried to force the Jews out with tear gas. Anielewicz and 140 others committed suicide rather than surrender. The capture of 18 Mila did not end the siege. On 16 May German troops were sent to Tlomackie Square. At 8.15 p.m., the grand synagogue and Jewish Institute were blown up in an explosion that shook all of Warsaw.[30] Later that evening, a chapel, mortuary and other buildings at the Jewish cemetery were also destroyed. Stroop's final cable, dated 24 May 1943, boasts that the Nazis sustained 16 dead and 90 wounded. They captured 56,065 persons, 7,000 of whom were shot immediately. Seven thousand more were sent to Treblinka. Another 6,000 died in 631 dugouts that were overrun. Seven hundred Polish Gentiles were also executed that summer.[31] Concluded the SS *Brigadeführer*, '*Es gibt keinen judischen Wohnbezirk in Warschau mehr!*' (There no longer is a Jewish living quarter in Warsaw).[32]

There were pockets of resistance within the ghetto area itself until the end of July. By then, the Nazis had tried to obliterate the memory of Jewish existence. Slave workers from Auschwitz tore down 3.4 million cubic yards of wall. All but eight buildings (police lodgings, a hospital and some factories) were demolished. At summer's end 1943, the landscape of the one-time ghetto, 445 acres of noise and merriment, pain and culture, resembled Hiroshima after the bomb.[33] When the Russians liberated the city in January 1945, they found 200 Jews living illegally among Poles.

What happened in Warsaw was not a massacre, as Allied prosecutors at Nuremberg would allege. Neither did it disrupt Nazi plans in World War II. Goebbels followed reports closely and commented that 'it [Warsaw] shows what is to be expected of the Jews when they are in possession of arms'. Hitler's propaganda minister considered the fighting to be 'exceedingly serious'.[34] Germany's top military men, however, considered Stroop's assignment little more than a trifle. As General Alfred Jodl later commented at Nuremberg, 'The dirty arrogant SS swine! Imagine writing a 75-page boastful report on a little murder expedition when a major campaign fought by soldiers against a well-armed enemy takes only a few pages.'[35]

The Warsaw Ghetto uprising was an heroic gesture on the part of men, women and children who knew they were doomed. As Marek Edelman noted in 1993, the term uprising may be inappropriate. 'We were planning the *defense* of the ghetto.'[36] The ghetto fighters succeeded, if only in small measure, in making the Nazis pay for the deportations of their brethren. The ghetto fighters did not stop the transports from running to the death camps. And most important, though their story is inspirational, it was not unique.

Before and after the destruction of the Warsaw Ghetto, Jews throughout Europe were striking back at the Nazis.[37]

THE *JUDENRATS*

At every level, Jews in eastern Europe offered resistance once they realized what relocation truly meant. While several prominent Jews may be reproached for their behavior, most *Judenrat* officials resisted Nazi demands. Delivery of one's kinsmen into the hands of the enemy violated the dictum 'if pagans should tell them [the Jews] "give us one of yours and we shall kill him, otherwise we shall kill all of you", they should all be killed and not a single Jewish soul should be delivered' (*Mishneh Torah*, 5:5). Officials in Zamosc, Lwow and Zolkiew tried to buy their way out of deportations. Rumkowski, Merin in Bedzin, Barash in Bialystok thought they could avert wholesale deportations by stressing the importance of Jewish labor. Gens in Vilna and Rumkowski thought it necessary to 'foul' their hands by sacrificing the aged, sick and young in order to save the greater number of Jews.[38] In Terezin, Leo Baeck withheld information from other internees, writing later: 'Living in expectation of death by gassing would only be harder.'[39]

Many councilors refused to cooperate before the large-scale deportations of 1942. Dr Joseph Parnas in Lwow, the lawyer Ciechanowski and eight colleagues in Nowogrodek, Marek Biberstein in Cracow, Leib Goldberg and his aide Apelbaum in Sandomierz, Dr Ignatz Duldig and Zygo Rechter in Przemysl, others in Kleck, Wlodzimeierz and Siedlce were shot for obstruction or sabotage. In Minsk Mazowiecki, Moshe Kramarz and three other Jewish leaders were executed after Kramarz tore up the Gestapo resettlement order. Dr Artur Rosenzweig, the first chairman of the Cracow ghetto, and Chaim Ringelblum, head of the Kolomyja *Judenrat*, were deported with their families when they refused to turn over deportation lists. Jewish officials in Baranowicze, Siauliai, Dabrowa, Zloczow, Kaluszyn and Zwiercie also refused. As Dr Weiler, head of the Ludmir *Judenrat*, declared: 'I am not god and I will not decide who will live or die.'

According to Yuri Suhl, 45 of 73 *Judenrats* in southeast Poland refused to hand over lists of their people or supply funds to cover the costs of deportation. Sixteen chairmen were executed, five committed suicide, four resigned and three went into hiding. In addition to Czerniakow, B. Szeps of Tomaszow Mazowiecki, Dr Reifeisen of Bolechow, Jacob Sucharczuk in Rovno and councilors in Miedzyrzec, Grodno, Szczebrzeszyn, Lomza, Kosow Poleski, Woldzimierz, Wolynski and Pruzana attempted suicide. Dr Wolf Chess in Borszczow refused to turn over money. In Piotrkow Trybunal-ski, Lenin, Radomsk, Kaunas and Minsk, the councils forged papers and encouraged contact with the underground. In Kovno, Dr Elkes, the head of the *Judenrat*, and Moshe Levin, chief of Jewish police, urged people to go into hiding. Following the destruction of the Warsaw Ghetto in 1943, Jewish leaders in Rohatyn, Czestochowa, Zdzieciol, Sasow, Nieswicz and Mir urged their people to flee to the woods.

Some Jewish leaders like Abraham Gepner in Warsaw, Lote Eisenbrod in Rubiezewicze, others in Brailov, Ozorkow, Siedlce and Kosow Poleski elected to stay with their people in the ghettos when they had an opportunity to join the partisans. Jewish councilors fought – at Tulczyn, Radomsk, Rovno, Slutsk, Minsk, Lublin, Sielce, Sosnowicz, Bedzin, Lida, Lvov, Tarnow, Stryzow, Tarnopol and Grodno. In September 1942, Berl Lopatyn urged his fellow Jews in Lachwa near Pinsk to arm themselves with knives and axes, to fight their way to freedom. That same month, at Tulczyn, Vice-Chair Meir Himmelfarb led 1,500 people to the woods after they torched the ghetto. When the time came, Jewish policemen in Stolin set fire to their ghetto. Jewish police also served as the core of the resistance in Barnowicze, Marcinkance, Vilna and Minsk.[40]

RESISTANCE IN THE GHETTOS

Two thousand of the 20,000 Poles catalogued by the Nazis as troublemakers in 1941–42 were Jews.[41] Polish Jews shared resources, information, even the name Jewish Fighting Organization (JFO). The Jews of Cracow conducted the first acts of sabotage in 1942, disrupting rail communications, burning storehouses and killing members of the SS. On 22 December 1942 they attacked the *Ziganeria*, a popular nightclub in the city, and several restaurants frequented by Germans, killing ten officers. The Nazis reacted by executing members of the resistance before liquidating the Cracow ghetto in March 1943.[42] Inspired by the Warsaw uprising, the Jewish Fighting Organization of Brody rebelled as the ghetto was cleared on 21 May 1943. Some Jews escaped, but 2,500 were deported.[43] During a bloody battle on 25–26 August, Czenstochowa's JFO fought to the death, when their ammunition ran out.[44]

Jews living in Vilna were at an added disadvantage, being removed from kinsmen in the Government General by hundreds of miles and two borders. Nevertheless, in January 1942 Vilna's ghetto youth created the *Vareinigte Partisaner Organizazje*, the United Partisan Organization (UPO). The UPO sent emissaries to other Jewish communities and smuggled weapons into the ghetto. Until midsummer 1943, the Vilna resistance was directed by a communist Itzig Wittenberg. Pursued by the Gestapo, Wittenberg was captured and shot. His successor Jechiel Scheinbaum and 40 members of the UPO were killed during the liquidation of the ghetto on 1 September 1943. Several hundred of their comrades led by Abba Kovner fled to the woods where they created their own guerrilla unit, *Nekomah* (Vengeance).[45]

Jews in Bialystok witnessed the deportation of 10,000 of their people. Through the early months of 1943, the Jewish Fighting Organization stockpiled guns and grenades. Their leader, Mordechai ('Tamarov') Tenenbaum, had no illusions about winning support from Gentile neighbors. Wrote Tenenbaum: 'There are naive people who believe in the humanity of this nation of hooligans, which rejoices in having Hitler purge Poland of the Jews.'[46] Sensing deportation to be imminent, the Jewish Fighting Organization secured work certificates for its members and convinced the Jewish Police to have nothing to do with further roundups. On 8 February, one of their number, Itzhak Malamed, was publicly hanged for assassinating an SS man.[47]

On 16 August 1943, the Nazis attempted to liquidate the Bialystok ghetto. Posters advised that all Jewish laborers were being transferred to Lublin. Members of Dror, a Zionist youth organization, made it clear that they would not leave the ghetto. Said Herschel Rosenthal, 'We must regard the ghetto as our Musa Dagh and add a glorious chapter to the history of Jewish Bialystok and of our movement.'[48] Hanoch Zeleznegora agreed: 'WE must have no illusions. WE may expect complete destruction to the last Jew. WE have two choices and both lead to death. The forest will not save us, neither will an uprising in the ghetto. We may as well die an honorable death.'[49] The Jewish Fighting Organization distributed weapons and assigned combat groups to key intersections.

Most Jews in Bialystok, however, started moving toward the transport center on Yuroviecka Street. Chaika Grossman was shocked to see whole families with their property piled upon a sagging child's carriage.[50] The Jewish fighters had to scrap their original plan. They improvised, mingling with the lines of deportees. The goal now was to force a breakout through the main gate. Young women signaled the start of the uprising. On Fabryehna Street, the canvas factory exploded in smoke and ash. On Ciepla Street, a haystack went up in flames. As Jews on Novgrouska and Smolna Streets rushed the barbed wire, Nazi machinegunners shot them down.[51] It took the Nazis a week, using tanks, artillery and aircraft, to subdue the Bialystok ghetto. Among the dead was Mordecai Tenenbaum, who took his own life.

THE CAMPS

Inspired by tales of heroism in the ghettos, *Sonderkommandos* in death camps fantasized about rebellions. In Treblinka, a group led by Dr Julian Chorazyski (a former Polish army officer), Dr Marius Leichert (professor of pathology at the University of Cracow), Samuel Rajman (who directed a rock-crushing unit), Yosef Gross (a maintenance worker), Eliahu Grinsbach (an electrician), a Czech army officer named Zielo, and Judah Klein (a worker in the hair factory) collected home-made bombs, blackjacks, knives, nooses and hid them in the latrines. They intended to act in April 1943 concurrent with the uprising in Warsaw. When Dr Chorazyski and Captain Zielo were transferred to another part of the camp, the attack was postponed. Their positions were assumed by Engineer Galewski of Lodz and Rudolf Masaryk. The latter, a non-Jew, had accompanied his Jewish wife to Treblinka. On the evening of 1 August 1943 the plotters stole three pistols and ten hand grenades from the arsenal. The plan was to strike at the guards when another transport arrived the next day. Grenades would be thrown at the main gate and gas chambers, as the masses rushed the perimeter fence. Beyond that, it was every man for himself. Forty men were apprised of the plot.

As scheduled, at 3:30 on the afternoon of 2 August 1943, a death train pulled alongside the Treblinka platform. Four thousand Jews were being unloaded in the presence of commandant Kurt Franz when Yosef Gross flung his first grenade at a watchtower destroying a machine gun. A second grenade killed six SS men near Franz, but missed the commandant. Gross was torn to pieces by Franz's dog. At that moment inmates at the hair factory strangled their guards. In the infirmary, Dr Leichert seized a rake that had been used to sift through human bones and struck a guard across the face. Leichert directed one group toward the SS barracks where grenades killed the sleeping men. Another group led by Rajzmann raided the armory, passing out guns and grenades. From Camp 2 there was a shout as the *Sonderkommando* broke for the main gate, led by Captain Zielo wielding an axe. At the loading platform, there was pandemonium. Some of the new arrivals were trying to reboard the cattle cars. Others were running in the opposite direction, tearing at the barbed wire. As the main gate was blown apart, the Nazis and Ukrainian guards shot at anything that moved.[52]

It all happened in 11 minutes. When it was over, 117 guards were dead or wounded. Eleven hundred Jews died in the breakout. Of 180 prisoners who made it to the woods, only 18 survived the war. Himmler ordered them to be hunted down by more than 1,000 guards, SS men and regular Wehrmacht troops. Though the fake railway buildings were burned and the death house apparatus damaged, Treblinka continued to process transports until October. With the advance of the Russians, the camp was decommissioned. Two hundred inmates transformed the camp into a model farm community. When their task was done, they were taken into the woods and shot.[53]

What happened in Treblinka, inspired the Jews of Sobibor. In a camp where the life expectancy was two months, it was not surprising that the inmate population of 600 would know the latest news from the outside. Some of the old-timers among the *Sonderkommandos* led by Leon Feldhendler had been discussing a tunnel or revolt for much of 1943. At the end of September, a group of Russian prisoners of war, all of them Jews, arrived in Sobibor to help recycle ammunition. One of these, Alexander Pechersky assumed command of the camp resistance. The plan, as in Treblinka, was simple. Hand-made weapons (knives, clubs, rope, bombs) were to be distributed among trusted members of the resistance. At a given signal, prisoners were to raid the arsenal, cut telephone wires, and then rush the main gate.[54]

Shortly before 5 p.m. on the afternoon of 14 October 1943, inmates in the tailor shop killed a Nazi officer with an axe. Three more were slain in Camp 1. Using captured pistols and grenades, the inmates returned fire from the guards. Some inmates were too stunned to move. Four hundred made it through the wire. SS General Jacob Sporrenberg, who had replaced Globocnik as Chief of police in the Lublin area, asked help from the Wehrmacht and Luftwaffe in tracking down the escapees. The Nazis managed to capture all but 60 of the escapees. Soon after the uprising, Sobibor was destroyed by Wehrmacht engineers. The gas chambers, prisoners barracks and SS villas were all dynamited.[55]

There are 17 cases where Jews rebelled in concentration camps, including Krusznya (December 1942), Krychow (August 1943), Kielce, Poniatow (8–10 November 1943), Trawniki (November 1943), Konin (a labor camp put out of commission when the inmates burned their huts in the summer of 1943), and Novaky. On 26 October 1944 Jewish *Sonderkommandos* blew up Crematoria 4 and damaged Crematorias 2 and 3 in Auschwitz. By way of contrast, there is not a single recorded instance of rebellion among the more than three and one-half million Russian prisoners of war during World War II.[56]

PARTISANS

Many of those who fled the ghettos joined partisan groups or formed their own bands in forests, swamps and mountains.[57] This was itself remarkable considering the fact that Jews were an urban people, unfamiliar with living off the countryside, and limited in their arms. (Only a third of the fighters had actual weapons.) Jewish guerrillas endured not only cold and hunger, Nazi patrols and also the hostility of Gentile peasants and partisans. It was risky to admit that one was Jewish, for many partisans boasted, '*Zhivem, zhidov boyem*' (We live and beat Jews).[58] Half of Tuczyn's 6,000 Jews went into the woods. Only 15 survived. The rest were hunted down and killed by the Germans and their Ukrainian allies. Virtually all those Jews who fled Czestochowa were annihilated by Polish collaborators.

Despite these obstacles Jewish partisans actively opposed the Nazis throughout eastern Europe. There were nearly 20,000 Jewish fighters in eastern Poland and the Soviet Union. Approximately 10,000 from Bialystok, Mir and Zhalel operated out of the Rudniki Forest. Among the more notable commanders in White Russia was Dr Yehezkel Atlas, a physician from Slonim, who lost his family to the deportations. In 1942, the Atlas group attacked a German garrison, destroyed a bridge, and seized an airplane that had made a forced landing.[59] The Belsky brothers (Tuvia, Zosa and Asoel) conducted sabotage against the Nazis and kept together a population of 1,200 men, women and children in the Naboliki forest. Their camp, replete with factories, hospital, schools and bakery, was dubbed 'Jerusalem'.[60] A

19-year-old girl from Vilna, Vitka Kempner, carried out the first major act of resistance in Lithuania, blowing up a German train in July 1942. Dozens of women from Bialystok were active in the resistance in the woods. In western and central Poland Jews under the command of Yehiel Grynzspan organized 28 battle groups and protected more than 3,000 refugees. The Bar Kochba group attacked Germans out of Hrubieszow.[61] There were more than 2,500 Jewish partisans in Slovakia, 6,000 in Yugoslavia, 4,000 in Greece.

As the Soviets advanced, they dissolved the Jewish fighting units and, in accordance with directives from Stalin, stressed the international nature of resistance to Hitler.[62] In his memoirs, Mishe Gildenman ('Uncle Misha'), commander of a battle group in Ukraine, clarified the nature of these combat units. At 5p.m. on 30 April 1943, a Jewish force of 70 men and women approached the town of Alexandrovka. They had only one mission: to wipe out 200 German troops garrisoned behind a dirt palisade and barbed wire. One of the guerrillas drove a wagon to the gate and leaped off, supposedly in pursuit of his hat. The wagon, loaded with dynamite, exploded. Jewish partisans came rushing through the gate, storming the barracks. The building went up in flames. As the attackers fled to the woods, they left a note with a village elder. Addressed to the German commandant, it read: 'Baron von Helman: Hitler will not destroy and annihilate the whole Jewish nation, but I and a very few other Jews destroyed the entire camp of the German garrison in Alexandrovka.' The message was signed: 'The Commander of the Jewish Partisan Group, the Jew Dida Mischa.'[63]

SPIRITUAL RESISTANCE

For every woman who tossed a grenade in the ghettos or donned the fur cap of a partisan, there were dozens who demonstrated a different kind of courage. Writers of the underground ghetto journals, diarists like Ringelblum and Anne Frank knew they were offering testimony to an unknown audience. Leo Haas, Bedrich Fritta, Karel Fleischmann and Otto Ungar sketched the suffering around them in Terezin and smuggled these images to Switzerland. When the SS discovered what they were doing, they shipped the artists to forced labor camps. Ungar was tortured, his hands broken in the *Kleine Festung*. He died holding a lump of coal, sketching scenes of a concentration camp upon a paper towel.[64] There were other heroes: the children of barracks L417, 410 and 414 in Terezin who left drawings and poems that were published by the Prague State Museum under the title, *I Never Saw Another Butterfly*;[65] Hans Krasa, Gideon Klein, Pavel Haas, Viktor Ullman, Raphael Schachter and Rudolf Freudenfeld, musicians who brought moments of rapture to that unhappy place; and the simple folk in concentration camps who did nothing more than share food and blankets with those less fortunate.

Genia Silkes lost her three-year-old child to typhus while serving as a teacher in the Warsaw Ghetto in 1942. Ms. Silkes expressed exasperation with people fixated upon armed resistance: 'You ask of resistance. To live one more day is resistance. Amidst the dysentery and typhus, the starvation, is resistance. To teach and learn is resistance. When the Nazis created the ghetto, it was illegal to have a school for Jewish children. If we were caught, it would be death for the rabbi, death for the teacher, death for the children.'[66] Silkes's sentiments are echoed by Vladka Meed, who served the ZOB. Writing on the fiftieth anniversary of the Warsaw Ghetto uprising, Meed saluted doctors who tried to heal under the most adverse conditions, the *Halutzim* who continued to train young Jews for a life they would never know in Palestine, workers for the Joint, Toropol, CENTOS, TOZ, ORT and a host of other Jewish self-help organizations. Said Meed: 'What must be remembered is that, throughout the Holocaust, every Jew in his or her own way resisted the Nazis; each act of resistance was shaped by its unique time and place. The soup kitchens, the secret schools, the cultural events in the ghettos and camps, constituted forms of resistance, the goals of which were survival with dignity, with *Menshlechkeit* [humanity].'[67]

19

Yugoslavia: The Dysfunctional State

YUGOSLAVIA 1941–45: A MILLION DEAD IN REPRISALS

Human decency was in short supply in eastern Europe. The peacemakers at Versailles hoped that a south Slav state would be a model of toleration among Orthodox Christians, Roman Catholics, Muslims, Jews and Greeks. The reality was that between the world wars, Yugoslavia was cursed with ethnic strife. Power was divided between Prince Paul (cousin of assassinated King Alexander) and cabinets dominated by Serbian nationalists.[1] With Paul's blessing, Dragisa Cvetkovic concluded a non-aggression pact with Nazi Germany on 25 March 1941. Two days later, a pro-Soviet junta seized control in Belgrade and Paul abdicated in favor of Alexander's son Peter.[2]

As an Austrian, Hitler harbored an abiding hatred of the Serbs. On 6 April, the Nazis launched a less-celebrated Blitz, leaving Belgrade, Dubrovnik and Ljubljana in flames and more than 5,000 dead. Peace terms dictated on 29 April were devastating. Bachka east of the Danube Bend was returned to Hungary; Skoplje, Pirot and Bitolj were ceded to Bulgaria. Albania took a slice of Kosovo. Croatia was given autonomy under Italian tutelage. Italy annexed the region around Ljubljana and much of the Dalmatian coastline. The Croatians and Germans shared control of Bosnia. Slavonia was incorporated into the Reich. Old Serbia fell under German military rule.

When Hitler's armies invaded the Soviet Union, they left three undermanned and overaged divisions in Yugoslavia. From the start, the Nazis and their allies had troubles with *komitaji* partisans under the command of Josef Broz Tito and the Chetniks of Drajlo Mihailovich.[3] Frustrated by the lack of cooperation from local officials, Field Marshal Wilhelm List, Commander of the Southeast Front, requested additional personnel. General Franz Bohme arrived in Serbia along with the battle-trained 342nd Division from France. When the Serbs failed to heed his warnings of hostage-taking or deportations to concentration camps, List instructed Bohme to burn villages and carry out public hangings.[4] In a series of ambushes during the first week of October, the communists captured 60 Germans and machine-gunned 31 others. Bohme retaliated with a decree calling for the execution of 100 Serbs for every single German killed, 50 Serbs for every German wounded.[5]

The Wehrmacht commanders believed that the execution of between 11,000 and 30,000 people would pacify the situation.[6] In the spring of 1942, however, Tito's partisans disrupted rail contact between Belgrade and Zagreb. The Nazis ordered their Ustashe allies into action. The Croatians panicked when they were attacked. As a result, General Friedrich Stahl was given command of Battle Group West Bosnia (the 714th and 737th Infantry). Stahl's forces encircled the partisans at Kozara by the first of June. After two months of bitter fighting, the German High Command rejected consideration of 'humanitarian drivel!' Anyone presumed to have taken part in the revolt was shot.[7] Healthy captives were shipped off to slave labor in Germany or Norway where they were worked to death in several months. The old and sick were eliminated by the Croatians. Some 68,000 Serbs from Kozara were massacred or deported to their deaths.[8] Twenty-nine Nazi officers were decorated for their part in this murder expedition. One of those awarded the Silver Medal of the crown of King Zvonimir was Lieutenant Kurt Waldheim, an Austrian officer who had arranged for trucks and railway cars to deport the Serbs.[9]

By war's end, more than one million Yugoslavs, one-tenth of the population, would be dead. Most were victims of reprisals carried out by the regular German military and their fascist allies. The killings were especially brutal in Croatia where Catholic zealots made assaults against Serbs into a religious crusade. Orthodox Christians were required to wear blue armbands marked with a P (*Pravoslavac*/Orthodox). Franciscan monks subjected communities to conversionary sermons. If the Serbs failed to abjure their faith, they were massacred. In several towns (Banja Luka, Bihac, Vukovar), the Serbs were given no choice at all. They were rounded up, marched out of town and slaughtered by Croatian or Bosnian nationalists shouting '*Za dom spremni!*' (Ready for the Fatherland!).[10] Milovan Zanic, Minister of Justice for Croatia, declared, 'There are no ways and means which we Croats will not use to make our country truly ours, and to cleanse it of all Orthodox Serbs. All those who came into our country 300 years ago must disappear.'[11]

SERBIA 1941: THE MASSACRE OF MALE JEWS

Yugoslavia's 75,000 Jews shared the fate of their Gentile countrymen. Jews made up less than one percent of Yugoslavia's 12 million people, only 4.5 percent of the university students. Most lived in cities and were merchants or artisans. The Constitution of 1869 promised (but did not deliver) equality for all Serbs. It would not be until December 1929, that King Alexander formally guaranteed the rights of Jews.[12] When the Nazis remade the map of eastern Europe, many of Yugoslavia's Jews found themselves living under new authorities. Bulgaria claimed 8,000, Croatia 21,000 and Bosnia 12,000. The Germans occupied Old Serbia with 12,000. To this number must be added 20,000 expelled by Hungary.

There were also 1,000 Jewish refugees who had been awaiting passage out of the country since leaving Austria aboard three Danubian river craft in October 1939.[13] The refugees proceeded as far as the port of Kladovo, where they were detained for the winter. In the spring of 1940, the passengers were transferred 300 miles west to Sabac on the Sava river while Zionist leaders tried to negotiate their release. They were supposed to return to Prahovo in the east, but neither rail nor boat transport could be arranged. Only 185 refugees from the Kladovo group (mainly children) would leave Yugoslavia shortly before the German invasion. The rest, 915 men and women, entered their second year in limbo.

The Germans followed their usual pattern of discrimination against Jews in Serbia. Following the invasion, Jewish stores and religious institutions were plundered. Rabbis were subjected to mock executions. Jews were ordered to register and don the Star of David. More than 800 shops in Belgrade as well as dozens of synagogues and libraries were burned or Aryanized. The Nazis confiscated estates valued at more than ten billion pre-war dinars as 'war reparations'.[14] Jews were barred from professions and schools. In May 1941 the Nazis instituted forced labor for Jewish men between the ages of 14 and 60, females between 14 and 40. The Jewish community in Belgrade, swollen to more than 25,000, was required to supply 40 hostages weekly.

When a 17-year-old Jewish boy set fire to a Wehrmacht truck in Belgrade on 29 July 1941, the Germans responded by seizing 1,200 hostages and shooting 100. SS *Gruppenführer* Harald Turner and Ambassador Pleni-potentiary Felix Benzler recommended that Serbia's Jews be deported to Romania. Franz Rademacher and Hans Luther favored methods employed by the Einsatzgruppen. That was the view of General List and his anti-partisan enforcer General Bohme. In Berlin, Keitel authorized reprisals, but it was Bohme who expanded the list of hostages to include communists, nationalists and Jews.[15]

As Nazi troops prepared for a *Strafexpedition* (punishment expedition) at Sabac and Valjevo on 22–23 September, Bohme reminded them that they were 'avengers' of Germans whose 'blood flowed in 1914 through the treachery of Serbs';[16] 1,136 Serbs were killed, another 20,000 rounded up in these punitive actions. Once blooded against Christians, the troops showed little remorse when they set out on *Judenerschiessungen* (shooting the Jews). On 9 and 11 October 449 Jews were killed at Topola. Jews and Gypsies were shot at Zasavica on 12 and 13 October. After conducting a house to house search in Kraljevo on 15–16 October, the Nazis killed 1,755 Jews and 'communists'. Over the next four days they massacred another 2,300 in Kragujevac, Grosnica and Mackovac. *Gruppenführer* Turner boasted to a friend in writing on 17 October that the Nazis killed more than 2,000 Jews and 200 Gypsies in the previous eight days. Another 2,000 would die in the next eight days in what Turner described as 'a beautiful job'. Hans-Dietrich Walther, commander of Infantry Regiment 433, informed his superiors: 'The shooting of Jews is simpler than the Gypsies. You must admit that the Jews go to their deaths very calmly. They stand very quietly while the Gypsies howl and scream and continue to move about [even] when they are standing at the shooting site. Some even leap into the grave and try to act dead before the salvo.'[17]

The single worst atrocity against Jews took place on 25 October 1941, in a remote location on the edge of the Sava River, not too far from Sabac. A farmer, Milorad Jelesic, described how the Germans led groups of Jews into a circle of wooden stakes. Guards passed by with a blanket, into which individuals were to toss their remaining valuables. Then, each Jew was shot in the neck by two soldiers. Jelesic testified:

> Immediately after we were ordered to double up to the ditch and to throw the murdered people into the ditch. After that the Germans ordered us to examine their [the Jews'] pockets and take out any valuables, like money or gold. We were also ordered to pull any rings off the fingers. Because many of the rings could not be pulled off, the Germans gave me a pair of pliers with which I cut the rings off which I gave them afterward. Also, before we threw the victims into the ditch I saw how the Germans tore out golden teeth from the murdered ones. because in some cases they did not succeed doing so, they trampled the teeth out by kicking with their boots.[18]

The killing lasted two days. When the detail returned the second day, dogs had gnawed some bodies in the uncovered ditches. Said one German, 'These too are dogs.' Then pointing at a dog which he shot, he declared, 'And this one is their brother.'[19] More than 1,200 civilians, mainly Jews, were killed in two days. After the war, the bodies were exhumed and passports confirmed most of the dead were from the Kladovo group.[20]

CAMP SEMLIN IN BELGRADE

Pressed by Benzler and Ribbentrop to resolve the Jewish problem in Serbia, Heydrich sent Franz Rademacher to 'clean out these people'. Heydrich agreed that the issue could only be settled 'on the spot', and not by deportation.[21] When Rademacher arrived in Belgrade in October 1941, he discovered that he was not really needed. The SS and army had already shot half of the able-bodied Jewish males (4,000) in Serbia. Another 1,500 would be dead by the end of the week. Twenty thousand elderly Jews, women and children, along with 1,300 Gypsies were vegetating in the old Gypsy quarter of Mistrovica Isle. Meanwhile 500 more Jewish workmen were preparing a replacement camp for Mistrovica which was perpetually under water.[22]

Wehrmacht General Heinrich Danckelmann, SS *Gruppenführer* Turner, Einsatzgruppe *Standartenführer* Wilhelm Fuchs, Ambassador Benzler and Franz Neuhausen, head of the Trusteeship Office rarely agreed on anything, but they threw their support behind the conversion of the fairground pavilions at Semlin (Sajmiste) into the new *Judenlager* in Belgrade.[23] Semlin was accessible to a multi-lane bridge through downtown Belgrade. On 8 December the Jews in the capital were ordered to report to Semlin with food and the keys to their apartments. The camp authority (headed by a 30-year-old woman named Sarfas) listed 5,291 Jews as of 15 December, 6,800 persons (including some Gypsies) by February.[24] They dwelt in two exposition halls that were partitioned for families by multi-tiered scaffolding. Some inmates worked at the suburban airfield of Zemun. A few risked punishment by sneaking out of the camp to obtain food. Apart from broths made with cabbage or potato peels, the daily ration of corn bread was 150 grams, and there were times when civil authorities did not deliver that.[25] The shortfall of milk and bread was acknowledged by the camp's first commandant SS *Scharführer* Edgar Enge who petitioned his superiors for additional supplies over the winter of 1941/42. Enge was succeeded in January by SS *Untersturm-führer* Herbert Andorfer. A genial Austrian from Salzburg, Andorfer met daily with leaders of the Jewish council, leaving them with the impression that Semlin was just a temporary stop for Belgrade's Jews.[26]

THE END OF SERBIAN JEWRY: *SAURERWAGEN*

According to the International Red Cross, the Jews of Serbia were sent to an unidentified concentration camp in 1942 and 'nothing further was heard of them'.[27] In fact, most of the Jews in Belgrade never left the city. Shortly after Semlin opened, Himmler sent *Standartenführer* Emanuel Schafer to Belgrade as *Judenreferat* (coordinator of Jewish affairs). A runty man with a Hitler mustache, Schafer was a veteran Nazi who participated in the Röhm purge. Shortly after the Wannsee Conference, Schaefer received a cable from Gestapo chief Müller which read: 'Subject: Jewish operation in Serbia. Commando with special *Saurer* truck underway overland with special assignment.'[28] Schaefer understood that the Jewish problem would be resolved with one of the gassing vans developed by Lange and his commando.[29]

In mid-March, two drivers, *Scharführers* Gotz and Meyer, arrived in Belgrade, bringing a *Saurerwagen* and a baggage truck. The Jews in Semlin were told they were being moved to another camp. As luggage was loaded on one truck, the guards passed chocolates to the children. Then the drivers, accompanied by Andorfer and Enge, four *Ordnungspolizei* from the 64th Reserve Police Battalion and seven Serbian prisoners motored across the Sava bridge. Once past the bridge, the drivers would stop, hook up the toxic exhaust pipes and continue their drive ten kilometers south to the Avala shooting range. Every day for two months, the same personnel murdered group after group of Jews. On 10 May 1942, the camp leadership in Semlin and their families were gassed. The Serbs, who had been promised they would be sent to Norway, were shot.[30]

By then the Nazis had mopped up most of the other Jews in Serbia, including 800 patients and medical personnel from the Jewish Hospital of Belgrade, as well as isolated communities.[31] On 29 May 1942 the German Foreign Office exulted, 'The Jewish question in Serbia is no longer acute. Now it is only a matter there of settling the legal questions concerning property.' Ten days later, Schaefer reported there was no longer a Jewish question in Serbia and that Belgrade was the only great city in Europe free of Jews. In August, Turner went even further and proclaimed in a report to General Loehr that 'Serbia is the only land in which the Jewish question and Gypsy question is solved' (*Serbia einziges Land, in dem Judenfrage und Zigeunerfrage geloest*).[32] The Nazis apparently thought so for shortly after they sent the gas van back to Berlin for repairs and closed the office of *Judenreferat* in Belgrade. The Nazis continued to use Semlin as a prison camp and perhaps 47,000 Serbs would die here before Belgrade was liberated. Six thousand Jews died on the way to Avala. Their remains were obliterated when Paul Blobel's Kommando 1005 retreated from Russia in December 1943.[33]

ETHNIC CLEANSING IN CROATIA

Ethnic cleansing was an essential feature of the government created in Zagreb when the Ustashis declared their independence on 10 April 1941. The Croat Revolutionary Organization known as the Ustashi (Insurrection) Party was founded by Ante Starcevic who preached that Serbs and other non-Catholics were 'a breed fit only for the slaughterhouse'.[34] The Ustashi members swore an oath to their *poglavnik* (leader) before a crucifix, dagger and pistol. From 1929 until 1945 that leader was Ante Pavelic, the man responsible for the assassination of King Alexander. Condemned to death for his role in the murder, Pavelic and his cohorts took sanctuary in fascist Italy. They established training camps, carried on anti-Yugoslav propaganda, and made an armed sally into the Lika district of Croatia in hopes of sparking a full-scale revolution.[35]

Pavelic opposed the *sporazum* (agreement) of 20 August 1939 between Prime Minister Cvetkovic and Vladko Macek, the leader of the Croatian Peasant Party. In an attempt to appease Croatian separatists, Cvetkovic agreed to the creation of the Banovina of Croatia. This new geographical entity would encompass Croatia, Slavonia, Dalmatia and Bosnia and include more than four million Serbs, one-fourth of the entire Serbian population in Yugoslavia. Croatia would have its own parliament and governor appointed by the king. The central government controlled foreign affairs, defense, transport and communications, but the Banovina would be responsible for fiscal matters.[36] When Hitler's armies entered Yugoslavia, Pavelic wired congratulations to Hitler and his 'invincible German troops' and promised that independent Croatia would 'tie her future to the New Order in Europe which you, *Führer*, and the Duce have created'.[37] On 15 May, Pavelic and 200 of his uniformed colleagues returned to Zagreb where they had to suffer the indignity of Aimone Duke of Spoleto, Victor Emmanuel's nephew, as head of state.

The Pavelic regime determined to resolve the Serbian question by taking a page from Tsarist bigots. As Dr Mile Budak, the Croatian Minister of Education, declared: 'The movement of the Ustashi is based on religion. For the minorities we have three million bullets. We shall kill one part of the Serbs. We shall transport another, and the rest of them will be forced to embrace the Roman Catholic religion; thus our new Croatia will become one hundred per cent Catholic.'[38] Interior Minister Andrija Artukovic was more blunt. To Chief of Police Franjo Truhar, Artukovic declared, 'Kill all the Serbs and Jews without exception.' And to the mayor of Cerin: 'If you can't kill Serbs or Jews you are an enemy of the state.'[39]

The forces of *Slavko* (Marshal) Eugene Kwaternik were unleashed against the Serbs. Orthodox churches were burned and villages destroyed. Three thousand persons were slaughtered in Virgin Most and Cemernica, 5,000 in the district of Sanski Most and Kljuc, another 3,000 in Vojnic. Twelve hundred were killed in the church of Glina. Before they died, many were mutilated. Photographs show people who were clubbed to death. At Korenica, people were bound with barbed wire, thrown into a pit, doused with gasoline and set afire. Some 2,800 Jews and Serbs shared a grave at Mitrovica. Five thousand Jews and 15,000 Serbs were drowned in the Dvina or Sava. German authorities were so embarrassed by the brutality of their allies that they disbanded the Croatian Black Legion in June 1942.[40]

JASENOVAC

At least 20 concentration camps were opened by Interior Minister Artukovic. The Ustashi funneled thousands of men, women and children into an old Austrian fort at Stara Gradiska, twin camps on Pag Island, a home for the aged at Loborgrad, a flour mill in Dakovo. A total of 3,336 children, many of them survivors of the Kozara massacre, passed through Jastrebarsko in little more than a year. Operated by the nuns of St Vincent DePaul, 'Jaska' was supposed to reeducate the children along Catholic lines; 768 children perished in 'the camp of diapers' before it was liberated by Yugoslav guerrillas in August 1942.[41]

The worst of the Ustashi camps was Jasenovac, a brick factory midway between Zagreb and Banja Luka. In February 1942, the Red Cross visited Jasenovac. Clean bedding was placed in the barracks, decent food served in the cafeterias. The mixed delegation from Germany, Hungary, Italy, Serbia and Croatia left Jasenovac, like Terezin, much impressed.[42] In reality, Jasenovac was a charnel house covering 220 acres. Newcomers were directed to a long barn (the 'Tunnel') where they wallowed in filth. Those unlikely to survive quarantine were taken to the Granik quay, to suffer execution by rifle butt or hammer. Conditions in the wooden huts of the main camp were no better. Prisoners lacked clothing, food, bedcovers and medicine. In one month 1,800 persons died of dysentery and typhus. In this camp, no one was safe. As Vladimir Cvija recalled:

> The most terrible scene I witnessed was when the Ustasha took a group of internees from Camp III/c. They looked more like skeletons … with swollen legs, complete physical and psychological wrecks after life behind barbed wire, under the open sky, in mud, with no food or water. They had been told they were going to pick plums. They passed before us with smiles on their faces, in which pity for us could be seen, because there would be plums where they were going, and that meant food. Clouds moved slowly across the sky, the camp was silent as a grave. Evening came and the gentle southern breeze brought desperate screams from Granik. The killers had started 'picking plums.'[43]

At Jasenovac, Croatians disemboweled their victims, gouged eyes, and ripped out tongues. The guards hanged young girls to trees by their hair, raped and tortured them. They killed with hammers and guns, walking upon the bodies of infants or smashing their skulls. They killed by setting prisoners against one another with sticks in mock gladiatorial combat. Ultimately, the guards devised their own form of competitive killing. Using a curved knife known as a *graviso*, they slashed throats and kept tallies. The record for one night by a single man was 1,360 achieved by Petar Brzica, a student at a Franciscan college.[44] Ljubo Milos, one-time governor of Jasenovac, boasted that his forces killed 3,000–4,000 people daily. His successor, Father Miroslav Filipovich-Maistorovic, claimed responsibility for the deaths of 40,000 persons in four months.[45] Vjekoslav Luburic, supervisor of all Croatian concentration camps, boasted in October 1942, 'We have slaughtered here at Jasenovac more people than the Ottoman Empire was able to do during its occupation of Europe.'[46] Catholic bishops in Slovenia made belated protests,[47] but were unable to halt the genocidal murders. Despite an inmate revolt in April 1943, Jasenovac continued to function until 2 May 1945. By that time over 600,000 Serbs had been massacred.[48]

THE MASSACRE OF CROATIA'S JEWS

Jews and Gypsies were not ignored in the killing process. One hour after the entry of German forces into Zagreb, Jews were attacked on the street by gangs of Croatian collaborators. Some of the victims were stripped and beaten. Others were forced to eat a mix of boiled rice and cigarette butts. Men, women and children were marched from the Danica factory in Drnja to clean latrines, ditches and channels with their bare hands. The great synagogue of Sarajevo was plundered on 16 April 1941. In Osijek, wealthy Jews paid a bribe of 20 million dinars to head off a pogrom.[49] At the end of April, the Ustashi government issued a host of racial decrees, defining Jews according to the Nuremberg laws and forbidding employment of female servants under the age of 45. Intermarriage was banned (even though Pavelic and General Kwaternik had Jewish wives). Jews were ousted from the professions and government service. On 4 June 1941, the wearing of the Yellow Star was decreed. In Bosnia, Muslims were permitted to attack and loot Jewish homes and businesses.

By the fall of 1941, Jews were being deported from Croatian cities for 'spreading false news' and speculation.[50] Sarajevo's Jews suffered a series of nighttime roundups between September 1941 and August 1942. An observer from Berlin commented about Zagreb:

> There are no more Jews in town. Previously there had been about 9,000, and in the principal streets they owned most of the shops. Meeting a man or a woman wearing the yellow insignia is now very rare. The Jews who were very powerful, economically speaking, have been done away with in Zagreb with lightning speed. The synagogue, of Moorish style, which lent such a foreign note and which one passed on entering the city, is completely gone.[51]

On 10 December, a number of Jews from Zagreb were taken to the banks of the Sava, tied with wire, shot and dumped into the water.[52]

There were 21,000 Croatian Jews temporarily interned in the camps of Jasenovac, Loborgrad, Dakovo, Tenje and Pag Island. Those without papers were liquidated at once. Many of the 1,000 women housed in Kruscica were raped. The 1,300 women and children in Loborgrad had to use cooking pans as chamber pots.[53] Those who could work were sent to salt mines at Karlovac and Jadovo. In the autumn of 1941, 4,500 Jews and Serbs were massacred before the Croatians turned Pag Island over to the Italians. Interior Minister Artukovic worked with Franz Abromeit, an Austrian-Croat in Eichmann's office, to arrange the deportation of 4,927 Croatian Jews to Nazi death camps in August–September 1942.[54] The Nazis established nine special camps for children (Lobor, Jablanac, Mlaka, Brocice, Ustici, Sisak, Jastrebarsko, Gornja Rijeka and Stara Gradiska). There was little chance of survival at Stara Gradiska. As Gordana Friedlender recalled:

> … Vrban (commander of the camp) ordered all children to be separated from their mothers and put in one room. Ten of us were told to carry them there in blankets. The children crawled about the room, and one child put an arm and leg through the doorway, so that the door could not be closed. Vrban shouted: 'Push it!' When I refused to obey, he banged the door and crushed the child's leg. Then he took the child by its whole leg, and banged it against the wall until it was dead. After that we continued carrying the children in. When the room was full, Vrban brought poison gas and killed them all.[55]

In February 1942, Artukovic boasted to the *Sabor* (parliament) how he was helping to write a glorious page in Croatian history. He told how Jewish capitalists, allied with the communists, sought to destroy the Croatian people. They had failed. 'The Croatian people, having reestablished their independence, could not do otherwise but to clean off the poisonous damagers and insatiable parasites – Jews, Communists, and Free-masons – from the national and state body.'[56] In addition to the Serbian dead, the Croatians were accountable for the deaths of 20,000 Gypsies and 50,000 Jews in World War II.[57]

THE ITALIANS IN DISTRICT II

With good reason, thousands of Serbs and Jews fled south to District II, the coastal zone that was under Italian control. The Italian military repeatedly intervened on behalf of the Croatians' victims, going so far as to send tanks to escort refugees to safety.[58] By mid-summer 1942, there were 4,500 Jews living in Dubrovnik, Spalato, Zebenico, Cattaro and Mostar. For the Nazis, Jews in the second zone constituted 'a great hindrance and their removal would ease matters generally'.[59]

The Croatian government offered to subsidize the shipment of its Jews and those in the Italian zone to Poland at a bounty of 30 marks per person. The Germans involved in negotiations – Luther, Ambassador Siegfried Kasche, and special liaison Otto von Bismarck – lamented the Italians' lack of cooperation. Said Luther, 'We have evidence of the effective resistance of the Italian authorities against the anti-Jewish measures of the Croatian Government, in favor of wealthy Jews.'[60] In October, Kasche complained, 'I keep getting the impression that the Italian attitude is intended to drag the matter.'[61] In the spring of 1941 Italian troops offered no objections to the bloodlust of their allies. Mobs were permitted to ravage synagogues in Susak and Split. There were 496 Jewish hostages seized in Korcula, another 1,250 interned at Kraljevica. There were no interventions when the Ustashis took prisoners from Pag Island and drowned them in the Adriatic. At the end of 1941, the Italians delivered 400 Jews from Kosmet to the *gaswagens* of Semlin.[62] But in the summer of 1942, when the Nazis demanded the Jews from Mostar, General Mario Roatta responded that it was impossible because all inhabitants of Mostar had been given assurances of equal treatment. Besides, Roatta informed the Inspector-General of the Todt Organization, such action was 'not in keeping with the honour of the Italian army'.[63]

After the Nazis sent Bismarck to Rome in August, the Italian Foreign Ministry prepared a background report on deportation for Mussolini. The document warned of a terrible fate for Jews if deportation were agreed to. Nevertheless, *Il Duce* jotted down the words *'nulla osta'* (not opposed). Italian diplomats and military officers were not ready to capitulate. They did intern numbers of refugees, creating a sense of despair on the part of some

Jews. Because of the presence of so many nationalities, the Italians announced they were going to conduct a census – ostensibly to determine which Jews were 'bound to territories' annexed by Italy. This counting went on till December. In that four-month period, the Italians did not turn over a single Jew.

When the Pavelic government suggested that Jewish refugees be transferred to Italy proper, the Marquis d'Ajeta exclaimed, 'Italy is not Palestine!' Even Mussolini backtracked after a less than pleasant visit from Ribbentrop early in 1943. Mussolini summoned General Robotti (commanding the Second Army), Pirzio Birolli (governor of Montenegro) and General Ambrosio (chief of the Headquarters General Staff) to the Palace Venezia. He explained that he had agreed to turn the Jews over to the Germans at Trieste. When General Robotti responded that aligning the Italians with the Ustashis and Nazis would have painful consequences among the Yugoslav population, Mussolini reversed himself, saying: 'True, I was compelled to consent to the expulsion, but you all think of whatever excuses you please, so as not to hand over even one single Jew. Say that we have no means of transport to take them to Trieste, and that transport by land is impossible.'[64]

Slowly, the Italians began shifting Jews to detention camps in mainland Italy. In March 1943 they concentrated the bulk of their 4,000 Jews at Porto Re in Istria and on the islands of Lopud and Arbe. When Mussolini's regime collapsed in July 1943, Augusto Rosso, the new Secretary-General of the Foreign Ministry, cabled the commander of the Second Army: 'We must avoid leaving behind the Croatian Jews or handing them over to the mercy of strangers, deprived of all protection, or exposed to the danger of repressions.'[65] Unfortunately, the Bagdolio government could not fend off a Nazi invasion or the entrapment of the remaining Jews on Arbe island.

By 1944, Pavelic realized that the Nazis could not win the war. His power reduced to the point that he was derided as 'the Mayor of Zagreb', the Croatian dictator initiated contacts with the Red Cross and Joint Distribution Committee. Ustashi apologists argue that many Jews managed to save their lives and property because of the actions of Pavelic and Archbishop Aloysius Stepinac of Zagreb. The latter, who condemned racism in March 1938 ('all of the nations are children of God'), offered several sermons in 1942 reminding his listeners of the unity of the human race. A year later, Stepinac condemned the 'shame, blot and crime' of Jasenovac and called upon Pavelic to repeal discriminatory laws. In fact, the last years of war brought no end of massacres of Serbs and Jews in Prijane, Halalpic, Dubrave, Deeljak, Podgreda and Travnik. Bishop Stepinac may have been a philo-Semite, but he was also a Croatian nationalist. In 1941 the Bishop welcomed Pavelic and his black-shirted Ustashi band to Zagreb and proclaimed the creation of the state of Croatia from the pulpit on Easter Sunday. Stepinac blessed the leaders of the Brotherhood of Crusaders, Catholic volunteers who participated in attacks upon Serbs and Jews in 1941–42. Stepinac approved the conversion campaign to 'take schismatics to its bosom' provided their return was sincere. The Archbishop also defended the Ustashi in a lengthy memorandum on atrocities prepared for Pius XII in the spring of 1943.[66] Stepinac ultimately was rewarded for his fealty by being raised to rank of Cardinal. As for Pavelic, his hope that he somehow might elude post-war prosecution was ill-founded. Named to the first list of the United Nations War Crimes Commission in 1945, the Ustashi Poglavnik fled to Austria. Aided by Catholic prelates who supplied 'Father Benarez' with false papers and a cassock, he escaped to Argentina. In December 1959, Pavelic died in a hospital in Spain. His obituary noted that he was implicated in the deaths of 700,000 Serbs and Jews.

Romania: The Hamans of Moldavia

Sodom is the term Simon Dubnow affixed to Romania.[1] Decades before the Holocaust, this Jewish historian described Romania as the most corrupt and anti-Semitic of all the successor states. Said Dubnow:

> Between Eastern and Western Europe stood a country that harbored the most ruthless hatred toward Jews, a country that concealed political barbarism under the mantle of constitutionalism. Under the cover of legitimacy, the government of the Rumanian kingdom created for Jews a hell of deprivation of rights and of subjugation on a par with neighboring Russia. An ignorant and uncultured mass of peasants who were being exploited by the gentry, a no less dark and fanatical Greek orthodox petty bourgeoisie that endeavored to oust Jews from the cities, and an officialdom that was downright mercenary from the policeman to the cabinet minister – such was Christian Rumania.[2]

Romania was created in the nineteenth century out of two Balkan principalities – Wallachia and Moldavia. Formal independence from Turkey was not granted until the Congress of Berlin in 1878. Though its monarchs were Hohenzollerns, Romania joined the Allies in World War I. Overrun by the Germans and forced to make a humiliating peace, Romania was rewarded for its efforts at Versailles with Bukovina, Transylvania, northern Banat and Bessarabia. Doubled in size, Romania's population grew from 7 million to 18 million, many of them Magyars, Ukrainians, Poles, Gypsies and Jews. People who had longed for liberation from Turkish or Russian guardianship reacted to their own freedom by proclaiming '*Romania Romanilor*' (Romania for Romanians) and treating other minorities as *Straini* (foreigners). Under King Carol, life for Christians who were not Romanian was difficult. For Jews, it was impossible.

There probably were Jewish traders in Romania in the earliest Roman period. The *voivods* may have paid tribute to Jewish kings of Khazaria in the eighth century. Jewish merchants and artisans came from Poland and Russia, lured by tax exemptions for synagogues, schools and burial grounds. They encountered peasants who blamed Jews for the death of Christ. Romania's middle class resented Jewish enterprise. Whenever a cabinet considered emancipating Jews, mobs would riot in Bucharest. In June 1867, Prime Minister Ion Bratianu (who referred to Jews as 'that leprosy') declared hundreds of

Jewish peddlers in Galatz vagabonds. They were taken by boat across the Danube where Turkish guards refused to accept them. As the refugees were shunted back and forth, the Romanians shouted, 'Out with the Jews into the heathen land of the Turks! Into the water with them!' Finally, after two people drowned, the Turks took them in.[3]

Before the Tsarist pogroms of 1881–82, there were massacres in Bucharest, Galatz and Jassy. The cry on the street was '*Afara cu jidani!*' ('out with the Jews'). Only 1,000 Jews achieved citizenship before the end of the century. But when the Jews tried to emigrate, the Romanian government made it difficult for them to obtain passports. Some 125,000, calling themselves 'the Wandering Jews', 'the Despairing', 'the Walkers', trudged overland to Hamburg in hopes of securing passage to England or America. On 11 August 1902, Secretary of State John Hay issued a circular letter to governments in Europe declaring that America could not remain 'a silent spectator of such an international injustice that is being perpetrated in Rumania'.[4] According to Hay, every conceivable restriction had been imposed upon this helpless people – political disabilities, denial of the right to own land or live in rural areas, requiring Jewish factory owners to hire two Romanian workers for every Jew. 'In short, by the cumulative effects of successive restrictions, the Jews have become reduced to a state of wretched misery.'[5] From Bucharest came a limp response that Romanian Jews refused to assimilate or conduct themselves in an honest fashion and most Romanian Jews were 'Mongol' converts who had been governed by the Austrians or Russians till 1828.

By 1900, Romania passed more than 200 anti-Semitic laws. Jews were barred from trading in liquor, tobacco or stocks. Quotas were established for doctors, lawyers and engineers. Denied access to Romanian hospitals, Jews could not build their own medical centers. When Jews responded to the *numerus clausus* by creating their own schools, the government decreed Sunday as the official day of rest. There were no Jewish representatives in parliament, none on municipal councils, and no Jewish officers in the Romanian army.[6] About the only concession made to these aliens was the abolition in 1909 of a degrading Jewish oath of allegiance dating to the Middle Ages.[7]

ROMANIA FROM VERSAILLES TO THE RUSSIAN WAR

During the inter-war years, Romania made a number of gestures designed to impress the democracies. At the urging of France, in 1921 it joined Czechoslovakia and Yugoslavia in a defensive alliance dubbed 'the Little Entente'. That same year, Foreign Minister Nicolae Titulescu resolved territorial disputes with Poland and the USSR. Romania signed the Kellogg–Briand treaty and became a member of the League of Nations. Its politicians promised to uphold the rights of minorities, including 350,000 Jews in the old kingdom,

150,000 in Transylvania and 300,000 in Bessarabia and Bukovina. The reality was something different.[8]

Old guard anti-Semites succeeded in amending Romania's constitution in 1923 requiring documents from Jews that were virtually unobtainable. Professor A.C. Cuza's National Christian Defense League (LANC) adopted the swastika as its symbol and the party's newspaper urged the killing of Jews. Between 1922 and 1927, the League of the Archangel Michael (*Garda de Fier*, Iron Guard) founded by the flamboyant Cornelius Codreanu carried out a number of murders of students, police officers and workmen that went unpunished. In 1927 synagogues and cemeteries in Bucharest, Oradea and Cluj were desecrated. During the Depression, Romania's anti-Semites concentrated on bankrupting the Jews by economic boycott.[9]

A Union of Jewish Communities headed by Dr Wilhelm Filderman contested the erosion of Jewish rights. Jews retaliated with their own boycott which proved successful in bringing down one nationalist regime. But they could not prevent the enactment of 89 anti-Jewish laws between 1938 and May 1942. Jews were dismissed from public service, law, medicine and pharmacy. Factory workers, clerks and teachers were fired without cause. Businesses were 'Romanized' at a fraction of their worth. By 1939 12,000 Jewish families who made their living through taverns could no longer sell liquor. Schools were closed and the translation of manuscripts into the Romanian language was prohibited.[10] In August 1940, the state revoked citizenship for Jews that could not prove their families resided in Romania in 1877.[11]

When Iron Guardists challenged Carol's authority in February 1937, the king suspended the constitution and arrested several leaders including Codreanu. After Munich, the Guardists again sparked pogroms and attempted to assassinate Carol. It was in this context that Codreanu and 13 of his colleagues were killed 'while trying to escape'.[12] Carol would not enjoy supremacy for long. On 24 November 1938, he visited Berlin and was informed that Germany desired closer ties with Romania. Four months later, Helmuth Wohltat and Wilhelm Fabritius dictated terms of an economic pact that gave Germany favored status in Romania's oil fields, agriculture and steel industry.[13] Carol was not around to witness the humiliation of his country. After Germany's defeat of France, he endorsed the New Order in Europe and took Romania out of the defunct League of Nations. His actions, however, did not win support from Hitler when Germany's other allies demanded the return of territories awarded to Romania after World War I.[14]

Between 28 June and 1 July 1940, the Romanians withdrew from Bessarabia and northwest Bukovina in a retreat marked by assaults against the Jewish populations. Two months later, Carol retroceded half of Transylvania to Hungary.[15] On 4 September, the king called upon General Antonescu to form a new cabinet. Antonescu agreed and made a deal with the Iron Guard, designating Codreanu's successor Horia Sima as Vice-Premier. On 7

September, Carol fled to Spain, taking with him $2.5 million in gold and leaving behind a 'Legionary state'. The Iron Guardists celebrated by looting Jewish businesses and murdering several moderate politicians. Antonescu promoted himself to the rank of Marshal and demanded to be called *Conducator* (Leader). In October 1940 he signed a military convention with Nazi Germany opening Romania to more than 600,000 German troops preparing for the invasion of Russia.

The delicate alliance between Antonescu and the Guardists could not be sustained. Believing they had the support of Wehrmacht General Erik Hansen, Sima and his followers tried to recreate Kristallnacht in Bucharest. On 21 January, Guardists stormed through the Jewish quarter, burning seven synagogues and tearing Jews from their homes. Some people were forced to drink gasoline mixed with Epsom salts. Others were doused with gasoline, then set afire. Eyewitnesses spoke of blackened corpses laying in the street with broken limbs, smashed noses, crosses cut into the skin of their backs. Hundreds of people were killed.[16] Robert St John, an American journalist, detailed what happened to some 200 Jewish men and women in Bucharest:

> The victims were taken to the abattoir on the edge of the city. There they were stripped naked, forced to get down on all fours, and were driven up the ramp of the slaughterhouse. Then they were put through all the stages of animals at slaughter until finally the beheaded bodies, spurting blood, were hung on iron hooks along the wall. As a last sadistic touch, the legionnaires took rubber stamps and branded the carcasses with the Romanian equivalent of FIT FOR HUMAN CONSUMPTION.[17]

After three days, 6,000 Jews lay dead and the popular saying on the street was, 'Kikes will be kikes: they like to pose as victims even after they've been murdered.'[18] Three hundred guardists were moved to Buchenwald because as General Hansen declared, 'Important military events are in the making.'[19]

ETHICAL PURIFICATION 1941

Elements of the Romanian Third and Fourth Armies accompanied the Germans when they invaded Russia. In this heady period, when the Nazis seemed invincible, Marshal Antonescu instructed his generals to detain 'all Yids and communist agents' until he decided how to deal with them.[20] Interior Minister Constantin Vasiliu advocated 'cleansing of the earth' through ghettoization and extermination of the Jews.[21] The clearest expression of the government's intentions came from the head of the Council of Ministers, Mihai Antonescu who declared: 'We find ourselves at an extremely favorable historical juncture ... for the ethical purification of our people from elements foreign to its soul, which grow like cancer and blacken our future.' Added Antonescu:

I am for the forced migration of the Jewish element in Bessarabia and Bukovina. They have to be thrown across the border. It is indifferent to me if we go down as barbarians in history ... a more favorable moment has never existed in our history ... The syrup-like, nebulous, philosophical humanitarianism is entirely out of place now. Let us take advantage of this historical moment and purge the soil of Romania and our nation of the misfortunes which were heaped upon this land in the course of the centuries. I tell you there is no law! Therefore, without any formality, entirely at your discretion, if it is necessary shoot with machine guns.[22]

Jews in the Regat (Old Romania) were punished before Romanian troops entered Soviet territory. Jassy was bombed during the last week of June. The city's 60,000 Jews were charged with having signaled Russian bombers and sniping at Romanian troops from the main synagogue.[23] A memorandum of the SS Feldgendarmerie dated 30 June 1941 states:

> *Sicherung der deutschen Truppen in Jasi Verhinderung jeder Agenten-verbindung von Jasi nach Rusland, Entwaffnung der Zivilbevolkerung und Sorge dafur zu tragen, die Bestattung der toten Zivilisten zu veranlassen. In Jasi war ein Aufstand der Juden versucht worden. Mit Waffengewalt wollten sie die Front durch Bedrohung der Soldaten in Jasi storen. Est hat etwa 2,500–5,000 Tote gegeben.* (The task of the German troops in Jassy was to prevent any contact between Jassy and Russia. Disarming of civil population and to ensure thereby the burial of the dead civilians. A group of Jews started an uprising with armed agitation in an attempt to disrupt the front by threatening soldiers in Jassy. This led to the deaths of some 2,500–5,000 Jews.)[24]

What actually happened was far more horrible. On 28 June, Jassy's Jews were summoned to Prefecture Square. Those who showed up were separated, women and children from men. Five hundred were shot and 5,000 more were packed into sealed railway cars and sent off. The trains were supposed to go to Poduloea on the Bessarabian border, but they simply moved back and forth with no destination. Every few hours, the cattle cars would be opened and stacks of people who had no air, food or water, spilled out onto the tracks. Italian journalist Curzio Malaparte described how peasants and Gypsies fought over shoes and underwear of the dead, demanding that the guards finish off any person found alive. In a group of 2,000, the only survivor was a baby of a few months. The situation was no better for the Jews remaining in Jassy. As Malaparte wrote:

> Up and down the narrow twisting streets leading toward the center of town, I heard all about me desperate barking, banging of doors, shattering of glass and of china, smothered screams, imploring voices calling *mama! mama!*, horrible beseeching cries of *nu, nu, nu!*... Hordes of Jews pursued by soldiers and maddened civilians armed with knives and crowbars fled along the streets; groups of policemen smashed in house doors with their

rifle butts; windows opened suddenly and screaming, disheveled women in nightgowns appeared with their arms raised in the air; some threw themselves from windows and their faces hit the asphalt with a dull thud.[25]

Twelve thousand Jews were massacred in Jassy. Within a week, most Bukovina towns were cleared of their Jews. One exception was Czernowitz (Cernauti), the provincial capital, where 45,000 survived a massacre on 5 July. In a 24-hour period, however, the city's main synagogue was burned and 2,000 Jews (including Chief Rabbi Dr Mark) were killed by Romanian troops assisting Einsatzgruppe D.[26] The Romanians were so brutal that Otto Ohlendorf and the German Legation in Bucharest complained of their excesses, in particular their habit of leaving dead bodies in the open.[27] Hitler commented to Goebbels that the Romanians seemed to be 'ahead' of the Germans in destroying Jews.[28] On 17 July, Romanians joined with German forces in ravaging Kishinev.[29] The pogrom lasted seven days and when it was over, 40,000 of Kishinev's 50,000 Jews were dead.[30] As the Romanian army advanced, it pushed Bessarabian Jews toward the Ukraine. When the refugees poured into the town of Atachi on the Dniester River, the Nazis, who occupied the other side of the river, permitted 25,000 Jews to cross 'the Bridge of Sighs'. But then the two fascist allies began shuttling boatloads of Jews back and forth across the Dniester, shooting people in the swampy water.[31] Eventually the Romanians set up makeshift camps in the border towns.[32]

Units of the 4th Romanian Army were welcomed by the Nazis into Odessa on 16 October. Six days later, Soviet saboteurs detonated a bomb at Romanian army headquarters on Engels Street, killing 61. In retaliation, 19,000 Jews were penned in the dockyard area. They were then sprayed with gasoline and burned alive. The next day, another 16,000 were massacred at trenches outside the city. Several thousand more, mainly women and children, were locked into four warehouses. These buildings were then set afire. As the Jews tried to escape, Romanian troops killed them with machine guns and hand grenades. According to eyewitnesses:

> Some of those inside appeared at the windows pointing at their head or heart for a bullet – the moment the soldiers raised their rifles to shoot, the victims disappeared. Then they reappeared ready to die. Women in an effort to save their children threw them out the window. There they were shot dead by the soldiers. One child with hands uplifted was seen running around for ten minutes – most soldiers had no heart to shoot at him.[33]

THE *TOITENWANDS* OF TRANSNISTRIA

Two months before the Odessa massacre (30 August 1941) the Germans and Romanians agreed to the Bug River as the border between their respective territories. Everything between the Dniester and Bug would become a new province – Transnistria – 16,000 square miles into which 140,000 Jews from

Bukovina and Bessarabia would be dumped.[34] Robbed of bank deposits and jewelry, the people moved 20 miles per day along yellow clay roads. Slackers were bayoneted, left to rot, or be picked over by crows and peasants.[35] Dr Mayer Teich, head of the Suceava Jewish community, noted the arrival of Jews at Atachi. 'Emaciated skeletons, clad in rags', their screams sounded like wild dogs. 'Their eyes bespoke the hunted animal's fear of death.'[36] Shaye Langer had been a delegate to the first Zionist Congress at Basel. Laying on a floor, the 92-year-old man asked: 'Dear Doctor, how is it possible that they drive me away from Suceava? I was born there ninety years ago. I took over my father's store and ran it for sixty years. I had been Imperial Councillor (under the Austrian regime), City Councillor, leader of the Congregation. I've never had any fight with anyone and was honored and liked by all.' Shortly after, Langer died. He was buried on the banks of the Dniester.[37]

As many as nine families were housed in a single hut with 'gutted walls and chimneys threatening to crumble any minute'.[38] Refugees who had passed this way earlier left their names inscribed on the walls in blood. They asked that *Kaddish*, the Jewish prayer for the dead, be recited for them.[39] *Toitenwand* (walls of death) is what the new occupants called these inscriptions and quite soon many of them would be making the same request. Only a few straggled into Moghilev where the engineer Siegfried Jagendorf organized the Jewish community.[40]

Even in Moghilev, life was precarious. Colonel Constantin Nasturas, a self-proclaimed poet, sent over 20,000 people to their deaths in Scazinetz, two rows of barracks where inmates were given nothing to eat but animal feed. Three thousand inmates at Peciora were reduced to eating excrement; 28 survived. Several thousand Jews accused of communist sympathies were imprisoned at Vapniarka and fed a poisonous vegetable that caused death in spasms. The Jews who entered Vertujen were told they would leave either dead or on all fours. They were fed a diet of cattle food that resulted in paralysis and death; 23,000 Jews died of starvation and typhus in Vertujen. Many of the 20,000 who died at Berhad could not be buried because the soil was frozen. In Tzibulovca, more than 1,800 confined in a single building succumbed to typhus. At Ladjin, none of the 4,800 deportees survived grueling work in a quarry. Colonel Modest Isopescu used a variety of methods to kill 70,000 Jews in Ukraine. At Bogdanovka, groups of men, women and children were taken into the woods where they were ordered to strip and stand in subzero temperatures. They were then pitched into a river or murdered with hand grenades. It took four days to kill 48,000 people in this manner.[41]

In October 1941, Romania's Chief Rabbi Alexandre Shafran and Dr Filderman appealed to Antonescu following the deportation of 1,500 Jews from Kishinev. Filderman had attended school with Antonescu and felt he could speak bluntly with the Marshal. Noting the plight of the aged and sick during eight days of travel in the snow, Filderman said, 'This is death, death, death without any other guilt than to be Jews!' Then: 'I implore you, Monsieur Marshal, do not permit such a crushing tragedy to happen.'[42]

Antonescu's response came on 19 October, three days before the Odessa massacre. He scored Filderman for taking the role of accuser when he had 'photos' showing Jews celebrating as Bukovina and Bessarabia were occupied by the Russians in 1940. Jewish criminals 'spat upon our officers, tore off their epaulets, ripped their uniforms, and when they could, beat and killed our soldiers like cowards'. During the occupation, they killed and mutilated, 'bringing grief and mourning into numerous Romanian homes'. They shed blood, 'very much blood' of Romanians. Antonescu admonished the Jewish leader: 'Do not pity, if you really have a soul, those who do not merit it; pity those who merit it.'[43]

Antonescu could have cared less what happened to Romania's Jews. On 16 December 1941, he informed his Council of Ministers: 'The Jewish Question is being negotiated in Berlin. The Germans will take all the Jews of Europe to Russia and settle them in certain regions. But the realization (of this) will take time. What should we do during this interval with them? Should we be waiting for what will be decided in Berlin? Should we wait for a decision in a matter which concerns us? Shall we try to shelter them? Put them in catacombs? Throw them in the Black Sea? I don't want to know anything. Perhaps 100 of them will die, perhaps 1,000 of them will die, perhaps they all will die.'[44] About the same time, he told a Spanish diplomat, 'This is war time, a good time to settle the Jewish problem once and for all.' Despite his agreements with the Nazis, Antonescu continued to expel Jews into German-held territory. In February 1942, Alfred Rosenberg, Reichsminister for Ukraine, complained about the arrival of 60,000 infected with typhus. More were forced across the Bug River that summer. The Nazis did not appreciate these 'wild' expulsions before killing centers in Poland were ready to process Jews.[45]

THE JEWS OF OLD ROMANIA

Dr Filderman and Rabbi Shafran were more successful in protecting those in the *Regat*.[46] The Antonescu government outlawed conversions of Jews in March 1941. That December, the Union of Jewish Communities was dissolved and replaced by the *Centrala Evreilor* (Central Office of Romanian Jews) headed up by Dr Nandor Gingold, a convert who would serve time in prison after the war. Gingold was a stooge for Radu Lecca, the fascist Commissar for Jewish Affairs, who periodically fined the Jewish community ($10 million in May 1942, $20 million in May 1943). Dr Filderman was deported to Moghilev for opposing the last fine. Before that, Filderman convinced government officials that 'alive, the Jews in Old Romania were more profitable than they were dead'. When in March–April 1941 the government began forcing Jews from Bucharest and surrounding communities into ghettos, Filderman reminded Antonescu of the danger this posed to real estate values. The order was canceled and shortly after the US unlocked $100,000 in Romanian assets and exchanged Romanian nationals for some

Jews. When Romanian propaganda denounced Jews as capitalists, he asked how they could also be Bolsheviks. When, in the summer of 1941, the government ordered Jews to wear the yellow star, Filderman pointed out that not even the Germans, Italians or Hungarians were requiring the badge at that time. The order was rescinded in September.[47]

Filderman's greatest coup (shared with Rabbi Shafran) was in stalling deportation of Jews from Wallachia/Moldavia to Poland. During the summer of 1942, Antonescu ordered the removal of Jewish communists to Vapniarka. At the same time, Lecca approved the transport of Transnistrian Jews beyond the Bug. In August, Antonescu and his Vice-Premier Mihai Antonescu agreed to Himmler's demands for all Jews from the old kingdom and Transylvania. Their destination would be Adjud, then Belzec. The entire process was supposed to take one year. Filderman and Shafran appealed to Queen Helena, Maria Antonescu, the Orthodox Patriarch Nichodemus, the Nuncio Monsignor Cassulo and Tit Semedrea, Metropolitan of Czernowitz.[48] On 15 September 1942, Shafran discussed the threat of deportation with Nicolae Balan, the anti-Semitic metropolitan of Transylvania. Balan was so upset by the news that as he was about to leave, he took the rabbi's hands, looked him in the eyes and told him to remember that day. Later that afternoon, Shafran received a call from Balan informing him that Antonescu had canceled the deportation plan.[49]

There was a price for their cooperation, however, and that was Transylvania. Antonescu and his colleagues resented the fact that this territory had been stripped away by Hungary in 1940. While Romania committed more than 500,000 troops to the struggle for the New Europe (nearly one-quarter of whom died in combat), Hungary made no comparable sacrifice.[50] The Romanians were further affronted when they received reports that Germany was claiming Transylvania based on the presence of so-called Saxons in the region.[51] Pressured by the Nazis, the Romanian government caved in, if only momentarily, on 10 October 1942. The Transnistrian Jews, who were going to die anyway, would now be sent to Poland. Later that same day, Antonescu reversed himself. Perhaps what was happening at El Alamein and Stalingrad prompted this change of heart. The Romanians also may have been influenced by a warning from Cordell Hull that America might retaliate against Romanian nationals living in the US if there were further deportations. Antonescu finally acknowledged what Dr Filderman had been stressing: Romania's Jews were more valuable as live hostages than as dead statistics.[52]

JEWS FOR SALE

In the last two years of the war, everyone, it seemed, had ideas how to profit from trading in Romanian Jews. Over the objections of Ambassador von Killinger, Radu Lecca informed the Allies early in 1943 that 75,000 Romanian

Jews could be purchased for less than $100 million. Five months later, the Nazis supposedly agreed to let 70,000 Romanian children go to Palestine if the Red Cross provided shipping. The figure was later changed to 35,000 contingent upon cooperation of the Bulgarian government. Then the number of children was dropped to 5,000, selected from the Lodz ghetto. Ambassador von Thadden insisted that the children be sent to England.[53]

Few people believed that Hitler would permit a handful of Jews to escape extermination. One group that did was the American-based Committee for a Jewish Army. Affiliated with the Irgun in Palestine, this militant organization was headed by Peter Bergson, Samuel Merlin and Ben Hecht. On 16 February 1943, the group purchased a four-column advertisement in the *New York Times*. Authored by Hecht, a celebrated playwright, the ad was addressed to 'the Four Freedoms, in care of the United Nations'. Hecht argued that Romania's offer had been endorsed by the *Manchester Guardian* and the inhabitants of Palestine. For those who fretted that there might be spies among the refugees, Hecht said, if any were discovered, 'You can shoot them.'[54]

One week after this ad appeared, Rabbi Stephen Wise informed the press that the State Department had received no confirmation of such an offer. The entire scheme, he wrote John Haynes Holmes was 'a hoax on the part of the Hecht group'.[55] In fact, Assistant Secretary of State Adolf Berle did receive a message from Gerhart Riegner of the World Jewish Congress in Bern on 10 February 1943 requesting earnest money of $3.5 million.[56] On 14 August 1943 Roosevelt informed Wise and Treasury Secretary Morgenthau that financial arrangements were being with America's representative in Bern, Leland Harrison. Still, there was no action because the plan had to be approved by the British.[57] It was not until 17 December that the British Foreign Office registered its assent. The next day, Breckinridge Long cabled Riegner telling him he could commence negotiations with the Romanians drawing on a fund of $25,000, a fraction of the sum Riegner had originally requested.[58]

Not surprisingly, few Romanian Jews managed to escape. As late as April 1944 Marshal Antonescu was offering to sell 7,000 orphans in Transnistria to the Red Cross. Hecht and Bergson blamed Wise and mainstream Zionist leadership in the US for down-playing the crisis. Wise, in turn, charged the State Department with bungling and callousness over 11 months during which time 'thousands of lives might have been saved and the Jewish catastrophe partially averted'.[59] Morgenthau concurred, noting that 'The State Department was usually among those who scoffed at economic warfare in other connections.' But Morgenthau reserved his chief criticism for the British. Of their December cable that finally approved rescue, Morgenthau snapped, 'The letter was a satanic combination of British chill and diplomatic double-talk, cold and correct, and adding up to a sentence of death.'[60]

LIBERATION

Nora Levin claims that by January 1943, Himmler and his aides 'had given up Romania as a co-partner in the Nazi program for the 'Final Solution'.[61] The Romanian government, reacting to threats of retribution, eased back on anti-Semitic propaganda.[62] Rabbi Shafran kept the Nuncio apprised of conditions facing Jews in outlying districts. In the spring of 1943, Monsignor Cassulo returned from a visit to Transnistria and registered a protest with Radu Lecca. That summer Antonescu approved a plan for repatriation of converts, veterans, war orphans, government prisoners, widows and aged; 40,000 of these refugees would be admitted to a convalescent camp that was established in Vijnita. With the Romanians seeking an armistice in November 1943, Antonescu informed his cabinet that he would not tolerate any more killings in Transnistria because 'these terrible murders' would give him 'a bad reputation'.[63]

A month later (16 December 1943) Antonescu permitted Charles Kolb and a delegation of the International Red Cross to visit the Jewish community in Shargorod. The delegation was supposed to see only well-fed prisoners living in clean houses. By accident, they stumbled across a windowless room where several hundred unattended children in rags were laying on the floor. A Romanian officer, Major Oraseanu, smacked the door shut with his whip. After the war, Kolb rationalized that it would have served no use to denounce the Romanians.[64] But in his memoirs he commented how for the deportees of Shargorod 'their only freedom was to die'.[65]

About the same time Kolb was at Shargorod, contacts were made in Istanbul between the Romanian Minister to Turkey and Ira Hirschmann, special representative of the United States War Refugee Board. Hirschmann offered immunity from war crimes prosecution to top-ranking Romanian officials if the Romanians would: disband the Transnistrian camps; release 5,000 Jewish children for Palestine; and halt all anti-Semitic persecutions. Amazingly, in March 1944 the Antonescu regime agreed. Jews in the Regat who lived in terror of deportation could now relax. King Michael took control of the government and ordered the arrest of Antonescu on 23 August 1944. The next week, Romania asked Russia for peace and joined the war against Germany.

In April 1946 Marshal Antonescu was executed by firing squad in Bucharest. He was condemned as much by his own words as his actions. In February 1944, he lamented that he had not completed the task of expelling Jews from Bessarabia and Bukovina 'for it has been conclusively proved to me that among those who remain are the greatest number of enemies of the State'.[66] Antonescu was not the only Romanian leader put to death at war's end. Joining him before the firing squad were his chief aide Mihai Antonescu, former Interior Minister Constantin Vasiliu and Gheorghe Alexianu, one-time governor of Transnistria. Radu Lecca, Commissar for Jewish Affairs, was spared at the last moment.

In 1946, the Anglo-American Committee of Inquiry regarding the Problem of European Jewry and Palestine put the number of Jews who perished in Romania at 530,000. Raul Hilberg estimated 430,000, Jacob Lestchinsky 425,000, Gerald Reitlinger 200,000. Fewer than 50,000 of the 300,000 Jews in Bessarabia or Bukovina were still alive. Most of Transylvania's Jews had been deported to Belzec or Auschwitz. Only the Jews of Old Romania had been spared the full onslaught of Nazi and Iron Guard terror, and even here perhaps 100,000 were gone.[67]

Greece: Destruction of a Sephardic Civilization

On the morning of 6 December 1942 Jews in Salonika, the major seaport in Macedonia, were startled to learn that 500 Greek workmen were proceeding toward the Jewish cemetery at the outskirts of town armed with pickaxes. Despite a municipal law passed at the turn of the century which made the burial grounds inviolate, despite a promise made to Jewish elders by Dr Alfred Merten, German administrator for Salonika, earlier that summer, the workmen were bound to raze the cemetery as part of a planned expansion of the neighboring University of Salonika.

The Jewish cemetery was a grand site, 350,000 square meters of shade trees that doubled as a public park. It contained 300,000 graves, the oldest of which was dated to 1493, a year after Sephardic refugees fleeing Spain were welcomed by the Ottoman Turks. The early markers were simple stones, crowded side by side, barely covering the actual coffins. As Jews prospered, families constructed ornate vaults or erected marble steles over brick pedestals. Some bore inscriptions in several languages. Scholars came here to converse in Castilian and listen as oldtimers spun tales of life in Toledo and Seville.

21. Salonika. Despoilation of a 500-year-old Jewish cemetery (Yad Vashem).

People boasted that if Columbus returned to the earth, he would be more at home in Salonika than in his birthplace of Palos. Twenty generations of rabbis, poets, merchants, shipbuilders and chandlers were laid to rest here. As one survivor from Salonika declared, 'No one dared disturb the repose of the dead.'[1]

Until December 1942. As the workmen applied themselves to leveling the cemetery, Jews pleaded with them not to do this awful thing. Within a few days, the cemetery was transformed into an expanse of broken stones. After the Germans used what they needed to line a swimming pool, some streets of Salonika are paved with marble tombstones.[2] Jews collected remains of the dead and reburied them in a cemetery at Vardar. For the rest, as one survivor from Salonika recounted, 'The bones of generations of Jews who had come to Greece seeking refuge in this tolerant country were thrown into the sea.'[3]

Jews had lived among Greeks on Aegean islands, on mainland peninsulas, in Athens, Corinth and Janina throughout the Diaspora. Their existence was never as idyllic as some Greek historians suggest.[4] Peasants harbored animosities that were grounded in Orthodox Christian beliefs. Relations worsened during the Greek war for independence when Jews in Salonika, Larissa and Smyrna were accused of pro-Turkish allegiance. The death of the Patriarch Gregory was attributed to the Jews and hundreds were massacred.[5] When the daughter of a Jewish tailor on Corfu was killed at Passover in 1899 Gentiles claimed she was a victim of ritual murder and carried out pogroms which lasted three weeks. Thousands of Jews left Corfu, Zanti and the Thessalian towns of Volos and Trikkala. And though 5,000 Jews served in Allied ranks during the First Balkan War, Jews suffered persecution at the hands of both Serbs and Greeks in 1912. Only the intervention of King George prevented wholesale massacres. The King assured the chief rabbi of Greece that Jews would be granted full equality. Prime Minister Venizelos took the same position in 1919 when he quashed another ritual murder accusation in Salonika.[6]

After Versailles, there were 75,000 Jews in Greece, 60,000 in Salonika where they constituted one fourth of the population.[7] Most were poor merchants and laborers. Disliked by Greek nationalists whose unoriginal rallying cry was 'Greece for the Greeks',[8] 4,000 Jews from Salonika volunteered to fight when Italy invaded Greece in October 1940. Of the first 500 men wounded in combat, 186 (37 percent) were Jews. One hero in the campaign against the fascists was Colonel Mordechai Frizis, a Zionist from Chalchis, who was killed by enemy aircraft while leading his men on horseback.[9]

LIBERTY SQUARE, 11 JULY 1942

Unfortunately, Hitler decided to alter the balance of power in the Balkans by declaring war against Yugoslavia and Greece on 6 April 1941. Greek collaborators cheered as German troops marched through the streets of Salonika on 9 April.[10] The Axis dictated an armistice to the right-leaning

22. Beating Jews, Liberty Square, July 1942 (Yad Vashem).

government of Prime Minister Constantin Logothetopoulos leaving the Italians in control of much of the country, including Athens. Bulgaria was awarded eastern Thrace and Macedonia. By taking Salonika, Germany inherited most of the Jews in Greece.

As in Yugoslavia and France, the Italians proved to be kindly toward Jews, offering refugees lodgings, documents, even financial assistance. It was in the German zone that most trouble occurred after 1941. The SS commandeered a synagogue and the 97-bed Jewish hospital for their use. They banned Jewish newspapers and sponsored a new anti-Semitic journal *Nea-Europi*.[11] The Bank of Salonika became a subsidiary of the Reichsbank. On 15 April, the Gestapo took all but two members of the Jewish Council (President Dr Halevi and Chief Rabbi Zvi Koretz were visiting Athens) away in handcuffs. Koretz and Halevi were arrested upon their return. Rabbi Koretz was jailed for eight months for 'anti-Nazi propaganda'. While he was gone, the invaders carried out several roundups ostensibly to punish communist provocateurs. They executed their first Jew in Salonika on 2 July 1941, for insulting a German soldier.[12] With the occupation, factories and docks closed and people were thrown out of work. The winter of 1941–42 proved especially difficult. 'Hideous phantoms' in rags begged on the street corners and rummaged through garbage cans. With cold and starvation came disease – typhus, scabies, tuberculosis. The death toll rose from a pre-war figure of 15 per day to more than 60. Corpses were stacked at the Jewish cemetery. The Nazis would not permit their burial.[13]

Salonika's *Kehillah* urged everyone to endure, to survive. The Jewish community maintained two orphanages, a Torah-trade school for boys and *Matanoth Laevionim* (Aid to the Needy) which distributed meals to 5,000 children daily. *Malbuch Arumim* (Clothing for the Poor) supplied clothing for children. *Yechua v' Rahamim* (Redemption and Compassion) supplied fuel to the needy. *Bikur Holim* (Aid to the Sick) treated 25,000 patients at three dispensaries. It was all in vain. As Max Revah commented, 'Our dear children, more than 12,000 were the prey of the flames of Auschwitz.'[14]

On 11 July 1942, Salonika's daily newspapers (*Nea-Europi* and *Apoye-matini*) instructed Jewish men to report the next morning at Independence Square *(Elefteria)*. Saby Saltiel who was serving as head of the Jewish Council, learned of the summons by reading the papers. Members of the Council were exempt, but all other Jewish men between the ages of 18 and 45 were to assemble at the spot where the Young Turks proclaimed their liberal revolution in 1908. Salonika's Jews were publicly degraded over the next four days. Photos in *Nea-Europi* showed Greek spectators laughing as Jews were forced to roll on the pavement like dogs.[15] Pepo Cohen, a professor of mathematics, recalled the terrible events of that first day:

> There was a crowd of 9,000 men at Liberty Square. The day was very hot. We had to stand in lines. The Nazis ringed the square with machine guns and small canons. It was forbidden to sit down, to break ranks, to screen the sun with a paper, or put on sunglasses. It was forbidden to light a cigarette, to make a friendly gesture to a brother, to a friend. The Nazi soldiers struck blows for the slightest infraction of their orders. They hit on the right and left side of the head, on the shoulders. They made us do useless calisthenics, to crawl in the dust, to roll over, to jump like frogs. All of this was accompanied by insults in German which were delivered with whips. On that day I learned how cruel people could be. I saw several friends faint. I also learned that this kind of activity could kill. These scenes of sadism very much amused the young German girls who were on the balconies of hotels at the Independence Square.[16]

The Nazis conscripted 3,500 men from the square for work on forti-fications and airfields. Shortly after the first contingent was sent off, Civil Administrator Merten appeared before Jewish leaders and offered to use his influence (as 'a friend of the Jews') to have the labor gangs released along with Jews who were in prison. He would need 3.5 billion drachmas[17] an impossible sum in view of relief costs. The Jews convinced Merten to take 2.5 billion drachmas (still more than one million dollars) in installments. Sacks of money were turned over to the Nazi administrator and his aide Meisner on the first of October, November, December 1942 and January 1943. When the fifth payment was due, Salonika's Jews had to appeal to coreligionists in Athens for assistance.[18]

The labor gangs did come back, but in a deplorable state. One in eight died in malarial swamps where the Nazis referred to inmates as *Stücken* (pieces). Upon their return to Salonika, survivors (60 percent of whom were sick) were given double rations and a fatty soup devised by dietitians. Some of the workers were restored to health, only to perish in Auschwitz. Merten made many promises to the Jews of Salonika. He promised to protect their precious cemetery. He told Yomtov Yacoel, a member of the council, that the Jews of Salonika would never be subjected to the Nuremberg Laws or the fate of other Jewish communities in Europe.[19] The same promise was made by Ioannis Rallis, the new prime minister of Greece, when he visited Salonika early in 1943. Rallis dissimulated. Merten lied.

THE INFERNO OF BARON HIRSCH

Dieter Wisliceny and Alois Brunner, the chief officers of *Sonderkommando fur Judenangelengenheiten in Salonika*, arrived in Salonika on 6 February 1943. They had been told by Eichmann that the Final Solution now meant 'the biological annihilation of the Jewish race in the Eastern Territories'.[20] Operating out of the basement of an elegant villa at #42 Vellisariou Street, Eichmann's assistants advised Dr Merten of the new policy on Jews. The chief administrator responded with a flurry of decrees. Order #1237 issued 6 February stipulated that Jews over the age of 5 were to wear the yellow star. Jewish businesses also had to be marked.[21] Merten's first decree restricted Jews to three areas of Salonika, the Mizrachi Street district, the region between Singru Street and Vardar, and the Baron de Hirsch refugee camp. A second order (#1517) issued 13 February, prohibited any change in residence without permission of the Gestapo. Anyone who violated curfew, used the telephone or rode streetcars would be shot. On 25 February 1943, Merten issued Order #2014, which expelled Jews from professional organizations and unions.[22]

The Jewish council met to discuss these measures, but 'nobody knew what to do because it all happened so quickly'.[23] Salonika's Jews donned the badge and competed for low-numbered work permits. (Rabbi Koretz was #1. Members of the Jewish police also had low numbers.) There were rumors that the Nazis were planning to ship 3,000 Jews to Auschwitz. Salonika's Jews celebrated Purim and prayed that they would avoid such a catastrophe. On 5 March, Rabbi Koretz told his co-religionists not to yield to panic.[24] When the SD issued a callup for the first transport on 14 March, Koretz, who was from Galicia, tried to bolster these unfortunates by telling them, 'The great community of Cracow affirms that it will look after your well-being. Each of you will get a job conforming to your needs, your aptitudes, your knowledge and your experience.'[25] (The reality was that at this time Cracow was being purged of its Jews.) Three days later, Koretz was nearly mobbed by doomed Jews when he declared, 'These are tough times, tragic. There is no way out but to gird our loins and go into exile.'[26]

Michael Molho and Joseph Nehama accuse Rabbi Koretz of naïveté. Raul

Hilberg called him 'an ideal tool for the German bureaucrats' and added 'rarely had a major operation been carried out so smoothly'.[27] In Koretz's defense, it should be noted that he had no confirmation of the death camps. He wanted desperately to believe that correspondence from the first deportees telling of land grants in Ukraine was true. Koretz did call upon Prime Minister Rallis to intervene so a community 'which had existed for two thousand years in Salonika would not be liquidated'.[28] When the Nazis asked for 3,000 workers who would remain in Greece, Koretz, recognizing that slave labor was preferable to deportation, recommended the number be increased to 15,000. He supported church officials who suggested Jews be interned on a Greek island. He thought he had reached a deal with Merten to halt the deportations in exchange for a bribe of 50 percent of the remaining wealth of Jews in Salonika.[29] And on numerous occasions, Koretz, who died in Belsen, urged people to flee to the mountains.[30]

The 400 Jews of nearby Florina were the first to go. They were moved to Baron Hirsch in Salonika. Named for a prominent French-Jewish philanthropist, this camp had been constructed for refugees fleeing Tsarist pogroms at the turn of the century. The camp was supposed to hold 2,000 persons. After February 1942, 10,000 Jews were stuffed into the dilapidated huts of Baron Hirsch. From watch towers, guards scanned the camp with searchlights. There were three gates, on the east and south funneling people in, the third leading to a railway station which took people away to Poland. The camp was commanded by a 23-year-old lieutenant E.D. Gerbin assisted by a renegade Jew Vital Hasson and his bodyguard Leon Sion.[31] The first residents of Baron Hirsch were the poor, the old and sick, and infants. They were joined by residents of the workers' ghetto, which supposedly was infested with communists. Then came the turn of middle class Jews.[32] Women from the finest families took turns sweeping streets and washing dishes, rabbis picked up trash, and young people got married in the overflowing huts of Baron Hirsch.[33]

On 11 March Merten and Wisliceny demanded that Jews turn over all personal property, furniture and valuables within four days. In return, they were given yellow vouchers payable to the Bank of Cracow. The exchange rate was 33 zlotys for 1,000 drachmas. Real property was catalogued by the Governor General and National Mortgage Bank before being transferred to Aryan owners. Jews who tried to conceal their wealth were taken to the basement of the villa on Vesalliou Street where they were pistol-whipped or dunked in the fancy fountains. The many jars overflowing with jewels and coins brought to mind the treasures of Ali Baba.[34] Meanwhile, in the evening, Cleobule Demetriades, a world-famous chef, prepared banquets for the SS and their lady friends.[35]

Merten, Wisliceny, Brunner, Gerblin and other SS leaders were present as the first convoy left Salonika at 11 a.m. on 15 March 1943. About 2,800 persons were squeezed into 40 cattle cars. Some were blind or legless war veterans. Another 150 were insane. A few were criminals. Seventy were more than 90 years old. The Jewish Council gathered food for the 15-day trip – bread, dried figs and raisins, black olives, orange marmalade and citrons. The Jews also carried quantities of halvah, chocolate and olive oil. Representatives of the International Red Cross supplied milk, sugar and semolina to nursing mothers and their babies. Every few days (15, 17, 19, 23 and 27 March) the cattle cars were filled with new victims. Recalled Sarina Saltiel-Venezia, 'The stay there was so hellish that departure inspired no fear. It was a relief. There was something of a hallucination in the air, as if the end of the world was near.'[36]

In the midst of this agony, Merten issued another edict on 21 March. Enraged by the activities of Dr Leon Cuenca, a Jewish physician who, with the blessing of Red Cross President Karl Burckhardt, was moving from one ghetto to another, Merten arrested Cuenca and his wife and placed them on the third convoy. Merten claimed that Cuenca had tried to run away. He also seized 25 Jews as hostages, warning they would be shot for the slightest infraction of rules. The Nazis meant what they said. All told, 600 hostages were executed.[37]

Such brutality did not go unnoticed by the Patriarch Theophilos Damaskinos in Athens. The highest official of the Greek Orthodox church registered a protest to Logothetopoulos on 23 March, as the fourth convoy was leaving Baron Hirsch. Damaskinos noted that the transports violated the armistice between Greece and Germany which guaranteed equal treatment to all Greek citizens. The patriarch evoked images of Jewish service to Greece on the battlefield, of Jewish children who were 'part of the national body'. He reminded the prime minister that 'our sacred religion does not recognize any difference of superiority or inferiority based on race or religion'. Damaskinos suggested that if Jews posed a threat to German security, they could be interned under Greek guard in Greece. The Patriarch asked the prime minister to submit a demarche to the Nazis offering 'the unanimous reprobation of the nation for the acts of deportation which have begun'.[38] Logothetopoulos's successor Rallis did offer such a protest the following month. It was ignored.

There would be 18 *Apostoli* (convoys) from Salonika before the last train carrying 2,000 Jews departed on 2 August. By the end of the year, there were only three Jews left in the city. The Jews from Salonika were in such deplorable condition when they reached Auschwitz (Rudolf Hoess complained how they were 'of such poor quality' that all but a few had to be killed immediately) that they sparked a typhus epidemic. As a result, transports had to be diverted to Sobibor and Majdanek for three weeks. Ninety-six percent of Salonika's Jews died in the Holocaust. When asked at his post-war trial why he signed the deportations, Merten offered the unoriginal defense, 'I was following orders. Besides, I was certain it would never be applied.'[39]

STROOP IN ATHENS

Prior to the degradation of Salonika's Jews, there had been 4,000 Jews in Athens. The Greek capital was in Italian hands. Following the lead of their countrymen in Croatia, General Carlo Geloso and Minister Plenipotentiary Pellegrino Ghigi refused to adopt German policies.[40] The Italians treated the Jews so decently (there was no ghetto, no yellow star or forced labor) that over the next year another 3,000 Jewish refugees made their way to the Italian zone. Once in Athens, Jews obtained false papers and financial assistance.[41] As one refugee recalled, 'Life wasn't easy but there was no difference between Jews and non-Jews.'[42]

That changed in September 1943 when the Nazis occupied all of Greece. Italian garrisons from Rhodes to Albania were disarmed. Real authority was shared by General Alexandre von Loehr, General Wilhelm Spedel and Minister Plenipotentiary Hermann Neubacher.[43] Directing police activities after his arrival in Athens was Jurgen Stroop, the *Brigadeführer* who had suppressed the Warsaw Ghetto uprising earlier in the year. For security reasons, the Nazis banned civilian traffic from streets near the docks and along the seacoast. Entire villages were evacuated. Borrowing from the Nuremberg Laws, the Nazis defined a Jew as anyone with three Jewish grand-parents. Jews were not to appear on the streets after 5 p.m. or before 7 a.m. Henceforth, the *Kehillah* in Athens would serve as the clearing house for Jewish interests in Greece. Moise Sciaky was appointed head of a new Jewish Council. Jews in the Athens area were given five days to register. Jews of foreign citizenship had to report by 8 a.m. on 18 October. Jewish males over the age of 14 would be required to report every other day at the Center. Those who failed to comply with these restrictions would be shot. Greeks who helped Jews would be sent to labor camps.[44]

The Nazis expected 8,000 Jews to register. The census netted only 1,200.[45] Perhaps 2,000 Jews from Athens joined EAM (*Ethnico-Apelertherotico Metopo*), the Greek Liberation Front in the mountains. They included Chief Rabbi Eliahu Barzilay, who refused to deliver the names and addresses of prominent Jews to the Gestapo. Five hundred others risked capture on the open seas by fleeing from Athens to Smyrna in Turkey. American sources reported that some police, like the Athenian Chief Angelos Evert, were sympathetic toward the Jews.[46] The Patriarch Damaskinos intervened for Jews married to Orthodox partners and their children. He also instructed priests to help Jews, just as he gave sanctuary in a convent to Rabbi Barzilay.[47]

In the winter of 1943–44, the SS caught two runaways from Salonika, Ida Angell and her nine-year-old son. They were taken to Gestapo headquarters on Marling Street, where Ida was beaten. When she refused to disclose the whereabouts of her husband, mother and child were sent to Haidari, a former military camp on the road to Eleusis.[48] The inmates of Haidari dug ditches that were filled with dirt again and built brick walls which had to be torn down the next day. There were some Greek criminals in Haidari. Despite the risks, the Greeks shared food parcels with the Jews. Said Ida Angell, 'They envied us. They said, "You are going to another camp. But if they take us away, it will be to the firing squad."' Even after the Nazis carried out a massive roundup on 24–25 March 1944, the Jews in Haidari were optimistic. 'Nobody among us', said Ida Angell, 'had heard talk of the existence of crematoria.'[49]

Errikos Servillias was one of several hundred Jews snared in the March 1944 roundup. It was Passover and officials announced that Jews could pick up flour for matzos at the *Etz Hayyim* synagogue. When Servillias and other 'law-abiding' Jews went to the old synagogue they were captured by the SS. They joined 3,000 men, women and children in the lice-infested barracks of Haidari. After a week, the Nazis loaded the 'emaciated, unshaven and dirty' Jews into trucks and transferred them to the main railway depot at Rouf. Sixty people were stuffed into each cattle car along with a barrel of drinking water and an empty barrel for elimination. The journey north took ten days and in that time several people grew sick and died. As Rebecca Fromer commented, 'The transports' grueling purpose was to subdue, humiliate, and disorient those about to be killed.'[50] When they reached Auschwitz 327 Jews in the convoy were selected to live.[51]

THE FINAL SOLUTION IN GREECE

Having achieved the *Judenreinerungen* of Salonika, the Nazis decided to clear out the remaining pockets on the mainland in the spring of 1944. They would be frustrated by partisans who blew bridges, supply depots, and generally disrupted rail traffic through Greece. More than 25,000 Greeks, including several thousand Jews, joined EDES (the right-wing movement headed by General Napoleon Zevos), ELAS (the communist front) or EAM (the national liberation front based in Athens). The Nazis were especially provoked by Jews like Eliahu Weiss, editor of *Il Messagero* who supplied the Allies with information on German troop movements or the medic Mitrani from Salonika who died in hand-to-hand fighting with the 36th partisan regiment. They were equally frustrated when the Christian population of Aicatherini, a little town near Salonika, outfitted its 33 Jews with food and ammunition and sent them into the hills to fight. Thirty of Aicatherini's Jews survived the war.[52]

Elsewhere, the results of the German roundups were mixed. Assisted by a Quisling, Christo Michaelides (real name Daniel Cohen), the SS encountered little difficulty clearing Jannina of 1,800 Jews and 360 of the 520 Jews from Trikkala in the spring of 1944.[53] In Larissa, an industrial town in Thessaly 200 miles from Athens, however, Rabbi Cassuto advised 1,120 Jews, 'Flee. Leave Larissa. Don't let yourselves be taken.' Only a handful were.[54] Many people joined the underground in Volo where the Nazis captured 645 of 872 Jews.[55] Half of the 325 Jews of Chalkis survived after Orthodox priests offered sermons reminding their parishioners, 'Don't forget. Christ was a Jew.' The Orthodox Archbishop Gregorius also saved seven torah scrolls in Chalkis.[56] The mayor and Metropolitan of Zante hid all 257 of the Jews on that island.[57]

The Nazis were more successful in the larger islands of the Adriatic and Aegean. On Crete, Corfu and Rhodes, Jewish communities were relatively oblivious to what was happening about them. In the spring of 1944, SS *Haupsturmführer* Anton Burger toured the Greek islands, as a prelude to the shipment of the Mediterranean Jews to Poland. Burger's first stop was Corfu, the gorgeous island which had been a retreat of Kaiser Wilhelm. There were four synagogues, 1,795 Jews speaking Ladino, Greek and Italian on the island. In April 1944, Corfu's Jews were confident that the Allies who had landed in Italy, would win the war. Meanwhile, Burger arranged for six coaling scows to dock in the harbor on 24 May. The deportation was postponed when he could not secure the needed personnel. To avoid a repeat of this error, Burger lined up local gendarmerie and SS stationed at Janina. He also obtained a promise from the German naval commander in western Greece, to have two freighters ready on 30 May.[58]

On 6 June 1944, the Nazis posted announcements in Kerkira, the principal city of Corfu, ordering the island's Jews to assemble at the public square in two days. Rossa Soussi, who was only six at the time, remembers 'the great fear' she felt on the day of the roundup. Rossa's mother, Eufenica was sent to Auschwitz with a newborn baby.[59] By noon on 8 October, the square was packed with families standing before Kommandant Emil Jaeger and his interpreter. As their names were read, the Jews went to an old fortress at one side of the square. After five days, the Jews of Corfu were loaded into coal barges and sent to the mainland. Esther Pitzon recalled, 'The heat was so great and we had nothing to drink. Several sick and old people died on the way. They threw their bodies into the sea.'[60] The vessel made several stops, at the island of Lefkada and the town of Patras before reaching Piraeus. At each spot, Greeks tossed the people bread or water. Members of the Red Cross offered medicine for the children. Then the survivors were taken to Haidari.

The Jews from Rhodes suffered a similar fate. In 1944 there were 2,000 Jews on the island, many of them descendants of fifteenth-century Spanish and Portuguese émigrés. Rhodian Jews, some of whom were prominent bankers, took pride in their rabbinical college. They also enjoyed good relations with their neighbors. As Salomon Galante remarked, 'We [the Jews] were established in the island for four centuries and hadn't experienced any persecution.'[61] That changed when the Wehrmacht occupied the island in September 1943. General Ulrich Kleemann confined Jews to the districts of Trianda, Climaso and Villanuovo. Then, in July 1944 Jewish males over the age of 15 were told to report to the *Kommandantur* in the basement of the Hotel du Soleil.

The roundup on 19 July was a repeat of the fiasco in Salonika. As the men gathered, a Greek interpreter told them that they would be detained before being transferred to a neighboring island. Their wives and children would join them within 12 hours.[62] After apprehending the men, women and children were forced into the hotel basement without food or water. When the freighters were finally available on Sunday, 24 July, the haggard mass of humanity was beaten to the ships. Erwin Lenz, a German artillery gunner, saw 200 Jews standing in the sun, their faces turned to a wall. When Greeks and Turks tried to bring them food, guards chased them off. Lenz remarked that the people seemed to have very little baggage. To which an SS guard responded, 'They don't need baggage, because they aren't going to live very long.'[63]

Twelve people who held Turkish citizenship were excused.[64] The rest were forced into three old scows. One survivor recalled the weeklong journey to Piraeus: 'Every third day, they tossed a little bread and some onions to us like animals. We had an intolerable thirst. The Germans would flash containers of water before us but did not let us drink from them. Finally, we were placed in the prison of Haidari.'[65] After a few days at Haidari, all Jews were sent to Poland. Salomon Galante left for Auschwitz with 1,200 persons. Because of partisan attacks, the trip took longer than usual, nearly two weeks. 'Every two or three days, the SS opened the doors and cried, 'Out with the dead!' We tearfully recited the *Kaddish* and put their cadavers in piles near the rails. It was 1944. The Reich was crumbling, but they still were sending Jews far away to death camps.'[66] There were 2,000 persons in Joseph Vitale's convoy which left Athens on 20 June. They traveled, 66 in a cattle car, with little more than sugar beets as nourishment before arriving at Auschwitz; 131 women and 446 men survived for the moment. Dr Miklos Nyiszli, one of the inmate doctors at Auschwitz, noted in his journal, 'All four crematoriums were working at full blast. Last night they had burned the Greek Jews from the Mediterranean island of Corfu, one of the oldest communities in Europe.'[67]

The Jews of Crete were spared the experience of Auschwitz. The Nazis managed to collect 260 Jews in an old prison a few miles outside Khania at the end of May. On 6 June, D-Day, these people were trucked to the port of Herakleon where they were loaded onto the SS *Danae*. Four hundred Greek hostages and 300 Italian soldiers were packed into the hold with them. The ship either capsized in high seas or was sunk by a U-boat near in the vicinity of Pholegandros.[68]

THE SPANISH JEWS OF GREECE

After June 1944, the only Jews still alive in Greece were those who fled to the mountains or those holding Spanish Jewish passports. Struck by the cruelty they had witnessed, Spanish consular officials (Solomon Ezrati in Salonika and Eduard Gasset in Athens) reminded officials in Madrid of a 1912 pact between Spain and Greece that awarded protection to descendants of Sephardic Jews.[69] The Nazis were irked when the Falange opened a special office in Athens on 1 April 1942, but they respected the appeals from Spain. None of the 400 Jews in Salonika who claimed Spanish ancestry were confined to ghetto sections in February 1943. That changed on 28 July, when Salonika's 'Spanish' Jews were called together at the Beth Shaul synagogue. They listened as Dieter Wisliceny told them how they were going to be repatriated to Spain. In all, 367 persons, including Vice Council Ezrati who was mistakenly included in the group, were confined at the Baron de Hirsch. On 2 August, a convoy carrying the Sephardic Jews moved out toward Germany. After 18 days, the train arrived at Bergen-Belsen outside Hanover. Eventually, two trainloads were transferred to the Spanish border (and then to Morocco and Palestine).

A few Jews holding Spanish papers fled to Athens in the summer of 1943. When the Italian zone came under Nazi control, they, too, were apprehended. Franco's brother Nicholas, Spain's ambassador to Portugal, inquired after Sephardim who were locked up in Haidari prison. This time, the Nazis responded that many had 'already been sent east' and others were dangerous saboteurs. As Eberhard von Thadden declared, 'Every Jew was an enemy of Germany, even if by chance he had a Spanish passport.'[70] Several hundred people bearing Spanish or Portuguese documents were sent to Belsen on 16 April. Many died of hunger or disease. When the camp was evacuated in March 1945, 155 Greek Jews made the march to camps in Magdeburg, then Stendahl, where they were liberated by American forces.

When the war ended 125 Jews returned to Corfu. Of 2,000 Jews deported from Rhodes, 150 survived the death camps. There were 20 Jews on the island in 1968. Athens counted 200 survivors out of 3,000 Jews. Only a handful of Salonika's Jews survived. In all, more than 67,000 Jews, almost 90 percent of the Jews in Greece, perished in World War II.

Co-Belligerents: Bulgaria and Finland

Two nations that fought alongside the Nazis have been praised for their handling of the Jewish Question during World War II. Bulgaria joined the Axis in March 1941 primarily to regain territories lost in the Balkan Wars. In the process, 10,000 of Bulgaria's 50,000 Jews were deported. The record of Finland is even more impressive. The Finns struggled alone against Russia in the Winter War of 1939–40. Then, adopting the novel designation of co-belligerent, they joined the Nazi assault against the Soviet Union in what Helsinki called 'the Continuation War' of 1941. Under Marshal Carl Mannerheim, only nine of 2,000 Jews in Finland were deported. The sagas of Bulgaria and Finland are inspiring. Unfortunately, the actual events have been overdrawn.

THE JEWS OF BULGARIA

Jews had resided in the Balkan hills since the Byzantine era. The empress Sarah, a Jew, converted when she married Bulgar Emperor Ivan Alexander in 1335.[1] Jewish exiles from Spain settled in Nikopolis, Vidin, Plevna, Silistria and Trnovo. Recognized as a *millet* (nationality), the Jews were organized in 40 consistories by the Ottoman Turks. There were 48,000 Jews in Bulgaria (29,000 in Sofia) in 1940.[2] Although Bulgaria's constitution of 1878 guaranteed equality, Jews had no illusions about their Orthodox neighbors. The Talmud was publicly denounced in Varna in 1885. The charge of ritual murder cropped up at Passover in Sofia (1884), Vratsa (1890), Parzardzhik (1898), Lom (1903) and Kiustendil (1904). Jews were accused of 'Gallicization' and Petur Gabe, the first Jewish representative, faced substantial opposition before he could take his seat in parliament.[3]

Bulgaria could hardly resist tilting toward Germany. The two nations were allies in World War I. Many of Bulgaria's top military men had been trained by the Germans. Their armaments came from Germany. During the inter-war period, Germany became the principal importer of Bulgarian goods. Boris III, the gnome-like man who assumed the throne in 1918, was a German prince, from the house of Saxe-Coburg. After seizing control of the government in 1935, Boris suspended parliament for three years, permitting only cabinets that mirrored his own views.[4] Alert to the threat of communism,

Boris sought to strengthen his nation by reclaiming disputed lands. The logical ally for such a program was Germany.

Pre-war Bulgaria was not lacking in fascist sympathizers. Alexander Tsankov of the University of Sofia created the Bulgarian National Social Movement. Tsankov served briefly as Prime Minister after his faction kidnapped and murdered agrarian reformer Alexander Stamboliski. The 1930s gave birth to two paramilitary organizations – the Union of Bulgarian National Legions (Legionnaires) and the Guardians (Ratnitsi).[5] On 15 February 1940, Bogdan Filov became Prime Minister. The German-educated Filov retained the anti-Semite Peter Gabrovski as Minister of Interior and brought right-wing ideologues Ivan Popov (Foreign Affairs), Ivan Bagrianov (Agriculture) and Dobri Bozhilov (Finance) into the cabinet. Before the government permitted German troops to enter its soil in February 1941, before Bulgaria joined the Tripartite Pact in anticipation of the invasions of Yugoslavia and Greece in March 1941, before it declared war on Great Britain in December 1941, Filov and his cronies had addressed the Jewish Question.

BULGARIA: THE ZZN AND KEV

The Law for the Defense of the Nation (*Zakon za zashtitata na natsiata*, ZZN) was submitted to the Sobranie (parliament) in July 1940. The scheme, to register Jews and restrict their economic activity, was the brainchild of Gabrovski and his top aide Alexander Belev. After months of debate, the bill was sent to Boris for his signature on 15 January 1941. Designated 'enemies of the state', Jews could not belong to political parties or serve in the civil service. Every Jew over the age of ten had to wear the Star of David.[6] To rectify 'over 60 years of exploitation', Jews were supposed to pay a special tax (25 percent) on property and transfer businesses at 50 percent of 1932 value. Personal wealth was to be deposited in blocked bank accounts of the Bulgarian National Bank. Implementation of the ZZN proved to be a nightmare. Converts, as recent as 1940, were exempt. So were Jews married to Gentiles and those who had served in the military. Jewish doctors, dentists, veterinarians and industrialists were also excused under the Law for Civilian Mobilization. So many complaints were lodged by embassies of Spain, Romania and Hungary on behalf of their own citizens in the next few months that the ZZN appeared useless.[7]

With coaxing from German ambassador Adolf Heinz Beckerle, Belev and Foreign Minister Popov worked to secure a more effective law. The second bill (26 August 1942) broadened the definition of Jew to include anyone with two Jewish grandparents. It also created a Commissariat for Jewish Questions (*Komisarstvo z evreiskite vuprosi*, KEV) with Belev as chief.[8] The KEV was divided into four bureaus: the Administrative Section which regulated Jewish housing; the Professional Section which enforced quotas and supplied labor gangs; the Agents and Police Section which enforced curfews and rationing laws; and the Economic Section which collect taxes on and liquidated Jewish property. After four years, the KEV managed to confiscate $54.7 million, much of which was lost through graft.[9] Such measures were temporary palliatives. In November 1941 and again in July 1942, the Filov government urged the Nazis to deport Bulgarian Jews from the Reich or territory controlled by Germany. In October 1942 Hans Luther offered to process all of Bulgaria's Jews for 250 DM per person, a sum deemed exorbitant by Bulgarian officials. Nevertheless, they agreed that something must be done.[10] As KEV director Belev declared: 'The radical solution of the Jewish problem in our country would be the deportation of the Jews and simultaneous confiscation of their property.'[11]

THE DANNECKER MISSION

In December 1942, SS *Haupsturmführer* Theodor Dannecker arrived in Sofia. Dannecker hoped to devise a plan that would eliminate Jews from Bulgaria. Meanwhile Jews in New York were trying to convince the British to accept 5,000 Bulgarian Jews in Palestine. The offer was contingent upon the co-operation of Turkey which did not want to give the refugees temporary haven.[12] On 22 February 1943, Belev and Dannecker reached an agreement. The Germans would accept 20,000 Jews 'in the new Bulgarian lands Thrace and Macedonia' for deportation. Twenty trains would be made available in Skopje, Bitol, Pirot, Gorna Dzhumaia, Duptnitsa and Radomir during the months of March and April. Jews exclusively were to travel in these transports, although Jews of mixed marriages were exempt. Likewise Jews with contagious diseases were not to travel. Jews would be stripped of their citizenship once they departed Bulgarian territory.[13] The deportees were to be detained in warehouses and schools. They would be told they were being removed to the interior or preparing to go to Palestine. Belev obviously intended the agreement to be the beginning of a much broader operation. There were not 20,000 Jews in the 'recently liberated territories'. The head of the KEV was already talking of removing 6,000 'undesirable' Jews from pre-war Bulgaria. Belev requested lists from subordinates of candidates based on wealth, prominence and subversive activity. He issued instructions dividing Bulgaria into five districts and drafted everyone from provincial governors to 'district agronomist' for the operation.[14]

Belev was tripped up by the cabinet which issued the 'warrants' for the 20,000 Jews. These documents signed by Interior Minister Gabrovski referred to Jews 'inhabiting the recently liberated territories'.[15] As Jews in Dupnitsa, Kiustendil, Varna and Plovdiv (all parts of pre-war Bulgaria) were placed under house arrest, it was impossible to ignore what was going on. Kiril, bishop of Plovdiv, wired the king, threatening to lie down on the railway tracks to block any trains leaving his city.[16] In Sofia, there were protests from the Holy Synod and writers unions. Gabrovski's brother-in-law divulged Dannecker's plan to a Jew from Kiustendil. As panicked members of the Sofia Jewish community made their last farewells, Iako Baruh, an official with the Zionist emigration agency, contacted several members of parliament who promised to help.

On 9–10 March, Dimitur Peshev, Sobranie vice-president and a fascist sympathizer, warned Prime Minister Filov he would make a public scandal if the deportations were not halted. In a petition cosigned by 42 of his colleagues (including the arch anti-Semite Tsankov), Peshev noted that old Bulgarian law stipulated that citizens of territory annexed by Bulgaria automatically became citizens of Bulgaria. The deportations would 'stain Bulgaria's reputation and place an unmerited blemish on her brow'. Filov caved in momentarily. He regained the initiative on 24 March when more than 100 members of parliament, not only endorsed the deportations, but censured Peshev and removed him from his post.[17] For the time being, there would be no transports from Sofia, but the trains were running from Thrace, Macedonia and Pirot.

DEPORTATIONS FROM THRACE

The Bulgarians may not have deported their own Jews, but they did not scruple to clear Jews from lands which constituted Greater Bulgaria. Following the three-week campaign against Greece in April 1941, the Nazis retained control of Didimoticon, Nea-Orestia and Soufli, but gave Serres, Cavalla, Drama, Xanthi, Comotini and Alexandropoulis to the Bulgarians. The Nazis appreciated the strategic importance of the Thracian Chalcidice, for they established naval bases throughout the region and operated a special seaplane unit out of Cavalla. There were 1,484 Jews among 50,000 Greeks in the town of Cavalla, 471 among 35,000 Gentiles in Serres, 589 of 30,000 in Drama, 526 of 25,000 in Xanthi, 1,000 of 9,000 people in Didimoticon, 800 in Comotini, 200 in Alexandropoulis, and 140 in Soufli.[18] Most of the Jews of Thrace were descended from Sephardic refugees. Several figured prominently in the tobacco industry. They knew terrible things were happening to Jews in Poland, but few thought of abandoning their homes even though Turkey was only 25 miles from Alexandropoulis.

Delighted with acquisitions that gave them access to the Aegean, the Bulgarians imposed their own brand of nationalism upon the Greeks. The conquered peoples were offered Bulgarian citizenship and Bulgarian became the language of instruction in schools, on street and business signs. Jews were invited to serve as informants against their Greek neighbors. When they refused, anti-Jewish decrees ensued. The Bulgarians ordered a census of Jews in every town, although as one survivor noted, 'It was unnecessary since everyone knew who was a Jew.'[19] That was followed by the wearing of the yellow star and marking of Jewish dwellings. The Bulgarians ordered a declaration of goods. For radios, jewels and other valuables turned in, the Narodnaja Bank (People's Bank) gave receipts which proved to be worthless.

On the night of 3–4 March 1943, the anniversary of Bulgarian independence, Bulgarian gendarmes descended upon the Jews in Thrace.[20] A Greek woman in Cavalla recalled how troopers broke down doors in her apartment complex and terrorized people with bayonets. When Jewish children began to weep, the Bulgarians told them, 'Don't cry. You will all be together. You are going on a trip.' The streets filled with people badly dressed against the subzero temperature. For the moment, their apartments would be locked. Later their possessions were looted or auctioned off.[21]

In Cavalla, Drama, Serres and Xanthi the Jews were taken to tobacco warehouses where they were held, pending the arrival of trains authorized by Commissar Belev. They stayed three days with little food or water. The Germans carried out a similar action in the western part of Thrace that same night. Adult males were summoned to synagogues where they were detained by armed guards. The next day, the prisoners were joined by their families. Some 2,500 Thracian Jews were sent by train to Gorna Dehumaia where they were placed in a warehouse and school gymnasium. Each building had one drinking faucet. Doctors tried to contain an outbreak of whooping cough. Fifteen hundred Greek Jews in a warehouse at Dupnitsa surrendered their valuables (all of $607).[22] A total of 4,706 Jews were deported from Thrace. Bulgarian and Greek collaborators confiscated $250,000 in Jewish property as a result of the March roundups.[23]

DEPORTATION FROM MACEDONIA AND SERBIA

The Jews in eastern Serbia and the province of Macedonia fared no better. From the fourteenth century, the region east of Lake Ochrid was known as the Valley of the Jews. Nearly three-quarters of the 800 Jewish families in Bitol (Greek Monastir) were living in poverty.[24] Writing in *Zhidov* (The Jew), the publication of Serbo-Croatian Zionists in 1936, Dr Rudolf Buchwald described the Jewish quarter of Bitol as 'a scene of utter neglect', with empty stores and empty display windows. Jewish homes, some no better than caves, reeked with 'mounting filth'. As for children (Jewish families often had nine or ten) all were 'pale and unhealthy'.[25]

After the Bulgarians arrived in 1941, Jews were ordered to liquidate their businesses. Jewish children were expelled from school. A property tax (20 percent) was levied and Jews could only withdraw small sums of cash from bank accounts. The Bulgarians forbade the use of Aryan names and eventually (August 1942) introduced the yellow star. Fifty-eight Jews were arrested and beaten by Bulgarian police in Pirot on 12 March.[26] The Jews of Bitol were also stuffed into tobacco warehouses where they were menaced by 'the Tatar', a policeman who lashed out at victims with a whip.[27] More than 7,000 Jews were shipped out of the Macedonian towns of Bitol, Skopje and Shtip.

A total of 1,393 persons were collected from the 'recently liberated territories' by the Bulgarians. Ambassador Beckerle reported to Berlin that the Macedonians Christians were pleased with the deportations.[28] Three trains departed from Skopje on 22, 25 and 29 March 1943. When Nazi troops appeared in the yard of the tobacco warehouse, a stunned Albert Zarfati realized: 'Until that very moment we believed that we would be sent to the central areas of Bulgaria. But when we saw the Germans we grasped that our die had been cast and that German trains would take us to Poland.'[29] The trains, carrying more than 2,300 Jews, traveled via Czestochowa, Piotrkov and Warsaw. During the seven-day trip, a number of individuals were 'amortized' on each transport. When they reached Treblinka 'the cargo was unloaded'.[30]

Nissim Behar remembers the last leg of the journey from Didimoticon: 'We were 80 in each wagon. 200 deported from Nea-Orestia joined our convoy. My sister, with a newborn baby, was sitting at my side. The child died during the journey. We left his body wrapped in a blanket in the wagon. Then it was Salonika, and then the infernal voyage to Poland.'[31] The other Thracian Jews were loaded into cattle cars and traveled across Bulgaria to the port of Lom on the Danube. A nurse, Nadeia Vasileva happened upon the trains sitting in the Lom station in March 1943. The people inside were pleading for food and water. She returned with members of the Red Cross and some Gypsies who gave them water, tea, cheese, bread, milk, fish and marmalade.[32] At Lom, 'the Germans took charge of the deportees and all trace of them disappeared'.[33]

Some non-Jews reported that the Jews of Thrace were loaded on old river barges which capsized in the river.[34] It was no mystery where the rest went. A post-war commission at Siedlce reported that the Greek convoys began arriving at Treblinka on 26 March. According to Yankel Wiernik, 'The Jews of Bulgaria were big and strong men. When you saw them, it was hard to believe that 20 minutes later they would no longer be alive. The executioners would not let these Jews who were so handsome die easily. They released a little amount of gas in the chambers and let them choke all night long. They suffered much before suffocating. They suffered a long time before entering the chambers.'[35]

After the war, there were only 30 Jews in Cavalla. The synagogue and cemetery were destroyed. All 600 Jews of Serres were killed. In Drama where only four Jews remained, the synagogue was converted into a private home, the Jewish school into a Christian one. The Jews of Xanthi disappeared 'without a trace'. Their synagogue became the seat of the Orthodox Religious League, the cemetery a vast ruin. There were 33 Jews in Didimoticon, none in Alexandropoulis or Comotini. Only 65 of the 7,144 Jews sent from

Macedonia survived the death camps. In 1971 there was only one Jew in Bitol. A cemetery maintained by the West German government and honoring German dead from World War I overlooked the ruins of the abandoned Jewish cemetery.

NEW THREATS TO THE JEWS OF SOFIA

Emboldened by successes in Macedonia and Thrace, and egged on by Ambassador Beckerle and Gestapo Attache Karl Hoffmann, Bulgarian anti-Semites renewed their efforts to eliminate the Jews of Old Bulgaria. Commissar Belev proposed to remove them from the capital in May 1943. Approved by Filov's cabinet, this decree generated great fear among the 20,000 Jews in Sofia. Rabbi Daniel Tsion tried to use his influence with the king who shared an interest in mysticism. Other Jewish leaders petitioned the Metropolitan Stefan. Some confronted Bulgarian police in the streets on St Methodius/Cyril Day. They were taken to a concentration camp at Samovit. As Jews of Sofia were evacuated to country sites, their apartments and possessions were auctioned off.[36]

To make matters worse, King Boris, perhaps the only figure who could have done something about all of this, died that August.[37] The king had just returned from a meeting with Hitler, where they discussed the possibility of an Allied invasion through the Balkans. A week later Boris suffered a heart attack while climbing Mt Mousalla, the highest peak in the Balkans. He died five days later. Disagreements between Hitler and Boris and the presence of three German physicians at the Bulgarian monarch's bedside, have given rise to the charge that Boris was eliminated by Hitler. The death did enhance the position of the pro-Nazi clique in the government. A regency for Prince Simeon was established with power vested in the hands of Filov, General Nikola Mihov and Prince Kiril, Boris's brother. By the end of August, the stage seemed set for the deportation of Bulgaria's remaining Jews.[38]

The transfer of power, however, worked in the Jews' favor. On 14 September 1943, Filov was replaced as prime minister by Dobri Bozhilov. More important, because of charges of corruption, Gabrovski was ousted from Internal Affairs. His crony Belev was transferred to another post. The new Commissar of Jewish Affairs was Hristo Stomaniakov, no friend of Jews but someone who eased their persecution. The anti-Jewish decrees remained in force and many Jews were still confined in labor camps. There were no more sales of property, however. And when Sofia was bombed for the first time in November 1943, Jews regarded their removal to the country as a mixed blessing.[39]

Anxious to prevent an invasion from Russia, Bulgaria shut down German shipbuilding activities at Varna in January 1944. Four months later, a new government headed by Prime Minister Ivan Bagrianov asked the Germans to stop bringing prisoners of war to Bulgarian territory. On 2 September, a pro-Western government headed by Konstantin Muraviev was installed and asked for an armistice. Responding to Allied demands that German forces be expelled, Bulgaria declared war on Germany. It was not enough. On 5 September, the Soviets declared war. Bulgaria was now fighting Germany, Russia, England and the United States. On 28 October 1944 another cabinet, handpicked by the Soviets signed an armistice with the Red Army.[40]

For Bulgaria's Jews, the nightmare seemed ended when, in one of its last official acts, the Bagrianov cabinet repealed the ZZN on 31 August 1944. The wearing of the badge, quotas, discriminatory taxes and ghettos were eliminated and all former rights were restored. The Muraviev government issued an amnesty on 7 September and Jews expelled from Sofia were permitted to return to their homes. The communist authorities tried to induce the Jews to stay by returning property and punishing wartime collaborators. Nothing, however, could erase the memory of years of pain and betrayal by former neighbors. When the opportunity presented itself after 1948 more than 40,000 Bulgarian Jews emigrated to Israel.[41]

BORIS AND THE JEWS

There are approximately 10,000 Jews in Bulgaria today. The synagogues in Sofia and Plovdi, as in Bitol or Salonika are nearly-deserted, the ancient cemeteries rank with weeds. Given the disposition of the principal political leaders (Filov, Belev, Gabrovski, Boshlov, Bagrianov) and the 'rubber stamp' 25th Sobranie, it is amazing that any Jews survived in Bulgaria. With the passage of the Law for the Defense of the Nation in 1940, Bulgarian anti-Semites embraced the ideology of Nuremberg. The Decree Law of August 1942 legitimized confiscation, ghettoization, marking with the badge. Bulgarian police herded people from their homes, terrorizing them in warehouses and guarded them aboard death trains. Bulgarians looted and auctioned off Jewish property. They planned to do the same thing in pre-war Bulgaria as late as September 1943. All that was missing were the German victories that would enable Bulgaria to fully enjoy the fruits of the Final Solution in Europe.

There remains the enigmatic figure of King Boris, who sanctioned the removal of his nation's Jews from the cities but not their deportation out of the country. Boris believed his destiny between 1938 and 1943 lay with Germany. If that meant authorizing anti-Semitic laws to placate his allies, so be it. If it meant the deportation of Jews rationalized as aliens, again he would let others take the responsibility. Says Frederick Chary, 'It is true that if Boris had desired to deport the Jews he could have, but it is not true that any desire to prevent deportation would succeed. His opposition did not save the Jews of Macedonia.'[42]

It is possible to construct a different picture of the Bulgarian king. It was Boris, after all, who controlled both the police and military. Boris outlawed the Macedonian IMRO, the communist party, and interfered with elections on several occasions. At any time, Boris could have called for the resignation of Filov government or some of his ministers. Although Bulgaria was never occupied, he joined the Axis and permitted the passage of German troops during invasions of Greece, Yugoslavia and Russia. Nazi forces subsequently operated out of Bulgarian bases on the Black and Aegean Seas. Boris affixed his signature to the Law for the Defense of the Nation (ZZN) and the August 1942 decree that created the Commissariat for Jewish Affairs. The king made no protest when in July 1942 the Nazis began deporting Bulgarians under German rule. When the Swiss ambassador opposed the deportation of Jews in the territories in March 1943, Boris told Prime Minister Filov to be 'firm'. Two months later, he told representatives of the International Red Cross that it was necessary to deport foreigners who were Poles. In his meeting with Hitler, he agreed to the arrest of communists and Jews within the original boundaries of Bulgaria. And on 15 April 1943, he informed his country's top clerics (Stefan of Sofia, Kiril of Plovdiv and Neofit of Vidin) that the Jewish question in Bulgaria was connected to the European solution of the question.[43]

Had Boris intervened on behalf of Jews, he might have been overthrown by more radical elements in his country. The Nazis might have occupied Bulgaria, as they did Hungary when that nation attempted to leave the fascist camp. More Jews might have been deported and exterminated. In that sense, by pursuing an expedient course, Bulgaria saved Jewish lives. That by no means justifies posthumous salutes toward Boris or any of his cabinets. Bulgaria was not Denmark which opposed Nazi occupiers. Rather, Bulgaria was France, a nation of collaborators, yielding its 'stateless' Jews and wishing it could give up the rest.

THE RESCUE OF FINNISH JEWRY

If the Bulgarians appear less heroic than self-serving, the same must be said for the Finns. Even before the end of the war, Field Marshal Mannerheim was accepting accolades for his role in preventing the deportation of 1,900 Jews who held Finnish citizenship and 300 refugees. Speaking at a Helsinki synagogue on Independence Day, 1944, the Finnish national hero declared, 'I have done nothing more than what every person with a sense of justice would be duty-bound to do.'[44]

Mannerheim was less self-effacing in his memoirs where he declared, 'Only much later have I learned that the opinions I made known within the hearing of certain members of the government have generally been regarded as having decisively influenced the final result in the treatment of this [Jewish] question.'[45] In fact, Mannerheim did little to influence the fate of Jews in the homeland. Mannerheim's pro-German sympathies were well known, even unavoidable. The Germans helped Finland win its independence from the Bolsheviks. Finnish *Jaegers* (light cavalry units), trained in Germany. General Rudiger von der Goltz accompanied Mannerheim into Helsinki in the spring of 1918. Von der Goltz would return 20 years later carrying the rank of SS *Obergruppenführer*. Allies against Russia, Mannerheim received Himmler at Mikkeli Airfield in June 1942 and awarded the *Reichsführer* Finland's Grand Cross of Freedom. A few days later, he greeted Adolf Hitler and Field Marshal Keitel, who came to bolster the alliance. In return, he was invited to Nazi command posts in Germany.[46] Asked to intervene on behalf of a group of Jews and non-Jews who were being shipped to Estonia (and Nazi hands) at the end of October 1942, Mannerheim declined, saying he had been assured that the individuals were 'spies' and that 'the government knew what it was doing'.[47]

Still the Jews of Finland were not deported and there is no shortage of individuals who claim credit. Philip Friedman devotes a chapter in *Their Brothers' Keepers* to Finnish resistance. Local Nazis who tried to introduce discriminatory legislation were quickly beaten down. Nazi Ambassador Wipert von Blucher tried to explain to his superiors in Berlin that the Finns would not tolerate the imposition of racial laws. When Himmler visited Helsinki, his goal was to press the Finns for a 'quick solution' of the Jewish problem. Finnish President Risto Ryti and Foreign Minister Witting stared down the *Reichsführer*. Witting supposedly told Himmler, 'Finland is a decent nation. We would rather perish together with the Jews. We shall not surrender the Jews!'[48]

The Finnish government was alerted to the nature of this visit by Dr Felix Kersten, the Finnish chiropractor who became Himmler's masseuse and confidant. Kersten claimed responsibility for winning the release of several thousand Jews to Sweden at Christmas 1944, brokering the transfer of another 1,000 women to Folke Bernadotte in 1945, and securing a pledge from Himmler to stop the killing of Jews on 12 March 1945. Kersten also claims that as a result of his warning, Finnish intelligence photographed dossiers in Himmler's valise which outlined plans of deportation and Finnish police sent 300 refugees to safety in Sweden. Philip Friedman and Nora Levin recite these claims without editorial comment.[49] The facts do not support Kersten's tale.

Some of Finland's 2,000 Jews were descendants of Cantonists settled here by Nicholas I. Others filtered in from Sweden. Most lived in Helsinki, Turku or Viipuri. Russians accused them of pro-Swedish tendencies. Finnish nationalists suspected them of being in league with Russian revolutionaries.[50] Jews were also targeted by a number of fascist parties. The Patriotic Peoples Movement (IKL) and Patriotic National Movement (PNM) never secured more than 14 seats in parliament, but they were cultivated by Abwehr, SD and Gestapo. Fearing a 'flood' of Jews in 1938 (less than 200 Jews arrived), Interior Minister Orho Kekkoen ordered the *Valpo* (State Police) to crack down on refugees. Those without passports were turned away. Those who could not show they were going elsewhere were rejected. Finland had its version of the SS *St Louis* – the steamship *Ariadne* was turned away with 50 Jewish passengers in August 1938. Immigrants who were admitted were watched closely. Before the war with Russia in 1939–40, the *Valpo* even exchanged information with the Gestapo.[51]

On 14 January 1940, the Finns ordered 'undesirable aliens' out of the country in 14 days. Lists of Jewish refugees were drawn up and males between the ages of 18 and 60 were sent to camps in Lappland where they were assigned to agriculture, logging and rail construction. Whether the camps at Kuusivaara, Kemijarvi or Suursaari should be called concentration camps or not,[52] for Jews interned under Finnish guard, life was harsh. Fear was widespread, especially after Finland joined Germany in the attack upon Russia.

THE *VALPO* AND THE EXTRADITION OF 6 NOVEMBER 1942

In February 1941 Arno Anthoni became head of the *Valpo* as pro-Nazi Finns clamored for the expulsion of Finnish Jews as well as refugees.[53] In October, a *Valpo* officer, Olavi Viherluoto, submitted a report describing the annihilation of 2,600 Jews by Einsatzgruppe A in the Estonian town of Tartu.[54] Anthoni traveled to Tallinn, the Estonian capital, in November 1941 and agreed to turn over lists of German deserters and Russian and Estonian prisoners of war to the Gestapo.[55] In April 1942, the Finnish police chief discussed the matter with SS *Gruppenführer* Heinrich Muller in Berlin and even visited the Sachsenhausen concentration camp. Shortly after, Himmler made his celebrated trip to Helsinki. The Nazi leader thought he had elicited a promise from Prime Minister J.W. Rangell to surrender Finland's Jews. When this had not occurred by the fall of 1943, Himmler exploded, 'What does that louse of a country think it is doing, fouling up the *Führer*'s plans? The *Führer* is not one to trifle with. If he so wishes, he could wring the Finns' necks any day at all.'[56] For his part, Rangell recalled Himmler asking, 'How is the situation with the Jews of Finland?' To which the Prime Minister replied, '*Wir haben keine Judenfrage*' (We have no Jewish problem).[57]

Whether the Nazis applied pressure or not, the *Valpo* did arrest several dozen 'alien undesirables' in the summer of 1942. When the *Neidenfels* sailed to Stettin on 17 June, there was one Jew, a Belgian named Georges Busch aboard. There were no Jews among the 26 Estonians and Russians deported to Tallinn on 28 August. Anthoni's police did compose lists of Jews in the fall of 1943. Jonas Adler, a businessman from Lemberg, 'showed himself to be an arrogant character, an actively anti-Nazi Jew'. Elija Zillbergas from

Lithuania was 'arrogant and refractory in his attitude toward officials'. Kurt-Paul Lipper of Czechoslovakia 'expressed disparaging opinions both orally and in writing about the authorities'. Wilhelm Werber, formerly of Vienna, 'made known his hope that Germany would lose the war'.[58] Rumors persisted that the Nazis detailed five ships to Helsinki. That could only mean one thing – the transport of all Jews from Finland.

On 30 October, Abraham Stiller, a prominent member of the Helsinki Jewish community, received word that nine foreign-born Jews had been arrested. Stiller appealed to a number of Finnish officials. *Valpo* officer Jalmari Sinivaara agreed the deportations would be 'dangerous to Finland, its future destiny and reputation'. Stiller was cheered by protests of foreign embassies (including the Swedes and Americans) and an editorial that appeared in the *Helsingin Sanomat* ('a state that no longer sees fit to grant the right of asylum does not live up to the image traditionally held of an independent nation').[59] Nevertheless, Field Marshal Mannerheim declined to intervene. When Stiller tried to reach President Risto Ryti, he was informed that the President 'was not giving audiences'. Stiller did speak with Vaino Tanner, who was serving as the head of Council of State. Tanner promised to help, but could not overcome objections offered by Foreign Minister Witting, Interior Minister Horelli and Police Chief Anthoni.[60]

The SS *Hohenhorn* left Helsinki bound for Tallinn on 6 November 1942, carrying 27 deportees. Nineteen of these passengers were Estonians and Russians. The other eight were Jews. They included Heinrich Huppert, a 46-year-old toy salesman from Austria, accused of smuggling, violating ration practices and 'engaging in [unspecified] practices endangering the security of the state'. Hans Korn was a technician convicted of two robberies and two swindles. Hans Szybilskij had been deported from Sweden for espionage after police found aerial photographs in his possession. Georg Kollmann, a medical student from Vienna, was accused of embezzlement and failure to renew his residence permit on time. Kollmann's wife and two children were expelled with him. From Estonia, the deportees were taken to Berlin. There, they joined a transport of 1,200 Jews who were sent to Birkenau. Of the eight Jews deported from Finland, only Georg Kollmann survived.[61]

Finns were appalled when they learned of these deportations. The nation's newspapers, church leaders and intellectuals joined the Swedes and foreign legations in condemning the action.[62] Belatedly, 300 Jews were welcomed into Sweden. In October 1943, Finns applauded Professor Eino Kaila, a noted psychologist-philosopher, who denounced the deportation of the Danish Jews. By mid-1944, Jewish refugees in Finland were granted citizenship. On 19 September, Finland agreed to an armistice with Great Britain and the Soviet Union.

After the war, *Valpo* Chief Anthoni fled temporarily to Sweden. Upon his return, he was arrested but never punished. Walter Laqueur argues that 'Anthoni had to know [about Nazi genocide] and that he had informed certain members of the Finnish government too' (notably Minister of Internal Affairs Toivo Horelli). The plain truth is that Finland did not protect all of its Jews. Just as Bulgaria and France, some foreign Jews were offered up to mollify the Nazis. The numbers do not matter. The deaths of seven Jews, four men, one woman and two children, may not mean much. Still, what happened to them and all other deportees stained the honor of Finland.

23

Italy: The Reluctant Ally

When the fascist government of Italy took a census in August 1938, it counted 47,000 native-born Jews, 0.1 percent of a population of 45 million. This figure did not include 10,000 foreign Jews who had taken refuge in Italy, 24,000 living in Libya, 37,000 Falashas in Ethiopia, 5,000 in the Dodecanese Islands or the thousands who were offspring of mixed parentage.[1] That any Jews resided in the Italian peninsula is remarkable considering the relationship between the Jewish people and Italians. After 1215, Jews in Rome were stigmatized with a badge and confined to a *vicus judaerum*, which in 1555 became a sealed ghetto. During carnival, 12 Jews ran a gauntlet from St Peter's to Castel San Angelo as the Pope looked on. In Pisa, on St Katherine's Day, Christians received the weight of the fattest Jew in candy and paper. There were pogroms in Savoy after a Jew from Venice 'confessed' his role in host desecration in 1348, more violence when Jews at Trent were accused of ritual murder in 1475. Mobs burned the Talmud in Rome in 1553 and pillaged anew when Napoleon was defeated.

Jews played a prominent role in the nineteenth-century Risorgimento. David Levi wrote the battle hymn of the movement. Isacco Artom was secretary to Count Cavour. Guiseppe Finzi served as one of Mazzini's military commanders and Daniel Marin led republican forces in Venice. Jews fought alongside Garibaldi and three Jews were elected to the national assembly in 1849.[2] Ernesto Nathan served as mayor of Rome from 1907 to 1913. Luigi Luzzatti served as finance minister five times, and was prime minister from 1908 to 1911. Baron Sidney Sonnino, a Protestant convert, was Prime Minister in 1905 and 1909–10 and headed the Foreign Ministry between 1915 and 1919. Giuseppe Ottolenghi was King Victor Emmanuel's tutor and Minister of War in 1902. One thousand Jews were decorated in World War I.

Jews, like other Italians, were duped when the liberal spirit of the Italian revolution was subverted by a dictator. On 30 October 1922, Benito Mussolini led his Black Shirted followers into Rome. Within two years, the fascists fused a one-party dictatorship and Mussolini ruled as *Il Duce* (absolute leader) until his deposition in July 1943. Among Mussolini's ardent supporters were Aldo Finzi, a convert who served on the Fascist Grand Council and in the Ministry of Interior, and Ettore Ovazza who helped edit *La Nostra Bandiera* (Our Banner), a nationalist journal between 1934 and 1938. (Both men were executed by the Nazis toward the end of the war.)[3] The fascist coup in 1922 was funded in part by Giuseppe Toeplitz, a Jew who headed the Banca Commerciale Italiana. Mussolini named another Jewish fascist, General Girogio Liuzzi, Chief of Staff in 1928. Four years later, he appointed Guido Jung Minister of Finance and Giuseppe Renzetti, who had a Jewish wife, as Ambassador to Germany.[4]

In those early years, Mussolini went out of his way to court Italy's Jews. He assured Angelo Sacerdoti, chief rabbi of Rome, Nahum Goldmann and author Emil Ludwig, 'Anti-Semitism does not exist in Italy.'[5] Mussolini mocked the Nazis' 'delirium of race', calling it barbarous and stupid. Following the assassination of Dollfuss, Mussolini declared, 'It would mean the end of European civilization if this country of murderers and pederasts were to overrun Europe. Hitler is the murderer of Dollfuss – a horrible sexual degenerate, a dangerous fool.'[6] The Duce contrasted his brand of autocracy with that of his northern neighbors: 'Thirty centuries of existence allow the Italians to look with some pity on certain doctrines which are preached beyond the Alps by those who were illiterate when we had Caesar, Virgil and Augustus.'[7]

An avowed 'Zionist', Mussolini met with Chaim Weizmann of the World Zionist Organization, and Zev Jabotinsky, leader of the militant Revisionists.[8] The Duce informed Goldmann, 'You must create a Jewish State. I am a Zionist myself and I told Dr. Weizmann so. I shall help you create a Jewish State.'[9] As proof of his intentions, Mussolini dedicated the Palestine (Zionist) pavilion at the Bari Fair in 1934. He opened a naval school for refugee Jews at Civitavecchia and permitted 151 Italian Jews to emigrate to the Holy Land between 1926 and 1938.[10]

When only a fraction (10 percent) of Italy's Jews embraced fascism, Mussolini's philo-Semitism evaporated. In a series of 'anonymous' essays, the one-time journalist denounced Zionism as utopian, a scheme of British imperialism, the product of an international conspiracy. Now he embraced the works of Luigi Pirandello, Roberto Farinacci and Giovanni Preziosi, editor of the journal *La Vita Italiana*, all of whom railed at the 'Jewish peril' in Italy.[11]

ETHIOPIA AND SPAIN: THE FIRST RACIST LAWS IN ITALY

Any thought of Jewish collaboration with fascism ended when Italian forces attacked Ethiopia in October 1935. Following the conquest of Ethiopia, the fascists banned sexual contact between Italians and Africans, including Jewish Falashas.[12] Over the winter of 1936–37, no more Jewish diplomats were sent to Germany and Jews were dismissed from fascist publications. Disgusted with Jewish politicians like Blum and bankers who opposed his imperial ventures, Mussolini commissioned Paolo Orano to write *Gli Ebrei in Italia* (The Jews in Italy), shortly before he visited Germany in the fall of

1937. Orano denounced Jewish claims to be 'a chosen people' and demanded that 'Italians of Jewish faith' renounce Zionist sympathies.[13] Not long after, Italian fascism embraced the very Nordic racism it had long deplored. On 14 July 1938, the government promulgated a *Manifesto degli scienziati razzisti*. This document was primarily the work of Guido Landra, a 25-year-old anthropology professor at the University of Rome. The manifesto declared that Italians were Aryans, a pure race since the time of the Lombards. Jews could not be Italian, hence there should be no intermarriage between the two peoples.[14] In December 1943 Mussolini referred to the law as 'a ponderous German essay translated into bad Italian'.[15] Four days after its publication, the Ministry of Interior opened an office of Race and Demography (*Demo-razza*) to conduct a census. The government also began publishing *La difesa della razza* (Defense of the Race), a journal similar to *Der Stürmer*.

The fascists dropped all pretense of fairness with the enactment of several anti-Jewish decrees on 1 September 1938. By law, a Jew was anyone born of parents who had been of the Jewish faith. Jews nationalized after 1 January 1919 were stripped of their citizenship. Stateless Jews were to leave Italian territory within six months and no more foreign Jews would be admitted. This decree was never implemented, but one barring Jews from teaching or studying at public institutions was. After 6 October 1938, Jews could no longer marry Aryans. They were barred from party membership and military service. Jews could not employ more than 100 workers, nor could they own more than 50 hectares of land.[16] Jews could not employ Gentile servants, belong to chambers of commerce, make use of public libraries or list their names in telephone directories. They could not own radios, publish books or give lectures. Jewish doctors and lawyers could only tend to their own people. Jewish ragpickers and dealers in second-hand clothing had their licenses revoked. Mussolini defended these edicts as 'not persecution but discrimination'.[17]

King Victor Emmanuel III expressed concern about the racial laws, warning Mussolini that 'the Jewish race is like a beehive – don't put your hand in it'.[18] Three members of the Grand Council (Italo Balbo, governor of Libya, Marshal Emilio de Bono and Luigi Federzoni) voted against them. Bruno Jesi, a Jew who had lost a leg in Ethiopia, flung his crutch through a café window which displayed a sign barring Jewish patronage. A Jewish officer in Turin called his unit to attention, pulled out his pistol and shot himself. Angelo Fortunato Formigini, a Jewish journalist who had written against fascism, leaped to his death from the Ghirlandini Tower in Modena as a protest against the racial manifesto.[19]

In the wake of anti-Jewish legislation, 4,000 Jews converted to Christianity. Their status and the ban on mixed marriages precipitated a crisis with the Catholic Church. If civil authorities did not recognize such unions, the Concordat would be compromised. Eventually, Mussolini backed down, extending a grace period for baptisms. A law passed in July 1939 empowered the Duce to Aryanize anyone he chose. The Office of Race and Demography was permitted to issue exemptions to individuals who could establish they were bona fide converts, as well as Jews who rendered meritorious service to the country in time of war or to the fascist PNF between 1922 and 1924. The *Demorazza* approved less than half of 5,800 applications by 1943. A separate office, the *Tribuna di Razza*, established in 1939, was receptive to bribes and approved certificates of Aryanization. The fascists encouraged emigration and another Jewish agency, the *Delegazione Assistenza Emigranti Ebrei* (*Delasem*) headed by Dante Almansi (former vice-prefect of Rome's police) and attorney Lelio Valobra managed, with funds from the Joint Distribution Committee and HIAS-HICEM, to send 5,500 Jews out of the country before the end of 1940.[20]

RELUCTANT ALLY: ITALY LOSES AT WAR

On 22 May 1939 Hitler and Mussolini signed a 'Pact of Steel'. The treaty pledged immediate aid in case of war. Unprepared when Germany invaded Poland, Mussolini was grateful that Hitler released him from his pledge. Over the winter of 1939–40, Mussolini blamed defeatists and Jews for Italy's reluctance to join the Nazis. That spring, he watched enviously as the Germans swept through Denmark, Norway, the Low Countries and France. Then, unable to resist any longer, he declared war on 10 June.

Almost immediately, synagogues were desecrated in Trieste, Turin, Leghorn, Ancona and Ferrara.[21] The government blocked Jewish bank accounts and expelled Jews from Sardinia, Sicily and the Austrian border. Jewish refugees were sent to 15 detention camps in the south. Typical of these was Ferramonti, a camp in the bogs of Calabria that held 1,400 inmates before it was closed in September 1943.[22] Jews volunteered for military service but were turned away. Instead, in May 1942 the fascists created a labor service for men between the ages of 18 and 55. Of 15,000 Jews who registered, 2,000 were sent to mills, forests, coal mines and road projects.[23]

Italy was a reluctant ally whose military efforts can best be termed inept. Marshal Rodolfo Graziani's forces invaded Egypt in September 1940. After four months, the Italians were chased 500 miles back into North Africa. Mussolini sent another army into Greece in October 1940. Two months later, the Italians lost a third of Albania. More than 200,000 men participated in the campaign against Russia. After two years, fewer than 10 percent straggled home and these were placed in detention camps to stem the spread of defeatism. The Italians also took a pounding in East Africa from British-Ethiopian forces. Weary of bluster, Marshal Pietro Bagdolio and 19 members of the Grand Fascist Council prevailed upon Victor Emmanuel to discharge Mussolini on 25 July 1943.

These were the same officials (Count Pietromarchi Luca in the Foreign

Ministry, Giuseppe Bastianini, governor of Dalmatia, Mussolini's son-in-law Count Ciano, and General Mario Roatta) that had shown little enthusiasm for the Nazi plan of genocide.[24] Mussolini performed a similar switch on the status of Jews in France under Italian protection. Pressed by Ribbentrop and Hans George von Mackensen, Germany's Ambassador to Rome, to expel these Jews, on 17 March 1943, Mussolini promised to give the French police 'a completely free hand' in this matter.[25] Three days later Bastianini informed Mackensen that Mussolini had decided to send his own agent, Police Inspector Guido Lospinoso to supervise actions in occupied France.

FROM ALPES-MARITIMES TO CÔTE D'AZUR

There were approximately 50,000 Jews in the eight French departments under Italian rule. The Italians would not allow anti-Semitic devices that were standard in other parts of Europe. Stamping passports with the word Jew or imposition of the yellow star was deemed 'irreconcilable with the dignity of the Italian army'.[26] The differences between French Quislings and the Italians came to a head in December 1942 when the Prefect of the Alpes-Maritimes ordered Jews out of his department. Responding to an appeal from Angelo Donati, former director of the Banque France-Italie, M. Calisse, the Italian Consul-General in Nice, asked Rome for instructions. On 29 December, the Italian Foreign Ministry wired Calisse that expulsion of Jews to territory occupied by the Germans was not permissible.[27]

Following this diplomatic victory, the Italians created another commission to coordinate Jewish food and housing problems with *Delasem*, the Italian-Jewish relief agency. Jewish schools were opened – some for children, others organized by ORT offering vocational training. When French police raided a refugee center across from the Nice synagogue, Colonel Mario Bodo sent carabinieri to the scene with orders to arrest the gendarmes if they tried to do it again.[28] Relations between Jews and the Italians on the Riviera were so good that Knochen complained, 'The best of harmony prevails between the Italian troops and the Jewish population. The Italians live in the homes of the Jews. The Jews invite them out and pay for them. The German and Italian conceptions seem here to be completely at variance.'[29]

When Guido Lospinoso, Mussolini's inspector, arrived in Nice to evaluate the situation, he met first with Donati, then with Father Benoit-Marie. The latter, a Capuchin monk who was hiding Jews, explained what was happening to the Jews in Poland and reminded Lospinoso that 'the God of the Jews is also the God of the Christians'. As a result of this meeting, Lospinoso virtually disappeared in the Côte d'Azur. Through much of April 1943, SD officials complained of their inability to contact him. On 26 May, the Italian Embassy in Paris claimed it knew nothing of Lospinoso's whereabouts. When Lospinoso finally did materialize at the end of May, he reneged on a promise to deliver 6,000 stateless Jews, claiming that he did not trust the French police.[30] His position was consistent with that of the general staff of the Fourth Italian Army. In March, Brigadier-General Carlo di Gualtieri informed Admiral Platon, Vichy Secretary of State, that 'the Supreme Italian command cannot give its approval to the measures which were taken by the Prefects in regard to the arrests and the interning of Jews living in the Italian occupation zone in France, whether they are Jews of Italian, French, or of foreign nationality'.[31] A month later, di Gualtieri annulled arrests and internments carried out by French officials in their zone.[32]

The Nazis sneeringly complained that 'Italy wants a humane solution of the Jewish problem'. When the Germans demanded more territory from the Italians, their allies simply transferred Jews to hotels in Megève and Nice and 'refused to hand them over'.[33] *Obersturmführer* Rothke summed up the frustrations of the Nazis in July 1943. Said Rothke, 'The attitude of the Italians is, and was incomprehensible. The Italian military authorities and the Italian police protect the Jews by every means in their power. The Italian zone of influence, particularly the Côte d'Azur, has become the Promised Land for the Jews in France.'[34] Four days later, supporters of Marshal Badoglio arrested Mussolini and relations between Germany and Italy came undone.

FROM BAGDOLIO TO SALO

All through the spring of 1943, there were rumors that Mussolini might be deposed. Churchill and Roosevelt welcomed talk of a separate peace with Italy and feelers were put out to several neutral nations. King Victor Emmanuel and Prince Humbert tried to disassociate themselves from the fascist regime. Ten days after the Allies landed on Sicily, Bagdolio replaced Mussolini. The new government was cheered in Naples and Sicily, but in northern Italy fascist militia incited street fighting. There was talk of the king seizing power if Bagdolio fell, of the king abdicating. Meanwhile the US Office of War Information insisted that Bagdolio and Victor Emmanuel were nothing but fascists themselves.

Both Germany and Japan were disturbed by the antics of their erstwhile ally. Tokyo warned Italy not to conclude a separate armistice with the Allies. In August, Berlin sent Ribbentrop and Keitel to meet with their Italian counterparts Foreign Minister Raffaele Guariglia and General Ambrosio. Publicly, these meetings resulted in promises of close ties between Germany and Italy. The King also indicated that Italy would honor its pledges. Privately, Bagdolio was preparing to take Italy out of the war. The Italians hoped to delay any announcements until they could ensure control of Rome and as much of Tuscany and the Po Valley as possible. They asked for an airborne assault on the outskirts of the capital to be followed by an amphibious landing of 15 Allied divisions. Angered by what he deemed stalling tactics, General Eisenhower announced peace terms on 8 September. Marshal Bagdolio had no other recourse but to acknowledge the armistice on the same day.[35]

American forces landed at Tarento and Salerno, well to the south of Rome on 9 September. By that time it was too late. When the fighting ended on Sicily in August, the Nazis pulled four divisions back to the mainland. They joined a German expeditionary force of 500,000 crack troops. Anticipating Italy's capitulation, Hitler authorized 'Operation Axis' which sent Field Marshal Rommel to occupy the Alpine passes. Field Marshal Albert Kesselring forced Bagdolio into flight and surrounded Rome. After playing a game of 'where in the world is Benito', the Nazis finally rescued Mussolini at a ski resort near Rome on 12 September. Following a brief reunion with Hitler at Rastenburg, the haggard Duce was installed as head of the *Republica Sociale Italiana* at Salo.

In France, the armistice was supposed to mean pulling back Italian troops and refugees to the Tinea–Var line. Donati assembled 22,000 Jews in Nice awaiting four vessels that would take them to North Africa.[36] Inadvertently, this facilitated the roundup of Jews. On 4 September 1943 Rothke, the SD specialist in Paris, called for the arrest of foreign Jews (including those naturalized after 1927). French police in Lyon and Marseille prepared assembly points in schools and factories. The Jews were to be sent to Drancy before proceeding east. Rothke was especially concerned about Jews in the Italian zone.[37] Unable to obtain lists of Jews in the resort towns, the SS stripped men on the streets, sending those who were circumcised to their deaths.

In Italy proper, Jews were heartened that the Nazis permitted the charade of an Italian government headed up by Mussolini and his Minister of Interior Guido Buffarini-Guidi. In fact, there was no real government for two months. Power was shared by the Wehrmacht, the German diplomatic corps and the police under SS *Obergruppenführer* Karl Wolff. Within days, SS units swept through quaint vacation towns along Lake Maggiore, killing 49 Jewish refugees and sending another 300 to their deaths at Auschwitz. What happened in Stresa, Arona and Meina was only a prelude to a much greater catastrophe for Italian Jewry.[38]

RANSOMING THE JEWS OF ROME: 50 KILOGRAMS OF GOLD

On 25 September, SS *Obersturmbannführer* Herbert Kappler, Gestapo chief in Rome, received a communiqué from the RHSA ordering the arrest of all Jews in the Italian capital. No figure was mentioned, but it was assumed that 12,000 persons would be transferred to Germany for 'liquidation'. To mask the *Judenaktion*, Kappler was advised to suspend anti-Jewish measures.[39] Kappler considered the order '*eine neue grosse politische Dummheit*' (a great new political blunder). His view was shared by Baron Ernst von Weizsacker, Germany's ambassador to the Vatican, and his aide Abrecht von Kessel, both of whom worried how the Pope might react to a roundup in his own backyard. Even before the order came down from Berlin, German diplomats tried to warn Rome's Jews, many of whom resided in a cluster of 500-year-old tenements along the Tiber. Only Rabbi Israel Zolli took such warnings to heart. He urged his colleagues to go into hiding. Zolli was denounced by Dante Almansi, head of Italy's united Jewish societies, and Ugo Foa of the Roman Jewish council for spreading 'discouragement'.[40]

Meanwhile, a copy of Kappler's cable was received by General Rainer von Stahel, Wehrmacht commander in Rome. Like Kesselring, Stahel believed an Allied invasion at Ostia was imminent. A roundup of Jews seemed frivolous when the fate of Italy was at stake. Stahel met with Eitel Frederick Moellhausen, acting German consul in Rome, and informed him of the proposed *razzia*. Moellhausen, who had been with Kesselring in Tunisia, where Kesselring conscripted Jews for labor, appealed to the Field Marshal to do the same in Italy. With Kesselring's consent, Moellhausen met with Kappler on 26 September and requested a postponement of the roundup while he sought clarification from Berlin.[41]

Kappler agreed to cooperate, but decided to protect himself by initiating another anti-Jewish action. That same day, he summoned Almansi and Foa to the Villa Wolkonsky. Because Rome's Jews were involved with the communist underground, said Kappler, they were being fined. The Jews had 36 hours to deliver 50 kilograms of gold to his office. Failure to do so would result in the arrest of 200 heads of families who would be transported to the Russian frontier where they would be 'rendered innocuous'.[42]

Almansi, Foa and journalist Luciano Morpurgo appealed to friends in the *Questura* and Italian Red Cross, but were told the fascists could do nothing. Resignedly, the Jewish leaders appealed for people to bring rings, jewelry and teeth to the great synagogue and called in a jeweler to serve as assayer. Some Gentiles volunteered their own treasures. Others sought to profiteer by selling gold at inflated prices. As the day went on, the Vatican agreed to *loan* any amount of gold, provided it was repaid in installments. The Vatican's gold was not needed. By noon of 28 September (the deadline had been extended one hour), the Jews had put together ten cartons, each containing five kilograms of gold, which were taken by taxi to Gestapo headquarters[43]

Kappler later claimed he demanded the ransom to prevent Jews from using the gold for bribes. The gold did not fall into his own pockets. Sent to Ernst Kaltenbrunner, it was found in the original cartons when Berlin was taken in 1945.[44] Neither did the gold spare the Jews of Rome further tribulations. On 29 September, the day after Kappler received his 50 pieces, SS officers ransacked the great synagogue, smashing the ark and tossing torah scrolls aside. More important, they carried off cabinets filled with reports of community meetings, index cards of Jews living in Rome, and a safe containing $20,000 in cash. Over the next two weeks, Nazi troops rummaged through the Biblioteca Communale and the Biblioteca del Collegio Rabbinico. Rabbi Zolli's apartment was looted on 2 October. On 13 October, the Nazis trundled two boxcars into position along the streetcar tracks of Lugotevere dei Cenci, and packed dozens of priceless manuscripts away for Munich.[45]

ATTESIMO

Though rumors of a roundup persisted, the attitude of most Roman Jews was expressed in one word – *attesimo* – wait and see. Whatever fears they might have felt when a number of Jews were arrested on 9 October were offset by the confident manner of Almansi and Foa who continued their daily routines. The Jews of Rome had good reason to be afraid. Early in October, SS *Hauptsturmführer* Dannecker arrived in the capital accompanied by 14 officers and NCOs and 30 soldiers of the Waffen SS, all veterans of the Einsatzgruppen. Dannecker poured over lists taken from the Jews and those supplied by Interior Minister Guido Buffarini and compared them with maps of the Roman ghetto.[46] Jews were living in all 26 sections of the city. Dannecker's unit required additional manpower and Kappler, whose forces were detailed to Rome's main prison, could not help. Fascist militia were unreliable. Eventually, Dannecker managed to secure a Waffen SS paratroop battalion from Stahel's command.[47]

Dannecker's mission was no secret. On 6 October, and again the following day, Consul Moellhausen cabled Ribbentrop asking that the liquidation of the Jews be canceled and that they be used for fortification work. Outraged, Ribbentrop telephoned a senior staff member at the Foreign Office and told him to stop Moellhausen from meddling. On 9 October, Eberhard von Thadden sent back a reply that the 8,000 Jews of Rome were being sent to Mauthausen as hostages 'on the basis of the *Führer*'s instructions'. A second note was issued instructing Moellhausen to 'keep out of all questions concerning Jews'.[48]

Meanwhile, Weizsacker was playing his own double game. Concerned about a possible statement from the Pope, Weiszacker exploited fears that the Nazis might, in turn, occupy the Vatican.[49] He urged Church leaders to offer sanctuary but to refrain from making public declarations. 'I know how our people react in these matters', said Weizsacker.[50] As a result, the Vatican limited its response to an inquiry sent from Bishop Alois Hudal, rector of the German Catholic Church in Rome, to Commandant Stahel on 16 October, and a statement printed in *L'Osservatore Romano* of 25–26 October. The latter recalled how the Pontiff tried to dissuade 'the Rulers of the peoples from having recourse to force of arms'. The statement concluded with reference to the charity of 'the Supreme Pontiff which knows neither boundaries, nor nationality, neither religion, nor race'. A delighted Weiszacker informed Berlin, 'There is no reason whatever to object to the terms of this message as only a very few people will recognize in it a special allusion to the Jewish question.'[51] Both Hudal's appeal and the 'very torturous and obscure' communiqué were issued too late. The great razzia in Rome had been completed three hours before Hudal's letter reached Stahel's office.

BLACK SABBATH

The action took place on a rainy Saturday, 16 October 1943, the same day the Allied armies crossed the Volturno River 90 miles south of Rome. At 5:30 a.m., the 365 SS men of Dannecker's special detail sealed off streets leading into the ghetto. Storm troopers (often no more than one to a complex) moved from floor to floor, waking the dazed Jews. Each family received a card telling them that they were being transferred to a labor camp. They were given 20 minutes to vacate. To prevent one batch from warning others, telephone lines in apartments were cut. (Public telephones still operated.) Soon, the streets were packed with columns of frightened men, women and children moving toward the Theater of Marcellus, the Augustan ruin near the Capitoline Hill. Piled into canvas-top trucks, they were then driven to a holding facility barely 200 yards from the Vatican – the Collegio Militare.[52]

It was impossible to conceal what was happening and 477 persons were granted sanctuary in the Vatican, another 4,238 in monasteries and convents about Rome. Roused by his secretary at 8 a.m., Ugo Foa protested about this 'premeditated crime' to the Ministry of Interior, Public Security and Fascist party. He then vanished. When the operation concluded at 2 p.m., the Nazis counted 1,259 persons in the courtyard of the military college on the Via della Lungara. Among those shunted to the straw-filled barracks were Admiral Augusto Capon, the 71-year-old father-in-law of Enrico Fermi; Lionello Alatri, owner of the largest department store in Rome; and 61-year-old Alina Cavalieri, who had received a silver medal for organizing nursing services in World War I.[53] After checking documents, the Nazis released 252 persons.[54]

At dawn on Monday, 18 October, 1,007 persons were trucked to the Tiburtina railway station where 20 closed boxcars were waiting. It took eight hours to load people who were told they were going for a trip. The deportees were heartened when fascist militia threatened to shoot the German *Schupos* (Security Police) if members of the Italian Red Cross were not permitted to tend to people's needs at Padua. Women of the German Red Cross distributed barley soup when the train stopped at Furth on 20 October, but offered no hint where the Jews were headed.[55] The transport reached Auschwitz at 11 p.m. on Friday, 22 October, too late for a selection. The next morning Dr Josef Mengele selected 450 men and women to live. Told they would have to walk ten kilometers to the camp, many chose to ride in trucks that went instead to the gas chambers. In all, 196 Jewish men and women from Rome (no children) entered the work camp. Of these, only 14 men and one woman survived.[56]

THE HOLOCAUST IN ITALY

Dannecker's unit continued its bloody work in a number of Italian cities that fall. There had been more than 3,000 Jews in Florence. Their rococo synagogue, gutted by the Nazis, was restored after the war. A marble wall standing in the garden bears the names of 243 Jews who were deported to Auschwitz between 6 November 1943 and 6 June 1944. Only 13 returned.[57] A detachment of Einsatz Reinhard was sent to Trieste where the Nazis set up La Risiera di San Sabba, the only camp in Italy with a gas chamber. Four hundred of 6,000 Jews in Trieste survived the war. Nine hundred Jews came from Milan, more than 400 from Turin, 200 from both Genoa and Venice. Three thousand Jews were shipped from Rhodes to Auschwitz and Buchenwald in July 1944. Eight hundred more Roman Jews would be arrested by the Nazis. They included 77 who were among 335 Italians shot in the Ardeatine Caves in retaliation for partisan attacks.[58]

The Nazi program in Italy was helped along by diehard *fascisti*. After years of seeking his niche, in April 1944 Giovanni Preziosi became Inspector-General of Race and promised to create a legion of fascist warriors. Instead he attracted ragtag elements like the Muti Legion in Milan along with bands of kidnappers headed by Major Carita in Florence and Pietro Koch in Rome. They were joined by the Guardia Nazionale Republicana, the dregs of the caribinieri, militia and African police, and the Brigate Nere, party members conscripted for a last-ditch fight in the summer of 1944. Twenty thousand Italians volunteered to serve in the Waffen SS in the last year of the war.[59]

Hoping to impress their Nazi overlords, the Salo government passed a wave of anti-Jewish laws. On 14 November, a law declared 'those of the Hebrew race are foreigners. While the war lasts, they are deemed of enemy nationality.'[60] Two weeks later, the Ministry of Interior called for the arrest of all Jews, including those of mixed marriages. Their property was liquidated by the *Ente Gestione e Liuidazione Beni Ebraici* (EGELI). In a feeble gesture, the carabinieri were given control of jails, Jewish centers and internment camps.[61] The largest was Fossoli di Campi, six kilometers from Modena. Designed for 100 prisoners of war, Fossoli held more than 1,000 Jews and Yugoslavs, some of them very old and gravely ill. Early in 1944, Friedrich Bosshammer replaced Dannecker and Fossoli became a transit camp on the order of Westerbork or Drancy.[62]

THE ITALIAN PSYCHE: *QUI REGI NON POTEST*

Ultimately 7,495 Jews, including 2,600 from Fossoli, were deported from Italy. Only 610 of the latter survived.[63] Historians suggest several reasons why 85 percent of Italy's Jews survived the Holocaust. There was no central *Judenrat*. It was easier for Jews to disappear into a countryside aswarm with all kinds of refugees. The Italians disliked the Germans who they regarded as invaders.[64] There was no long-standing tradition of anti-Semitism in Italy. Italians, even Mussolini, considered racism beneath them. Early on Mussolini had dismissed Hitler as 'an idiot, a rascal, an insufferable talker, a joke who would be over in a few years'.[65] Much as Hitler at the end lamented having treated Italy as an equal, Mussolini regretted the Race Manifesto and claimed in February 1944 that he was not an anti-Semite.[66]

There is another reason that goes to the very psyche of the Italian people.[67] All kinds of words in Latin describe the Italians – *effenatio* (unbridled), *incitatio* (impulsive), *indomitus* (unrestrained). Cicero spoke of a people *animi impotentis* (motivated by unbridled impetuosity) and his contemporaries offered the expression, *qui regi non potest* (whoever rules has no power). From the ancient struggles with the mountain folk of Samnium to contemporary troubles in Sicily, Italians have proven independent and cantankerous. As Alan Cassels has written, 'This attribute has been the bane of every regime to govern in Rome.'[68]

In the final analysis, the behavior of people in this most Catholic of nations cannot be explained in scientific terms. As Susan Zuccoti writes, the Italians acted to save lives, 'not the lives of friends, neighbors, coreligionists, or countrymen. Just lives.'[69] Villagers, priests and farmers in Nonantolla risked their lives to hide 92 Jewish children in the Villa Emma. Mayors and police chiefs from Bologna to Naples burned registration books rather than turn lists of Jews over to the Nazis. More than 1,000 fascists were dismissed from the party for the crime of '*pietismo*' (sympathizing with Jews, associating with them, assisting them in circumventing racist laws). During Black Saturday, a Catholic woman from the Via della Luce Assunta Fratini risked her life by snatching a young Jewish boy. Emanuele Sbaffi, director of the Wesleyan Methodist Church in Italy, hid two Jewish women in his home. One of those Christians arrested by mistake during the 16 October roundup in Rome was a nurse who was caring for a Jewish boy, an epileptic. She chose to stay with him to Auschwitz.[70] Giuseppe Tiburzio saved a 9-year-old Belgian Jewish girl from deportation. Asked why he acted the way he did, Tiburzio replied, 'What I did appeared then, as now, perfectly natural and I believe that in my place many others would have done the same.'[71] Of such people, Zuccotti writes, 'They were brave, decent, and far too few.'[72]

24

The Humanitarians: The Vatican and the Red Cross

At 11 a.m. on 19 July 1943, the first of 500 American planes started bombing locations in and about Rome. The expressed targets of the attack were the Ciampino airfield and the Littorio railway yards. H.L. Matthews of the *New York Times* accompanied the raiders and testified that their objectives were legitimate.[1] Before the bombardment was over, however, the holy city sustained casualties of 1,400 dead and 5,000 wounded. Much of the damage took place in the vicinity of San Lorenzo Fuori Le Mura, one of seven principal churches of Rome, 500 yards from the freight yards. The basilica lay in ruins. Some gravesites (including the sepulcher of Pius IX) were also damaged.

Shortly before 6 p.m. that same day, Pope Pius XII motored to the scene of the air raid. His white garments spattered with blood, the Pontiff 'imparted words of solace to the stricken neighborhoods'. Pius prayed at San Lorenzo (a mass of ruins 'beyond repair') and the cemetery (which contained the graves of several of his relatives). He walked among the crowds, comforting residents of the working-class district. Then he returned to the Vatican where he blessed another frightened throng. As Rome radio charged that only one bomb had hit a military target, rumors circulated that the Pope was sending an 'energetic' reprimand to Churchill and Roosevelt.[2]

Over the next several days, the Vatican received letters of support from Germany, Spain, Ireland and Argentina, but no protest was sent to the Allies. Instead, on 20 July, Pius drafted a 1,500-word message to Cardinal Marchetti-Salvaggiani, vicar-general of Rome. The missive was prompted, said Pius, by an 'unusual affliction'. In this war, he had tried to get belligerents to respect 'the inviolability of peaceful citizens and monuments of faith and civilization'. Ignoring the pain that Italy caused innocent civilians in Ethiopia, Spain, Albania and Greece, Pius fixed upon the violation of Rome. With rapture, he wrote of this 'ancient city', 'guardian of precious documents and relics', 'the holy city of Catholicism, exalted to new and more brilliant glory in the name of Christ', city of religious institutes, basilicas and art treasures, 'where men forgather from all parts of the world to learn not only religion but also the faith and wisdom to which men look as to a beacon of civilization founded on Christian virtues'.

Because of Rome's extraordinary importance, the Vatican had hoped it would remain inviolate. 'But, alas, this so reasonable hope of ours has been disappointed.' Pius mentioned the destruction of San Lorenzo Fuori le Mura, and added, 'As we contemplated the ruins of that famous temple, the words of the Prophet Jeremiah came to mind: "How is the gold become dim, the finest color is changed, the stones of the sanctuary are scattered."' (Except that the Pope's words were in Latin, not Hebrew: *Quomodo obscuratum est aurum; mutatus est color optimus, dispersi sunt lapides sanctuarii.*) Pius went on to note his own efforts to bring relief to 'the piteous people'. He closed with prayers for peace for the 'convulsed world'.[3]

Such expressions were remarkable for a Pope noted for reticence. Pius had not condemned the Nazi occupation of Prague in March 1939, the invasion of Poland six months later, aggression against Lithuania, Norway or Denmark in the following months.[4] The closest Pius came to a denunciation of tyranny was in *Summi Pontificatus* on 20 October 1939 where he mentioned the 'inexpressible' suffering of the Poles. His Christmas message in 1939 denounced atrocities 'committed by whatever side'.[5] His words of sympathy to the monarchs of Belgium, Luxembourg and Holland in the spring of 1940 spoke not of invasion but of 'territory exposed to war'. His so-called declaration of war on totalitarians in October 1940 concerned itself more with agnosticism and apostasy.[6] He issued no condemnation when Serbs were slaughtered in Croatia.[7] Instead, Pius informed the Lithuanian minister to the Vatican that he would not allow the Church to become involved in 'temporal controversies and territorial rivalries among states'. His efforts on behalf of priests were limited to transferring those in custody from extermination camps to labor camps and the recovery of remains once they were dead.[8] His Christmas message of December 1941 complained about restrictions on church activity.[9]

If the Pontiff mentioned the plight of Jews, his statements came in vagaries that bemused the oppressors and confounded their victims.[10] Pius thought he was being perfectly clear in his Christmas message of 1942 where he vowed to help widows, orphans, exiles and 'the hundreds of thousands of people, who, through no fault of their own and sometimes only on grounds of nationality or origin are destined for death and slow deterioration'.[11] Mussolini found the speech so full of platitudes it 'might just as easily be by the priest of [my home village] Predappio'.[12] The Vatican's lone statement on the Black Sabbath roundup was printed in the 24/25 October *L'Osservatore Romano* stipulating that papal charity 'knew neither boundaries nor nationality, neither religion nor race'. Pius's Christmas message issued on 27 December 1943, two months after Black Sabbath, condemned 'all atrocities' perpetrated against 'innocent victims'.

Church historians claim that Pius intended to make a vigorous speech decrying German violations of human rights.[13] In August 1944 Pius made quiet overtures to the Nazis and was ignored.[14] Only after the war ended, did the Pope feel free to speak. Robert Lieber, Pacelli's secretary of 34 years, maintains he had only piecemeal evidence of genocide in 1942–43. Monsignor Alberto Giovannetti notes that even the Allies were skeptical of reports they received at the time. Little more could be expected of the Vatican which was isolated and threatened with the prospect of occupation.

Actually, a wealth of data was channeled to Secretary of State Luigi Cardinal Maglione who briefed the Pontiff daily. Diplomats from two dozen nations made Rome a center of current information. The Catholic church maintained nunciatures in Berlin, Vichy, Budapest, Bratislava, Bucharest, Berne, Madrid and Lisbon, as well as five special apostolic delegations during the war. It received information from 1,300 bishops and countless missionaries.[15] Pius was aware of the Slovakian Jewish Code, Ustashi persecution of Jews and Vichy's Statute of Jews.[16] As early as February 1940 Archbishop Cesare Orsenigo in Berlin advised that Jews were being deported to Poland in a cruel manner. Orsenigo followed with a report on the imposition of the yellow star in September 1941.[17] One month later, Monsignor Giuseppe Burzio in Bratislava informed Maglione that the Nazis were systematically shooting Jews in Slovakia. In August 1942 Archbishop Valerio Valeri, questioned whether the large numbers of sick, aged and children leaving France could really be going to work camps. The Vatican received memoranda from Archbishop Filippo Bernaradini, Nuncio in Berne (19 March 1942) and chaplain Pirro Scavizzi in Poland (May 1942) telling of the massacre of two million Jews. By the end of the year, Rome had reports from Andreas Szeptycki, Archbishop of Lwow and Anthony Springovics, Archbishop of Riga, telling of the annihilation of Jews in their respective cities.[18] Researchers have uncovered a memorandum dated 5 May 1943 in Cardinal Maglione's office. Drafted during the death pangs of the Warsaw Ghetto, it told how the Jewish population had shrunk from 650,000 to 20,000. Most of these had been transported by cattle car to 'special death camps near Lublin (Treblinka) and near Brest-Litovsk. It is told that they are locked up several hundred at a time in chambers where they are finished off with gas.'[19] Verification of these procedures came from eyewitnesses. Pius had two briefings with Admiral Canaris, head of German Intelligence. Kurt Gerstein, an SS officer, related details of mass murder in Belzec to officials of the Berlin Archdiocese in August 1942. Two years later Rudolf Vrba and Alfred Wetzler brought the Auschwitz Protocol from Bratislava.[20]

Eugene Cardinal Tisserant had been urging Pius to issue an encyclical on the duty of the individual to obey the dictates of conscience ('this is the vital point of Christianity') since November 1939.[21] Through 1942, ambassadors of Brazil, Great Britain, Poland, Uruguay and Yugoslavia pressed the issue of atrocities. One week after the Pope issued his Christmas message, Wladislaw Raczkiewicz, President of the Polish Government in Exile, 'implored' the Vatican to 'show clearly and plainly where the evil lies and to condemn those in the service of evil'.[22] Pius did no such thing. He issued no instructions to priests to intervene on behalf of Jews in any European country. He did not threaten to break diplomatic relations with Germany as his predecessor had done with Czechoslovakia in 1925. Pius did not suspend the concordat with Hitler, threaten excommunication or ban of interdict upon Germany. As Harold Tittmann reported to Washington in 1942, the Pope was fearful that any statement might cause the deaths of more people. Should Germany lose the war, its people would accuse the Church of being, in part, responsible.[23]

Such muddled thinking prompted Rolf Hochhuth, a young editor from Eschwege/Werra to write *The Deputy (Der Stellvertreter)*, a searing attack upon the Vatican in 1963. The core of the play deals with an encounter between Father Ricardo Fontana (a character based on Provost Lichtenberg and Maximilian Kolbe) and the Pontiff shortly after the roundup of Jews in October 1943. The meeting was arranged by Ricardo's father, a nobleman with influence at the Vatican. Ricardo had told his father: 'A deputy of Christ who sees these things and nonetheless permits reasons of state to seal his lips – who wastes even one day in thought, hesitates even for an hour to lift his anguished voice in one anathema to chill the blood of every last man on earth – that Pope is a criminal.'[24]

In the long scene at the papal palace, the young priest appeals for an intervention from the Vatican. Instead, the Pope rambles on about the Allied bombardment of San Lorenzo and Monte Cassino ('It is extremely bad behavior!'). Pius recites passages from his last Christmas message and warns 'whoever wants to help must not provoke Hitler'. He calls the persecution of the Jews 'loathsome', but hastens to note that 'Hitler alone ... is now defending Europe' from 'this new assault from the East'. Pressed to issue a protest, the Pope agrees with the advice of a cardinal who suggests something 'not so direct and not so detailed' for 'the Holy See must continue to shelter the spirit of neutrality'. In the end, Pius, his hands stained after signing an official document, washes away the ink in an action evocative of Pontius Pilate.

Defenders of Pius were outraged by this portrayal. They claim that a break with the Germans would have had no impact upon the Nazis. Not since Canossa had the Church been able to influence affairs of state. Writing in *La Civilta Cattolica*, Father Martini noted how little impact the Church had upon Elizabeth I or Nicholas of Russia when they flouted rules of morality. The Church was a universal institution better served in the moral reconstruction that would come from the ashes of war. How could the Holy Father condemn Nazi atrocities without citing Russia's aggression against Finland or the Katyn massacre which left hundreds of Polish officers dead at the start of World War II?[25] The Vatican was equally opposed to cutting off innocent Catholics from the sacraments. As Pius told the journalist Eduardo Senatro, 'Dear friend, do not forget that millions of Catholics serve in the German armies. Shall I bring them into conflicts of conscience?' Pius took as his inspiration Benedict XV who was neutral during World War I. Another role model was Pius XI, author of *Mit Brennender Sorge*, the man who had declared that spiritually all men are Semites.[26]

One of the Pope's staunchest advocates was the Rev. Robert Graham, S.J., editor of an 11-volume series of documents on Vatican activities during World War II. Graham notes how the Pope intervened to repatriate Italian prisoners of war, asked for the release of inmates in concentration camps who were suffering from tuberculosis and malaria, pleaded for a halt of bombardments in Turin, Bologna, Milan and other cities in northern Italy. He highlighted church efforts to reverse deportation orders in Romania, Slovakia, France and Hungary and cited Jews (Dr Joseph Lichten and Pinchas Lapides) who argued that 'prudent deeds' were more effective than 'loud words'.[27] Speaking on NBC radio, Father Robert Graham likened Pius XII's behavior to Jesus Christ who 'did not condemn all the evils of his time'.[28]

In 1976, the Vatican published a 688-page book detailing assistance rendered by the Church to Jews in and outside Italy. It mentioned the Brazilian visa project which helped more than 1,000 baptized Jews leave Europe in 1939–40. It spoke of the efforts of Nuncio Andreas Cassulo to help 50,000 converts in Romania and Cassulo's visits to Jews in Transnistria and Transylvania. It mentioned the rescue work of Father Benoit-Marie and protests of French bishops. It chronicled efforts of papal representatives to stay the deportation of converts from Pressburg and Budapest.[29] It told how Angelo Roncalli negotiated the release of several thousand children from Bulgaria. The report claimed that 15 kilograms of the 50 kilograms of gold demanded of Roman Jews in October 1943 was supplied by the Vatican.[30] The Nazis may have whisked away 1,000 Jews from Rome, but the Pope saved more than 7,000 others.[31] Speaking of the Pope's response to Black Sabbath, Monsignor Graham offers the remarkable conclusion: 'In the absence of documentation … one is left to surmise that the Pontiff intervened personally, as he had on so many earlier occasions.'[32]

Such arguments are flawed. The achievements of individual churchmen like Archbishop Saliege, Father Benoit-Marie or Don Raimondo Viale of Borgo San Dalmazzo cannot be claimed by Pius. It was Monsignor Cassulo who tried to repatriate Jews to the Regat of Romania in January 1944. The Vatican Charge in Bratislava, Monsignor Burzio tried to ameliorate the suffering of Slovak Jews later that year. It was the Nuncio Angelo Rotta who pleaded with the Arrow Cross in Hungary in the winter of 1944–45. In Germany, Cardinal Faulhaber and Bishop von Galen helped unravel the T-4 program while Archbishop Bertram and Bishop Berning made inquiries on behalf of 'non-Aryan' Catholics who had been deported. These individuals may not have acted without papal approval, but there is no documentation to that effect. Carlo Falconi rejects the idea that multiple acts of charity redeem the Vatican. 'The Church is not the International Red Cross,' wrote Falconi. 'Silence amounted to complicity with iniquity.'[33]

The Pope's choice of role models is also flawed. Until the creation of the modern state of Italy the Popes were very much involved in Europe's political disputes. Benedict XV witnessed a war, one in which adversaries used poison gas, Turks massacred Armenians, and innocent civilians were pillaged from Flanders to Finland, yet he was silent. Pius XI may have intended to denounce totalitarianism before his death in 1939, but there is no specific reference to fascism in his encyclical *Non Abbiamo Bisogno*, issued in 1931. Pius XI was silent when the Nazis opened their first concentration camps in 1933 and when they promulgated the Nuremberg Laws. He offered no protest against the *Anschluss*, Munich or Kristallnacht. Readers would find only two possible reproaches to the Nazis (denouncing 'whoever exalts race' and labeling those who reject the Old Testament as blasphemers) in his celebrated encyclical of 1937. Most important, the speech about Catholics being spiritual heirs of Jews was made behind closed doors and went unrecorded by the *Osservatore Romano*[34] According to Gunther Lewy, the Vatican had no intrinsic objection to discriminatory legislation prior to the Holocaust.[35]

Not even Cardinal Maglione, the Pope's liaison to the Germans, comes off well upon scrutiny of the Vatican documents. At the height of the terror in Italy, in 1943, Maglione informed the Papal Nuncio in Washington, that the Vatican would frown upon the use of Palestine as a refuge for Jews. The church could not support Zionist claims and warned 'If Palestine fell under the rule of the Jews, it would give birth to new and grave international problems and make the Catholics of the world unhappy. It would cause righteous complaints of the Holy See and would poorly reciprocate the charitable concern that the Holy See has had and continues to have for non-Aryans.'[36]

Pius XII may have been all the things his supporters declared (affable, wise, impartial, pure, warm and gentle) but it borders on sacrilege to compare him to Christ.[37] Michaelis argues that he was simply a diplomat guided by the principle of *ad maiora mala vitanda* (avoid greater evils).[38] Zuccotti says he allowed others to take great risks while he fulfilled his institutional mandate at the expense of moral leadership.[39] While conceding that a 'flaming protest' might have been useless, Lewy claims the Pope did not speak out because 'he did not view the plight of the Jews with the real sense of urgency and moral outrage'.[40] Perhaps the fairest evaluation came from Hochhuth, who called Pius 'one of the most intelligent men of the first half of this century'. Hochhuth concluded, however, that Pius was 'a fence sitter, an overambitious careerist who, having attained his goal, wasted his time on inconsequential trifles while the tormented world waited in vain for a word of spiritual leadership from him'.[41] Early in his pontificate, Pius had said that the greatest obligation he owed his Holy Office was *testimonium perhibere veritati* (to give testimony to the truth).[42] Through this terrible period, the Church threatened to withhold sacraments from individuals who engaged in duels or practiced cremation, but it offered no reproach to the SS (23 percent of whom were Catholics).[43] As the death trains rolled inexorably to Auschwitz and Treblinka, the spiritual leader of 400 million Catholics promulgated the dogma of the Immaculate Heart of the Blessed Virgin.[44]

In March 1998, after two years of preparation, a Vatican commission issued a 14-page document dealing specifically with the *Shoah*. It called upon all the sons and daughters of the Church to remember the 'the worst suffering' perpetrated upon the Jewish people. It outlined the torment suffered by Jews for 2,000 years and pointed out how Nazism flourished in a neo-pagan regime. The Church publicly apologized for its errors and failures. But in the course of evoking *memoria futuri*, the document again defended the courage of Pius XI and XII.[45]

COMITÉ INTERNATIONAL DE LA CROIX ROUGE (CICR)

'The Church is not the International Red Cross,' wrote Carlo Falconi. Yet these two great humanitarian institutions resembled one another in attitude and behavior during World War II. Since its inception in 1863, the CICR, a non-governmental agency founded and based in Switzerland, concerned itself with the care of prisoners of war and (after 1929) wounded soldiers. From this benevolent idea evolved scores of national societies which co-operated with one another in times of natural disaster or epidemics. Meeting at Tokyo in 1934, representatives of the national societies discussed broadening the mandate to include civilians. A formal vote was postponed until 1939, by which time it was too late. Belligerents would only agree to protect their own nationals and not civilians living in occupied territories. When the war broke out, the CICR declared itself neutral regarding politics, religion or race.[46]

In his semi-official history of the CICR, André Durand lists the many interventions offered by representatives of the International Red Cross to Axis officials throughout Europe. In 1935 Karl Burckhardt (one-time League High Commissioner in Danzig) met with Heydrich, hoping to gain entry into German forced labor camps. This was the first of four such requests before 1938 that were rejected for reasons of 'state security'.[47] Between 1940 and January 1943, delegates of the CICR asked permission to visit Dutch deportees in Buchenwald and Spanish refugees in Mauthausen. They appealed to the OKW (High Command of German Armed Forces) when Polish reserve officers were arrested and when Hitler issued his *Nacht und Nebel* decree on 7 December 1941. On 24 August 1942 and one month later, on 24 September 1942, the Red Cross *demanded* information on prisoners of war and interned civilians. Its demarches were ignored or answered by statements that such matters were being handled by 'competent authorities'.[48]

Officials of the CICR made two general appeals (in March and May 1940) urging restraint in aerial attacks and the taking of hostages.[49] Moved by the suffering of west Europeans under Nazi occupation, in 1941 the CICR created a special relief committee that distributed blankets, clothing, medicines and food to refugees in France, Holland, Latvia, Poland, Slovakia, Slovenia and Italy.[50] The CICR claims to have sent more than one million packages to inmates of concentration camps and civilians between 1939 and 1945. When Germany capitulated, the Red Cross had 21 depots with more than 100,000 tons of supplies at its disposal.[51]

The Red Cross tried to contact the commandants of Ravensbruck, Sachsenhausen, Dachau, Buchenwald and Flossenburg in 1944. On 2 October, CICR President Max Huber sent a harsh note to Nazi Foreign Minister Ribbentrop. Huber's 'minimum' demands included lists of all detainees and their location, permission for them to receive parcels, and the right of entry into concentration camps for delegates of the CICR. All of this was to be done *sans distinction de nationalité ni de lieu d'internement.*[52] The Nazis did allow parcels, but refused to open the camps.

THE NON-STATEMENT OF 1942

Because there were no clauses pertaining to race in existing conventions, the CICR would not refute the Nazi argument that Jews, Gypsies and others were *Schutzhaftlinge* (criminals beyond international protection). By mid-summer 1942, the CICR was being pressed by the Jewish Bund, the Polish Government in Exile and World Jewish Congress to react to reports of mass murder. At the end of August, a draft was circulated to members of the International Committee. The statement opened with a reminder of the committee's traditional neutrality and its commitment to prisoners of war and civilian internees. Beside these unfortunates, however, 'certain categories of diverse nationalities had been deprived of their liberty, deported or taken as hostages for acts for which they often were not the authors'. Invoking terms of the Tokyo Project, the draft called for guarantees of the life and health of such persons, notification of their place of detention, the right to correspond with families and to receive packages.[53]

No Swiss government official believed that the committee would actually approve such protest. They were stunned when 21 of 23 correspondents approved the protest.[54] Embarrassed, but not stymied, the Swiss government convened a meeting of the CICR in Geneva on 14 October 1942. Several delegates suggested that the statement be buried in an innocuous journal. Chairman Edouard Chapuisat permitted only opponents of the measure to speak. Karl Burckhardt questioned whether actions contrary to the goals of the Red Cross could be termed 'courageous'. Then Eduard Haller fretted about the sensitivities of belligerents, noting 'every appeal would be regarded as a judgment'. Instead of a general proclamation, Haller recommended that the CICR continue to act confidentially as it had done with hostages and prisoners of war. After he spoke, the CICR unanimously approved quiet interventions in specific cases.[55]

The CICR did publish a statement on the Jewish Question in its obscure *International Review* on 23 July 1943. After reciting its traditional commitments, the CICR called upon all belligerents to refrain from unjustifiable destruction or actions proscribed by international law. By March 1944, 22 states (including the US, France, Italy and most Latin American countries) had responded favorably to the appeal. Great Britain, Nazi Germany and the Soviet Union did not.[56]

THE RED CROSS: AN ASSESSMENT

Between 2 September 1939 and 21 May 1945, the CICR sent out 39 notes, telegrams, letters and appeals to league affiliates. Some were misdirected to the German Foreign Ministry, Wehrmacht, or the DKR (German Red Cross) when they should have petitioned Himmler or Heydrich. In August–September 1940, the CICR made formal inquiry about *Schutzhaftlinge* and protested the categories of Jews and political prisoners detained in concentration camps.[57] About the same time, Dr Max von Wyss tried to send supplies to Jews in the Government-General.[58] On 20 May 1942, the CICR protested against the deportations of Jews from Drancy, Compiegne and North Africa. Eleven days later, Huber asked Dr Ernst Grawitz, President of the German Red Cross, to intervene on behalf of Jews deported from Vught in Holland.[59] Such requests were deemed 'inadmissible' by the Nazis.[60]

The CICR was somewhat more successful with Hitler's allies. George Dunand went to Bratislava in the summer of 1942, carrying with him a request from Huber to inspect Slovakian internment camps. Tiso allowed Dunand to visit Marianna after most of the Jews were removed to Poland. Unable to convince Alois Brunner to call off the hunt for Slovak Jews in October 1944, the CICR concluded that the only solution for Jews was to hide.[61] After 1943, delegates of the International Committee established a working relationship with Saly Mayer, representative of the Joint Distribution Committee in Switzerland. Dr de Salis in Rome, Karl Kolb in Bucharest[62] and Colonel Edouard Chapuisat in Sofia all offered funds, provisions and medicine to their Jewish communities.[63]

The efforts of the CICR in Hungary especially deserve comment. When Jean de Bavier arrived in Budapest in October 1943, his principal concern was for Allied prisoners of war and civil internees. The latter included Hungarian Jews. De Bavier's reports, warning of grave risks to 800,000 Jews in February 1944, prompted a letter of protest from CICR President Huber to Admiral Horthy. Following the Arrow Cross coup of October 1944, Red Cross delegates intervened with the Ministry of Interior to stop the pillaging. Buildings and hospitals occupied by the international committee temporarily were granted extraterritorial status and the CICR cooperated with foreign consulates organizing care and feeding of ghetto residents. When the Nazis started deporting Jews to Germany, CIRC doctors visited the Altofeuer brickyards, snatching 7,000 potential victims (most of them women) from the death marches.[64]

During the last months of war, officials of the Red Cross (Dr Burckhardt, Count Folke Bernadotte and Dr Marti) arranged the release of some inmates of concentration camps. The Nazis permitted the CICR to set up depots at Uffing, Moosburg and Lubeck, and to establish offices at Wagenitz, northwest of the capital. As the war wound down, the number of Red Cross requests for access to concentration camps multiplied. Red Cross supplies were admitted to Dachau days before the camp was liberated on 29 April. Albert de Cocatrix accepted the surrender of Ravensbruck. And after a month of negotiations, on 5 May, Dr Paul Dunant and Dr Otto Lehner accepted the keys to the Kleine Festung at Terezin.[65]

Durand says the CICR rescued 5,500 deportees in April–May 1945. The CICR claims to have spent more than 250 million Swiss francs on relief and to have saved more than four million lives.[66] Writing in 1946, Jacques Cheneviere rationalized that the CICR worked in silence but 'with all its energy' for the deportees.[67] In 1947 the International Committee explained that it shied away from publicly condemning the Nazis because: 'every protest is a judgment'; 'the indicted party will either keep its own public in ignorance of the protest or present it in one-sided fashion, whilst the opposing side will be free to use it for purposes of propaganda'; public protests would produce a 'stiffening' of the indicted country's attitude toward the CICR; and such protests might be construed as a challenge to German national sovereignty.[68] Durand's semi-official history offers the same excuses. Since its representatives were not permitted to enter the camps, the CICR had no means of verifying what went on at extermination facilities. To expect the Nazis to suddenly honor protests was naive. The CICR considered its duty 'to carry out what was practical and effective'. Durand concedes that other decisions might have been more effective, but the CICR saved thousands of lives in the final phase of hostilities.[69]

Claude Favez, rector of Geneva University, suggests that the International Committee was hamstrung by its close identification with the Swiss government. At that time 3,500 Swiss citizens worked for the Red Cross. Fifty-five percent of its wartime budget was supplied by Switzerland. The Swiss government issued diplomatic passports and made its cable lines available to members of the International Committee.[70] The committee depended upon affiliated groups to implement policy and in Germany they were confronted with an inflexible government. Jews were the most tragic of war's victims, living 'on the margin of interventions founded on human rights'. If the CICR did not act in 1941–42 it was because no one, not even the Allies or the Vatican, could imagine 'the unimaginable' at that time.[71]

Having said that, however, Favez scores the Red Cross for failing to issue the statement it contemplated in 1942. The CICR had issued complaints to various governments in World War I, reminding them of their obligations under the Convention of 1906. It condemned the use of poison gas on 6 February 1918. While the tonnage of food and medical supplies assembled by the CICR in World War II is impressive, Favez concurs with Meir Dworczecki that 'the help extended was absolutely inadequate when measured in terms of the needs at the time'.[72] Favez labels such aid 'modest' and says that the 'sum of the individual acts' of Red Cross delegates in Berlin, Budapest, Croatia, Italy and Slovakia 'does not constitute a policy'.[73] The CICR adhered to nineteenth-century conventions made obsolete by the ideological warfare of the new century. He concludes: 'In the use of international law, the CICR, confronted with juridically unnamed victims who turned to it, often sought not the means to act, but on the contrary, a justification for not acting, so as not to disturb the conventional missions on which, in its eyes, its very existence stood.'[74]

In 1989, officials of the International Committee conceded: 'The ICRC feels that the meager results yielded by the considerable efforts made at the time and in the prevailing circumstances represent the worst defeat in the history of its humanitarian mission and exemplify the failure of an entire civilization.'[75]

The European Neutrals

In the brief interlude before his attack upon the Soviet Union, Hitler held sway over the European continent. Those countries that were not formally aligned with the Axis were either sympathetic to totalitarianism (Spain, Portugal) or fearful of invasion (Switzerland, Sweden). Though each of these nations claimed they resisted Hitler and aided the beleaguered Jews, it is clear when the New Order seemed transcendent they all willingly collaborated.

SWITZERLAND: EUROPE'S PORCUPINE

There were 20,000 Jewish citizens in Switzerland in 1939 and they were no more popular here than elsewhere in Europe. Accused of spreading the Black Death, Jews had been expelled in the fourteenth century. A few cattle dealers filtered back to the valley towns of Lengnau and Endigen during the Thirty Years War. Switzerland was the last country in western Europe to grant Jews civic rights (in 1866) and even then its 22 cantons moved slowly in extending citizenship.[1] In 1919, the state parliament of Zurich considered imposing a 20-year residence requirement before 'Ostjuden' could apply for citizenship.[2]

During the Depression, the press blamed alien Jews for the country's economic suffering (124,000 workers were unemployed by 1936). Jews were assaulted on the street and the great synagogue of Zurich was vandalized. Johann Baptist Rusch, C.A. Loosli and Theodor Fischer reprinted *The Protocols of the Elders of Zion* and Henry Ford's *International Jew*. In the summer of 1933, the principal Jewish organization in Switzerland, the *Schweizerischen Israelitischen Gemeindebund* (SIG), sued the publishers of the *Protocols*, charging them with violating Swiss law that barred the sale of 'indecent writing'. The trial in Berne lasted almost two years before the court affirmed that the *Protocols* constituted *Schundliteratur* (trash). Said Judge Meyer: 'I hope to see the day when nobody will be able to understand why otherwise sane and reasonable men should have had to torment their brains for fourteen days over the authenticity or the fabrication of the *Protocols of Zion*. I regard the *Protocols* as ridiculous nonsense.'[3]

During the 1930s, a number of proto-fascist groups (*Schweizer Heimatwehr*, *Vereiningung Schweizerischer Republikaner*, *Schweizerischer Volksbund fur Freiheit und Recht*, *Kreuzwehr*) hoped to emulate Hitler's success. The most prominent clique was the National Front (NF) which claimed 40,000 members by September 1939. (A more reasonable estimate is 9,200.[4]) The Front staged demonstrations – in Zurich after the assassination of Nazi leader Gustloff, at Berne on 23 May 1937, in Lucerne that same year. Its message was readily discerned in signs that squealed, 'Immigrants Out. The Jews are our misfortune. *Die Schweiz den Schweizern.* Switzerland for the Swiss.' Front demagogues claimed Jewish refugees were profiteers, their children were flooding the schools. The NF urged a boycott of Jewish businesses and demanded that the government close the borders to Jewish refugees.[5]

By 1939, Switzerland counted 7,100 refugees, 5,000 of them Jews. A number been dumped upon Switzerland by the Germans who refused to take them back. Shortly after he attended the Evian conference, Swiss Police Chief Heinrich Rothmund met Hans Globke, a German race specialist in Sachsen-hausen and proposed that the Nazis stamp Jewish passports with a 'J' to make it easier for border guards to repulse such undesirables.[6] Jews who managed to secure entry permits were sustained by agencies like the SIG, JDC, OSE as the government showed 'little interest in supporting refugees'.[7] In 1939 1,000 Jewish men were sent to labor camps where they toiled on roads and farms and endured taunts from Swiss guards and Gentile refugees who also had been interned. Most Swiss agreed with federal counselor Edward Steiger, who likened Switzerland to a life raft that could only rescue so many people. Said Steiger, 'The boat is full.'[8] In 1942 Rothmund shut down access to refugees fleeing France. Several committed suicide.[9] In all, 23,000 desperate people were sent away from Switzerland's borders.[10]

Mindful of what had happened to Denmark, Norway and Belgium, Switzerland would do nothing that might provoke Germany. In June 1940 President Marcel Pilet-Golaz saluted the New Order in Europe and called for authoritarian rule in Switzerland. Two months later, General Henri Guisan, commander of the Swiss army, apologized for having called for resistance against a German invasion, in mountain redoubts if necessary. In November, 200 business leaders circulated a petition calling for press censorship and judicial reforms that emulated Nazism. Switzerland followed German orders on blackouts and ignored violations of its air space by German aircraft. Such behavior was somewhat surprising. Though no match for the Wehrmacht, Switzerland's army could expand from a standing force of 100,000 to 450,000. Its aircraft were state of the art Messerschmitts. The railway tunnels that linked central Europe with the Adriatic could be mined. Valleys and gorges could be transformed into defensive bastions.[11] If Denmark were Hitler's canary, Switzerland liked to think of itself as Europe's porcupine.

A rather tame beast at that, for Switzerland depended upon its neighbors for more than 7.5 million tons of food. Rationing (even for chocolate) was instituted in 1939 along with meatless days. Gasoline was in short supply. Switzerland shipped 220,000 tons of iron ore per year to Germany, rationaliz-ing that the economy might be destroyed if it did not cooperate. In the last year of the war, the Swiss did hold back ball bearings, fuses, electric motors, timber and dairy products while sending precision parts and instruments through the Nazi blockade to the Allies.[12] What most concerned the Swiss was the prospect of a German invasion. The military felt this was imminent on several occasions – when the Allies collapsed in June 1940, in October 1940 (when the Nazis did have plans for 'Operation Tannenbaum'), in March 1943 when Italy capitulated, and after D-Day. Each time the Nazi high command weighed the cost of a mountain campaign and rejected such plans.

Individual Swiss acted courageously during wartime. Paul Gruninger, police chief of St Gallen, was dismissed for trying to assist Jews. Reverend Paul Vogt offered a sermon read in every church in Switzerland in 1944 asking God's forgiveness for his people's inaction. Karl Lutz, the Swiss consul in Budapest, supplied more than 10,000 passports to Hungarian Jews. The Romanian-born George Mantello handed out 50,000 documents in 1944 before he was forced to flee Budapest. During World War II, 400,000 stateless persons passed through Switzerland, far more than Turkey, Spain or Sweden. Among them were 100,000 Jews, subsidized by the small Swiss Jewish community. When the war ended in May 1945, 115,000 refugees were in temporary camps.

SWISS BANKS/JEWISH GOLD

Because of its fabled neutrality, Switzerland became a center of international finance. The Swiss asked no questions of funds deposited and under Article 47 of the Federal Code offered no answers.[13] After March 1940, German officials shipped an estimated $378 million in gold bullion from the Reichsbank primarily to the Swiss National Bank in Bern.[14] Much of this had been confiscated from Poland, Italy, Belgium, Luxembourg, France and Czechoslovakia. The transfers, approved by the Bank for International Settlements (BIS) enabled Nazi Germany to obtain trade credits and currency exchange. Thomas Mckittrick, an American who headed the BIS, rationalized that such currency exchanges were inevitable. Switzerland was, as some put it, 'a garden surrounded by blood'.[15]

In January 1943, 17 Allied nations issued a warning to Europe's neutrals to stop laundering money for the Nazis. That same year, Switzerland accepted $120 million in gold from Germany after Sweden rejected the transfer.[16] The Swiss proved to be equally obstinate when a post-war commission (consisting of representatives of the United States, Great Britain and France) insisted upon return of confiscated national funds. Dr Walter Stucki, Undersecretary of Foreign Affairs, agreed to repayment of $58.4 million, a fifth of what the Tripartite Commission estimated. The process was interminably slow, with some individuals waiting until the 1980s for reimbursement.[17]

In 1996, the World Jewish Congress claimed that the Swiss government had concealed the fact that it accepted wealth confiscated from Jews for more than a half century. Elan Steinberg of the WJC demanded that Swiss banks offer restitution to Holocaust survivors and their relatives. When the US Senate Banking Committee, chaired by Alphonse d'Amato, began holding hearings, the Swiss remained nonplused. Carlo Jagmetti, Switzerland's ambassador to the US, dismissed the notion there might be unclaimed fortunes in Swiss bank accounts, citing the case of New Yorker Greta Beer, whose family, Jagmetti claimed, discovered such funds had already been claimed by relatives. In fact, they had done no such thing and Jagmetti subsequently resigned. Relations with the Swiss did not improve when the outgoing President of the Swiss Confederation, Jean-Pascal Delamuraz labeled calls for restitution 'blackmail'. That same month (January 1997) a watchman in Switzerland's largest bank revealed that employees were working through the night shredding wartime documents.[18]

On 7 May 1997 a task force appointed by President Clinton issued a preliminary study on the issue of German gold and Swiss banks. The 200-page report concluded that Switzerland had indeed accepted huge amounts of Nazi loot and that the operation involved 11 agencies. Some $400 million had been deposited in Switzerland's protected banking system (more than $4 billion by current standards). Some of this was in the form of wedding bands, glasses, gold fillings and jewelry taken from concentration camp inmates and melted into gold bars. Stuart Eizenstadt, committee Chair and Undersecretary of Commerce, said that by doing 'business as usual' the Swiss had prolonged the Nazi war effort. While allowing that the Swiss may have been unaware of the origins of such gold, the report concluded that 'neutrality collided with morality'.[19]

The Swiss response was predictable. Foreign Minister Flavio Cotti said the US report lacked 'measured recognition' of Switzerland's difficult position in wartime. The little country had been compelled to make 'a tightrope walk between adaptation and resistance'. The government insisted that all but $68 million in former Nazi accounts had been returned.[20] According to the Swiss, the Americans and British retrieved the bulk of Nazi gold confiscated from Jews ($252 million) from caves in Thuringia, near Salzburg, and La Fortezza, Italy.[21] Having provoked the civilized world, in 1996 Switzerland agreed to fund a study of Jewish and German bank accounts through the US Holocaust Museum. In August 1998, the government reached a class action settlement with survivors, promising compensation in the amount of $1.25 billion.[22]

SPAIN: THE WISDOM OF A GALICIAN OX

Unlike Switzerland, Spain was heavily indebted to the Axis. Italy and Germany had sent troops to aid the right-wing nationalists during the Civil War. The *Falangist Española* was modeled after Mussolini's Black Shirts. Generalissimo Franco called himself *Caudillo* (leader) and repaid fascist support by granting

Italy and Germany trading privileges in 1936 and 1937. Spain was Germany's source of wolfram ore (essential for steel and precision instruments) and mercury. Franco permitted Nazi U-boats to refit at ports on the mainland and Canary Islands. The Germans flew reconnaissance missions from Spanish bases in planes bearing Spanish markers. The Gestapo could even arrest and deport suspects from Spain.[23]

When France surrendered, Franco announced that Spain was changing its status from neutral to 'nonbelligerent'. The term, used by Mussolini before his declaration of war, offered several advantages. On 14 June, Franco sent 3,000 troops to seize the Moroccan port of Tangier, which since 1928 had been administered by an international condominium. At the end of July, Franco welcomed Admiral Wilhelm Canaris and a team of German intelligence officers to develop 'Operation Felix', the assault on Gibraltar. No mean task, this projected siege would require a force of more than 65,000 men who were training in the Jura mountains.[24]

Hitler invited Franco to join the Axis in 1940, but the Spanish leader demurred. More than 170 cities had been flattened during the Civil War; 170,000 people had been killed or wounded; 250,000 were in concentration camps, another 300,000 had fled to France. At a meeting with Hitler on the French border in October 1940, the Spanish dictator outlined a number of material needs (700,000 tons of food, trucks, railway cars) and territorial demands (Gibraltar, French Africa to the bay of Guinea) in exchange for a declaration of war. Franco argued that he was more valuable to the Germans as a non-belligerent since the British might attack the Spanish coastline or seize the Azores, Madeira and Cape Verde Islands.

Unknown to the *Führer*, his own emissary Canaris was advising the Spanish to stay out of the conflict. The issue became academic when the Nazis diverted troops intended for the Gibraltar campaign to the Balkans in the spring of 1941. Hitler was pleased when Spain offered 47,000 troops against the Soviet Union. (Spain justified its involvement on the Eastern Front as retaliation for Russia's intervention in the Civil War.) Integrated in the Wehrmacht to protect Spain's 'non-belligerency', members of the Blue Legion fought around Leningrad before being recalled in July 1943. Only half returned home.[25]

Franco may have come from Spanish hill country, but he was no fool and events vindicated his caution. When the Americans seized Morocco, he began to tilt toward the Allies. The Germans could not send troops through Spain to fight in North Africa and shipments of wolfram were cut back. On 1 October 1943, Franco abandoned 'non-belligerency', taking Spain back to 'neutrality'. The Nazis reacted by massing troops at the Pyrennees. 'Operation Ilona', the occupation of both Spain and Portugal, was postponed until the spring of 1943. Redubbed 'Operation Gisela', the invasion was canceled by Hitler who believed the Spanish (the 'only tough Latins') would fight to the death in their mountainous homeland. The *Führer* instructed

Schellenberg to undermine Franco with more radical Falangists such as Foreign Minister Ramón Serrano Suñer and General Augustin Munoz Grandes, commander of the Blue Legion. When the 'Galician Ox' learned of the plot, he replaced Serrano Suñer with Francisco Jordana, an aristocrat with a pro-British bias.[26]

FALANGIST SPAIN AND THE JEWS

No less likely havens could be imagined than Spain or Portugal. These were the lands identified with the Inquisition and the forced conversion of tens of thousands of Jews. Spain expelled all of its professing Jews in 1492, Portugal followed suit five years later. The *limpieza de sangre*, the certificate of blood that established one's station in society, originated in Iberia. Efforts to rescind the edict of expulsion in 1797 failed, but reformers did succeed in guaranteeing freedom of religion to residents between 1854 and 1876. Small numbers of Jews returned when Spain annexed parts of Morocco. A few were granted asylum after the Russian pogroms in 1881–82.[27] There were no synagogues in Spain until 1909.

When Greek nationalists attacked Jews in Salonika in 1912, the Spanish consul intervened on their behalf. Four years later, Spain enrolled Sephardic Jews under its protection. Senator Angelo Pulido Fernández worked for more than four decades to increase cultural and economic ties with Jews. Pulido Fernandez believed that Sephardic Jews were *Españoles sin patria* (Spaniards without homeland).[28] On 20 December 1924, the government of General Miguel Primo de Rivera ruled that persons who could establish Spanish descent might be enrolled as a Spanish national.[29] The 1931 constitution of the new republic guaranteed freedom of conscience, ended church control of education, and granted citizenship to residents of Spain after two years. By 1939, there were 6,000 Jews in mainland Spain, half of them refugees. Despite expressions of support from President Niceto Zamora and diplomats Luis de Zulueta and Salvador de Madariaga, Spanish Jews had good reason to be wary. The Catholic Church fought against every modification of its powers or improvement of the rights of Jews. As in France, the clergy had strong allies in monarchists, reactionary politicians and the military.

Falangist General Gonzalo Queipo de Llano declared Spain's civil war a contest 'for western civilization against world Jewry'. When the nationalists won, synagogues in Barcelona and Madrid were closed. 'Scholars' began distinguishing between Sephardic Jews (who allegedly possessed some Aryan blood) and Ashkenazim (who had none). Some refugees, fearing another expulsion, opted for conversion.[30] Newspapers blamed the outbreak of World War II upon Jews. History texts lionized Ferdinand and Isabella for their solution of the Jewish Problem and José Luna, Vice-Secretary of the Falange, revived the concept of expulsion in 1942. In December 1943, Franco told

German Ambassador Hans Dieckhoff that 'thanks to God and the clear appreciation of the danger by our Catholic kings, we have for centuries been relieved of that nauseating burden'.[31]

In June 1940 Franco ordered the borders closed. Sympathetic patrols looked the other way as refugees continued to cross the Pyrenees. After September 1940 individuals were admitted if they possessed travel documents for another country. Women and children were shunted to provincial jails, men to the concentration camp of Miranda de Ebro near Burgos. Between 1,500 and 3,000 men were housed in squalor at Miranda.[32] Prisoners received limited assistance from the American Red Cross, Quakers, the Joint and the wife of US Ambassador Alexander Weddell.[33]

Spanish officials made no distinction between Jewish and Gentile refugees until November 1942. If anything, Spain made representations on behalf of certain Jews. In September 1940, Bernardo Rolland, Consul-General in Paris, managed to exempt 6,000 Jews from wearing the yellow star or paying the Jew tax to the UGIF.[34] Rolland eventually was replaced by Alfonso Fiscovich, who was less sympathetic to Jews. Foreign Minister Jordana instructed him to apply the most rigid standards of documentation to individuals who claimed Spanish citizenship. A total of 877 Sephardic Jews, mostly Greeks, were deported from Drancy on 9 November 1942.[35]

Eduardo Gasset, consul in Salonika, and Sebastian Radigales, ambassador in Athens, tried to impress upon Madrid the seriousness of the threat facing Jews in Greece. Spain had intervened on behalf of Salonika's Jews in 1912, 1916 and 1936. When the Nazis started shipping Jews from the Baron Hirsch camp in March 1943, Spain's ministers were instructed to rescue persons who claimed Spanish citizenship. Because of disagreements between Madrid and Berlin, two transports of 'Spaniards' were delayed at Bergen-Belsen for several months.[36] Elsewhere, it was the same pattern of misplaced hope and bureaucratic delay. In the summer of 1943, Renee Reichman, a Jewish refugee in North Africa, arranged to have Sephardic children transferred from Budapest to Spanish Morocco. Pressed by the Szalasi regime to take 'his' people out, Angel Sanz Briz, the Spanish chargé in Hungary, managed to save not only 1,898 Jews who claimed Sephardic ancestry but also issued 2,750 protective documents to non-Spanish Jews in the last weeks of 1944.[37]

On 10 July 1944 the Spanish government instructed its diplomats 'to render all possible assistance to Jews and other persons in immediate danger of death or persecution, regardless of nationality.'[38] In Casablanca, Consul General Jaime Jorro issued thousands of travel documents. In Zurich, Simon Marin helped initiate the rescue of 10,000 refugees. In Romania, José Rojas Moreno interceded on behalf of a small number of Jews during the pogroms of 1940–41. As in France, these individuals were spared the wearing of the yellow star, confiscation of property and deportation.[39] Consuls in Sofia, Bratislava and Vienna all issued bogus visas and hid Jews. The Spanish also helped 500 Jews from the Mirrer Yeshiva reach Shanghai.

At least 30,000 Jewish refugees came to Spain during the war years.[40] According to Rabbi Chaim Lipschitz, Spain's achievements outstrip those of Denmark, Great Britain or the United States.[41] In a 1949 White Paper, the Spanish government explained that it was motivated by 'Christian charity to a neighbor ... caught in the ruthless wheels of totalitarian materialism'.[42] Franco mouthed the same platitudes ('we acted because of an elementary feeling of justice and charity') in an interview with Rabbi Lipschitz in July 1970. Many of the other arguments (Franco was influenced by the Vatican, he acted to embarrass the Nazis and the Allies, he sought financial gain, he was descended from Marranos, he was interested in securing his place in history) may also be disputed.[43]

In fact, the numbers rescued by Spain are substantially lower than those claimed by the Franco government. According to Haim Avni, 6,000 Jews reached Spain by the end of 1943,[44] no more than 11,535 thereafter.[45] At any given moment there were less than 2,000 refugees in Spain. Franco had to be cajoled to take a handful of Jews from France. Warned that the Germans would deport 700 'Spanish' Jews in the summer of 1943 Franco's government bedeviled the Nazis with trivial details. In the next year Sephardic Jews from Athens, Bulgaria and Italy were sent to concentration camps. Diplomats like Rolland, Radigales and Sanz Briz were frustrated by their government, which insisted upon documents that were unobtainable or made admission of new groups of Jews contingent upon others moving out of the country. There was no altruism in the actions of Franco and his cronies. Like Switzerland, Spain steered a course between adversaries, watching as fortune favored one side, then the other. By pleading Spain's inability to make war, Franco managed to avoid being swept down with other fascist leaders. When it became obvious that the Allies would determine the course of a post-war world, he set about repairing Spain's image.

PORTUGAL

If Franco's efforts were late and insincere, even less may be said of his neighbor in Portugal. Antonio de Oliveira Salazar established the first fascist regime in the Iberian peninsula in 1932. By gauging diplomatic winds, the one-time finance minister remained in office for more than 35 years. During World War II, Salazar, like Franco, feigned neutrality, openly sympathizing with the Nazis in the early phases of the war, then cheering on the Allies. Between 1940 and 1943, Lisbon became the port of embarkation for persons with entry visas to the United States or some other country in the western hemisphere.[46] Like Franco, Salazar worried about occupation. After reinforcing his outposts in the Azores in 1941, Salazar granted an air base to the British and Americans on the island of Terceira in the fall of 1943.

Rarely did Portuguese diplomats issue visas to groups of Jews. One who did was Aristes de Sousa Mendes, Consul General in Bordeaux. Thousands of Jews fled to this coastal city in the summer of 1940. Many lined up at the Portuguese consulate, hoping for a miracle. While Salazar declared he would accept 'no Jews under any circumstances', De Sousa Mendes welcomed Rabbi Chaim Kruger into his house and revealed that he was descended from a New Christian family. De Sousa Mendes worked three days with little rest, distributing 10,000 visas before Salazar recalled him. On the drive back to Portugal, de Sousa Mendes encountered another crowd at the Portuguese consulate in Bayonne. He issued several thousand more life-saving papers.[47]

For Jews who managed to secure visas for London, Haiti or some other haven, the wait in Portugal seemed interminable. A Polish teenager wrote: 'Lisbon in those days of the spring of 1942 seemed less like a city and more like a waiting room. It was crowded with people who were in transit. They were all waiting for planes and boats. There was no land route of escape for them, for the land led back to where they all had come from, what they were running away from.'[48] A Jewish Agency office was opened in Lisbon in 1944 and it was through Portugal that the Zionist underground smuggled hundreds of adults and children to Palestine. By war's end, nearly 30,000 Jews passed through Portugal.[49]

SWEDEN/TRANSITANIA

More than Switzerland, less than Spain, neutral Sweden tilted toward the Axis for much of World War II.[50] Sweden honored normal shipments of iron ore (8 million tons annually) to Germany in exchange for 5.7 million tons of coal/coke. In 1940, the Swedes increased the German allotment, arguing that the excess would have gone to Czechoslovakia or Poland. The Swedish firm SKF shipped hundreds of thousands of precision ball bearings to the Nazis.[51] When Hitler invaded Norway, Sweden permitted shipment of 'humanitarian' supplies (food and medicine) to German troops even after boxes were found to contain ammunition and other contraband. During the battle for Narvik, the Swedes agreed to let one train carrying a few artillery pieces cross their territory. The Nazis upped the request to three trains carrying everything from ack-ack to machine guns. Soon, the Germans were demanding the right to fly across Swedish air space; to dock their vessels in Swedish harbors longer than the 24 hours sanctioned by international law; and to rotate troops out of Norway.[52] Observers discovered that the Germans were sending far more troops into Norway than were coming out. In preparation for Operation Barbarossa, the Nazis requested permission to move the 163rd Engelbrecht Division across to Finland. More than 75,000 railway cars carrying German troops and military supplies (2 percent of all Swedish railway traffic) traversed what the Allies mockingly called 'Transitania' between June 1940 and August 1943.[53]

Unlike Norway's Haakon, who went into exile, or Denmark's King

Christian, who appeared daily in Copenhagen to inspire his countrymen, Sweden's King Gustav V was a doddering septuginarian who spent much of his time doing needlepoint. Gustav criticized the Nazis regime when he visited Germany in 1933, but seven years later this son of a German princess threatened to abdicate unless the government agreed to German demands on transshipment of war *matériel*.[54] Erling Eidem, Archbishop of the Swedish Lutheran Church, was equally brave before the war. Like the king, he urged Hindenburg to rein in the Nazis when he visited Germany in 1934. Privately, Eidem condemned 'Germany's monstrous blood guilt'. But fearful of 'godless communism', in November 1942 Eidem would only authorize a general statement by Sweden's bishops denouncing 'race prejudice' without any specific reference to Jews.[55]

The government of Prime Minister Per Hansson was equally timid. Though Hitler dangled Narvik and Petsamo before them in 1941, the Swedes avoided war with the Soviet Union. Sweden did send food, timber, military supplies and 8,000 volunteers to help the Finns in the winter of 1939–40.[56] The government repealed a law that permitted refugees without visas to stay in the country for three months. In the spring of 1940, the Swedes also restricted books and newspapers that endangered state security. About the same time, police raided communist party headquarters and sent their leaders to labor camps.

After the war, Swedes offered a tale of an indomitable people that was prepared to do battle in the Arctic Circle if the Germans invaded. Faced with runaway inflation, unemployment and shortages of fuel and food, the Swedes leased half of their fleet to Great Britain. The Swedes loaded British 'pocket freighters' with high-grade steel in 1943 and continued to send iron ore and ball bearings to the British and Americans even after they halted shipments to Germany in 1944.

Swedes also fashioned a positive perspective on the Jewish Question. Foreign Minister Rickard Sandler and publisher Torgny Segerstedt criticized Nazi Germany during the 1930s. Sweden accepted 800 of Norway's 1,700 Jews, 8,000 Jews and converts from Denmark.[57] After arranging the exchange of 10,000 Allied and German PWs in 1944, the king's nephew Count Folke Bernadotte secured the transfer of 13,000 Scandinavians early in 1945. In April 1945 Bernadotte obtained the release of 21,000 prisoners, including 6,500 Jews.[58] All told, Sweden may have helped 45,000 Jews during the war.[59]

There is, of course, another view. In 1939 there were 7,000 Jews in Sweden. Anti-foreign, anti-Jewish sentiments existed among the upper classes, church leaders, university students and 186,000 unemployed workers.[60] Eugenicists like Hermann Lundborg worried whether Sweden was becoming 'an international garbage can'.[61] One hundred right-wing groups came into existence, including the National Socialist League, the Right Front and the Swedish National Party (none of which won seats in the *Riksdag*).[62] The Swedish people may not have been receptive to blatant anti-Semitism, but they were supportive of the Conservatives and Farmers' Parties, essential parts of Hansson's coalition, which included restrictionists, corporatists and polite bigots.[63]

Because of such hostility, Sweden admitted just 3,000 Jewish refugees from Austria, Germany and Czechoslovakia.[64] In the summer of 1938, the government seconded Switzerland's call for a special marking of Jewish passports. In September, Sigfrid Hansson, the Prime Minister's brother, called for the border to be closed to Jews. The Hansson government was notoriously slow responding to a proposal that would have provided refuge to 200 Finnish Jews in 1943. Of the 185,000 refugees that entered Sweden during wartime, more than half (108,000) were Finns, 50,000 Norwegians, 18,000 Danes.[65] Sweden suppressed news of Nazi policies toward Jews, even when it possessed confirmation of genocide. Swedish missionaries (the Church under the Cross) accompanied the Nazis during the invasion of Russia and witnessed atrocities perpetrated by Einsatzgruppen.[66] In July 1942, Sven Norrman and four other Swedish businessmen brought back film of the Warsaw ghetto. A month later, while traveling from Warsaw to Berlin, Baron Goran von Otter was briefed by Kurt Gerstein on extermination procedures at Belzec. Von Otter's report went to Staffan Soderblom of the Swedish Foreign Ministry, who spiked the story as 'too risky to pass … from one belligerent country to another'.[67]

The Swedish Lutheran Church issued a general condemnation of wartime brutality in December 1942. Despite their avowed sympathy for Jews, neither the crown nor the Hansson government offered a statement. The excuses are familiar (small nations can achieve more through quiet negotiation, the Nazis might invade Sweden, the only nation that would profit was the Soviet Union) and they are invalid. The Swedes, like the Spanish, Swiss and Portuguese, were guided by expedience. When it appeared the Nazis were winning, they cooperated with Germany. When it was evident the Allies would win, the Swedes made the most of their democratic traditions. For most of the war, however, they were silent, and 'the silence also confirmed German suspicions that other states tacitly approved of their Jewish policies'.[68]

WALLENBERG

One last chapter on Sweden must be related. Raoul Wallenberg was a scion of one of the most prestigious families in Sweden.[69] Something of a playboy, Wallenberg graduated from the University of Michigan, but his degree was not honored in Sweden. His grandfather arranged for Raoul to work with an import-export firm in Capetown in 1933, then with the Holland Bank in Haifa. Upon returning to Sweden, he volunteered for Finnish relief. His uncles referred him to Koloman Lauer, a Hungarian Jew who was the largest food supplier in central Europe. In 1942 young Wallenberg was sent by Lauer to France where he witnessed the *razzias* in Paris. He spent the following year in Budapest.

In the spring of 1944, the American War Refugee Board sent Ivor Olsen to Stockholm to win the release of Hungary's Jews. Someone had to act as an intermediary with the Hungarians and the Nazis. The assignment went to Raoul Wallenberg. A man with no diplomatic training, Wallenberg impressed US Ambassador Herschel Johnson and Marcus Ehrenpreis, the chief rabbi of Stockholm. And so in July 1944 the young Swede presented his credentials to Admiral Horthy. In his early reports, Wallenberg suggested that warnings of post-war punishment be balanced with clemency. Wallenberg also corroborated details of the Auschwitz Protocols that had been in western hands since April 1944.

Wallenberg was especially impressed with the efforts of Swedish legation secretary Per Anger and Professor Valdmar Langlet of the Swedish Red Cross, who invented 'letters of protection' and 'provisional passports'. Wallenberg designed his own blue and yellow document bearing the emblem of the Swedish throne and a refugee's photograph. This *Schutzpass* certified that the bearer was under Swedish protection and was permitted to travel to Sweden. Ambassador Carl Danielsson told the Hungarians he authorized 4,500 such passports, but the actual number was more than 20,000. Wallenberg's actions inspired Swiss, Spanish and Portuguese diplomats to devise their own documents.

During that summer, Wallenberg expanded his staff from 40 to more than 400. He funded two hospitals with 40 physicians and set up a soup kitchen for refugees. When Eichmann demanded the deportation of 50,000 Jews in 25 August, Wallenberg convinced Angelo Rotta, the Papal Nuncio, the Portuguese, Spanish and Swiss chargé d'affaires, and Minister Danielsson to intervene. Eichmann would have his revenge. In late July, he deported 1,500 prominent Jews over the protests of Cardinal Seredi, Protestant Bishop Vilmos Apor and the neutral legations.[70]

When the Arrow Cross seized control of the government in October 1944, the Swedes offered sanctuary to more than 15,000 Jews in 32 buildings while the Swiss maintained 72 bearing the yellow star. When the Nazis organized death marches in early November, Wallenberg and his aides rescued as many Jews as possible with passes typed on the spot. When deportations by rail were resumed, Wallenberg set up an office at the terminal, distributing passes to all who asked for exemptions. He felt responsible for 53,000 Jews in the ghetto and offered the stiffest protests to Erno Vajna, the Hungarian fanatic whose 'troops' committed atrocities. But not even Wallenberg was able to prevent the murder of Arthur Weisz, owner of the Glass House, which sheltered 2,500 Jews, the Zionist leader Otto Komoly or Miklos Szego and Janos Gabor of the Jewish Council. As he traveled from building to building in the last days, Wallenberg told a comrade, 'They are looking for me.' He meant the Hungarian fascists. 'They' turned out to be the Soviets.[71]

Righteous Gentiles: Denmark and Norway

Many nations puffed up their humanitarian achievements in World War II. Two that had no need of fabrication were Denmark and Norway. Fiercely independent peoples, once part of the same empire, Danes and Norwegians shared much in common. Both were from the Nordic stock of which Hitler raved so much and both were conquered by the Germans in the spring of 1940. Both were Protestant Christian nations – overwhelmingly Lutheran. And after the war, both were acknowledged among the Righteous of Nations by the State of Israel and Yad Vashem.

DENMARK: HITLER'S CANARY

Among all of Europe's conquered nations, only Denmark was permitted to retain its government. Ambassador Cecil von Renthe-Fink promised that Germany would never encroach upon the sovereignty of the kingdom. Seventy-year-old Christian X of Denmark was permitted to retain his throne. The Danish parliament under Prime Minister Thorvald Stauning continued to function. Likewise Denmark's foreign ministry and military. While Danes termed their actions 'the policy of negotiation', Stauning conceded, 'We will be forced to do many things for which people will afterward spit at us, if we are to bring Denmark unscathed through this period.'[1]

Denmark was Germany's *Musterprotektorat* (model protectorate) or, as Winston Churchill dubbed it, 'Hitler's Canary'. Wehrmacht Generals Erich Luedke, L. Kaupisch and Hermann von Hannecken were not governors, merely troop commanders. Renthe-Fink and the man who replaced him in November 1942, Dr Werner Best were Ministers Plenipotentiary. Denmark was privileged for several reasons. Strategically, it controlled access to the Baltic which the Nazis intended to make their own lake. Economically, Denmark funneled foodstuffs, aircraft parts, armored cars and diesel vehicles, as well as iron and ball bearings from Sweden. Mythically, Hitler believed that Jutland, the peninsula that constitutes the bulk of Denmark, was the ancestral home of the Nordic race.[2]

There was an underground in Denmark, but initially it did little more than distribute leaflets criticizing the oafish behavior of Nazis. Some taxi drivers ignored the hale of German troops. Danish pranksters slashed tires on German autos. For a brief spell, students donned beanies with designs that resembled RAF insignia. Until 1943, most Danes were apathetic about the occupation. In that year, food shortages and dock strikes became more widespread. News of Nazi military setbacks prompted more Danes to join cells of the Freedom Council. They received weapons from British intelligence and supplied information for bombing runs. The Danes carried out more than 2,000 acts of sabotage, disrupting railways and destroying bridges. In the last days of the occupation, 87 persons died and 664 others were wounded in anti-German riots. Leo Goldberger estimates that 15,000 men and women actively participated in the resistance; 6,000 were arrested; and 600 of these died in prison.[3]

Relations between the Danes and Germans reached a critical point in the last week of August 1943. Best returned from a meeting in Berlin with instructions to proclaim a state of emergency. To prevent flight to Sweden, the Germans confiscated rowboats and stepped up coastal patrols. Any Dane found in possession of a weapon would be executed. Danish troops were confined to their barracks and the Danish navy was ordered to join the Axis fleets. Instead, Admiral Vedel instructed his commanders to scuttle their vessels: 29 ships were put out of commission, 13 others fled to Sweden. In retribution, on 29 August, the Nazis seized hostages from among Danish army and navy officers. When the Danish parliament was suspended, Prime Minister Scaevenius and most of his cabinet resigned. A number of high-ranking Danish officials were arrested and Nazi guards were dispatched to Amalienburg Castle where King Christian called himself a prisoner of war.[4]

For three years, the Danes had put up with rationing, air raid sirens, bombings, life in underground shelters. Now they had no government and their beloved king was a hostage. On the heels of these indignities, the Nazis decided to deport Denmark's Jews. As Leo Goldberger has written, 'for a peace-loving country, with its famous facade of good humor', persecution of Jews 'signified the proverbial last straw'.[5]

THERE IS NO JEWISH PROBLEM IN DENMARK

There were 7,800 Jews in Denmark in 1943. Most were congregated in Copenhagen: 345 were engaged in business, 35 were lawyers, 21 artists, 14 editors. There were no Jews in Parliament. Sixteen hundred could trace their lineage to the expulsions from Spain or Portugal; 3,350 had fled Russian pogroms after 1903; and 1,500 were recent refugees from Germany, Austria and Czechoslovakia. Perhaps 1,300 were children of mixed marriages.[6] Although Jews developed a host of religious and political organizations (schools, a B'nai B'rith lodge, Hakoah, Jewish bowling team), the emphasis, even among refugees, was on blending into Danish society. As one correspondent for the *Jodisk Familieblad* (the monthly publication of the Danish Jewish community) put it in January 1934, 'Assimilation was and is a fact'.[7]

Apparently the Danes felt the same way. In 1690, the Danish parliament rejected the concept of a ghetto as 'an inhuman way of life'. In 1814 Parliament outlawed all forms of racial or religious discrimination.[8] Jews organized as a consistory with rabbis appointed by the state. Jews were granted immunity from taxes to the state church in the Danish Constitution of 5 June 1849. The criminal law provided for fine or imprisonment of anyone inciting hatred on the basis of religion, origin or citizenship. Aage Andersen, the foremost anti-Semitic propagandist in Denmark, was sentenced to 80 days imprisonment and his writings confiscated for such offenses.[9]

One of the first nations to abolish the slave trade, Denmark developed what Samuel Abrahamsen termed *livkunst*, the art of living and caring for others. This philosophy was attributed to N.F.S. Grundtvig (1783–1872), 'the greatest spiritual force in Danish History'. It was Grundtvig, the founder of the folk high school and author of 1,000 hymns, who emphasized the community of man. According to Grundtvig, man had to recognize that he was a human being first, then a Christian, and that mercy should be given to all.[10] This lesson was emphasized during the early phase of the occupation by Hal Koch from the University of Copenhagen. In a series of lectures, in articles published by the Union of Danish Youth in their journal *Lederbladet*, and in a pamphlet titled *The Day and the Way*, Koch stressed that Nazism and fascism represented the antithesis of democracy. He urged Danish youth to commit themselves to humanism and Christianity. As for the Jewish question, Koch noted that 'justice and freedom in Danish life are at stake'. The popular professor reminded his readers that the country's fate would not be decided by outside powers 'but by the extent to which we are able to maintain truth, justice and freedom by being ready to pay the price'.[11]

When the Nazis occupied Denmark, Karl Rademacher and Hans Luther badgered Renthe-Fink to introduce discriminatory laws like those that operated in Poland or Holland. Renthe-Fink, who was not a Nazi ideologue, informed Ribbentrop that the Danes would not tolerate such interference. Imposition of the Nuremberg Laws, the yellow star, even the stamping of a 'J' on Jewish identity cards, he said, might incite protests by thousands of Danish Aryans and could jeopardize recruitment of Danes into the Waffen SS. General Luedke agreed. In February 1941, Hans Hedtoft, the leader of the Social Democratic party, declared that anti-Jewish decrees would be unacceptable in Denmark. Hedtoft's position was endorsed by Christmas Moller, head of the Conservatives, and Vilhelm Buhl, Prime Minister in an interim government.[12] On 20 January 1942, the day of the Wannsee Conference, Renthe-Fink advised his superiors that the Danish population lagged behind the Germans. Unless Berlin was prepared to deal with disturbances, 'We should not entertain the idea that a solution of the Jewish problem is possible in Denmark.' Renthe-Fink recommended only that Jews not be appointed to posts in government and that Danish citizenship be withheld from refugees. Colonel Rudolph Mildner of the Gestapo also warned Berlin that the Danes might revolt if anti-Jewish laws were imposed.[13]

Through 1942, a number of experts (Wilhelm Stuckart of the Interior Ministry, Einsatzgrupp leader Otto Ohlendorf, Eichmann, Rademacher) either visited Denmark or offered memoranda on the Jewish Question. Rademacher agreed with Danish Nazi Frits Clausen who recommended that the issue be dealt with 'at once' and solved 'radically'. Half-heartedly, Renthe-Fink proposed the elimination of Jews from the Danish economy through Aryanization and the withdrawal of fuel and coal from Jewish firms during the winter.[14]

Renthe-Fink did not know it at the time, but he would be replaced shortly. On 26 September 1942, one week after Renthe-Fink sent Ribbentrop his last report, Christian X celebrated his 72nd birthday. Hitler wired the king congratulations and received a curt response: 'My utmost thanks. Christian Rex.' Angered, Hitler recalled his minister. It was at this point that he decided to force the issue of the Danish Jews. In November he dispatched a Gestapo veteran, Dr Best and General Hermann von Hanneken to Denmark.

Soon, Best was being criticized by Ribbentrop, Goering, Ohlendorf and Eichmann for following the soft policies of his predecessor. During the winter of 1942/43, Best warned of the negative consequences of anti-Semitic decrees and suggested instead that 31 Jews in public administration be ousted and that Germans no longer deal with Jewish firms. The Danes might tolerate publication of *Kampftegnet*, an anti-Semitic journal. Several hundred joined the *Hipos* (auxiliary police). But there was no enthusiasm for Nazi ideology. (The fascist parties won 5 percent of the vote in the elections of March 1943.)[15] Most Danes seemed to agree with Police Chief Thune Jacobsen who informed Himmler in April 1941: 'If the *Reichsführer* SS thinks that 5,000 Jews here in Denmark constitute a problem, then of course we have a problem, but the Danish population does not consider this topic a problem.'[16]

Danish goodwill was manifest repeatedly during the occupation. The centenary of Jewish critic Georg Brandes on 3 February 1942 turned into a rally on behalf of Danish Jews. When, late in 1942, someone tried to torch the main synagogue in Copenhagen, the Danish police authorized special patrols of Jewish auxiliaries. In January 1943 Gjorslev University students petitioned to hold a public demonstration where they would sing two anthems dear to the hearts of Danes. The Nazis, thinking that one of the melodies would be *Deutschland uber Alles*, granted the request. The students sang the Danish national anthem, then they unfurled the Zionist flag and sang *Hatikvah*.[17] Theologian Frederick Torm offered lectures against Nazism. Even King Christian was outspoken. There was no Jewish Question in Denmark, said the aging monarch, 'There is only my people.' Christian's sympathies were so pronounced that several myths grew up about him. It was said that he visited the synagogue in Copenhagen to bolster Jewish confidence (he had attended a service on 12 April 1933, on the 100th anniversary of the synagogue). It was rumored that he threatened to abdicate if anti-Jewish laws were introduced. And when the Nazis proclaimed the wearing of the yellow star, the king supposedly pinned one to his chest and rode through the streets of Copenhagen. In fact, Christian warned that if the Nazis imposed a ghetto and badge, he would move his palace to the Jewish zone and would regard the wearing of the badge as an honor.[18] Christian did take a daily outing on horseback, but the Nazis never instituted the badge or ghetto in Denmark.

EINE RECHT KLEINE AKTION

On 31 August 1943, the offices of the Jewish center in Copenhagen were raided and community records disappeared. No one was deceived by this break-in, not the Danish government and certainly not the Jews. They knew that deportation was always a possibility. The Nazis kept reassuring Danish leaders like Bishop Fuglsang Damgaard, Hedtoft and H.C. Hansen that nothing was in the works and these men in turn reassured the Jews. However, on 8 September, Best, the Nazis' top official in Denmark, cabled Ribbentrop that the time was propitious for a roundup.[19] On 17 September, Nazi troopers seized additional files from the offices of archivist Josef Fischer. That same day, Best called in Denmark's Foreign Minister Niels Svenningsen and told him the Germans intended to conduct 'a little legal action' against saboteurs at the end of the month. The next day, a contingent of SS commandos from the Eichmann Office arrived in Copenhagen. When General Hannecken complained to Jodl that such an action would interfere with Wehrmacht operations, Jodl replied, 'Nonsense'.

The plan was to strike at Denmark's Jews on 1–2 October while they congregated for Rosh Hashanah services. The Jews would be shipped via three freighters docked in Copenhagen's Langelinie harbor to a port some-where in the east. They would then be transferred by trains to Terezin. The Nazis commissioned Georg Ferdinand Duckwitz, a German coffee dealer who had been trading in Denmark since 1928, to arrange the details. On 28 September Werner Best wired Hitler that Denmark was about to become *Judenrein*.[20]

The little cleansing action did not materialize. The Nazis had not antici-pated how distressed Duckwitz would become. He contacted Swedish Prime Minister Per Hansson and asked Sweden to accept 8,000 Jews. Hitherto, the Swedes had been reluctant to welcome refugees. In March 1943 several youths demonstrated the feasibility of flight in a fishing vessel. The celebrated physicist Niels Bohr, a half-Jew, also was enlisted to press the Swedes for a reversal of their policies. On Tuesday, 28 September, Duckwitz met with several Danish Social Democrats (former Prime Minister Wilhelm Buhl, H.C. Hansen, Herman Dedichen and Hans Hedtoft) and informed them,

'The disaster is going to take place.'[21] Hedtoft then informed C.B. Henriques of the Jewish community:

> The action against the Jews which we feared is about to be carried out. The procedure will be like this: on the night between the 1st and 2nd of October, the Gestapo will raid all Jewish homes and then bring all Jews to ships in the harbor. You will have to warn every single Jew in this town immediately. It is obvious that we are ready to give you all the assistance we possibly can.

Henriques was disbelieving at first because Svenningsen had given him his word that the roundup was intended only for trouble-makers. But a communication from the Swedish government agreeing to accept Jews changed his mind.[22] Hedtoft proceeded to Rabbi Marcus Melchior, acting spiritual leader of the Copenhagen congregation. Melchior's son, Werner, had been urging companions in Zionist youth groups to prepare for flight. Rabbi Melchior, who had been assured by five cabinet under-secretaries there was no cause for alarm, dismissed his son's actions as premature. On the morning of 30 September, he advised 150 congregants in his synagogue:

> There will be no services this morning ... Last night I received word that tomorrow the Germans plan to raid Jewish homes throughout Copenhagen to arrest all the Danish Jews for shipment to concentration camps. They know that tomorrow is Rosh Hashanah and our families will be home. We must take action immediately. You must leave the synagogue now and contact all relatives, friends and neighbors you know are Jewish and tell them what I have told you ... You must also speak to all your Christian friends and tell them to warn the Jews ... By nightfall tonight we must all be in hiding.[23]

The news quickly spread across Copenhagen. Jorgen Knudsen, an ambulance driver from the Bisbejerg Hospital, exclaimed, 'So the bastards have finally decided to do it. God damn them!'[24] Then he grabbed a telephone directory and went off to round up Jews on his own. At the hospital, Dr Karl Koster and his wife hid more than 300 Jews in a chapel, the psychiatric wing and nurses' quarters.[25] Overnight Jewish patients were discharged and 'Christians' with identical ailments were admitted to the same beds. (The Nazis eventually caught on to this ruse. A few days later an armed gang of the SS, looking for Jews, shot up a surgery unit.) So many of the staff at the *Kommunehospitalet* in Copenhagen were involved in the rescue, they were dubbed 'the White Brigade'.[26] More than 1,100 Jews passed through the home of Dr Jorgen Gersefelt, a physician from Rungsted.

Denmark's Christians mobilized for what some called 'Little Dunkirk'. Professor Richard Ege of the Rockefeller Institute brought several Jewish colleagues to his house. When a frantic passenger on a Copenhagen streetcar told the conductor he was a Jew and had no place to go, the conductor took the stranger home. King Christian protested in writing to Best of the grave consequences that would follow any action against Denmark's citizens. Officials at the Seamen's Church on the Copenhagen waterfront and the Trinity Church hid Jews and Torah scrolls. On Sunday, 3 October 1943 Denmark's Lutheran ministers issued a pastoral letter that affirmed: 'Despite different religious views, we shall struggle to ensure the continued guarantee to our Jewish brothers and sisters of the same freedom we ourselves treasure more than life itself.' Wherever Jews were persecuted, 'it is the duty of the Christian Church to protest against such persecution because it is in conflict with the sense of justice inherent in the Danish people and inseparable from our Danish Christian culture through centuries'.[27] A Lutheran minister Ivar Lange put it more succinctly, 'I tell you I would rather die with the Jews than live with the Nazis.'[28]

Groups of self-proclaimed 'pimpernels' ferreted Jews out of the city to hiding places in lofts, brick factories and the Tesdorpf estate whose owner declared, 'We must do everything we can to help the Jews.' Members of the 'Elsinore Sewing Club' fed the Nazis false tips. Like the time they called the Gestapo to say a Jew had taken a room at a fancy inn in the country. The Germans descended upon the place and battered the man before they discovered he was, in fact, a Danish Nazi.[29] Many of these young people were shot dead or died in Neuengamme after being betrayed. A widow, Ellen Nielsen, was sent to Ravensbruck for hiding Jews.[30] The underground supplied Jews with forged papers, blank baptismal forms, cash and cyanide pills and escorted them to the countryside. Taxis whisked Jews to a staging center at the rear of a bookstore across from Dagmarhaus, Gestapo headquarters. To prevent discovery, children were drugged and their mouths were taped. The Danes also confounded German dogs patrolling harbor areas by smearing rags or posts with a mix of blood and cocaine.[31]

One group was especially important in the rescue effort – the fishermen. They risked inspections by the Gestapo and Wehrmacht on the docks and ran the gauntlet of German patrol boats. Their task was eased by soldiers who permitted trucks carrying Jews to pass[32] and the Danish coast guard which refused to participate in the patrols. Initially, some of the fishermen agreed to take Jews across to Sweden for a price of 2,000 kroner. That changed as the fishermen soon took on families who could pay very little or nothing. Peder Hanson, a codfisherman, agreed to take eight people to safety. In the end he took more than 400. Another fishing boat captain agreed to take a score of refugees but was concerned that two new crew members might not be reliable. He gave a gun to one of the men below deck. At a given moment, the passengers were to come out and commandeer the vessel. The Jews were extremely nervous about using a weapon. When they appeared in mid-straits, the captain and other members of the crew shouted, 'Don't shoot. We'll take you to Sweden.' (It turned out the new crew members were also sympathetic.)[33]

Some people did lose heart at the last moment. Rabbi Melchior arranged to have his family transported in a rowboat near Elsinore Castle.[34] The coast of Sweden was only 2,000 yards away, six hours at most, but his oarsmen dawdled fearfully the entire night. Finally, the Rabbi seized the oars himself and rowed to safety. Melchior was more fortunate than Moritz Oppenheim, a barrister who once represented the German embassy. Oppenheim's vessel foundered in the crossing. A Danish fisherman notified the Nazis who sent a patrol boat to arrest him and his family. Oppenheim was more fortunate still than a young scientist who was hiding with his family and others in the woods, waiting to be ferried across. Somebody reported that the Germans were near and panic spread through the group. The scientist slashed the throats of his wife and three children and tried to kill himself. There was no German patrol. His wife and children died, he recovered.[35]

During the first few days of the roundup, the Nazis managed to catch 202 Jews. An 84-year-old woman said the Germans would not bother with her. On her transport, she met another lady who was 102. One woman had to be dragged out of her house protesting that her dishes were not clean. Another man, a refugee from Poland, was tired of running from land to land and simply waited to be arrested.[36] Two other ladies volunteered themselves to Gestapo headquarters a day early and were told to wait at home until they were summoned. The Germans paid informants and succeeded in capturing 60–70 Jews who had taken refuge in the loft of the Gilleleje church.[37] They offered bribes to the government – an exchange of three military hostages for every Jew (the Danes replied, 'We do not swap one Dane for another') – and even promised to end the military emergency. The Nazis also lobbied with Sweden to stop receiving the refugees. Swedish newspapers published touching accounts of the arrivals. As the fishing boats neared shore, people aboard the vessels started singing *Du gamla, du fria* (the Swedish national anthem). Wrote one Swedish journalist, 'It is almost more than you can bear. Tears run down the cheeks of tall, hefty men standing on the beach, watching. Here they come, hunted from home and house, driven from their jobs and sometimes torn away from relatives, and here they come, singing, as if they were approaching the gates of paradise, from death to life.'[38] Not all Swedes were thrilled. Some Jews hid aboard an empty ferry train from Elsinore until a Swedish newspaper published an account of their flight. At least one fishing boat was rammed by a Swedish patrol boat. There were also several anti-Semitic parades staged in Stockholm following the arrival of the Danish Jews.

VELKOMMEN TIL DANMARK

By the end of October the Nazis captured 472 men, women and children, less than 5 percent of the Jews in Denmark. They were assembled at Horserod prison, actually two camps, located on a plantation nine kilometers west of Elsinore. Previously, this remote location had housed communists and

Danish officials. Jews were penned temporarily in a companion camp behind barbed wire in the woods of north Zeeland.[39] Transferred to Terezin, the Jews of Denmark became the aristocrats of the paradise ghetto. They generally had better quarters and more food. King Christian and his government badgered the Nazis with questions about their welfare. The Danish Red Cross made several attempts to look into the status of Jews at Terezin. Gentile relatives and friends sent letters, money and parcels of food or clothing by registered mail to 'Aunts' or 'Uncles' and the officious Germans passed along the correspondence. In the fall of 1943 the Danes even established a rescue corps of drivers and cooks to assist the Jews upon their return. As Jorgen Haestrup writes, 'At no time did the administration in Copenhagen give up its hope of bringing those deported back.'[40]

On 13 April 1945 Count Bernadotte arranged the repatriation of 425 Danish Jews from Terezin. The Danes were turned over to Red Cross agents and loaded into white vans bearing Swedish license plates. The busses eventually crossed the Danish-German border at a small town Padborg. As the vans passed through Denmark, people waved flags, tossed food and flowers, and sang the Danish national anthem. There were signs proclaiming *Velkommen til Danmark!*[41] Survivors and refugees would grasp the meaning of those words only upon returning from Sweden after the war. Unlike those in Poland, Slovakia, France or Holland, Denmark's Jews found their homes and personal belongings intact, clean, with flowers in vases and four days of food in the pantries. Even their pets and plants had been cared for. Those with businesses discovered that their employees had drawn salaries and banked the rest against the day when the Jews came home.

Ninety-eight percent of the Jews of Denmark survived the Holocaust. Scholars offer a number of explanations. Jewish numbers were small, no real threat to Gentile Danes. There was no deep-rooted tradition of anti-Semitism in the country. Hitler and his subordinates mistakenly believed that Denmark would embrace the Nazi ideology and therefore sent few officers of the Gestapo and SS to this land. Jews were concentrated in one locale, hence warnings could be issued immediately. Neutral Sweden was close by, accessible. The timing of the Nazi purge, coming so late in 1943, was fortuitous. Yahil offers another factor: the special character and moral stature of the Danish people and their love of freedom. Goldberger agrees, noting the many sociopolitical milestones of Danish history.[42] Whether the Danes were better people than their contemporaries we may never know. Certainly, they took their religious obligations seriously. Mr and Mrs Richard Ege risked their lives to save Jews. Afterward Vibeke Ege explained:

> We helped the Jews because it meant that for once in your life you were doing something worthwhile. There has been a lot of talk of how grateful the Jews should be to their fellow Danes for having saved their lives, but I think that the Danes should be equally grateful to the Jews for giving them an opportunity to do something decent and meaningful.[43]

NORWAY AND THE JEWS

Norway also distinguished itself during World War II. Within days of the British departure from Narvik, the resistance was distributing stenciled newspapers in towns on the Atlantic. Some 3,500 Norwegians sailed to freedom in the British Isles; 500 returned to direct the central resistance organization (R Group).[44] Members of the Supreme Court announced their resignation on 12 December 1940. Five months later (9 April 1941), the anniversary of the invasion, all of Norway shut down for one-half hour despite warnings from the Nazis. Children donned red woolen caps marked with an 'H7' in honor of exiled King Haakon. The 300,000 members of sporting clubs shunned Norway's *Nasjonal Samling* (NS, Nazi movement). Students resisted interference with their curricula and ultimately shut down Oslo University on 30 November 1943.[45]

No group was more inspirational than the Norwegian Protestant Church and its leader Bishop Odd Bergvald. The Lutheran Church issued a number of directives (*paroles*) advising teachers, trade unionists and others to resist being coopted by the Nazis. Only 50 of 850 clergy embraced the NS ideology. In January 1941, Bishop Bergvald delivered a letter to the government, noting that the Church as 'guardian of men's consciences' must oppose violence and injustice. On Easter Sunday, 5 April 1942, congregations listened as their pastors read the clergy's defense of teachers (1,000 of whom were imprisoned by the Nazis). 'If any person is harassed and persecuted for the sake of his convictions', read the impassioned expression of faith, 'then the Church as guardian of conscience must stand beside the persecuted.'[46] Norway's seven bishops (representing 90 percent of the population) even threatened Quisling with resignation.[47] When the Nazis began rounding up Jews, the bishops reminded Quisling of fundamental rights which Jews enjoyed as God's children and as longtime citizens of Norway. If Jews committed crimes, they should be punished according to law, but the race hatred and persecution must stop. Prayers were said on behalf of Jews for two weeks.[48] Members of the resistance did more than light candles. Many risked their lives, escorting 50–60 persons per week through the snow from Oslo or across the Skagerrak. By the end of 1942, 1,100 Norwegians and Jews reached neutral Sweden.[49]

Norway's accomplishments must be measured against its own short-comings. For whatever reason (deicide, distrust of business practices, contempt for *Ostjuden*), Jews had never been welcome. When the Viking state gained independence in 1814, its *Storting* (parliament) voted 92 to 7 to bar Jews. The ban was lifted in 1851 after an exhausting campaign by poet-politician Henrik Wergeland. Fifty years later there were 642 Jews in Norway, many of them refugees from Tsarist pogroms. By 1939, their numbers had grown to 1,400 (including 200 refugees from Germany and central Europe.)[50] They endured job discrimination, interference with their religious practices and attacks from traditional anti-Semites. Knut Hamsun, a Nobel laureate in literature, and Dr Jon Mjoen, who created a race-hygiene institute in Oslo after World War I, lent a cachet to bigotry. Vidkund Quisling (Minister of Defense 1931–33) tried to exploit Jew-hatred without much success. His nationalist movement failed to elect a single member to parliament.[51]

Quisling and his followers (who numbered 54,651 by 1945) welcomed the Germans in April 1940. Quisling headed a rump government for six days before the Nazis opted for an administrative council comprised of seven leaders more acceptable to the Norwegians. After battling over the role of parliament and whether to force the abdication of Haakon the council was abolished on 25 September 1940. Quisling was brought back as Minister President, but true authority rested with *Reichskommissar* Josef Terboven. On the day he abolished the administrative council, Terboven issued a general amnesty and assured Norwegians their rights would be guaranteed. Some people who had fled to Sweden, took Terboven at his word and returned home.[52]

Many Norwegians adjusted to defeat. Samuel Abrahamsen criticizes members of the NS ('one cannot stress too much their collaboration'), but also indicts the civil administration, church and police. There was no protest from parliament when Jews were ordered to turn in radios on 10 May 1940 or when anti-Jewish placards appeared on walls. The church did not speak out when the Nazis dismissed Jewish professionals and Aryanized their businesses. Bishop Bergvald did protest a ban on marriages with Jews and Lapps and Protestant ministers hid torah scrolls in Trondheim and Oslo. But they could not prevent synagogues from being vandalized or being converted to storehouses. Jews were berated on the streets, vilified in the collaborationist press, ousted from land ownership, abandoned by government co-workers who signed an Aryan attestation, and stigmatized with identity cards stamped with a 'J'.[53]

Worst of all were members of the police, reorganized by Jonas Lie. What Norwegian criminologist Per Ole Johansen said of the Quisling bureaucracy ('they did the job for the SS without lifting a finger in defense of the Jews')[54] could just as easily be said of the STAPO (state police), GREPO (border police) and KRIPO (criminal police). Despite their obligation to protect the rights of citizens, the national police watched in June 1941 as the Nazis rounded up Jews in northern Norway and detained them in a camp at Tromso. There was no outcry the next year when the Nazis arrested individual Jews (including Julius Samuel, chief rabbi of Oslo) and whisked them off to camps operated by Norwegians at Falstad, Vollan, Bredtveit, Berg and Grini.

Confronted with broad opposition to their racist policies, the Nazis and the NS seized upon a botched escape to justify the deportation of Norway's Jews. On Thursday, 22 October 1942 nine young Jews tried to flee to Sweden by passenger train. When a border policeman questioned their papers, their escort, a Norwegian fireman, shot the man dead. Eight youths were arrested at the next station. The fireman and two others who jumped off the train, were caught soon after. The fireman and one Jew were executed by the Germans. The day after the incident, K.A. Marthinsen, chief of state police, demanded complete lists of Jews remaining in Norway. Using a law that provided for the detention of anyone suspected of pursuing goals in conflict with the interests of state, Marthinsen issued warrants for the arrest of all Jewish males over the age of 15.

The first raids began at dawn in Oslo on 26 October. Operating in teams of two, 124 Norwegian police pounded on doors and dragged terrified Jews to a holding facility at 23 Kirkeveien. That day 260 men were arrested and sent to the Berg concentration camp outside Tonsberg.[55] Over 300 Norwegian police participated in a second razzia on 24–25 November. Only persons holding passports from the US, Great Britain, neutral nations or those allied to Germany were exempted.[56] Prisoners at the Berg camp were called to the Appelplatz, then loaded on trucks that took them to the harbor in Oslo. There, SS *Sturmbannführer* Helmut Reinhard had secured transport to Stettin. The SS *Donau* was a filthy scow, ill-equipped to accommodate 50 passengers, let alone the 900 Reinhard hoped to pack aboard with 'scanty' provisions (potatoes, sardines, herring). Meanwhile, screaming men, women and children were hoisted aboard in a cattlesling. When the *Donau* sailed at 2.55 p.m. on 25 November, its manifest counted 532 Jews. There were protests from the Norwegian underground, the Swedish press, the Protestant Church and Trygve Lie, foreign minister of the Government in Exile in London. To no avail. The *Donau* made land at Stettin on 30 November. The Jews were then shipped east by cattle car. The commandant of Auschwitz acknowledged their arrival and official reports told how 186 prisoners were given numbers in the camp. '*Die ubrigen wurden vergasst.*'[57]

There would be several other deportations from Norway. A small number were shipped out on the SS *Monte Rosa* before the end of the year. On 24 February 1943, 158 Jews, including a 14-month-old infant, traveled aboard the SS *Gotenland*. Their journey took them from Oslo to Stettin, Berlin, and finally to Auschwitz. More than half of Norway's pre-war Jewish population survived the Holocaust. Of 761 Jews who were deported, 24 came back.[58]

The Middle East

THE FORGOTTEN GENOCIDE: THE SAGA OF THE ARMENIANS

For most of the past 400 years, much of the Middle East was ruled by the Ottoman Turks. By the start of the twentieth century, a series of unsuccessful wars left the empire $1 billion in debt and in the hands of a receivership.[1] As Britain, France and Italy nibbled away most of North Africa, the Ottomans gravitated into the German sphere. Although harboring grudges against Austria-Hungary and Bulgaria, Turkey joined the Central Powers in the fall of 1914. Four years later, the empire lay in shambles. When the Turks agreed to an armistice on 30 October 1918, British forces were in Jerusalem, Amman, Damascus and Baghdad. Arab shaykhs in Riyadh, Mecca and Asir had declared themselves independent. Turkey's army sustained a million casualties and the population of Anatolia was reduced by 20 percent.[2]

Some of those victims were massacred by the Turks themselves. Having failed to deliver a promised victory over the Russians in the winter of 1914–15, Minister of War Enver Pasha resorted to a favorite device of tyrants – scapegoatism. In Turkey that role was filled by Armenians. An urban minority envied for their mercantile skills and despised for their religion, the Armenians agitated for autonomy in 1893–94 and were promptly suppressed by the Turks.[3] Between 25,000 and 100,000 Armenians were killed while their avowed benefactors, the British, did little to alleviate these or later incidents.

In 1915, Enver blamed his defeat upon the Christian Armenians, whose spiritual leader, the Catholicos, resided across the border. A decree to remove Armenian troops to 'labor battalions' was issued on 18 February. The actual massacres did not begin until 24 April when 600 prominent Armenians in Istanbul were hanged. Thereafter, entire city populations were slaughtered. Armenians from Tebizond were taken out to the Black Sea on rafts and drowned.[4] Four thousand villagers near the Cilician mount of Jebel Musa withstood a Turkish siege for 53 days before being withdrawn by a French naval squadron.[5] Armenians from Konya, Sivas and Zeitun were beaten along roads to the Syrian desert. An American missionary, Dr Samuel Ussher, told of seeing 55,000 bodies in the province of Van in May 1915. When the refugees reached Deir-ez-Zor, they cooked grass, ate dead birds, and died – 50,000 burned to death in caves called 'the Place of Darkness'.[6]

By the time the killing was done, nearly one million Armenians were dead.

One country that could have mitigated the suffering was Imperial Germany. On 10 June 1915, the German consul at Mosul wired his embassy in Istanbul that the Tigris River was clogged with bodies. Eight days later, the German consul at Erzerum reported the murder of 25,000 men, women and children in a gorge. German missionaries described how people were drawn and quartered or sexually mutilated at Erzinjan. In May 1915, Ambassador Hans von Wangenheim wired Berlin, 'I think we ought to mitigate the form the hardships take, but not to attempt to prevent them on principle. The work of the Armenian undermining, nourished by Russia, has assumed dimensions which menace the existence of Turkey.' And to a German newspaper, he declared, 'I think that the Turks are entirely justified. The weaker nation must succumb.'[7] The failure of civilization to address this tragedy emboldened other tyrants. Discussing the fate of the Jews in 1941, Adolf Hitler is reputed to have asked, 'Who remembers the Armenians today?'[8]

AUTHORITARIAN TURKEY: ATATURK, INONU AND THE JEWS

The Turks accepted their defeat in World War I until Greek troops began landing at Smyrna in the summer of 1920. At that point, Mustapha Kemal, known as Ataturk, rallied his countrymen for a two year conflict that repulsed the Greeks. Determined to make Turkey strong, Ataturk established a republic on paper but retained dictatorial power until his death in November 1938.[9]

Ataturk and his handpicked successor Ismet Inonu also proved to be rather adept at the game of diplomacy. Territorial awards to Greece, Italy and France were canceled at Lausanne in July 1923. In return for the cancellation of capitulatory treaties which granted foreign nations extraterritorial privileges, Turkey ceded the oil-rich vilayet of Mosul.[10] In February 1934, Turkey joined Yugoslavia, Greece and Romania in a Balkan non-aggression pact. Yet Turkey refrained from helping Greece when it was attacked by Italy in 1940 or Yugoslavia when it was invaded in 1941. In May 1939, the Turks pledged their 800,000 man army to the Allies in case of a war involving Italy.[11] Pressed by British Ambassador Hugh Knachtbull-Hugessen to honor its commitments, then warned by German Ambassador Franz von Papen if it did, Turkey signed a separate treaty with Germany in June 1941 guaranteeing Hitler supplies of copper and chromite. Turkey declined to join the Axis after Germany's victory over France or when Rommel sent his Afrika Korps against Egypt. Neither did it align itself with the Allies when the Americans landed in North Africa and the British routed Rommel at el-Alamein.[12]

Though the overwhelming majority of Turkey's 70,000 Jews were loyal to Ataturk, political and trading enemies accused them of working for Austrian, Hungarian or Italian interests. After 1933, Jews were expelled from Adrianople and the Straits. Following Ataturk's death, Inonu promoted propaganda directed at eliminating Jews from the Turkish economy.[13] Yet when the war ended, Inonu recited the following humanitarian accomplishments: hundreds of scholars, physicians and artists granted sanctuary before 1939; 16,474 Jews who passed through Turkey on the way to Palestine; another 75,000 unofficial refugees admitted to Turkish territories; rescue of 10,000 Jews who claimed Turkish citizenship in France; and cooperation with Apostolic delegate Angelo Roncalli, Chaim Barlas of the Jewish Agency, US Ambassador Laurence Steinhardt and Ira Hirschmann of the War Refugee Board aiding Jews from Hungary, Romania and Bulgaria.[14] The Turks claim they might have done more but for the opposition of the British, Greeks (who 'outdid the Nazis and British in working to prevent escape of Jewish refugees') and Armenians accused of plotting an uprising.[15]

ARAB NATIONALISTS AND EUROPEAN IMPERIALISTS

Elsewhere in the Middle East, Arab nationalists flirted with fascism as independence was deferred or never fully granted. Syrian Arabs complained that France dismembered the fatherland by granting Lebanese Maronites 'independence' in 1926. Syrian nationalists rallied behind Taj al-Din, chief judge of Damascus, forming *al-Kutlah al-Wataniyyah* (the National Bloc) when the French returned Alexandretta to Turkey. In 1940 extremists in Damascus led by Zaki al-Arsuzi, Saladin al-Bitar and Michel Aflaq created the *Ba'ath* (Arab Socialist Resurrection Party) which stressed Arab unity, racial purity and militarism.[16]

The British fared no better in their protectorates. They molded Iraq out of the vilayets of Mosul, Baghdad and Basra, then had to suppress a revolt that cost $100 million and 10,000 lives. For the next two decades, England tried to coddle nationalists in the oil-rich state, dangling a constitution before them in 1924 and 'independence' in 1932, while retaining control of strategic sites.[17] The English also pretended that Egypt was a sovereign nation after 1922, but whenever elections were held there would be street violence and movement toward independence halted. Egypt's servile status was evident in the treaty dictated to its teenaged king Farouk in April 1936. Egypt yielded control of the Suez canal, seaports, airfields and was bound to assist the British against common aggressors. By 1939 many Egyptian nationalists abandoned moderation for more radical views propounded by the Muslim Brotherhood or the fascist Saadists and Blue Shirts.[18]

Frustrated Arabs shared a common foe – the Jews. Before World War II there were one million Jews from Morocco to Persia. Jews in the Islamic world were *dhimmi* (protected persons) required to pay a special tax (*jizyah*).[19] Under the rule of Umar, a social code dating to the seventh century, they were not supposed to serve in the military, touch the Quran, criticize the Prophet, make use of signet rings, cummerbunds and canes, or ride in honorable conveyances. In 1946, the sight of Jews riding in a jeep provoked riots in the streets of San'a, Yemen. Cautioned to practice their religion quietly, Jews were barred on pain of death from the Temple Mount in Jerusalem and the cave of the Patriarchs at Hebron. Some of their synagogues were gutted or converted to mosques. Jews in Smyrna, Damascus, Cairo and Istanbul lived in *haras*, ghettos that existed since the Middle Ages. In Libya and parts of the Atlas mountains they lived in caves. Jews were also required to wear garb that distinguished them from Muslims. The badge had its origins in the yellow armband decreed by al-Mutawakkil in the ninth century.[20]

PALESTINE BETWEEN THE WARS

During the inter-war period, Jews faced their greatest hostility in Palestine. In 1920, Haj Amin al-Husseini, head of one of the wealthiest clans in Palestine, was designated Grand Mufti of Jerusalem (controlling Islamic institutions and religious patronage in the Holy Land). Through the inter-war period, the Mufti raged against Jewish immigrants who allegedly were dispossessing the indigenous population. A charismatic spokesman, Haj Amin provoked anti-Jewish riots in the spring of 1919, 1920 and 1921. Crowds chanting *adawlah ma'ana* ('the government is with us'), raced through the old city of Jerusalem for three days at Passover 1920 killing nine and wounding 200. The following year another 100 persons were murdered.[21]

Concern for regional stability prompted the British to reassess the pledge made in the Balfour Declaration and incorporated in the League of Nations Mandate to promote a national home for the Jewish people. Britain severed two-thirds of Palestine to create Trans-Jordan in 1921. Jewish immigration was restricted to 1,000 per month and land purchases in the Beit Shean and Huleh districts were prohibited. Despite the success of such measures (Jewish emigration outstripped immigration in 1927) Arab nationalists were not satisfied. Using a trumped-up accusation that Zionist militants planned to seize the temple compound, the Mufti incited a new wave of violence during the summer of 1929. These Wailing Wall riots resulted in deaths of more than 500 persons and the dispatch of two parliamentary commissions that exonerated the British and blamed Palestine's problems on Jewish immigration.[22]

When Hitler came to power, there was a surge of refugees from Germany. Between 1933 and 1939 200,000 Jews entered Palestine, increasing their share of the population to 30 percent. In April 1936 the Arab Higher Committee headed by the Mufti called for a general strike. Rail and telephone communications were disrupted. More than 200,000 citrus and forest trees were destroyed, 4,000 acres ruined. Arabs who had come to Palestine seeking higher wages, better food and improved health care were thrown out of work.[23] Over the next three years, 3,000 Arabs, Jews and Englishmen lost their lives, including several village mukhtars and labor leaders who opposed the Mufti.

Documents from the German High Command reveal that the Nazis supplied weapons and financial support to the nationalists. Adolf Eichmann, Baldur von Schirach and Dr Fritz Grobba, the Nazi ambassador to Baghdad, met with Haj Amin in 1937. When Muhammad's birthday was celebrated in May, pictures of Hitler and Mussolini as well as German and Italian flags were displayed by Arabs as nationalist newspapers hailed this 'significant gesture of sympathy and respect with the Nazis and fascists in their agony and trials at the hands of Jewish intrigues and international financial pressure'. The Allies concluded, 'Only through funds made available by Germany to the Grand Mufti of Jerusalem was it possible to carry out the revolt in Palestine.'[24]

True to form, the British sent another commission headed by Lord William Robert Peel, former Secretary of State for India. In July 1937, the Peel Commission issued a 404-page report. It concluded that an irrepressible conflict existed between Arabs and Jews. Arab claims of excessive Jewish immigration and land acquisitions were not legitimate. The Commission noted, 'The large import of Jewish capital into Palestine has had a general fructifying effect on the economic life of the whole country.' Peel recommended partition of Palestine with most of the land going to the Arabs while the British retained control of Haifa, Jaffa and Aqaba as well as a land bridge from Jaffa to Jerusalem. Jewish immigration would be limited to 50,000 over five years.[25]

Haj Amin rejected the plan, noting that Arabs predominated in lands awarded to Jews.[26] The World Zionist Congress meeting in Zurich also rejected Peel, arguing that 35,000 square miles of the original mandate had been sliced away to form Jordan. Frustrated, the British convened another conference in London in February 1939. The Chamberlain government invited representatives of Egypt, Iraq, Jordan, Saudi Arabia, Yemen and the Mufti while denying credentials to Revisionist Zionists. When the Arabs refused to meet with Jews, the British held separate sessions with the two groups. Chaim Weizmann pleaded for a Jewish state in a cantonist federation, arguing that the lives of six million Jews hung in the balance. The Arabs would only offer guarantees on the order of those enjoyed by Jews in Romania.

The British suspended negotiations on 17 March, about the same time Hitler marched into Prague. Two months later (17 May 1939), the British announced their solution to the Palestine problem in a government White Paper. Jewish immigration would be limited to 75,000 over the next five years. The figure could be lower and would be tied to the absorptive capacity of the Holy Land. Jews could not constitute more than one-third of Palestine's population. Land purchases were to be severely restricted. After five years, no more Jews would be admitted unless the Arabs agreed. In ten years, the British would grant independence to an Arab-dominated Palestine.[27]

When the White Paper was laid before Parliament it was roundly condemned. Herbert Morrison denounced Colonial Secretary Malcolm McDonald, saying,

I should have more respect for him if he had frankly admitted that the Jews were to be sacrificed to the incompetence of the government in the matter, to be sacrificed to its inability to govern, to be sacrificed to its apparent fear, if not indeed, its sympathy with violence and these [Arab] methods of murder and assassination – that the Jews must be sacrificed to the government's preoccupation with exclusively imperialist rather than human considerations.

Lt Commander Fletcher added, 'The government are now joining in the hunt of the Jews which is going on in Europe. Last year, to get out of a difficulty, they did not hesitate to sell the Czechs down the river. This year, we see them prepared to sell the Jews down the river.' Winston Churchill also labeled the policy 'another Munich' and suggested that the Chamberlain government 'file a petition in moral and physical bankruptcy'. Parliament voted 268 to 179 against the White Paper.[28]

Prior to the debate, Chaim Weizmann confronted Colonial Secretary McDonald, who stammered that the document did not represent the government's final position. In June, the League Mandates Commission declared that 'the policy set out in the White Paper was not in accordance with the interpretation which the Commission had always placed upon the Palestine mandate'.[29] Once war broke out, the White Paper became official policy for Palestine.

MYTHS OF ASSISTANCE

In November 1974, Yasser Arafat addressed the General Assembly of the United Nations. Bedecked in *keffiyah*, pistol in side holster, Arafat declared, 'While we [presumably the Arabs] were vociferously condemning the massacres of Jews under Nazi rule, Zionist leadership appeared more interested, at the time, in exploiting them as best it could in order to realize its goal of immigration to Palestine.'[30] The reality is that 135,000 Jewish men and women in Palestine volunteered for Britain's armed forces during World War II. Some 32,000 carried out missions against the Italians and manned isolated oases in Libya. Some, like Moshe Dayan, repulsed attacks from Syria. Moshe Sneh devised the 'Carmel Plan', which called for Palestine's Jews to delay the Afrika Korps at the ridge overlooking Haifa long enough for the British to regroup in Iraq. When the tide of war turned, the British created a Jewish Legion that distinguished itself in Crete, Greece, Abyssinia, Iraq, Italy, the Low Countries and Austria. Countless Jewish civilians operated radar installations, worked as stevedores, manned hospitals and maintained oil refineries.[31]

Arabs contributed to the war effort, but not to the degree implied by Arafat. Algerian and Moroccan troops fought with the Free French, but they, like Muslims from the Indian sub-continent, were conscripted. What happened in May 1941 offers a truer gauge of Arab sentiments. With Syrian

nationalists attacking Palestine, the Golden Square in Iraq declared war
against Great Britain. Rashid Ali al-Gailani received congratulatory telegrams from Hashim Atassi, President of Syria, Riad as-Sulh, premier of
Lebanon, and King Farouk. Anti-British mutinies erupted in Jordan.
Lamented John Bagot Glubb, commander of Abdullah's Legion, 'Every Arab
force previously organized by us mutinied and refused to fight for us, or faded
away in desertions.'[32] The British recruited 12,455 Arabs in Palestine where
Arabs outnumbered Jews two to one. The number was reduced by 50 percent
due to discharges and desertions.[33]

As Rommel's tanks menaced Egypt, mobs in Alexandria and Cairo were
preparing to welcome their perceived liberators. King Farouk refused to
honor terms of the Anglo-Egyptian defense pact and was placed under house
arrest. The king's father-in-law Zulfikar Pasha (Egypt's ambassador to Iran),
Siri Oman Bey (one of Farouk's confidants), and Farouk's uncle, Abbas
Hilmi expressed hope for a German victory. While the battle of El Alamein
raged, veteran nationalist leader Aziz Ali al-Misri tried to defect to enemy
lines. On 6 July 1942, Egyptian Defense Minister Ahmed Saudi Hussein was
shot down by German anti-aircraft, even as he tried to carry British defense
plans to the Nazis. The British removed Azzam Pasha, head of the Territorial
Army, and jailed a number of younger officers, including Anwar Sadat, as
pro-fascist collaborators.[34]

In August 1943, the victorious British called several Middle Eastern leaders
to Cairo. The guests included members of the Arab Higher Committee, the
Prime Minister of Iraq, and the kings of Jordan, Saudi Arabia and Egypt.
No Zionists were invited. Some Arab leaders feared they were being lured
into a trap. Instead, they marveled at the treatment they were accorded. Said
one, 'Personally, I rather expected to be imprisoned upon the defeat of the
Germans. But then, here I am, the honored guest of His Britannic majesty!'
At which point, King Abdullah 'chuckled till the tears rolled down his cheeks,
and the whole company burst into uncontrollable fits of laughter'.[35]

THE UBIQUITOUS MUFTI

The presence of a representative of the Palestinian Arab Higher Committee
at this conference, as well as London in 1939, demonstrates the importance
of Haj Amin al-Husseini. A self-styled Palestinian patriot, Haj Amin would
later claim that he never spoke against the Allies, never advocated destruction
of the Jews. The facts are otherwise. Unwelcome by the French in Beirut, he
sought refuge in Baghdad where he was treated as an honored personality.
He received a stipend of £18,000 from the Iraqi parliament and officials were
ordered to tithe 2 percent of their salaries on his behalf. Haj Amin also
received a subsidy of £100,000 from the Germans and Italians. OKW files
reveal that his mission was to assist German Ambassador Grobba and Prime

Minister Gailani in fomenting an Iraqi revolt against Great Britain. The Nazis were prepared to send parachutists to ensure success of the operation.[36]

As the German war machine rolled from one victory to another, the Mufti began to dream of returning to Palestine, perhaps even of reviving the Caliphate. In July 1940, the Iraqi Foreign Minister carried a letter, offering the Mufti's 'sincerest felicitations' for Germany's victory over France, to von Papen in Istanbul. Shortly after, the Mufti sent his personal secretary to Rome and Berlin to propose an alliance with the Axis. Germany and Italy would be granted economic privileges and would 'recognize the right of the Arab countries to solve the question of the Jewish elements in Palestine and other Arab countries in a manner that conforms to the national and ethnic interests of the Arabs and to the solution of the Jewish question in the countries of Germany and Italy'.[37] In January 1941, the Mufti sent another communiqué to Hitler, assuring 'the great *Führer*' of the 'friendship, sympathy and admiration' of the Arab people. He pledged that Arabs everywhere were 'prepared to act as is proper against the common enemy and to take their stand with enthusiasm on the side of the Axis and to do their part in the well deserved defeat of the Anglo-Jewish coalition'.[38] He proclaimed the Iraqi insurrection in May 1941 a Jihad (holy war). When the rebellion failed, the Mufti incited a pogrom in Baghdad on 1–2 June 1941 that left 110 Jews dead.[39]

The Mufti turned up later that summer in Teheran, where he encouraged an anti-Allied revolt on the part of Shah Reza Khan and Iranian nationalists. When the British and Russians occupied Iran, the Mufti fled to Italy. On 20 November 1941, he was granted a 90-minute audience with Adolf Hitler in Berlin. Impressed with the Haj Amin's 'Aryan' attributes (Hitler believed the red-haired, blue-eyed Mufti was descended from Roman stock), the *Führer* dubbed Haj Amin 'the man to direct the Arab force' at the end of the war. It was, however, premature to speak of boundaries of projected Arab states at this point.[40]

Supplied with two villas outside Berlin, the Mufti was put on the Nazi payroll at 75,000 marks per month heading the *Buro des Grossmufti*. A major function of this agency, according to the captured diary of Abwehr General Erwin Lauhousen, was sabotage. The Nazis opened centers in Athens and the Hague to train Arab agents who were supposed to disrupt communications and oil operations in the Middle East.[41] Using Axis radio stations in Berlin, Bari, Rome, Athens and Tokyo, Haj Amin called upon Muslims in India and Indonesia to rebel. Pledging the support of 70 million Arabs, he said: 'The Arab nation has great sympathy for the Axis powers and much confidence in them. The Arab nation is ready and willing, during and after the current war, to work together with the Axis powers.'[42] The Mufti called upon North Africans to stop fighting 'your brothers, the Germans'. Early in 1942, he eulogized the Japanese as 'champions of the liberation of the Asiatic peoples from the yoke of British and Jewish capitalists and Bolsheviks'.[43] The Mufti also promised to raise an army of 500,000 Muslims for the Waffen SS.

Twenty thousand Bosnian 'Mujo' legionnaires murdered thousands of Serbs and Jews in Croatia and killed more civilians in Lithuania. For these actions, Marshal Tito branded Haj Amin and 38 of his officers war criminals.[44]

After the war, Haj Amin told *Life Magazine*: 'We don't mean at all to eliminate the Jews. Not at all. We have no idea of wiping them out. The Jews lived among us for thirteen centuries as a minority and we protected them. This idea you mention is not in our thought and has never been in our history. We Moslems were always known for tolerance with minorities.'[45]

During the Holocaust, Haj Amin demonstrated more than a passing acquaintance with the Jewish Question. He praised the *Führer* as a descendant of the Prophet, 'the savior of Islam' and called upon Arab Americans to rise up in revolt to stop 'FDR and his Jewish ambitions'. He reminded his listeners that the Jews were a corrupt, immoral people, 'incapable of being trusted', 'the most evil minded toward Muslims', cursed for having tried to poison the Prophet. From Berlin on Muhammad's birthday in March 1943, he warned Muslims around the world that the Jews, bolstered by bands of gangsters from Chicago, had designs on the shrines of al-Aqsa and the Dome of the Rock. America's invasion of North Africa was a deception, concealing the goal of a second Jewish state that would be populated by 'European Jews and Negroes'. When the Nazis held symposia on the menace of world Jewry at Frankfurt in April 1943, at Cracow in 1944, the Mufti lectured on Palestine as a center for Jewish domination plans.[46]

On the anniversary of the Balfour Declaration, Haj Amin asked for and received anti-Zionist pledges from Nazi Foreign Minister Ribbentrop and Heinrich Himmler. He urged the bombing of Tel Aviv, the Dead Sea Potash Works, the Jewish Agency in Jerusalem, the Rutenberg Electric Works and the harbor at Haifa. As he told one Nazi official: 'The Jewish national home must disappear and the Jews get out.' He did not care where they went. 'They are free to go to Hell,' he said.[47]

Whenever one of Hitler's puppets contemplated releasing Jews, the Mufti presented a stumbling block. When Boris of Bulgaria indicated a willingness to release 5,000 Jewish children to Palestine in May 1943, the Mufti protested that the children 'present a degree of danger to Bulgaria whether they remain in Bulgaria or be permitted to depart from that country'. Later that month, the Mufti reacted against a proposal of the Romanian government to release 70,000 Jews. In separate notes, he demanded that Italy and Hungary rescind grants of Jewish emigration and suggested that if Jews did leave these countries they should be sent to Poland 'where they are under active supervision'. The German Foreign Office agreed that Palestine 'was an Arab country' and few of the Jewish refugees escaped.[48]

While the Nazis were transporting the useless and useful to murder camps, Haj Amin declared, 'The Arab nation awaits the solution of the world Jewish problem by its friends, the Axis powers.' He was aware of what the Nazis meant by *Endlosung*. As Dieter von Wisliceny reported: 'The Grand Mufti has repeatedly suggested to the Nazi authorities, including Hitler, Ribbentrop and Himmler, the extermination of European Jewry. He considered this a comfortable solution to the Palestine problem.'[49] The Mufti was especially fond of Himmler, calling him 'an understanding, great and energetic man'.[50] In July 1944, when 400,000 Hungarian Jews were being transported to Auschwitz, Haj Amin complained to Himmler that the Nazis were too lenient with the Jews. He asked that the German government make no more exchanges of Palestinian Germans for European Jews and urged a speedup of deportations as a gesture of 'good will' toward the Arabs.

On 9 November 1944, the Mufti made an entry in his diary – 'very rare diamond, the best savior of the Arabs' – and under that the name 'Eichmann'. The man who boasted he would leap into Hell laughing because he was responsible for killing six million Jews admitted at his trial in Jerusalem in 1961 that he had met the Grand Mufti on several occasions. Their first meeting took place in 1937 when the Mufti was receiving a German stipend for anti-British activities and Eichmann was expediting Jewish emigration from Germany. According to Eichmann, they renewed acquaintance some time late in 1942 or early 1943. The Mufti, accompanied by three Arab aides, visited Buro IVA4b, Eichmann's section in the Reich Security Office which specialized in the extermination of the Jews. The Palestinians were shown the catalog room where Eichmann amassed statistics on European Jews. The Nazi leader later testified: 'I received the order to open everything to them, to let them look everywhere, also state secrets.'[51]

According to von Wisliceny, 'Eichmann was strongly impressed by the personality of the Mufti. He told me then and often repeated later that the Mufti had also made a strong impression on Himmler and exerted considerable influence in Arabic-Jewish affairs.' The Mufti reciprocated Eichmann's admiration, telling Himmler, 'I hope you will lend me Eichmann after the victory. He will be very useful to us, with his methods, for applying the Final Solution in Palestine.'[52] Haj Amin also lavished praise on Rudolf Hoess, commandant of Auschwitz, Franz Ziereis of Mauthausen, Siegfried Seidl of Theresienstadt, and Josef Kramer of Bergen-Belsen. There is evidence he witnessed killings in Auschwitz and Majdanek.[53] Accused of war crimes in 1945, the elusive Arab leader slipped through the hands of the British and French, returning to Cairo, then Beirut. Haj Amin continued to direct Palestinian liberation operations till 1949. After several vain efforts to win diplomatic recognition at the United Nations, he faded into obscurity until his death in 1974.

SAGA OF THE *STRUMA*

Between July 1942 and April 1944, the British welcomed 45,000 Yugoslavs, Greeks and Poles to the Egyptian Delta, Sinai and Cyprus.[54] There were no Jews among these refugees. Mindful of activities of anti-Jewish attitudes of

Arabs from the Maghreb to Yemen, the British cleaved to policies outlined in the White Paper of 1939, limiting Jewish immigration to Palestine. Fewer than 40,000 'legal' refugees were admitted, as Mandatory authorities suspended Jewish immigration during the winters of 1939–40 and 1940–41.

Chamberlain was Prime Minister when British patrols attacked the refugee-laden *Aghios Nikolaos* in March 1939, when the SS *Rim* burned stranding 800 Jews at Rhodes in June of that year and when the *Uranus* was halted at Kladovo in October. Chamberlain's staff approved the policy of boarding vessels and interning illegals away from Palestine. Thus in February 1940, 2,175 passengers aboard the *Sakarya* were detained at Tenedos before being escorted to makeshift camps near Haifa. Churchill barred shipload after shipload of 'illegal' Jews from the shores of Palestine over the next four years. After their vessel faltered near Kamili island in September 1940, 514 starving Jews aboard the *Pentscho* were interned by the Italians. The following month passengers from the *Atlantic, Pacific* and *Milo* were intercepted by the British who placed 1,900 of them aboard another ship, the *Patria*. While docked at Haifa, there was an explosion (never explained) and 254 Jewish refugees died. The survivors were sent to the leper colony of Mauritius. Of 327 Jewish passengers aboard the *Salvador*, 204 drowned when their boat sank in December 1940.

The most egregious incident was that of the SS *Struma*, a tiny (180 tons) wooden freighter built in 1830. Jews from Constanza, Romania, chartered the vessel to take them to Palestine in December 1941. There were 770 passengers aboard, including 269 women and 70 children under the age of 13. The list included 20 doctors, ten engineers, 15 lawyers and 30 businessmen, five of whom held legal permits to enter Palestine. All had paid handsomely for their passage aboard the *Struma*. Yet as they assembled for the journey on 8 December, the refugees had to endure further indignities, strip searches at the hands of Iron Guardists who confiscated personal valuables, food, medication.

The actual trip proved no better. The ship's engine, dredged from the bottom of the Danube where it lay for ten years, repeatedly broke down. There was only one functioning water closet, no water for laundering clothes or personal hygiene aboard the *Struma*. The vessel carried no lifeboats, no life preservers. It had no lights, no radio, no heliograph system. On 13 December, the passengers scraped together $1,000 to pay the captain of a passing Romanian ship who tinkered with the engine. The journey to Istanbul (normally 14 hours) lasted four days.

When the ship limped into Istanbul harbor on 16 December, the Turks would not permit the passengers to disembark. The British raised a number of objections: they might constitute a drain on resources in Palestine; some of the passengers might be spies; and admitting this group might encourage a spate of illegal ships, jeopardizing the war effort. Representatives of the Jewish Agency and the Joint tried to counter these arguments, noting that passengers represented the cream of the middle class in Constanza. There was no chance any of these people might be a Nazi agent. The humanitarian agencies could now, however, guarantee that there would be no more refugees. As a result, the passengers were left to molder, beyond Christmas when foreign diplomats cruised past the darkened slave ship, beyond 20 January 1942 when Heydrich chaired the Wannsee conference, beyond 15 February 1942 when the British agreed to accept children between the ages of 11 and 16.

Before that could be arranged, on 24 February Turkish sea patrols surrounded the *Struma* and towed it out into the Black Sea. The vessel had no food or water, no fuel. Its engine was sputtering and it was listing badly. A sheet marked 'SOS' was draped over one side. Later that day, the Jewish Agency announced 'with grief and horror' the sinking in the Black Sea of the SS *Struma* with 750 Jewish men, women and children aboard, refugees from Roumania.[55]

The actual number of casualties was 769. One man, David Stoliar survived. To this day, there is speculation over what may have happened. The British did change their policy following this disaster, allowing people who reached Palestine to be interned. But the words of British member of Parliament D.L. Lipson still ring true, 'Had the *Struma* carried Germans, Japanese or Italians – that is, citizens of enemy countries – they would not have been *sentenced to death. They would have been taken ashore and at worse interned.* The only reason the *Struma*'s travelers died was because they were Jews.'[56]

THE MIDDLE EAST STATES GO TO WAR AGAINST THE AXIS

Delegates of Saudi Arabia, Jordan, Iraq, Egypt and Lebanon signed the charter of the United Nations at San Francisco in April 1945. Yemen was the first state admitted to the organization. Of this group, only Jordan declared war against the Axis in 1939. The Hashemite Kingdom was a dependency of Great Britain. Its king was subsidized by the British crown, its army officered by British soldiers. Following suppression of its anti-British putsch, Iraq became the second Arab state to declare war against Germany in January 1943. The rest of the Muslim nations remained neutral, like Turkey, until the last week of February 1945 when an Allied victory was assured. They joined the United Nations, not so much from an affection for western democracy as a desire to participate in the post-war reconstruction of the world.

Among people given to street demonstrations, there were no expressions of solidarity with Jews, no denunciations of genocide. Quite the contrary. In 1942, John Gunther reported that 'the greatest contemporary hero is probably Hitler'. In Palestine, the peasants were being told by their mukhtars and mullahs: 'Now go and sell your land to the Jews and be quick about it, for in a month Hitler will be in Jerusalem and you will not only have your land back but everything the Jews possess! Let the knives be sharpened! The great day is about to dawn!'[57]

In the end, acts of appeasement neither saved Jewish lives nor did they mollify the Arabs. Instead of bringing peace to the Middle East, a second world war paved the way for more hatred, more killing in this troubled region.

28

Great Britain and the United States

THE RIEGNER MESSAGE: GENOCIDE CONFIRMED

On 29 August 1942, Rabbi Stephen Wise received a cable from Samuel Silverman of the World Jewish Congress in Great Britain. It contained the following message from Gearhart Riegner, the WJC representative in Geneva:

> HAVE RECEIVED THROUGH FOREIGN OFFICE FOLLOWING MESSAGE FROM RIEGNER GENEVA STOP (RECEIVED ALARMING REPORT THAT IN FUHRERS HEADQUARTERS PLAN DISCUSSED AND UNDER CONSIDERATION ALL JEWS IN COUNTRIES OCCUPIED OR CONTROLLED GERMANY NUMBER 3½ TO 4 MILLION SHOULD AFTER DEPORTATION AND CONCENTRATION IN EAST AT ONE BLOW EXTER-MINATED TO RESOLVE ONCE FOR ALL JEWISH QUESTION IN EUROPE STOP ACTION REPORTED PLANNED FOR AUTUMN METHODS UNDER DISCUSSION INCLUDING PRUSSIC ACID STOP WE TRANSMIT INFORMATION WITH ALL NECESSARY RESERVATION AS EXACTITUDE CANNOT BE CONFIRMED STOP INFORMANT STATED TO HAVE CLOSE CONNEXIONS WITH HIGHEST GERMEN [sic] AUTHORITIES AND HIS REPORTS GENERALLY RELIABLE STOP INFORM AND CON-SULT NEW YORK STOP FOREIGN OFFICE AS NO INFORMA-TION BEARING ON OR CONFIRMING STORY.[1]

It had been more than a year since Jan Ciechanowski, ambassador of the Polish Government in Exile, delivered a White Paper to Secretary of State Cordell Hull, charging the Nazis with 'compulsory euthanasia' against the Jews. The Jewish Bund in Poland spoke of a German campaign of 'physical extermination of the Jewish people on Polish soil'. On 17 July, Israel Goldstein of the Synagogue Council of America delivered a memorandum to Secretary Hull telling how the ghetto populations of Warsaw, Cracow and Lodz had been thinned. Shortly after, several Slovak Jews escaped from Poland, bringing with them the Auschwitz Protocol that detailed killings in the camps.[2]

Gearhart Riegner spent the summer of 1942 trying to convince Howard Elting, America's Vice-Consul in Geneva, that the Allies should respond to these atrocities. Elting's superiors, Leland Harrison and Elbredge Durbrow, dismissed such tales as 'war rumor inspired by fear'. On 17 August, the State

Department instructed officials in Geneva to confine themselves to information involving 'definite American interests'.[3] Sumner Welles asked Wise to delay going public with the Riegner message until he could check its contents with Vatican sources. Ten weeks later (4 November) Welles called in the rabbi and confirmed his ' deepest fears'.[4] As Church leaders, newspaper editors and humanitarian groups denounced Nazi genocide, the British proposed another conference on refugees.[5] The Allies agreed to meet at the well-insulated site of Hamilton, Bermuda. The lone Jewish official invited was George Backer, a member of the board of the Refugee Economic Corporation and president of the Organization for Rehabilitation through Training (ORT). Titillated daily with talk of sanctuaries in Madagascar, Mauritius, Ethiopia, Kenya, Argentina, Mexico, Jamaica and the Isle of Man, newsmen who attended the meeting took to calling Bermuda 'the no-news conference'.[6]

Little should have been expected from an American delegation that included Democrat loyalists Senator Scott Lucas and Congressman Sol Bloom, R. Borden Reams, Robert Alexander, George Warren, and George Brandt of the State Department. The delegation was headed by Harold Willis Dodds of Princeton after Supreme Court Justice Owen Roberts, Myron Taylor and the Presidents of Yale and Johns Hopkins begged off. Richard Law, Parliamentary Undersecretary for Foreign Affairs, headed the British contingent. He was accompanied by Osbert Peake, Undersecretary of State at the Home Office, G.H. Hall, financial secretary to the Admiralty, and A.W.G. Randall of the Foreign Office. Shortly before the Americans departed, Rabbi Wise told Dodds that Jews 'expected great things' from the meeting.[7] He was unaware that Dodds had been instructed to avoid discussion of US immigration laws or British policy in Palestine. Dodds agreed to perform his duties, but swore he would 'never work for that man [FDR] again'.[8]

THE MOCKERY OF BERMUDA

The Anglo-American Conference on Refugees opened on 19 April 1943 with Dodds's announcement that the British hoped to revive the all but defunct IGCR, the 'result of Roosevelt's thought'.[9] Dodds had barely finished reading his remarks when the *New York Times* lashed out against the conference calling it 'pitifully inadequate' and 'designed to assuage the conscience of the reluctant rescuers rather than to aid the victims'.[10] The *Washington Post* blamed the British and their 'stupid "White Paper" policy' with having prevented refugees from getting to the one place where they would have been welcomed and needed.[11] Journals in Palestine condemned the conference as 'a screen to conceal inactivity' and 'a second version of the Evian Conference'.[12] Frank Kingdom called Bermuda 'a shame and a disgrace'.[13] To Rabbi Goldstein it was a mockery.[14]

After going through the motions for ten days, the delegates issued a final communiqué on 29 April. This document was an exercise in self-congratulation. Alert to the dangers posed to refugees 'of all races and nationalities', the allies considered every possibility 'however remote'. Questions of shipping, food and supply were measured against military considerations. About the only thing the British and Americans revealed was a plan to revive the intergovernmental committee.[15]

The combination of Allied inaction and news of the destruction of the Warsaw Ghetto was too much for Smuel Zygelboim, one of two Jews in Sikorski's cabinet. On 12 May, he addressed a note to the Polish people, the Allies and 'the conscience of the world'. Said Zygelboim:

> News recently received from Poland informs us that the Germans are exterminating with unheard-of savagery the remaining Jews in that country. Behind the walls of the Ghetto is taking place today the last act of a tragedy which has no parallel in the history of the human race. The responsibility for this crime – the assassination of the Jewish population in Poland – rests above all on the murderers themselves, but falls indirectly upon the whole human race, on the Allies and their governments, who so far have taken no firm steps to put a stop to these crimes. By their indifference to the killing of millions of hapless men, to the massacre of women and children, these countries have become accomplices of the assassins.[16]

The agonized note continued:

> I cannot remain silent. I cannot live while the rest of the Jewish people in Poland, whom I represent, continue to be liquidated. My companions of the Warsaw Ghetto fell in a last heroic battle with their weapons in their hands. I did not have the honor to die with them but I belong to them and to their common grave. Let my death be an energetic cry of protest against the indifference of the world which witnesses the extermination of the Jewish people without taking any steps to prevent it. In our day and age human life is of little value; having failed to achieve success in my life, I hope that my death may jolt the indifference of those, who, perhaps even in this extreme moment, could save the Jews who are still alive in Poland.

Concluding with a wish for a free Poland in a world of justice, Zygelboim committed suicide.

CHURCHILL AND ROOSEVELT: FAULTY ADVICE AND CONSENT

Jews expected more from Great Britain and the United States. Presidents from Grant to Wilson, Prime Ministers like Disraeli and Balfour had threatened sanctions when Jews were persecuted in Romania and Tsarist Russia. Both nations produced influential Jewish leaders: Oscar Straus, Jacob Schiff, Louis Brandeis, Henry Morgenthau Sr. and Felix Frankfurter in the US, Herbert Samuel, Alfred Mond, Harold Laski and Leslie Hore-Belisha in England. What most inspired confidence were the giants who led the Allies through the perilous days of World War II – Winston Churchill and Franklin Roosevelt. Churchill denounced Russian pogroms and the Aliens Act, which restricted Jewish immigration. As Colonial Secretary he declared that Jews were in Palestine 'as of right, not sufferance'. According to Bernard Wasserstein, no British statesman had 'a more emphatic record of sympathy for Jewish refugees and support for Zionism' than Churchill.[17]

Roosevelt made common cause with tenement reformers in 1910. In 1928, he was elected governor of New York by 25,000 votes. His Republican opponent, Albert Ottinger, was a Jew and it is fair to say that FDR's margin in 1928, just as his victory in New York's presidential poll of 1940 (plurality of 200,000 votes), Illinois (plurality of 100,000) and Pennsylvania in 1944 (plurality of less than 50,000) resulted from Jews who voted for him at a rate of nine-to-one.[18] During the Holocaust, Churchill and Roosevelt opened their doors to Jewish leaders but managed to play factions off one another. Driven by public opinion polls, the two men were determined to do nothing that would compromise their chances of winning the war or retaining power.

During the inter-war period, Britain's policies in Palestine were guided by imperialists like Gertrude Bell and Charles Ashbee or anti-Semites like Ronald Storrs, Ernest Richmond and Harold MacMichael. Of Anthony Eden, his private secretary Oliver Harvey noted, 'Unfortunately A.E. is immovable on the subject of Palestine. He loves Arabs and hates Jews.'[19] That may be a bit harsh, but there is no denying that Eden halted Jewish immigration to the Holy Land as Jews in Hungary were being deported. He delayed negotiations for Bulgarian, Polish and Romanian Jews. He dismissed Wise's proposals at Bermuda as 'fantastic' and 'impossible'.[20] And when he authorized the creation of a Jewish Legion in 1944, he named Brigadier L.A. Hawes in place of Orde Wingate and stipulated that the unit do its fighting away from the Middle East.

Whether Eden was 'tinged' with anti-Semitism,[21] there is no question that others about him were biased. Lord Moyne (Deputy Resident in the Middle East), Malcolm MacDonald and Lord Lloyd all recommended that the government do nothing to offend the Arabs.[22] In 1942 Moyne regaled the House of Lords with theories how intermarriage with Hittites and Slavs had diluted Jewish blood and created an inferior European breed.[23] Sir John Shuckburgh of the Colonial Office, wrote in 1940: 'I am convinced that in their hearts they (the Jews of Palestine) hate us and have always hated us; they hate all Gentiles.' A colleague, H.F. Downie, reacting to an article by Hayyim Greenberg, commented, 'This sort of thing makes one regret that the Jews are not on the other side in this war.'[24]

There was outright anti-Semitism operating among the high echelons of the Ministry of Information, which instructed subordinates to downplay the plight of the Jews, in the Home Ministry, which released fascist leader Oswald Moseley, in the War Ministry, where Sir Alexander Cadogan opposed the appointment of Hore-Belisha as minister because he was a Jew and where other officials grumbled about Jewish black-marketeering. The *eminence grise* of British obstructionism was A.W.G. Randall, refugee specialist for the Foreign Office. Randall dismissed the Romanian offer to trade 70,000 Transnistrian Jews. He regarded American interest in the Brand mission as pandering to the Jewish vote during a presidential election. Most important, it was Randall who in December 1943 offered the basic reason why the British could not endorse any rescue scheme involving Jews: 'Once we open the door to adult male Jews to be taken out of enemy territory, a quite unmanageable flood may result.'[25]

Fear of a wave of Jewish refugees also disturbed US policy makers. Some officials, like Hull, Welles, Adolf Berle and Edward Stettinius were honorable men who believed the only way to stop the atrocities was winning the war. Speaking in Boston in May 1943, Berle said, 'The only cure for this hideous mess can come through Allied armies.' Hull also emphasized the importance of victory in a July message to the Emergency Conference to Save the Jews of Europe: 'You will readily realize that no measure is practicable unless it is consistent with the destruction of Nazi tyranny; and that the final defeat of Hitler and the rooting out of the Nazi system is the only complete answer.'[26]

The motivations of other officials were a bit murkier. Avra Warren (head of the Visa Division), Warren's top aide Robert Alexander, Elbredge Durbrow, consuls Leland Morris in Berlin and James Stewart in Zurich, George Brandt, executive assistant to Assistant Secretary of State Breckinridge Long, even Long himself have been accused of everything from insensitivity to Jew hatred. Long related how much better he would feel about the future 'if we could get rid of all groups, blocks, and special interests'.[27] Asked about the *Struma* incident, he replied, 'It was a terrible thing to happen, but it was one of those things that do happen.'[28] Long ordered the Visa Division to reject 292 German-Jewish refugees in England because 'they are pacifists'. He shared British concerns for Muslim sensibilities in North Africa and Palestine and repeatedly opposed bringing Jews to these regions. His temporizing killed Swedish and Transnistrian rescue schemes in 1943. Whether a spiteful conservative or an anti-Semite, in the words of Henry Morgenthau Jr., Long obstructed rescue.[29]

The worst obstipant in the State Department was R. Borden Reams, an ex-salesman with three years of college education, who somehow became the expert on Jewish questions in the Division of European Affairs by 1942. Reams derided suggestions for an Allied declaration on genocide, noting that the statement did not contain Jewish tales of 'soap, glue, oil and fertilizer factories'.[30] He persuaded Congressman Hamilton Fish and President Rafael Calderon of Costa Rica to withdraw statements on behalf of Europe's Jews. At Bermuda, he opposed negotiations with the Germans, instead, as Acting

Secretary of the IGCR, urging revival of this organization. When the Swedish government agreed to offer temporary refuge to 20,000 Jewish children in May 1943, Reams and his cronies at State dragged out negotiations for seven months, by which time only a handful could be saved. Reams opposed rescue of the Transnistrians warning that the government was granting relief to 'a special group of enemy aliens' that was denied to Allied peoples. He opposed inter-blockade shipments to Jews because many were 'enemy aliens'.

Reams likened himself to a master sergeant who was defending the nation from fifth columnists.[31] The British, too, were panicked by the notion of Nazi agents, 20,000 of them in the home islands according to the press. Internment camps were set up and an elaborate system of review established to determine who should be arrested. The reality was that just as in America, British intelligence had done such a good job exposing Nazi spies, German espionage in Great Britain was dubbed 'the double cross system'. Nevertheless, the British shipped more than 8,000 Jews with Germans to detention camps in Canada and Australia.[32]

RATIONALIZATIONS FOR INACTION

Rabbi Wise and others suggested a number of ways the free world might have alleviated the plight of Europe's Jews: creative use of British and American immigration laws; exchanging Jews for interned German citizens; ransom of Jewish populations in Poland, Romania or Hungary; trans-blockade shipping of food and medical supplies; opening Palestine or North Africa as a temporary haven; transporting refugees across the Atlantic in returning troop ships; bombing rail lines to death camps and the camps themselves; and threatening retribution for Nazi genocide.

Herbert Morrison vetoed immigration reform in England when, at the end of December 1942 he declared that England could accept no more than 2,000 refugees. The Home Secretary's statement came after Parliament stood in silence to the Jews of Europe, after Foreign Minister Eden publicly acknowledged the Nazi attempt to exterminate 'persons of Jewish race', and before a special Cabinet Committee on the Reception and Accommodation of Jewish Refugees was reformed to delete the word 'Jewish'.[33]

America's preoccupation with its immigration laws was legendary. Yet Congress made exceptions to accommodate Mexican farm laborers and Chinese between 1926 and 1943. There were loopholes in existing laws that provided temporary admission for ministers, professors, their families and students 15 years of age.[34] The officers responsible for implementing such policy (Long, Reams, Alexander, Warren) were the strongest opponents of reform. After Bermuda, Hull wrote President Roosevelt: 'I cannot recommend that we bring in refugees as temporary visitors and thus lay ourselves open to possible charges of nullification or evasion of the national origins provisions embodied in the quota law.'[35] The President concurred 'I agree with you that we cannot open the question of our immigration laws. I agree with you as to bringing in temporary visitors. We have already brought in a large number.'[36]

Though Hull would later claim that the State Department did not have the money or personnel to negotiate with the Germans,[37] there were face-to-face encounters between the Allies and their enemies during the war. Representatives of the International Red Cross brokered five exchanges of British and Italian citizens in 1943. Before war's end, more than 15,000 persons would be exchanged.[38] The British had no problems trading German civilians, nurses, members of the Templar community and wounded PWs for their own people. Stateless refugees were another matter. The Nazis and their allies offered to trade Jews on several occasions – with the Working Group in Bratislava in 1942, for Romanians and Poles a year later, through Joel Brand for Hungarians in 1944. There were all kinds of ramifications attached to these schemes, but money was not one of them. By 1941, the Joint had raised more than $40 million for relief. When Antonescu dangled 70,000 Jews before the Allies in February 1943, the JDC pledged $3.5 million, more than enough to cover this scheme and one involving 20,000 children in Sweden. Later that year, Henrik Kaufmann pledged $20 million in Danish accounts toward Jews in Sweden.

Neither the British nor the Americans were enthusiastic about trans-blockade feeding. Such a plan was rejected at Bermuda in April 1943. Four months later Nahum Goldmann urged a $10 million undertaking through the Red Cross. The proposal was killed as a result of a memo from Reams warning there would be no control over the disbursement of food. Reams was supported by Bloom who noted that efforts to supply Greece and other Nazi-occupied lands in 1941–42 failed when the Germans seized most of the goods.[39] What Reams and Bloom did not say was that the US was sending 18,000 tons of food each month to Greece in 1943. Through international affiliates, the American Red Cross supplied Belgium with $340,000 in drugs between December 1941 and October 1943. Twenty million units of insulin were distributed in France. Countless garments had been passed to the persecuted in Poland, Yugoslavia, Norway and the Netherlands by the International Red Cross and Swedish Relief Commission.

Ultimately it all came down to Randall's conundrum: what were the Allies to do if a million people were suddenly released by the Nazis? Transporting them across the Atlantic was impossible. Neutral shipping was inadequate. Noting that few Spanish or Portuguese masters risked the wrath of German U-boats, Breckinridge Long told Congress in 1943, 'There just is not any transportation.' Ships from Lisbon came to the US carrying less than 10 percent of their potential passengers.[40] That same year (1943), however, Churchill informed Congress that the German submarine menace was ended.[41] The American navy carried eight million troops aboard liners and converted Liberty ships between December 1941 and December 1945. Many of these vessels returned as 'empty bottoms'. In all, 146,246 civilians, government officials, dependents, employees and Axis PWs came to the US in the fall of 1944. The government also ferried 400,000 enemy prisoners of war (371,000 Germans, 50,000 Italians and 5,400 Japanese) to the US by the end of May 1945, but not refugees.[42]

REFUGE IN PALESTINE AND NORTH AFRICA

When the British desired, they found shipping – to transport pilgrims to Mecca in the spring of 1943, for 100,000 prisoners of war to East Africa and the West Indies. Travel to such destinations presented more difficulties than escape from Spain, Portugal, Bulgaria or Romania. The trip across the Straits of Gibraltar to North Africa by ship took a matter of hours, a day from Istanbul to Palestine. The problem was that the British did not want them there. As 400,000 Hungarian Jews were being shipped to Auschwitz, the British shut down immigration to Palestine. At this terrible moment, a group of Jewish extremists in Palestine known as the Stern Gang tried to kill British High Commissioner Sir Harold MacMichael. The attempt on 8 August 1944 failed. Three months later two young Sternists murdered Lord Moyne in Cairo.[43]

The British came under criticism from the American press and members of Congress for their policies in Palestine, but they could count upon support from State Department Arabists. In the fall of 1943, Wallace Murray advised Goldmann that the government would appreciate quiet during the visit of the son of Saudi King. Samuel Rosenman informed Wise and Goldmann that the President was 'disturbed' by an advertisement taken in the *Washington Post* by the Emergency Committee for the Rescue of European Jews.[44] Following the Presidential election of 1944, Roosevelt killed a bi-partisan measure sponsored by Senators Wagner and Taft calling for Jewish immigration to Palestine. In February 1945, Roosevelt met with Ibn Saud aboard the cruiser *Quincy* at Suez. Returning from Yalta, the President told Congress: 'I learned more about the whole problem, the Muslim problem, the Jewish problem, by talking with ibn Saud for five minutes than I could have learned in the exchange of two or three dozen letters.'[45]

The British and Americans proved solicitous of Arab feelings in North Africa. Following the Allied invasion in November 1942, General Eisenhower and his civilian advisor Robert Murphy wanted to bring 4,000 refugees from Spain to Morocco. Middle East experts raised a howl. Major General George Strong noted that Jewish refugees would divert personnel, material and shelter at a time when every man was needed for combat and many American soldiers were without adequate supplies.[46] On 14 November 1942, Allied Headquarters in London warned against 'any further trouble in

Morocco which will stir up tribes with disastrous effects'. In February 1943, Thomas Lamont said that any attempt to aid the Jews would 'provoke a grave crisis which would interfere with the speedy outcome of the military campaign'. On 20 March Harold Hoskins of Army Intelligence indicated that a large army of occupation might be required if Jews were brought to North Africa. Ultimately, Roosevelt informed Hull: 'I agree that North Africa may be used as a depot for these refugees from Spain, but not a permanent residence without full approval of all authorities. I know, in fact, that there is plenty of room for them in North Africa, but I raise the question of sending large numbers there. That would be extremely unwise.'[47]

American authorities offered no objections when the Free French issued lesser rations to Moroccan Jews, discriminated against Jews in their ranks and established quotas for Jewish professionals. By January 1944, the entire zone was closed to Jewish refugees. A disgusted Undersecretary Stettinius wrote Hull on the 8th of that month: 'If that is a true expression of military policy, and I question if it can represent the considered opinion of high military leaders, we might as well shut up shop on trying to get additional refugees out of occupied Europe.'[48]

THE BOMBING OF AUSCHWITZ AND RAILWAY LINES

In 1944, a number of Jewish leaders appealed for some form of interdiction against transports bound for Auschwitz.[49] Military planners in England and the United States reviewed the situation and submitted negative evaluations to their civilian bosses. On 4 July Assistant Secretary of War John McCloy labeled the request for bombing 'technically unfeasible' and added that it could be executed 'only by the diversion of considerable air support essential to the success of our forces and … would not amount to a practicable project'.[50] This statement led British historian Martin Gilbert to ascribe responsibility for inaction to the Americans.[51] Other scholars (David Wyman, Michael Berenbaum, Leni Yahil, Michael Marrus) argue that such raids were feasible. The Allies knew a great deal about Auschwitz by 1944 from the Auschwitz Protocol (see pages 343, 378). Aerial photographs taken in the spring of 1944 showed lines of people winding into the gas chambers. The camp was within range of heavy bombers and lighter aircraft. The I.G. Farben fuel and rubber factory at Buna four miles from the main death camp was bombed on 13 September 1944. Allied field manuals permitted strikes against targets of opportunity, including places 'occupied by a combatant military force'. Yet the main sites at Auschwitz were not bombed.

While the OSS possessed a great deal of information on the Auschwitz complex, much of this was flawed.[52] Four large chimneys at the northeast corner of the camp were identified as the smokestacks of crematoria when in fact the buildings were located at the opposite side of the camp. Sources gave no information on anti-aircraft emplacements. (Monowitz/Buna had 79 guns.) There were also problems with any of the attack scenarios. Bombing railway lines was feasible, but useless. Damage done by a 250-pound bomb could be repaired in six hours. Allied bombers turned railway yards in Bingen, Frankfurt, Munich, Salzburg and Linz into 'moonscapes' and still the Nazis managed to keep their trains rolling.[53] If the US Air Force had deployed B-17 Flying Fortresses and B-24 Liberators, perhaps a third of the 500-pound bombs would have fallen within camp housing areas. Based upon a similar raid conducted against a V-2 guidance works factory outside Buchenwald in August 1944, 3,000 inmates might have been killed.[54]

Use of high-level bombers in a low-level attack might have recreated the disaster of the August 1943 raid over Ploesti where the Americans suffered 30 percent losses. Mixing B-25s with B-17s and B-24s made little sense because the B-25s required heavy fighter support, and had neither the fuel capacity, speed nor ceiling of the high-altitude bombers. The VB-1 Azon bomb was an unreliable guided weapon that went astray half the time. Which left only one other alternative – low-level attack by Lockheed P-38s and British Mosquitos. Swift fighter-bombers that distinguished themselves in sorties across the English Channel, neither plane was equipped for the 1,300-mile round trip above the Alps and Tatra Mountains.[55]

Some Allied planners argued that any raid resulting in deaths of civilians was unacceptable. In July 1944, Leon Kubowitzki, head of the Rescue Department of the World Jewish Congress, claimed that raids that killed Jews would only contribute to Hitler's propaganda. In 1985 Lewis Powell affirmed that position, saying, 'I am perfectly confident that General [Carl] Spaatz would have resisted any proposal that we kill the Jewish inmates in order temporarily to put an Auschwitz out of operation. It is not easy to think that rational persons would have made such a recommendation [to bomb Auschwitz].'[56] Apart from nagging suspicions that the British and Americans were influenced by indifference, if not anti-Semitism, there was the problem of Stalin and the Russians. The Russians permitted Allied aircraft to land and refuel, but they wanted no diversionary attacks against the death camps. For Stalin, who was already weighing post-war considerations, the integrity of rail lines was more important than Jewish lives.

Neither British nor American decision-makers were privy to the thoughts of the people in the concentration camps. Many hoped that Allied bombers would destroy the camps, even if it meant their own deaths. In the last days of the war, Bill Vegh endured air raids at Platling: 'Every day at noon the American planes came bombing the big cities, railroads and airfields. We were very happy when they used to come, because we had to rush into the shelters and stay there till the airplanes left.'[57] Sam Hollander was in Buchenwald working on the Bavarian redoubt when the Americans came: 'We were working on the bomb shelters when all of a sudden we saw American planes bombing. We were happy. We knew that the Germans were losing the war.'[58]

Alex Gross learned to pray while digging bomb shelters at Buna: 'We used to be proud as hell to watch the planes coming over, nice silver, shining things dropping bombs on our warehouse. I remember one of the holidays we were dovening as we were digging bunkers for the civilians. The sirens were on and the planes were coming. Quite frankly, we were praying that the bombs would come and hit us and kill us and take us out of our misery.'[59]

A MESSAGE OF HOPE

If the Allies were unwilling to direct assaults against the death camps, they could at least have threatened retribution for Nazi genocide. 'Worse than fear, torture, even humiliation', writes Elie Wiesel, 'is the feeling of abandonment, that you don't count.'[60] When in 1940 the Polish government in exile urged a declaration denouncing atrocities in eastern Europe, the British Foreign Office deleted reference to Jews. In October 1941 Eden omitted Jewish victims from a statement on terrorism drafted for the cabinet. Three months later, Allied representatives meeting at St James's Palace again omitted reference to Jews. According to General Sikorsky, explicit mention might 'be equivalent to an implicit recognition of the racial theories which we all reject'.[61] Asked why Jews were not mentioned in Churchill's addresses, Embassy First Secretary W.G. Hayter offered the disingenuous excuse that Churchill looked over the map and 'could think only of specific countries seized by Hitler. The Jews, of course, were not on that map, and they were overlooked.'[62]

Churchill's oversight apparently was contagious. Between May 1942 and February 1943, Under Secretary Welles delivered a host of speeches from Arlington Cemetery to the University of Toronto. Welles paid tribute to the 28 nations fighting for liberty, 'the glorious men and women of the Soviet Union', 'British flyers' and their Commonwealth compatriots, 'peace-loving peoples of Belgium, Denmark, Sweden, Switzerland and Norway', 19 Latin American republics, Yugoslav Chetniks, guerrillas in Greece, and patriots of occupied Poland, Czechoslovakia, Holland, Luxembourg and Occupied France 'who are murdered daily by the agents of the Gestapo'. Welles never mentioned Jews.[63]

Having denounced Nazi oppression for a rally at Madison Square Garden on 21 July 1942, and endorsed the Allied declaration on German extermination of 'the Jewish race' (17 December 1942),[64] Roosevelt felt no need to elaborate his position. Requests from the Emergency Conference to Save the Jews (September 1943), the Independent Jewish Press Service (spring 1944), Senator Guy Gillette who was hosting a banquet for Albert Einstein (August 1944) and representatives of New York's Jewish parochial schools (December 1944) were shunted aside with form letters that indicated the President was unavailable ('out of town') or that FDR had given 'tangible evidence of his determination to aid Jewish victims of Nazi oppression'.[65]

Jews were hard pressed to find 'tangible evidence' in the declaration issued by the Allies on 1 November 1943, that threatened punishment for Nazi atrocities against the French, Poles, Dutch, Belgians, Norwegians and Italians. There was no mention of Jews in that document, but there was in one issued by Roosevelt in the summer of 1944. Secretaries Morgenthau, Stimson and Stettinius submitted a draft which began, 'One of the blackest crimes in history, the systematic murder of the Jews of Europe, continues unabated.' When the final paper was issued, it spoke of the sufferings of Warsaw, Lidice, Kharkov, Nanking, the Filipinos, Norwegian, Dutch, Danes, Greeks, Russians and US servicemen. Jews were not mentioned until the middle of the second page.[66] Reacting to this strange laconism at 'the assassination of a people', Abba Silver told a ZOA audience in October 1944, 'A spiritual palsy seemed to have attacked the world and the mildewed spirit of this moldering age found all sorts of excuses for doing so little.'[67]

THE WAR REFUGEE BOARD

Actually the White House had not been completely inactive. On 16 January 1944, Treasury Secretary Morgenthau, accompanied by General Counsel Randolph Paul and Foreign Funds Division Chief John Pehle, delivered a blistering 18-page critique of State Department policies to the the President. Six days later, Roosevelt authorized the creation of the War Refugee Board (WRB), an agency that would not be hampered by provisions of the Trading with the Enemy Act. The WRB was Roosevelt's way of conceding that the IGCR was defunct, buried amid bureaucracies like the Office of Foreign Relief and Rehabilitation Operations, the Foreign Economic Administration and the United Nations Relief and Rehabilitation Agency.[68]

In January 1944 John Pehle was appointed to lead the WRB. He would be assisted by Ira Hirschmann in Turkey, Robert Dexter in Lisbon, Ivor Olsen in Stockholm, Leonard Ackermann in Egypt, and Roswell McClelland in Switzerland. There was no specific charge concerning Jews, but it was clear that Jewish agencies were shouldering the brunt ($16 million) of $20 million spent by the WRB. Five weeks after his appointment, Pehle reported that: Romanian authorities were permitting a few Jews to leave Constanza; France and Spain had agreed to let Jewish refugees travel to Morocco; Spain, Switzerland, Sweden, the Vatican were urging Slovakia, Hungary and Bulgaria to refrain from deporting more Jews; and fascist allies of Hitler had been warned of punishment for war crimes. Agents of the WRB were so faithful in their work that some of the closet bigots in the State Department wondered whether Pehle, Josiah Dubois and McClelland were themselves Jewish.[69]

During the spring of 1944 Pehle and his assistants proposed creation of 'free ports' along the East Coast. Just as merchandise could lie duty free while awaiting transshipment, so human beings would be admitted to the United

States for the duration, with the understanding that they would leave at war's end. When the government announced it was establishing a camp at Fort Ontario in Oswego, New York, the President received a letter of 'deep appreciation' from that town's Citizens' Committee. There was talk of bringing thousands of refugees from camps in Italy to the United States, 984 were admitted to Fort Ontario, the lone free port ever created.[70]

Working with the Joint, the War Refugee Board saved thousands of Jews in the Balkans and Baltic regions. It smuggled funds into France to sustain Jews in hiding, subsidized those in camps in North Africa and Italy, and secured passports to South America for many in Switzerland. The WRB was able to detour a few death trains from their destinations. Its final report contradicted what Long and Hull had said about the feasibility of negotiating with the Germans. The board 'purchased' 50,000 Jewish lives from the Nazis before the European war ended.[71]

Between 1933 and 1939 the United States welcomed 57,000 refugees (Jews and non-Jews) from Germany. During World War II, another 70,000 refugees were admitted.[72] British officials speak of 56,000 refugees from Hitler (90 percent of them Jews) who arrived in England before the start of World War II. An estimated 10,000 more came between 1939 and 1945.[73] In Britain, there was no agency comparable to the War Refugee Board.

The Last Chapter: Hungary

THE JEWS IN MAGYARORSZAG

There were 750,000 Jews (6 percent of the total population) in what was left of Hungary after the treaty of Trianon;[1] 250,000 lived in Budapest which some anti-Semites disparaged as 'Judapesht'. Sixty-one percent of the printers in Hungary, 55 percent of the physicians, 49 percent of the lawyers, 37.5 percent of the chemists, 32 percent of the journalists, 27 percent of those in arts and literature were Jews.

Such status had not been won easily. Although most Hungarian Jews supported Lajos Kossuth's liberal revolution in the spring of 1848, mobs that ravaged Budapest's Jewish quarter forced Kossuth to postpone discussion of Jewish emancipation.[2] Only when Russian and Austrian forces surrounded the capital did the diet acknowledge the rights of Jews. Emancipation lasted less than a year. The victorious Hapsburgs decided Jews had been the principal trouble-makers and fined them two million gulden.[3] Efforts to elevate Judaism to the status of 'accepted religion' were resisted by Church spokesmen who reminded the emperor of the 'profound' differences between Christianity and 'Mosaism'. In parliament, Hungarian anti-Semites, led by Geza Onody, charged that the Talmud instructed Jews to seek Christian blood.[4] In March 1882, again in 1899, Hungarian Jews endured pogroms following ritual murder accusations.[5]

Jews were encouraged when Count Mihaly Karolyi invited all elements to join his provisional government at the end of October 1918. The dream did not last long. Just as Germany, Hungary was subjected to blockade into the summer of 1919. There were shortages of food, fuel and clothing. Accused of being a 'Jewish stooge', Karolyi could not mollify Czech, Serbian and Romanian nationalists and would not carry out land reform. When the French threatened to invade Hungary unless it ceded Transylvania to the Romanians, Karolyi resigned.[6] For the next 130 days (March–July 1919), Hungary was ruled by a Soviet-style politburo. Eighteen of its 29 leaders had been born Jews, including Prime Minister Bela Kun (Berele Kohn). Once a Social-Democrat, Kun became a communist after he came in contact with disciples of Lenin in a Russian PW camp during World War I. In Budapest, Kun lashed out against all religious sects (44 of the 342 victims of the regime were Jews). Following an unsuccessful clash with Romania, Kun and his followers fled to Vienna, leaving Hungary's practicing Jews to bear the brunt of his legacy.[7]

As the Romanian army crossed into Hungary, it was accompanied by royalists who created a national army at Szeged in May 1919. Six months later, the 'men of Szeged' reached Budapest and reconstituted the monarchy under a regent Admiral Miklos Horthy de Nagybanya. More than 3,000 Jews were killed and 30,000 Galicians expelled.[8] In return the Catholic Church blessed the White terror. On 22 August 1919, a Synod of Bishops, noting 'the terrible rampaging of Bolshevism [that] has shocked the public conscience', appointed Bishop Ottokar Prohaszka to write a Shepherd's Epistle. Justifying the post-Kun massacres, Prohaszka called the Jews 'red demons' whose goal was to create Hell on Earth. He concluded this epistle with a prayer asking that the God of Peace 'swiftly trample Satan under his feet'.[9]

Virtually every aspect of Hungarian society directed hostility toward Jews during the inter-war period. Teaching faculties, students and medical associations complained about swarms of Jews. 'Christian' newspapers editorialized against Jews as 'sewer rats'. A number of super patriotic organizations came into being: Bishop Prohaszka's *Etelkozi Szovetseg*; Karoly Wolf's Christian Socialist Party; the Blood Alliance of the Double Cross; the Blue Cross; and the green-shirted Arrow Cross. Created by Ferenc Szalasi in 1936, the Arrow Cross received 750,000 votes in the national elections of 1939, making it the second most popular party in Hungary.[10]

In 1920 the diet passed the first *numerus clausus* in post-war Europe, capping Jews in educational institutions at 6 percent. Diplomats who protested against this violation of minority guarantees were stonewalled by Pal Telecki's short-lived cabinet. During the ten-year ministry of Count Stephan Bethlen (1921–31), Hungary was more concerned with economic revival than body counts in schools.[11] Adrift in financial chaos, in October 1932 the ruling Government Party designated Gyula Gombos Prime Minister. Once Minister of Defense, Gombos left the army in 1920 to establish MOVE (*Magyar orszagos vedero Egyesulet*/Hungarian Association for National Defenses), one of the chauvinist groups that provoked pogroms. An inveterate anti-Semite, Gombos had been implicated in a plot to overthrow the government. He also authored a book calling for the expulsion of Jews. Hungarians were surprised when Jews were not mentioned in the 95-point program presented by Gombos to Parliament on 6 October. Until his death in 1936, Hungary passed no more anti-Jewish legislation.[12] Gombos experienced no spiritual conversion.[13] A political opportunist, he was willing to work with wealthy Jews as long as such cooperation advanced the nationalist program.[14]

LAWS TO GUARANTEE 'A BALANCED SOCIAL AND ECONOMIC LIFE'

During the inter-war period, nearly two-thirds of Hungary's Jews identified as modernist and belonged to the *Neolog*, the Reform *Kehillah* headed by Samu Stern in Budapest. Perhaps 30 percent were Orthodox, mainly Hasidim in the rural regions. Only a small number belonged to Zionist organizations.

When central Europe boiled over in 1938, these blocs set up relief agencies to assist refugees. In 1939, the Welfare Bureau of Hungarian Jews (*Magyar Izraelitak Partfogo Irodaja*, MIPI) and the National Hungarian Jewish Assistance Campaign (*Orszagos Magyar Zsido Segito Akcio*, OMZsA) were charged by the National Central Alien Control Office (*Kulfoldieket Ellenorzo Orszagos Kozponti Hatosag*, KEOKH) with helping out in camps at Garany, Ricse, Csorgo, Sarvar and Kistarcsa.[15]

After Hitler's success in Germany, Hungarian extremists agitated for more anti-Jewish restrictions. Early in 1938 Prime Minister Kalman Daranyi and his successor Bela Imredy championed a bill 'for the more effective guarantee of a balanced social and economic life' by limiting Jews in the professions to 20 percent.[16] While Parliament debated the fate of Jews, members of the Arrow Cross attacked Jews on the streets. In March 1939 Prime Minister Imredy was forced to resign when it was revealed he had a Jewish great-grandmother. His successor, Pal Teleki, presided over the adoption of a second Jewish bill on 4 May 1939.[17] This 'law to limit the expansion of the Jews in the public and economic domain' was far more sweeping than the one passed the previous year. It set a limit of 6 percent in all professions, university admissions and trading licenses. The number of Jews in banking, industry and commerce was reduced to 12 percent. Jews were ordered to divest themselves of 1.4 million acres of agricultural property. Jews who had entered Hungary after 1914 were denationalized. As a result of this legislation, more than 30,000 persons converted; 20,000 jobs were transferred to Christians; 200,000 Jews were impoverished.[18]

Under Teleki, Hungary played a dangerous game, snipping off land that belonged to Poland, while supporting Hitler and respecting the territorial integrity of Yugoslavia. When Horthy and Foreign Minister Laszlo Bardossy pledged Hungary's participation in the expedition against Yugoslavia at the end of March 1941, Teleki committed suicide. The note he left read: 'We have committed perjury. We signed a pact of perpetual friendship with the South Slavs and yet out of cowardice we have now allied ourselves with criminals. I accuse myself and consider myself guilty of not having been able to prevent the decisions taken by your Excellency. It may well be that I shall render the nation a service by my death.'[19]

If anything, Teleki's death paved the way for more severe anti-Jewish activity. With Bardossy as Prime Minister, Parliament adopted a law defining sexual contact between a Jew (anyone with two Jewish grandparents) and a Christian woman (except prostitutes) as *fajgyalazas* (racial shame). When Hungary declared war against Russia on 27 June, 22,000 'stateless' Jews were expelled to Podolia. They were murdered by *Einsatzgruppen* and Ukrainian auxiliaries outside Kamenetz-Podolsk. Some Hungarian troops witnessed the slaughter but it would not be long before these units would do their own killing – in Novi Sad, where 10,000 Jews were shot, in a hospital at Korasten where 500 typhoid patients were machine-gunned, at Titel where dozens were clubbed to death in the icy waters of the Tisza, in the sports stadium at Ujvidek where Jews were forced to race, having been promised that winners would be spared. (All 250 were shot.)[20]

Since 1919, the Hungarians had press-ganged asocial elements into labor battalions. A new corps of *Munkaszolgalat* was created in July 1939. By the summer of 1943, 800,000 Jews and non-Jews received summonses to units bound for Serbia or the Ukraine. With uniforms and boots in short supply, many Jews wore civilian clothes. They were identified by yellow armbands. About 130,000 Jewish men below the age of 60 were drafted to clean roads, dig trenches, chop trees, work in copper mines or act as human mine sweepers. Hungarian guards imposed concentration camp rules and amused themselves by hosing down prisoners in subzero temperatures, forcing them to swing from trees, burying some alive, or chaining others together and throwing them into bonfires.[21]

One of those sent to Russia in 1941 was Karl Klein, the son of a leather worker from Ferherg Yarmat. A veteran of two years in the Hungarian army, Klein was drafted into a company of 220 Jews at the end of 1941. Klein endured burns, starvation and frostbite before being taken prisoner at Kharkov:

> I was in leather shoes. You can't wear leather shoes in bitter cold – 30–35–40 below. My toes were frozen, and I didn't know. The last day before we arrived at the railroad we took a rest in a Russian home. I took off my shoes, together with the toes. There was no flesh, just the bones. A Russian woman used pliers and clipped the bones. I lost four toes. There was no doctor and I didn't feel anything. I didn't know what to do. I asked for warm water and put it on. I nearly killed myself. The pains – I thought I would die. The Russian woman gave me some clothing to put around my legs. I didn't have the shoes anymore. I walked in the rags.[22]

General Gusztay Jany led 250,000 men of the 2nd Hungarian Army into Russia. They were accompanied by 50,000 Jews in labor gangs. He had been told to bring the Jews back in an attaché case (return only with their names). Perhaps 70,000 Hungarian soldiers managed to straggle back. Fewer than 7,000 Jews returned.[23]

KALLAY AND THE QUESTION OF EXPULSION

Unwilling to accept Horthy's son Istvan as successor to the regent, Bardossy was fired in March 1942. Hungary's new Prime Minister, Nicholas Kallay, was an aristocrat who referred to Jews as allies of Russian-Asian Bolshevism, an impermeable stratum in Hungarian society. He had long advocated taxing or confiscation of Jewish property. The first ghettos in Hungary were created under Kallay. Parliament decreed the expropriation of forests, farmland and estates owned by Jews. On 29 July 1942, the reactionaries repealed the act of 1895 that granted Judaism protected status. Kallay saluted General Jany's efforts and expanded the labor battalions in the Soviet Union. While visiting the town of Ungvar, Kallay warned, 'Let Jewry engrave on the tablet of its heart: the Jews must give up all hope!'[24] He elaborated in a speech before the National Congress: 'I know there is no final solution to the problem other than the removal of the Jews, who number 800,000 people ... In the meantime, the Jews must be removed from each and every socially and nationally important position – until such time as the final solution becomes feasible.'[25]

After the war Kallay claimed that he was trying to deceive the Nazis.[26] According to Kallay, 'It also meant that the 800,000 Jews would be there (in Hungary) until after the war and that until then they would not be harmed.'[27] During his two years as Prime Minister, Kallay did refuse to mandate the badge and other anti-Jewish laws. When German emissaries pressed for the implementation of the Final Solution in Hungary, Kallay responded that Jews were vital to industrial production, 80 percent of which was being diverted to German use. Upset with Hungarian policies, Hitler met with Admiral Horthy near Salzburg in April 1943. The *Führer* reminded the Regent, 'Where the Jews were left to themselves, as for instance, in Poland, the most terrible misery and decay prevailed.' This had changed. 'If the Jews there did not work, they were shot. They had to be treated like tuberculosis bacilli, with which a healthy body may become infected. This was not cruel, if one remembers that even innocent creatures of nature, such as hares and deer, have to be killed, so that no harm is caused by them.'[28]

For his part, through the year 1943 Prime Minister Kallay tried to avoid falling deeper into the arms of the Germans. The campaign in Russia had turned disastrous. Like the Italians, Kallay fantasized surrendering to the western Allies, while avoiding occupation by the Red Army. He contacted American diplomats in Turkey and the Zionist underground. While Dome Sztojay, his Ambassador in Berlin, continued to call for deportation of Jews to the so-called Polish reserve, Kallay steadfastly refused, stating in May 1943, 'So long as the basic prerequisite of the solution, namely the answer to the question where the Jews are to be resettled is not given.'[29]

Hitler's rage boiled over in February 1944 when Kallay and Horthy recalled their forces from Russia. Rather than leave a strategic flank exposed, Hitler decided to move against Hungary and share the remains with more loyal allies – Slovakia, Croatia and Romania. The Nazi leader again invited Horthy to Schloss Klessheim. On 19 March 1944, the regent was informed that the Germans had sent two mechanized divisions into Budapest. Within hours these troops occupied the houses of government and airports and arrested 3,500 Jews and dozens of opponents. Kallay fled the country and the Nazis named Dome Sztojay to replace him. From Vienna came Adolf Eichmann with his retinue of specialists. When Horthy returned to Budapest, he informed Sztojay that he would no longer review Jewish legislation.[30]

PASSOVER 1944: THE DEPORTATIONS BEGIN

Despite reports from forced labor units, the Polish Government in Exile, World Jewish Congress, the Working Group in Bratislava and the BBC that their kinsmen were being exterminated, the Jews of Hungary refused to believe they were in danger. They were shocked when the new government introduced more discriminatory regulations. In the interest of 'public security' Jews over the age of six were ordered to wear the yellow star.[31] Jews were no longer permitted to enter public bathhouses or parks. They could not possess radios, automobiles, jewelry and gold coins. Jewish bank accounts were frozen and debts owed by Gentiles were canceled. Libraries were confiscated. Jewish pharmacies, publishing houses, legal offices were closed, though the operators were still obligated to pay their Gentile workers. Jews received ration coupons which entitled them to lesser quantities of sugar, fat or oil.[32]

To calm their victims, the Nazis created a new Jewish Council headed by Samu Stern and Baron Philipp von Freudiger. On 31 March Eichmann met with the Jewish leaders and assured them that all measures relating to Jews would last only for the duration of the war. Afterward, 'Everything will be as before.' Eichmann promised that he would not tolerate abuse of Jews by German soldiers. For the moment, however, the Nazis intended to remove some Jews to labor colonies. They would need complete listings of Jewish residences and businesses.[33] When the Germans made demands for silverware, paintings, women's lingerie and perfume, the Council complied.[34] Stern later explained that Jewish leaders cooperated because they believed the war was ending and they were 'in a race with time'.[35]

Under arrangements negotiated in April 1944 100,000 Jewish men were to be shipped to factories in the Reich. Some of the first to go were internees from the Kistarcsa concentration camp on the outskirts of Budapest. As mothers, children and 100-year-old women were deported, it became evident that *all* Jews were being sent away. The scheme worked out by *Sondereinsatzkommando* Eichmann was simple. Hungary was divided into six zones. While assuring the Jews of Budapest that nothing would be done to them, the Nazis gathered Jews from rural regions in ghettos in the provincial capitals, from which they were taken to Poland. Once Carpatho-Ruthenia, northern Transylvania, northern Hungary, Szeged and Debrecen, Szombathely and Pecs were cleared, the Jews of Budapest would be purged.[36]

Eichmann had fewer than 200 bureaucrats, and no order police at his disposal.[37] On 7 April, State Secretary Laszlo Baky volunteered the assistance of every public servant, including Hungarian police, gendarmerie, firemen and postal workers. Said Baky, 'It is the patriotic duty of every Hungarian who knows or learns of any Jews attempting to disregard regulations to report to the nearest police station.' Eberhard von Thadden, Edmund Veesenmayer (German Minister Plenipotentiary in Hungary), Wisliceny and

General Winckelmann also praised farmers who carted Jews out of their villages, professional associations, common laborers, clerks and trainmen who helped plot the route from Munkacs to Stryj, Lemberg, Przemysl and Auschwitz.[38] Said Adolf Eichmann: 'Hungary was the only European country to encourage us relentlessly.'[39]

Survivors recall with bitterness the brutality of the 'Feathers', Hungarian gendarmes under the command of Lt. Col. Laszlo Ferenczy. For Frida Weiss, who lived in a small village near Munkacs, the *Nyilas* who sent them to a brick factory in Polonak were 'pharaoh's army'.[40] For 15-year-old Jim Elephant from Sarospatak, the gendarmes who beat people with truncheons were 'bastards'. To Manci Feig from Sighet, they were 'regular Nazis with black uniforms'.[41]

The deportations began on 15 May 1944. In the next 46 days 430,000 Hungarian Jews would be deported to 'Waldsee', a mythical reservation by the sea. Despite lading tickets on the boxcars that read 'Auschwitz', Hungarian Jews were somewhat naive concerning what was to befall them. Jim Elder showed one of the tickets to a friend who worked with the *Judenrat*. He said, 'Boy, that Auschwitz. It has a bad reputation.'[42] Many Hungarians reacted to the deportations the way they had to the German occupation – with *ennui*. In the town of Veszprem they celebrated. Minister Laszlo Endre asked General Winckelmann to increase the number of transports from two per day to six. Endre emptied refugee camps, prisons and sanitariums, demonstrating how more Jews could be squeezed into boxcars if people stood with their arms stretched above their heads.[43]

Several bishops (Aron Marton in Kolozsvar, Vilmos Apor of Gyor, Endre Hamyas of Csanad and Sandor Kovacs of Szombathely) did make representations to Sztojay. They were undermined by Cardinal Justinian Seredi whose sole concern was for Jews who had converted to Christianity. Seredi insisted upon preferential treatment for converts as opposed to practicing Jews who 'executed a wickedly destructive influence on the Hungarian economic, social and moral life'. Seredi threatened the government with censure if bona fide converts were mistreated. He offered no comment on massacres or deportations of Jews.[44]

On 7 July, Horthy acting with the support of his Crown Council put a halt to further deportations. Deputy Foreign Minister Mihaly Arnothy-Jungerth, former prime minister Stephan Bethlen, and Horthy's son apparently had read portions of the Auschwitz Protocols. The Regent received an appeal from the Pope on 25 June, King Gustav of Sweden on 30 June. Horthy also received notes from Roosevelt and Hull that warned of saturation bombing of Hungarian cities and post-war prosecutions if the deportation of Jews did not cease. Angered by German newsreels highlighting Hungarian involvement in the roundups and facing a coup planned by Baky and Endre, Horthy finally acted. By the time he did, more than half of Hungary's Jews had been shipped to the death camps in Poland.[45]

THE BRAND MISSION

During the spring of 1944 agents of several wealthy Jewish families contacted Kurt Becher, chief of Himmler's economic staff in Hungary, offering to trade their holdings for passage to a neutral country. When the transfer was completed, 47 individuals were permitted to go to Portugal. As Becher pursued other ransom schemes, Wisliceny negotiated with the *Vaadah Ezra va Hazalah* (Council for Assistance and Rescue) organized in January 1943 under the leadership of Otto Komoly, Dr Rezso Kastner and Samuel Springmann. Wisliceny offered to halt deportations of European Jews for $2,000,000. When the council came up with 10 percent of this sum, the Nazis permitted 70 Jews to leave the country.

On 25 April 1944 Eichmann summoned a representative of the Vaad to his offices at the Hotel Majestic. Joel Brand, a 37-year-old ne'er-do-well from Transylvania, managed to ingratiate himself to Zionist leadership.[46] Eichmann stunned Brand by declaring:

> I suppose you know who I am. I was in charge of the actions in Germany, Poland, and Czechoslovakia. Now it is Hungary's turn. I have already investigated you and your people of the Joint and the Jewish Agency, and I have verified your ability to make a deal. Now then, I am prepared to sell you one million Jews. Not the whole lot – you wouldn't be able to raise enough money for that. But you could manage a million. Goods for blood; blood for goods. You can take them from any country you like, wherever you can find them. From Hungary, Poland, the eastern provinces, from Terezin, from Auschwitz – wherever you want. Whom do you want to save? Men who can beget children? Women who can bear them? Old people? Children? Sit down and talk.[47]

Eichmann offered to release a million Jews in exchange for 10,000 trucks and a hodge-podge of supplies including two million cakes of soap, 200 tons of cocoa, 200 tons of tea and 800 tons of coffee. The winterized vehicles would be used on the Eastern Front against the Russians. Out of deference to the Arabs, Eichmann would allow only a few Jews to emigrate to Palestine. An unlimited number could leave through Spain. The offer, which was to be communicated to the Jewish Agency and Allied officials in Turkey, was made three weeks before the deportations from Hungary began. If Brand were not successful, Eichmann threatened to deport all remaining Jews, including Brand's family. Said Eichmann, '*Ich lasse die Mühle in Auschwitz arbeiten*' (I will let the mill in Auschwitz work).[48]

On 19 May, Brand and Andor Grosz, an agent of the Hungarian secret service, flew to Istanbul. Brand thought he would be meeting Chaim Weizmann. Instead, his contact was Chaim Barlas, a middle level official of the Jewish Agency, who offered him little hope of success. Brand traveled to Aleppo where he was arrested by the British. Subsequently, he was transferred to a jail in Cairo. While there he told his story to Moshe Shertok, a confidant of David Ben-Gurion, and Ira Hirschmann, Roosevelt's emissary from the War Refugee Board. They reported to the British and American governments, which, in turn, contacted the Russians. On 20 June, Deputy Soviet Foreign Minister Andrei Vishinsky responded that it was 'neither expedient nor permissible to negotiate with the Germans on such a matter'.[49]

If Washington harbored any notion of following up on the proposal, the British made it clear they would have none of it. In an *aide-mémoire* from the British Embassy (5 June 1944), the British raised a host of objections, apart from the betrayal of an ally. Allowing Hitler to determine the nature and place of the exchange would be a dangerous precedent. Taking responsibility for one million refugees was like asking the Allies to suspend essential military operations. The British would not, however, reject 'genuine proposals' or discussions with Spain and Portugal that did not prejudice the war effort.[50]

While Brand vegetated in an Egyptian jail, Rudolf Kastner, the Vaad's agent, continued to meet with Eichmann. As a goodwill gesture, Eichmann directed 21,000 Jews to Strasshof, a camp near Vienna. Most of these people were placed in special quarantine barracks and survived the war.[51] Through that summer, Kasztner managed to increase the original number of Jews bound to Switzerland to 1,600. They included industrialists, rabbis, scientists, writers, friends and relatives of Vaad officials, including the Komoly and Kasztner families. The first group of 318 made a stop at Bergen-Belsen before proceeding to Switzerland. There were no more deals when the other 1,300 followed in December. Hitler was upset when he read of the arrival of these refugees in Switzerland. According to Becher, the *Führer* declared, '*Ein deutscher Jude kommt nicht mehr in Ausland*' (No German Jew goes out ever again).[52] Himmler agreed, saying, '*Ich muss dem Führer treue bleiben*' (I must remain true to the *Führer*).[53]

OCTOBER 1944: THE END OF HORTHY

The 200,000 Jews of Budapest were spared deportation, but not many other indignities that summer. There was no ghetto in Budapest until December 1944 because of Allied threats of bombing if Jews were confined. Instead, the Sztojay regime placed them in buildings scattered through the city. Jews who once occupied more than 26,000 apartments were now restricted to fewer than 3,000 houses marked with a yellow Star of David. Hundreds of people were hustled off to internment camps and more inane decrees were enacted (segregating Jews and Gentiles in air raid shelters, reminding people of basic hygiene).[54]

While anti-Semites burned books and beat Jews on the streets of Budapest, Horthy permitted the departure of 7,800 Jews to neutral lands. Diplomatic personnel from neutral nations and the Vatican began issuing protective passports (*Schutzpass*) or protective letters (*Schutzbriefe*) to Jews. They were assisted by Otto Komoly, liaison between the Vaad and Department A of the International Red Cross and Halutz leaders who encouraged 7,000 young men and women to risk *Tiyul* (flight) through Romania to Turkey and Palestine.[55] By the end of October there were more than 100,000 Jews and Jewish converts in Budapest claiming foreign protection.

Angered by such ruses, Eichmann decided to clear Budapest of 50,000 'Galician' and 'infiltrated' Jews. On 23 August, the Red Army broke through Romanian lines in Bessarabia and the government of King Paul capitulated. The next day, 24 August, Horthy replaced Sztojay with General Geza Lakatos. When Eichmann asked for gendarmes to carry out the roundup, he was told none were available. Eichmann threatened to take the city with SS units if 10,000 Jews were not given over, but Horthy also refused. That same day, Himmler ordered deportations be halted and Wisliceny telephoned Kasztner saying, 'You have won, Herr Kasztner. Our staff is leaving.'[56]

Hungary's old guard had not reckoned with the desperation of the Nazis and their Arrow Cross allies. On 15 October the Germans sent the 24th Panzer Division, 40 tanks and three other divisions to Budapest to depose the Regent. *Operation Panzer Faust* (Armed Fist) was led by SS *Obergruppenführer* Erich von dem Bach-Zelewski, who had commanded anti-partisan units in Russia and Poland, and SS Major General Otto Skorzeny, the six foot five inch warlord who rescued Mussolini the previous winter. Skorzeny captured Horthy's son, forcing the regent to step down on 16 October. Horthy was taken to a castle in Germany and on 17 October the offices of Prime Minister and Regent were fused into one. The new *Führer* of Hungary was Ferenc Szalasi, founder of the Arrow Cross. Cardinal Seredi met with Szalasi at the end of October and instructed teachers to take an oath of allegiance to the fascist leader.[57] With the Nyilas in control, Eichmann was welcomed back to Budapest to finish the decimation of Hungarian Jewry.

WINTER 1944–45: MASSACRES ALONG THE DANUBE

The return of the Nazis was celebrated by pogroms in Budapest and the few outlying towns where there were still some Jews. In the capital, Andras Kun, a priest carrying a crucifix and a gun, led hoodlums through the streets beating Jews. An entire company of Jewish labor-service men was butchered in Pusztvam. A favorite technique was to bind three victims together with wire at the banks of the Danube, shoot the one in the middle, and watch as all three plunged to a drowning death in the waters below. When Jews offered resistance at Telecki Square, dozens were dragged from their homes and massacred. At least 6,000 more were confined to synagogues for days without food or medical attention. On 18 October, Gabor Vajna, the new Minister of the Interior, announced he would no longer recognize the validity of foreign passports. Forced to back off, he granted 7,800 visas to Switzerland, 4,500 to Sweden, 2,500 to the Vatican, 700 to Portugal and 100 to Spain.[58]

That same day, 18 October, Eichmann demanded that the deportations resume. Szalasi promised to supply 70,000 slave laborers from battalions that were digging trenches about the capital. The first deportees, many of them women conscripted off the streets wearing light clothes and heels, set out by foot on 10 November. Few survived the cold, beatings and shootings of the 120 mile death march to Hegyeshalom on the Austrian border. Foreign diplomats who intervened to save a handful of deportees described them as in a state where 'all human appearances and all human dignity have completely left them'.[59]

On 18 November, the fascist government defied the Allies by ordering the creation of a formal ghetto in Budapest. The old Orthodox quarter, where 3,500 Jews lived in less than one-tenth of one square mile, counted 70,000 residents after 10 December. Food, water, fuel and medicine were all in short supply. Corpses piled up in makeshift morgues as hundreds of people died of disease, starvation and brutality.[60] In those last weeks, members of the Arrow Cross engaged in a frenzy abusing people in buildings under the protection of foreign diplomats. At one point grenades were thrown into the Glass House. Jews caught on the street were mutilated. The head of the Institute of Forensic Medicine reported victims whose eyes had been shot out or who had been scalped. Bodies retrieved from the street bore signs of bruised faces, broken bones and abdominal knife wounds. On Christmas Eve, gangs terrorized children from the Jewish orphanage on Munkacsi Mihaly Street, forcing two-year-olds to stand in the cold before dispersing them to gunfire. On 28 December, the Nyilas broke into the Bethlen Square hospitals, shooting patients in beds. Nuns and priests who tried to intercede were tortured. Ninety-two doctors, nurses and patients from the Maros Street Hospital were shot at trenches on 11 January. The personnel and patients of the Orthodox Hospital in Buda were murdered on 14 January. The Nyilas followed up by killing 90 residents of the Orthodox almshouse on 19 January. Eichmann left Budapest on Christmas Eve, but the killing continued until 13 February 1945 when the city came under Russian control. In four months of rule, the Szalasi regime murdered 80,000 Jews.[61]

HANNAH SENESH

Just as Anne Frank symbolized the tragedy of Jews in Holland, so another young woman put the face of humanity to the more than 500,000 Jews from Hungary who perished in World War II. Hannah Senesh was born in Budapest in 1921. Her father Bela was a popular columnist during the Bethlen era. He died of a heart attack at the age of 33 in 1927, leaving a widow, a son and a daughter. Hannah grew up in a comfortable middle-class existence. She loved opera and read voraciously – Maeterlinck, Thackeray, Zweig, Lewisohn, Dostoevsky and Tolstoy. Though the family vacationed in Switzerland, she had problems with French. Like Anne Frank, she loved movies and, like the remarkable girl from Amsterdam, she left a diary filled with poems and great insight. With prescience Hannah wrote in 1936, 'I would like to be a great soul. If God will permit.'[62]

On 27 October 1938 she declared herself a Zionist, a term which meant 'I now consciously and strongly feel I am a Jew and am proud of it.' She applied for an entry permit to Palestine and began polishing her Hebrew. After arriving in the Holy Land in September 1939, Hannah tried to buoy the spirits of her mother with letters that proclaimed, 'I am home.' Privately, she expressed doubt and loneliness. Though she hoped to be a teacher or politician, she worked all day in her kibbutz chicken coops and laundry room. In July 1940, she visited the hills of Kfar Giladi and noted, 'In the mountains one involuntarily hears the query: "Whom shall I send?" And the answer, "Send me to serve the beautiful and the good."' A few months later, she wrote that God had entrusted her with a mission. Finally in January 1943 that mission became clear: 'I was suddenly struck by the idea of going to Hungary. I feel I must be there during these days in order to help organize youth emigration, and also to get my mother out.'

Hannah Senesh volunteered for a unit of Jews being trained for guerrilla activity in the Balkans. On 13 March 1944, six days before the Nazis installed the Sztojay regime in Budapest, the commandos boarded a British plane for the 13-hour trip to the Adriatic. There were 32 Jews in the group, most of whom shared a kibbutz background.[63] By design, the Palestinians parachuted into Yugoslavia, not Hungary. They made contact with Croatian nationalists who were fighting the Nazis. Fearing these partisans might be anti-Semites, the Hebrew-speaking Jews told the Croatians they were Welshmen. While the Jews offered instruction and moral support to the Yugoslavs, Hannah personally was troubled. When Eichmann came to Budapest, she wrote, 'What will happen to all of them – to the million Jews in Hungary. They're in German hands now – and we're sitting here – just sitting.'[64]

On 9 June 1944 Hannah and her companions crossed the border into Hungary. When one of the commandos panicked, they were all captured. A few days later, Catherine Senesh was summoned to police headquarters in Budapest. Questioned, Catherine insisted Hannah was in Palestine. At that point, the girl was dragged into the room. She had been tortured, beaten black and blue, several of her teeth knocked out. Both women were incarcerated that summer. When Catherine was released, she sought an attorney for her daughter.

On 28 October, a military tribunal found Hannah guilty of spying. Ten days later, as Hannah's attorney was preparing an appeal, the prosecuting officer, entered her cell and informed her that she had been sentenced to death. A prison orderly described how Hannah refused to ask for clemency from 'hangmen and murderers'. Given permission to write two letters, she asked forgiveness from her mother. Of her fellow commandos, she urged: 'Continue on the way, don't be deterred. Continue the struggle till the end, until the day of liberty comes, the day of victory for our people.'[65] A few moments later, she was killed by firing squad.

Hannah Senesh is remembered mainly for a poem that is recited around the world during Yom Ha-Shoah memorials and Hanukkah. Inscribed in May 1944 just days before her group crossed into Hungary, *Ashrei ha-gafrur*, translates:

> *Blessed is the match consumed in kindling flame.*
> *Blessed is the flame that burns in the secret fastness of the heart.*
> *Blessed is the heart with strength to stop its beating for honor's sake.*
> *Blessed is the match consumed in kindling flame.*

Hannah Senesh was 23 years old when she was executed in Budapest.

Extermination: Auschwitz

ANOTHER PLANET

The final destination for the Hungarians and many other European Jews was Oswiecim, a concentration camp situated in the industrial heartland of Upper Silesia. Once an Austrian military base, Auschwitz, as the Germans called it, would become synonymous with genocide. Eighteen miles southeast of Katowice, the camp was easily accessible by rail from Cracow 50 kilometers away, Prague and Vienna 350 kilometers to the west, Warsaw 286 and Berlin 500 kilometers north. The first prisoners (200 Jews and 30 Gentiles) were brought here in May 1940. Another 700 Jews came from Cracow the following month. German criminals transferred from Sachsenhausen became the first Kapos in a camp designed to hold 10,000 prisoners.

Following the invasion of Russia, Auschwitz became more than a forced labor camp like Dachau and less a killing center on the order of Treblinka. In mid-summer 1942, Himmler instructed Commandant Rudolf Hoess to prepare for 100,000–125,000 prisoners. Residents of the town and neighboring villages were relocated. In their place, the Nazis created an industrial complex covering 40 square kilometers. Prisoners considered themselves fortunate if they were assigned to Auschwitz I or any of a score of subsidiary camps where inmates had a chance to stay alive through slave labor. Most Jews, Gypsies and Slavs were sent to die in Birkenau (Auschwitz II) or Monowitz (III), two clusters of barracks a few miles south of the main camp.[1]

The trains arrived daily, bearing a fatigued, polyglot population. Some, like 3,000 Jews of Tarnow who had been confined in wagons for four days at the end of July 1944, were already dead. Bill Vegh was 14 when his town in the Carpathians was cleared in April 1944. After staying one night in an aerodrome, the Jews of Apsa rode three days and nights in cattle cars. Says Vegh, 'An old man in our car looked out a little opening way up high on the wall. The train was going and he said, "We're going home. I can already see our town. I can see my neighbor's apartment. We shall be home soon." We were going in the other direction. He never saw his home again.'[2]

Dazed and unaware of where they were, people hoped this was the reservation they had heard so much about. Said Bill Vegh, 'When the train pulled into Birkenau, it was actually beautiful. It was right by the crematorium, but we didn't know what it was.'[3] Eva Fugman was deported from

Pionki in August 1944. Arriving in the daytime, she was unimpressed. As Eva wrote later: 'If any one ever wanted a good description of Hell, Auschwitz was the place, with its flames shooting up high from the crematoria, the smell of human burning flesh, the screams that were heard miles around, and the thousands of thousands of walking corpses.'[4]

Jews formed lines and paraded before SS doctors. Individuals too frail or sick, the aged, underweight, mothers with children were motioned to one side while those able to work were sent to the other. Esther Bittman was a teenager when she, her mother and sister came before Dr Josef Mengele at Passover 1944: 'He never touched anybody with his hands – always pointing with that stick, to go to the side. We knew there was something wrong with the people who were chosen out of the crowd.'[5] Facial scars, acne, the slightest physical impediment could signal a death sentence. Lola Hollander was sent to a labor camp at Gabersdorf. Mengele visited the camp once. When he left, an aide took away a 13-year-old girl. 'She was the most beautiful thing you ever saw in your life', recalled Lola. 'She was perfect. He noticed that her one arm was maybe $\frac{1}{10}$th of a centimeter longer than the other. He took her out and she went to Auschwitz.'[6]

If the SS discovered infants hidden in valises, they sent mother and child directly to the gas chambers. Before coming to Auschwitz, Eva Fugman had cared for the children of her uncles (two girls, aged 7 and 3, and a little boy of one):

> They were trained that if anyone knocked at the door, all three would crawl under the bed. One day when there was an inspection by a Gestapo official from a different city, the three children and I spent a very uncomfortable eight hours in a water tank in the attic. One day the children had to be brought to the shop because the camp was inspected thoroughly. Normally they did not inspect the shops. We were warned just in time. All I could do was take the children to an outhouse. The oldest stood there very pale looking, her little legs trembling, but did not say a word in two hours. The little boy was over 2 then, and all he did was press his tiny fingers to his lips whispering, 'Sh, sh, sh.' But the little girl was getting impatient and sick to her stomach. I remember her saying, 'I hope they catch us this time, I'm getting sick and tired of running and hiding.' She wasn't the only one because I felt the same way. But she at least was honest.[7]

Only a handful of children survived in the camps.[8] Germaine Tillion, a French anthropologist related how guards in Ravensbruck induced labor on a pregnant Jewish woman. The newborn infant was then taken and drowned, a process that took 20 minutes.[9] Esther Shudmak recalls how the guards took an infant away from a woman in Block 14 of Auschwitz. 'She used to sit and sing lullabies to her baby. She was mad. She always pretended to have the baby in her hand.' Fifteen-year-old Jimmy Elder arrived with his father, mother, nine-year-old sister and aunt in 1944. Jim managed to convince the SS doctor that he was 17. 'I found later from my cousin that mother was first sent to the other side (the safe side) and my sister stayed with my aunt. The child began crying, so my mother crossed. She might have survived, but she wanted to be with her daughter.'[10]

IN THE BARRACKS

By day pillars of smoke, at night pillars of flame rose above the camp.[11] Camp veterans warned this was the only way anyone left Auschwitz. Jim Elder was sent near an open pit cremation. 'They made you run there and you could see the fire. It wasn't more than 200 yards away. There is nothing like the smell, not even a slaughterhouse. It's comparable to a burnt tire, like burnt oil cloth. This guy had a full loaf of bread and a mixed fruit preserve, a delicacy made mostly from sugar beets. I remember I took a bite of it and vomited right on the spot because of the stench.'[12] Those who passed the first selection were shaved and tattooed. Then they were given ill-fitting gray dresses or tick striped clothes with wooden clogs. Said Esther Bittman: 'We marched into a camp where we could see nothing except long barracks with chimneys and people standing behind bars. We thought those were people who were mentally sick. You couldn't tell the difference between the men and the women. It didn't take long, and we ended up looking the same way.'[13]

A few peasant huts were used to house women. These sod and brick buildings were small, dark and unsanitary. The regular wooden barracks were 120 feet long, 30 wide, and eight or nine feet high. The roofs, made of boards covered with felt, gave little protection from rain. The floors were of clay. There was no insulation, thin walls shielded the summer sun, a pot-bellied stove offered heat in the winter. There were no beds, just planks of wood with

23. Barracks at Auschwitz-Birkenau.

24. Auschwitz – the main camp where medical experiments were conducted.

blankets distributed to groups of four or eight. The buildings had no latrines. Mornings and evenings, inmates would take their turn at an open row of seats. Modeled after stables and fit for 52 horses, each of the buildings held 750 human beings. Rats ran among the sick and dying, who were covered with lice and fleas.[14]

At first, there was no hospital, but later two blocks held as many as 1,000 sick inmates. Given minimal treatment, the 'patients' lay on straw until they died. The main camp contained several innocuous-looking brick buildings where medical experiments were conducted. And while sexual relations between Jews and Germans was technically forbidden, in 1944 the Nazis designated for Hungarian girls a dozen units known as 'Mexico' or 'Puff' where the forbidden occurred.[15]

Belongings left on the loading platform were taken to 30 barracks dubbed 'Canada'. Anything that might be useful for winter relief was shipped back to Germany. Currency and jewelry were supposed to go to the WVHA in Berlin. Watches were reconditioned at Sachsenhausen for use by frontline troops. Six warehouses contained prostheses, eyeglasses and tons of human hair intended for packing torpedoes or as felt lining in overcoats. Inmates froze for lack of clothing and watched their feet bleed and rot in wooden clogs, while mountains of leather shoes and jackets were stacked up. Between 1 December 1944 and 15 January 1945, the SS processed 222,269 sets of men's clothing and underwear, 192,652 women's and 99,952 sets of children's apparel.[16]

WITHERING AWAY THROUGH LABOR

Auschwitz was the culmination of everything the Nazis had been working toward – extermination through violence, starvation, disease, gas and forced labor. Just as at Dachau, the sign over the entry into the camp proclaimed *Arbeit Macht Frei*. Every morning at 4 a.m. inmates were called to the Appelplatz while the dead were removed and counted. Esther Bittman recalled a young girl in her barracks who turned blue and died. She was wrapped in a blanket at the door of her barrack. A truck came and picked the dead up. 'When it was over, we started to work.'

Work assignments fell under the domain of SS *Gruppenführer* Pohl and the WVHA. Generally, artisans such as masons, carpenters and plumbers were spared. Some tailors and seamstresses were lucky enough to work indoors. People employed in I.G. Farben's Buna plants were also fortunate, even though the factories never produced any rubber or fuel. A few hundred women in Rajsko were assigned to greenhouse research on the Koksoghyz dandelion. Men in the carbonizing plant at Jawischowitz, foundries at Gleiwitz, or small factories like Weichsel-Union, Hindenburg A.C., Furstengrube GmbH had a longer life expectancy than inmates assigned to coal mines, quarries or construction. If heavy labor did not kill them then the shot-happy guards did.

Here *Sportmachen* meant having the inmates stand in the cold, singing '*Im Lager Auschwitz war ich zwar so manchen Monat so manches Jahr*'. The guards forced individuals to kneel, holding bricks in each hand above their heads. On the night of 5 October 1942, guards attacked a group of French Jewish women in the camp of Budy, killing 90 with rifle butts and axes.[17] At

25. Entry at Auschwitz proclaiming 'work gives freedom'.

Auschwitz Sergeant Moll selected 20 girls from each transport and shot them. A female guard, Irma Grese, picked out well-endowed Jewesses and beat them across the breasts until they collapsed. Robert Clary, a teenager from Paris, was sent to Blechhammer, a satellite camp of Auschwitz. There he encountered an SS guard nicknamed 'Tom Mix' who rode about on a bicycle, shooting Jewish prisoners:

> One day, this sadistic Tom Mix saw an inmate grab a useless piece of wire that was on the ground, to make a belt out of, because his pants were falling. He grabbed that inmate and two inmates standing next to him who had absolutely nothing to do with him and hit them. The Kapo who was responsible for the three inmates was a marvelous man from Belgium, went to that guard and said, 'What are you doing? It's a useless piece of wire.' He hit that Kapo, too. And these four people that same night when we came back to the camp were hanged. We had to stand two and one-half hours on roll call – not to steal anything, not to be caught stealing anything, not to stand next to someone stealing anything.[18]

MUSSELMÄNNER

Prisoners received grain coffee and two slices of ersatz bread in the morning. Lunch and supper was doled from 120-pound vats by red-kerchiefed cooks. The soup might contain turnips, kale, potato peels, macaroni, barley, millet or rye. The diet contributed to dysentery, which was rampant in the camps. Women believed the Nazis doctored their food with something that halted menstruation. The prisoners received less than an ounce of margarine or cheese each day and the little meat that was included came from old, steerly cattle. People who received 700 calories per day had to be on good terms with the soup distributors. Whether one's ration was scooped from the top or bottom of the barrel made the difference between slow starvation and survival.[19]

Everything was calculated to reduce inmates to the level of animals. Eugene Heimler, once a psychiatric social worker, wrote: 'Five of us ate off one plate. If one of the five took one bite more than his due, we flew at one another and then literally licked up the food that spilled on the floor. There were even some who killed in their hunger. I had known these people at home. Once they had been respectable, cultured citizens, members of charitable societies and select clubs.'[20] Said Leon Wells: 'If we could have died during the night! Again the cursed day. Oh God! What did we do to deserve this?'[21]

There was a name for victims who accepted death – *Musselmen*. According to Dr Wadyslaw Fejkiel, there was something different about their facial expressions (clouded eyes sunk deep in their sockets) and movements (slow and undirected). Their pale gray skin became paper thin and hard. Their hair was unkempt, matted and brittle and they were susceptible to scabies. Edema made breathing difficult. As body temperature lowered, the *Musselmen* developed tremors and lost interest in all activity about them. Curled up in their beds, in the final stages of starvation, Fejkiel said, 'they looked like praying Arabs'. Desire Haffner and Otto Wolken noted how men six feet tall shriveled up to 25–30 kilograms. Dr Robert Waitz of Monowitz confirmed that the first eight to ten days were critical in determining if one would survive. Eduard de Wind wrote: 'I saw young men waste away into a totally pathetic condition in a few days. A Dutch doctor sprained his ankle. He lay in bed and died after four days without showing any significant symptoms of illness. You could call it a form of suicide.'[22]

Sometimes death was not so peaceful. Janina Kowalczykowa told of a woman whose feet were gnawed by rats as she lay in her bunk. Some pathetic automatons stumbled to the electrified barriers to end their suffering. The sight of people 'touching wire' became so common, it aroused no emotion. As one survivor from Terezin recalled: 'Death ... lost its glory. It was grotesque, horrifying dying. We referred to it merely as ex.'

HUMAN GUINEA PIGS

SS doctors who killed German children and adults had few scruples about exterminating Jews. Peer pressure, belief in Nazi racial theories, and the recognition that ruthlessness led to promotions made it easier to participate in camp selections. Once an SS doctor compromised his ethics, subsequent *Selekzias* became automatic. Because the Jews were vermin, responsible for the war, doctors rationalized they could be used like rats in a laboratory. Prisoners were exposed to gangrene and frostbite to observe the effects of experimental drugs. In Dachau, Dr Kurt Schilling injected 2,000 prisoners with malaria bacteria and watched as they perished. In the same camp, Dr Sigmund Rascher dunked subjects in freezing water, hoping to develop techniques that would serve downed German airmen or sailors. Some inmates were forced to drink sea water. Dozens underwent high altitude experiments in pressure chambers where, unprotected, their eardrums ruptured. At Block 46 in Buchenwald, experiments were conducted on the storage of blood, the affects of yellow fever, smallpox, diphtheria, poison gas, phosphorous and incendiary bombs. Prisoners in Mauthausen were subjected to chlorine gassing, with and without masks. At Natzweiler, 30 women were blinded as Nazi doctors conducted experiments with leprosy, cholera and bubonic plague. In 1942, 115 inmates from Natzweiler were killed to accommodate Dr August Hirt's request for skulls of 'Bolsheviks'.[23]

Between 1943 and 1945, Dr Mengele frequented the sidings of Auschwitz-Birkenau, sending thousands to their deaths. When typhoid struck the camp in May 1943, he ordered the extermination of 1,600 Gypsies in a two-day period. To contain an outbreak of typhus, he had 600 women prisoners killed.

At the end of 1944, Mengele was in charge of 40,000 women subsisting on a ration of 600 calories in Birkenau. He arranged the gassing of all 40,000 over ten days in November. That same year, he approved the killing of 1,000 young boys who could not touch the top of a soccer goal.[24] A disciple of Ottmar von Verschuer of the Frankfurt Institute for Heredity, Mengele tried to alter the eye color of brown-eyed prisoners by injecting their irises with dye. Not surprisingly, many were blinded. Guards and kapos were instructed to pull *Zwillinge* (twins) from the ranks of incoming prisoners and take them to Mengele's clinic. After enduring painful procedures, these 'depot prisoners' were sent to the gas chambers to make way for new specimens.[25]

Nazi physicians violated the Hippocratic oath in other ways. Karl Clauberg and Horst Schumann sterilized hundreds of men and women in a single day by exposing their testicles or ovaries to X-rays for as long as eight minutes.[26] Dr Johann Kremer and a Polish assistant Wladislaw Dering performed surgical resections upon otherwise healthy prisoners without anesthesia.[27] In Auschwitz, Nazi doctors bled 700 young women from both arms in order to obtain plasma. Eyewitnesses described victims 'lying on the ground, faint, deep rivers of blood flowing around their bodies'.[28] Frida Weiss was deported to Auschwitz at Passover 1944. Two weeks later Frida and her sister became part of the Nazi blood-letting:

> I didn't know what they were taking me for. I had never given blood before. They had a whole laboratory with girls lined up. German nurses and doctors worked on me. They told my sister and me to lie down on tables. We were strapped down with both arms. They massaged both my arms, then they put needles in both arms and the blood started. They pumped blood out simultaneously from both arms. There were two bottles. That bottle was so guarded, no *Haftling* was around it. It was their property.[29]

SONDERBEHANDLUNG

In Auschwitz, death had a name – *Sonderbehandlung* (special treatment). The SS experimented with several means of execution (shooting, hand grenades, flame thrower, gassing with carbon monoxide). After 1942 the favored method was Zyklon B (hydrogen cyanide), a poison gas used to fumigate naval vessels. Experiments with 250 Russian prisoners and sick inmates in the fall of 1941 demonstrated that the white crystals evaporated quickly in rooms at 27 degrees centigrade. The first Jews from Upper Silesia were murdered in an underground bunker on 15 February 1942. Between 1941 and 1943, the use of Zyklon B in concentration camps was so widespread that the Degesch company (German Society for Pest Control) tripled its profits.

Himmler monitored the killing process at Auschwitz, beginning with the conversion of two farmhouses to gas chambers at the end of 1941. Polish and Slovak inmates worked day and night to transform a morgue into a third gas chamber the following year. Working with designs suggested by AEG, a German electrical firm, Fritz Kammler incorporated gas chamber and crematoria into death houses #4 and #5 near Birkenau in the summer of 1943. By this time, Auschwitz could 'process' 5,000 people each day.[30] After undressing, they entered a larger room with concrete walls (about 600 square feet) with shower heads protruding from the ceiling. Commandant Hoess claimed that 3,000 people could be squeezed into this second room. Then, with the air-tight door closed and locked, gas was pumped in like a spray. Said Hoess:

> It was possible to see through the peephole in the door that the persons nearest the intakes fell dead immediately. Nearly one third died at once. Others would mill around, shout and gasp for air. But soon the shouting would give place to a death-rattle and a few minutes later all were prone. After twenty minutes there was hardly a stir from anybody. The effect of the gas showed in five to ten minutes. Those shouting, the old, the sick, the weak and the children fell quicker than the healthy and young.[31]

The procedure was quick and, arguably, efficient. Once the gas chamber was vented, teams of prisoner *Sonderkommandos* removed the dead. This was a particularly grisly task as the victims, seeking air, had formed a tangled pyramid. Some were foaming at the mouth, others bleeding from noses. There was excrement and urine everywhere. Occasionally, the *Sonderkommando* found a child or adult who survived. The person would be included with the next batch to be gassed.[32] As the *Sonderkommandos* worked, they noted fingernail marks cut in the concrete walls.

Disposal of bodies was always a problem. The SS tried burial but when decomposing corpses polluted the water table around Auschwitz and even bubbled back to the surface, Himmler ordered the burning of bodies. Large trenches were dug and petroleum dumped on the corpses. But this, too, proved to be demoralizing and inadequate. (There were cases when men assigned to the *Sonderkommando* discovered bodies of their loved ones at the pits later the same day.) The firm of J.A. Topf and Sons from Erfurt built the five crematoria or 'Bakeries'. By means of hooks, carts and elevators, the dead were moved upstairs to the retorts. Forty inmates scrutinized their teeth for gold before they were consigned to the flames. The burning corpses supplied energy to operate the gas chambers. The ashes produced from burning (more than 100 tons) were sold to various agricultural firms as fertilizer.[33]

When the Red Army overran the camp in February 1945 they discovered 18 inches of human fat in one of the chimneys. The Poles estimated the death count in Auschwitz at close to four million, two million of them Jews. Franticek Piper and Yehuda Bauer estimate the number slain in Auschwitz at between 1.1 and 1.5 million. According to Bauer these include 83,010 Polish victims (3,665 gassed, 79,345 murdered in the camp); 11,685 Russians who were gassed; 20,000 Gypsies (6,430 gassed, 13,825 who died in the camp);

and 1,323,000 Jews who were murdered by gassing and 29,980 who died in the camp.[34]

RESISTANCE IN AUSCHWITZ

There were frequent attempts to escape from Auschwitz and its satellite camps,[35] culminating in April 1944 with the delivery of the so-called 'Auschwitz Protocol', an exposé of Nazi genocide by Alfred Wetzler and Walter Rosenberg (aka Rudolf Vrba). Those who could not flee offered defiance, even in their last moments. Efraim Stiebelmann told how during a selection of Jews from Lodz, a mother refused to be separated from her 13-year-old daughter. When Mengele intervened, the woman bit and scratched him. The Nazi doctor shot both of them and ordered the entire transport gassed, cursing, '*Weg mit der Scheisse!*' (Away with the shit!)[36] In February 1944, 41 Poles were sent to Crematorium IV. From their midst, stepped a young woman. Facing the SS guards, she cried that the world knew of their crimes and promised that they would be punished. As her group entered the gas chambers, they shouted 'Poland is not yet lost!' and 'To the barricades!'[37] A 12-year-old boy from Kaunas counseled 30 comrades as they were about to be gassed: 'Don't cry, children! Be brave! You have seen how your mothers and fathers were murdered. Do not have fear of death! Today we go to our deaths, but we are sure that they too will bite the dust.'[38] In October 1943, a group of Polish-Jewish women were returned to Auschwitz from Belsen. Holding passports to Latin American countries, they thought they were going to be liberated. Instead they were taken to Crematoria II and III where they were ordered to undress. One woman attacked an SS sergeant, grabbed his pistol and shot him three times. Others joined the melee, scratching and biting the guards. Reinforcements drove them into the gas chambers.[39]

One who gave his life for another was Maximilian Kolbe, a 47-year-old priest from the Lodz area. An anti-Semite before the war, he opened his monastery to Jewish refugees and was imprisoned in Auschwitz in February 1941. Six months later, following an escape, *Standartenführer* Frisch selected ten men to die of starvation in an underground 'hunger bunker'. Two days into the punishment Father Kolbe volunteered to replace Francizek Gajowniczek, a Pole with a family and children. After several days, Kolbe and three of his comrades were given lethal injections. The 82-year-old Gajowniczek was among 150,000 persons in Rome when Pope John Paul II canonized Kolbe in October 1981.[40]

Ultimately resistance in Auschwitz came to mean a full-fledged rebellion by members of the *Sonderkommando*. Informed that they were about to be snuffed out, 663 members of the death squads (many of them deportees from Greece) attacked their guards on 7 October 1944. Using hammers, axes and homemade knives, the men managed to kill three SS men and tear up part of the fence around Birkenau. They succeeded in blowing up two crematoria. Crematorium IV was permanently disabled, but the killing process continued. There were 250 *Sonderkommandos* killed in the uprising, 200 more were gassed along with 2,000 men, women and children from Trieste and Terezin and 2,000 unregistered female Jews.[41]

DEATH MARCHES AND DEATH PITS

When the camps in Poland were abandoned, some survivors were taken back to Germany. In January 1945 Robert Clary was evacuated with 4,000 others from Blechhammer. 'We walked 15 days and nights. I was with two friends in front of the line, so we wouldn't see what was happening. There was an order to kill anyone if they sat on the road.'[42] Three weeks later 1,200 survivors straggled into Buchenwald. About the same time Bill Vegh left Platling with 400 inmates. Lacking food, the prisoners picked from garbage along the way. Bill walked with two teenaged brothers. After eight days, the younger boy collapsed. An SS guard told the older brother to move on. 'A few seconds later, I heard a shot and I knew that his troubles were over. You should have seen his little brother crying. He could not help himself. If he hadn't left his brother, he would have been shot too.'[43]

Inmates from Gross Rosen, Helmbrechts and Dachau were shuttled back and forth on rail lines that were supposed to take them to a Nazi 'redoubt' in Bavaria.[44] Thousands died on death marches. The trip from Flossenburg to Regensburg 80 miles south zigzagged 250 miles. Jewish inmates of Beerga covered 170 miles before they reached the town of Plauen just 40 miles away. Of 12,000 prisoners who set out from Ohrdruf at the end of March, 74 reached their destination. On 6 April, 3,000 Jews were shot in several large pits outside Buchenwald. A week later, prisoners from camp Dora were taken to Gardelegen, a town just north of Magdeburg. The weary band was forced into the Isenschnibbe barn. SS men and units of the *Volksturm* then sealed all doors of the brick building and set it afire. The Nazis pounded the building with hand grenades and machine-gun fire. Soldiers of the American 102nd Infantry Division counted 1,016 victims when they entered Gardelegen on 14 April.[45] The next day, 300 prisoners were murdered in Thekla, a small camp near Leipzig. Sixty of them were lured into a barrack with the promise of soup. Once more, the SS sealed the building, then set it afire. The Americans took photos of what appeared to be blackened topiary figures and what in reality were the scorched, still smoking bodies of humans.

When units of the Third Armored Division entered Nordhausen-Dora, they found deportees of every nationality draped in rags, suffering from typhus and tuberculosis, dying on the campgrounds. 'Only a handful could stand on rickety, pipestem legs ... their eyes were sunk deeply into their skulls and their skins under thick dirt were a ghastly yellow. Some sobbed great dry sobs to see the Americans.'[46] Thirty thousand were dead, another 2,000 lay unburied in the tunnels of Dora. General Patton was physically sickened after visiting one of the compounds at Ohrdruf. Gene Barnett, a soldier from Barberton, Ohio summed up the mixed emotions of liberation:

> A man, I would say he was in his late thirties, walked up to me and looked me in the eye. I was trying to speak my poor Yiddish. What do you learn in Barberton, Ohio? A little smattering. My parents didn't want me to know. What are you going to tell this guy? What my parents didn't want me to know? So I tried to explain to him and he heard me mumbling this Yiddish of mine and he asked a question: *Du bist a yid* [are you a Jew]? Well, I knew what that meant. When he said it to me, I said to him as we have that prerogative, 'Du bist a yid?' And he said, 'I am a Yid.' With that, I hugged and I kissed and I cried because I had found a Jew. He insisted that he take me on to show me some more Jews. And God in his infinite wisdom – I don't know if he did right or wrong – but they took me to a three-car garage which had two wooden doors, a wooden arm that came down on a hasp, and he said, 'I'm going to show you Jews.' And with that, he told me to lift up this wooden bar, but to run back. When I lifted up the bar – it took three of us to push it up because it was locked against the hasp – we pushed it up and ran back. Because out fell upon me *bones*. You know in Ezekiel 37 it says, 'dry bones, dry bones.' Well, these were not only dry bones – these were dry bones, wet bones, partly with sinew, and partly with flesh. And I ran back and kissed my newfound buddy. And I said, 'by the grace of God and the foresight of my grandfather these bones could have been mine and my brothers.'[47]

MORAL DILEMMAS

Everyone who walked through the gates of Auschwitz had to choose between maintaining a spark of decency or sinking into barbarism. There were 6,000 guards in Auschwitz, fewer than 1,000 of whom have been identified.[48] These men patrolled the perimeters of the camp and unleashed attack dogs against prisoners. Some unloaded cattle cars and supervised labor details. They were responsible for ridiculing the inmates, depriving them of basic medical care, forcing people into gas chambers. Yet every night they returned to their barracks or homes outside the camps. They joked and sang, ate and drank. Officers employed prisoners as nannies for their children.[49] The men of the SS made love, petted dogs, and exchanged Christmas presents while human beings were turned into sewers, then murdered. Like the doctors in the camp, they had sworn vows of loyalty to Adolf Hitler and were convinced they were dealing with subhumans.

Those individuals dubbed Kapos viewed their appointments as a mixed blessing.[50] Esther Bittman recalls one named Laura, a woman in her 40s who carried a baton and struck prisoners for the slightest pretext. If somebody reported late to Appel or stole a potato they were given 25 lashes. If a girl did not clean latrines properly, 'she made them eat human waste'.[51] Jim Elder owed his survival to an Austrian who picked him to clean the barracks. Bill Vegh was protected in Barrack 13 of Auschwitz by a Jewish Kapo who told him to volunteer for transfer to any work camp. In Buchenwald Robert Clary was helped by a Frenchman Yves Darriet and a Czech Jiri Zak. Gypsies viewed their positions as a form of societal leveling.[52] One thousand Hungarian Jewish children under Gypsy Kapos in Auschwitz, were spared temporarily for entertainment and medical experiments.

Those experiments have generated serious ethical debates.[53] The methodology was unscientific, cruel. Information obtained was unreliable, inaccurate, even irrelevant. Twenty years ago, Robert Pozos, a physician in Minnesota, applied techniques developed by Sigmund Rascher in treating hypothermia. Ethicists denounced Pozos and demanded that such information be rejected. Survivors urged that details of Nazi experiments be restricted, if not permanently censored. Some physicians equivocated, noting that such information, however improperly obtained, might give meaning to those who had been slain. Dr Velvl Greene, an epidemiologist from Ben Gurion University said, 'In Jewish life, the sanctity of human life is the first principle. In matters of life and death it is not permitted to suppress information if it is already available.'[54]

One key member in the killing process was tormented by his role and tried to do something about it. Kurt Gerstein joined the Nazi party to bear witness against the regime. (His sister-in-law was gassed at Hadamar during the T-4 program.) In the summer of 1942, Gerstein was instructed by Globocnik to deliver a cargo of Zyklon B to a 'prisoner of war' camp in Poland. One hundred kilos of prussic acid were to be used for disinfecting clothing in Belzec. Instead, Gerstein and August Wirths watched as 6,000 Jews from Lemberg were gassed. When he returned from Belzec, Gerstein tried to contact the Papal Nuncio, and was turned away. He passed reports along to the Dutch underground, to Cardinal Preysing, Archbishop of Berlin, and Baron Gorran von Otter of the Swedish Embassy, but none of these messages was made public until after the war. Instead of resigning his post, Gerstein told his father, 'I never lent a hand in any of this. Whenever I received orders, I not only didn't carry them out but saw to it that they were disobeyed. I did it from principle and a sense of decency.'[55]

For Jews, the horrific experience created a debate over the existence of God. Simon Wiesenthal had a friend in Mauthausen. 'Arthur', a cynic had a response to those who wondered how a merciful God could permit such misery. 'Where is God?' he asked. Answering his own question, he declared, 'God is on vacation.' Arthur died in Wiesenthal's arms during a typhus epidemic.[56] Martin Buber talked of 'the eclipse of God'. Speaking for the Orthodox, Eliezer Berkowitz said, 'We must believe, because our brother Job believed.' Berkowitz offered no answer for the cruelties of Auschwitz because there were none. Better than asking 'Where was God?' he asked, 'Where was man?' This stolidity is echoed by Elie Wiesel who has written 'where God is concerned all is mystery'[57] and Emil Fackenheim who says that a 'commanding Voice' is heard from Auschwitz issuing a 614th commandment: 'Jews are forbidden to grant posthumous victories to Hitler.' Perhaps the most disturbing assessment came from Rabbi Richard Rubenstein who in 1966 suggested that God had perished in Auschwitz. Rubenstein was restating what has become a widespread view that God is neither watchful nor interactive. Traditional theology rationalized attacks against Jews somehow as punishment for sin or suggested that God operated with a different level of intelligence or purpose. Said Rubenstein, 'I fail to see how this position can be maintained without regarding Hitler and the SS as instruments of God's will. To see any purpose in the death camps, the traditional believer is forced to regard the most demonic, anti-human explosion in all history as a meaningful expression of God's purposes. The idea is simply too obscene for me to accept.'[58] For Rubenstein, the message of Auschwitz is clear. Writing in *The Cunning of History*, he warned that modern technology combined with a politicized bureaucracy made the Holocaust possible. This time the Jews were the victims of mass murder. The next time it could be anyone.

31

Punishing the Guilty

Nazi Germany surrendered on 7 May 1945. Meeting at Potsdam two months later, Stalin, Truman and Attlee affirmed the Allies would deal with the legacy of a decade of horror. War crimes would be prosecuted for the salutary affect they would have upon Europe. Not everyone agreed. In November 1945, 30 prominent Germans, including Cardinal Faulhaber, Wilhelm Hoegner in Bavaria, and Professors Alfred and Marianna Weber of Heidelberg questioned the wisdom of 'retroactive' punishment.[1] Ohio Senator Robert Taft agreed that such trials violated the *ex post facto* clause of the US Constitution. Speaking at Kenyon College, Taft argued that such procedures amounted to victors punishing the vanquished. By cloaking vengeance in legal procedure, Taft worried that America would discredit the idea of justice for years to come.[2]

Taft's speech drew rebuke from Herbert Lehman, Claude Pepper, Thomas Dewey and Jacob Javits, and Willis Smith, President of the American Bar Association. John Parker, an alternate jurist at Nuremberg, noted: 'Things that were done violated the fundamental laws of human nature, the laws against murder and robbery and enslavement which have been universally recognized as crimes from time immemorial.'[3] Germany had sworn to resolve disputes peaceably at Locarno, then renounced offensive warfare by signing the Kellogg–Briand pact. The Hague Convention of 1907, the Geneva Protocol of 1925 and the Geneva Convention of 1929 required respect for rights of property. International law forbade execution of hostages, deportation of civilians, forced labor or impressment into military service. As Article 46 of the Hague Convention declared: 'the honor and the rights of the family, the life of individuals, private property, as well as religious beliefs and the practice thereof must be respected.'[4]

In view of atrocities perpetrated at Warsaw, Maly Trostinec, Treblinka, Jasenovac, Lidice and Apeldoorn, the question was not should there be war crimes trials, but who should be prosecuted and how were they to be punished. John Simon, legal advisor to Churchill and Eden, raised the issue in the summer of 1942. Simon spoke of punishing 'ringleaders or actual perpetrators' of crimes committed against Allied nationals. (There was no mention of stateless persons such as Jews.)[5] One hundred Axis leaders would

26. Warsaw. The Rapoport memorial to Jewish resistance
in the heart of the ghetto.

be labeled 'world outlaws' and executed within six hours of their capture. After weeks of haggling, British officials could agree to only five names (Hitler, Himmler, Goering, Goebbels and Ribbentrop). Any list without Japanese names was unacceptable to the Americans. The Russians could not have cared less about the Pacific, but wanted Hess and Wehrmacht generals charged.[6]

In March 1943, Roosevelt announced the creation of the UN War Crimes Commission. The Allies promised to track the masterminds of genocide and 'the little men' who committed atrocities 'to the uttermost ends of the earth'.[7] Yet when the UNWCC held its first session in London, the Soviets did not attend. Instead, Russia executed three German soldiers and a collaborator after a three-day trial in Kharkov.[8] Obstructed by their respective governments which refused to release documents for 'security reasons', America's delegate Herbert Pell and UNWCC Chair Sir Cecil Hurst would resign from the UN Commission within a year.

Whenever it attempted to draw up lists of war criminals, the UNWCC received conflicting signals. At Teheran, Stalin challenged the Allies to pursue 'at least 50,000 of them'. US War Department handbooks for the occupation of Germany mentioned 250,000 officials who were to be arrested. The lists did not include members of the SS or Wehrmacht, millions who voted for Hitler, or east European fascists, perhaps 13 million people in the US zone. The Russians put 500,000 persons into stockades and executed more than 100,000 before the end of 1946. Meanwhile, the UNWCC in London came up with names of 184 major war criminals in the summer of 1944. Ultimately the list would grow to 25,000.[9]

On 5 September 1945, the Allies agreed to form an International Military Tribunal (IMT) composed of judges from the four major powers. Sitting in Nuremberg, the IMT would try persons accused of: crimes against the peace (violation of treaties); war crimes (mistreatment of prisoners of war and civilians); and crimes against humanity (deportation, enslavement, murder and extermination).[10] A fourth count, conspiracy to commit crimes against the peace, would be added. Twenty-one Nazi leaders were brought to trial in the fall of 1945. They included Hermann Goering, Rudolf Hess, Joachim Ribbentrop, Ernst Kaltenbrunner, Alfred Rosenberg, Hans Frank, Hans Fritsche, Walther Funk, Baldur von Schirach, Albert Speer, Artur Seyss-Inquart, Julius Streicher, Wilhelm Keitel, Alfred Jodl, Karl Doenitz, Erich Raeder, Fritz Sauckel, Wilhelm Frick, Hjalmar Schacht, Constantin von Neurath and Franz von Papen. Martin Bormann was tried in absentia. Adolf Hitler, Heinrich Himmler and Joseph Goebbels were all dead, killed by their own hands in the last days of the war.

Witness after witness offered testimony of acts of inhumanity. Samples of tattooed human skin and shrunken skulls were displayed as evidence. Newsreels showed the methodical reduction of the Warsaw Ghetto. As the trial droned on, certain defenses emerged. Like the general public, none of the accused (not even Goering, source of the July 1941 Final Solution order) had knowledge of genocide. Most were sympathetic toward Jews and co-operated with Zionists in arranging emigration. The British and French encouraged Hitler by appeasing him. The Russians enabled him to make war by signing the Molotov–Ribbentrop pact and perpetrated their own atrocities. The men in the dock were loyal officials or soldiers, following orders issued by the real architects of war and genocide – Himmler, Bormann, Heydrich, Eichmann, Mueller, and above all, Adolf Hitler.

Obedience to authority would be the refuge of 185 Germans indicted in cases involving the Einsatzgruppen, I.G. Farben and Krupp, the Nazi judiciary, Oswald Pohl and the concentration camp bureaucracy, industrialists of the Flick combine, medical doctors, the RSHA, German diplomats and generals on the southeast front and Russia. The defense would have little merit. Nine of the principal Nazi war lords tried at Nuremberg were hanged. (Goering committed suicide shortly before the executions.) Twenty-five of those in the second group were also executed, 20 were sentenced to life in prison, 97 to terms of up to 25 years.[11]

END OF DENAZIFICATION

In a country where 92 percent of the schoolteachers, 60 percent of the police and 800 judges and prosecutors had been members of the Nazi party, denazification was supposed to last ten years. In the US zone, 72 percent of those chargeable were amnestied without trial. Of 955,000 who had hearings,

320,000 were exonerated. By January 1951, fewer than 50 convicted Nazis remained in prison.[12] There were several explanations for this uneven prosecution. Some of the victorious troops in the West found the Germans amiable, industrious people. It made little sense to 'persecute' them for past mistakes. Some military personnel were poorly trained, unwilling to investigate incidents in Russian territory. In the Cold War, America needed Germany. Gene Bramel of Army Intelligence declared, 'It would have been impossible for us to operate in southern Germany without using Nazis. We were Americans. I spoke pretty good German, but by the time I got through ordering dinner they would have suspected I was American. And who knew Germany better than anyone else? Who were the most organized? Who were the most anti-communist? Former Nazis. Not to use them would mean complete emasculation. And we used them, the British used them, the French used them, and the Russians used them.' The Russian threat prompted one of the judges in the I.G. Farben case to tell Josiah Dubois, 'We have to worry about the Russians now; it wouldn't surprise me if they overran the courtroom before we get through.' When communist troops attacked across the 38th parallel in June 1950, Farben executive Ter Meer walked out of jail, gloating, 'Now that they have Korea on their hands, the Americans are a lot more friendly.'[13]

ODESSA

The new arrangement benefited the old Nazis. A number were deemed too frail to undergo prosecution. Many were rehabilitated. Werner Best, sentenced to death by Denmark, became legal advisor to the Hugo Stinnes trust in the Ruhr. Franz Six, liquidation officer in Smolensk, became advertising manager for Porsche-Diesel. Rudolf Bilgner, assistant to Eichmann, was counselor to the administrative court in Mannheim. Johannnes Thummler, Gestapo chief in Katowice, became an executive of the Carl Zeiss Foundation. Hermann Raschhofer, an aide to Hans Frank, taught international law at Wurzburg University. Franz Nusstein, hanging judge in Prague, was named Consul-General in Barcelona. Heinz Lammerding, commander of the SS division that perpetrated the massacre of Oradour, became an engineer-contractor in Dusseldorf.[14]

Lammerding was a leader of HIAG (*Hilfe und Interessengewanschaft der Angehorigen der Waffen SS*). Like the *Brudershaft* of General von Manteufel, *Stille Hilfe* (Silent Help Society), *Kameradschaft* in Austria, HINAG in Holland, *Dansk Frontkampfer Forbindet* (Denmark) and the St Martin Fund (Belgium), HIAG was a brotherhood of former SS. These groups held reunions aimed at promoting their image as noble soldiers. They offered aid to families in need. They also were part of ODESSA,

Organization der ehemaligen SS Angehorigen (Association of former SS members), the network of inveterate Nazis headed by Otto Skorzeny until his death in 1975.[15]

ODESSA's origins may be traced to the summer of 1943 when Juan Peron seized power in Argentina. German nationals offered cash to Peron in exchange for 7,000 passports that would be needed in case Germany lost the war.[16] During the collapse of 1945, Nazis fled Germany using a complex system known as *Die Schleusse* (the Locks). Airplanes out of Madrid, submarines from the Baltic, carried them to Argentina. With the assistance of Franciscan monks, CARITAS (Catholic relief) and Bishop Hudal of Rome, Nazis moved through the Allgau to Rome, Genoa or Naples. Over 2,500 persons utilized the *Vatikanissiche Hilfslinie* between 1947 and 1953.[17]

Among the Nazis who eluded capture: Gestapo chief Heinrich Mueller, rumored to be in Central America or the USSR; Richard Baer, Hoess's successor at Auschwitz; Walther Rauff, inventor of the gas vans; Harst Schumann and Karl Babor, physicians whose experiments inspired Leon Uris's novel *QB VII*; Johannes von Leers, Goebbels's number two man in the Ministry of Propaganda, who fled to Egypt where he was known as Amin Omar von Leers. A number of ex-Nazis found a new faith in Egypt, including General Dirlewanger (renamed Hassan Souleman); Leopold Gleim (Naam el Nahar), one-time Gestapo chief in Warsaw, and Heinrich Sellmann (Hamide Souleiman), Gestapo chief in Ulm. Paul Gorke, Rolf Engel and Wolfgang Pilz worked on rockets that were supposed to rain nuclear waste over Israel.

The Middle East harbors the most notorious war criminal from World War II. Alois Brunner lives in a villa near the port of Latakia protected by Syrian police. It was Brunner who shipped 47,000 Austrian Jews to Terezin and Riga in 1942. He assisted Wisliceny in clearing Salonika in 1943. He was commandant of Drancy at the time of the largest deportations from Paris. He helped sweep the Riviera when the Italian zone was occupied in 1943. The following year, Brunner shipped 14,000 Slovakian Jews to Auschwitz. SS *Hauptsturmführer* Brunner was responsible for the deaths of more than 100,000 Jews and 60,000 non-Jews. Warrants for his arrest had been issued by West Germany, Austria, Czechoslovakia, Greece and Israel.

In 1954, Alois Brunner entered Syria under the name of Georg Fischer. Until his death, Syria's President Hafez al-Assad rejected inquiries about Brunner, saying, 'I know nothing about the man and this is not a productive line of questioning.' In fact, for many years, Brunner served as advisor to the various cliques who ruled Syria. Separate letter bomb incidents cost him two fingers and the sight of one eye. Over 80 years old as of this writing, Brunner lives off a small Syrian government stipend and complains that 'the Federal Republic owes me a lot for my pension'. In 1987, Eichmann's 'craftsman' told Charles Ashman and Robert Wagman, 'They [the Jews] deserved to die and I would do it all over again because they were human garbage.'[18]

THE CASE OF JOSEF MENGELE

Like many Nazis, Brunner managed to escape at the end of the war by doffing his uniform and mixing with troops captured by the Allies. Hermann Krumey, a member of Eichmann's staff, went home to manage a drugstore. Wilhelm Koppe, a higher SS leader in Poland, was serving as director of a chocolate factory in Bonn when he was arrested in 1960. The West Germans and Allies share responsibility, however, for the escape of the man who was for many years the world's most wanted war criminal. That dubious distinction went to Josef Mengele, the 'Angel of Death' from Auschwitz.

A member of a wealthy family that produces farm equipment in Bavaria, Mengele joined the Nazi party at the age of 18. He earned a Ph.D. in anthropology, then a medical degree from the University of Munich in 1936. In June 1940, he was posted to the Race and Resettlement Office. Between 1943 and 1945, Mengele served at Auschwitz where he may have sent 500,000 persons to their deaths. He returned to Germany in January 1945 carrying notes on genetics experiments. Five months later, he was taken into custody by British forces. Since their prisoner had no tattoo like other members of the SS (and the British lacked a copy of the Allied watch list) he was released. In 1948, Mengele's father arranged for his son to go to Buenos Aires. Upon arriving in Argentina, Joseph requested a German passport in his own name. He opened a pharmaceutical firm and was untroubled for the next decade.

That tranquility was shaken by the kidnapping of Adolf Eichmann. This Nazi had lived under the assumed name Ricardo Klement in a Buenos Aires suburb. Believing that the Argentines would not approve extradition, the Israelis sent a team of Mossad agents to Buenos Aires. In May 1960 they swooped down on Eichmann as he returned from work.[19] The subsequent publicity prompted Mengele to flee to Paraguay. German and Israeli authorities believed he spent the next 30 years among German colonists in the fascist state. Mengele was rumored to have visited Cairo in 1961, his wife and son after that. German police may have unwittingly tipped off Mengele's family as the Israelis were close to seizing him in 1964.

Mengele's family declared him dead on four occasions as the bounty for his capture reached $5 million. In fact, he was living in Sao Paulo, Brazil until he allegedly drowned in 1979.[20] In 1985, the family permitted forensics experts to exhume a corpse which they claimed was Josef's. It was evident there were numerous discrepancies between the body and known facts about Mengele. The body was an inch taller than Mengele. There was no evidence of ostyeomylitis, hip or leg deformity. There were differences between teeth, ears, and fingers on his left hand. Death had also come in a curious way for a 66-year-old man who was not fond of swimming. At the time, Simon Wiesenthal disputed whether the body, described as 'Caucasoid', was Mengele's. For members of CANDLES (Children of Auschwitz Nazi Deadly Laboratory Experiments Survivors), the twins abused by this man, Mengele may never die. He is the bogeyman who governs their thoughts and haunts their dreams.

At the end of World War II, the Allies established a Central Registry of War Crimes and Security Suspects (CROWCASS) in Obereursel. As of 1988, 91,160 investigations yielded 6,482 convictions. The average sentence was eight years and actual time served less than four years; 75 percent of these prosecutions took place when German courts were still under Allied supervision. No central tracking unit was established in West Germany until 1956, none in Austria until 1963. As Hannah Vogt noted, Germans regarded the Holocaust as 'a small error' that would be forgotten in a few years.[21]

Pressed by the Allies to do the work they would not do, Germany created a *Zentrallstelle* for war crimes in 1956. By 1965, the *Zentrallstelle* accumulated the names of 170,000 suspects. There was outrage when one, Erwin Schule, accused of participating in a massacre at Zhitomir, turned out to be the head of the *Zentrallstelle*. (Schule resigned.) After much discussion in 1964, the statute of limitations on war crimes was extended to September 1969, again till 1979. That year, NBC's docudrama 'Holocaust: The Story of the Family Weiss' convinced lawmakers to extend the statute indefinitely. Observers criticized punishments meted out by German juries. Adolf Petsch, Waffen SS officer in Stolin and Pinsk where 9,000 Jews were murdered, was sentenced to 15 years in jail. Ludwig Hahn, Gestapo chief of Warsaw also was sentenced to 15 years. It took eight years and three trials before Eichmann's aide Franz Novak was sentenced to nine years in prison. He served six. Novak secured transport for 1.7 million people exterminated in concentration camps. His sentence came to 20 seconds per victim.[22] The writer Robert Neumann refused to return from exile because, 'too many criminals are walking the streets free in the German Federal Republic'.[23]

The new Germany would not countenance capital punishment and made it practically impossible to convict anyone for the crime of murder. To establish murder (as opposed to manslaughter) prosecutors had to show 'cruelty, iniquity, lust for murder and base motives'. Proof of cruelty existed if 'the perpetrator ... had imposed special pain or torture on the victims out of a mentality entirely devoid of feeling or mercy'.[24] In 1983, the US asked the Germans to accept jurisdiction over Bohdan Koziy, a Ukrainian who served as a policeman with the Nazis. Eye-witnesses from Lisets testified how they saw Koziy drag a Jewish child across the town square in the fall of 1943. Said one, 'With his right hand he held either the neck or the hair: from the back I did not see exactly. She was [Monica Zinger] the daughter of the Jewish doctor Zinger. She was three or four years old. She was dressed in a coat, without a head cover. The girl was crying and saying in Polish, "Mother he is taking me to kill me. I want to live."' Another witness added, 'I saw that he carried the child into the yard and put her next to the foundation of the police station, not far from the well. The girl was saying something to him in Polish, but I was too far away to hear her words; she was surely pleading with him to spare her. He put her down, stepped back several paces, drew his pistol, and killed her with two shots.'[25] The Americans also claimed Koziy had murdered members of another Jewish family.

While conceding Koziy participated in the two incidents, the German Foreign Ministry noted that 'the witnesses' statements do not make any reference ... [as] to what motives may have formed the basis for his actions. They are limited to this extent to solely their optical and acoustical impressions gained during the process of the shootings as such.'[26] In other words, the Germans claimed the eyewitnesses could not say what was going through Koziy's mind when he was killing these people. Since there was no evidence of 'cruelty' or 'base motive', West Germany refused to issue a warrant. As US officials wondered what to do with this quiet old man who ran a motel in Boca Raton, Koziy and his wife fled to Costa Rica, where they took up residence in a large hacienda 15 miles west of San José.[27]

OLD NAZIS IN AMERICA: THE CASE OF ARTHUR RUDOLPH

If Bohdan Koziy illustrated the failure of German justice, then Arthur Rudolph symbolizes what was wrong in America. Between 1951 and 1960, Rudolph worked at the Redstone Arsenal, helping to launch America's first satellite into space. Later, he headed the Pershing missile program and served as chief engineer for the Saturn 5 booster that sent Apollo astronauts to the moon. For these efforts, Rudolph received NASA's highest award, the Distinguished Service Medal. He became an American citizen in 1954. To his neighbors and colleagues he was a good friend. Yet in 1984, the Office of Special Investigation of the US Immigration and Naturalization Service forced Rudolph to renounce his citizenship and leave the US.

The facts are that Arthur Rudolph joined the Nazi party in Germany in 1931, five years before the date (1936) utilized to identify active Nazis. Rudolph remembered those pre-war years as 'really marvelous ... the best years in Germany'. In September 1943, Rudolph was assigned to the V-2 rocket project in the Harz mountains. By shifting their base 250 miles south of Peenemunde, the Nazis hoped to avoid Allied bombers. Sixty thousand inmates from Buchenwald cleared 46 underground tunnels with their bare hands and pickaxes. One hundred men died each day of beatings, exposure and starvation. When the Allies liberated camp Dora, they found 30,000 dead stacked in tunnels. All deaths were reported by the SS to General Walter Dornberger, Werner von Braun, camp production director Georg Rickhey and Rickhey's deputy – Arthur Rudolph.[28]

To his death in 1996 Rudolph insisted he had done no wrong, that the dead were victims of Allied 'smart bombs'. Back in 1945–46, the Allies accepted no excuses from administrators who worked slaves to death. Rudolph's former boss, Rickhey was returned to Germany and tried as a war criminal. When US forces ran a background check on Rudolph in June 1945, they noted '100 percent Nazi, dangerous type, security threat ... suggest internment'. Nine months later, that evaluation was toned down to 'not a war criminal, but an ardent Nazi'. Because Rudolph's knowledge of rocketry was deemed valuable, another evaluation was prepared, this one stating 'nothing in his records indicated he was a war criminal, an ardent Nazi, or otherwise objectionable'.

How had this metamorphosis occurred? In 1945, President Truman authorized 'Operation Paperclip', providing for the admission of Nazi scientists. Both the West and Soviets appreciated that the Germans were ahead in the development of space weaponry. Truman stipulated, however, that no member of the Nazi party or active supporter of Nazism should be brought to the United States. Colonel Walter Rozamus was Deputy Director of the Pentagon office responsible for implementing Paper Clip. He later admitted telling subordinates to delete references to Nazi associations. Said Rozamus: 'I felt by changing a sentence or two and to get these people and their knowledge over here, that we could use to our benefit, I think that's a smart way to do it. Change a sentence or two. That's all it takes.'[29]

Rudolph was one of 642 rocket scientists who entered the United States between 1945 and 1952 under Paper Clip. Among the others were General Dornberger, who overnight was transformed from 'a menace to security' to 'not an ardent Nazi'; Herbert Wagner, chief of the V-2 works at Nordhausen; Werner von Braun, who held the rank of colonel in the SS; and Walter Schreiber, who conducted experiments upon inmates at Dachau and who later headed America's School of Aviation Medicine at Randolph Field in San Antonio. Paper Clip was just one of several programs designed to benefit American security.[30] 'Operation Pajamas' excused Nazi economists and east European analysts, 'Project Dwindle' Nazi cryptographers. 'Apple Pie' admitted officials from the Reichs Security Office and 'Project Pan Handle' called upon the anti-Soviet intelligence networks established by the Abwehr.[31]

OSI AND THE CASE OF JOHN DEMJANJUK

Anxious to alleviate the suffering of Europe's displaced persons, the US passed the Stratton Act of 1947 providing for the admission of 400,000 refugees. A second Refugee Relief Act in 1953 settled 214,000 aliens. Unfortunately, these laws benefited many people against whom the US had been fighting. Forty percent of the visas authorized by the Stratton Act were reserved for persons living beyond the Curzon Line who were in jeopardy under Soviet rule. Thirty percent were reserved for 'proven agriculturalists'.

Of the 339,698 visas issued under the Stratton Bill 2,500 went to Jews. Most of the others went to Germans (54,000 *Volksdeutsch* admitted between 1950 and 1952), Hungarians, Poles, and Balts, many of whom were as anti-Semitic as they were anti-communist. In 1949 Congress also permitted the CIA to bring in 100 individuals each year, if they were deemed essential to national security. Understaffed and overworked officials skimmed applications from persons who slipped by on guile, lies and assistance from their kinsmen.

It was not until 1973 that the immigration service established a bureau to deal with the problem of war criminals. Renamed the Office of Special Investigations (OSI) in 1977, it was transferred to the Criminal Division of the Justice Department in 1979. The OSI soon discovered a pattern of insensitivity and dereliction of duty. Among those granted sanctuary in the United States were Andrija Artukovic, the Croatian Minister of Interior; Dr Hubertus Strughold, superintendent of American space medicine, suspected of having participated in freezing, typhus and mustard gas experiments at Dachau and Natzweiler; Gustav Hilger, Ribbentrop's aide who in 1944 approved the deportation of Jews from Trieste and other regions of Italy; Vincent Brizgys, auxiliary bishop of Kaunas, who forbade any assistance to Jews when they were being massacred in 1941; Boleslaw Maikowskis, who as chief of police in Reshnitza Latvia supervised the killing of 15,000 Jews and Gypsies; Wladimir Osidach and Miroslav Stassiw, Ukrainian police who murdered 14,000 Jews in Rawa Ruska; Edgars Laipineks of San Diego, responsible for the murder of Jews in the central prison of Riga; Alexander Lehmann, deputy police chief of Zaporozhe; and Karl Linnas, sentenced to death *in absentia* by Latvia for massacres at the Tartu camp.[32]

Each of these cases required months of investigations before the INS could initiate extradition proceedings. Even then, it took years before a defendant was expelled. Simon Wiesenthal discovered Hermine Braunsteiner-Ryan, the most notorious female guard at Majdanek and Ravensbruck, living in Queens in 1964. Mrs Ryan was not extradited to Germany until 1975. Vladimir Sokolov was praised as one of the best linguists at Yale when he joined that faculty in 1959. In 1976, critics released anti-Semitic articles Sokolov had published in Voronezh during the war. Another decade would pass before he was ordered out of the country. Valerian Trifa, bishop of the Romanian Orthodox Church, was condemned to death *in absentia* for inciting pogroms in Bucharest in 1941. Exposed in 1974, he fled to Portugal in 1984 and lived there until his death in 1987. Fedor Federenko, accused in 1977 of being a guard at Treblinka and Sobibor, was deported to the Soviet Union and executed in 1987.

Years after an accused war criminal was stripped of his citizenship, there might still be no resolution of his case. The most celebrated example was that of John Demjanjuk, a Ford plant worker from Cleveland, accused of being 'Ivan the Terrible', the sadistic guard who tormented prisoners and operated diesel machinery at Treblinka. In 1975 a pro-Soviet Ukrainian-language newspaper in New Jersey published a list of Nazi collaborators living in America. It was not until August 1977 that Demjanjuk was summoned to the US District Attorney's office. Denaturalization proceedings began on 10 February 1981.[33]

The evidence against Demjanjuk was impressive. Nine survivors of Treblinka picked out his picture in pretrial investigations. Five of these identified him in court as Ivan the Terrible. The government introduced an index card from the Trawniki training center for SS guards which contained Demjanjuk's photo, signature, vital statistics and special features ('scar on back'). Watermarks, seals, signatures of camp officials and other indicia convinced Heinrich Schaefer, one-time paymaster at Trawniki and Israeli intelligence that the card was authentic. Demjanjuk's supporters discounted eyewitness accounts after 36 years. Evidence from the Soviet Union was unacceptable, for the communists had been waging war against Ukrainians since 1917. The case was moot since the Jewish author Jean Steiner had recounted how Ivan the Terrible died during the Treblinka uprising in August 1943.[34] (Steiner's book was fiction.)

Ultimately, Demjanjuk was done in by his own testimony which was riddled with vagaries and inconsistencies. The Nazis captured him at Kerch, then took him to Romno in 1942 or 1943 ('I don't remember exactly'). His group worked on the railroad lines ('perhaps a few weeks') before they were taken to a PW camp at Chelm. 'About 1943 or 1944' they were moved to Graz. After another 'three or four weeks' ('I think it was 1944') Demjanjuk and fellow farm laborers were taken to Oelberg, then Bischenshofen. When the Americans came, the Ukrainian PWs were assigned to Regensburg, where Demjanjuk stayed 'about two years'.[35] Georgia Professor Earl Ziemke noted that Demjanjuk could not have been in a PW camp at Chelm as the town was in Russian hands early in 1944. Wolfgang Scheffler pointed out that only the SS, including camp guards, were tattooed under the armpit as Demjanjuk. It was equally unlikely that as a prisoner Demjanjuk never had a haircut in three years. The Nazis had been scrupulous about shaving the heads of inmates since the earliest days of Dachau and Oranienburg. The prosecution pointed out how fortuitous it was that he was working near Sobibor, Treblinka and Majdanek when those death camps were doing their bloodiest work. Demjanjuk could not explain how he learned to operate heavy equipment like that used for ditch-digging. Nor could he account for discrepancies on his International Refugee Organization application, where he listed his place of birth as Kiev, his nationality as Polish, and offered a jumbled listing of his whereabouts between 1937 and 1945.

The Displaced Persons Act of June 1950, the McCarran–Walter Immigration Act of 1952, the amendment to that act passed on 30 October 1978 (as well as Paragraph 19, Section 1182, Title 8 of the US Code) exclude aliens who by fraud or willfully misrepresenting a material fact gained entry into the United States. Paragraph 33 of the same laws bars any alien who between

23 March 1933 and 8 May 1945, 'under the direction of or in association with the Nazi government in Germany ... ordered, incited, assisted, or otherwise participated in the persecution of any person because of race, religion, national origin or political opinion'. On 25 June 1981, District Judge Frank Battisti ruled that Demjanjuk concealed the fact that he had assisted the Nazis in persecuting civilians, actions which would have warranted denial of admission to the US. Battisti concluded that Demjanjuk had illegally procured his citizenship and ordered that his naturalization be canceled.

Dreading extradition to the Soviet Union, Demjanjuk was sent to Israel in February 1986. Again he faced Treblinka survivors who identified him as Ivan the Terrible. After 14 months, a three man panel of judges invoked Israel's rarely used death penalty against him. Four more years passed as Israeli attorney Yoram Sheftell exhausted the appeals process. By then, Revisionists, conservative pundit Pat Buchanan and the newsprogram '60 Minutes' were claiming the real Ivan was another Ukrainian who was dead. Confronted with doubt as to the identity of 'Ivan the Terrible', the Israeli Supreme Court reversed the judgment against Demjanjuk. Because of errors committed by the INS deemed intentional by an appellate court in Cincinnati, Demjanjuk was readmitted to the US in 1992. Five years later, his citizenship was restored. Allan Ryan, the one-time head of the OSI, insists, 'I have studied the evidence for ten years. I looked into his [Demjanjuk's] eyes as prosecutor and observer. I have no doubt that Demjanjuk is Ivan the Terrible. Seven judges in two countries reached the same conclusion.'[36] In the summer of 1999, the INS announced plans to proceed with a new denaturalization hearing.

LET BYGONES BE BYGONES

Critics ask why should individuals be charged after such a long time? Would it not be better after all these years to forgive and forget? Precisely such questions were raised in the case of George Lindert, a retired factory worker from Canfield, Ohio, who was targeted for deportation in 1992. According to the OSI, the Austrian-born Lindert served as an SS guard at Mauthausen when he was 19. He made no effort to conceal this fact from his 1955 immigration application. The INS felt, however, that service at the camp constituted a violation of American law. Lindert's attorneys countered that his youth and the fact that he was drafted mitigated charges against him. For the umpteenth time, the government pointed out that no one was drafted into the SS – it was a volunteer, criminal organization. As for evidence of brutality, there was the precedent of Fedor Federenko. Federenko admitted to being a guard at Sobibor, but argued that he never mistreated anyone. During the trial, Robert Jay Lifton pointed out that guards were 'given license to indulge atrocities as long as they advanced the ideological and political purpose of the camp'. Charles Sydnor also testified that promotion was tied to 'readiness to carry out persecution with thoroughness and dispatch'.[37] District Judge Anne Aldrich rejected the government's case, stating, 'Lindert's credible testimony that he never touched, threatened, or shot at a prisoner is supported by the massive volumes of records from the camp, none of which indicate any specific actions taken by Lindert.'[38] Finding no moral turpitude, Aldrich permitted the 72-year-old Lindert to return to Canfield.

That kind of myopia is not limited to the United States or Germany. For decades, Austria attempted to avoid responsibility for the Holocaust. Austria did not restore citizenship to expellees or compensate them ($7,000) until 1993. One-time Chancellor Bruno Kreisky brought four ex-Nazis into his government, including Vice-Chancellor Friedrich Peter. When Simon Wiesenthal exposed Peter as a former officer in an SS unit that murdered thousands, Kreisky denounced him as 'a Jewish fascist' and 'Mafioso'.[39] Kreisky also defended Kurt Waldheim, whose wartime dossier had been concealed by the United Nations. Kreisky attributed Waldheim's problems to 'Holocaust-obsessed' American Jews. The one-time President of Austria remains on the State Department watch list, barring Nazis from entering the US.[40] Italy also suffered a memory lapse. In August 1996, an Italian jury released Erich Priebke, charged with the massacre of 335 civilians in the Ardeatine caves. Italy secured Priebke's extradition from Argentina only to have a panel find no cruelty and premeditation in the executions. (Public outcry forced the Italians to rearrest Priebke, causing a protest from his attorney.) An earlier jury released Wilhelm Kappler, the Gestapo officer responsible for the roundup of Jews in Rome.

For humanitarian reasons, 8,000 Ukrainian and 15,000 German prisoners of war were permitted to remain in England at the end of the war. A large number of Latvian refugees were also admitted to the British Isles. It was not until 1986 that the British, responding to publicity generated by the Waldheim case, began to look into the background of some of these individuals and not until 1988 that the government created a commission to prosecute war criminals.[41] The record of the Commonwealth nations was equally embarrassing. In 1961, a West German court convicted Helmut Rauka, an SS officer who directed the murder of 10,000 Jews in Kaunas, *in absentia*. In 1981 Sol Littman of the Wiesenthal Center informed the Royal Canadian Mounted Police that Rauka had been living in Toronto under his own name since 1950. Rauka died in 1983 while his case was pending. Littman also reported that 2,000 members of the 14th Galician SS Division were holding annual reunions in Canada.[42] Meanwhile, the Deschenes Commission on War Criminals could only guess at the number of Nazi suspects (between 218 and 778) in Canada. They included Imre Finta, commander of the Szeged ghetto; Ivan Chrabatyn, who helped kill 10,000 Jews at Stanislav in October 1941; and a host of Vichy French collaborators protected by one-time Prime Minister Louis St Laurent.[43] Even Australia has its problems, as Prime Minister Robert Hawke discovered. After the war that nation opened its doors to 170,000 displaced persons. Fifty thousand came from the Baltic states, 50,000 from Germany. When the Australian government conducted a review of such immigrants in 1987, it identified more than 250 suspects, none of whom were ever expelled.[44]

Those who wonder why governments still pursue war criminals should consider what Justice Robert Jackson said at the opening of the Nuremberg Tribunal on 20 November 1945: 'The wrongs which we seek to condemn and punish have been so calculated, so malignant and so devastating that civilization cannot tolerate their being ignored because it cannot survive their being repeated.' In April 1980 Elizabeth Holtzmann reminded a Youngstown State audience that war criminals had no right to the fruits of a democratic society. In the name of justice, the American people were obliged to pursue such individuals and, through due process of law, make them leave.

27. An Israeli tour group at Mila 18, headquarters of the Jewish fighting organization in the Warsaw Ghetto.

32

Final Thoughts

Fifty million people died during World War II. Six million Jews, one million Yugoslavs, at least 200,000 Gypsies, 250,000 handicapped, 10,000 homosexuals and 5,000 Jehovah's Witnesses were among the victims. Who was responsible for all of this? In 1945, the answer came easily – the Germans. Not just the Nazi hierarchy, but all Germans, and they had to be punished. From a calmer perspective, today we know it makes as much sense to impose collective guilt upon 'the Germans' as it did historically to stigmatize 'the Jews'. Many Germans fled their homeland rather than subscribe to the Nazi system. Others who stayed behind participated in resistance movements like the White Rose student group or the Stauffenberg plot to kill Hitler in 1944. While most Germans endorsed Hitler when he was victorious and blocked out the existence of concentration camps, they were not all Nazis and they were not alone when it came to the killing. Collaborators from France to Ukraine, 'Hitler's lickspittle' as Winston Churchill once called them, expedited the extermination process. Polish schmaltzovniks and Croatian Ustashis attacked Jews and Serbs. Ukrainian auxiliaries and Hungarian 'Feathers' assisted the Einsatzgruppen. Lithuanian Askaris and Greek police rousted Jews from ghettos. Romanians, Bulgarians and Slovaks divided confiscated goods. Belgian, French, Dutch and Czech trainmen made certain that the transports moved on time. There were guards and Kapos of every background in the death camps.

The list of those complicit did not end there. At Nuremberg, the principal Nazi leaders protested that the Russians should have been sitting in the dock with them. For four decades, the Soviet Union would trumpet its losses (20 million dead) during the Great Patriotic War. Yet the Russians had very little to say about the Molotov–Ribbentrop pact, which enabled Hitler to go to war, Russia's aggression against Poland, Finland and the Baltic states, Russian assistance to the Germans during the invasion of western Europe in 1940, atrocities perpetrated by the Red Army before its betrayal by the Nazis in 1941, or the extent of Stalin's own slave system in Siberia. The top Nazis at Nuremberg must have been bemused when Allied prosecutors at Nuremberg read from Hitler's pre-war speeches or *Mein Kampf* to establish a conspiracy against the peace. Such proclamations were public record and available in translation for all to read. Instead of stopping Hitler from reviving the armed forces, marching into the Rhineland, Austria, the Sudetenland or Bohemia, western diplomats dallied. Instead of addressing pre-war persecution of Jews (pogroms in 1933, the Nuremberg Laws, No Man's Lands, Kristallnacht), the western democracies appeased Hitler. Before, during and after the war, British Commonwealth and Latin American states demonstrated their hostility to Jews by refusing to open their doors to this group that had been targeted for destruction by the Nazis. Fixated with their own nationalist aspirations, Arabs, too, refused to show the basic humanity commanded in such a crisis. The responses of international agencies like the League of Nations, the International Red Cross and the Vatican must also be labeled failures.

A portion of responsibility, no matter how small, must be borne by the US government and the American people. Several high-ranking policy-makers were, if not outright anti-Semites, at least indifferent to the plight of the Jews. Others who were friendly (including Hull and Roosevelt) were swayed by public opinion which, while sympathetic toward Jews, was decidedly against any bold ventures on their behalf. No man in the twentieth century was more idolized by Jews than Roosevelt. His name was a magic talisman to millions in ghettos and concentration camps. The starving and the strangled believed that if only the United States and Roosevelt knew about the murders, something would be done to stop the Nazis. Roosevelt was troubled by the agony of Jews in Europe, but consistently avoided acknow-ledging their singular persecution between 1933 and 1945. Confronted with spatting Jewish groups, some of whom demanded action against the Nazis as early as 1933 while others counseled quietism, some of whom believed the Romanian offer of 70,000 Jews for sale in 1943 was bona fide, while others did not, the President equivocated. Before and during the war, Roosevelt used his influence to persuade Jewish leaders that it was in their best interests to mute advocacy of their own people.

Some historians contend that during the age of Hitler, the American Jewish community was powerless to effect more substantial rescue measures in this country. A small community (six million), recently arrived (most could only trace their lineage back one generation), easily distinguishable, and generally unpopular, American Jews could not overcome the additional obstacles of the Great Depression and reconciling diversionary schemes with the war effort. Arthur Morse notes they had also been deliberately mis-informed by the State Department. They were, in effect, victims of what Earl Raab labeled the Rule of Marginal Effect (the sentiment of a minority will influence American foreign policy only to the extent that it makes no substantial difference to what are otherwise perceived as the best foreign-policy interests of the nation).[1]

In 1983, Gearhart Riegner stated, 'Let me say, nobody did enough. In such a situation nobody does enough. It is very difficult to admit this, too, and nobody wants to.'[2] Nahum Goldman suggested, 'This may sound naive today, but I still believe as I did then, that a desperate, unconventional gesture might have achieved something. Besides, in certain situations leaders have a moral duty to make quixotic gestures.'[3] Elie Wiesel once suggested that American Jews should have engaged in hunger strikes, marches against the White House, 'should have shaken heaven and earth, echoing the agony of their doomed brethren'.[4] American Jews did a great deal during this period. Rabbi Steven Wise organized countless demonstrations in New York City. Orthodox Jews held vigils in Washington. Wise, Goldmann and Abba Silver met with leading figures of both parties, while Jewish congregations in Tulsa, Charleston, Schenectady and Bayonne oversubscribed their annual campaigns by as much as 180 percent. And yet it was not enough.

The wartime experience of American Jews should serve as a lesson to other minorities to be resolute in the pursuit of their goals. Leaders lead best, when they are not co-opted by the system. Roosevelt was very good at making people believe they were important cogs in the official decision-making process. Co-optation soothed egos and neutralized opposition from minorities. Stephen Wise confessed consternation over his own role when he wrote to Felix Frankfurter on 16 September 1942, 'I don't know whether I am getting to be a Hofjude, but I find that a good part of my work is to explain to my fellow Jews why our Government cannot do all the things asked or expected of it.'[5] Roosevelt, as we have seen, was also good at playing off one set of personalities against another. As Chayim Greenberg complained, 'Every "Committee" cherishes its own committee interests, its sectarian ambitions, its exclusively wise strategy, and its "power-position" in the teapot of Jewish communal competition.'[6] Instead of squabbling among themselves, American Jews might have pressed for immigration reform and the opening of Palestine as a refuge. They could have argued that there was nothing incompatible between a statement specifically relating to the plight of the Jews and the war effort. And, if necessary, they should have threatened to withhold their votes as a bloc from support of the Democratic candidate for President. Instead, they were put off with 'empty words of sympathy, praise or the denunciation of Hitler or Nazi persecution'.[7] Long before the Holocaust, the Psalmist warned, 'put not your trust in princes'. He might just as well have been writing of Franklin Roosevelt.

ON REMEMBERING

While the overwhelming burden of guilt for what happened in World War II devolves directly upon Nazis of every shape and nationality, all of humanity was, to some degree, complicit. In the spring of 1945, a world which had doubted atrocity tales coming out of eastern Europe, gazed upon the horrors of Nazi concentration camps and vowed, 'Never again.' Not to Jews, nor anyone else. Monuments were erected around the world inscribed with the word 'Zachor' (remember). A few astute observers wondered how long it would be before the passing of time would blur these images. The narrator in Alain Resnais's celebrated film *Night and Fog*, warns: 'War slumbers, with one eye always open ... Who among us watches over this strange observatory to warn of the new executioners arrival? ... we who pretend to believe that all this happened in one time and in one place, and who do not think to look around us, or hear the endless cry.' A decade later, a tormented Anatoly Kuznetsov pointed to the thousands of experts who argue about totalitarianism, authoritarianism, national-socialism, chauvinism, communism, fascism and other 'isms' and concluded that people will 'put their trust in absolutely anybody – in Lenin or in Stalin, in Hitler or in Khrushchev, in Mao Tse-tung or Brezhnev, and in all sorts of Fidel Castros lower down the scale'. In the past, such blind faith resulted in Babi Yars, Oswiecims, Hiroshimas, Kolymas and Patmas and 'there is no guarantee whatever that even more sinister events will not occur tomorrow'. Said Kuznetsov: 'The world has learnt nothing. It has become only a more gloomy place. It is crammed with misguided puppets and unthinking blockheads who, with the light of fanatical conviction in their eyes, are ready to shoot at any target their leaders may command, and trample underfoot any country they are sent to; and it is frightful to think of the weapons they have in their hands today.'[8]

With the breakup of the Soviet Union in 1989–90, some pundits advised that 'peace was breaking out all over the world'. The reality is that 58 years after the end of World War II, the lessons of that conflict still have not been learned. Starving children from Mauritania to Somalia evoke images of waifs in the Warsaw Ghetto, yet the civilized world cannot meet the needs of millions in the Sahel (sub-Saharan Africa). Millions more killed in China, India, Zaire, Biafra, Uganda, Indonesia, El Salvador, Peru, Chile, Nicaragua and Guatemala have been written off as victims of civil war. When the forces of Ho Chi Minh conquered Vietnam, the world proved incapable of helping a second wave of boat people – 700,000 Chinese set adrift from their adopted land. There was little anyone could or would do for tens of thousands of refugees from Laos festering in refugee camps in Thailand. For a time there was even denial when the first reports of two million dead came from Cambodia. People prayed and signed petitions for inmates of the Soviet Gulag and slaves in southern Sudan. We watched as Iraqis and Iranians killed one another for ten years. Even today, no one knows how to deal with the violence in Northern Ireland, Bosnia and Kosovo, Lebanon where more than one million people have been displaced, Rwanda or Burundi, where Hutus and Tutsis murdered one another with impunity. Racism and hate, uniformed bands armed with machine guns or teenagers in T-shirts carrying machetes, politicians urging revenge against a scapegoat, violence, torture and killing, these seem to be the hallmarks of our age.

For years now, some scholars proposed using a grid of some ten or 15 factors as an early warning system (EWS) for societies imperiled by totalitarianism that may breed genocide.[9] The concept is laudable but flawed. For one thing, in its original form the early warning system focused solely upon western democracies. The real problem is not so much what might happen if a Jörg Haider or Jean-Marie Le Pen seizes control in Austria or France. Many nations have laws which are proactive to fascist threats and it is doubtful that their neighbors would tolerate the existence of such a system. The EWS scheme offers no suggestions how to deal with existing right wing or communist tyrannies. Nor does the grid offer instructions how to distinguish between uniformed groups like the American Legion, which some considered a para-military threat when it paraded in uniforms and with arms during the 1930s, and Louis Farrakhan's well-attired Fruit of Islam, who supposedly carry no weapons. Name-calling, bias, neighborhood mayhem against people deemed outsiders are lamentable but universal patterns of behavior. It takes more than this to set off alarm bells. The mass killings in Liberia, Haiti, Burundi and Rwanda should have commanded more immediate response from the civilized world, but it is doubtful that any of these tragedies could have been predicted.

After what they have experienced in the past century, Jews should require no early warning system. Emil Fackenheim once declared that since 1933 an ongoing war has been waged against every Jew on this planet. Lucy Dawidowicz incorporated that concept in the title of her text on Holocaust and was taken to task by some scholars. Yet it is undeniable that some 50 years after the end of World War II, the only victims of Nazism that continue to be the object of spite and warfare are Jews. No one is persecuting Jehovah's Witnesses or conducting experiments upon the terminally ill. Homosexuals are not being rounded up and tortured in concentration camps. The French and Germans who made war for 400 years now share profits in the European Union. Only the Jews remain targets of an international campaign of vilification – from the old-fashioned right which lionizes Hitler, the left which equates Zionism with racism, Christian reactionaries who refuse to accept the message of Vatican II, and Muslim states that deny the existence of a Jewish people. Five times in the past 50 years, the state of Israel has had to defend itself against its Arab neighbors. Israel's population includes children of survivors, refugees who fled anti-Semitic persecution in the Soviet Union, and descendants of Jews degraded in other Middle Eastern states. Jews are still denounced in the Arab press, and Jews *qua* Jews are targeted for murder by self-proclaimed holy warriors.

The Torah instructs, 'Neither shalt thou stand idly by the blood of thy neighbor' (Lev. 19:16). As elaborated in Maimonides's *Mishneh Torah* 1:14 and the *Shulchan Aruch* 184:8, 'If one person is able to save another and does not save him, he transgresses the commandment.' Similarly, if a person sees another drowning in the sea or being attacked by bandits or wild animals, and though able to rescue him either alone or by hiring others and does not rescue him, he violates the commandment. Most importantly: 'if one hears heathens or informers plotting against another or laying a trap for him and does not ... let him know, he transgresses the commandment.' After Dachau and Auschwitz, the message is clear. People need not sacrifice their wealth and well being for others. They need not risk their lives. But no human being can ignore harm done to another.

In the end, the image of one man looms over the wreckage of the Holocaust – Adolf Hitler. He had expressed his loathing for Jews in speeches at street corners and mass rallies, in *Mein Kampf* and in personal asides to top aides and diplomats, at the podium of the Reichstag and through schemes like Nisko, Madagascar or Waldsee, when he signed the euthanasia decreee, in his declaration of war against the US and in his final testament pecked out in the rubble of Berlin. A half-century later, docudramas refer to him as a 'monster' or 'psychopath'. Quite the contrary, Hitler could be absolutely clear, cynical or obtuse as he elected. If, he were inhuman, deranged, incompetent, what does that tell us of 11 million Nazis who proclaimed Hitler their leader? Or the other Germans who cheered as he gave them jobs and quick victories on the battlefield? What does that suggest about millions more from Spain to the Baltic who applauded his vision of a New Order? Or the tens of millions who even now would not be troubled by a second *Entfernung* of Jews? The Nazis who stood in the prisoners' dock at Nuremberg claimed they were following the orders of one man. Nazi sympathizers and onlookers feigned ignorance of what Hitler planned. If guards and generals were not guilty because everything could be traced to a man not competent, then once more in the words of Alain Resnais, 'Who is responsible?'

Some may forgive what happened during the Holocaust. Many want to forget. In Friedrich Duerrenmatt's novel, *The Quarry*, the mythic figure Gulliver acknowledges the Jew's singular obligation to history when he says:

> But I do not want to forget anything, and not only because I am a Jew – the Germans have killed six million of my people, six million – no, because I am still a human being, even though I live in my underground holes with the rats. I refuse to make a distinction between peoples and speak of good and bad nations, but a distinction between human beings I have to make. That was beaten into me and from the first blow that cut into my flesh, I have distinguished between torturers and tortured. I don't deduct the new cruelties of new guards in different countries from the bill I present to the Nazis, I add them to it. I take the liberty of not distinguishing between those that torture. They all have the same eyes. If there is a God, Commissar, and my defiled heart hopes for nothing more, He will recognize not nations but only individuals and He will judge each one by the measure of his crimes and acquit each one by the measure of his own justice.[10]

Notes

Preface

1. The transition to Holocaust occurred as a result of the translation of the scriptures into Greek (Septuagint) by Hebrew scholars for Ptolemy II. See Roland de Vaux, *Ancient Israel* (New York: McGraw-Hill, 1965), Vol. II, pp. 415–56.
2. *Shoah* has also been translated as ruin (Is. 47:11, Job 30:14) and desolation (Zeph. 1:14, Job 38:27).
3. Yisrael Gutman and Shmuel Krakowski, *Unequal Victims: Poles and Jews during World War II*, tr. T.E. Gorelick and Witold Jedlicki (New York: Holocaust Library, 1986), p. iii.
4. Emil Fackenheim, *The Jewish Return into History: Reflections in the Age of Auschwitz and a New Jerusalem* (New York: Schocken, 1978), p. 27.
5. Peter Novick's *The Holocaust in American Life* (Houghton-Mifflin, 1999) is the latest book to address our fascination with that terrible era. The release of government documents in the late 1960s prompted a flurry of texts dealing with American and British policy toward Jewish refugees. Stanley Milgram's disturbing book, *Obedience to Authority* (New York: Harper & Row, 1974), published during the Vietnam War era, made us reevaluate ourselves. Twenty years ago, the so-called Institute for Historical Review attempted to challenge the veracity of the Holocaust and this challenge was quickly refuted by legitimate historians. Ronald Reagan's visit to the military cemetery at Bitburg in 1985 prompted additional debate about the role of the regular German Army in the mass killings of World War II. Apart from the much-ballyhooed Goldhagen thesis, in the past decade scholars have also debated the disposition of accused war criminal John Demjanjuk, the authenticity of what proved to be forged Goebbels diaries, the exact moment when Adolf Hitler decided to kill all the Jews of Europe and the moral dilemmas raised by the movie *Schindler's List*.

Chapter 1. The Jews: A History of Persecution

1. *Grimms' Tales for Young and Old*, tr. Ralph Manheim (Garden City, NY: Doubleday and Co., 1977), pp. 380–3.
2. Joshua Trachtenberg, *The Devil and the Jew* (JPS, 1937), and Joseph Gaer, *The Legend of the Wandering Jew* (New York: New American Library, 1981).
3. *The German Legends of the Brothers Grimm*, Donald Ward (ed.) (Philadelphia: Institute for Study of Human Issues, 1981), Vol. I, pp. 279–80.
4. Jacob and Wilhelm Grimm, *Deutsches Wörterbuch* (Leipzig: Verlag von S. Hirzel, 1877), IV, pp. 2351–8.
5. Maria Tatar, *The Hard Facts of the Grimms' Fairy Tales* (Princeton University Press, 1987), p. 21; Alan Dundes, 'Interpreting Little Red Riding Hood Psychoanalytically', in James McGlathery (ed.), *The Brothers Grimm and Folktale* (Urbana: University of Illinois Press, 1988), pp. 16–51.
6. Louis Snyder, 'Nationalistic Aspects of the Grimm Fairy Tales', *Journal of Social Psychology* (1951), XXXIII, pp. 220–2.

7. Ruth Bottigheimer, *Grimms' Bad Girls and Bold Boys: The Moral and Social Vision of the Tales* (New Haven: Yale University Press, 1987), p. 142.
8. Gordon Allport, *The Nature of Prejudice* (New York: Addison-Wesley, 1954), p. 49.
9. Ashley Montagu, *The Nature of Human Aggression* (New York: Oxford, 1976), p. 21; Anthony Storr, *Human Destructiveness* (New York: Basic Books, 1972), p. 13; Rollo May, *Power and Innocence* (New York: Norton, 1972), pp. 165–79.
10. Miller, *Incident at Vichy* (New York: Bantam, 1965), p. 105.
11. Gustave LeBon, *The Crowd: A Study of the Popular Mind* (London: T. Fisher Unwin, 1897); T.W. Adorno *et al.*, *The Authoritarian Personality* (New York: Harper, 1950); Wilhelm Reich, *The Mass Psychology of Fascism*, tr. V. Carfagno (New York: Farrar, Straus & Giroux, 1971); Stanley Milgram, *Obedience to Authority* (New York: Harper & Row, 1974).
12. Storr, *Human Destructiveness*, p. 86.
13. Irenaus Eibl-Eibesfeldt, *Love and Hate: The Natural History of Behavior Patterns*, tr. Geoffrey Strachan (New York: Holt, Rinehart, Winston, 1971), pp. 99–102.
14. Erich Fromm, *The Nature of Human Destructiveness* (New York: Holt, Rinehart & Winston, 1973), pp. 271–88.
15. Leon Pinsker, *Auto-Emancipation* (Berlin: 1882), p. 5.
16. Hans Toch, *Violent Men: An Inquiry into the Psychology of Violence* (Chicago: Aldine, 1992), pp. 211–12.
17. Renae Cohen, 'What We Know, What We Don't Know About Antisemitism: A Research Perspective', in Jerome Chanes (ed.), *Antisemitism in America Today* (New York: Carol Publishing, 1995), pp. 65–9. See also Charles Glock and Rodney Stark, *Anti-Semitism in America* (New York: Free Press, 1979).
18. Werner Sombart, *Jews and Modern Capitalism*, tr. M. Epstein (Glencoe: Free Press, 1951), p. 175.
19. On Francis Galton see *Hereditary Genius* (London: Macmillan, 1869), *Inquiries into Human Faculty* (London: Macmillan, 1883), and *Natural Inheritance* (London: Macmillan, 1889). See also Diane Paul, *The Politics of Heredity: Essays on Eugenics, Biomedicine and the Nature–Nurture Debate* (Albany: SUNY Press, 1998); and William Tucker, *The Science and Politics of Racial Research* (Chicago: University of Illinois Press, 1996).
20. Poliakov, *Aryan Myth*, pp. 157–61, 279.
21. Ibid., pp. 162, 249–50, 264; and Mosse, *Toward the Final Solution*, pp. 21–2, 26–7.
22. Arthur de Gobineau, *The Inequality of Human Races*, tr. Adrian Collins (New York: Putnam, 1915).
23. Malcolm Hay, *The Foot of Pride: The Roots of Christian Anti-Semitism* (Boston: Beacon Press, 1950); Edward Flannery, *The Anguish of the Jews: Twenty-Three Centuries of Anti-Semitism* (New York: Macmillan, 1965); Joshua Trachtenberg, *The Devil and the Jews: The Medieval Conception of the Jew and Its Relation to Modern Anti-Semitism* (New York: Meridian, 1961).
24. Israel Abrahams, *Jewish Life in the Middle Ages* (Philadelphia: JPSA, 1958).
25. P. Borchsenius, *Behind the Wall: The Story of the Ghetto*, tr. R. Spink (London: Allen & Unwin, 1964), p. 118.
26. *Luther's Works: The Christian in Society*, II, W. Brandt (ed.) (Philadelphia: Muhlenberg, 1962), pp. 199–229.
27. Ibid., p. 200.
28. Borchsenius, *Behind the Wall*, p. 118.
29. *Luther's Works: Lectures on Titus, Philemon and Hebrews*, Jaroslav Pelikan (ed.) (St Louis: Concordia Publishing, 1968), pp. 6, 35, 41, 49, 60.
30. *Luther's Works: The Christian in Society*, Vol. III, p. 186.
31. *Luther's Works: Table Talk*, ed. and tr. by Theodore Tappert (Philadelphia: Fortress Press, 1967), p. 43.
32. Hay, *The Foot of Pride*, pp. 167–8.
33. *Luther's Works: The Christian in Society*, Vol. III, p. 64.

34. *Luther's Works: Table Talk*, p. 239.
35. Ibid., p. 455.
36. Jacob Marcus, *The Jews in the Medieval World* (New York: Meridian Books, 1960), pp. 167–9.
37. Jacob Goldberg, 'The Privileges Granted to Jewish Communities of the Polish Commonwealth as a Stabilizing Factor in Jewish Support', in Chimen Abramsky, Maciej Jachimczyk and Antony Polonsky (eds), *The Jews of Poland* (Oxford: Basil Blackwell, 1986), pp. 31–54.
38. Alexander Gieysztor, 'The Beginnings of Jewish Settlement in the Polish Lands', pp. 15–21, and Daniel Tollet, 'Merchants and Businessmen in Poznan and Cracow, 1588–1668', pp. 22–30 in *The Jews of Poland*.
39. Simon Dubnov, *History of the Jews in Russia and Poland*, tr. I. Friedlaender (Philadelphia: JPSA, 1916), Vol. I, pp. 144–58. See also, Dubnov, *History of the Jews*, tr. Moshe Spiegel (South Brunswick: T. Yoseloff, 1971), IV, pp. 9–37, and Bernard Weinryb, *The Jews of Poland*, pp. 181–205.
40. Roman Vishniac, *A Vanished World* (New York: Schocken, 1975); Lionel Reiss, *A World at Twilight: A Portrait of the Jewish Communities of Eastern Europe before the Holocaust* (New York: Macmillan, 1971); M. Zborowski and E. Herzog, *Life Is With People: The Culture of the Shtetl* (New York: Schocken, 1971); and Diane and David Roskies, *The Shtetl Book* (New York: Ktav, 1975).
41. *Di Farshvundene Velt*, Raphael Abramavich (ed.) (New York: Forward Association, 1947), pp. 97–106; Ezra Mendelsohn, 'Interwar Poland: Good for the Jews or Bad for the Jews?', in Chimen Abramsky, Maciej Jachimczyk and Antony Polonsky (eds), *The Jews of Poland* (Oxford: Basil Blackwell, 1986), pp. 130–9.
42. 'Hasidism', *Encyclopedia of the Jewish Religion*, R.J. Zwi Werblowsky and Geoffrey Wigoder (eds) (New York: Holt, Rinehart & Winston, 1965), pp. 174–6.
43. Jacob Presser, *The Destruction of the Dutch Jews*, tr. Arnold Pomerans (New York: Dutton, 1969), p. 359.
44. Rezo Kastner, *Der Bericht des judischen Rettungskomittees aus Budapest 1942–1945* (Geneva: 1946), pp. 67–8.
45. Itzhak Zuckerman and Moshe Basak, *The Fighting Ghettos*, tr. and ed. Meyer Barkai (Philadelphia: Lippincott, 1962), p. 8; Jozef Garlinski, *Fighting Auschwitz: The Resistance Movement in the Concentration Camp* (London: J. Friedmann, 1975).
46. James Glass, *Life Unworthy of Life* (New York: Basic Books, 1997), p. 193.
47. Miriam and Saul Kuperhand, *Shadows of Treblinka* (Urbana: University of Illinois Press, 1998), pp. xii–xiii.
48. Ronald Headland, *Messages of Murder: A study of the Reports of the Einsatzgruppen of the Security Police and the Security Service 1941–1943* (London: Associated University Presses, 1992), pp. 110–25.

Chapter 2. Rehearsal for Destruction: The Jews of Tsarist Russia

1. Salo Baron, *The Russian Jews under Tsar and Soviets* (New York: Macmillan, 1964), p. 9. See also Heinrich Graetz, *History of the Jews* (Philadelphia: Jewish Publication Society of America, 1895), IV, p. 633, V, 114–15, 472–3; and Lois Greenberg, *The Jews in Russia* (New Haven: Yale University Press, 1951).
2. Isaac Levitats, *The Jewish Community in Russia, 1772–1844* (New York: Octagon Books, 1943) and John Klier, *Russia Gathers Her Jews: The Origins of the 'Jewish Question' in Russia 1772–1825* (Dekalb: Northern Illinois University Press, 1986).
3. Michael Stanislawski, *Tsar Nicholas I and the Jews: The Transformation of Jewish Society in Russia, 1825–1855* (Philadelphia: JPS, 1983); John Klier, *Imperial Russia's Jewish Question, 1855–1881* (Cambridge: Cambridge University Press, 1995); Erich Haberer, *Jews and Revolution in Nineteenth-Century Russia* (Cambridge: Cambridge University Press, 1995).

4. J.B. Weber and Dr W. Kempter, *Report of the Commissioners of Immigration upon the Causes which Incite Immigration to the U.S.* (Washington: GPO, 1892), pp. 34ff.; and Leo Errera, *The Russian Jews: Extermination or Emancipation*, tr. Bella Lowy (Westport: Greenwood Press, 1975 [1894]), pp. 29–30, 115–16.
5. Michael Florinsky, *Russia: A History and an Interpretation* (New York: Macmillan, 1947), II, pp. 879–87.
6. Ibid., p. 119.
7. K. Pobedonostsev, *Reflections of a Russian Statesman* (Ann Arbor: University of Michigan Press, 1965 [1898]).
8. Florinsky, *Russia*, II, pp. 1086–117.
9. John Klier and Shlomo Lambrozo (eds), *Pogroms: Anti-Jewish Violence in Modern Russian History* (Cambridge: Cambridge University Press, 1992); Hans Rogger, 'The Formation of the Russian Right', pp. 188–211; and 'Was There a Russian Fascism?', pp. 212–32, in *Jewish Policies and Right-Wing Politics in Imperial Russia* (Berkeley: University of California Press, 1986).
10. Ismar Elbogen, *A Century of Jewish Life* (Philadelphia: JPS, 1944), pp. 205–8; and Hans Rogger, 'Russian Ministers and the Jewish Question, 1881–1917', in *Jewish Policies and Right-Wing Politics*, pp. 56–112.
11. *The Times*, 11 January 1882, p. 4, 13 January 1882, p. 4, 4 February 1882, p. 5.
12. I. Michael Aronson, 'The Anti-Jewish Pogroms in Russia in 1881', pp. 44–61; Moshe Mishkinsky, '"Black Repartition" and the Pogroms of 1881–1882', pp. 62–97; Erich Haberer, 'Cosmopolitanism, Anti-semitism, and Populism', pp. 98–134 in *Pogroms: Anti-Jewish Violence in Modern Russian History*, John Klier and Shlomo Lambroza (eds) (Cambridge: Cambridge University Press, 1992); Michael Ochs, 'Tsarist Officialdom and anti-Jewish pogroms in Poland', pp. 164–90 in Klier and Lambroza, *Pogroms*; Irwin Aronson, *Troubled Waters: The Origins of the 1881 Anti-Jewish Pogroms in Russia* (Pittsburgh: University of Pittsburgh Press, 1990); Stephen Berk, *Year of Crisis, Year of Hope: Russian Jewry and the Pogroms of 1881–1882* (Westport: Greenwood Press, 1985).
13. Elbogen, *Century of Jewish Life*, p. 220.
14. Lucien Wolf (ed.), *The Legal Sufferings of the Jews in Russia: A Survey of Their Present Situation, and a Summary of Laws* (London: T. Fisher Unwin, 1912).
15. Shlomo Lambroza, 'The Pogroms of 1903–1906', pp. 195–247, and Robert Weinberg, 'The Pogrom of 1905 in Odessa', pp. 248–90, in John Klier and Shlomo Lambrozo (eds), *Pogroms: Anti-Jewish Violence in Modern Russian History*. See also Michael Davitt, *Within the Pale: The True Story of Anti-Semitic Persecutions in Russia* (New York: Arno Press reprint, 1975).
16. Alexander Tager, *The Decay of Czarism: The Beiliss Trial* (Philadelphia: Jewish Publication Society, 1935); Maurice Samuel, *Blood Accusation: The Strange History of the Beiliss Case* (New York: Knopf, 1966); Bernard Malamud, *The Fixer* (New York: Farrar, Straus & Giroux, 1966).
17. Norman Cohn, *Warrant for Genocide: The Myth of the Jewish World-Conspiracy and the Protocols of the Elders of Zion* (New York: Harper Torch, 1969) and US Congress. Senate Judiciary Committee, 'Protocols of the Elders of Zion', report of Sub-committee to Investigate the Internal Security Act (Washington: GPO, 1964).
18. Cohn, *Warrant for Genocide*, pp. 208–9.
19. Binjamin Segel, *Der Weltkrieg und das Schicksal der Juden*; Egmont Zechlin, *Die deutsche Politik und die Juden im Ersten Weltkrieg*; Werner Angress, 'Das deutsche Militär und die Juden im Ersten Weltkrieg', *Militär geschichtlische Mitteilungen*, XIX (1976), pp. 77–146.
20. *New York Times*, 7 April 1919, p. 2.
21. Elia Tcherikover, *Di ukrainer pogromen in yor 1919* (New York: YIVO, 1965); Elias Haifetz, *The Slaughter of the Jews in the Ukraine in 1919* (New York: T. Seltzer, 1921); I.B. Schechtman, E. Tcherikover, N. Tsatkis and I. Motzkin (eds), *The Pogroms in the Ukraine under the Ukrainian Governments 1917–1920* (London: Comité des

Delegations Juives, 1927).

22. *The Massacres and Other Atrocities Committed against the Jews in South Russia* (New York: American Jewish Congress and the Committee on Protest against Massacres of Jews in Ukrainia, 1920), pp. 58–71.

23. A. Resutski, Alphabetic list of victims at Proskurov, File 398, Tcherikover Archive, YIVO Institute for Jewish Research, New York. See also A.I. Hillerson, 'Le pogrome de Proskurov', report to the Kiev Central Committee for the Relief of Pogrom Victims, File 466 and reports of Drs Goloubev and Hornstein for Danish Red Cross, File 407, Tcherikover Archive.

24. Zvi Gitelman estimates 150,000 deaths in *Jewish Nationality and Soviet Politics: The Jewish Sections of the CPSU 1917–1930* (Princeton, 1972), p. 162. Lionel Kochan places the figure at 180,000–200,000, with another 60,000–70,000 killed in White Russia, in *Jews in Soviet Russia since 1917* (Oxford, 1970), p. 298. Elias Haifetz estimates 70,000 due to Ukrainian forces, another 50,000 victims of White Russians in the *Encyclopedia Judaica*, XIV, p. 1027, and Sachar, *Course of Modern Jewish History*, p. 303.

25. *New York Times*, 8 August 1920, Section viii, p. 20.

26. Saul S. Friedman, *Pogromchik: The Assassination of Simon Petlura* (New York: Hart, 1976).

27. Henry Alsburg, 'Situation in the Ukraine', *Nation*, CIX (1 November 1919), pp. 569–70. See also Peter Kenez, 'Pogroms and White Ideology in the Russian Civil War', pp. 293–313, in Rogger, *Pogroms*.

28. Nachman Syrkin, 'The Jewish Problem and the Socialist-Jewish State' (1898), in Arthur Hertzberg, *The Zionist Idea* (New York: Atheneum, 1971), p. 346.

29. Hyman Lumer (ed.), *Lenin on the Jewish Question* (New York: International Publishers, 1974).

30. Solomon Schwarz, *The Jews in the Soviet Union* (Syracuse: Syracuse University Press, 1951) and William Korey, *The Soviet Cage: Anti-Semitism in Russia* (New York: Viking, 1973).

Chapter 3. The Witches' Brew of Fascism

1. Jean-Denis Bredin, *The Affair: The Case of Alfred Dreyfus*, tr. J. Mehlman (New York: Braziller, 1986); Alfred Dreyfus, *Cinq Années de Ma Vie* (Paris: Maspero, 1982); Norman Kleeblatt (ed.), *The Dreyfus Affair: Art, Truth and Justice* (Berkeley: University of California Press, 1987).

2. Michael Curtis, *Three Against the Third Republic: Sorel, Barres, and Maurras* (Westport: Greenwood Press, 1959).

3. Alexander Bein, *Theodor Herzl* (New York: Atheneum, 1942, 1962), p. 115.

4. Erich Fromm, *Escape from Freedom* (New York: Holt, Rinehart & Winston, 1941), p. 8.

5. J. Christopher Herold, *The Age of Napoleon* (New York: Harper & Row, 1963), p. 414.

6. Fromm, *Escape from Freedom*, pp. 39, 51, 59, 63, 99, 111, 113, 117, 119.

7. Bruno Bettelheim, *The Informed Heart: Autonomy in a Mass Age* (Glencoe: Free Press, 1960), pp. 54–7.

8. Herold, *Age of Napoleon*, p. 415.

9. John Halsted, *Romanticism* (New York: Walker, 1969), pp. 9–15.

10. *Giuseppe Mazzini: Selected Writings*, N. Gangulee (ed.) (London: Lindsay Drummond, 1945), p. 105.

11. Roy Porter and Miklaus Teich (eds), *Romanticism in National Context* (Cambridge: Cambridge University Press, 1988), p. 99.

12. Hannah Arendt, *The Origins of Totalitarianism* (Cleveland: World Publishing, 1958), p. 232.

13. Ibid., pp. 104–13.
14. *Garibaldi*, ed. Denis Smith (Englewood Cliffs: Prentice-Hall, 1969), p. 85.
15. Ibid., p. 82. See also Giuseppe Garibaldi, *Memorie autobiografiche*, tr. A. Werner (New York: Fertig, 1971).
16. Stanley Payne, *A History of Fascism, 1914–1945* (Madison: University of Wisconsin, 1995), pp. 62–3, 93; and Gaetano Salvemini, *The Origins of Fascism in Italy* (New York: Harper & Row, 1973), pp. 222–34.
17. Philip Morgan, *Italian Fascism 1919–1945* (New York: St Martin's Press, 1995), p. 14.
18. Salvemini, *Origins of Fascism*, pp. 372–86.
19. Simonetta Falasca-Zamponi, *Fascist Spectacle: The Aesthetics and Power in Mussolini's Italy* (Berkeley: University of California Press, 1997), pp. 90–113; and Mabel Berezin, *Making the Fascist State: The Political Culture of Interwar Italy* (Ithaca: Cornell University Press, 1997), pp. 199–244.
20. Stanley Payne, *Fascism: Comparison and Definition* (Madison: University of Wisconsin Press, 1980), pp. 16–21. See also Hermann Rauschning, *Revolution of Nihilism* (London: Heinemann, 1939), pp. 232–40; Hans Morgenthau, 'Nazism', in J.S. Roucek (ed.), *Twentieth Century Political Thought* (New York: Philosophical Library, 1946), p. 132.
21. Payne, *History of Fascism*, p. 7.
22. Helmut Kuhn, *Freedom: Forgotten and Remembered* (Chapel Hill: University of North Carolina Press, 1943), p. 110. See also Fromm, *Escape from Freedom*.
23. Irving Horowitz, *Radicalism and the Revolt against Reason* (London: Routledge, Kegan Paul, 1961).
24. Martin Blinkhorn, *Mussolini and Fascist Italy* (London: Metuant, 1989), pp. 29–32.
25. Mussolini, 'Doctrine of Fascism', in Adrian Lyttelton (ed.), *Italian Fascisms from Pareto to Gentile*, tr. Douglas Parmee (New York: Harper & Row, 1973), pp. 40–57.
26. Payne, *Fascism*, p. 76.
27. Martin Blinkhorn, *Fascists and Conservatives* (London: Unwin Hyman, 1990), p. 8.
28. *Human Dynamite: The Story of Europe's Minorities* (New York: Foreign Policy Association, 1939).
29. George Mosse and Walter Laqueur, *International Fascism* (London: Sage, 1979); Hans Rogger and Eugen Weber (eds), *The European Right* (Berkeley: University of California Press, 1965); Bela Vago, *The Shadow of the Swastika: The Rise of Fascism and Anti-Semtism in the Danube Basin, 1936–1939* (Farnborough: Saxon House, 1975).
30. Frank Golczewski, 'Rural Anti-Semitism in Galicia before World War I', in Abramsky *et al.*, *The Jews of Poland* (Oxford: Basil Blackwell, 1986), pp. 97–105.
31. Sachar, *Course of Modern Jewish History*, p. 363.
32. Mendelsohn, 'Interwar Poland: Good for the Jews or Bad for the Jews', in *The Jews of Poland*, pp. 130–9; and Celia Heller, *On the Edge of Destruction* (New York: Columbia University Press, 1977).
33. Dieter Pohl, *Nationalsozialistische Judenverfolgung in Ostgalizien 1941–1944* (Munich: Oldenburg Verlag, 1996), p. 27.
34. Bernard Weinryb, 'Poland', in Peter Meyer *et al.* (eds), *The Jews in the Soviet Satellites* (Westport: Greenwood Press, 1953, 1971), pp. 250–321.

Chapter 4. The Metapolitics of Nazism

1. Erich Fromm, *The Sane Society* (New York: Rinehart, 1955), pp. 30–4; and *Escape from Freedom* (New York: Holt, Rinehart & Winston, 1972, 1941), pp. 114–15.
2. Jay Gonen, *Utopian Barbarism: Deciphering Hitler's Ideology* (Lexington: University of Kentucky Press, 2000); and Weiss, *Ideology of Death: Why the Holocaust Happened in Germany* (Chicago: Ivan Dee, 1996).

3. Goldhagen insists that the principal perpetrators were Germans, acting in the name of Adolf Hitler. *Hitler's Willing Executioners* (New York: Knopf, 1996).

4. 'Religion and Philosophy in Germany', in *Heinrich Heine: A Biographical Anthology*, Hugo Bieber (ed.) (Philadelphia: Jewish Publication Society, 1956), p. 331.

5. Heinrich Treitschke, *History of Germany in the Nineteenth Century*, tr. Eden and Cedar Paul (London, 1914–19), II, pp. 37–76; E.L. Stahl, *Heinrich von Kleist's Dramas* (Oxford: Basil Blackwell, 1961); and Ernst Arndt, *Ausgewählte Gedichte und Schriften* (Berlin: Union Verlag, 1969).

6. Robert Adamson, *Fichte* (Freeport, NY: Books for Libraries Press, 1903, 1969), pp. 85–91.

7. Jacob Katz, *From Prejudice to Destruction: Anti-Semitism, 1700–1933* (Cambridge: Harvard University Press, 1980), pp. 13–22.

8. J.G. Fichte, *Beitrag zur Berichtigung der Urteile des Publikums uber die franzosische Revolution* (Jena, 1793), pp. 188, 101.

9. Alfred Low attributes the jibe at Jews to a 'youthful indiscretion'. *Jews in the Eyes of the Germans* (Philadelphia: Institute for Study of Human Issues, 1979), pp. 143–54.

10. Ibid., pp. 87–99, 154–64.

11. Peter Viereck, *Metapolitics: The Roots of the Nazi Mind* (New York: Capricorn, 1965, 1951), pp. 62–89.

12. Treitschke, *History of Germany*, V, pp. 529–30. See also 'Die Politik', in H.W. Davis, *The Political Thought of Heinrich von Treitschke* (London: Constable, 1914), pp. 148–62.

13. Adolf Hausrath, *Treitschke: His Doctrine of German Destiny and of International Relations* (New York: Putnam's, 1914), p. 113; and Andreas Dorpalen, *Heinrich von Treitschke* (New Haven: Yale University Press, 1957).

14. Treitschke, *History of Germany*, III, p. 44ff, IV, pp. 531–68.

15. Weaver Santaniello, *Nietzsche, God and the Jews* (Albany: SUNY Press, 1994), pp. 124–9.

16. *Selected Letters of Frederich Nietzsche*, ed. and tr. Christopher Middleton (University of Chicago Press, 1969), pp. 54, 80, 102, 295, 298, 301, 304–5.

17. Joachim Kohler, *Nietzsche and Wagner* (New Haven: Yale University Press, 1998), pp. 118–38.

18. Michael Tanner, *Nietzsche* (Oxford: Oxford University Press, 1994), p. 77.

19. Santaniello, *Nietzsche, God and the Jews*, p. 146.

20. Viereck, *Metapolitics*, p. 183. See also the *Nietzsche–Wagner Correspondence*, Elizabeth Foerster-Nietzsche (ed.) (New York: Liveright, 1921), pp. xiii–xvii.

21. 'Thus Spake Zarathustra', in *The Philosophy of Nietzsche* (New York: Modern Library, 1937), pp. 27–8, 33–4; and *The Will to Power*, tr. Walter Kaufman and R.J. Hollingdale (New York: Vintage, 1968).

22. Nietzsche, *Beyond Good and Evil*, tr. Marianne Cowan (Chicago: Gateway, 1955).

23. Crane Brinton, *Nietzsche* (Cambridge: Harvard University Press, 1940), p. 222.

24. Steven Aschheim, *The Nietzsche Legacy in Germany 1890–1990* (Berkeley: University of California Press, 1992), p. 9; and R. Hinton Thomas, *Nietzsche in German Politics and Society 1890–1918* (Manchester University Press, 1983), pp. 128, 130.

25. Weaver Santaniello claims the Nazis embraced Nietzsche as 'a means of silencing him'. *Nietzsche, God and the Jews*, p. 151.

26. *Selected Letters of Nietzsche*, p. 264.

27. Houston Stewart Chamberlain, *Foundations of the Nineteenth Century*, tr. John Lees (New York: John Lane, 1892), pp. 395, 457.

28. Ibid., pp. 329–44.

29. Ibid., pp. 474–83.

30. Ibid., pp. 352–411.

31. Ibid., p. 389.

32. Ibid., p. 331.

33. Ibid., p. 491.

34. Ibid., pp. 211–15.

35. Viereck, *Metapolitics*, p. 148.
36. Nicholas Goodrick-Clarke, *The Occult Roots of Nazism* (New York: New York University Press, 1992), pp. 33–105.
37. Leon Poliakov, *The Aryan Myth: A History of Racist and Nationalist Ideas in Europe*, tr. Edmund Howard (New York: New American Library, 1974, 1971), p. 309.
38. Ibid., p. 92.
39. Otto Weininger, *Sex and Character* (New York: Putnam's, 1906), pp. 303–4.
40. Viereck, *Metapolitics*, p. 93.
41. Ibid., p. 115.
42. See Ernest Newman, *The Life of Richard Wagner* (Cambridge: Cambridge University Press, 1976, 1933–1946), I, pp. 3–18, II, 608–13. See also Robert Gutman, *Richard Wagner: The Man, His Mind and His Music* (New York: Harcourt, Brace & World, 1968); and Ronald Taylor, *Richard Wagner: His Life, Art and Thought* (New York: Taplinger, 1979).
43. Marc Weiner, *Richard Wagner and the Anti-Semitic Imagination* (Lincoln: University of Nebraska Press, 1997), pp. 195–260.
44. Proudhon, *Carnets*, P. Haubtmann and Marcel Rivier (eds) (Paris, 1960), Vol. II, No. VI, p. 337.
45. Jacob Katz traces his animosity to rebuffs from Meyerbeer. *The Darker Side of Genius: Richard Wagner's Anti-Semitism* (Hanover: University Press of New England, 1986), pp. 49–50.
46. Ibid., p. 27.
47. *Judaism in Music*, in *Richard Wagner's Prose Works*, tr. William Ellis (London: Kegan Paul, Trench, Tubner, 1897), III, p. 91. Leon Stein, *The Racial Thinking of Wagner* (New York: Philosophical Library, 1950), p. 108.
48. *Judaism in Music*, in *Richard Wagner's Prose Works*, III, p. 81. Katz, *The Darker Side of Genius*, pp. 33–46, and Stein, *Racial Thinking of Wagner*, pp. 105–14.
49. Ellis, *Wagner's Works*, III, p. 85.
50. *Judaism in Music*, p. 32.
51. *The Authentic Librettos of the Wagner Operas* (New York: Crown, 1938).
52. Viereck, *Metapolitics*, p. 92. Most scholars agree with Viereck's assessment of Wagner. Paul Rose, *Wagner: Race and Revolution* (New Haven: Yale University Press, 1992) and *Revolutionary Anti-Semitism in Germany from Kant to Wagner* (Princeton: Princeton University Press, 1992); Thomas Mann, *Pro and Contra Wagner*, tr. A. Blunden (London: Faber, 1985); Theodor Adorno, *In Search of Wagner*, tr. R. Livingston (London: New Left Books, 1981); David Aberbach, *Richard Wagner's Religious Ideas* (Lewiston: Edwin Mellen Press, 1996); and Stein, *Racial Thinking of Richard Wagner*.
53. While noting possible Jewish stereotypes in Wagnerian operas, Michael Tanner finds Wagner's work free of anti-Semitism. *Wagner* (Princeton: Princeton University Press, 1996), pp. 26–30.
54. Weiner is specific with his criticisms about sexual threats (pp. 185–93), noses (pp. 117–23), impaired gait and other deformities (pp. 261–306). *Wagner and the Anti-Semitic Imagination*.
55. John Jackson, *The Bayreuth of Wagner* (New York: J.W. Lovell, 1891).
56. Richard DuMoulin-Eckart, *Cosima Wagner*, tr. Catherine Phillips (New York: Knopf, 1930). See also *Correspondence of Wagner and Liszt*, tr. Francis Hueffer (New York: Scriber & Welford, 1889).
57. Stein, *Racial Thinking of Wagner*, pp. 33–4.
58. 'Against Vivisection', in Ellis, *Wagner's Prose Works*, VI, pp. 195–210, and Paul Rose, *Wagner: Race and Revolution* (New Haven: Yale University Press, 1992), p. 144.
59. 'What Boots This Knowledge', in Ellis, *Wagner's Prose Works*, VI, pp. 253–363.
60. 'Know Thyself', in Ellis, *Wagner's Prose Works*, VI, pp. 264–74.
61. Rose, *Wagner: Race and Revolution*, pp. 153–8.
62. 'Heroism and Christendom', in Ellis, *Wagner's Prose Works*, VI, pp. 275–84.

63. Viereck, *Metapolitics*, pp. 126–43, Gutman, *Wagner, The Man, His Mind and His Music*, pp. 422–9, and Robert Waite, *Psychopathic God: Adolf Hitler* (New York: Basic Books, 1997), pp. 128–35.
64. 'Know Thyself', in Ellis, *Wagner's Prose Works*, VI, p. 274; and Rose, *Wagner*, pp. 143–52.

Chapter 5. Hitler and the End of Weimar

1. Peter Phillips, *The Tragedy of German Democracy* (New York: Pegasus, 1970), pp. 59–60.
2. John Hiden, *Germany and Europe 1919–1939* (New York: Longman, 1993), pp. 7–31, and Samuel William Halperin, *Germany Tried Democracy* (New York: Crowell, 1946), pp. 100–3 and 137–53.
3. Detlev Peukert, *The Weimar Republic: The Crisis of Classical Modernity*, tr. Richard Deveson (New York: Hill & Wang, 1987), pp. 52–70.
4. Ibid., pp. 70–7.
5. Michael Burleigh, 'Scholarship, State and Nation,1918–1945', in John Breuilly (ed.), *The State of Germany* (London: Longman, 1992), pp.128–40, and Richard Hunt (ed.), *The Creation of the Weimar Republic: Stillborn Democracy* (Lexington, MA: Heath, 1969).
6. William Pelz, *The Spartakusbund and the German Working Class Movement, 1914–1919* (Lewiston, NY: E. Mellen Press, 1988); J.P. Nettl, *Rosa Luxemburg* (New York: Oxford University Press, 1966).
7. James Corum, *The Roots of Blitzkrieg: Hans von Seeckt and the German Military Reform* (Lawrence: University Press of Kansas, 1992).
8. Johannes Erger, *Der Kapp-Lüttwitz-Putsch: Ein Beitrag zur deutschen innenpolitik, 1919–1920* (Düsseldorf: Droste, 1967).
9. Johannes Mattern, *Bavaria and the Reich* (Baltimore: Johns Hopkins University Press, 1923).
10. Alois Hudal, *Die Grundlagen des Nationalsozialismus* (Leipzig and Vienna: Gunther, 1937), pp. 21ff; Dietrich Orlow, *The History of the Nazi Party, 1919–1945* (Pittsburgh: University of Pittsburgh Press, 1969–73); and Detlev Peukert and Jürgen Peukert (eds), *Alltag im Nationalsozialismus* (Wuppertal: Peter Hammer Verlag, 1981).
11. *The Speeches of Adolf Hitler*, tr. and ed. Norman Baynes (New York: Howard Fertig, 1969), I, pp.103–7.
12. Recommended biographies include: Alan Bullock, *Hitler: A Study in Tyranny* (Harmondsworth: Penguin, 1962); Joachim Fest, *Hitler* (New York: Random House, 1975); John Toland, *Adolf Hitler* (Garden City, NY: Doubleday, 1976); William Carr, *Hitler: A Study in Personality and Politics* (London: Edward Arnold, 1978); and Rainer Zitelmann, *Hitler: Selbstverständis eines Revolutionärs* (Hamburg: Berg, 1987).
13. Walter Langer, *The Mind of Adolf Hitler* (New York: Basic Books, 1972), pp. 43–4.
14. Robert Waite, *The Psychopathic God: Adolf Hitler* (New York: Basic Books, 1977), pp. 79–81.
15. Ibid., pp. 70–1, 131–2.
16. Brigitte Hamann, *Hitler's Vienna: A Dictator's Apprenticeship*, tr. Thomas Thornton (New York: Oxford University Press, 1999), pp. 42–72.
17. Ian Kershaw, *Hitler: 1889–1936* (New York: Norton, 1998), p. 11.
18. Langer, *Mind of Hitler*, p. 157, and Rudolph Binion, *Hitler Among the Germans* (New York: Elsevier, 1976), pp. 131–4.
19. Waite, *Psychopathic God*, pp. 194–7.
20. Hamann, *Hitler's Vienna*, pp. 10–11, and Kershaw, *Hitler*, pp. 15–18.
21. Langer, *Mind of Hitler*, pp. 116–18.
22. Hamann, *Hitler's Vienna*, pp. 28–36.

23. Kershaw, *Hitler*, pp. 52–6.
24. Hamann, *Hitler's Vienna*, pp. 117–31.
25. Peter Pulzer, *The Rise of Political Anti-Semitism in Germany and Austria* (New York: Wiley, 1964), pp. 112–25.
26. Felix Salten, *Vom österreichische Antlitz* [Austria's Face] (Berlin, 1909), pp. 135–6.
27. Hamann, *Hitler's Vienna*, pp. 347–52, and Kershaw, *Hitler*, pp. 60–7.
28. Hamann, *Hitler's Vienna*, pp. 325–59.
29. Ibid., pp. 253–61.
30. Kershaw, *Hitler*, pp. 95–101.
31. Waite, *Psychopathic God*, pp. 241–6. A Jewish officer recommended him for the award.
32. Binion, *Hitler Among the Germans*, pp. 5–14.
33. Kershaw, *Hitler*, pp. 97–105.
34. Langer, *Mind of Hitler*, pp. 125–30.
35. Hannah Vogt, *The Burden of Guilt*, tr. Herbert Strauss (New York: Oxford University Press, 1964), pp. 163–6.
36. Fromm says Hitler was anal sadistic with women he deemed inferior, masochistic with those he admired.
37. Kershaw, *Hitler*, pp. 109–26.
38. See Richard Koenigsberg, *Hitler's Ideology* (New York: Library of Social Science, 1974), pp. 10–14.
39. Waite, *Psychopathic God*, p. 25.
40. Adolf Hitler, *Mein Kampf* (Harrisburg: Stackpole Sons, 1939), I, p. 294.
41. *Hitler's Speeches*, 28 July 1922, I, p. 30, and 20 April 1923, p. 59.
42. Ibid., p. 316.
43. *Mein Kampf*, I, p. 317.
44. *Hitler's Speeches*, April 1922, I, pp. 19–20.
45. Ibid., 1 May 1923, p. 69.
46. Joachim Fest, *The Face of the Third Reich* (New York: Pantheon, 1970); Michael Kater, *The Nazi Party: A Social Profile of Members and Leaders, 1919–1945* (Cambridge: Harvard University Press, 1983); Ronald Smelser and Rainer Zitelmann (eds), *The Nazi Elite*, tr. Mary Fischer (New York: New York University Press, 1993).
47. According to psychologist Felix Gilbert, who tested them at Nuremberg, IQs ranged between 120 and 140, with one exception – Julius Streicher.
48. Max Gallo, *The Night of the Long Knives* (New York: Harper & Row, 1972).
49. Ernest Bramsted, *Goebbels and National Socialist Propaganda, 1925–1945* (East Lansing: Michigan State University Press, 1965); Helmut Heiber, *Goebbels*, tr. John Dickinson (New York: Hawthorn Books, 1972).
50. R.J. Overy, *Goering, The Iron Man* (London: Routledge and Kegan Paul, 1984) and Leonard Mosley, *The Reich Marshal: A Biography of Hermann Goering* (Garden City: Doubleday, 1974).
51. Richard Breitman, *The Architect of Genocide: Himmler and the Final Solution* (New York: Knopf, 1991); Roger Manvell and Heinrich Fraenkel, *Himmler* (New York: Putnam, 1965); and Peter Padfield, *Himmler* (New York: Henry Holt, 1991).
52. Gunther Deschner, *Reinhard Heydrich: Statthalter der totalen Macht* (Esslingen am Neckar: Bechtle Verlag, 1977); Shlomo Aronson, *Reinhard Heydrich und die Frühgeschichte von Gestapo und SD* (Stuttgart: Deutsche Verlag-Anstalt, 1971).
53. Roger Manvell and Heinrich Fraenkel, *Hess: A Biography* (London: MacGibbon, 1971).
54. J.V. Lang and Claus Sibyll, *The Secretary; Martin Bormann, the Man Who Manipulated Hitler* (Athens: Ohio University Press, 1978).
55. Randall Bytwerk, *Julius Streicher: The Man Who Persuaded a Nation to Hate Jews* (New York: Stein & Day, 1983).
56. Fritz Nova, *Alfred Rosenberg: Nazi Theorist of the Holocaust* (New York: Hippocrene Books, 1986).

57. *The Ribbentrop Memoirs* (London: Wm. Heinemann, 1956).
58. Albert Speer, *Inside the Third Reich* (New York: Macmillan, 1970), and *Spandau: The Secret Diaries* (New York: Macmillan, 1976).
59. Harold Gordon, *Hitler and the Beer Hall Putsch* (Princeton: Princeton University Press, 1972); and Ernst Hanfstaengl, 'Fiasco at the Feldherrenhalle', *Hitler: The Missing Years* (London: Eyre & Spottiswood, 1957), pp. 91–109.
60. D.J. Goodspeed, *Ludendorff: Soldier, Dictator, Revolutionary* (London: Hart-Davis, 1966).
61. Hannah Vogt, *Schuld oder Verhängnis* (Frankfurt: Verlag Moritz Diesterweg, 1961), p. 51.
62. Ian Kershaw (ed.), *Weimar: Why Did German Democracy Fail?* (New York: St Martin's, 1990); Helmut Heiber, *The Weimar Republic*, tr. W.E. Yuill (Oxford: Blackwell, 1993); and Eberhard Kolb, *The Weimar Republic*, tr. P.S. Falls (London: Unwin Hyman, 1988).
63. Henry Turner, *Stresemann and the Politics of the Weimar Republic* (Princeton: Princeton University Press, 1963).
64. Andreas Dorpalen, *Hindenburg and the Weimar Republic* (Princeton: Princeton University Press, 1964).
65. Max Kele, *Nazis and Workers, 1919–1933* (Chapel Hill: University of North Carolina Press, 1972); Michael Dobkowski and Isidor Walliman (eds), *Towards the Holocaust: The Social and Economic Collapse of the Weimar Republic* (Westport: Greenwood Press, 1983).
66. Michael Burleigh and Wolfgang Wippermann, *The Racial State: Germany 1933–1945* (Cambridge: Cambridge University Press, 1991), p. 276, and Thomas Childers, *The Nazi Voter: The Social Foundations of Fascism* (Chapel Hill: University of North Carolina Press, 1986).
67. Halperin, *Germany Tried Democracy*, pp. 447–526; Martin Broszat, *Hitler and the Collapse of Weimar Germany* (Leamington Spa: Berg, 1987); and Peter Stachura (ed.), *The Nazi Machtergreifung* (London: Allen & Unwin, 1983).

Chapter 6. Gleichschaltung: The Nazi Consolidation of Power

1. Jeremy Noakes and Geoffrey Pridham (eds), *Documents on Nazism 1919–1945* (New York: Viking, 1974), pp. 188–95.
2. Nico Rost, 'Concentration Camp Dachau', tr. Captain Bernard Hanauer (Brussels: Comite International de Dachau), pp. 13–16, and Paul Berben, *Dachau 1933–1945: The Official History* (London: Latimer Trend, 1975).
3. Saul S. Friedman, *Amcha: An Oral Testament of the Holocaust* (Hanover: University Press of America, 1979), p. 201.
4. 'Dachau 1933–1945', report of US 7th Army (1945), pp. 36–7.
5. Olga Wormser-Migot, *Le Système Concentration Nazi (1933–1945)* (Paris: Presses Universitaires de France, 1968), pp. 80–8.
6. Charles Sydnor, *Soldiers of Destruction: The SS Death's Head Division, 1933–1945* (Princeton: Princeton University Press, 1990), pp. 27–35.
7. Ibid., p. 391.
8. Eugen Kogon, *The Theory and Practice of Hell* (New York: Farrar, Straus, Giroux, 1950), pp. 251–7. See Eugene Heimler, *Concentration Camp* (New York: Pyramid, 1959); Pierre Julitte, *Block 26: Sabotage at Buchenwald* (New York: Doubleday, 1971); and Elie Wiesel, *Night* (New York: Avon, 1969).
9. Konnilyn Feig, *Hitler's Death Camps: The Sanity of Madness* (New York: Holmes & Meier, 1981), p. 121.
10. Typed confession of Erich Ziereis, 24 May 1945. (See Feig, *Hitler's Death Camps*.)
11. Feig, *Hitler's Death Camps*, pp. 178–9.
12. Michael Burleigh and Wolfgang Wippermann, *The Racial State: Germany 1933–1945*

(Cambridge: Cambridge University Press, 1991), pp. 68–72.

13. Saul S. Friedman, *The Oberammergau Passion Play* (Carbondale: Southern Illinois University Press, 1984), p. 126.

14. William S. Allen, 'Objective and Subjective Inhabitants in the German Resistance to Hitler', in Franklin Littell (ed.), *The German Church Struggle and the Holocaust* (Detroit: Wayne State University Press, 1974), p. 121.

15. Max Gallo, *The Night of Long Knives*, tr. Lily Emmet (London: Souvenir Press, 1973), p. 92.

16. Heinrich Bennecke, *Die Reichswehr und der 'Röhm-Putsch'* (Munich: G. Olzog, 1964).

17. One of the executioners was Theodor Eicke.

18. Adolf Kober, 'Germany', *Universal Jewish Encyclopedia*, Isaac Landman (ed.) (New York: Universal Jewish Encyclopedia, 1941), IV, pp. 441–2.

19. Jacob Marcus, *The Jew in the Medieval World* (Philadelphia: Jewish Publication Society of America, 1960), pp. 115–58.

20. Peter Pulzer, *The Rise of Political Anti-Semitism in Germany and Austria* (New York: John Wiley & Sons, 1984), pp. 44–68, 108–11, 116–20.

21. W.E. Mosse, *Jews in the Germany Economy: The German-Jewish Economic Elite, 1820–1935* (Oxford: Clarendon Press, 1987), pp. 20–8, 179, 211–14.

22. Peter Pulzer, *Jews and the German State* (Cambridge, MA: Blackwell, 1992), p. 120.

23. Ibid., p. 23. See also Shulamit Volkov, 'Kontinuität und Diskontinuität im deutschen Antisemitismus 1878–1945', *Vierteljährshefte für Zeitgeschichte*, 1985, Heft 2, p. 224.

24. Sidney Bolkosky, *The Distorted Image: German Jewish perceptions of Germans and Germany 1918–1934* (New York: Elsevier, 1975), pp. 1–29; George Mosse, *Germans and Jews: The Right, the Left and the Search for a Third Force in Pre-War Nazi Germany* (New York: Fertig, 1970).

25. Pulzer, *Jews and German State*, p. 7.

26. Hannah Vogt, *The Burden of Guilt*, tr. Herbert Strauss (New York: Oxford University Press, 1964), pp. 136–40.

27. Saul S. Friedman, *No Haven for the Oppressed: United States Policy toward Jewish Refugees, 1938–1945* (Detroit: Wayne State University Press, 1973), p. 46.

28. Karl Schleunes, *The Twisted Road to Auschwitz: Nazi Policy toward German Jews, 1933–1939* (Urbana: University of Illinois Press, 1990, 1970), pp. 77–8.

29. Ibid., pp. 92–118.

30. George Mosse, *Nazi Culture: Intellectual, Cultural and Social Life in the Third Reich* (New York: Grosset & Dunlap, 1966), pp. 317–18.

31. Schleunes, *Twisted Road to Auschwitz*, p. 108.

32. Robert Proctor, 'Nazi Biomedical Policies', in Arthur Caplan (ed.), *When Medicine Went Mad: Bioethics and the Holocaust* (Totowa, NJ: Humana Press, 1992), p. 36.

33. John Mendelsohn (ed.), *The Holocaust: Selected Documents* (New York: Garland, 1982), I, pp. 24–32.

34. Friedman, *Oberammergau Passion Play*, pp. 82–3.

35. *Hitler's Secret Conversations 1941–1944* (New York: Octagon Books, 1972), p. 457.

36. *The Passion Play of Oberammergau*, 1934, p. 10 (Village of Oberammergau, 1934).

37. Friedman, *Oberammergau Passion Play*, pp. 128–46.

38. Richard Mandell, *The Nazi Olympics* (New York: Macmillan, 1971); Saul S. Friedman, 'The Olympics: Flawed Ideals', *Congress Monthly*, 45 (September–October 1978), pp. 10–13.

39. Within the week, Glickman ran against Germany's best sprinter, Erich Buchheimer, in Hamburg and defeated him handily.

40. Brundage was instrumental in returning the games to Munich in 1972. That year 11 Israeli athletes were kidnapped by PLO terrorists and killed in a bungled rescue operation.

41. Led by athletes in gymnastics, women's track, canoeing, equestrian and pistol shooting, Germany won more than 70 medals in the summer games.

Chapter 7. The Year of Decision: 1938

1. *American Jewish Yearbook 1939–1940*, p. 261.
2. Erich Maria Remarque, *Flotsam*, tr. Denver Lindley (Boston: Little, Brown, 1941).
3. Alfred Low, *The Anschluss Movement 1931–1938 and the Great Powers* (New York: Columbia University, 1985).
4. Gottfried Kindermann, *Hitler's Defeat in Austria, 1933–1934: Europe's First Containment of Nazi Expansionism*, tr. Sonia Brough and David Taylor (Boulder, CO: Westview Press, 1988).
5. Kurt von Schuschnigg, *The Brutal Takeover*, tr. Richard Barry (New York: Athenaeum, 1971), p. 255.
6. Gordon Brook-Shepherd, *The Anschluss* (Philadelphia: Lippincott, 1963), pp. 119–20.
7. Dieter Wagner and Gerhard Tomkowitz, *Anschluss: The Week Hitler Seized Vienna*, tr. Geoffrey Strachan (New York: St Martin's, 1968), pp. 102, 115.
8. Saul S. Friedman, interview with Walter Beck, Youngstown, 20 August 1975, in *Amcha: An Oral Testament of the Holocaust* (Lanham, MD: University Press of America, 1979), pp. 78–9.
9. Schuschnigg, *Brutal Takeover*, pp. 265–77.
10. Wagner and Tomkowitz, *Anschluss*, p. 228.
11. Brook-Shepherd, *Anschluss*, p. 195.
12. 'Sack of Austria' and 'The Locust Strikes Again', *National Jewish Monthly*, 52 (April 1938), pp. 266, 281ff.
13. Ibid., p. 266.
14. Radomir Luza, *Austro-German Relations in the Anschluss Era* (Princeton: Princeton University Press, 1975), p. 227.
15. *Völkischer Beobachter*, 15 May 1939, p. 1.
16. Interview with Walter Beck, *Amcha*, pp. 83–4.
17. *Speeches of Adolf Hitler, Apr. 1922–Aug. 1939*, Norman Baynes (ed.) (New York: Fertig, 1969), I, p. 727.
18. *Public Papers and Addresses of Franklin D. Roosevelt* (New York: Random House, 1938–50), 7: 170.
19. John Hope Simpson, *Refugees: A Review of the Situation since September 1938* (London: Royal Institute of International Affairs and Oxford University Press, 1939), pp. 5–6, 52–9, 114.
20. Author interview with Dodds, Washington, 2 June 1968.
21. *Public Papers of FDR*, 7: 172.
22. League of Nations, International Bureaux, *Nansen International Office for Refugees: Report of the Governing Board for the Year Ending June 30th 1938* (XII. B, 1–3), 1938, p. 3.
23. Louis Holborn, 'The League of Nations and the Refugee Problem', *Annals of the American Academy of Political and Social Science*, 203 (May 1939), pp. 126–33.
24. Saul S. Friedman, *No Haven for the Oppressed: United States Policy toward Jewish Refugees, 1938–1945* (Detroit: Wayne State University Press, 1973), p. 31.
25. Ibid., pp. 20–2.
26. Ibid., pp. 22–6.
27. Martin Gumpert, 'Immigrants by Conviction', *Survey Graphic*, 30 (September 1941), p. 463.
28. Minutes of Meeting, 16 May 1938, President's Advisory Committee on Political Refugees, Wise Papers.
29. *Proceedings of the Intergovernmental Committee, Evian, July 6 to 15, 1938. Verbatim Record of the Plenary Meetings of the Committee, Resolutions and Reports* (July 1938), pp. 12–13, 16, 20.
30. Ibid., pp. 21–5.
31. Mark Wischnitzer, *The Historical Background of the Settlement of Jewish Refugees in Santo Domingo* (New York, 1942), pp. 46–7.

32. Interview with Licci Habe, Ascona, Switzerland, 18 May 1988.
33. Hans Habe, *The Mission*, tr. Michael Bullock (New York: Coward-McCann, 1966).
34. Friedman, *No Haven for the Oppressed*, pp. 63–4.
35. Welles to Rublee, 21 Dec. 1938, *FRUS* I: 878–9.
36. *Public Papers of FDR*, 8: 364.
37. Jeremy Noakes and Geoffrey Pridham (eds), *Documents on Nazism, 1919–1945* (New York: Viking Press, 1974), pp. 301–4.
38. R.A.C. Parker, *Chamberlain and Appeasement: British Policy and the Coming of the Second World War* (New York: St Martin's, 1993), pp. 156–81; Shiela Grant Duff, *Europe and the Czechs* (London: Penguin, 1939); Martin Gilbert and Richard Gott, *The Appeasers* (London: Weidenfeld & Nicolson, 1963).
39. Beneš, *From Munich to New War and New Victory*, tr. Godfrey Lias (New York: Arno Press, 1972), pp. 8, 38, 63–72.
40. Celia Heller, *On the Edge of Destruction* (New York: Schocken, 1977), pp. 175–9.
41. John Mendelsohn (ed.), *The Holocaust: Selected Documents* (New York: Garland Press, 1982), III, pp. 1–5.
42. The note was deposited without comment in Presidential files.
43. Rita Thalmann and Emmanuel Feinermann, *Crystal Night*, tr. Gilles Cremonesi (New York: Coward, McCann & Geoghegan, 1974), p. 48.
44. Some of the Grynszpan claim Herschel was killed by the Nazis, while others believe he took another name at the end of the war.
45. Mendelsohn, *Holocaust*, I, pp. 136–45; and Zosa Szajkowski, *An Illustrated Sourcebook on the Holocaust* (New York: Ktav, 1977).
46. Thalmann and Feinermann, *Crystal Night*, pp. 56–62; Mendelsohn, *Holocaust*, III, pp. 78–170; and International Military Tribunal, *Trial of the Major War Criminals* (New York: AMS Press, 1971, 1949), IX, pp. 90–3, and XIII, p. 122.
47. Thalmann and Feinermann, *Crystal Night*, pp. 63, 128.
48. Ibid., pp. 64–85.
49. Interview with Sonja Schulmann Schwartz, 13 July 1979, in *Amcha*, pp. 62–3.
50. Interview with Settie Sonnenborn, 10 September 1974, in *Amcha*, p. 46.
51. 'An Official Nazi Report on the November (1938) Pogroms in Vienna', *Yad Vashem Bulletin*, No. 2 (December 1957), p. 28.
52. Friedman, *Amcha*, pp. 54–5.
53. Mendelsohn, *Holocaust*, III, p. 278.
54. Thalmann and Feinermann, *Crystal Night*, pp. 117–26.
55. Ibid., p. 127.
56. Prentiss Gilbert, Chargé d'Affaires to Hull, 6 December 1938, in Mendelsohn, *Holocaust*, I, p. 158.
57. Youngstown, *Vindicator*, 19 November 1938, p. 5.
58. Friedman, *No Haven for the Oppressed*, p. 85.
59. Youngstown, *Vindicator*, 16 November 1938, p. 13.
60. Friedman, *No Haven for the Oppressed*, pp. 85–6.
61. *Public Papers of FDR*, 7: 597.
62. Ibid., 602–4.
63. Witt and Thomas, *Voyage of the Damned*, p. 303.

Chapter 8. World War II Begins: The Polish Ghettos

1. Anthony Reed and David Fisher, *The Deadly Embrace: Hitler, Stalin and Nazi-Soviet Relations, 1939–1941* (New York: Norton, 1988); Peter Kleist, *Zwischen Hitler und Stalin, 1939–1945* (Bonn: Athenaeum, 1950).
2. Youngstown, *Vindicator*, 2 September 1939, pp. 1–2.
3. Yisrael Gutman, *The Jews of Warsaw 1939–1943* (Bloomington: Indiana University Press, 1982), p. 11.

4. *Meczenstwo, Walka, Zaglada, Zydow w Polsce, 1939–1945* (Warsaw: Polish Ministry of Information, undated), pp. 26–42.
5. Michael Burleigh and Wolfgang Wippermann, *The Racial State: Germany 1933–1945* (Cambridge: Cambridge University Press, 1991), p. 100.
6. Jacob Apenszlak (ed.), *The Black Book of Polish Jewry* (New York: American Federation for Polish Jews and Association of Jewish Refugees and Immigrants from Poland, 1943), p. 24. See also pp. 8–9.
7. Gutman, *Jews of Warsaw*, pp. 27–8.
8. Apenszlak, *Black Book of Polish Jewry*, pp. 5–6.
9. Ibid., pp. 28–69.
10. Philip Friedman (ed.), *Martyrs and Fighters: The Epic of the Warsaw Ghetto* (New York: Praeger, 1954), pp. 166–7.
11. Simon Segal, *The New Order in Poland* (New York: Knopf, 1942), pp. 5–25.
12. Nora Levin, *The Holocaust: The Destruction of European Jewry 1933–1945* (New York: Schocken, 1973), pp. 171–6.
13. Gutman, *Jews of Warsaw*, pp. 77–83.
14. Dieter Pohl, *Von der 'Judenpolitik' zum Judenmord: Der Distrikt Lublin des General-gouvernement 1939–1944* (Frankfurt: Peter Lang, 1993), pp. 79–84.
15. Gutman, *Jews of Warsaw*, pp. 72–7.
16. Ibid., pp. 86–90, and Friedman, *Martyrs and Fighters*, pp. 78–82.
17. Pohl, *Judenpolitik zum Judenmord*, p. 47.
18. Götz Aly, *Final Solution: Nazi Population Policy and the Murder of the European Jews*, tr. B.L. Cooper and A. Brown (London: Arnold, 1999), pp. 20–1.
19. Ibid., p. 19.
20. Ibid., pp. 42, 143.
21. Ibid., pp. 45, 61, 151.
22. Gerald Reitlinger, *The Final Solution* (London: Beechhurst Press, 1953), p. 41.
23. Segal, *New Order in Poland*, pp. 40–69.
24. Levin, *Holocaust*, pp. 181–3.
25. Christopher Browning, *The Path to Genocide* (New York: Cambridge University Press, 1992), pp. 10–11, and Pohl, *Judenpolitik zum Judenmord*, pp. 48–9.
26. Apenszlak, *Black Book of Polish Jewry*, pp. 44–5.
27. Ibid., pp. 282–314.
28. Gutman, *Jews of Warsaw*, pp. 60–3.
29. Friedman, *Martyrs and Fighters*, pp. 58–65; Gutman, *Jews of Warsaw*, p. 64; and Apenszlak, *Black Book of Polish Jewry*, pp. 36–9, 45–6, 195–204.
30. Apenszlak, *Black Book of Polish Jewry*, p. 186. See also Segal, *New Order in Poland*, pp. 181–97.
31. Apenszlak, *Black Book of Polish Jewry*, p. 186. Others estimate the daily rations for Poles at 699 calories and Jews at 184. C. Manojczyk, *Polityka III Rzesy w okupowaney Polsce* (Warsaw 1970), II, p. 171.
32. Gutman, *Jews of Warsaw*, pp. 94–100, and Charles Roland, *Courage under Siege: Starvation, Disease and Death in the Warsaw Ghetto* (Oxford: Oxford University Press, 1992).
33. Apenszlak, *Black Book of Polish Jewry*, pp. 46–9, 184–6.
34. Friedman, *Martyrs and Fighters*, p. 90.
35. Gutman, *Jews of Warsaw*, pp. 91–3.
36. Friedman, *Martyrs and Fighters*, pp. 111–41, and Gutman, *Jews of Warsaw*, pp. 102–6.
37. Ringelblum, *Notes from the Warsaw Ghetto*, ed. and tr. Jacob Sloan (New York: McGraw-Hill, 1958), pp. 233–4.
38. *Janusz Korczak: Ghetto Diary* (New York: Holocaust Library, 1978), p. 176.
39. Apenszlak, *Black Book of Polish Jewry*, pp. 66–73.
40. Interview with Sam Eilenberg, in *Amcha*, p. 113.
41. Alan Adelson and Robert Lapides (eds), *Lodz Ghetto: Inside a Community under Siege* (New York: Viking, 1989), p. 373.

42. Ibid., pp. 368, 391.
43. Apenszlak, *Black Book of Polish Jewry*, p. 199.
44. *Lodz Ghetto*, p. 328.
45. Ibid., p. 330.
46. Interview with Eilenberg, *Amcha*, p. 117.
47. *Lodz Ghetto*, p. 494.
48. Ibid., pp. 83–6.
49. Pankiewicz, *Cracow Ghetto Pharmacy*, p. 96.
50. Ibid., pp. 107–20.
51. Ibid., pp. 124–31.
52. Interviews, Eva Fugman, Youngstown, 10 February 1972, 10 June 1974, 7 August 1975.
53. Interview, Mrs Rosenzweig, 15 June 1973, in *Amcha*, p. 149.
54. Ibid., pp. 152–3.
55. Ibid., p. 153.
56. Apenszlak, *Black Book of Polish Jewry*, p. 201.
57. *Life Magazine*, 12 (23 February 1942), pp. 26–7.

Chapter 9. Blitzkreig in the West: Holland

1. *New York Times*, 5 April 1940, pp. 1, 3.
2. *New York Times*, 4 April 1940, pp. 1, 3.
3. *New York Times*, 7 April 1940, p. 1.
4. Frederic S. Pearson, *The Weak State in International Crisis: The Case of the Netherlands in the German Invasion Crisis of 1939–1940* (Washington: University Press of America, 1981) and Eeko Nicolas van Kleffens, *Juggernaut over Holland* (New York: Columbia University Press, 1941).
5. Len Deighton, *Blitzkrieg: From the Rise of Hitler to the Fall of Dunkirk* (New York: Knopf, 1980) and Larry Addington, *The Blitzkrieg Era and the German General Staff, 1865–1941* (New Brunswick: Rutgers University Press, 1971).
6. Interview with Siep Jongeling, 10 August 1974, in Friedman, *Amcha*, p. 170.
7. Interview with Eva Fugman Jacobs, 7 August 1975.
8. Cecil Roth, *History of the Marranos* (Philadelphia: JPSA, 1932) and Heinrich Graetz, *History of the Jews* (Philadelphia: JPSA, 1956, 1894), IV, pp. 76–86.
9. Bob Moore, *Victims and Survivors: Nazi Persecution of the Jews in the Netherlands, 1940–1945* (London: Arnold, 1997), p. 25.
10. Werner Warmbrunn, *The Dutch under German Occupation, 1940–1945* (Stanford: Stanford University Press, 1963), pp. 83–96; Gerhard Hirschfeld, *Nazi Rule and Dutch Collaboration* (Oxford: Berg, 1988), pp. 250–310; Franz Neumann, *Behemoth: The Structure and Practice of National Socialism 1933–1944* (1944).
11. IMT, *Trial of Major War Criminals* (New York: AMS Press, 1971, 1947), V, p. 350.
12. Jacob Presser, *The Destruction of the Dutch Jews*, tr. Arnold Pomerans (New York: Dutton, 1969), p. 41, and Hirschfeld, *Nazi Rule*, pp. 118–31.
13. Presser, *Destruction of Dutch Jews*, pp. 325–6, and Hirschfeld, *Nazi Rule*, pp. 225–42. See also Walter Maas, *The Netherlands at War* (Amsterdam: Abelard-Schumann, 1970); Gerhard Hirschfeld, 'Collaboration and Attentism in the Netherlands, 1940–1941', *Journal of Contemporary History*, 16 (July 1981), pp. 467–86; Henry Mason, *The Purge of Dutch Quislings: Emergency Justice in the Netherlands* (The Hague: Nijhoff, 1952); and N.W. Posthumus (ed.), *The Netherlands During German Occupation* (Philadelphia: American Academy of Political and Social Science, 1946).
14. Presser, *Destruction of Dutch Jews*, pp. 33–8.
15. Moore, *Victims and Survivors*, pp. 57–9.
16. Joseph Michman, 'The Controversial Stand of the Joodse Raad in the Netherlands', *Yad Vashem Studies*, 10 (1974), p. 12, and Moore, *Victims and Survivors*, pp. 29–30.

17. Ibid., p. 6. See also 'The Controversy Surrounding the Jewish Council in Amsterdam', in Yisrael Gutman and Cynthia Haft (eds), *Patterns of the Jewish Leadership in Nazi Europe* (Jerusalem: Yad Vashem, 1977), pp. 235–57.
18. Michman, 'Controversial Stand of Joodse Raad', p. 32.
19. Presser, *Destruction of Dutch Jews*, pp. 78–93.
20. Moore, *Victims and Survivors*, pp. 82–3.
21. Ibid., pp. 75, 112.
22. See Moore's detailed evaluation of the *Joodse Raad*, pp. 106–15.
23. Warmbrunn, *Dutch under German Occupation*, pp. 66–7, and Moore, *Victims and Survivors*, 118–45.
24. Presser, *Destruction of Dutch Jews*, pp. 274–5.
25. Warmbrunn, *Dutch under German Occupation*, pp. 177–84, and Moore, *Victims and Survivors*, pp. 106–15.
26. Ibid., pp. 106–11, 113–18.
27. Interview with Jongeling, *Amcha*, pp. 169–70.
28. Ibid., pp. 171–2.
29. IMT, *Trial of Major War Criminals*, VII, pp. 99–104.
30. Ibid., p. 59.
31. Moore, *Victims and Survivors*, pp. 206–11.
32. Ibid., pp. 199–205.
33. Presser, *Destruction of Dutch Jews*, pp. 328–63.
34. Raul Hilberg, *The Destruction of the European Jews* (New York: Quadrangle, 1951), p. 381.
35. Philip Mechanicus, *Year of Fear: A Jewish Prisoner Waits for Auschwitz* (New York: Hawthorn Books, 1968); Hilde Verdoner-Sluizer, *Letters from Nazi Transit Camp Westerbork, 1942–1944*, Yoka and Francisca Verdoner (eds) (Washington: Acropolis Books, 1990); Marietta Moskin, *I Am Rosemarie* (New York: Dell, 1972); Etty Hillesum, *Letters from Westerbork*, tr. Arnold Pomerans (New York: Pantheon, 1986).
36. Jacob Boas, *Boulevard des Misères: The Story of Transit Camp Westerbork* (Hampden, CT: Archon Books, 1985), pp. 111–28.
37. Ibid., pp. 50–1.
38. Ibid., pp. 20–8.
39. Ibid., pp. 35–42.
40. Moore, *Victims and Survivors*, p. 94.
41. Presser, *Destruction of Dutch Jews*, p. 142.
42. Boas, *Boulevard des Misères*, pp. 85–110.
43. Moore, *Victims and Survivors*, p. 102.
44. Presser, *Destruction of Dutch Jews*, p. 457.
45. Ibid., pp. 178–84.
46. Warmbrunn, *Dutch under German Occupation*, pp. 185–220.
47. Moore, *Victims and Survivors*, pp. 89–90.
48. Ibid., pp. 146–90.
49. Philip Friedman, *Their Brother's Keepers* (New York: Crown, 1957), pp. 64–7, and Marie Syrkin, *Blessed Is the Match: The Story of Jewish Resistance* (Philadelphia: Jewish Publication Society, 1947), p. 286.
50. Interview with Jongeling, *Amcha*, p. 174.
51. Author interview with Paul van Kessel, Kent, Ohio, 2 May 1994. See also Warmbrunn, *Dutch under German Occupation*, pp. 173–7.
52. *Anne Frank: The Diary of a Young Girl*, tr. B.M. Mooyart (New York: Washington Square Press, 1967, 1952). See also *The Diary of Anne Frank: The Critical Edition*, ed. David Barnouw and Gerrold Van der Stroom, tr. Arnold Pomerans and B.M. Mooyart-Doubleday (New York: Doubleday, 1986). Doubleday recently published a 'definitive' edition with additional materials.
53. Bruno Bettelheim, *The Informed Heart* (New York: Free Press, 1960), pp. 248–9.

54. Interview with Bettelheim, Youngstown State University, 16 October 1986.
55. *Diary of Anne Frank: Critical Edition*, pp. 200–1. For Margot's plans to become a midwife in Palestine see pp. 636–7.
56. Ibid., p. 316.
57. Ibid., p. 600.
58. David Barnouw, 'The Play', *Diary of Anne Frank: Critical Edition*, pp. 78–83; Cynthia Ozick, 'Who Owns Anne Frank?', *New Yorker* (6 October 1997), pp. 76–87; Meyer Levin, *The Fanatic*; Lawrence Graver, *An Obsession with Anne Frank: Meyer Levin and the Diary* (Berkeley: University of California Press, 1996); and Ralph Melnick, *The Stolen Legacy of Anne Frank* (New Haven: Yale University Press, 1997).
59. Simon Wiesenthal, *The Murderers Among Us* (New York: Bantam, 1967), pp. 172–80.
60. *Diary of Anne Frank: Critical Edition*, p. 694.
61. Friedman, *Brothers' Keepers*; Peter Hellman, *Avenue of the Righteous* (New York: Atheneum, 1980).
62. *ZINS Weekly News Bulletin*, 31 December 1976, p. 3.

Chapter 10. Belgium and Luxembourg

1. Maxime Steinberg, *L'Étoile et Le Fusil: La Question Juive 1940–1942* (Brussels: Vie Ouvrière, 1983), pp. 155–6.
2. Ibid., pp. 144–8; Harold Callender, 'Fascism in Belgium', *Foreign Affairs*, 15 (April 1937), pp. 554–63; Werner Warmbrunn, *German Occupation of Belgium, 1940–1944* (New York: Peter Lang, 1993), pp. 149–69.
3. Steinberg, *La Question Juive*, pp. 168–9, and Jacques Willequet, *Le Belgique sous la botte: Résistances et collaborations 1940–1945* (Paris: Editions Universitaires, 1986).
4. Falkenhausen's father had been Governor-General of Belgium in World War I. Paul Struye, 'Policy of Occupation', in *Belgium under Occupation*, ed. and tr. Jan-Albert Goris (New York: Moretus Press, 1947), pp. 19–20.
5. Steinberg, *La Question Juive*, pp. 20–1.
6. Jean van Houtte, 'War Damages', in Goris, *Belgium under Occupation*, p. 105. See Marcel Thirry, *La Belgique pendant la guerre* (Paris: Machette, 1947); Gaby Warris, *Het bloedbad van Abbeville: 20 Mei 1940* (Antwerp: Hadewijch, 1994); Jacques de Launay, *Hitler en Flandres* (Brussels: Byblos, 1975).
7. John Gillingham, *Belgian Business in the Nazi New Order* (Ghent: Jan Dhondt Foundation, 1977), pp. 45–6.
8. Ibid., p. 48.
9. Ibid., pp. 163, 142–53, 189; and R. Ardenne, *German Exploitation of Belgium*, Brookings Pamphlet 35 (Washington: The Brookings Institution, 1942).
10. *We Suffer in a Thousand Ways: Letters from Occupied Belgium* (Belgian Information Center, 1942), p. 28.
11. Steinberg, *La Question Juive*, pp. 43–8.
12. Ibid., pp. 88–91.
13. Interview with Anita Maroko, 26 August 1975, in *Amcha*, pp. 181–2.
14. Nathan Ausubel, *Pictorial History of the Jewish People*, pp. 193–4; *La Grande Synagogue de Bruxelles* (Brussels: Communauté Israelite de Bruxelles, 1978); Ludo Abicht, *De joden van Antwerpen* (Antwerp: Hadewijch, 1993).
15. Jan-Albert Goris, *Belgium in Bondage* (Antwerp: NV Standaard-Boekhandel, 1946), p. 35.
16. *We Suffer in a Thousand Ways*, pp. 10–11.
17. Michel Deveze, 'Human Rights: Violation of the Rights of Man', in Goris, *Belgium under Occupation*, pp. 216–17, and Betty Garfinkels, *Les belges face à la persecution raciale 1940–1944* (Brussels, 1965).
18. Steinberg, *La Question Juive*, p. 106.

19. Ibid., p. 64.
20. Goris, *Belgium in Bondage*, pp. 100–1.
21. Jean Vanwelkenhuyzen, *Les universités belges sous l'occupation allemande* (Brussels, no date).
22. Edmond-Francis Leclef, canon St Rombaut's Cathedral, *Le Cardinal J.E. van Roey et l'occupation allemande en Belgique* (Brussels: Editions Goemaere, 1945), pp. 53–5, 85–7.
23. Steinberg, *La Question Juive*, pp. 36–7.
24. Ibid., pp. 90–1.
25. Ibid., pp. 36–9.
26. Ibid., p. 208.
27. Lucien Steinberg, *Le Comité de défense des Juifs en Belgique 1942–1944* (Brussels: Éditions de l'Université de Bruxelles, 1973), pp. 54–5.
28. Ibid., p. 57.
29. Friedman, *Amcha*, p. 183.
30. Goris, *Belgium in Bondage*, pp. 39–42, 78; Joseph Bondas, 'Forced Labor and Deportations', in Goris, *Belgium under Occupation*, pp. 84–96; Mathias Haupt, *Der 'Arbeiteinsatz' der belgischen Bevölkerung wahrend des zweiten weltkriegs* (Bonn, 1970).
31. Steinberg, *Comité de défense des Juifs*, p. 39; Bondas, 'Forced Labor', in Goris, *Belgium under Occupation*, p. 87.
32. Steinberg, *La Question Juive*, pp. 144–5.
33. Edmond-Francis Leclef, 'The Catholic Church', in Goris, *Belgium under Occupation*, p. 164.
34. Leclef, *Cardinal van Roey*, pp. 115–62.
35. Ibid., pp. 141–4.
36. Maxime Steinberg, *L'Étoile et le Fusil: Les Cent Jours de la Déportation des Juifs en Belgique* (Brussels: Vie Ouvrière, 1984), pp. 197–9.
37. Ibid., pp. 171–2.
38. Breendonck was a fort on the outskirts of Antwerp. Prisoners were often clubbed or placed in punishment cells. Three hundred and fifty were shot, 15 hanged and 500 died because of the brutal treatment. Deveze, 'Violations of the Rights of Man', in Goris, *Belgium in Bondage*, pp. 218–19.
39. In August 1941, Leizer Krant tossed two fascists out of his shop. A year later, Krant was killed by one of the men and his wife was sent to Auschwitz. Steinberg, *Cent Jours de la Déportation*, p. 206.
40. Ibid., p. 214.
41. Yvonne de Ridder Files, *The Quest for Freedom: Belgian Resistance in World War II* (Santa Barbara: Fithian Press, 1991), pp. 30–3.
42. Goris, *Belgium in Bondage*, p. 67.
43. Steinberg, *Cent Jours de la Déportation*, p. 219.
44. Ibid., pp. 220–1.
45. Steinberg, *Comité de défense des Juives*, pp. 56–7.
46. Henri Sonnenbluck, *J'Avais 16 ans à Auschwitz* (Brussels: Cercle d'Éducation Populaire, 1990), pp. 15–17.
47. Few Jews sent their children back to school. Steinberg, *Cent Jours de la Déportation*, pp. 223–4.
48. Reminiscences of Nahum Mitteslbach, Microfilm 400, #213, Hebrew University Oral History Collection, Pt II, Holocaust Resistance and Rescue (Glen Rock, NJ: Microfilming Co., 1975), pp. 2–5.
49. Steinberg, *Le Comité de défense des Juifs en Belgique*, pp. 162–3.
50. Leclef, *Cardinal van Roey*, p. 231.
51. Ibid., p. 232.
52. Ibid., p. 234.
53. Ibid., p. 233.
54. Ibid., p. 236.

55. Leclef, 'The Catholic Church', in Goris, *Belgium under the Occupation*, pp. 165–6.
56. Steinberg, *Comité de défense des Juives*, p. 102.
57. Leclef, *Cardinal van Roey*, pp. 211–29.
58. Steinberg, *Comité de défense des Juives*, pp. 102–3, and Philip Friedman, *Their Brother's Keepers* (New York: Crown, 1997), pp. 70–1.
59. Steinberg, *Comité de défense des Juives*, pp. 84–5.
60. Goris, *Belgium in Bondage*, pp. 113–17; Roger Motz, *Belgium Unvanquished* (London: Drummond, 1942); *The Underground Press in Belgium* (London: Belgian Government-in-Exile, 1944); Pierre Jacquet, *Brabant Wallon 1940–1944, Occupation et Résistance* (Paris: Editions Duculot, 1989).
61. Steinberg, *Comité de Défense des Juives*, pp. 36–7.
62. Friedman, *Brother's Keepers*, pp. 68–9.
63. Steinberg, *Comité de Défense des Juives*, pp. 120–1.
64. Ibid., p. 70.
65. Maxime Steinberg, *La Traque des juifs, 1942–1944* (Brussels, 1986), pp. 218–29.
66. Steinberg, *Cent Jours de la Déportation*, p. 229. See also Maxime Steinberg, *Dossier Bruxelles Auschwitz: La police SS et l'extermination des juifs de Belgique* (Brussels, 1980).
67. Colonel Rémy (no first name listed), *Une Epoque de la Résistance* (Paris: Grange Batelière and Brussels: Erasme, 1976), pp. 1–2. See also Government of Luxembourg, *Luxembourg and the German Invasion, Before and After* (London: Hutchinson, 1942); Georges Heisbourg, *Le gouvernement Luxembourgeoios en exil* (Luxembourg: Saint Paul, 1986).
68. Remy, *Une Epoque de la Résistance*, III, pp. 23–4, 133, 285, and *Die Faschistische Okkupationspolitik in Belgien, Luxemburg und den Niederlanden (1940–1945)* (Berlin: Deutscher Verlag, 1990); Paul Weber, *Geschichte Luxemburgs im zweiten Weltkrieg* (Luxembourg: Buck, 1947).
69. Remy, *Une Epoque de la Résistance*, I, pp. 190–2.
70. Ibid., III, p. 138.
71. Ibid., III, pp. 134–8.
72. Marcel Engel, *Hinzert: Das SS Sonderlager im Hunsruck* (Sankt-Paulus Drückerei, 1983), pp. 528–40.
73. Remy, *Une Epoque de la Résistance*, II, pp. 73-4.
74. Reitlinger, *Final Solution*, p. 494, and Gilbert Trausch, *Le Luxembourg a l'époque contemporaine* (Luxembourg: Editions Bourg-Bourger, 1975), p. 159.

Chapter 11. Vichy France

1. Michael Marrus and Robert Paxton, *Vichy France and the Jews* (New York: Schocken, 1981), pp. 34–49.
2. Paula Hyman, *From Dreyfus to Vichy: The Remaking of French Jewry, 1906–1939* (New York: Columbia University Press, 1991). See also *Histoire des Juifs en France* (Toulouse: Commission Française des archives Juives, 1972), pp. 380–3, and Philippe Bourdrel, *Histoire des Juifs en France* (Paris: Albin Michel, 1974), pp. 315–35.
3. Paul Webster, *Pétain's Crime: The Full Story of French Collaboration in the Holocaust* (Chicago: I.R. Dee, 1991); Geoffrey Warner, *Pierre Laval and the Eclipse of France* (London: Eyre & Spottiswoode, 1968).
4. Marcel Ophuls, *The Sorrow and the Pity*, tr. Mireille Johnston (New York: Berkeley Windhover, 1972), p. 50.
5. Jacques Adler, *The Jews of Paris and the Final Solution* (New York: Oxford, 1987), pp. 3–14.
6. George Wellers, *L'Étoile Jaune à l'Heure de Vichy* (Paris: Fayard, 1973), pp. 63–4.
7. Dannecker committed suicide at the end of the war.
8. Marrus and Paxton, *Vichy France and the Jews*, pp. 104, 153–60, 294. See also Adler,

Jews of Paris and Final Solution, pp. 15–31, and Bourdrel, *Histoire des Juifs en France*, pp. 358–68.

9. Jacob Kaplan, 'French Jewry under the Occupation', *American Jewish Yearbook 1945–46*, XLVII (Philadelphia: JPSA, 1945), pp. 77–9; Adler, *Jews of Paris and the Final Solution*, pp. 32–49, and Bourdrel, *Histoire des Juifs en France*, pp. 346–54, 368–80.
10. Wellers, *L'Étoile Jaune*, p. 50.
11. Marrus and Paxton, *Vichy France and Jews*, pp. 87–8.
12. Jean Laloum, *La France antisémite de Darquier de Pellepoix* (Paris: Syros, 1979).
13. Joseph Billig, *Le Commissariat général aux questions juives (1941–1944)* (Paris: Editions du Centre, 1955–1960). See also Bourdrel, *Histoire des Juifs en France*, pp. 414–26.
14. Jeremy Josephs, *Swastika over Paris* (New York: Arcade, 1989), pp. 38–9.
15. Wellers, *L'Étoile Jaune*, pp. 86–9.
16. Ibid., p. 95.
17. Ibid., p. 57. Cynthia Haft, *The Bargain and the Bridle: The General Union of Israelites of France* (Chicago: Dialog Press, 1983); Adler, *Jews of Paris*, pp. 81–164, and Bourdrel, *Histoire des Juifs en France*, pp. 380–4.
18. Kaplan, 'French Jewry under Occupation', pp. 74–5; Richard Cohen, *The Burden of Conscience: French Jewish Leadership during the Holocaust* (Bloomington: Indiana University Press, 1992); and Bourdrel, *Histoire des Juifs en France*, pp. 394–7.
19. Jean Jacques Bernard, *Le Camp de la mort lente: Compiègne, 1941–1942* (Paris: Albin Michel, 1944); Lion Feuchtwanger, *The Devil in France: My Encounter with Him in the Summer of 1940* (New York: Viking, 1941) and André Fontaine, *Le Camp d'étrangers des Milles 1939–1943* (Aix-en-Provence: Edisud, 1989).
20. Serge Klarsfeld, *Le Mémorial de la déportation des Juifs de France* (Paris: Beate & Serge Klarsfeld, 1978).
21. Kaplan, 'French Jewry under Occupation', p. 81. Protests were mounted, to no avail, pp. 88–9.
22. Wellers, *L'Étoile Jaune*, pp. 106–13, and Bourdrel, *Histoire des Juifs en France*, pp. 408–14.
23. Wellers, *L'Étoile Jaune*, p. 137.
24. Ibid., p. 382.
25. Ibid., p. 244, and Richard Golsan (ed.), *Memory, The Holocaust and French Justice: The Bousquet and Touvier Affairs* (Hanover: University Press of New England, 1996).
26. Wellers, *L'Étoile Jaune*, pp. 389–90.
27. Dannecker to Eichmann in Wellers, *L'Étoile Jaune*, p. 386.
28. Marrus and Paxton, *Vichy France and the Jews*, pp. 263–4. See also Claude Levy and Paul Tillard, *Betrayal at the Vel d'Hiv*, tr. Inea Bushnaw (New York: Hill & Wang, 1969), pp. 89–97.
29. Memorandum, 16 July 1942, by Röthke, in Wellers, *L'Étoile Jaune*, pp. 392–3.
30. Wellers, *L'Étoile Jaune*, p. 390.
31. Levy and Tillard, *Betrayal at the Vel d'Hiv*, pp. 44–54; Donald Lowrie, *The Hunted Children* (New York: Norton, 1963).
32. Ibid., pp. 395–6.
33. Ibid., pp. 103–5.
34. Ibid., pp. 126–7. See also Levy and Tillard, *Betrayal at the Vel d'Hiv*, pp. 146–50.
35. Wellers, *L'Étoile Jaune*, pp. 128–9.
36. Ibid., pp. 130–1.
37. Ibid., pp. 140–1.
38. Ibid., p. 144, and Levy and Tillard, *Betrayal at the Vel d'Hiv*, pp. 156–7.
39. Wellers, *L'Étoile Jaune*, pp. 145–7.
40. Ibid., p. 245.
41. Andre Schwarz-Bart, *The Last of the Just*, tr. Stephen Becker (New York: Athenaeum, 1961), pp. 351, 364–5.
42. Josephs, *Swastika over Paris*, p. 72.

43. Wellers, *L'Étoile Jaune*, p. 403.
44. Marrus and Paxton, *Vichy France and the Jews*, pp. 302–8; Kaplan, 'France under the Occupation', pp. 84–5; Bourdrel, *Histoire des Juifs en France*, pp. 450–74; and Donna Ryan, *The Holocaust and the Jews of Marseille* (Urbana: University of Illinois Press, 1996).
45. Marrus and Paxton, *Vichy France and the Jews*, pp. 266–9.
46. Hans Safrian, *Die Eichmann-Männer* (Vienna: Europowerlag, 1933), pp. 261–9.
47. Marrus and Paxton, *Vichy France and the Jews*, p. 344.
48. Nora Levin, *The Holocaust: The Destruction of European Jewry 1933–1945* (New York: Schocken, 1973), p. 200.
49. Eugene Hevesi, 'Hitler's Plan for Madagascar', *Contemporary Jewish Record*, 4 (August 1941), p. 381.
50. Lucy Dawidowicz, *The War against the Jews* (New York: Holt, Rinehart & Winston, 1975), pp. 118–19.
51. Hevesi, 'Hitler's Plan for Madagascar', p. 389.
52. Discussion with Wiesenthal, Youngstown, 14 November 1979. See also Hilberg, *Destruction of European Jews*, pp. 259–61, and Reitlinger, *Final Solution*, pp. 21–2.
53. Hilberg, *Destruction of European Jews* (1985), II, p. 399.
54. Reitlinger, *Final Solution*, pp. 76–9, and Hevesi, 'Hitler's Plan for Madagascar', p. 394. See also Leni Yahil, 'Madagascar – Phantom of a Solution for the Jewish Question', in Bela Vago and George Mosse (eds), *Jews and Non-Jews in Eastern Europe, 1918–1945* (New York: Wiley, 1974), pp. 315–34.
55. Reitlinger, *Final Solution*, p. 79.
56. Henri Michel, *Histoire de la résistance* (Paris: Presses Universitaires de France, 1975) and Harry Kedward, *Resistance in Vichy France* (New York: Oxford University Press, 1978).
57. Lucien Lazare, *Rescue as Resistance: How Jewish Organizations Fought the Holocaust in France*, tr. J. Green (New York: Columbia University Press, 1996).
58. Kaplan, 'France under the Occupation', pp. 100–3; Adler, *Jews of Paris*, pp. 165–95; and Bourdrel, *Histoire des Juifs en France*, pp. 507–10.
59. Marrus and Paxton, *Vichy France and the Jews*, p. 204.
60. Philip Hallie, *Lest Innocent Blood Be Shed: The Story of the Village of Le Chambon and How Goodness Happened There* (New York: Harper & Row, 1978); Violette Mouchon *et al.*, *Quelques actions des protestants de France en faveur des juifs persécutés sous l'occupation allemande, 1940–1944* (Paris: CIMADE, 1945).
61. Marrus and Paxton, *Vichy France*, pp. 197–202.
62. Ibid., pp. 271–7.
63. Ibid., pp. 86–7.
64. Ophuls, *Sorrow and Pity*, pp. 139–40.

Chapter 12. Fear of Fascism: America before Pearl Harbor

1. US Congress, House, *Investigation of Un-American Activities*, 76th Cong., ed. Sess., 1938, H. Rept. 1476, p. 16.
2. Leo Lowenthal and Norbert Guterman, *Prophets of Deceit: A Study of the Techniques of the American Agitator* (New York: Harper & Bros., 1949); and Ralph Lord Roy, *Apostles of Discord: A Study of Organized Bigotry and Discrimination on the Fringes of Protestantism* (Boston: Beacon, 1953).
3. Gustavus Myers, *History of Bigotry in the United States* (New York: Capricorn, 1943), pp. 319–42; Leland Bell, *In Hitler's Shadow: The Anatomy of American Nazism* (Port Washington, NY: Kennikat Press, 1973); and Donald Strong, *Organized Anti-Semitism in America: The Rise of Group Prejudice during the Decade 1930–1940* (Washington: American Council on Public Affairs, 1941), pp. 21–40.
4. John Roy Carlson (pseud.), *Under Cover: My Four Years in the Nazi Underworld in*

America (New York: Dutton, 1943), pp. 27–30, 108–20.

5. Myers, *History of Bigotry*, pp. 343–59; Harold Lavine, *Fifth Column in America* (New York: Doubleday, Doran, 1940), pp. 171–80, and William Dudley Pelley, *The Door to Revelation* (Asheville: Foundation Fellowship, 1939).

6. 'The Question of Anti-Semitism and the Problem of Fascism', in Allen Brinkley, *Voices of Protest: Huey Long, Father Coughlin and the Great Depression* (New York: Knopf, 1982), pp. 269–83; *Father Coughlin: His 'Facts' and Arguments* (New York: General Jewish Council, 1939); *The Fine Art of Propaganda: A Study of Father Coughlin's Speeches*, Alfred and Elizabeth Lee (eds) (New York: Harcourt, Brace, 1939); and Charles Tull, *Father Coughlin and the New Deal* (Syracuse: Syracuse University Press, 1965).

7. Tull, *Father Coughlin and the New Deal*, p. 195.

8. Gary Marx, *The Social Basis of the Support of a Depression Era Extremist* (Berkeley: Survey Research Center, 1962), pp. 16, 111.

9. Myers, *History of Bigotry*, p. 350.

10. George Seldes, *Lords of the Press* (New York: Julian Messner, 1939), pp. 20–86.

11. George Seldes, *You Can't Do That* (New York: Modern Age Books, 1938), pp. 154–5, and Lavine, *Fifth Column in America*, pp. 54–5.

12. Seldes, *You Can't Do That*, pp. 114–25, and Carlson, *Under Cover*, pp. 285–6.

13. Hadley Cantril (ed.), *Public Opinion 1935–1946* (Princeton: Princeton University Press, 1951), pp. 384, 1081.

14. Herbert Hoover, *Further Addresses upon the American Road, 1938–1940* (New York: Scribner's, 1940), p. 244.

15. 'The Evacuation of Refugee Children Our Responsibility', *Social Service Review*, 14 (September 1940), pp. 543–4.

16. Saul S. Friedman, *No Haven for the Oppressed: United States Policy toward Jewish Refugees 1938–1945* (Detroit: Wayne State, 1973), p. 110.

17. Seldes, *You Can't Do That*, pp. 173–84.

18. Carlson, *Under Cover*, pp. 137–9.

19. James M. Burns, *Roosevelt: The Lion and the Fox* (New York: Harcourt, Brace, 1956), p. 422.

20. *New York Times*, 7 February 1941, p. 6.

21. *New York Times*, 2 July 1941, p. 2.

22. *New York Times*, 30 May 1941, p. 8.

23. *New York Times*, 7 February 1941, p. 5.

24. *New York Times*, 16 June 1940, p. 1.

25. Ibid., p. 37.

26. *New York Times*, 12 September 1941, p. 2.

27. Ibid., p. 2.

28. 'Wartime Journals of Charles A. Lindbergh', *American Heritage*, 21, 6 (October 1970), pp. 32–7.

29. Strasser, 'Hitler on the River Plata', *Current History*, 53 (May 1941), pp. 27–8; Lubell, 'War by Refugee', *Saturday Evening Post*, March 1941, pp. 12–13; and Donald Keyhoe and John Daly, 'Hitler's Slave Spies in America', *American Magazine*, 131 (April 1941), pp. 14–15.

30. *New York Times*, 28 August 1940, p. 2.

31. *New York Times*, 21 August 1940, p. 9.

32. *PM*, 11 February 1941, p. 7.

33. Friedman, *No Haven for the Oppressed*, pp. 118–21.

34. *The War Diary of Breckinridge Long*, Fred Israel (ed.) (Lincoln: University of Nebraska Press, 1966), p. 108.

35. *Department of State Bulletins*, 4 (28 June 1941), pp. 761–4.

36. Steinhardt to Long, 8 May 1941, Refugee Movement and Nationality Groups File, Long Papers.

37. Long to Roosevelt, 20 August 1941, Political Refugees File, Roosevelt Library.

38. Minutes of the 50th Meeting, 4 September 1941. President's Advisory Committee on Political Refugees File, Wise Papers.
39. US Congress, House, *Hearings before the House Committee on Foreign Affairs on HR 350 and HR 352: Resolutions Providing for the Establishment by the Executive of a Commission to Effectuate the Rescue of the Jewish People of Europe*, 78th Cong., 1st sess. (1943), p. 21.
40. US Congress, House, *Hearings before House Committee on Immigration and Naturalization on HR 2190: To Admit 400,000 Refugees into the U.S.*, 80th Cong., 1st sess. (1947), p. 303.
41. Earl Harrison, 'Axis Aliens in an Emergency', *Survey Graphic*, 30 (September 1941), pp. 465–8.
42. O. John Rogge, *The Official German Report* (New York: T. Yoseloff, 1961).
43. Editors of *Look Magazine*, *The Story of the FBI* (New York: Dutton, 1947), p. 226.

Chapter 13. Germany: Purge of the Contragenics

1. Robert Proctor, 'Nazi Biomedical Policies', in Arthur Caplan (ed.), *When Medicine Went Mad: Bioethics and the Holocaust* (Totowa, NJ: Humana Press, 1992), pp. 29–30.
2. 'Handicapped', pamphlet of US Holocaust Memorial Museum, Washington, n.d., p. 3. See Henry Friedländer, *The Origins of Nazi Genocide* (Chapel Hill: University of North Carolina Press, 1995), p. 123; James Glass, *Life Unworthy of Life: Racial Phobia and Mass Murder in Hitler's Germany* (New York: Basic Books, 1997); and John Michalczyk (ed.), *Medicine, Ethics and the Third Reich* (Kansas City, MO: Sheed and Ward, 1994).
3. 'Lynchburg', PBS, 1994.
4. Michael Burleigh and Wolfgang Wippermann, *The Racial State: Germany 1933–1945* (Cambridge: Cambridge University Press, 1991), p. 58, and Friedländer, *Origins of Nazi Genocide*, pp. 39–85.
5. Telford Taylor, 'Opening Statement of the Prosecution, December 9, 1946', in George Annas and Michael Grodin (eds), *The Nazi Doctors and the Nuremberg Code* (New York: Oxford University Press, 1992), pp. 90–1.
6. Burleigh and Wippermann, *Racial State*, pp. 128–30.
7. Benno Müller-Hill, 'Eugenics: The Science and Religion of the Nazis', in Caplan, *When Medicine Went Mad*, pp. 44–6. See also Paul Weindling, *Health, Race and German Politics between National Unification and Nazism* (Cambridge: Cambridge University Press, 1989), pp. 399–439, 442–57.
8. Lifton, *The Nazi Doctors* (New York: Basic Books, 1966), pp. 46–7, and Friedländer, *Origins of Nazi Genocide*, pp. 14–22.
9. In 1935 Nobel Laureate Alexis Carrel suggested that criminals and mentally ill persons be 'humanely and economically disposed of' by gas, see Proctor, 'Nazi Biomedical Policies', p. 34.
10. Burleigh and Wippermann, *Racial State*, p. 142. See also Gotz Aly, P. Chroust and C. Pross, *Cleansing the Fatherland: Nazi Medicine and Racial Hygiene*, tr. Belinda Cooper (Baltimore: Johns Hopkins University Press, 1994), p. 54.
11. Friedländer, *Origins of Nazi Genocide*, p. 39.
12. Ibid., pp. 86–110, and Lifton, *Nazi Doctors*, pp. 43–6, 55–62.
13. Lifton, *Nazi Doctors*, pp. 70–2. See also 'Selected Letters of Doctor Friedrich Mennecke', in Aly *et al.*, *Cleansing the Fatherland*, pp. 238–95.
14. Burleigh and Wippermann, *Racial State*, pp. 150–4.
15. Aly, 'Medicine against the Useless', in Aly *et al.*, *Cleansing the Fatherland*, p. 34.
16. Lifton, *Nazi Doctors*, pp. 80–90, and Friedländer, *Origins of Nazi Genocide*, pp. 113–14.
17. Burleigh and Wippermann, *Racial State*, p. 153.
18. Aly *et al.*, *Cleansing the Fatherland*, p. 39.
19. Friedländer, *Origins of Nazi Genocide*, pp. 151–63.

20. Gotz Aly, *Final Solution: Nazi Population Policy and the Murder of the European Jews*, tr. B. Cooper and A. Brown (London: Arnold, 1999), p. 72.

21. Friedländer, *Origins of Nazi Genocide*, p. 148.

22. Christine King, 'Jehovah's Witnesses under Nazism', in Michael Berenbaum (ed.), *A Mosaic of Victims: Non-Jews Persecuted and Murdered by the Nazis* (New York: New York University Press, 1990), pp. 188–90.

23. *Jehovah's Witnesses*, pamphlet of United States Holocaust Memorial Museum, p. 7.

24. Eugen Kogon, *Theory and Practice of Hell* (New York: Farrar, Strauss, Giroux, 1950), pp. 40, 118.

25. *Jehovah's Witnesses*, pamphlet of United States Holocaust Memorial Museum, p. 14.

26. Ibid., p. 13.

27. Kogon, *Theory and Practice of Hell*, p. 40.

28. James Steakley, *The Homosexual Emancipation Movement in Germany* (New York: Arno Press, 1975), p. 84; Jack Porter, *Sexual Politics in Nazi Germany: Persecution of Homosexuals during the Holocaust* (Spencer, 1995); Scott Lively and Kevin Abrams, *Pink Swastika: Homosexuals in the Nazi Party* (Newton, MA: Keizer, OR: Founders, 1998).

29. Richard Plant, *The Pink Triangle: The Nazi War against Homosexuals* (New York: Holt, 1986), p. 99.

30. Warren Johannson and William Percy, 'Homosexuals in Nazi Germany', *Wiesenthal Center Annual*, 7 (1990).

31. See 'Homosexuals', pamphlet of US Holocaust Memorial Museum, Washington, n.d.

32. Plant, *Pink Triangle*, p. 45.

33. Ibid., p. 110.

34. Ibid., pp. 137–42.

35. Ibid., p. 117.

36. Ibid., p. 166.

37. Burleigh and Wippermann, *Racial State*, pp. 182–97.

38. Heinz Heger, *The Men with the Pink Triangle*, tr. David Fernbach (Boston: Alyson, 1980), pp. 41–2.

39. Ibid., p. 43.

40. 'Homosexuals', pamphlet of US Holocaust Memorial Museum, Washington, p. 4.

41. Heger, *Men with Pink Triangle*, p. 181.

42. 'Sinti & Roma', pamphlet of US Holocaust Memorial Museum, Washington, n.d.; David Crowe and John Kolsti, *The Gypsies of Eastern Europe* (New York: M.E. Sharpe, 1991).

43. Hoess claimed that as a child he was saved from Gypsies. Michael Zimmermann, *Rassenutopie und Genozid: Die nationalsozialistische 'Lösung der Zigeunerfrage'* (Hamburg: Christians Verlag, 1996), pp. 68–9.

44. Donald Kenrick and Grattan Puxon, *The Destiny of Europe's Gypsies* (New York: Basic Books, 1972), pp. 18–41.

45. Angus Fraser, *The Gypsies* (Oxford: Blackwell, 1992), p. 249, see also pp. 10–69.

46. Zimmermann, *Rassenutopie*, p. 69.

47. Jacob Marcus, *The Jew in the Medieval World* (New York: Meridian Books, 1960), p. 92.

48. Ian Hancock, *Pariah Syndrome: An Account of Gypsy Slavery and Persecution* (Ann Arbor: Karoma Publishers, 1987), pp. 30–7.

49. Fraser, *The Gypsies*, pp. 254–7, and Hancock, *Pariah Syndrome*, p. 47.

50. Benno Mueller-Hill, *Murderous Science: Elimination by Scientific Selection of Jews, Gypsies and Others, Germany 1933–1945* (Oxford: Oxford University Press, 1980), p. 57.

51. Ian Hancock, *Pariah Syndrome*, p. 67. See also 'Sinti and Roma', pp. 4–7; Burleigh and Wippermann, *Racial State*, pp. 118–22; and Zimmermann, *Rassenutopie*, pp. 94–7.

52. After the war, Ritter resumed work at the University of Tubingen. In 1950 he committed suicide.
53. Friedländer, *Origins of Nazi Genocide*, p. 257.
54. Zimmermann, *Rassenutopie*, p. 87.
55. Kenrick and Puxon, *Destiny of Europe's Gypsies*, pp. 76–84, Sybil Milton, 'Nazi Policies toward Roma and Sinti, 1933–1945', *Journal of the Gypsy Lore Society*, 2 (1992), p. 7, and Zimmermann, *Rassenutopie*, pp. 174–8.
56. Kenrick and Puxon, *Destiny of Europe's Gypsies*, p. 86.
57. Hancock, *Pariah Syndrome*, p. 62.
58. Ibid., p. 128.
59. Zimmermann questions the accuracy of Gypsy deaths in most European lands. The figures for Croatia, Hungary and Romania are 'uncertain and controversial', numbers from France, Belgium and Holland are 'not exact', those from the USSR 'hardly precise' and 'requiring further study'. Zimmermann allows 1,000 documented deaths in Serbia, 8,000 in Poland (which 'will probably go higher'). Only those reported in the Crimea and Baltic are 'relatively accurate'. Zimmermann, *Rassenutopie*, pp. 381–3.
60. Zimmermann, *Rassenutopie*, p. 189.
61. Kenrick and Puxon, *Destiny of Europe's Gypsies*, pp. 87–8.
62. Reports of Einsatzgruppe A, C and D in Zimmermann, *Rassenutopie*, pp. 260–2.
63. Ibid., p. 297, and Milton, 'Nazi Policies', p. 8.
64. Kenrick and Puxon, *Destiny of Europe's Gypsies*, pp. 88–94. A handful of Gypsy children were spared for Eva Justin's doctoral research, Friedländer, *Origins of Nazi Genocide*, p. 294.
65. Milton, 'Nazi Policies', p. 7.
66. On the Gypsies in Auschwitz see Zimmermann, *Rassenutopie*, pp. 293–358.
67. Kenrick and Puxon, *Destiny of Europe's Gypsies*, p. 156.
68. Rudolf Hoess, *Kommandant in Auschwitz* (Stuttgart: Deutsche Verlag, 1958), pp. 105–7.
69. Ibid., p. 109.
70. O. Kraus and E. Kulka, *Death Factory* (Oxford: Pergamon, 1966), p. 204; B. Naumann, *Auschwitz* (London: Pall Mall Press, New York: Praeger, 1966), p. 114; I. Aldesberger, *Auschwitz* (Berlin: Lettner, 1953), p. 110; and Miriam Novitch, 'The Gypsy Camp in Auschwitz-Birkenau', ms., Wiener Library, PC8, VII, 96E, n.d.
71. Brenda and James Lutz, 'Gypsies as Victims of the Holocaust', *Holocaust and Genocide Studies*, 9 (Winter 1994), p. 359.

Chapter 14. The Last Jews of Germany

1. Robert Gellately, *The Gestapo and German Society: Enforcing Racial Policy 1933–1945* (Oxford: Clarendon Press, 1990), pp. 115ff.
2. *American Jewish Yearbook 1941–1942*, pp. 205–10.
3. Kurt Jacob Ball-Kaduri, 'Leo Baeck and Contemporary History', *Yad Vashem Studies*, 6 (1967), p. 126. See also Ernst Simon, 'Comments on the Article on the Late Rabbi Baeck', *loc. cit.*, pp. 131–4.
4. Albert Friedländer, *Leo Baeck: Teacher of Theresienstadt* (New York: Holt, Rinehart & Winston, 1968).
5. Kurt Jacob Ball-Kaduri, 'Berlin Is Purged of its Jews: The Jews in Berlin in the Year 1943', *Yad Vashem Studies*, 5 (1963), p. 292.
6. Henry Huttenbach, *The Destruction of the Jewish Community of Worms 1933–1945* (New York: Memorial Committee of Jewish Victims of Nazism from Worms, 1981), p. 26.
7. Michael Burleigh and Wolfgang Wippermann, *The Racial State: Germany 1933–1945* (Cambridge: Cambridge University Press, 1991), pp. 92–4.

8. Telegram from Leland Morris, chargé d'affaires, US Berlin Embassy, to Secretary of State, 30 September 1941, in John Mendelssohn (ed.), *The Holocaust: Selected Documents* (New York: Garland Press, 1982), II, pp. 280–1.

9. Landgericht Frankfurt 1950, in *Justiz und NS-Verbrechen: Sammlungen deutscher Strafurteile wegen nationalsozialistischer Toetungsverbrechen* (Amsterdam, 1968), pp. 1407–8, and Henry Friedlaender, 'The Deportation of the German Jews: Postwar German Trials of Nazi Criminals', *Leo Baeck Institute Yearbook*, 29 (1984), p. 224.

10. Jonathan Friedman, *The Lion and the Star: Gentile–Jewish Relations from the Perspective of the Jewish Communities in Frankfurt Am Main, Giessen, and Geisenheim, 1919–1945* (Lexington: University of Kentucky Press, 1998), p. 330.

11. Michael Müller-Claudius estimated only 5 percent approved of extreme measures, 5 percent were opposed and 69 percent were indifferent to the fate of Jews. Martin Kitchen, *Nazi Germany at War* (New York: Longman, 1995), p. 206.

12. Robert Gellately, *Gestapo and German Society: Enforcing Racial Policy, 1933–1945* (Oxford: Clarendon Press, 1990), pp. 180–3.

13. SD Bericht: Versuche der Kirchen, die judengegnerische Haltung der Bevölkerung durch die konfessionelle Gegenarbeit zu untergraben, Report Nr. 240, 24 November 1941, in Heinz Boberach, *Meldungen aus dem Reich: Auswahl aus dem geheimen Lageberichte 1939–1944* (Berlin, 1965), pp. 195–6, Bertram to German bishops, Breslau, 17 September 1941; and Michael Phayer, *Protestant and Catholic Women in Nazi Germany* (Detroit: Wayne State University Press, 1990), pp. 210, 211, 271.

14. K. Scheurenberg, *Ich will Leben: Ein autobiographischer Bericht* (Berlin: Oberbaumverlag, 1982), pp. 78–81; E. Bukofzer, *Laws for Jews and Persecution of Jews under the Nazis* (Berlin, 1946), p. 11; 'Recollections of Leo Baeck', in Erich Boehm, *We Survived: The Stories of Fourteen of the Hidden and Hunted of Nazi Germany* (New Haven, 1949), p. 288; 'Memoirs of Jacob Jacobsen', in Monika Richarz, *Juedisches Leben in Deutschland* (New York, 1981), p. 402; Inge Deutschkron, *Ich trug den gelben Stern* (Cologne, 1978), pp. 85–8; and David Bankier, *The Germans and the Final Solution* (Cambridge, MA: Basil Blackwell, 1992), pp. 124, 125, 182.

15. Kurt Heyne, 'Judenverfolgung in Giessen und Umgebung 1933–1945', in *Mitteilungen der Oberhessischen Geschichtsvereins Giessen*, 69 (1984), p. 119.

16. Frances Henry, *Victims and Neighbors: A Small Town in Nazi Germany Remembered* (South Hadley, MA: Bergin & Garvey, 1984), p. 88.

17. Huttenbach, *Destruction of Worms*, p. 28.

18. Leon Gross, *The Last Jews of Berlin* (New York: Simon & Schuster, 1982), pp. 9–10.

19. Memorandum from Alexander Kirk to Hull, 5 March 1940, in Mendelssohn, *Holocaust*, II, pp. 130–1.

20. Leni Yahil, *The Holocaust: The Fate of European Jewry, 1932–1945*, tr. Ina Friedman and Haya Gallai (New York: Oxford, 1990), p. 234.

21. Gotz Aly, *Final Solution: Nazi Population Policy and the Murder of European Jews*, tr. B. Cooper and H. Brown (London: Arnold, 1999), p. 124. By July 1942, the number had grown to 200,000.

22. Nora Levin, *The Holocaust: The Destruction of European Jewry 1933–1945* (New York: Schocken, 1973), pp. 185–8.

23. Aly, *Final Solution*, p. 116.

24. Ibid., pp. 117–18.

25. Peter Longerich (ed.), *Die Ermordung der europäischen Juden: Eine umfassende Dokumentation des Holocaust 1941–1945* (Munich: Piper, 1989), p. 157.

26. Rogers Brubaker, *Citizenship and Nationhood in France and Germany* (Cambridge, MA, 1992), p. 167.

27. Frankfurt Zuzug und Abwanderung der Juden von 1 Oktober 1939 bis 30 September 1944. Zusammengestellt nach den Halbjahresberichten den Polizeipräsidenten an den Oberbürgermeister, Document IX 21, in DGF, 420.

28. Lina Katz, 'Deportationen 1941 and 1942: Geschrieben 1961', Document XIV 1, in *Spuren des Faschismus in Frankfurt: Das Alltagsleben in Frankfurt am Main 1933–1945* (Frankfurt, 1968).
29. Bankier, *The Germans and the Final Solution*, pp. 106, 178.
30. Ella Lingens-Reiner, *Prisoners of Fear* (London, 1948), p. 119.
31. Hersh Smolar, *The Minsk Ghetto* (New York: Holocaust Library, 1989), pp. 38–42.
32. Kube expedited the killing of 55,000. Ernst Klee, Willi Dressen and Volker Reiss, *Those Were the Days: The Holocaust through the Eyes of the Perpetrators and Bystanders*, tr. Deborah Burnstone (London: Hamish Hamilton, 1991), pp. 180–94.
33. Andrew Ezergailis, *The Holocaust in Latvia 1941–1944* (Riga: Historical Institute of Latvia and Washington/US Holocaust Memorial Museum, 1996), pp. 239–48.
34. Ibid., pp. 249–52.
35. Ibid., p. 186. Arajs managed to evade punishment until 1975 when a German court sentenced him to life imprisonment. He died in 1988.
36. Ibid., pp. 253–9.
37. Affidavit of Alfred Winter, Nuremberg, 15 October 1947, in Mendelssohn, *Holocaust*, X, pp. 230–3.
38. Ezergailis, *Holocaust in Latvia*, p. 355.
39. Ibid., pp. 365–6; Winter affidavit, pp. 230–3; and statement of Josef Grunberg, in Longerich, *Ermordung der europäischen Juden*, p. 161.
40. Ezergailis, *Holocaust in Latvia*, pp. 358–61. See also Winter affidavit, pp. 231–2, and Gertrude Schneider, 'The Two Ghettos in Riga, Latvia, 1941–1943', in Lucjan Dobroszycki and Jeffrey Gurock (eds), *The Holocaust in the Soviet Union* (London: M.E. Sharpe, 1993), pp. 181–93.
41. Smolar, *Minsk Ghetto*, pp. 102–3.
42. *The Goebbels Diaries, 1942–43*, ed. Louis Lochner (Garden City: Doubleday, 1948), pp. 92, 376.
43. Ibid., pp. 147–8.
44. Ibid., p. 211.
45. Ber Mark, 'The Herbert Baum Group', in Yuri Suhl (ed., tr.), *They Fought Back: The Story of the Jews' Resistance in Nazi Europe* (New York: Crown, 1967), pp. 55–68. See also Allan Merson, *Communist Resistance in Nazi Germany* (Atlantic Highlands, NJ: Humanities Press, 1986), p. 243.
46. Gross, *Last Jews of Berlin*, pp. 146–65, 170–2, 256–65.
47. The worst of these were Rolf Isaakson and Stella Kübler, responsible for betraying 2,300 persons. Gross, *Last Jews of Berlin*, pp. 173–5.
48. *Goebbels Diaries*, pp. 261, 290.
49. Ball-Kaduri, 'Jews in Berlin in 1943', pp. 286–8.
50. Ibid., pp. 274–5.
51. *Goebbels Diaries*, p. 294.
52. Nathan Stoltzfus, *Resistance of the Heart: Intermarriage and the Rossensstrasse Protest in Nazi Germany* (New York: Norton, 1996).
53. *Goebbels Diaries*, p. 294.
54. Gross, *Last Jews of Berlin*, p. 113.
55. Ibid., p. 191.
56. Report of Hans Lammers, 12 October 1941, Mendelssohn, *Holocaust*, II, pp. 282ff.
57. Jeremy Noakes, 'The Development of Nazi Policy towards the German-Jewish Mischlinge 1933–1945', *Leo Baeck Institute Yearbook*, 34 (1939), p. 343, and Ursula Buettner, 'The Persecution of Christian-Jewish Families in the Third Reich', *Leo Baeck Institute Yearbook*, 34 (1939), pp. 67–90.
58. Gross, *Last Jews of Berlin*, p. 267.
59. See also Larry Orbach, *Soaring Underground: A Young Fugitive's Life in Nazi Berlin* (Washington: Compass Press, 1996); Hertha Nathorff, *Das Tagebuch der Hertha Nathorff* (Munich: Oldenburg, 1987); and *Jüdisches Leben in Pankow: Eine Zeitgeschichtliche Dokumentation* (Berlin: Edition Hentrich, 1993).

60. George Berkeley, *Vienna and its Jews: The Tragedy of Success 1880s–1980s* (Cambridge, MA: Abt Books, 1988), p. 318.
61. Ibid., pp. 301–18.
62. Ibid., p. 303.
63. Paul Burmetz, *Our Share of Morning* (Westport: Greenwood Press, 1961), p. 29.
64. Hans Safrian, *Die Eichmann-Männer* (Vienna: Europowerlag, 1993), p. 29.
65. Berkeley, *Vienna and its Jews*, pp. 278–83.
66. Hannah Arendt, *Eichmann in Jerusalem* (New York: Viking, 1963), p. 26.
67. Hilberg, *Destruction of European Jews*, pp. 545–6.
68. William Perl, *The Four-Front War* (New York: Crown, 1978), pp. 10–12.
69. Arendt, *Eichmann in Jerusalem*, pp. 32–3.
70. Wolfgang von Weis, *The Jews of Austria*, ed. J. Fraenkel (London: Mitchell, 1967), p. 169.
71. Berkeley, *Vienna and its Jews*, pp. 296–314.
72. Ibid., pp. 296–314.
73. Ibid., pp. 312, 319–20.
74. There were 80,000 Jews in Germany in the summer of 1999, 70 percent of whom were immigrants from Russia. Akron, *Beacon-Journal*, 10 July 1999, p. A11.

Chapter 15. The Invasion of Russia: Einsatzgruppen

1. Gotz Aly, *Final Solution: Nazi Population Policy and the Murder of the European Jews*, tr. B. Cooper and A. Brown (London: Arnold, 1999), p. 199.
2. Barton Whaley, *Codeword Barbarossa* (Cambridge, MA: MIT Press, 1973); John Erickson, *The Road to Stalingrad* (London: Weidenfeld & Nicolson, 1975); H.W. Koch, 'Operation Barbarossa – The Current State of the Debate', *Historical Journal*, 31 (June 1988), pp. 377–90; and Louis Rotundo, 'Stalin and the Outbreak of War in 1941', *Journal of Contemporary History*, 24 (April 1989), pp. 277–300.
3. Alan Seaton, *The Russo-German War, 1941–45* (London: Barker, 1971); and Earl Ziemke and Magna Bauer, *Moscow to Stalingrad: Decision in the East* (Washington: US Army Center of Military History, 1987).
4. Generals Leeb, Bock and von Rundstedt protested these orders, but Brauchitsch failed to transmit their objections to his superiors. Aly, *Final Solution*, pp. 80–1.
5. Ibid., pp. 117–18.
6. Dieter Pohl, *Von der 'Judenpolitik' zum Judenmord: Der Distrikt Lublin des General-gouvernements, 1939–1944* (Frankfurt and New York: Peter Lang, 1993), p. 98.
7. Hannes Heer, 'Killing Fields: The Wehrmacht and the Holocaust in Byelorussia', *Holocaust and Genocide Studies*, 11 (Spring 1997), p. 80.
8. Andreas Hillgruber, *Staatsmänner und Diplomaten bei Hitler* (Munich, 1970), p. 556.
9. Goering to Heydrich, 31 July 1941. Mendelsohn, *The Holocaust: Selected Documents*, XI, p. 39.
10. 'Anlage zu: Verb. St.D. OKW/Wi Ru Amt beim Reichsmarschall v.14.841', NA Wi/ID 1420 in National Archives, College Park, Maryland, in Browning, 'The Decision Concerning the Final Solution', in Francois Furet, *Unanswered Questions: Nazi Germany and the Genocide of the Jews* (New York: Schocken Books, 1989), pp. 105, 342.
11. Reitlinger, *Final Solution*, pp. 44–5.
12. Gerald Fleming, *Hitler and the Final Solution* (Berkeley: California Press, 1984), pp. 172–3.
13. David Irving claims Hitler had little knowledge of the extermination scheme. *Hitler's War* (New York: Viking, 1977). Saul Friedlaender replies: 'In essence, the known evidence indicates a clear Hitler-intention of mass extermination, in whatever form the intention was expressed and transmitted to those directly in charge of planning and execution – Himmler, Heydrich, and the various SS agencies.' Fleming, *Hitler*

and Final Solution, pp. xxviii–xxix, in Browning, 'The Decision Concerning the Final Solution', in Furet, *Unanswered Questions*.

14. Dawidowicz, *War against the Jews* and Eberhard Jaeckel, *Hitler's World View* (Middletown, CT: Wesleyan University Press, 1972).
15. Krausnick and Martin Broszat, *Anatomy of the SS State* (Cambridge: William Collins, 1968).
16. Browning, *The Final Solution and the German Foreign Office: A Study of Referat DIII of Abteilung Deutschland, 1940–43* (New York: Holmes & Meier, 1978); Uwe Dietrich Adam, *Judenpolitik im dritten Reich* (Düsseldorf, 1972); Martin Broszat, 'Hitler and the Genesis of the Final Solution: An Assessment of David Irving's Thesis', *Yad Vashem Studies*, 13 (1979), pp. 73–125; and Arno Mayer, *Why did the Heavens Not Darken? The Final Solution in History* (Princeton: Princeton University Press, 1989).
17. Dawidowicz, *War against the Jews*, p. 120.
18. *The American Heritage Picture History of World War II*, p. 101.
19. Philip Friedman, 'The Lublin Reservation and the Madagascar Plan: Two Aspects of Nazi Jewish Policy During the Second World War', in Joshua Fishman, *Studies in Modern Jewish Social History* (New York: Ktav Pub. House, 1972), p. 174.
20. Aly, *Final Solution*, pp. 166–7.
21. Ibid., p. 174.
22. Ibid., p. 215.
23. Friedländer, *Origins of Nazi Genocide*, p. 284.
24. Richard Breitman, *The Architect of Genocide: Heinrich Himmler and the Final Solution* (New York: Knopf, 1991), p. 148.
25. Jürgen Forster, 'The Wehrmacht and the War of Extermination against the Soviet Union', *Yad Vashem Studies*, 14 (1981), p. 11.
26. Heer, 'Killing Fields', pp. 80–1.
27. Reitlinger, *Final Solution*, p. 82.
28. Ronald Headland, *Messages of Murder: A Study of the Reports of the Einsatzgruppen of the Security Police and the Security Service 1941–1943* (Rutherford: Fairleigh Dickinson University Press, 1982), pp. 24–5, and Yitzhak Arad *et al.* (eds), *The Einsatzgruppen Reports* (New York: Holocaust Library, 1988).
29. Dieter Pohl, *Nationalsozialistische Judenverfolgung in Ostgalizien 1941–1944* (Munich: R. Oldenbourg Verlag, 1996), pp. 31–4.
30. 'From Dust and Ashes', PBS Documentary, April 1983.
31. Fleming, *Hitler and Final Solution*, pp. 109–10.
32. Ibid., p. 31.
33. Ibid., p. 2.
34. Hilberg, *Destruction of European Jews*, p. 192.
35. Ernst Klee, Willi Dressen and Volker Reiss, *Those Were the Days: The Holocaust through the Eyes of Perpetrators and Bystanders*, tr. Deborah Bunstone (London: Hamish Hamilton, 1991), pp. 24–34.
36. Smolar, *Minsk Ghetto*, p. 73; and Lucjan Dobroszycki and Jeffrey Gurock (eds), *The Holocaust in the Soviet Union* (Armonie, NY: M.E. Sharpe, 1993).
37. Pohl, *Nationalsozialistische Judenverfolgung*, p. 32.
38. Interview with Joshua Abelow, 15 June 1973, in *Amcha*, p. 208.
39. Headland, *Messages of Murder*, pp. 136–7.
40. Heer, 'Killing Fields', p. 82.
41. Dressen, 'Role of Wehrmacht and Police', p. 296.
42. Ibid., p. 303, and Heer, 'Killing Fields', pp. 85–7.
43. Heer, 'Killing Fields', pp. 83–92, and Nachum Albert, *Destruction of Slonim Jewry* (New York: Holocaust Library, 1990).
44. Dressen, 'Role of Wehrmacht and Police', pp. 296–7, and Headland, *Messages of Murder*, pp. 141–2.
45. Pohl, *Nationalsozialistische Judenverfolgung*, p. 59.

46. Headland, *Messages of Murder*, p. 145.
47. Kuznetsov, *Babi Yar*, tr. Jacob Guralsky (New York: Dial Press, 1967), pp. 65–79.
48. Hans Safrian, *Die Eichmann-Männer* (Vienna: Europowerlag, 1993), p. 138.
49. Nora Levin, Shimon Kiipnis, Dr Leon Friedman *et al.*, *Book of Remembrance* (Philadelphia: Committee for Babi Yar Book of Remembrance, 1983).
50. Kuznetsov, *Babi Yar*, pp. 303–6. See also testimony of Yasha Kaper, *Book of Remembrance*, p. 133.
51. In 1991, Ukraine dedicated a ten-foot menorah in memory of the Jews who died here.
52. Taras Hunczak, 'The Ukrainian Losses during World War II', in M. Berenbaum (ed.), *A Mosaic of Victims: Non-Jews Persecuted and Murdered by the Nazis* (New York: NYU Press, 1990), pp. 116–27.
53. Pohl, *Nationalsozialistische Judenverfolgung*, p. 49.
54. 'Ukraine during World War II' and 'The Ukrainians in German-occupied Territory', in *A Concise Encyclopedia* (Toronto: University of Toronto Press, 1963–1971). See also Yaroslav Halan, *Lest People Forget* (Kiev: Dnipro, 1986); *History Teaches a Lesson* (Kiev: Olividav Ukraini Publishers, 1986); *Nazi Crimes in Ukraine 1941–1944* (Kiev: Naukova Dumka Publishers, 1987).
55. Aharon Weiss, 'The Holocaust and the Ukrainian Victims', in *Mosaic of Victims*, pp. 109–15.
56. Pohl, *Nationalsozialistische Judenverfolgung*, p. 58.
57. Hilberg, *Destruction of European Jews*, pp. 205–8.
58. Ibid., pp. 60–4.
59. Philip Friedman, 'Ukrainish-Yidishe Batziungen in der Zeit fun Natzishere Okupatzie', *YIVO Bleter*, 41 (1957–58), pp. 247–8.
60. Hilberg, *Destruction of European Jews*, p. 208.
61. Kornbluth, *Sentenced to Remember: My Legacy of Life in Pre-1939 Poland and Sixty-Eight Months of Nazi Occupation*, ed. Carl Calendar (Bethlehem: Lehigh University Press, 1994), pp. 81–2.
62. Weiss, 'Holocaust and Ukrainian Victims', p. 110.
63. Friedman, 'Ukrainish-Yidishe Batziungen', p. 249.
64. Ibid., p. 250.
65. Pavel Shandruk, *Arms of Valor*, tr. Roman Olesnicki (New York: Speller, 1959), and Basil Dmytryshyn, 'The Nazis and the SS Volunteer Division "Galicia"', *American Slavic and East European Review* (1956), pp. 1–10.
66. Sol Littman, 'The Ukrainian Halychyna Division: A Case Study of Historical Revisionism', in Saul Friedman (ed.), *Holocaust Literature: A Handbook of Critical, Historical and Literary Writings* (Westport: Greenwood, 1993), p. 282.
67. Ibid., p. 283.
68. Ibid., p. 284. Szymon Datner *et al.*, *Genocide, 1939–1945* (Warsaw: Wydawnictwo Zachodnie, 1962).
69. Michael Hanusiak, *Lest We Forget* (Toronto: Progress Books, 1976), *passim*. Simon Wiesenthal reported on their activity 25 years ago. Bulletins of Wiesenthal Center, no. 12, 31 Jan. 1972, pp. 4, 6; no. 13, 31 Jan. 1973, p. 7; no. 14, 31 Jan. 1974, p. 6; no. 16, 31 Jan. 1976, p. 8; no. 21, 31 Jan. 1981, p. 3.
70. Philip Friedman, *Their Brothers' Keepers* (New York: Crown, 1957), pp. 133–6.
71. Ibid., p. 212.
72. Pohl, *Nationalsozialistische Judenverfolgung*, pp. 66–7.
73. Anna Simaite risked her life hiding Jews in Lithuania. Betrayed by a neighbor, she was sent to a concentration camp. After the war, she was recognized as a Righteous Gentile and given a home in Israel. Friedman, *Brothers' Keepers*, pp. 136–41.
74. Zvi Kolitz, 'The Physical and Metaphysical Dimensions of the Extermination of the Jews in Lithuania', in Dobroszycki and Gurock (eds), *The Holocaust in the Soviet Union*, pp. 195–204.
75. Headland, *Messages of Murder*, pp. 124–7; Nancy and Stuart Schoenburg, *Lithuanian Jewish Communities* (North Vale, NJ: Aronson, 1997); Gertrude Schneider (ed.), *The*

Unfinished Road: Jewish Survivors of Latvia (Westport: Greenwood, 1991); B.F. Sabrin (ed.), *Alliance for Murder: The Nazi–Ukrainian Nationalist Partnership in Genocide* (New York: Sarpedon, 1992); Zvi Gitelman (ed.), *Bitter Legacy: Confronting the Holocaust in the USSR* (Bloomington: Indiana University Press, 1997).

76. Levin, *The Holocaust*, p. 363.
77. Weiss, 'Holocaust and Ukrainian Victims', p. 113.
78. File T-175-94, National Military Archives, Washington, DC.

Chapter 16. Wannsee: The Saga of Czech Jewry

1. Gunther Deschner, *Reinhard Heydrich: A Biography*, tr. Sandra Bance, Brenda Woods and David Ball (New York: Stein & Day, 1981), p. 289.
2. Jan Wiener, *The Assassination of Heydrich* (New York: Grossmann, 1969), pp. 197–204.
3. *The Jewish Communities of Nazi-occupied Europe* (New York: Fertig, 1972 [1944]). See pp. 3–4.
4. George Kennan, *From Prague after Munich: Diplomatic Papers, 1938–1940* (Princeton: Princeton University Press, 1968).
5. Josef Korbel, *Twentieth-Century Czechoslovakia: The Meaning of Its History* (New York: Columbia University Press, 1977), pp. 74–8.
6. Livia Rothkirchen, 'The Jews in Bohemia and Moravia, 1938–1945', in Avigdor Dagan (ed.), *The Jews of Czechoslovakia* (New York: Society for the History of Czechoslovak Jews, 1984), III, pp. 26–8.
7. *Jewish Communities of Nazi-occupied Europe*, pp. 20–3.
8. Gerald Fleming, *Hitler and the Final Solution* (Berkeley: California Press, 1984), p. 67.
9. Erich Kulka, 'The Annihilation of Czechoslovak Jewry', in Dagan, *Jews of Czechoslovakia*, III, p. 270.
10. Minutes of Prague Conference on Solution of Jewish Problem, 17 October 1941, in *Jews of Czechoslovakia*, III, p. 31.
11. *New York Times*, 12 December 1941, p. 4.
12. Christian Gerlach, *Krieg, Ernahrung, Vokermord: Forschungen zur deutschen Vernichtungspolitik im Zweiten Weltkrieg* (Hamburg: HIS Verlag, 1998), p. 124.
13. Deschner, *Reinhard Heydrich*, p. 289.
14. Fleming, *Hitler and Final Solution*, p. 71. See also Friedländer, *Origins of Nazi Genocide*, pp. 68–72.
15. *Nazi Mass Murder: A Documentary History of the Use of Poison Gas*, ed. Eugen Kogon, Hermann Langbein and Adalbert Ruckerl, tr. Mary Scott and Caroline Lloyd-Morris (New Haven: Yale University Press, 1993), pp. 38–9.
16. Ibid., pp. 52–3, and Friedländer, *Origins of Nazi Genocide*, pp. 208–14.
17. *Nazi Mass Murder*, pp. 57–72.
18. Fleming, *Hitler and Final Solution*, p. 74.
19. *Nazi Mass Murder*, pp. 73–101. See also Konnilyn Feig, *Hitler's Death Camps: The Sanity of Madness* (New York: Holmes & Meier, 1981), pp. 266–74 and Jacob Apenszlak (ed.), *The Black Book of Polish Jewry* (New York: Roy, 1943), pp. 115–18.
20. Aly, *Final Solution*, pp. 223–4, and Friedländer, *Origins of Nazi Genocide*, pp. 296–302.
21. Mendelsohn, *The Holocaust: The Wannsee Protocol*, XI.
22. Ibid., pp. 19–25.
23. Ibid., p. 26.
24. Ibid., p. 31.
25. Ibid., pp. 27–8.
26. Vojtech Mastny, *The Czechs under Nazi Rule: The Failure of National Resistance, 1939–1942* (New York and London: Columbia University Press, 1971), p. 191.
27. Eleanor Wheeler, *Lidice* (Prague: Orbis, 1962); Callum MacDonald, *The Killing of*

SS Obergruppenführer Reinhard Heydrich (London: Odham, 1962); Miroslav Ivanov, *Not Only Black Uniforms* (Prague: Nase Vojsko, 1964).

28. Nora Levin, *The Holocaust: The Destruction of European Jewry 1933–1945* (New York: Schocken, 1973), pp. 527–47; Hilberg, *Destruction of European Jews*, pp. 458–73, and Ladislav Lipscher, *Die Juden im slowakischen Staat 1939–1945* (Munich and Vienna: Oldenbourg Verlag, 1980).

29. *Jewish Communities of Nazi-Occupied Europe*, pp. 18–24; and Lipscher, 'Jews of Slovakia', pp. 173–80.

30. Hans Safrian, *Die Eichmann-Männer* (Vienna: Europowerlag, 1993), p. 210.

31. Shiela Duff Grant, *A German Protectorate: The Czechs under Nazi Rule* (London: Cass, 1970) and Lipscher, 'Jews of Slovakia', pp. 191–9.

32. Safrian, *Die Eichmann-Männer*, p. 212.

33. Lipscher, 'Jews of Slovakia', pp. 200–1.

34. Ibid., p. 213.

35. Joan Campion, *In the Lion's Mouth: Gisi Fleischmann and the Jewish Fight for Survival* (Lanham, MD: University Press of America, 1987); and Rabbi Michael Weissmandel, *Min Hameitzar: Zichronot Misnot 1941–1945* (From the Depths: Reminiscences from the Years 1941–1945) (New York: Emunah Press, 1960).

36. Levin, *Holocaust*, pp. 535–40; and Poliakov, *Harvest of Hate*, pp. 254–9.

37. Weissmandel, *Min Hameitzar*, p. 200.

38. Merlin, 'The Europa Plan: A Real Opportunity, A Fantasy or Trap?', in Arthur Goldburg and Seymour Finger (eds), *American Jewry during the Holocaust* (New York: American Jewish Commission on the Holocaust, 1984), p. 4.

39. Rothkirchen, 'The Europa Plan', p. 18.

40. Jorgen Haestrup, *European Resistance Movements 1939–1945* (Westport: Meckler, 1981); and Eugen Steiner, *The Slovak Dilemma* (Cambridge: Cambridge University Press, 1973).

41. Safrian, *Die Eichmann-Männer*, pp. 293–311.

42. Reitlinger, *Final Solution*, pp. 392–4, and Lipscher, 'Jews of Slovakia', pp. 227–32.

43. Ibid., p. 240. For a nationalist view, see Francis Vnuk, *Dr. Josef Tiso, President of the Slovak Republic* (Sydney: Association of Australian Slovaks, 1967); Milan Durica, 'Dr. Jozef Tiso and the Jewish Problem in Slovakia', *Slovakia*, 8 (1947), pp. 1–22; J.M. Kirschbaum, 'Dr. Joseph Tiso, The Prelate Politician Who Died on the Gallows for his People', *Slovakia*, 22 (1972), pp. 5–20.

44. Levin, *Holocaust*, pp. 476–93; Reitlinger, *Final Solution*, pp. 165–75; Hilberg, *Destruction of European Jews*, pp. 227–84; Norbert Troller, *Theresienstadt: Hitler's Gift to the Jews*, tr. S.E. Cernyak-Spatz (Chapel Hill: University of North Carolina Press, 1991); Saul Friedman, 'The Holocaust in Czechoslovakia: A Survey of the Literature', in *Holocaust Literature*, pp. 261–8.

45. Rothkirchen, 'Jews of Bohemia and Moravia', p. 31.

46. Rena Rosenberger Memoir, summer 1945, Beit Terezin Archives, Microfilm III, pp. 2, 10.

47. Trude Herzl File, Beit Terezin Archives, Microfilm III.

48. Oliva Pechova *et al.*, *Arts in Terezin 1941–1945*, tr. Hana Kvicalova (Prague: Memorial Exhibition, 1973); Gerald Green, *The Artists of Terezin* (New York: Hawthorn Books, 1969); Jacob Jacobson, *Terezin: The Daily Life, 1943–45* (London: Jewish Central Information Office, 1946); Joiza Karas, *Music in Terezin 1941–1945* (New York: Pendragon, 1975); and Vaclav Novak, *Terezin: Dokumenty* (Prague: Terezin Museum, 1975).

49. Letter of Dr Ruth Ornstein, undated, Ornstein File, Beit Terezin Archive, Microfilm III.

50. *The Terezin Diary of Gonda Redlich*, ed. Saul Friedman (Lexington: University Press of Kentucky, 1992), p. 62; and *The Book of Alfred Kantor* (New York: McGraw-Hill, 1971).

51. 'Problemen der Raumwirtschaft an die Leitung', 22 August 1942, Raumwirtschaft

File, Beit Terezin, p. 1.
52. Zdenek Lederer, *Ghetto Theresienstadt* (New York: Howard Fertig, 1983), p. 45.
53. Twelve-page report of Dr Ruth Ornstein, Prague 1945, Beit Terezin Archive, III, p. 5.
54. Rosenberger Memoir, p. 18.
55. H.G. Adler, *Theresienstadt, 1941–1945: Das Antlitz einer Zwangsgemeinschaft: Geschichte, Soziologie, Psychologie* (Tubingen: Mohr, 1980), pp. 534–6.
56. Weglein memoir, p. 14.
57. Lederer, *Ghetto Theresienstadt*, p. 49.
58. Ibid., pp. 100–5; Weglein memoir, pp. 35–6.
59. *Redlich Diary*, p. 135.
60. Ibid., pp. 146–50.
61. Rosenberger memoir, p. 20, and Weglein memoir, pp. 43–5.
62. Lederer, *Ghetto Theresienstadt*, pp. 119–21.
63. Dr Theodor Mobs, *Theresienstadt: Eine Philatelistische Studie*, tr. Dr Carl Praeger (Frankfurt: Philip Kohler, 1965), pp. 6–7.
64. Ornstein report, p. 9.
65. Weglein memoir, p. 45.
66. Erich Kulka, 'The Annihilation of Czech Jewry', in *Jews of Czechoslovakia*, III, pp. 295–9.
67. Kathe Starke, *Der Führer schenkt den Juden eine Stadt* (Berlin: Haude und Spener, 1975), p. 160.
68. Seven-page report of Holzer, 1945, Feuerwerk file, II, Beit Terezin Archive, p. 2.
69. Rosenberger memoir, p. 27.
70. Holzer report, p. 2.
71. Rosenberger memoir, p. 28; Lederer, *Ghetto Theresienstadt*, p. 21, and Novak, *Terezin, Dokumenty*, p. 71.
72. David Altshuler (ed.), *The Precious Legacy* (New York: Summit, 1983), pp. 19–29.
73. Holzer report, p. 2.

Chapter 17. *Aktion Reinhard*

1. Yitzhak Arad, *Belzec, Sobibor, Treblinka: The Operation Reinhard Death Camps* (Bloomington: University of Indiana Press, 1987), pp. 8–16.
2. Christopher Browning, *Ordinary Men: Reserve Police Battalion 101 and the Final Solution in Poland* (New York: Harper Collins, 1992) and Daniel Goldhagen, *Hitler's Willing Executioners: Ordinary Germans and the Holocaust* (New York: Knopf, 1996), pp. 208–9.
3. Twelve policemen begged out of the Jozefow massacre. Browning, *Ordinary Men*, pp. 55–71, and Goldhagen, *Hitler's Willing Executioners*, pp. 211–19.
4. Browning, *Ordinary Men*, pp. 78–89; and Goldhagen, *Willing Executioners*, pp. 222–30.
5. Goldhagen, *Willing Executioners*, pp. 232–3.
6. Thomas Blatt, *From the Ashes of Sobibor: A Story of Survival* (Evanston: Northwestern University Press, 1997), p. 236.
7. G.M. Gilbert, *Nuremberg Diary* (New York: Farrar, Straus, 1947), p. 251.
8. Arad, *Belzec, Sobibor, Treblinka*, pp. 47–8.
9. Philip Friedman, *Martyrs and Fighters: The Epic of the Warsaw Ghetto* (New York: Praeger, 1954), pp. 146–8. See also Melech Neustadt (ed.), *Hurbn un oyfstand fun di Yidn in Varshe* (Tel Aviv: Histadrut and Jewish National Workers Alliance, 1948), pp. 69–73.
10. Wladyslaw Bartoszewski, *The Warsaw Ghetto: A Christian's Testimony*, tr. Stephen Cappellari (Boston: Beacon, 1987), pp. 27–8, and Yitzhak Zukerman, *Fighting Ghettos*, tr. Meyer Barkai (Philadelphia: Lippincott, 1962), p. 8.
11. Ibid., p. 21.

12. Diary of Joshua Perle, in Albert Nirenstein, *A Tower from the Enemy* (New York: Orion, 1959), pp. 16–17. See also Calel Perechodnik, *Am I A Murderer? Testament of a Jewish Ghetto Policeman*, ed. and tr. Frank Fox (Boulder, CO: Westview Press, 1996).
13. Jacob Apenszlak (ed.), *The Black Book of Polish Jewry* (New York: Roy, 1943), pp. 123–30.
14. Emmanuel Ringelblum, *Notes from the Warsaw Ghetto*, tr. and ed. Jacob Sloan (New York: McGraw-Hill, 1958), pp. 331–5.
15. *The Warsaw Diary of Adam Czerniakow*, ed. Raul Hilberg, Stanislaw Staron and Joseph Kermisz (New York: Stein & Day, 1979).
16. Neustadt, *Hurbn un oyfstand fun di Yidn in Varshe*, p. 674.
17. Marek Edelman, *The Ghetto Fights* (*In di yorn fun yidishn hurbn*) (New York: American Representation of the General Jewish Workers Union of Poland, 1946), pp. 26–7.
18. Arad, *Belzec, Sobibor, Treblinka*, p. 52.
19. Edelman, *The Ghetto Fights*, pp. 24–5.
20. Ringelblum, *Notes from the Warsaw Ghetto*, p. 312.
21. *Janusz Korczak: Ghetto Diary* (New York: Holocaust Library, 1978).
22. Ibid., p. 139.
23. Ibid., pp. 104–7.
24. Ibid., pp. 160–3.
25. Ringelblum, *Notes from the Warsaw Ghetto*, p. 322.
26. *Janusz Korczak*, pp. 31–41.
27. Interview with Genia Silkes, 28 April 1979, in Friedman, *Amcha*, p. 141.
28. *Janusz Korczak*, p. 76. See also Joseph Hyams, *A Field of Buttercups* (London: Muller, 1970).
29. Seidman, *Tagebuch fun Varshever ghetto* (Buenos Aires: CFPJ, 1947), pp. 66–7.
30. Wladyslaw Szpilman, *Smierc miasta: The Death of a City, A Diary, 1939–1945*, ed. Jerzy Waldorf (Warsaw: Wiedza, 1946), pp. 101–2.
31. Bartoszewski, *Warsaw Ghetto*, p. 34.
32. Jan Sehn, *Auschwitz-Birkenau*, tr. Klemens Keplicz (Warsaw: Wydwan, Prawnicze, 1961), p. 134.
33. Konnilyn Feig, *Hitler's Death Camps: The Sanity of Madness* (New York: Holmes &d Meier, 1981), pp. 323–5.
34. Ibid., p. 325.
35. Report of Stanislaw Mikolajczyk, Vice-Premier of Polish Government in Exile, *Black Book of Polish Jewry*, p. 96.
36. Jozef Marszalek, *Majdanek: Konzentrationslager Lublin* (Warsaw: Verlag Interpress, 1984), pp. 131–5.
37. Jozef Marszalek, *Majdanek: Geschichte und Wirklichkeit* (Hamburg: Rowohlt, 1981); Ingrid Muller-Munch, *Die Frauen von Majdanek* (Hamburg: Rowohlt, 1982); Arnold Goldstein, *The Shoes of Majdanek* (Lanham: University Press of America, 1992); Czeslaw Rajca, *Majdanek: Concentration Camp*, tr. Anna Zagorska (Lublin: State Museum Majdanek, 1983); *Rywka Rybak: A Survivor of the Holocaust* (Cleveland: Tricycle Press, 1993); *The State Museum at Majdanek*, tr. Tomasz Kranz (Lublin: Museum of Majdanek, 1949); and Edward Gryn and Zofia Murawska, *Majdanek Concentration Camp*, tr. Jan Gaczo (Lublin: Wydawn, Lubelskie, 1966).
38. Miriam Novitch, *Sobibor: Martyrdom and Revolt* (New York: Holocaust Library, 1980), p. 81.
39. *Black Book of Polish Jewry*, p. 136, and Feig, *Hitler's Death Camps*, pp. 275–83.
40. Novitch, *Sobibor*, p. 25.
41. Ibid., pp. 50, 138.
42. Ibid., p. 107.
43. Ibid., p. 55.
44. Ibid., p. 144.
45. Ibid., pp. 157–8.

46. Nirenstein, *Tower from the Enemy*, pp. 57–8.
47. Feig, *Hitler's Death Camps*, pp. 293–312.
48. *Black Book of Polish Jewry*, p. 145.
49. Yankel Wiernik, 'A Year in Treblinka Horror Camp', in *Anthology of Holocaust Literature*, ed. Jacob Glatstein, Israel Knox and Samuel Margoshes (Philadelphia: Jewish Publication Society, 1969), p. 184.
50. Arad, *Belzec, Sobibor, Treblinka*.
51. Bernard Goldstein, *The Stars Bear Witness* (New York: Viking, 1949), p. 118.
52. Friedman, *Martyrs and Fighters*, pp. 181–3, and Jan Karski, *Story of a Secret State* (Boston, 1944).
53. Ibid., pp. 320–1.
54. Ibid., p. 310.
55. Bartoszewski, *Warsaw Ghetto*, pp. 36–7.
56. Ringelblum, *Notes from Warsaw Ghetto*, p. 296–7.
57. Friedman, *Martyrs and Fighters*, pp. 216–17.

Chapter 18. Jewish Armed Resistance

1. Nirenstein, *A Tower from the Enemy* (New York: Orion, 1959), p. 77.
2. Home Army Information Bulletin #4, 28 January 1943 in Wladyslaw Bartoszewski, *The Warsaw Ghetto: A Christian's Testimony*, tr. Stephen Cappellari (Boston: Beacon, 1987), p. 68.
3. Unpublished ms. of Miriam Novitch titled 'Spiritual Resistance: Their Last Voices: The Underground Press in the Warsaw Ghetto, 1940/43'. See 'Why We Love Peretz', *Nowa Mlodziez* (New Youth), Feb. 1942, pp. 59–61. The Maurois quote is from *The Voice of Youth*, 13, Nov. 1941, in Yiddish, p. 50. Review of Asch in *Suffering and Courage*, a special anthology of *Dror* (Aug. 1940), p. 22. See also *Sturm*, 1 (5 July 1942), p. 77.
4. Anielewicz maintained that the happiest day in his life was when the Jewish rebellion broke out. S. Friedman, *Amcha*, p. 142.
5. Yisrael Gutman places the number of fighters at 750: 500 with the ZOB and 250 with the ZZW. *The Jews of Warsaw 1939–1942* (Bloomington: Indiana University Press, 1982), p. 365.
6. Emmanuel Ringelblum, *Notes from the Warsaw Ghetto*, tr. and ed. Jacob Sloan (New York: McGraw-Hill, 1958), pp. 338–44.
7. Bartoszewski, *Warsaw Ghetto*, p. 63.
8. Nirenstein, *Tower from the Enemy*, pp. 58, 68–71.
9. Malvina Graf, *The Krakow Ghetto and the Plaszow Camp Remembered* (Tallahassee: Florida State University Press, 1989).
10. Bartoszewski, *Warsaw Ghetto*, pp. 70–2.
11. Wdowinski, 'The Answer', IV, 6 (Warsaw, June 1946), pp. 18–22.
12. Philip Friedman, *Martyrs and Fighters: The Epic of the Warsaw Ghetto* (New York: Praeger, 1954), p. 225.
13. Photos confirm the deployment of tanks. Gutman also notes that both were burned during the initial battle. *Jews of Warsaw*, p. 373.
14. Yuri Suhl, *They Fought Back* (New York: Crown, 1967), p. 99.
15. Gutman, *Jews of Warsaw*, p. 372.
16. Ibid., p. 373.
17. Reported by Stroop and cited in Gutman, *Jews of Warsaw*, p. 374.
18. Nirenstein, *Tower from the Enemy*, pp. 213–14.
19. Stroop Report, Document 1061-PS, *International Military Tribunal, Nuremberg 1945–1946, Trial of the Major War Criminals*, Vol. XXVI, pp. 628–93.
20. Ibid., p. 659.
21. Ibid., p. 654.

22. Ibid., p. 648.
23. Nirenstein, *Tower from the Enemy*, pp. 109–10.
24. Nirenstein says the Poles did very little, *Tower from the Enemy*, pp. 106, 117. For another view, see David Engel, *Facing a Holocaust: The Polish Government in Exile and the Jews, 1939–1945* (Chapel Hill: University of North Carolina Press, 1993).
25. Gutman, *Warsaw Ghetto*, p. 76.
26. Zvia Lubetkin, *In the Days of Destruction and Revolt* (Tel Aviv: Beit Lohamei hagettaot, 1981), p. 216.
27. Ibid., p. 139.
28. Stroop Report, *Nuremberg Tribunal*, p. 680.
29. Ibid., p. 688.
30. Nirenstein, *Tower from Enemy*, p. 133.
31. Bartoszewski, *Warsaw Ghetto*, p. 82.
32. Stroop Report, *Nuremberg Tribunal*, p. 628.
33. One photo was marked, 'So sicht es in ehemaligen judischen Wohnbezirk nach der Vernichtung aus' (thus appears the former Jewish living area after the destruction).
34. *Goebbels Diaries*, pp. 343, 350–1, 364, 388.
35. G.M. Gilbert, *Nuremberg Diary* (New York: Farrar, Straus, Giroux, 1947), p. 69.
36. 'A Resistance Fighter Looks Back: An Interview with Marek Edelman', *Dimensions*, 7, 2 (1993), p. 18.
37. According to Gutman, 'The Germans had indeed been defeated in battle and suffered losses in equipment, lives and – far more serious (from their point of view) – pride and prestige.' *Jews of Warsaw*, p. 376.
38. Isaiah Trunk, *Judenrat: The Jewish Councils in Eastern Europe under Nazi Occupation* (New York: Stein & Day, 1977), pp. 388–400. The Maimonides rule is discussed on pp. 426–30, see also pp. 447–50.
39. Gerald Green, *The Artists of Terezin* (New York: Hawthorne Books, 1969), p. 148.
40. See Trunk, *Judenrat*, pp. 437–71. On the Jewish police and their role in resistance, ibid., pp. 519–26.
41. Jacob Apenszlak, *The Black Book of Polish Jewry* (New York: Roy, 1943), p. 232.
42. Yitzhok Zukerman, *Fighting Ghettos*, tr. Meyer Barkai (Philadelphia: Lippincott, 1962), pp. 98–105.
43. Ibid., pp. 109–17.
44. Ibid., pp. 118–25.
45. Marie Syrkin, *Blessed Is the Match* (New York: Knopf, 1947), pp. 246–54.
46. Nirenstein, *Tower from the Enemy*, pp. 256–7.
47. Nirenstein credits anti-Nazi Germans with rescuing many Jews of Bialystok by furnishing them money, ration cards and arms. *Tower from the Enemy*, p. 248.
48. Ibid., p. 274.
49. Ibid., p. 275.
50. Chaika Grossmann, *The Underground Army: Fighters of the Bialystok Ghetto* (New York: Holocaust Library, 1987), pp. 281–3.
51. Ibid., pp. 285–90.
52. Michael Elkins, *Forged in Fury* (New York: Ballantine, 1971), pp. 106–19. See also testimonies of Stanislaw Kon, 'Story of the Battle of the Ghettos', in Nirenstein, *Tower from the Enemy*, pp. 296–302; Samuel Willenberg, *Surviving Treblinka*, ed. Wladyslaw Bartoszewski, tr. Naftali Greenwood (Oxford: Blackwell, 1989), pp. 127–50; and Yitzhak Arad, *Belzec, Sobibor, Treblinka: The Operation Reinhard Death Camps* (Bloomington: University of Indiana Press, 1987), pp. 286–99.
53. Miriam Novitch, *Sobibor: Martyrdom and Revolt* (New York: Holocaust Library, 1980), p. 31.
54. Testimony of Pechersky in Novitch, *Sobibor*, pp. 89–99, and Arad, *Belzec, Sobibor, Treblinka*, pp. 299–342.
55. Novitch, *Sobibor*, pp. 30–1.
56. Zukerman, *Fighting Ghettos*, pp. 292–357.

57. See Isaac Kowalski, *Anthology on Armed Jewish Resistance*, I, pp. 522–630; II, pp. 472–622; III, pp. 129–384; and IV, pp. 441–560; and Harvey Rosenfeld and Eli Zborowski (eds), *A Legacy Recorded: An Anthology of Martyrdom and Resistance* (New York, 1989).
58. Syrkin, *Blessed is the Match*, p. 259. See Moshe Kahanowitz, 'Why No Separate Jewish Partisan Movement was Established during World War II', *Yad Vashem Studies*, 1 (1957). On difficulties faced by Jews in hostile populations, see Arad, *Belzec, Sobibor, Treblinka*, pp. 342–8.
59. Zukerman, *Fighting Ghettos*, pp. 217–40.
60. Syrkin, *Blessed Is the Match*, pp. 255–6.
61. Suhl, *They Fought Back*, pp. 226–59.
62. Emil Knieza, 'The Resistance of the Slovak Jews', in Suhl, *They Fought Back*, pp. 176–81.
63. Zukerman, *Fighting Ghettos*, pp. 265–70.
64. See Green, *Artists of Terezin*.
65. Hana Volavkova (ed.), *I Never Saw Another Butterfly*, tr. Jeanne Nemcova (New York: McGraw-Hill, 1964).
66. Interview with Genia Silkes, *Amcha*, pp. 137, 145.
67. Meed, 'Jewish Resistance in the Warsaw Ghetto', *Dimensions*, 7, 2 (1993), p. 15. See also Herbert Druks, *Jewish Resistance during the Holocaust* (New York: Irvington, 1983); Arnold Geier, *Heroes of the Holocaust* (Berkeley: University of California Press, 1998); and Julien Hirshaut, *Jewish Martyrs of Pawiak* (New York: Holocaust Library, 1982).

Chapter 19. Yugoslavia: The Dysfunctional State

1. Edmond Paris, *Genocide in Satellite Croatia, 1941–1945: A Record of Racial and Religious Persecutions and Massacres*, tr. Lois Perkins (Chicago: American Institute for Balkan Affairs, 1961), pp. 30–41.
2. *New York Times*, 23 April 1941, p. 1.
3. Reports of Army Kommando 12 to the General Staff, 8 July–9 October 1941, in Peter Longerich, *Die Ermordung der europaischen Juden: Eine umfassende Dokumentation des Holocaust 1941–1945* (Munich: Piper, 1989), pp. 285–7.
4. Sentenced to life imprisonment for war crimes, an ailing List was released after serving six years.
5. As Bohme phrased it, the reprisals were in response to the 'bestial' killings of Germans. Longerich, *Die Ermordung der europaischen Juden*, p. 287.
6. Reports listing 11,164 persons killed in reprisals do not take into account 20,000 in uncounted reprisals. Christopher Browning, *Fateful Months: Essays in the Emergence of the Final Solution* (New York: Holmes & Meier, 1985), p. 55.
7. Robert Herzstein, *Waldheim: The Missing Years* (New York: Paragon, 1988), pp. 71–6.
8. Ibid., p. 75.
9. As Secretary-General of the United Nations, Waldheim would recall nothing of his time in Yugoslavia, Greece or the Italian occupation zone. Waldheim subsequently was elected president of Austria and was one of the few national leaders placed on a watch list by the US State Department.
10. By June 1941, it was estimated that 180,000 Serbs and Jews, including three bishops and 100 priests, had been killed in Croatia. Paris, *Croatia*, p. 88. See also pp. 59–61, 80–3, 102–14, 188–9. Muslims of Bosnia were co-opted to help in the slaughter, pp. 119–26.
11. Ibid., p. 83.
12. Harriett Freidenreich, *The Jews of Yugoslavia* (Philadelphia: Jewish Publication Society, 1979), pp. 55–71.
13. William Perl, *The Four-Front War* (New York: Crown, 1978), p. 193.
14. Zdenko Lowenthal, *The Crimes of the Fascist Occupants and Their Collaborators*

against Jews in Yugoslavia (Belgrade: Federation of Jewish Communities, 1957), pp. 8–9.

15. Browning, *Fateful Months*, p. 50.
16. Ibid., p. 46.
17. Ibid., pp. 90–1.
18. Perl, *Four-Front War*, p. 210.
19. Ibid.
20. Hana Weiner, *Dead-End Journey: The Tragic Story of the Kladovo-Sabac Group*, tr. Anna Barber (Lanham, MD: University Press of America, 1996) and Gabriele Anderl, *Gescheiterte Flucht: der Judische 'Kladovo-Transport' auf dem Weg nach Palestine, 1939–42* (Vienna: Verlag fur Gesellschaftskritik, 1993).
21. Browning, *Fateful Months*, p. 46.
22. See Rademacher's report of meetings with Benzler and Turner, Longerich, *Die Emordung der europaischen Juden*, pp. 288–9.
23. Browning, *Fateful Months*, p. 71.
24. Ibid.
25. *Crimes of Fascist Occupants*, pp. 3–5.
26. Browning, *Fateful Months*, p. 81.
27. *Report of Activities of CIRC in Second World War* (Geneva, 1948), II, p. 251.
28. Browning, *Fateful Months*, p. 77.
29. Longerich, *Die Emordung der europaischen Juden*, pp. 293–4.
30. Browning, *Fateful Months*, pp. 80–1.
31. *Crimes of Fascist Occupants*, pp. 5–6.
32. Longerich, *Die Ermordung der europaischen Juden*, pp. 294–5; Walter Manoschek, *Serbien ist judenfrei: militarische Besatzungspolitik und Judenvernichtung in Serbian 1941/42* (Munich: Oldenburg, 1993); and *Die zwei intellektuellen SS-Generale die verantwortlich waren fur die Ermordung der Juden in Jugoslawien und in Danzig, 1941–1943* (Haifa: Israel Documentation Instituter, 1996).
33. Browning, *Fateful Months*, pp. 82–3.
34. Howard Blum, *Wanted: The Search for Nazis in America* (New York: Quadrangle, 1977), p. 159.
35. Paris, *Croatia*, pp. 17–29.
36. Alex Dragnich, *Serbs and Croats: The Struggle in Yugoslavia* (New York: Harcourt Brace, 1992), pp. 92–3.
37. Blum, *Wanted*, p. 162.
38. Ibid., p. 160.
39. Ibid., p. 164. In 1951 Artukovic came to the United States. Extradition failed when a federal judge ruled that the US treaty was operative only with Serbia. Artukovic was extradited to Yugoslavia in 1986 and convicted of war crimes in 1987. He was sentenced to death by firing squad.
40. Paris, *Croatia*, pp. 102–6, 188–9.
41. See Milan Bulajic, Antun Miletic and Dragoje Lukic, *Never Again: Ustashi Genocide in the Independent State of Croatia (NDH) from 1941–1945*, tr. Vida Jankovic and Svetlana Raicevic (Belgrade: Ministry of Information, 1992), pp. 28–9. Another partisan polemic on this subject is Vladimir Dedijer, *The Yugoslav Auschwitz and the Vatican*, tr. Harvey Kender (Buffalo: Prometheus, 1988).
42. Paris, *Croatia*, pp. 139–41.
43. Radovan Trivuncic, *Memorial Place Jasenovac* (Zagreb: Turistkomerc, 1975), p. 58.
44. Blum, *Wanted*, p. 163.
45. Paris, *Croatia*, pp. 134–7.
46. Ibid., p. 132.
47. Ibid., pp. 162–4.
48. Franjo Tudjman, President of Croatia, offered his view of Jasenovac in *Bespucapovjesne zbitjnosti* ('Wastelands – Historical Truth'), tr. Vida Jankovic and Svetlana Raicevic (Zagreb: Nakladni zavod Matice Hrvatske, 1989). Tudjman

believes the number of victims have been 'monstrously' multiplied. Jasenovac was supposed to be a legitimate labor camp with factories. Inmates, mostly Jews, controlled the camp. 'Witnesses' claimed Jews killed Gypsies, Serbs and partisans (pp. 316–20). According to Tudjman, Jews suffer from historical unreasonableness and narrowness. A people that suffered so much should know better than conducting 'a genocidal policy towards the Palestinians that they can rightly be defined as Judeo-Nazis' (pp. 160–1). Milan Bulajic, *Tudjmans 'Jasenovac Myth' Ustasha Crimes of Genocide* (Belgrade: Ministry of Justice, 1992); Slobodan Kljakic, *A Conspiracy of Silence: Genocide in the Independent State of Croatia and Concentration Camp Jasenovac* (Belgrade: Ministry of Information, 1991).

49. *Crimes of the Fascist Occupants*, pp. 10–12.
50. Ibid., p. 11.
51. Paris, *Croatia*, p. 117.
52. *Crimes of the Fascist Occupants*, p. 14.
53. Ibid., pp. 15–16, and Bulajic *et al.*, *Never Again*, pp. 28–9.
54. See Longerich, *Die Ermordung der europaischen Juden*, pp. 307–8, and Safrian, *Die Eichmann-Männer*, pp. 214–17.
55. Paris, *Croatia*, p. 133.
56. Blum, *Wanted*, pp. 157–8; Longerich, *Die Ermordung der europaischen Juden*, pp. 303–4.
57. Olga Njemirovski, *The Holocaust and the Jews of Yugoslavia* (Jerusalem and Hewlett, New York: Gefen House, 1996); Jasa Romano, *Jevreji jugoslavije 1941–1945, zrtve genocida i ucesnici NOR* (Jews of Yugoslavia 1941–1945, Victims of Genocide and Freedom Fighters) (Belgrade: Savez jevrejskih opstina Jugoslavije, 1980); Zdenko Levental, *Aug gluhendem Boden: ein judisches Uberlebensschicksal in Jugoslawien 1941–1947* (Konstanz: Hartung-Gorre, 1994).
58. Jacques Sabille, 'Attitude of the Italians to the Persecuted Jews in Croatia', in Léon Poliakov and Jacques Sabille, *Jews under the Italian Occupation* (New York: Howard Fertig, 1983), p. 133.
59. Ibid., pp. 164–5.
60. Ibid., p. 164.
61. Ibid., p. 172.
62. *Crimes of Fascist Occupants and Collaborators*, pp. 22–5.
63. Sabille, 'Attitude of Italians', p. 164.
64. Ibid., pp. 147–8.
65. Ibid., p. 149.
66. Ibid., pp. 55–66, 193–7; Josip Stilinovic, 'A Patriot, Not a Nationalist', *Catholic World* (Fall 1998), pp. 38–9.

Chapter 20. Romania: The Hamans of Moldavia

1. Simon Dubnow, *History of the Jews*, tr. Moshe Spiegel (South Brunswick: T. Yoseloff, 1973), V, p. 805.
2. Ibid., pp. 627–8.
3. Ibid., pp. 385–7.
4. Ibid., p. 804.
5. Ismar Elbogen, *A Century of Jewish Life* (Philadelphia: JPSA, 1944), p. 364. Gary Best, *To Free a People: American Jewish Leaders and the Jewish Problem in Eastern Europe, 1890–1914* (Westport: Greenwood Press, 1982).
6. Ibid., pp. 631–3.
7. Henry Roberts, *Rumania: Political Problems of an Agrarian State* (New Haven: Yale University Press, 1951), and Stephen Fischer-Galati, *Twentieth-Century Rumania* (New York: Columbia University Press, 1970).
8. Fischer-Galati, 'Fascism, Communism and the Jewish Question in Romania', in Bela Vago and George Mosse (eds), *Jews and Non-Jews in Eastern Europe, 1918–1945*

(New York: Wiley, 1974), pp. 157–61.

9. Radu Ioanid, *The Sword of the Archangel: Fascist Ideology in Romania* (New York: Columbia University Press, 1990); Avigdor Shachan, *Burning Ice: The Ghettos of Transnistria* (Boulder: East European Monographs, 1996), pp. 6–16.; Randolph Braham, 'Romanian Nationalist and the Holocaust: A Case Study in History Cleansing', *Holocaust and Genocide Studies* (Winter 1996), pp. 211–51; and Ezra Mendelssohn, *The Jews of East Central Europe between the World Wars* (Bloomington: Indiana University Press, 1983), pp. 171–212.

10. *Statutul evreilor din Romania* (Bucharest, 1941); Carol Iancu, *L'Emancipation des juifs de Roumanie (1913–1919)* (Montpellier: Centre de recherches et d'études Juives et hebraiques, 1992).

11. Jacob Geller, *Tsemihatah u-sekiatah shel kehilah: ha-Yehudim ha-Askenazim veha-Sefaradim be-Romanyah 1919–1941* (The Rise and Fall of a Community: Ashkanazic and Sefardic Jews in Romania) (Tel Aviv: Hotsaat 'Moreshet', 1985); and Hildrun Glass, *Zerbrochene nachbarschaft: das deusch-judische Verhaltnis in Rumanien 1918–1938* (Shattered Friendship: German–Jewish Relations in Romania) (Munich: Oldenbourg, 1996).

12. Eugen Weber, 'Romania', in Hans Rogger and Weber (eds), *European Right* (Berkeley: University of California Press, 1966), pp. 501–74, and Radu Ioanid, *The Sword of the Archangel: Fascist Ideology in Romania*, tr. Peter Heinegg (Boulder: East European Monographs, 1990).

13. Julius Fisher, *Transnistria: The Forgotten Cemetery* (South Brunswick: T. Yoseloff, 1969), p. 28.

14. Andreas Hillgruber, *Hitler, Konig Carol and Marschall Antonescu: Die deutsch-rumanischen Beziehungen 1938–1944* (Wiesbaden, 1954).

15. Fisher, *Transnistria*, pp. 24–5, and Shachan, *Burning Ice*, pp. 18–21.

16. US Consul Franklin Gunther reported on these atrocities. *Foreign Relations of the United States* 2: 860. See Emil Dorian, *The Quality of Witness: A Romanian Diary 1937–1941* (Philadelphia: JPSA, 1982), pp. 136–8.

17. Robert St John, *Foreign Correspondent* (Garden City, NJ: Doubleday, 1957).

18. Reitlinger, *Final Solution*, p. 395, and Dorian, *Quality of Witness*, p. 143.

19. Fisher, *Transnistria*, p. 30.

20. Order of Antonescu, 19 June 1941, in Jean Ancel (ed.), *Documents Concerting the Fate of Romanian Jewry During the Holocaust* (New York: Beate Klarsfeld Foundation, 1986), VI, pp. 424–40.

21. Statement of Vasiliu, Ancel, *Documents*, VI, pp. 441–5.

22. Statement of Antonescu, 8 July 1941, in Ancel, *Documents*, VI, pp. 199–218.

23. Reitlinger, *Final Solution*, p. 396.

24. Memorandum of Feldgendarmerie, Ancel, *Documents*, V, p. 14.

25. Curzio Malaparte, *Kaputt*, tr. Cesare Foligno (New York: Dutton, 1946), p. 138.

26. Longerich, *Ermordung der europaischen Juden*, pp. 310–11, and Shachan, *Burning Ice*, pp. 58–67, 89–93, 141.

27. Einsatzgruppe D report, Ancel, *Documents*, V, pp. 25–6.

28. Levin, *Holocaust*, p. 572.

29. Einsatzgruppe D Report, Ancel, *Documents*, V, pp. 28–30.

30. Fisher, *Transnistria*, p. 40.

31. Reports of Gendarmerie Inspectorate at Czernowitz, Hotin and Soroca, and Pretor of Third Army, Ancel, *Documents*, V, pp. 35–8.

32. Fisher, *Transnistria*, pp. 45–53. See also Order of Army Headquarters to Service of High Pretor, Ancel, *Documents*, V, p. 47, and Shachan, *Burning Ice*, pp. 71–89.

33. *Procesul Marii Tradari Nationale*, Trial of the Great National Betrayal: Stenographic Record of the Antonescu Government Trial before the People's Tribunal Bucharest 1946, pp. 287ff. See also Dora Litani, 'The Destruction of the Jews of Odessa in the Light of Rumanian Documents', *Yad Vashem Studies*, 6 (1967), p. 139.

34. Shachan, *Burning Ice*, pp. 121–34, 153–8.

35. Fisher, *Transnistria*, p. 61.
36. Meir Teich, 'The Jewish Self-Administration in Ghetto Shargorod (Transnistria)', *Yad Vashem Studies*, 2 (1958), p. 224.
37. Fisher, *Transnistria*, pp. 95–8.
38. Teich, 'Ghetto Shargorod', p. 223.
39. Shachan, *Burning Ice*, pp. 173, 208–12.
40. *Jagendorf's Foundry: Memoir of the Romanian Holocaust 1941–1944*, ed. Aron Hirt-Manheimer (New York: HarperCollins, 1991), pp. 95–8.
41. Fisher, *Transnistria*, pp. 122–5.
42. Ibid., p. 70.
43. Ibid., pp. 73–4, and I.C. Butnaru, *Waiting for Jerusalem: Surviving the Holocaust in Romania* (Westport: Greenwood Press, 1993), p. 11.
44. Fisher, *Transnistria*, p. 41.
45. Reitlinger, *Final Solution*, pp. 401–2.
46. Theodore Lavi, 'Documents on the Struggle of Rumanian Jewry for its Rights during the Second World War', *Yad Vashem Studies*, 4 (1960), pp. 260–15; Alexandre Shafran, 'The Rulers of Fascist Rumania whom I had to Deal With', *Yad Vashem Studies*, 4 (1963), pp. 175–80; and Shafran, *Resisting the Storm, Romania, 1940–47*, ed. Jean Ancerl (Jerusalem: Yad Vashem, 1987).
47. Butnaru, *Waiting for Jerusalem*, p. 18.
48. Reitlinger, *Final Solution*, pp. 401–2, and Lavi, 'Documents on Struggle of Rumanian Jewry', p. 263.
49. Butnaru, *Waiting for Jerusalem*, pp. 113–14.
50. Randolph Braham, *Genocide and Retribution: The Holocaust in Hungarian-ruled Northern Transylvania* (Boston: Kluwer-Nijhoff, 1983).
51. Butnaru, *Waiting for Jerusalem*, pp. 107–12.
52. Ibid., pp. 116–21.
53. Ibid., pp. 124–42, and Shachan, *Burning Ice*, pp. 311–13.
54. Saul S. Friedman, *No Haven for the Oppressed: United States Policy toward Jewish Refugees 1938–1945* (Detroit: Wayne State, 1943), p. 149.
55. *The Personal Letters of Stephen Wise*, ed. Justine Wise Poler and James Waterman Wise (Boston: Beacon, 1956), p. 265.
56. Ben Hecht, *Perfidy* (New York: Julian Messner, 1961), p. 192.
57. 'The Morgenthau Diaries: VI, The Refugee Run-Around', *Collier's* (1 Nov. 1947), CXX, pp. 23, 62. See also Arthur Morse, *While Six Million Died* (New York: Random House, 1967), pp. 73–86.
58. Memorandum by Long for Hull, 28 October 1943, Relief File, Long papers. Long to Riegner, 18 December 1943, ibid.
59. Stephen Wise, *Challenging Years: The Autobiography of Stephen Wise* (New York: Putnam's, 1949), p. 279.
l60. 'Morgenthau Diaries', p. 62.
61. Ibid., p. 585.
62. Longerich, *Ermordung der europaischen Juden*, p. 315.
63. *Jagendorf's Foundry*, pp. 183–5.
64. Teich, 'Ghetto Shargorod', pp. 245, 252.
65. Butnaru, *Waiting for Jerusalem*, pp. 65–6.
66. Theodore Lavi, 'The Vatican's Endeavors on Behalf of Rumanian Jewry during the Second World War', *Yad Vashem Studies*, 5 (1963), p. 416.
67. Matatias Carp, *Holocaust in Rumania: Facts and Documents on the Annihilation of Rumania's Jews 1940–44*, tr. Sean Murphy (Budapest: Primor, 1994); I.C. Butnaru, *The Silent Holocaust: Romania and Its Jews* (Westport: Greenwood Press, 1992); Randolph Braham (ed.), *The Tragedy of Romanian Jewry* (Boulder: Social Science Monographs, 1994); Sabin Manuila, *Populatia evreiasca din Romania in timpul celui deal II-les razboi mondial* (The Jewish Population in Romania during World War II) (Jassy: Romanian Cultural Foundation, 1994).

Chapter 21. Greece: Destruction of a Sephardic Civilization

1. Testimony of Madame Malah, April 1959, in Miriam Novitch (ed.), *Passage des Barbares: Contribution à l'Histoire de la Déportation et de la Résistance des Juifs grecs* (Haifa: Ghetto Fighters House, 1982), pp. 41–3. See also Michael Molho and Joseph Nehama, *In Memoriam: hommage aux victimes juives des Nazis en Grèce* (Jewish Community of Salonika, 1973), pp. 71–4.
2. Mark Mazower, *Inside Hitler's Greece: The Experience of Occupation 1941–44* (New Haven: Yale University Press, 1993), p. 248.
3. Novitch, *Passage des Barbares*, p. 42.
4. Contrast Nikos Stavroulakis, *The Jews of Greece: An Essay* (Athens: Talus Press, 1990) and L.S. Stavrianos, 'The Jews of Greece', *Journal of Central European Affairs*, 8 (1948), pp. 256–69, with George Mavrogordatos, *Stillborn Republic: Social Coalitions and Party Strategies in Greece, 1922–1936* (Berkeley: University of California Press, 1983), Joshua Plaut, *Greek Jewry in the Twentieth Century, 1913–1983: Patterns of Jewish Survival in the Greek Provinces before and after the Holocaust* (Madison, NJ: Farleigh Dickinson University Press, 1996), and Bernard Pierron, *Juifs et chrétiens de la Grèce moderne: histoire des relations inter-communautaires de 1821 à 1945* (Paris: Harmattan, 1996).
5. Dubnov, *History of the Jews*, tr. Moshe Speigel (South Brunswick: T. Yoseloff, 1973), V, p. 391.
6. Ibid., pp. 635–8, 809. See also Stanford Shaw, *The Jews of the Ottoman Empire and the Turkish Republic* (New York: New York University Press, 1991).
7, Alexander Kitroeff, 'Documents: The Jews in Greece, 1941–1944 – Eyewitness Accounts', *Journal of the Hellenic Diaspora*, 12 (Fall 1985), p. 10.
8. Elias Petropouos, *A Macabre Song: Testimony of the Goy Elias Petropulos Concerning Anti-Jewish Sentiments in Greece*, tr. John Taylor (Paris: Atelier Merat, 1985).
9. Testimony of Isaac Aruh, Athens, 17 March 1959, in Novitch, *Passage des Barbares*, p. 21.
10. Testimony of Hella Cougno, Salonika, 12 March 1959, in Novitch, *Passage des Barbares*, p. 58.
11. Molho and Nehama, *In Memoriam*, pp. 32–3.
12. Novitch, *Passage des Barbares*, p. 58.
13. Revah in Novitch, *Passage des Barbares*, pp. 27–31.
14. Ibid., p. 23.
15. John Katris, *Eyewitness in Greece: The Colonels Come to Power* (St Louis: New Critics Press, 1971), p. 81.
16. Peppo Cohen, Salonika, March 1959, in Novitch, *Passage des Barbares*, p. 16. The women were actresses from Strength thru Joy.
17. Cecil Roth reckoned it at $40,000 in 'The Last Days of Jewish Salonica', *Commentary* (July 1950), p. 51.
18. Molho and Nehama, *In Memoriam*, pp. 63–7.
19. Yacoel was killed in the revolt of the Sonderkommando at Crematoria III along with 130 others.
20. Hans Safrian, *Die Eichmann-Männer* (Vienna: Europowerlag 1993), pp. 230–1.
21. Ibid., pp. 236–7.
22. Molho and Nehama, *In Memoriam*, pp. 75–80, 153–8.
23. Novitch, *Passage des Barbares*, p. 24.
24. Safrian, *Die Eichmann-Männer*, p. 239.
25. Molho and Nehama, *In Memoriam*, pp. 86, 97, and Safrian, *Die Eichmann-Männer*, p. 242.
26. Nathan Eck, 'New Light on the Charges against the Last Chief Rabbi of Salonica', *Yad Vashem Bulletin*, 17 (December 1965), pp. 9–10.
27. Raul Hilberg, *The Destruction of the European Jews* (New York: Quadrangle, 1951), pp. 444, 447.

28. Mazower, *Inside Hitler's Greece*, p. 243.
29. Molho and Nehama, *In Memoriam*, p. 97.
30. Safrian, *Die Eichmann-Männer*, p. 244; Levin, *Holocaust*, p. 521; Molho and Nehama, *In Memoriam*, pp. 103–4.
31. Molho and Nehama, *In Memoriam*, pp. 106, 110.
32. Mazower, *Inside Hitler's Greece*, p. 243; Hilberg, *Destruction of European Jews*, p. 445; and Molho and Nehama, *In Memoriam*, pp. 30, 87, 106.
33. Safrian, *Die Eichmann-Männer*, p. 241.
34. Ibid., p. 240.
35. Molho and Nehama, *In Memoriam*, pp. 92–6.
36. Testimony of Sarina Saltiel-Venezia, Salonika, April 1959, in Novitch, *Passage des Barbares*, p. 52.
37. Novitch, *Passage des Barbares*, pp. 12, 32.
38. Ibid., pp. 117–19; Molho and Nehama, *In Memoriam*, pp. 134–5.
39. Novitch, *Passage des Barbares*, p. 13.
40. Mazower, *Inside Hitler's Greece*, p. 248, and Molho and Nehama, *In Memoriam*, pp. 138–42, 166–8.
41. Ibid., pp. 128–32.
42. Testimony of Ida Angell, in Novitch, *Passage des Barbares*, p. 100.
43. After the war, von Loehr was executed. Spedel and Neubacher each received 20-year prison terms.
44. See Report No. 1746 (R0–1616) dated 11 November 1943 of Burton Berry, American Consul General, and Regulations in Dispatch No. 1601 (R–1483), 22 October 1943 of Stroop, in Kitroeff, 'Documents', pp. 22–4.
45. Hilberg claims 1,200 reported to the authorities. *Destruction of European Jews*, p. 450. A confidential report No. 13270 dated 'before Dec. 7, 1943' places the number at 200. Kitroeff, 'Documents', p. 31.
46. Kitroeff, 'Documents', pp. 6, 31.
47. Testimony of Baruch Chibi, March 1959, Salonika, in Novitch, *Passage des Barbares*, p. 38. Also Molho and Nehama, *In Memoriam*, pp. 171–5.
48. Testimony of Ida Angell, in Novitch, *Passage des Barbares*, p. 100.
49. Ibid., pp. 101–2.
50. Fromer, *Holocaust Odyssey*, p. 28.
51. Errikos Servillias, *Athens-Auschwitz*, tr. Nikos Stavroulakis (Athens: Lycabettus Press, 1983), pp. 3–23.
52. Isaac Kabelli, 'The Resistance of the Greek Jews', *YIVO Annual of Jewish Social Sciences*, 8 (1943), pp. 281–8; and Novitch, *Passage des Barbares*, pp. 40, 57.
53. Rachel Dalven, *The Jews of Ioannina* (Philadelphia: Cadmus Press, 1986); Molho and Nehama, *In Memoriam*, pp. 218–20.
54. Novitch, *Passage des Barbares*, p. 97.
55. Ibid., p. 96.
56. Ibid., pp. 98–9.
57. Mazower, *Inside Hitler's Greece*, p. 258.
58. Memorandum of Jaeger, 17 June 1944, NOKW 1915; Novitch, *Passage des Barbares*, p. 106. See also Mazower, *Inside Hitler's Greece*, pp. 253–6; and Safrian, *Die Eichmann-Männer*, pp. 275–80.
59. Testimony of Rosa Soussi in Novitch, *Passage des Barbares*, p. 105.
60. Testimony of Estir Pitzon, Corfu, June 1968, in Novitch, *Passage des Barbares*, p. 106.
61. Testimony of Salomon Galante, April 1952, in Novitch, *Passage de Barbares*, p. 108; interview with Victoria Soriano, Rhodes, 24 June 1968, *loc. cit.*, p. 112; and Molho and Nehama, *In Memoriam*, pp. 231–3.
62. Ibid., p. 110. See Safrian, *Die Eichmann-Männer*, pp. 282–3.
63. Deposition of Lenz, 5 October 1947, NOKW 1715, Process of von Leeb, in Novitch, *Passage de Barbares*, p. 108.
64. Soriano in Novitch, *Passage des Barbares*, p. 112.

65. Galante in Novitch, *Passage des Barbares*, p. 109.
66. Novitch, *Passage des Barbares*, p. 111.
67. Miklos Nyiszli, *Auschwitz: A Doctor's Eyewitness Account*, tr. Tibere Kremer and Richard Seaver (Greenwich, CT: Fawcett, 1960), p. 83.
68. Ibid., p. 111. Mazower suggests the boats were sunk by British torpedoes. *Inside Hitler's Greece*, p. 256.
69. S. Haim Avni, 'Spanish Nationals in Greece and Their Fate during the Holocaust', *Yad Vashem Studies* 8 (1970), pp. 31–68; Molho and Nehama, *In Memoriam*, pp. 111–14; and Novitch, *Passage des Barbares*, pp. 33, 45.
70. Hilberg, *Destruction of European Jews*, pp. 447–8.

Chapter 22. Co-Belligerents: Bulgaria and Finland

1. Vicki Tamir, *Bulgaria and Her Jews: The History of a Dubious Symbiosis* (New York: Sepher-Hermon Press, 1979), pp. 36–44.
2. Marshall Miller, *Bulgaria during the Second World War* (Stanford: Stanford University Press, 1975), p. 93. See also Wolf Oschlies, *Bulgarien – Land ohne Antisemitismus* (Bulgaria: Land without Anti-Semitism) (Erlangen: Ner Tamid Verlag, 1976).
3. Frederick Chary, *The Bulgarian Jews and the Final Solution 1940–1944* (Pittsburgh: University of Pittsburgh Press, 1972), pp. 32–3.
4. Tamir, *Bulgaria and Her Jews*, pp. 123–6, 161.
5. Miller, *Bulgaria during the Second World War*, pp. 3–5, 17–19, and Tamir, *Bulgaria and Her Jews*, pp. 126–32.
6. For a complete list of restrictions, see Tamir, *Bulgaria and Her Jews*, pp. 170–2.
7. Miller, *Bulgaria during the Second World War*, pp. 94–6, and Tamir, *Bulgaria and Her Jews*, pp. 173–4.
8. Ibid., pp. 174–5.
9. Chary, *Bulgarian Jews and Final Solution*, pp. 59–64. See also A.J. Fischer, 'Bulgarian Ferment', *Central European Observer*, 19 (6 February 1942), pp. 39–40; Benyamin Arditti, *Yehude bulgaryah bi-shenot hamishtar ha-Natsi 1940–1944* (Jews of Bulgaria under the Nazi Regime, 1940–1944) (Holon: J. Arditti, 1961).
10. Chary, *Bulgarian Jews and Final Solution*, p. 77; Tamir, *Bulgaria and Her Jews*, pp. 184–7; and Hans-Joachim Hoppe, *Bulgarien – Hitlers eigenwilliger Verbundeter: eine Fallstudie zur natonalsozialistichen Sudosteuropapolitik* (Bulgaria – Hitler's Voluntary Ally: A Case Study in National Socialist Southeast European Politics) (Stuttgart: Deutsche Verlags-Anstalt, 1979).
11. Natan Grinberg, *Dokumenti* (Sofia: Central Consistory of Jews in Bulgaria, 1945), p. 7.
12. Nir Baruch, *ha-Kofer: Bulgaryah vi-Yehudehah be-mesheskh ha-dorot* (The Ransom) (Tel Aviv: Shevilim, 1990).
13. *Rettung der bulgarischen Juden 1943: eine Dokumentation*, Dieter Ruckhaberle, Christiane Ziesecke (eds) (Berlin: Publica, 1984); Tamir, *Bulgaria and Her Jews*, pp. 190–3; and Miller, *Bulgaria during Second World War*, pp. 99–100.
14. Chary, *Bulgarian Jews and Final Solution*, pp. 84–5.
15. Ibid., pp. 211–13.
16. Ibid., p. 90.
17. Miller, *Bulgaria during Second World War*, pp. 101–3, and Tamir, *Bulgaria and Her Jews*, pp. 198–204. See also Gay Block and Malka Drucker, *Rescuers: Portraits of Moral Courage in the Holocaust* (New York: Holmes & Meier, 1992).
18. Michael Molho and Joseph Nehama, *In Memoriam: hommage aux victimes juives des Nazis en Grèce* (Jewish Community of Salonika, 1973), pp. 118–26.
19. Testimony of Maurice Benveniste, Cavalla, April 1959, in Miriam Novitch (ed.), *Passage des Barbares: Contribution à l'Histoire de la Déportation et de la Résistance*

de Juifs grecs (Haifa: Ghetto Fighters House, 1982), p. 79.

20. Testimony of Nissim Alkalay, Athens, March 1959, in Novitch, *Passage des Barbares*, p. 90.
21. Ibid., p. 80.
22. Chary, *Bulgarian Jews and Final Solution*, pp. 101–13.
23. Molho and Nehama, *In Memoriam*, p. 120.
24. Uri Oren, *A Town Called Monastir* (Tel Aviv: Imud, 1971), p. 54.
25. *Zhidov* (13 November 1936), p. 1.
26. Chary, *Bulgarian Jews and Final Solution*, pp. 114–16, and Tamir, *Bulgaria and Her Jews*, p. 195.
27. Oren, *A Town Called Monastir*, pp. 196–7.
28. Miller, *Bulgaria during Second World War*, pp. 125–6; Chary, *Bulgarian Jews and Final Solution*, p. 141; and Molho and Nehama, *In Memoriam*, pp. 121–3.
29. Oren, *A Town Called Monastir*, p. 198.
30 Ibid., pp. 198–200.
31. Testimony of Nissim Behar, Tel Aviv, 1959, in Novitch, *Passage des Barbares*, p. 94.
32. Nadejda Vasileva, 'On the Catastrophe of the Thracian Jews', *Yad Vashem Studies*, 3 (1959), pp. 295–301.
33. Testimony of Moise Pessah, Drama, April 1959, in Novitch, *Passage des Barbares*, p. 84.
34. Testimony of Abraham-Salomon Ovadia, Athens, 25 March 1959, in Novitch, *Passage des Barbares*, p. 83.
35. Jankel Wiernik, *A Year at Treblinka*, published by Polish clandestine press in Warsaw, 1944, cited in Novitch, *Passage des Barbares*, p. 88.
36. Chary, *Bulgarian Jews and Final Solution*, pp. 143–52, and Tamir, *Bulgaria and Her Jews*, pp. 179–81.
37. Miller, *Bulgaria during Second World War*, pp. 135–48.
38. Tamir, *Bulgaria and Her Jews*, p. 215.
39. Chary, *Bulgarian Jews and Final Solution*, p. 169.
40. Tamir, *Bulgaria and Her Jews*, pp. 212–18.
41. Guy Haskell, *From Sofia to Jaffa: The Jews of Bulgaria and Israel* (Detroit: Wayne State University Press, 1994).
42. Chary, *Bulgarian Jews and Final Solution*, pp. 185–7.
43. Ibid., pp. 129–44.
44. Ms. of Jack Weinstein, Helsinki, 1956, p. 19, cited in Hannu Rautkallio, *Finland and the Holocaust: The Rescue of Finland's Jews*, tr. Paul Sjoblom (New York: Holocaust Library, 1987), p. 57.
45. *The Memoirs of Marshal Mannerheim*, tr. Count Eric Lewenhaupt (New York: Dutton, 1954).
46. Wilhelm Tieke, *Das Finnische Freiwilligen-Bataillon der Waffen SS* (Osnabruck: Munin, 1979); Waldemar Erfurth, *Warfare in the Far North* (Washington: US Army Center of Military History, 1987); and Hans Peter Krosby, *Finland, Germany and the Soviet Union 1940–1941* (Madison: University of Wisconsin Press, 1968).
47. Rautkallio, *Finland and the Holocaust*, p. 212.
48. Philip Friedman, *Their Brothers' Keepers* (New York: Crown, 1957), pp. 143–8.
49. Levin, *Holocaust*, pp. 399–400.
50. Wipert von Blucher, *Gessandter zwischen Diktatur und Demokratie* (Wiesbaden: Limes Verlag, 1951).
51. Rautkallio, *Finland and the Holocaust*, pp. 39–83.
52. Ibid., p. 118.
53. Ibid., p. 129.
54. Ibid., p. 136.
55. Martin Sandberger, Gestapo chief in Estonia, disputed whether Anthoni visited any mass grave.
56. Achim Besgem, *Der Stille Befehl, Medizeinalrat Kersten, Himmler und das Dritte Reich* (Munich, 1950), p. 220.

57. Rautkallio rejects Kersten's 'colorful stories', *Finland and the Holocaust*, pp. 166, 168.
58. Ibid., pp. 201–3.
59. Ibid., p. 217.
60. Ibid., pp. 211–13.
61. Ibid., pp. 229–36.
62. Eino Murtorinne, *Die finnisch-deutschen Kircenbeziehungen 1940–1944* (Gottingen: Vandenhoeck & Ruprecht, 1990).

Chapter 23. Italy: The Reluctant Ally

1. Renzo de Felice, *Storia degli ebrei italiani sotto il fascismo* (Turin: Giulio Einaudi, 1972), pp. 5–14.
2. Susan Zuccotti, *The Italians and the Holocaust: Persecution, Rescue and Survival* (New York: Basic Books, 1987), pp. 15–17, and Nathan Ausubel, *Pictorial History of the Jewish People* (New York: Crown, 1965), p. 199.
3. Collaborators betrayed Ovazza and his family in October 1943. Alexander Stille, *Benevolence and Betrayal: Five Italian Jewish Families under Fascism* (New York: Summit Books, 1991), pp. 19–89.
4. Douglas Radcliff-Umstead, 'The Fascist Betrayal of the Italian Jews', in Franklin Littell, Irene Shur, and Claude Foster (eds), *The Holocaust: In Answer* (West Chester: Sylvan Publishers, 1988), pp. 140–2.
5. Emil Ludwig, *Talks with Mussolini* (London: Allen & Unwin, 1932), p. 74; Nahum Goldmann, *Memories* (London: Weidenfeld & Nicolson, 1969), pp. 154–63.
6. Ibid., p. 74.
7. De Felice, *Storia degli ebrei italiani*, pp. 138–9.
8. Weizmann, *Trial and Error: The Autobiography of Chaim Weizmann* (Philadelphia: JPSA, 1949), II, pp. 25–6; and Joseph Schechtman, *Fighter and Prophet: Vladimir Jabotinsky's Story: The Last Years* (New York: T. Yoseloff, 1961).
9. Meir Michaelis, *Mussolini and the Jews* (Oxford: Clarendon Press, 1978), p. 69.
10. Sam Wagenaar, *The Pope's Jews* (La Salle, IL: Open Court, 1974), pp. 296–7.
11. De Felice, *Storia*, pp. 54–6, and Harry Fornari, *Mussolini's Gadfly: Roberto Farinacci* (Nashville: Vanderbilt University Press, 1971).
12. Mussolini was distressed by a novel, *Amore Negro*, which talked of miscegenation, Michaelis, *Mussolini and Jews*, p. 115. See also Esmonde Robertson, 'Race as a Factor in Mussolini's Policy in Africa and Europe', *Journal of Contemporary History*, 23 (1988), pp. 37–58.
13. An earlier book by Giulio Cogni, *Il razzismo* (1935), borrowed from Nazism.
14. De Felice, *Storia*, p. 231.
15. Michaelis, *Mussolini and Jews*, p. 397.
16. De Felice, *Storia*, pp. 347–50; Michaelis, *Mussolini and Jews*, pp. 169–71; Zuccotti, *Italians and Holocaust*, pp. 36–9.
17. Galeazzo Ciano, *Diario 1937–43*, ed. Renzo de Felice (Milan: Rizzoli, 1980), 15 July 1938, p. 158.
18. Collier, *Duce*, p. 148. Jews were devoted to the House of Savoy and a king who did little to help them. Zuccotti, *Italians and Holocaust*, p. 51.
19. Stille, *Benevolence and Betrayal*, p. 77.
20. Wagenaar, *The Pope's Jews*, pp. 383–5.
21. Ibid., p. 293.
22. Carlo Sparataco Capogreco, 'The Internment Camp of Ferramonti-Tarsia', tr. Ruth Feldman, in Ivo Herzer, Klaus Voigt and James Burgwyn (eds), *The Italian Refuge: Rescue of Jews during the Holocaust* (Washington: Catholic University, 1989), pp. 161–77.
23. Zuccotti, *Italians and Holocaust*, pp. 61–4.
24. Note to *Standartenführer* Knochen from Rothke, undated, Leon Poliakov and Jacques

Sabille (eds), *Jews under the Italian Occupation* (Paris: Centre de Documentation Juive Contemporaine, 1955), pp. 93–6.

25. Mackensen Telegram, 18 March 1943, in Poliakov and Sabille, *Jews under Italian Occupation*, pp. 68–70.
26. *The Times*, 21 January 1943.
27. Poliakov, 'The Jews under the Italian Occupation in France', p. 23.
28. Ibid., p. 28.
29. Eichmann to Mueller, 12 February 1943, in Poliakov and Sabille, *Jews under the Italian Occupation*, p. 62.
30. Hagen to Himmler, 29 June 1943, Paris, in Poliakov and Sabille, *Jews under the Italian Occupation*, pp. 99–100.
31. Ibid., p. 86.
32. Note from General Gualtieri to General Bridoux, Secretary of State for Defense, Vichy, 27 April 1943, in Poliakov and Sabille, *Jews under the Italian Occupation*, p. 88.
33. See telegram from Barbie to RHSA IVB in Paris, 15 May 1943, in Poliakov and Sabille, *Jews under the Italian Occupation*, p. 81.
34. Note for *Obersturmbannführer* Dr Schmidt, Paris, 21 July 1943, in Poliakov and Sabille, *Jews under the Italian Occupation*, p. 106.
35. *New York Times*, 9 September 1943, p. 1.
36. Zuccotti, *Italians and Holocaust*, pp. 88–91.
37. Rothke to Hagen, Paris, 4 September 1943, in Poliakov and Sabille, *Jews under the Italian Occupation*, pp. 119–21.
38. Nicola Caracciolo, *Gli ebrei e l'Italia durante laguerra 1940–45* (Rome: Bonacci, 1986), and Giuseppe Mayda, *Ebrei sotto Salo: La persecuzione antisemita, 1943–1945* (Milan: Feltrinelli, 1978).
39. Robert Katz, *Black Sabbath: A Journey through a Crime against Humanity* (New York: Macmillan, 1969), pp. 53–4.
40. Ibid., pp. 19, 33.
41. Ibid., pp. 59–62.
42. Ibid., pp. 62–5.
43. Katz, *Black Sabbath*, pp. 85–96; Michaelis, *Mussolini and Jews*, pp. 385–6, and Zuccotti, *Italians and Holocaust*, p. 110.
44. Katz, *Black Sabbath*, pp. 101–2.
45. Ibid., pp. 105–8, 118–20, 123–5, 147–51. See also Zuccotti, *Italians and Holocaust*, p. 115, and Michaelis, *Mussolini and Jews*, pp. 358–9.
46. Liliana Picciotto Fargion, 'The Jews during the German Occupation and the Italian Social Republic', tr. Susan Zuccotti, in Ivo Herzer *et al.* (eds), *The Italian Refuge* (Washington: Catholic University, 1989), pp. 119–20.
47. Katz, *Black Sabbath*, pp. 155–8.
48. Ibid., pp. 134–5; Zuccotti, *Italians and Holocaust*, pp. 12–29; Michaelis, *Mussolini and Jews*, p. 364.
49. There is no basis for Zuccotti's claim (p. 134) that Hitler wanted to create his own Papacy in Germany.
50. Zuccotti, *Italians and Holocaust*, pp. 130–1.
51. Michaelis, *Mussolini and Jews*, pp. 365–71.
52. Katz, *Black Sabbath*, pp. 174–84.
53. Zuccotti, *Italians and Holocaust*, pp. 103–4, and Katz, *Black Sabbath*, pp. 189–90.
54. Zuccotti, *Italians and Holocaust*, pp. 116–19.
55. Katz, *Black Sabbath*, pp. 239–68.
56. Ibid., pp. 268–73, and Zuccotti, pp. 120–5.
57. 'Florence', *Encyclopedia Judaica*, VI (Jerusalem: Keter, 1971), p. 1360.
58. Jonathan Katz, *Death in Rome* (London: Jonathan Cape, 1967).
59. Ricciotti Lazzero, *Le SS italiane: Storia dei 20,000 che giuranorono fedelta a Hitler* (Milan: Rizzoli, 1982), and Lazzero, *Le brigate nere: Il partito armato della republica di Mussolini* (Milan: Rizzoli, 1983).

60. De Felice, *Storia*, p. 446.
61. Fargion, 'Jews during Social Republic', pp. 126–34.
62. Primo Levi, *Survival in Auschwitz*, tr. Stuart Woolf (London: Collier, 1973), p. 11.
63. De Felice, *Storia*, pp. 465–6.
64. Zuccotti, *Italians and Holocaust*, pp. 97–100.
65. Michaelis, *Mussolini and Jews*, p. 69.
66. Ibid., p. 397.
67. Jonathan Steinberg, *All or Nothing: The Axis and the Holocaust 1941–1943* (London: Routledge, 1990), p. 229; and Joseph LaPalombara, *Democracy, Italian Style* (New Haven: Yale University Press, 1987).
68. Alan Cassels, 'Italy and the Holocaust', in S. Friedman (eds.), *Holocaust Literature* (Westport: Greenwood, 1993), p. 399.
69. Zuccotti, *Italians and Holocaust*, p. 100.
70. Katz, *Black Sabbath*, pp. 186, 194, 212.
71. Zuccotti, *Italians and Holocaust*, p. 94.
72. Ibid., p. 100.

Chapter 24. The Humanitarians: The Vatican and the Red Cross

1. *New York Times*, 21 July 1943, p. 3.
2. *New York Times*, 20 July 1943, pp. 1–2.
3. *New York Times*, 22 July 1943, p. 4.
4. Saul Friedlaender, *Pius XII and the Third Reich*, tr. Charles Fullman (New York: Knopf, 1966), pp. 15–47.
5. Carlo Falconi, *The Silence of Pius XII*, tr. Bernard Wall (Boston: Little Brown, 1965), p. 40.
6. Camille Cianfarra, *The Vatican and the War* (New York: Dutton, 1944), p. 197.
7. Ibid., pp. 275–310.
8. Friedlaender, *Pius XII and Third Reich*, pp. 47–55.
9. Anthony Rhodes, *The Vatican in the Age of the Dictators 1922–1949* (New York: Holt, Rinehart & Winston, 1975); Robert Graham, *Vatican Diplomacy: A Study of Church and State on the International Plane* (Princeton: Princeton University Press, 1959).
10. Leon Poliakov, 'Pope Pius XII and the Nazis', *Jewish Frontier*, 31 (April 1964), pp. 7–13; Poliakov, 'The Vatican and the Jewish Question', *Commentary*, 10 (November 1950), pp. 439–49; Rev. Edward Flannery, 'Vatican Diplomacy during the Holocaust', *Conservative Judaism*, 33 (Summer 1980), pp. 84–8; Barry Schwartz, 'The Vatican and the Holocaust', *Conservative Judaism*, 18 (Summer 1964), pp. 27–50; and Solomon Grayzel, 'The Ties that Bind Synagogue and Church', *Reconstructionist*, 33 (14 April 1967), pp. 22–36.
11. Falconi, *Silence of Pius XII*, pp. 43–4.
12. Rolf Hochhuth, *The Deputy*, tr. Richard and Clara Winston (New York: Grove Press, 1964), p. 349.
13. Falconi, *Silence of Pius XII*, p. 88.
14. Meir Michaelis, *Mussolini and the Jews* (Oxford: Clarendon Press, 1978), p. 395.
15. Writing while the war was still raging, Cianfarra said the Vatican was probably the best-informed power in the world, *Vatican and the War*, p. 67.
16. Friedlaender, *Pius XII and Third Reich*, pp. 93–8. Tisserant might have been a more sympathetic advocate. John Cornwell, *Hitler's Pope* (New York: Viking, 1999), p. 259.
17. John Morley, *Vatican Diplomacy and the Jews during the Holocaust 1939–1943* (New York: Ktav, 1980), pp. 107–11.
18. Ibid., pp. 135–7.
19. Ibid., p. 142.
20. Falconi, *Silence of Pius XII*, pp. 46–60.
21. Friedlaender, *Pius XII and Third Reich*, pp. 54–5.

22. Ibid., p. 132.
23. Ibid., pp. 122–5, and Falconi, *Silence of Pius XII*, pp. 74–92.
24. Hochhuth, *The Deputy*, p. 102.
25. On Pius's fear of communism, see Cornwell, *Hitler's Pope*, p. 328.
26. Guenter Lewy, 'The Role of the Papacy', pp. 151–7, Joseph Lichten, 'A Question of Judgment: Pius XII and the Jews', pp. 157–61, Father Robert Leiber, 'On Hochhuth's Historical Sources', pp. 161–4, and Father A. Martini, 'The Historical Truth and Rolf Hochhuth's *The Deputy*', pp. 164–81, in Earl and Dolores Schmidt (eds), *The Deputy Reader: Studies in Moral Responsibility* (Chicago: Scott, Foresman, 1965).
27. Pinchas Lapides, *Three Popes and the Jews* (New York: Hawthorn, 1967), pp. 267–9; Lichten, 'A Question of Judgment', in Schmidt, *The Deputy Reader*; and Alexander Randall, *The Pope, the Jews and the Nazis* (London: Catholic Truth Society, 1963).
28. Interview by Frank McGee, in Schmidt, *The Deputy Reader*, p. 213, and Graham, *Pius XII's Defense of Jews and Others 1944–45* (Milwaukee: Catholic League Publication, n.d.).
29. Morley, *Vatican Diplomacy*, pp. 23–48, 48–70.
30. According to Cornwell, not an ounce of gold came from the Vatican, *Hitler's Pope*, p. 302.
31. *New York Times*, 24 January 1976, p. 1.
32. Graham, *Pius XII's Defense of Jews and Others*, p. 15.
33. Falconi, *Silence of Pius XII*, p. 72. Cornwell concludes that Pius was a flawed human being and a hypocrite, *Hitler's Pope*, p. 297.
34. Falconi, *Silence of Pius XII*, pp. 94–5.
35. Guenter Lewy, *The Catholic Church and Nazi Germany* (New York: McGraw-Hill, 1964), p. 297. See also M. Mashberg, 'The Unpublished Encyclicals of Pius XI', *National Jewish Monthly*, 92 (April 1978), pp. 40–6.
36. Morley, *Vatican Diplomacy*, pp. 93, 201–7.
37. Cornwell labels him vain and preoccupied with self-image as the 'angelic shepherd', *Hitler's Pope*, pp. 220–43, 291.
38. Michaelis, *Mussolini and Jews*, p. 377.
39. Susan Zuccotti, *The Italians and the Holocaust: Persecution, Rescue and Survival* (New York: Basic Books, 1987), p. 135.
40. Lewy, *Catholic Church and Nazi Germany*, pp. 303–5.
41. Hochhuth, *The Deputy*, p. 352.
42. Falconi, *Silence of Pius XII*, p. 17.
43. Lewy, *Catholic Church and Nazi Germany*, p. 292.
44. Arthur Gilbert, *The Vatican Council and the Jews* (Cleveland: World Publishing, 1968), pp. 271–9.
45. VIS (Vatican Press Release), 16 March 1998. The church conceded that 'erroneous and unjust interpretations of the New Testament' may have contributed to the Shoah. The Israeli government and Jewish scholars deemed the statement inadequate.
46. Jean-Claude Favez, *Une Mission Impossible? Le CICR, les déportations et les camps de concentration Nazis* (Lausanne: Editions Payot Lausanne, 1988), pp. 10–11; and Meir Dworzecki, 'The International Red Cross and Its Policy vis-à-vis the Jews in the Ghettos and Concentration Camps in Nazi-Occupied Europe', in *Rescue Attempts during the Holocaust* (Jerusalem: Yad Vashem, 1974), pp. 72–3.
47. André Durand, *Histoire du Comité International de La Croix-Rouge: De Sarajevo à Hiroshima* (Geneva: Institut Henry-Dunant, 1978), p. 502.
48. Ibid., pp. 505–11.
49. Favez, *Mission Impossible*, p. 158.
50. Ibid., p. 180.
51. Ibid., p. 167.
52. Durand, *Histoire du Comité*, p. 514.
53. Ibid., pp. 158–61.
54. Ibid., p. 158.

55. Ibid., pp. 162–3.
56. Ibid., pp. 165–6.
57. Ibid., p. 504.
58. Dworzecki, 'International Red Cross', p. 95.
59. Durand, *Histoire du Comité*, p. 508.
60. Favez, *Mission Impossible*, pp. 178–80.
61. Durand, *Histoire du Comité*, p. 490, and Dworzecki, 'International Red Cross', pp. 104–5.
62. Favez, *Mission Impossible*, pp. 181–90.
63. Durand, *Histoire du Comité*, pp. 493–500.
64. Ibid., pp. 496–9.
65. Ibid., pp. 517–27.
66. Dworzecki, 'International Red Cross', pp. 109–10. See also Aryeh Tartakower, 'Where the Red Cross Failed', *Congress Weekly*, 13 (3 May 1946), pp. 9–10; and S.Z. Kantor, 'The International Red Cross Was Silent', *Jewish Frontier*, 12 (May 1945), pp. 17–20.
67. Favez, *Mission Impossible*, p. 166.
68. *Documents sur l'activité du Comité International de la Croix-Rouge en faveur des civils détenus dans les camps de concentration en Allemagne (1939–1945)* (Geneva, 1947); and *Seventeenth International Red Cross Conference, Report of the International Committee of the Red Cross on its Activities during the Second World War* (Geneva, 1948), 1, pp. 19, 36.
69. Durand, *Histoire du Comité*, pp. 529–30.
70. Favez, *Mission Impossible*, pp. 45–6.
71. Ibid., pp. 367–70.
72. Dworzecki, 'International Red Cross', p. 109.
73. Favez, *Mission Impossible*, p. 373.
74. Ibid., pp. 374–5.
75. *Washington Post*, 17 February 1989, p. A29.

Chapter 25. The European Neutrals

1. Willy Guggenheim, 'The Jews of Switzerland', fact sheet, SIG, Jewish Community of Zurich, May 1988.
2. Florence Guggenheim-Grunberg, Ralph Weingarten, Willy Guggenheim and Rabbi Jakob Teichman, *Juden in der Schweiz: Glaube – Geschichte – Gegenwart* (Zurich: Kusnacht, 1983), p. 70.
3. Norman Cohn, *Warrant for Genocide: The Myth of the Jewish World-Conspiracy and the Protocols of the Elders of Zion* (New York: Harper Torch, 1969), pp. 220–31.
4. Beat Glaus, *Die Nationale Front: Eine Schweizer Faschistischen Bewegung 1930–1940* (Cologne: Benziger Verlag, 1969), pp. 170–1, 375.
5. Ibid., p. 284.
6. Werner Rings, *Schweiz im Krieg, 1933–1945* (Zurich: Kindler Verlag, 1974); Karl Ludwig, *Die Fluchtlingspolitik der Schweiz in den Jahren 1933 bis 1945* (Bern: Lang, 1957); and 'Origins of the "J" Passport: A Controversy in Switzerland', *Wiener Library Bulletin*, 8 (May 1954), p. 20.
7. Guggenheim-Grunberg *et al.*, *Juden in der Schweiz*, p. 85.
8. Alfred Hasler, *Das Boot ist voll* (Zurich: Fretz and Wasmuth Verlag, 1968).
9. Karl Ludwig, *Die Fluchtlings-politik der Schweiz in den Jahren 1933 bis 1945* (Bern: Lang, 1957); 'Origins of the "J" Passport', p. 20.
10. Mathias Knauer and Jurg Frischknecht, *Die unterbrochene Spur: Antifaschistiche Emgraten in der Schweiz von 1933 bis 1943* (Zurich: Limmat Verlag Genossenschaft), 1983.
11. Denis de Rougemont and Charlotte Muret, *The Heart of Europe* (New York: Duell,

Sloan & Pearson, 1941), p. 213.

12. Denis Fodor, *The Neutrals* (New York: Time-Life Books, 1982), pp. 28–62.

13. Jean Ziegler, *Switzerland: The Awful Truth*, tr. Rosemary Sheed Middleton (New York: Harper & Row, 1976), pp. 47–52. Ziegler's approach is shrill, but her criticism rings true.

14. Arthur Smith, *Hitler's Gold: The Story of the Nazi War Loot* (New York: Berg, 1989), p. 155.

15. Ziegler, *Switzerland*, p. 41.

16. Smith, *Hitler's Gold*, p. 80.

17. Ibid., p. 82.

18. *USA Today*, 28 January 1997, p. A6.

19. CNN World News, 7 May 1997.

20. *USA Today*, 8 May 1997, p. A1.

21. Smith, *Hitler's Gold*, p. 101.

22. *USA Today*, 24 January 1997, p. A4.

23. Hugh Thomas, *The Spanish Civil War* (New York: Harper & Row, 1961); Robert Whealey, *Hitler and Spain: The Nazi Role in the Spanish Civil War 1936–1939* (Lexington: University Press of Kentucky, 1989); Max Gallo, *Spain Under Franco*, tr. J. Stewart (New York: Dutton, 1974).

24. Fodor, *Neutrals*, p. 82.

25. Haim Avni, *Spain, Franco and the Jews* (Philadelphia: JPS, 1982), pp. 60–1.

26. Chaim Lipschitz, *Franco, Spain, the Jews and the Holocaust* (New York: Ktav, 1983), pp. 21–35, 92.

27. Avni, *Spain, Franco and Jews*, pp. 6–17.

28. Ibid., pp. 21–6.

29. Ibid., pp. 21–32.

30. Ibid., pp. 68–71.

31. Nehemiah Robinson, 'The Spain of Franco and Its Policies Toward the Jews' (New York: Institute of Jewish Affairs, 1944), p. 8.

32. Avni, *Spain, Franco and Jews*, pp. 73–6, 98–9, 100–14; Lipschitz, *Franco, Spain, Jews and Holocaust*, p. 127.

33. Avni, *Spain, Franco and Jews*, pp. 114–17.

34. Lipschitz, *Franco, Spain, Jews and Holocaust*, pp. 39–47.

35. Michael Molho and Joseph Nehama, *In Memoriam: Hommage aux victimes juives*, pp. 204–6.

36. Ibid., pp. 149–60.

37. Lipschitz, *Franco, Spain, Jews and Holocaust*, pp. 52–70.

38. Letter from Butterworth to Hull, FRUS, 10 July 1944.

39. Federico Ysart, *Espana y los judios* (Barcelona: Dopesa, 1973), pp. 124–32.

40. Lipschitz, *Franco, Spain, Jews and Holocaust*, p. 143

41. Ibid., p. 146.

42. Ibid., p. 164.

43. Stanley G. Payne, *The Franco Regime 1936–1957* (Madison: University of Wisconsin Press, 1987), p. 68.

44. Avni, *Spain, Franco and Jews*, p. 126.

45. Ibid., p. 136.

46. Antonio Costa Pinto, 'The Radical Right in Contemporary Portugal', pp. 108–28, in Luciano Cheles *et al.* (eds), *Far Right in Western and Eastern Europe* (New York: Longman, 1991).

47. Harry Ezratty, 'The Portuguese Consul and the 10,000 Jews', *Jewish Life* (September 1964), p. 17.

48. Maia Wojciechowska, *Till the Break of Day* (New York: Harcourt, Brace, Jovanovich, 1972), p. 137.

49. Avni, *Spain, Franco and Jews*, pp. 186–94.

50. W.M. Carlgren, *Swedish Foreign Policy during World War II*, tr. Arthur Spencer (New

York: St Martin's, 1977); and Paul Levine, *From Indifference to Activism: Swedish Diplomacy and the Holocaust 1938–1944* (Upsala: Almqvist & Wiksell, 1996).

51. Gerald Aalders and Cees Wiebes, *The Art of Cloaking Ownership: The Secret Collaboration and Protection of the German War Industry by the Neutrals: The Case of Sweden* (Amsterdam: Amsterdam University Press, 1996).

52. Joachim Joesten, *Stalwart Sweden* (Garden City: Doubleday Doran, 1943); and Bo Widfeldt, *The Luftwaffe in Sweden 1939–1945* (Boylston, MA: Monogram Aviation Publishers, 1983).

53. Henrik Nissen (ed.), *Scandinavia during the Second World War*, tr. Thomas Munch-Petersen (Minneapolis: University of Minnesota Press and Oslo: Universeitets forlaget, 1983), p. 105.

54. O. Fritjof Ander, *The Building of Modern Sweden* (Rock Island, IL: Augustana Library Publishers, 1958).

55. Steven Koblik, *The Stones Cry Out: Sweden's Response to the Persecution of the Jews 1933–1945* (New York: Holocaust Library, 1988), pp. 103–4.

56. Ibid., pp. 26–39; Dankwart Rustow, *The Politics of Compromise* (Princeton: Princeton University Press, 1955); and Joseph Board, *The Government and Politics of Sweden* (Boston: Houghton-Mifflin, 1970).

57. Koblik, *Stones Cry Out*, pp. 60–3.

58. Ralph Hewins, *Count Folke Bernadotte* (Minneapolis: Denison, 1950); and *Bernadotte, Instead of Arms* (Stockholm: Bonniers, 1948).

59. Koblik, *Stones Cry Out*, p. 78.

60. Ibid., pp. 50–4.

61. Ulf Lindstrom, *Fascism in Scandinavia, 1920–1940* (Stockholm: Almqvist & Wikssell, 1985), pp. 56–9.

62. Ibid., pp. 6–14.

63. Ibid., p. 59.

64. Helmut Mussener, *Die deutschsprachige Emigration in Schweden nach 1933* (Stockholm: Holmqvists Reprotryck, 1971).

65. Fodor, *Neutrals*, pp. 138–9.

66. Koblik, *Stones Cry Out*, pp. 88–9.

67. Soderblom later accepted the Soviet contention that Wallenberg died in Lubianka Prison in 1947.

68. Koblik, *Stones Cry Out*, p. 154.

69. Per Anger, *With Raoul Wallenberg in Budapest* (New York: Holocaust Library, 1981); Elenore Lester, *Wallenberg, The Man in the Iron Web* (Englewood Cliffs: Prentice Hall, 1982); Sharon Linnea, *Raoul Wallenberg: The Man Who Stopped Death* (Philadelphia: Jewish Publication Society, 1993); Kati Marton, *Wallenberg* (New York: Random House, 1982).

70. Lester, *Wallenberg*, p. 106.

71. Ibid., pp. 125–7.

Chapter 26. Righteous Gentiles: Denmark and Norway

1. Leni Yahil, *The Rescue of Danish Jewry* (Philadelphia: JPS, 1969), pp. 32–3.

2. Harold Flender, *Rescue in Denmark* (New York: Holocaust Library, 1963), pp. 20–6.

3. Leo Goldberger (ed.), *The Rescue of the Danish Jews: Moral Courage under Stress* (New York: NYU Press, 1987), pp. 144–51.

4. Flender, *Rescue in Denmark*, p. 43.

5. Goldberger, 'Explaining the Rescue of the Danish Jews', *Rescue of Danish Jews*, pp. 204–5.

6. Report of Julius Margolinsky, Statistke Underogelser over Alders og Konsfordeling blandt Flygtninge fra Danmark i Sverige (Stockholm, 1945), in Goldberger, *Rescue of Danish Jews*, p. xxi.

7. Rabbi Melchior, 'The Danish Jews in the 20th Century', in Goldberger, *Rescue of Danish Jews*, pp. 58, 62.
8. Flender, *Rescue in Denmark*, p. 30.
9. Jorgen Haestrup, 'The Danish Jews and the German Occupation', in Goldberger, *Rescue of Danish Jews*, pp. 30–2.
10. Jaroslav Pelikan, 'Gruntvig's Influence', in Goldberger, *Rescue of Danish Jews*, pp. 173–83.
11. Yahil, *Rescue of Danish Jewry*, p. 42.
12. Haestrup, 'Danish Jews', pp. 30–2.
13. Yahil, *Rescue of Danish Jewry*, p. 60.
14. Ibid, pp. 71–2.
15. Haestrup, 'Danish Jews', p. 37.
16. Yahil, *Rescue of Danish Jewry*, p. 43; and Haestrup, 'Danish Jews', in Goldberger, *Rescue of Danish Jews*, p. 28.
17. Flender, *Rescue in Denmark*, pp. 32–3.
18. Philip Friedman, *Their Brothers' Keepers* (New York: Crown, 1957), p. 151.
19. Haestrup, 'Danish Jews', pp. 43–4.
20. Flender, *Rescue in Denmark*, pp. 46–9.
21. Goldberger, *Rescue of Danish Jews*, p. 82.
22. Aage Bertelsen, *October '43*, tr. Milly Lindholn (New York: Putnam's, 1954), pp. 18–19.
23. Marcus Melchior, *A Rabbi Remembers* (New York: Lyle Stuart, 1968), and Flender, *Rescue in Denmark*, p. 15.
24. Flender, *Rescue in Denmark*, pp. 54–5.
25. Ibid., pp. 116–24.
26. Dr Steffen Lund, 'Den hvide Brigade: Danske Leagers Modstand' (The White Brigade: The Resistance of Danish Physicians), in Goldberger, *Rescue of Danish Jews*, p. 90.
27. Haestrup, 'Danish Jews and German Occupation', p. 6.
28. Flender, *Rescue in Denmark*, p. 69.
29. Ibid., pp. 145–67.
30. Ibid., pp. 183–5.
31. Ibid., p. 199.
32. Goldberger, *Rescue of Danish Jews*, pp. 87–92.
33. Ibid., pp. 98–101, 168–76, 199–206.
34. Ibid., pp. 103–4.
35. Ibid., p. 156.
36. Ibid., p. 60.
37. Christian Tortzen, *Gilleleje Oktober 1943* (Copenhagen: Fremad, 1970).
38. Goldberger, *Rescue of Danish Jews*, p. 93.
39. Memoir of Valdemar Koppel, in Goldberger, *Rescue of Danish Jews*, pp. 107–8; and Flender, *Rescue in Denmark*, pp. 204–20.
40. Haestrup, 'Danish Jews', p. 52.
41. Flender, *Rescue in Denmark*, pp. 249–54.
42. Goldberger, *Rescue of Danish Jews*, p. 206.
43. Flender, *Rescue in Denmark*, p. 144. See also Jergen Barfod, *Escape from Nazi Terror: A Short History of the Persecution of Jews in Denmark and Norway and the Danish Underground Refugee Service* (Copenhagen: Forlaget for Faglitteratur, 1968); and Richard Pettrow, *The Bitter Years: The Invasion and Occupation of Denmark and Norway* (New York: Morrow, 1974).
44. Philip Paneth, *Haakon VII: Norway's Fighting King* (London: Alliance Press, 1944); Olav Riste and Berit Nokleby, *Norway 1940–45: The Resistance Movement* (Oslo: Tanum, 1970); Leif Hovelsen, *Out of the Evil Night*, tr. John Morrison (London: Blandford Press, 1959); and Maynard Cohen, *A Stand against Tyranny: Norway's Physicians and the Nazis* (Detroit: Wayne State University Press, 1997).

45. Tore Gjelsvik, *Norwegian Resistance 1940–45*, tr. Thomas Derry (London: C. Hurst, 1979), pp. 15–33.
46. Oskar Mendelson, *The Persecution of the Norwegian Jews in World War II* (Oslo: Norges Hjemmefrontmuseum, 1991), p. 8; and Gjelsvik, *Norwegian Resistance*, pp. 63–4. See also Bjarne Hooye and Trygve Ager, *The Fight of the Norwegian Church against Nazism* (New York: MacMillan, 1943).
47. Tor Mykelbost, *They Came as Friends* (Garden City, NY: Doubleday, Doran, 1943), pp. 271ff.
48. Samuel Abrahamsen, *Norway's Response to the Holocaust* (New York: Holocaust Library, 1991), pp. 141–3; and Mendelson, *Persecution of Norwegian Jews*, p. 18.
49. Gjelsvik, *Norwegian Resistance*, p. 70.
50. Ibid., pp. 35–6.
51. Ralph Hewins, *Quisling: Prophet without Honour* (New York: John Day, 1965); Oddvar Hoidal, *Quisling, a Study in Treason* (Oslo: Norwegian University Press, 1989); and Richard Landwehr (ed.), *Frontfighters: The Norwegian Volunteer Legion of the Waffen SS* (Madison: Hunt, 1986).
52. Abrahamsen, *Norway's Response*, p. 109.
53. Mendelson, *Persecution of Norwegian Jews*, pp. 10–11.
54. Abrahamsen, *Norway's Response*, p. 78.
55. Mendelsohn, *Persecution of Norwegian Jews*, p. 16.
56. Abrahamsen, *Norway's Response*, pp. 117–18.
57. Mendelsohn, *Persecution of Norwegian Jews*, pp. 20–2.
58. Abrahamsen, *Norway's Response*, p. 148; Axell Strom, *Norwegian Concentration Camp Survivors* (New York: Humanities Press, 1968); and Herman Sachnowitz, *Ein Norwegisciher Jude uberlebte* (Frankfurt: Buchergilde Gutenberg, 1980).

Chapter 27. The Middle East

1. Halil Inalcik, 'The Emergence of the Ottomans', *Cambridge History of Islam* (Cambridge: Cambridge University Press, 1970); Lord Eversley and Sir Valentine Chirol, *The Turkish Empire from 1288 to 1914* (New York: Howard Fertig, 1969); and Lord Kinross, *The Ottoman Centuries: The Rise and Fall of the Turkish Empire* (New York: Morrow, Quill, 1977).
2. W.E.D. Allen and Paul Muratoff, *Caucasian Battlefields* (Cambridge: Cambridge University Press, 1953).
3. George Filian, *Armenia and Her People* (Hartford: American Pub. Co., 1896); James Nazer, *The Armenian Massacre: Excerpt from the First Genocide of the Twentieth Century* (New York: T and T Publ., 1970); Gerard Chaliand, *The Armenians, From Genocide to Resistance* (London: Zed Press, 1983); Stanley Kerr, *The Lions of Marash: Personal Experiences with American Near East Relief 1919–1922* (Albany: SUNY Press, 1973).
4. *Living Age* (5 February 1916) CCLXXXIII, pp. 370–3.
5. Franz Werfel, *The Forty Days of Musa Dagh* (New York: Carroll & Graf, 1933).
6. Donald and Lorna Miller, *Survivors: An Oral History of the Armenian Genocide* (Berkeley: University of California Press, 1993), pp. 80–8.
7. Howard Sachar, *Emergence of the Middle East: 1914–1924* (New York: Knopf, 1969), p. 105; Akaby Nassibian, *Britain and the Armenian Question 1915–1923* (New York: St Martin's Press, 1984); and Richard Hovannisian, *Armenia on the Road to Independence* (Berkeley: University of California Press, 1967).
8. Rubina Peroomian, *Literary Responses to Catastrophe* (Georgia: Scholars Press, 1993); Robert Melson, *Revolution and Genocide: On the Origins of the Armenian Genocide and the Holocaust* (Chicago: University of Chicago Press, 1992); and Florence Mazian, *Why Genocide? The Armenian and Jewish Experiences in Perspective* (Books on Demand, 1990).

9. H.C. Armstrong, *Gray Wolf: The Life of Kemal Ataturk* (New York: Capricorn, 1933); and Lord Kinross, *Ataturk: The Rebirth of a Nation* (London: Weidenfeld & Nicolson, 1964).

10. Frank Weber, *The Evasive Neutral: Germany, Britain and the Quest for a Turkish Alliance in the Second World War* (Columbia: University of Missouri Press, 1979), p. 9.

11. Ibid., p. 32.

12. Denis Fodor, *The Neutrals* (Alexandria, VA: Time-Life Books, 1982), p. 172.

13. Weber, *The Evasive Neutral*, pp. 22–3.

14. Stanford Shaw, *Turkey and the Holocaust* (New York: NYU Press, 1992), pp. 4–8, 46, 257–77, 288–303.

15. Ibid., pp. 38–50, 278–88.

16. Stephen Longrigg, *Syria and Lebanon under French Mandate* (London: Oxford University Press, 1958); and Albert Hourani, *Syria and Lebanon* (London: Oxford University Press, 1946).

17. Stephen Longrigg, *Iraq 1900–1950* (Oxford: Oxford University Press, 1953); Reeva Simon, *Iraq between the Two World Wars* (New York: Columbia University Press, 1983); A.S. Stafford, *The Tragedy of the Assyrians* (London: Allen & Unwin, 1966).

18. Janice Terry, *The Wafd, 1919–1952: Cornerstone of Egyptian Political Power* (London: Third World Center, 1982); and Marius Deb, *Party Politics in Egypt: The Wafd and its Rivals, 1919–1939* (London: Ithaca Press, 1979).

19. D.F. Green (ed.), *Arab Theologians on Jews and Israel*, 4th Conference of Academy of Islamic Research, al-Azhar, Cairo (Geneva: Editions de l'Avenir, 1971).

20. Andre Chouraqui, *Between East and West: A History of Jews of North Africa* (Philadelphia: JPSA, 1968); Joan Peters, *From Time Immemorial: the Origins of the Arab–Jewish Conflict over Palestine* (New York: Harper & Row, 1984); Joseph Schechtman, *On Wings of Eagles: The Plight, Exodus and Homecoming of Oriental Jewry* (New York: T. Yoseloff, 1961); Bat Ye'or, *Dhimmi Peoples: Oppressed Nations* (Geneva: Editions de l'Avenir, 1978).

21. Joseph Schechtman, *The Mufti and the Führer* (New York: T. Yoseloff, 1966).

22. Naomi Cohen, *The Year after the Riots* (Detroit: Wayne State University Press, 1988); and William Ziff, *The Rape of Palestine* (New York: Longmans, Green, 1938).

23. Fred Gottheil, 'Arab Immigration into Prestate Israel: 1922–1931', pp. 13–22; Moshe Aumann, 'Land Ownership in Palestine 1880–1948', pp. 5–12; and Frederick Kisch, 'Arab–Jewish Contacts in Palestine, 1923–1931', pp. 23–6, *Middle East Information Series*, APPME, East, XXV (Fall 1973).

24. Howard Sachar, *Europe Leaves the Middle East 1936–1954* (New York: Knopf, 1972), pp. 37–9, 66–71.

25. *Palestine, Royal Commission Report*, Cmd. 5479 (London: HMSO, 1937).

26. Kenneth Stein, *The Land Question in Palestine 1917–1939* (Chapel Hill: North Carolina Press, 1984).

27. *Palestine: Statement of Policy* (White Paper), Cmd. 6019 (London: HMSO, 1939).

28. Pierre Van Paassen, *Forgotten Ally* (New York: Dial, 1943), pp. 282–5.

29. Oscar Janowsky, *Foundations of Israel* (Princeton: D. Van Nostrand, 1959), p. 142.

30. *Palestine Lives: Address by Arafat, 13 November 1974* (Washington: Free Palestine, 1974), pp. 19–20.

31. Van Paassen, *Forgotten Ally*, pp. 175–236.

32. Howard Sachar, *The Course of Modern Jewish History* (Cleveland: World, 1958), p. 461.

33. Van Paassen, *Forgotten Ally*, p. 180.

34. Jean Lugol, *Egypt and World War II*, tr. A.G. Mitchell (Cairo: Société Orientale de publicité, 1945).

35. Van Paassen, *Forgotten Ally*, p. 253.

36. Schechtman, *Mufti and Führer*, pp. 95–115; Sachar, *Europe Leaves the Middle East*,

pp. 163–73; and Fritz Grobba, *Iraq* (Berlin: Junker & Dunnhaput, 1984).

37. Elias Cooper, 'Forgotten Palestinian: The Nazi Mufti, Roots of the Bitterness in the Arab–Israeli Conflict', *American Zionist*, 68 (March–April 1978), p. 15.

38. Lukasz Hirszowicz, *The Third Reich and the Arab East* (Toronto: University of Toronto Press, 1966), p. 109.

39. Reeva Simon, *Iraq between the Two World Wars*, pp. 138–41, 158–9.

40. *The Arab Higher Committee: Its Origins, Personnel and Purposes* (New York: United Nations and Nations Associates, May 1947), pp. 30–2; and Hirszowicz, *Third Reich and Arab East*, pp. 218, 262.

41. Friedman, 'Arab Complicity in the Holocaust', *Jewish Frontier*, 42 (April 1975), pp. 9–18. See also Francis Nicosia, *The Third Reich and the Palestine Question* (London: Tauris, 1985).

42. Cooper, 'Forgotten Palestinian', p. 15.

43. Schechtman, *Mufti and Führer*, p. 133.

44. Hirszowicz, *Third Reich and Arab East*, pp. 250–311; John Roy Carlson, *Cairo to Damascus* (New York: Knopf, 1951).

45. 'The Mufti Speaks', *Life*, 33 (27 October 1952), p. 151.

46. *The Arab Higher Committee*, pp. 58, 68, 69; and Schechtman, *Mufti and Führer*, p. 148.

47. Schechtman, *Mufti and Führer*, pp. 152, 157, 163.

48. Hirszowicz, *Third Reich and Arab East*, p. 312; and *Arab Higher Committee*, pp. 58–64.

49. Maurice Pearlman, *Mufti of Jerusalem: The Story of Haj Amin el-Husseini* (London: Gollancz, 1947), p. 73.

50. Cooper, 'Forgotten Palestinian', p. 21.

51. Ibid., p. 28.

52. Michael Bar Zohar, *The Avengers*, tr. Len Ortzen (New York: Hawthorn, 1969), p. 144.

53. Simon Wiesenthal, *Grossmufti – Grossagent der Achse* (Salzburg, 1947), pp. 51, 53, 54.

54. Friedman, *No Haven for Oppressed*, p. 38.

55. Van Paassen, *Forgotten Ally*, p. 258.

56. Sarah Honig, 'Forgotten Shame: The Last Voyage of the Struma', *Jerusalem Post*, 1 February 1992, pp. 12–13.

57. Gunther, *Inside Asia* (New York: Harper, 1939); and Friedman, 'Arab Complicity in the Holocaust', p. 17.

Chapter 28. Great Britain and the United States

1. Cable from Samuel Silverman to Stephen Wise, 29 August 1942, World Jewish Congress.

2. 'Chronicles', *Contemporary Jewish Record*, 5 (August 1942), p. 426; Goldstein to Hull, 17 July 1942, State Department Records; and *Bulletin on Refugees Abroad and at Home*, 12 (16 October 1942), p. 1.

3. Elting to Hull, 10 August 1942, Harrison to Hull, 11 August 1942, Durbrow to Culbertson, 13 August 1942, Welles to Harrison, 17 August 1942, and memo of Durbrow, 11 August 1942, State Department Records.

4. Stephen Wise, *Challenging Years: The Autobiography of Stephen Wise* (New York: Putnam's, 1949), p. 275.

5. Halifax to Hull, 20 January 1943, *Foreign Relations of the United States, Diplomatic Papers*, I, pp. 134–7.

6. Friedman, *No Haven for the Oppressed*, p. 169.

7. *Program for the Rescue of Jews from Nazi Europe*, memo of the Joint Emergency Committee for European Jewish Affairs, 19 April 1943, YIVO, 3/48486.

8. Interview with Dodds, 2 June 1968.

9. Herbert Emerson, 'Postwar Problems of Refugees', *Foreign Affairs*, XXI (January

1943), p. 216, and Taylor to Hull, 26 August 1943, State Department Records.

10. *New York Times*, 19 April 1943, p. 18.
11. *Washington Post*, 20 April 1943, p. 20.
12. Translations of editorials, 12 and 14 April, in State Department Records, 548.G1/180.
13. *New York World-Telegram*, 28 April 1943, p. 2.
14. *New York Herald-Tribune*, 28 April 1943, p. 8.
15. US Department of State Bulletin, VIII (May 1943), p. 388.
16. Albert Nirenstein, *A Tower from the Enemy* (New York: Orion, 1959), pp. 217–19.
17. B. Wasserstein, *Britain and the Jews of Europe 1939–1945* (Oxford: Clarendon, 1979), p. 33.
18. Friedman, 'The Power and/or Powerlessness of American Jews, 1939–1945', in Arthur Goldberg and Seymour Finger (eds), *American Jewry during the Holocaust* (American Jewish Commission on the Holocaust, 1984), p. 12.
19. Wasserstein, *Britain and the Jews*, p. 34.
20. Friedman, 'Power/Powerlessness of American Jews', p. 22.
21. Wasserstein, *Britain and the Jews*, p. 351.
22. Ibid., p. 278.
23. Ibid., p. 117.
24. Ibid., p. 50.
25. Ibid., p. 248.
26. 'Chronicles', *Contemporary Jewish Record*, 5 (August 1943), p. 394; and *New York Times*, 26 July 1943, p. 19.
27. Long to Hull, May 1943, Refugee Movement and Nationality Groups File, Long Papers.
28. Ibid., p. 44.
29. Louis Rapoport, *Shake Heaven and Earth: Peter Bergson and the Struggle to Rescue the Jews of Europe* (New York: Gefen, 1999).
30. Arthur Morse, *While Six Million Died* (New York: Random House, 1967), p. 34.
31. Ibid., p. 32.
32. Wasserstein, *Britain and the Jews*, p. 108.
33. Ibid., pp. 173, 183.
34. Friedman, *No Haven for Oppressed*, p. 172.
35. Hull to Roosevelt, 7 May 1943, State Department Records.
36. Roosevelt to Hull, 14 May 1943, State Department Records.
37. *Memoirs of Cordell Hull* (New York: Macmillan, 1948), II, p. 1539.
38. Morse, *While Six Million Died*, pp. 378–81.
39. Friedman, *No Haven for Oppressed*, p. 192.
40. Ibid., p. 194.
41. *Washington Post*, 20 May 1943, p. 1.
42. Friedman, 'Power/Powerlessness of American Jews', p. 34.
43. Gerold Frank, *The Deed* (New York: Simon &d Schuster, 1963), pp. 190–1.
44. Friedman, 'Power/Powerlessness of American Jews', pp. 21–2.
45. Robert Sherwood, *Roosevelt and Hopkins* (New York: Harper, 1948), pp. 871–3.
46. Friedman, *No Haven for Oppressed*, pp. 155–60.
47. US Department of State Bulletin, VIII (May 1943), p. 388.
48. Stettinius to Hull, 8 January 1944, Breckinridge Long Records, Refugee File, Library of Congress.
49. Dino Bugioni, 'Why World War Photography Interpreters Failed to Identify Auschwitz-Birkenau', *Martyrdom and Resistance*, 10 (September–October 1983), pp. 5, 12; Herbert Druks, 'The Allies and Jewish Leadership on the Question of Bombing Auschwitz', *Tradition*, 19 (Spring 1981), pp. 28–34; L. Tursky, 'Could the Death Camps Have Been Bombed?', *Jewish Frontier*, 31 (September 1964), pp. 19–24.
50. Friedman, *No Haven for Oppressed*, p. 228.
51. Martin Gilbert, *Auschwitz and the Allies* (New York: Holt, Rinehart & Winston, 1981), p. 341.

52. James Kitchens, 'The Bombing of Auschwitz Reexamined', *Journal of Military History*, 58 (April 1994), pp. 233–66.
53. Ibid., pp. 262–3.
54. Ibid., pp. 252–4.
55. Ibid., pp. 258–60.
56. Ibid., pp. 264–5.
57. Interview with Bill Vegh, 10 July 1974, in *Amcha*, pp. 362–3.
58. Interview with Sam Hollander, 27 June and 3 July 1974, in *Amcha*, p. 408.
59. Interview with Alex Gross, 10 August 1974, in *Amcha*, pp. 309–10.
60. Elie Wiesel, 'The Struggle to Reconcile the Reality of Evil with Faith in God', *Chronicle of Higher Education* (13 April 1983), p. 22.
61. Wasserstein, *Britain and the Jews*, p. 165.
62. Minutes of meeting of W.G. Hayter and Henry Montor, 8 December 1941, United Palestine Appeal Folder, 11–23, Manson Files, Silver papers.
63. Welles, *The World of the Four Freedoms* (New York: Columbia, 1943).
64. *Documents on American Foreign Relations*, V, July 1942–June 1943, ed. Leland Goodrich and Marie Carroll (Boston: World Peace Foundation, 1944), pp. 178–9.
65. Bohlen to Early, 24 March 1944, and Berle to Hasset, 4 August 1944, Church Matters, Jewish File, Roosevelt Library, Hyde Park, New York.
66. FDR Memorandum, undated, Refugee Folder, Roosevelt Library.
67. Abba Silver, *Vision and Victory: A Collection of Addresses by Dr. Abba Hillel Silver, 1942–48* (New York: ZOA, 1949), p. 65.
68. Allan Nevins, *Herbert H. Lehman and His Era* (New York: Scribner's, 1963).
69. Friedman, *No Haven for the Oppressed*, pp. 214–16.
70. Ibid., pp. 217–20.
71. *Final Summary Report of the U.S. War Refugee Board* (Washington, 1945).
72. Arieh Tartakower and Kurt Grossmann, *The Jewish Refugee* (New York, 1944), pp. 196–7.
73. A.J. Sherman, *Island Refuge: Britain and Refugees from the Third Reich 1933–1939* (London: Elek, 1973), pp. 264–5.

Chapter 29. The Last Chapter: Hungary

1. 'Hungary', *Encyclopedia Judaica*, VIII, pp. 1088–110.
2. Simon Dubnov, *History of the Jews*, tr. Moshe Spiegel (South Brunswick: T. Yoseloff, 1968), V, pp. 295–8.
3. Ibid., pp. 299–301.
4. Oskar Jaszi, *The Dissolution of the Hapsburg Monarchy* (Chicago: Chicago University Press, 1929), pp. 273ff.
5. Ismar Elbogen, *A Century of Jewish Life* (Philadelphia: JPSA, 1944), pp. 179–81.
6. *Memoir of Michael Karolyi: Faith without Illusion* (London: Jonathan Cape, 1956).
7. Rudolf Tokes, *Bela Kun and the Hungarian Soviet Republic* (New York: Praeger, 1967).
8. Miklós Horthy, *Memoirs* (New York: Robt, Speller & Sons, 1957), pp. 99–115.
9. Moshe Herczl, *Christianity and Holocaust of Hungarian Jewry*, tr. Joel Lerner (New York: NYU Press, 1993), pp. 21–9.
10. Randolph Braham, *The Politics of Genocide: The Holocaust in Hungary* (New York: Columbia University Press, 1981), pp. 20–3, 56–69.
11. Nathaniel Katzburg, *Hungary and the Jews, Policy and Legislation, 1920–1943* (Ramat Gan: Bar Ilan University Press, 1981). See also Randoph Braham and Bela Vago, *The Holocaust in Hungary Forty Years Later* (New York: Columbia University Press, 1985), pp. 3–73.
12. Braham, *Politics of Genocide*, pp. 22–3, 44–57.
13. Mendelsohn, *Jews of East Central Europe*, pp. 114–15.
14. C.A. MaCartney, 'Hungarian Foreign Policy during the Inter-War Period with

Special Reference to the Jewish Question', in Bela Vago and George Mosse (eds), *Jews and Non-Jews in Eastern Europe 1918–1945* (Jerusalem: Keter, 1974), pp. 132–4.

15. Asher Cohen, 'The Last Tragedy of the Shoah: The Jews of Hungary', in Friedman, *Holocaust Literature*, pp. 218–22. See also Braham, *Politics of Genocide*, pp. 84–96.
16. Braham, *Politics of Genocide*, pp. 118–35.
17. Ibid., pp. 142–3.
18. Ibid., pp. 147–56.
19. Jeno Levai, *Black Book on the Martyrdom of Hungarian Jewry*, ed. Lawrence Davis (Zurich: Central European Times Pub., 1948), p. 23.
20. Braham, *Politics of Genocide*, pp. 201–15, and Safrian, *Die Eichmann-Männer*, p. 294.
21. Braham, *Politics of Genocide*, pp. 285–361.
22. Friedman, *Amcha*, p. 273.
23. Randolph Braham, *The Hungarian Labor Service System, 1939–1945* (New York: Columbia, 1977).
24. Herczl, *Christianity and Holocaust of Hungarian Jewry*, p. 165.
25. Ibid., pp. 145–52.
26. Miklós Kallay, *Hungarian Premier: A Personal Account of a Nation's Struggle in the Second World War* (London, 1954), p. 73.
27. Ibid., p. 99.
28. Levin, *Holocaust*, pp. 607–8.
29. Hilberg, *Destruction of European Jews*, pp. 525–6.
30. Randolph Braham, 'The Rightists, Horthy and the Germans', in Vago and Mosse, *Jews and Non-Jews in Eastern Europe*, pp. 137–43. See also Braham, *Politics of Genocide*, pp. 374–82.
31. Levai, *Black Book*, p. 119.
32. Braham, *Politics of Genocide*, pp. 480–511.
33. Safrian, *Die Eichmann-Männer*, p. 296.
34. Levai, *Black Book*, p. 81.
35. Braham, *Politics of Genocide*, pp. 419–24, 720–4.
36. Ibid., pp. 529–35, 604–76, and Safrian, *Die Eichmann-Männer*, pp. 297–8.
37. Levai, *Black Book*, p. 136, and Braham, *Politics of Genocide*, pp. 402–12.
38. Braham, *Politics of Genocide*, pp. 608–12.
39. Levai, *Black Book*, p. 217.
40. Interview with Frida Weiss, 19 August 1975, in *Amcha*, p. 256.
41. Interview with Manci Feig, 23 July 1978, in *Amcha*, p. 375.
42. Interview with Jim Elder, 11 September 1974, in *Amcha*, pp. 287–8.
43. Levai, *Black Book*, p. 151.
44. Herczl, *Christianity and Holocaust of Hungarian Jewry*, p. 224.
45. Braham, *Politics of Genocide*, pp. 752–6.
46. Andre Bliss, *A Million Jews to Save: Check to the Final Solution: Joel Brand's Story* (London: Hutchinson, 1973), pp. 35–42.
47. Alex Weissberg, *Desperate Mission* (Cologne, 1956), pp. 91–2.
48. Interrogation transcript of Kurt Becher, 7 July 1947, Pretrial Interrogation series collected for US Military Tribunals at Nuremberg, Interrogation Nr. 929. John Mendelssohn, *The Holocaust: Relief in Hungary and the Failure of the Joel Brand Mission* (New York: Garland, 1982), Vol. XV, p. 67.
49. Mendelsohn, *Holocaust Documents*, XV, p. 133.
50. Ibid., pp. 92–5.
51. Braham, *Politics of Genocide*, pp. 622–9, 649–53.
52. Becher interrogation, 7 July 1947, in Mendelssohn, *Documents*, XV, p. 69.
53. Ibid., p. 72.
54. Braham, *Politics of Genocide*, pp. 732–41.
55. See Asher Cohen, *The Halutz Resistance in Hungary 1942–1944* (New York: Columbia University Press, 1986); and Gilles Lambert, *Operation Hazalah*, tr. Robert Bullen and Rosette Letellier (Indianapolis: Bobbs-Merrill, 1974).

56. Levin, *Holocaust*, p. 652.

57. Herczl, *Christianity and Holocaust of Hungarian Jewry*, pp. 73–4.

58. Safrian, *Die Eichmann-Männer*, pp. 306–7; and Arieh Ben-Tov, *Facing the Holocaust in Budapest: The International Committee of the Red Cross and the Jews in Hungary 1943–1945* (Boston: M. Nijhoff, 1988).

59. Braham, *Politics of Genocide*, p. 842; and Theo Tschuy, *Carl Lutz und die Juden von Budapest* (Zurich: Verlag Neue Zurcher Zeitung, 1995); and Levai, *Black Book*, pp. 372–3.

60. Braham, *Politics of Genocide*, pp. 856–67.

61. Levai, *Black Book*, pp. 402–6.

62. *Hannah Senesh: Her Life and Diary* (New York: Schocken, 1972), p. 25.

63. Reuven Dafne, 'The Last Border', *Senesh Diary*, p. 173.

64. Ibid., p. 175.

65. Yoel Palgi, 'How She Fell', *Senesh Diary*, pp. 199–200.

Chapter 30. Extermination: Auschwitz

1. *Auschwitz: Geschichte, Rezeption und Wirkung* (Frankfurt: Fritz Bauer Institut and New York: Campus, 1996); Hermann Langbein, *Menschen in Auschwitz* (Vienna: Eurpoaverl, 1972); *Oswiecim: hitlereowski oboz masowej zaglady* (Warsaw: Wydawn, Interpress, 1981); Danuta Czech, *Kalendarium wydarazen w Obozie Koncentracy jnym Auschwitz-Birkenau 1939–1945* (Auschwitz: Wydawan, Panstwowego Muzeum w Oswiecim-Birkenau, 1992); Charlotte Delbo, *Auschwitz et apres* (Paris: Editions de Minuit, 1970); and Wieslaw Kielara, *Anus mundi: Five Years in Auschwitz*, tr. Susanne Flatauer (London: Allen Lane, 1981).

2. Interview with Bill Vegh, Youngstown, 10 July 1974, in *Amcha*, p. 351.

3. Ibid., p. 352.

4. Eva Jacobs, 'More Luck than Brains', unpublished ms., 1957.

5. Interviews with Esther Shudmak, 10 November and 17 November 1973, in *Amcha*, p. 329.

6. Interview with Lola Hollander, 27 June and 3 July 1974, in *Amcha*, p. 415.

7. Interviews with Eva Jacobs, 10 February 1972, 14 August 1972, 10 March 1973, in *Amcha*.

8. Alwin Meyer, *Die Kinder von Auschwitz* (Gottingen: Lamuv, 1990); and Wolf Wagner, *Wo die Schmetterllinge Starben: Kinder in Auschwitz* (Berlin: Dietz, 1995).

9. Germaine Tillion, *Ravensbruck: An Eyewitness Account of a Women's Concentration Camp*, tr. Gerald Satterwaite (New York: Anchor Press, 1975), p. 77.

10. Interview with Jim Elder, 11 September 1974, in *Amcha*, p. 290.

11. See Alfred Kantor, *The Book of Alfred Kantor* (New York: McGraw-Hill, 1971), pp. 34–5.

12. Ibid., p. 291.

13. Ibid., p. 325.

14. Jan Sehn, *Oswiecim-Birkenau Concentration Camp*, tr. Klemens Keplicz (Warsaw: Wydawan, Prawnicze, 1961), pp. 45–6.

15. Karola Cetynski, *House of Dolls*, tr. Moshe Kohn (New York: Simon & Schuster, 1944); Germaine Tillion, *Ravensbruck*, pp. 62–70, 73; Dr Antoni Makowski, 'Organization, Growth and Activity of the Prisoners' Hospital at Monowitz', in Jan Mikulski (ed.), *From the History of KL Auschwitz* (Panstwowego Muzeum w Oswiecim, 1976), pp. 178–80.

16. Sehn, *Oswiecim-Birkenau*, pp. 121–3.

17. Czech, *Auschwitz Chronicle*, p. 249.

18. 'A5714: Robert Clary: A Memoir of Liberation'.

19. Memoir of Paul Cooley, Youngstown, November 1980–September 1981, p. 48.

20. Eugene Heimler, *Night of the Mist* (Bodley Head, 1959), in Albert Friedlander (ed.), *Out of the Whirlwind: A Reader of Holocaust Literature* (New York: UAHC, 1968), p. 193.

21. Leon Wells, *Janowska Road*, in *Out of the Whirlwind*, p. 243.
22. Langbein, *Menschen in Auschwitz*, pp. 113–16.
23. Gotz Aly, Peter Chroust and Christian Pross, *Cleansing the Fatherland*, tr. Belinda Cooper (Baltimore: Johns Hopkins University Press, 1994); Hugh Gallagher, *By Trust Betrayed: Patients, Physicians, and the License to Kill in the Third Reich* (New York: Holt, 1990).
24. Philippe Aziz, *Doctors of Death*, tr. Edouard Bizub and Philip Haentzler (Geneva: Ferni Publishers, 1976); Gerald Posner and John Ware, *Mengele: The Complete Story* (New York: McGraw-Hill, 1986).
25. Lucette Matalon Lagnado, *Children of the Flames: Dr. Josef Mengele and the Untold Story of the Twins of Auschwitz* (New York: Morrow, 1991); *C.A.N.D.L.E.S.: The Story of the Mengele Twins* (PBS, 1990); Miklos Nyiszli, *Auschwitz: A Doctor's Eyewitness Account*, tr. Tibere Kremer and Richard Seaver (New York: Fawcett, 1960), pp. 50–6, 61–3, 69, 85, 100–3, 130, 215–28; Christian Bernadac, *Les Médecins Maudits: Les experiences medicales humaines dans les camps de concentration* (Paris: Editions France Empire, 1967), pp. 101–20.
26. Czech, *Auschwitz Chronicle*, pp. 400–19.
27. *Trials of War Criminals before the Nuremberg Military Tribunals, October 1946–April 1949*, II (US GPO), pp. 1–352; Alexander Mitscherlich and Fred Mielke, *Doctors of Infamy: The Story of the Nazi Medical Crimes*, tr. Heinz Norden (New York: Henry Schuman, 1949); Bernadac, *Les Médecins Maudits*; Jan Mikulski, 'Pharmacological Experiments in the Concentration Camp at Auschwitz-Birkenau', in *From the History of KL Auschwitz*, II, pp. 197–227.
28. Dr Gisela Perl, *I Was a Doctor in Auschwitz* (New York: International University Press, 1948), pp. 73–5; *Trial of the Major War Criminals before the International Military Tribunal, Nuremberg 14 November 1945–1 October 1946* (New York: AMS Press, 1971), XX, p. 543; Whitney Harris, *Tyranny on Trial: The Evidence at Nuremberg* (Dallas: SMU Press, 1954), pp. 431–2; *From the History of KL Auschwitz*, pp. 48, 69, 79, 161; and Nyiszli, *Auschwitz*, pp. 46–7, 57.
29. Interview with Frida Weiss, 19 August 1975, in *Amcha*, pp. 257–8.
30. *Nova*, 7 February 1995.
31. Rudolf Hoess, *Commandant of Auschwitz*, tr. Constantin FitzGibbon (London: Pan Books, 1959).
32. Nyiszli, *Auschwitz*, p. 88.
33. Jean-Claude Pressac, *Les crématoires d'Auschwitz: la machinerie du meurtre de masse* (Paris: CNRS Editions, 1993).
34. Bauer, 'Auschwitz: The Dangers of Distortion', *Jerusalem Post International Edition*, 30 September 1989, p. 7.
35. Czech, *Auschwitz Chronicle*, pp. 430, 442, 450, 456, 493, 590, 597, 656, 666, 677.
36. Langbein, *Menschen in Auschwitz*, p. 143.
37. Czech, *Auschwitz Chronicle*, p. 591.
38. Ibid., p. 720.
39. Ibid., p. 513.
40. *New York Times*, 11 October 1982, pp. 1, 8.
41. Czech, *Auschwitz Chronicle*, pp. 725–8.
42. Clary video.
43. Friedman, *Amcha*, p. 365.
44. Goldhagen, *Hitler's Willing Executioners*, p. 356.
45. *Dora-Nordhausen Labor Concentration Camps*, information for Nordhausen War Crimes Case (US Prosecution Staff, Dachau, Germany, August 1947), pp. 28–39.
46. Ibid., p. 31.
47. Testimony of James Barnett, Kent State Holocaust Conference, April 1982.
48. Wiesenthal lecture, Youngstown State, 7 November 1979.
49. Czech, *Auschwitz Chronicle*, p. 398.
50. Charles Liblau, *Les kapos d'Auschwitz* (Paris: La Pensée universelle, 1974).

51. Friedman, *Amcha*, pp. 332–3.
52. Ibid., p. 263.
53. George Annas and Michael Grodin, *The Nazi Doctors and the Nuremberg Code* (New York: Oxford University Press, 1992); Arthur Caplan (ed.), *When Medicine Went Mad: Bioethics and the Holocaust* (Totowa, NJ: Humana Press, 1992); Paul Hoedeman, *Hitler or Hippocrates: Medical Experiments and Euthanasia in the Third Reich*, tr. Ralph de Rijke (Sussex; Book Guild, 1991).
54. Faye Sholiton, 'Perspective America: The Nazis and the Laboratory', *Hadassah Magazine*, 71 (Aug.–Sept. 1989), p. 15.
55. On 25 July 1945, Gerstein was found hanging in his cell in a military prison in Paris.
56. Simon Wiesenthal, *The Sunflower* (New York: Schocken, 1976), p. 13.
57. Wiesel, *Memoirs: All Rivers Run to the Sea* (New York: Knopf, 1995), p. 104.
58. Richard Rubenstein, *After Auschwitz* (Indianapolis: Bobbs-Merrill, 1966), p. 153.

Chapter 31. Punishing the Guilty

1. *New York Times*, 1 November 1945, p. 8.
2. *New York Times*, 6 October 1946, p. 1.
3. *New York Times*, 8 October 1946, p. 15.
4. Michel Deveze, 'Violations of Human Rights', in Jan-Albert Goris (ed.), *Belgium under Occupation* (New York: Moretus Press, 1947), pp. 203–17. See also Howard Levie, *Terrorism in War: The Law of War Crimes* (Dobbs Ferry, NY: Oceana Publishers, 1993); Geoffrey Best, *Nuremberg and After: The Continuing History of War Crimes and Crimes against Humanity* (Reading: University of Reading, 1984).
5. Charles Ashman and Robert Wagman, *The Nazi Hunters* (New York: Pharos, 1988), pp. 52–3.
6. *New York Times*, 19 February 1943, p. 10, and 11 March 1943, p. 4.
7. *New York Times*, 2 November 1943, p. 14.
8. *New York Times*, 5 December 1943, p. 24, and 14 December, p. 3.
9. Ashman and Wagman, *Nazi Hunters*, pp. 60–6.
10. Ibid., p. 46.
11. Hilberg, *Destruction of European Jews*, pp. 687–99. See also *Trial of the Major War Criminals, Nuremberg 1945–1946* (International Military Tribunal); United States Army Investigation and Trial Records of War Criminals, microform, April, 1945–June 1958 (National Archives Microfilm Pubs., 1979); Bradley F. Smith, *Reaching Judgment at Nuremberg* (New York: Basic Books, 1977); Wilborn Benton and Georg Grimm (eds), *Nuremberg: German Views of the War Trials* (Ann Arbor: University Microfilms, 1993).
12. Michael Elkins, *Forged in Fury* (New York: Ballantine, 1971), pp. 281–2.
13. *New York Times*, 26 August 1950, p. 7.
14. National Front des Demokratischen Deutschland, *Brown Book: War and Nazi Criminals in West Germany* (Verlag Zeit im Bild, 1965), p. 118.
15. Charles Foley, *Commando Extraordinary* (New York: Putnam, 1955).
16. Simon Wiesenthal, *The Murderers Among Us* (New York: Bantam, 1967), pp. 76–94.
17. Michael Bar-Zohar, *The Avengers*, tr. Len Ortzen (New York: Hawthorn Books, 1967), pp. 124–5.
18. Ashman and Wagman, *Nazi Hunters*, pp. 17–30. See also T. Friedman, *Eichmanns-rechte Hand: das ist Alois Brunner, der Morder von 125,000 Juden* (Haifa: Institute of Documentation in Israel for Investigation of Nazi War Crimes, 1991); Jeremy Josephs, *Swastika over Paris: The Fate of the Jews in France* (New York: Arcade, 1989); Jewish Telegraph Agency, *Daily News Bulletin*, 7 August 1989, p. 4; UPI Wire Services, 11 January 1989, pp. 23–4; Reuters, 11 January 1990, p. 8, 12 January 1990, pp. 5–6, and 17 May 1990, p. 5.
19. Hannah Arendt, *Eichmann in Jerusalem: A Report on the Banality of Evil* (New York:

Viking, 1963); Towiah Friedman, *The Hunter*, ed. and tr. David Gross (Garden City: Doubleday, 1961); Isser Harel, *The House on Garibaldi Street* (New York: Bantam, 1975); Gideon Hausner, *Justice in Jerusalem* (Herzl Press, 1977); Moshe Pearlman, *The Capture and Trial of Adolf Eichmann* (New York: Simon & Schuster, 1963); Jacob Robinson, *And the Crooked Shall be Made Straight: The Eichmann Trial, the Jewish Catastrophe and Hannah Arendt's Narrative* (New York: MacMillan, 1965).

20. Gerald Astor, *The Last Nazi: The Life and Times of Dr Joseph Mengele* (New York: Fine, 1985); US, Congress, Senate, Committee on Judiciary, Subcommittee on Juvenile Justice, 'Searching for Josef Mengele' (Washington: GPO, 1986).

21. Hannah Vogt, *The Burden of Guilt*, tr. Herbert Strauss (New York: Oxford, 1964), p. 286.

22. See *Law Reports of Trials of War Criminals: The Belsen Trial, Prepared by the United Nations War Crimes Commission* (New York: Fertig reprint of HMSO, 1947, 1983); Dick de Mildt, *In the Name of the People: Perpetrators of Genocide* (The Hague: Martinus Nijhoff, 1996).

23. Yuri Suhl, *They Fought Back* (New York: Crown, 1967), p. 50.

24. Ashman and Wagman, *Nazi Hunters*, p. 267.

25. Ibid., p. 155.

26. Ibid., p. 267.

27. Ibid., pp. 180–3. German justice was equally incomprehensible in the case of Max Taubner. A former SS officer, court martialled in 1941 for the unauthorized massacre of civilians in the Ukraine, Taubner was pardoned by Himmler. The Federal Supreme Court blocked a new prosecution in 1972, claiming *res judicata*. Willi Dressen, 'Role of Wehrmacht and Police', p. 305.

28. *The Dora-Nordhausen War Crimes Trial* (OMGUS, 1947) and Tom Bower, *The Paperclip Conspiracy* (Boston: Little Brown, 1987).

29. 'The Nazi Connection', *Frontline*, PBS (24 February 1987).

30. Michael Bar-Zohar, *The Hunt for German Scientists*, tr. Len Orizen (New York: Hawthorn, 1967).

31. Christopher Simpson, *Blowback: America's Recruitment of Nazis and Its Effects on the Cold War* (New York: Weidenfeld & Nicolson, 1988), pp. 66–79; and John Loftus, *The Belarus Secret* (New York: Paragon, 1989).

32. See Howard Blum's *Wanted! The Search for Nazis in America* (New York: Quadrangle, 1977).

33. Tom Teicholz, *The Trial of Ivan the Terrible: State of Israel vs. John Demjanjuk* (New York: St Martin's Press, 1990); Willem Wagenaar, *Identifying Ivan: A Case Study in Legal Psychology* (Cambridge: Harvard University Press, 1988); and Yoram Sheftel, *The Demjanjuk Affair*, tr. Haim Watzman (London: Gollancz, 1994).

34. Jean Steiner, *Treblinka*, tr. Helen Weaver (New York: Simon & Schuster, 1967), p. 296.

35. Demjanjuk courtroom testimony, US District Court, Cleveland, 4 March 1981.

36. Ryan lecture, Youngstown State, 29 October 1990.

37. In 1980 I asked a colleague to reckon the odds that a guard in the camps refrained from brutality toward prisoners. After several days of factoring in the number of guards, duties, peer pressure, etc., he indicated the odds were a googol to one.

38. *Plain Dealer*, 19 September 1995, pp. 1, 9A.

39. Robert Herszstein, *Waldheim: The Missing Years* (New York: Arbor House, 1988), p. 250.

40. Eli Rosenbaum and William Hoffer, *Betrayal: The Untold Story of the Kurt Waldheim Investigation* (New York: St Martin's Press, 1993); Richard Mitten, *The Politics of Antisemitic Prejudice: The Waldheim Phenomenon in Austria* (Boulder: Westview, 1992); and Hillel Seidman, *United Nations, Perfidy and Perversion* (New York: M.P. Press, 1982).

41. Ashman and Wagman, *Nazi Hunters*, pp. 256–65.

42. Littman lecture, Youngstown State, 29 October 1990.

43. Ashman and Wagman, *Nazi Hunters*, pp. 239–43.

44. Ibid., pp. 250–3.

Chapter 32. Final Thoughts

1. Raab, 'The Deadly Innocences of American Jews', *Commentary* (December 1970), p. 32; and James Rosenau, *Domestic Sources of Foreign Policy* (New York: Free Press, 1967), p. 250.
2. Aviva Cantor, 'Did US Jews Do Enough to Stop the Holocaust?', *Buffalo Jewish Review*, 22 April 1983, pp. 8, 9.
3. *Autobiography of Nahum Goldmann*, p. 203.
4. Wiesel, 'Telling the Tale', *Dimensions in American Judaism*, 2 (Spring 1968), p. 11.
5. Carl Hermann Voss, 'Let Stephen Wise Speak for Himself', *Dimensions in American Judaism*, 3 (Fall 1968), p. 139.
6. Chayim Greenberg, '6,000,000 or 5,000', *Midstream*, 10 (March 1964), p. 8.
7. Silver, *Vision and Victory: A Collection of Addresses by Dr Abba Hillel Silver, 1942–48* (New York: ZOA, 1949), p. 7.
8. Kuznetsov, *Babi Yar*, pp. 391–2.
9. Littell introduced the concept at a conference on genocide in Tel Aviv in 1982. Yehuda Bauer, *History of the Holocaust* (New York: Franklin Watts, 1982), p. 333.
10. Friedrich Duerrenmatt, *The Quarry*, tr. Eva Morreale (Greenwich: New York Graphic Society, 1961), pp. 42–3.

Index

References to illustrations are in italics.